A LIBERALISM SAFE FOR CATHOLICISM?

The Review of Politics Series

A. James McAdams and Catherine Zuckert
Series Editors

A Liberalism Safe FOR Catholicism?

Perspectives from *The Review of Politics*

EDITED BY DANIEL PHILPOTT AND RYAN T. ANDERSON

University of Notre Dame Press
Notre Dame, Indiana

University of Notre Dame Press
Notre Dame, Indiana 46556
www.undpress.nd.edu
All Rights Reserved

Copyright © 2017 by University of Notre Dame

Published in the United States of America

Library of Congress Cataloging-in-Publication Data

Names: Philpott, Daniel, 1967– editor.
Title: A liberalism safe for Catholicism? : perspectives from the Review of politics /
edited by Daniel Philpott and Ryan T. Anderson.
Other titles: Review of politics.
Description: Notre Dame : University of Notre Dame Press, 2017. |
Series: The Review of politics series |
Identifiers: LCCN 2017018504 (print) | LCCN 2017019355 (ebook) |
ISBN 9780268101725 (pdf) | ISBN 9780268101732 (epub) |
ISBN 9780268101701 (hardcover : alk. paper) |
ISBN 9780268101718 (pbk. : alk. paper) |
ISBN 026810171X (pbk. : alk. paper)
Subjects: LCSH: Liberalism—Religious aspects—Catholic Church. |
Christianity and politics—Catholic Church. |
Catholic Church—United States—History. | Liberalism—United States.
Classification: LCC BX1396.2 (ebook) | LCC BX1396.2 .L525   2017 (print) |
DDC 261.7088/282—dc23
LC record available at https://lccn.loc.gov/2017018504

∞ *This paper meets the requirements of*
ANSI/NISO Z39.48-1992 (Permanence of Paper).

Contents

Introduction: The *Review of Politics* and the Story of American Catholicism   1
Daniel Philpott and Ryan T. Anderson

CHAPTER 1.
Jacques Maritain, "The End of Machiavellianism" (1942)   37

CHAPTER 2.
Alvan S. Ryan, "The Development of Newman's Political Thought" (1945)   68

CHAPTER 3.
Heinrich Rommen, "Church and State" (1950)   100

CHAPTER 4.
Josef Pieper, "The Social Meaning of Leisure in the Modern World" (1950)   120

CHAPTER 5.
Yves R. Simon, "Common Good and Common Action" (1960)   131

CHAPTER 6.
Ernest L. Fortin, "The New Rights Theory and the Natural Law" (1982)   171

CHAPTER 7.
John Finnis, "Grounding Human Rights in Natural Law" (2015, response to Fortin)   194

CHAPTER 8.
Paul E. Sigmund, "The Catholic Tradition and Modern Democracy" (1987)   234

CHAPTER 9.
David C. Leege, "Catholics and the Civic Order: Parish Participation, Polities, and Civic Participation" (1988) — 253

CHAPTER 10.
Thomas R. Rourke, "Michael Novak and Yves R. Simon on the Common Good and Capitalism" (1996) — 285

CHAPTER 11.
Michael Novak, "A 'Catholic Whig' Replies" (1996) — 312

CHAPTER 12.
Thomas R. Rourke, "Response to a 'Catholic Whig'" (1996) — 319

CHAPTER 13.
Michael J. Baxter, "Catholicism and Liberalism: Kudos and Questions for *Communio* Ecclesiology" (1998) — 322

CHAPTER 14.
Michael Novak, "Liberal Ideology, an Eternal No; Liberal Institutions, a Temporal Yes? And Further Questions" (1998) — 342

CHAPTER 15.
David L. Schindler, "*Communio* Ecclesiology and Liberalism" (1998) — 352

CHAPTER 16.
Joseph A. Komonchak, John Courtney Murray, Samuel Cardinal Stritch, and Francis J. Connell, "'The Crisis in Church-State Relationships in the U.S.A.': A Recently Discovered Text by John Courtney Murray" (1999) — 364

CHAPTER 17.
Carson Holloway, "Christianity, Magnanimity, and Statesmanship" (1999) — 402

CHAPTER 18.
James V. Schall, "*Fides et Ratio*: Approaches to a Roman Catholic Political Philosophy" (2000) — 424

CHAPTER 19.
Gary D. Glenn and John Stack, "Is American Democracy Safe for Catholicism?" (2000) — 449

CHAPTER 20.
Glenn Tinder, "The Core of Freedom: Public or Private?" (2000) — 472

CHAPTER 21.
Clarke E. Cochran, "Robust Tension over Safety" (2000) — 475

CHAPTER 22.
Michael Novak, "Democracy Unsafe, Compared to What? The Totalitarian Impulse of Contemporary Liberals" (2000) — 479

CHAPTER 23.
Gary D. Glenn and John Stack, "Response to Our Critics" (2000) — 484

CHAPTER 24.
William A. Barbieri, Jr., "Beyond the Nations: The Expansion of the Common Good in Catholic Social Thought" (2001) — 490

CHAPTER 25.
Thomas S. Hibbs, "MacIntyre, Aquinas, and Politics" (2004) — 520

CHAPTER 26.
Paul S. Rowe, "Render Unto Caesar . . . What? Reflections on the Work of William Cavanaugh" (2009) — 545

CHAPTER 27.
William T. Cavanaugh, "If You Render Unto God What Is God's, What Is Left for Caesar?" (2009) — 571

Introduction
The Review of Politics *and the Story of American Catholic Liberalism*

DANIEL PHILPOTT AND RYAN T. ANDERSON

A fortnight of freedom! Such was the rallying cry of the United States Conference of Catholic Bishops in 2012 in warning American Catholics about growing threats to the freedom of the church. In their "Statement on Religious Liberty," the bishops pointed to a series of laws, administrative policies, and court decisions in recent years that, they urged, threatened the consciences of religious believers in the United States. They called for two weeks of reflection, education, prayer, and protest.[1]

To convey the bishops' views on what was in danger of being lost, the statement offered a history of what had been accomplished: a constructive partnership between the American Catholic Church and liberal institutions as set forth by the U.S. Constitution, most importantly, the First Amendment's provision for religious freedom. This partnership, the bishops argued, had allowed the church to flourish in the United States but was now fraught with tensions.

The pages of the *Review of Politics* since its founding in 1939 can be read as a chronicle of this partnership—its development, its heyday, its encounter of travails, its ongoing virtues, and its persistent flaws. Indeed, the partnership has been fraught with controversy over its true extent, its robustness, and its desirability. Many secular liberals and some Catholics insist that the bishops' narrative is roseate and that tensions alleged to be recent are in fact historically typical. Others side with the bishops' history of harmony.

If the American church was warm to the partnership, as the bishops suggest, the church in Rome was wary of it in the nineteenth century and well into the twentieth. Pope Gregory XVI had called liberty of conscience an "absurd and erroneous proposition" in his encyclical of 1832, *Mirari Vos*. Pope Pius IX affirmed this condemnation in his 1864 encyclical, *Quanta Cura*, asserted the right of the state to punish those who violate church law, and in the renowned appendix of that encyclical, the Syllabus of Errors, condemned "progress, liberalism, and modern civilization." Pope Leo XIII endorsed both of his predecessors' condemnations of civil liberties.[2] In his 1895 encyclical addressed to the American church, *Longinqua Oceani*, Leo rhapsodized about the flourishing of the church on American shores but warned that the First Amendment's combination of religious freedom and nonestablishment was not to be considered universally valid; it was rather a compromise that the church should accept only where it must. The Vatican's wariness toward liberalism persisted into the early years of the publication of the *Review of Politics*.

Why did the Vatican find liberalism objectionable? First, popes, especially those of the nineteenth century, associated civil and political rights and democratic institutions with religious relativism—what Gregory XVI called "latitudinarianism" and "indifferentism." Second, the church in Rome saw itself directly attacked through the political enactment of this relativism in the French Revolution and in later regimes based on the Revolution's ideals in France, Italy, Mexico, and several other European and Latin American countries. Third, less defensively, the church sought to preserve a medieval model by which church and state upheld each other's prerogatives and worked together to promote a thoroughly Christian society, including through the state's enforcement of religious uniformity. Given Rome's views, American liberals and Protestants have not lacked grounds for their historic suspicion of American Catholics' professed friendliness to American liberal institutions.

For their part, voices in the liberal tradition have a long history of viewing the Catholic Church as liberty's archenemy, casting further doubt on claims of partnership. A strong current of thought in the West holds that liberal democracy could emerge only when politics was freed from traditional Christianity. This view is exemplified by contemporary thinkers such as John Rawls and Mark Lilla and lamented by Pierre Manent.[3] For Enlightenment thinkers, it was the Catholic Church in particular that posed problems for liberty. (Some, like John Locke, were favorable to Protestantism and its moral doctrines, whereas others, like Jean-Jacques Rousseau, wanted to replace Christianity altogether with a new civil religion.) They considered the Catholic Church an obstacle to political freedom on account of its hierarchical authority, its surfeit of supernatural doctrines, its opposition to free thought, its teaching that the state ought to enforce orthodoxy, and its status as a foreign power that channeled popular loyalties away from the nation state. The Inquisition represented what the Catholic Church offered for politics.

In the United States, liberals and Protestants have taken up this critique of Catholicism at least since the days of the American Revolution. Thomas Jefferson quipped that "history, I believe, furnishes no example of a priest-ridden people maintaining a free civil government." Opposition to the church's role in public life runs through the history of the republic. It was expressed in the Blaine Amendments of the late nineteenth century, which denied public funding to Catholic schools, in the opposition to the presidential candidacies of Al Smith and John F. Kennedy, in the heated rhetoric of Paul Blanshard's 1949 book *American Freedom and Catholic Power*, and in numerous other episodes. Historian Arthur Schlesinger Sr. has called anti-Catholicism "the deepest-held bias in the history of the American people."[4]

A very different line of reasoning among Catholics also emerged from the battle royal between liberalism and Catholicism. It affirmed a partnership of the sort that the U.S. bishops described in their 2012 statement and that, as we shall see, was expressed vividly and repeatedly in the first two decades of the *Review of Politics*. Its proponents endorsed liberal democratic institutions, civil and political liberties, including religious freedom, and democratic elections. Differences among them existed, with some supporting civil and political liberties, for instance, while remaining wary of popular rule. What is most important about Catholic political liberals, though, is that the reasons they gave for their support were drawn from the Catholic tradition and consistent with the church's authoritative teachings. Unlike their secular counterparts, they did not endorse free institutions because they were skeptical of religious faith, suspicious of religious authority, or doubtful of any of the church's traditional theological claims. They were not appealing to autonomous reason in their arguments. That is to say, Catholic liberals were not liberal Catholics. This position—an endorsement of liberal rights and institutions from a traditional Catholic standpoint—we shall herein call "Catholic political liberalism."

The earliest strong articulators of Catholic political liberalism were found in France, chief among them the exuberant priest and writer Felicité de Lamennais. It was during the middle portion of Lamennais's career, from the mid-1820s to the early 1830s, that his thought fit the Catholic liberal description. Earlier he was a Catholic but not a liberal; subsequently, after papal demands for conformity, he was a liberal but not a professed Catholic. Although Lamennais allied himself with "ultramontanists" of the time in supporting a bolstered papacy, he also urged that the church become independent of state authority so that it could bring about the moral and spiritual renewal that he thought France badly needed after the Revolution. Lamennais also opposed Gallicanism, a different form of close collaboration between state and church that elevated the state and eroded papal authority. Lamennais remained strongly loyal to the pope even as he became convinced, in the late 1820s, that the best guarantee of the Catholic Church's freedom and influence was through liberal politics: liberty of conscience for people of all religions, freedom of education, freedom of the press, freedom of association, universal suffrage, and a decentralization of the state.[5] Lamennais and his followers thus became "liberal ultramontanists," as political philosopher Emile Perreau-Saussine has termed them.[6] Sadly, Pope Gregory did not return Lamennais's support. In *Mirari Vos*, he condemned Lamennais's liberalism, and he demanded Lamennais's full agreement. Embittered, Lamennais left the church.

In France, Lamennais's followers included his colleagues Charles Montalembert and Henri-Dominique Lacordaire, as well as Bishop Felix Dupanloup. The political writings of their contemporary Alexis de Tocqueville, also a Catholic, contain many of the commitments of Catholic political liberalism. In the nineteenth century, Catholic political liberalism found allies across the English Channel in John Henry Newman and Lord John Acton; in Germany, it was articulated by Bishop Wilhelm von Ketteler; in the Netherlands, by Herman Schaepmann; and across Europe, by numerous lesser-known voices. In the early twentieth century, Fr. Luigi Sturzo, one of the founders of the Italian Christian Democratic Party, espoused Catholic political liberalism.

Critical for the story at hand, Catholic political liberalism also found strong expression in the United States. Charles Carroll, the only Catholic signer of the Declaration of Independence, can be viewed as an early Catholic political liberal. By the late nineteenth century, it was apparent that the Catholic Church was growing and flourishing in the United States with very little legal restriction. Despite the anti-Catholicism that pervaded the culture and shaped politics, the First Amendment to the U.S. Constitution blocked the kind of harsh restrictions on the church typical of liberal republican regimes elsewhere in the world. In 1887, Monsignor Denis O'Connell observed:

> Americans never suppressed a religious order, never confiscated a sou of church property, never suppressed the salary of a bishop, never sent a semi-

narian into the army, never refused permission to open a Catholic university, never forbade anyone to become a religious, never forbade a meeting of bishops nor claimed a voice in naming them. In the United States the government of the Church is not carried on by the state over the heads of the bishops.[7]

Nineteenth-century intellectuals such as Orestes Brownson (whose perspective admittedly shifted over his career) articulated a Catholic basis for American institutions and made direct reference to Catholic liberals on the European continent. Importantly, American prelates, perhaps most prominently James Cardinal Gibbons, archbishop of Baltimore in the late nineteenth century, argued similarly. In the twentieth century, the French émigré Jacques Maritain drew from the Thomist tradition of natural law thought in formulating his defense of human rights and democratic institutions. The Jesuit theologian John Courtney Murray argued from the 1940s through the 1960s that the American Constitution could be defended on grounds of Catholic thought and that the church had good reason to "develop its doctrine" and embrace the First Amendment's guarantee of religious freedom.

Murray's arguments played a pivotal role in bringing about a momentous development—the embrace of what we have called Catholic political liberalism by the magisterium of the Catholic Church in Rome. Intimations of such an embrace had arisen sporadically in previous decades, for instance, in Leo XIII's encyclical *Rerum Novarum* of 1891, which endorsed certain natural rights, as well as in Pope Pius XII's Christmas Address of 1944, which praised democracy. The embrace became far more thorough, however, at the Second Vatican Council of 1962–1965. Pope John XXIII's encyclical of 1963, *Pacem in Terris*, wholeheartedly endorsed human rights. Little noticed was the inclusion of one human right that the church had not officially proclaimed before—that of religious liberty. It took another document, *Dignitatis Humanae*, promulgated by the council on its penultimate day, December 7, 1965, to spell out the case in full for religious freedom, which it declared to be a human right. *Dignitatis Humanae*, the church's declaration on religious liberty, was the most important statement of Catholic political liberalism at the council, for it dramatically taught in favor of a right that the church had previously refrained from asserting.

Catholic political liberalism, as described above, involves support for liberal institutions on grounds consistent with traditional Catholic teaching, not on grounds of secular Enlightenment philosophy or religious relativism. The development of a rationale for religious freedom along these lines by the architects of

Dignitatis Humanae was critical for the development and passage of the declaration. The document was much debated, and it evolved through several versions. Bishops who stood by the arguments of the nineteenth-century popes that religious freedom would invite the kind of intellectual, moral, and political chaos provoked by the French Revolution were skeptical. They both shared the previous popes' views and worried that in endorsing religious liberty, the church would break continuity in its dogmatic teaching. Their skepticism was overcome only when the declaration's supporters developed arguments for religious freedom that swung free of Enlightenment relativism and avoided contradicting previous church teaching—indeed, that grew out of and developed previous church teaching. Critically, supporters insisted, the declaration would endorse not a right to error but rather the right of every person to search for and embrace religious truth without coercion. Such a basis for religious freedom was different from the arguments rejected by the nineteenth-century popes and was consistent with the Catholic tradition's long-standing stress on the centrality of conscience and freedom of the will in the act of faith.[8]

Over centuries, then, through a kind of Hegelian dialectic, a rapprochement between political liberalism and Catholicism came about. The Hegelian thesis was liberal rights and institutions, grounded in Enlightenment thought. The antithesis was the rejection of liberalism by the nineteenth-century magisterium. The synthesis was the political liberalism of Catholics who looked to their tradition for what they thought were older, better groundings for liberal rights and democratic institutions. The Catholic Church could still reject Enlightenment thought but also embrace liberal institutions, for distinctively Catholic reasons. Triumphing at the Second Vatican Council, this synthesis has been continued in subsequent magisterial teaching, which has affirmed religious liberty and liberal democratic institutions grounded in natural law and the dignity of the person created in the image of God. The United States played a critical role in paving the way for this synthesis by providing an environment where the church flourished under legally protected religious liberty, thus showing that such a combination was possible. This synthesis, as realized both in the Catholic Church in general and in the United States, is what the American Catholic bishops celebrated in their statement of 2012—and its unraveling is what they fretted about. In terms of this introductory essay, they saw a robust Catholic political liberalism being threatened by a liberalism that emphasized personal autonomy, religious skepticism, a rejection of natural law and its view of human nature, and a devaluation of religious liberty.

Again, the story of the rapprochement between liberalism and Catholicism—its rise and its subsequent tensions—can be found in the pages of the *Review of Politics*. The dramatis personae are some of the greatest Catholic political philosophers of the past century. The rest of this essay introduces the selections in this volume in subsections that deal with this theme in different ways.

Catholicism and Liberal Democracy

The original stance of the *Review of Politics* on the Catholic political liberal synthesis arose in large part from the émigré experience of its founding editor, Waldemar Gurian, and of several of its early authors, including Jacques Maritain, Heinrich Rommen, and Yves Simon. Having experienced European fascism firsthand, these intellectuals were convinced liberal democrats and wanted to find a Catholic foundation for their politics. They were also enthusiastic about the United States and its example of a religion-friendly democracy. From its founding up to the present, the *Review of Politics* has published articles stressing the complementarity of Catholicism and liberal democracy.

One of the earliest and most exemplary of these pieces is a 1945 essay on the English Catholic intellectual John Henry Newman, "The Development of Newman's Political Thought," by Alvan S. Ryan, then a young scholar of English literature who had just completed a dissertation on Newman. Ryan presents Newman as a Catholic political liberal. He shows that Newman admired French Catholic liberals such as Lamennais, Dupanloup, Montalembert, and Lacordaire, and he makes connections between Newman's thought and that of Jacques Maritain and Luigi Sturzo.

Like most Catholic political liberals, Ryan explains, Newman rejected "religious liberalism" root and branch, considering it one of his life's purposes to fight against it. In his politics, Newman was more open to the liberal state, although he wanted to keep it limited in its power. He was a Tory at heart, a Burkean who preferred to hold on to traditions and who harbored a skepticism of revolutionary democracy and the idea that power should reside in the people. Yet as England developed and expanded liberal democratic institutions in the nineteenth century, Newman thought that the church should also adapt.

While he was still an Anglican and a leader in the Oxford Movement during the 1830s, Newman opposed Erastianism, the state control of the Anglican Church that had arisen in the English Reformation. The most recent manifestation had been the state's imposition of liberal theology on the church.

After Newman became a Catholic, several themes in his thought bore a politically liberal stamp. First, he vigorously affirmed the basic rights of the person against the state. Second, he strongly valued the conscience of the individual, which he connected to the dignity of the person, and thought that everyone is called to form his conscience according to the truth. In his renowned *Letter to the Duke of Norfolk*, he wrote that "conscience has rights because it has duties." Thus, in the political and social sphere, Newman thought that the rights of conscience must be protected. In answer to William Gladstone's claim that Catholics could not be loyal citizens of a national liberal democracy, he argued that papal authority did not override conscience. Third, Newman had a strong appreciation for national and cultural traditions. He did not think that ultramontanism (the assertion of papal authority over and against national bishops and governments) or a politically established Catholic Church would serve England well. Instead, the Catholic Church in England should accept its pluralistic setting and seek to preserve its freedom.

Although Newman did not reject any of the church's teachings or its teaching authority, his politically liberal spirit is apparent in his reservations about certain papal actions. He affirmed the doctrine of papal infallibility, but he questioned the prudential wisdom of Pope Pius IX's reassertion of papal authority in the Syllabus of Errors, his declaration of papal infallibility at the First Vatican Council, and his adamant protest at the loss of the church's temporal power.

The first essay in this collection, "The End of Machiavellianism," is by Jacques Maritain, one of the most important Catholic philosophers of the twentieth century and one of Catholic political liberalism's most influential proponents. Maritain was a leader in the revival of Thomism in the twentieth century and drew from this foundation to ground human rights and democracy. In doing so, he helped pave the way for the acceptance of these concepts in magisterial teaching, particularly at the Second Vatican Council. True to the Catholic political liberal pattern, Maritain was deeply skeptical of Enlightenment philosophy and expressed strong reservations about the Rousseauian view of democracy. Instead, he believed that liberal democracy should be based on natural law and the concept of the common good as found in the Thomist tradition.

In this essay, which Maritain wrote during World War II and with an eye toward the war, these commitments are strongly reflected. Machiavelli was an important turning point in Western political thought, Maritain argues, insofar as he severed politics from morality, made the strength of the state the primary criterion for success in politics, and placed morality at the service of the state.

Machiavelli thus departed from the Western tradition that politics was answerable to morality. Over subsequent centuries, this fissure between morality and politics has widened. First came moderate Machiavellianism, the realpolitik of Cardinal Richelieu in the seventeenth century, which retained the common good as a moral goal but allowed the politician to depart from morality. Then, in the nineteenth century, came absolute Machiavellianism, for which power and success are the supreme moral criteria. This version, which is realized in ideologies of fascism and communism, led to the crisis that Maritain observes in this 1942 essay.

According to Maritain, Machiavellianism contains the seeds of its own demise. When justice, righteousness, and the common good are not the moral criteria for politics, then politics will collapse under the weight of its own evil. In calling for a politics governed by morality, Maritain did not reject the idea of the modern state or of a just war; he thought that the Second World War was certainly just. He viewed modern democracies based on freedom as the ground of hope for a politics based on law and right. By contrast, the totalitarianisms he observed around him were the products of Machiavellianism. As a Catholic political liberal, Maritain placed his hope in liberal institutions based in natural law and Christianity.

The rise of Catholic political liberalism is the central theme of the essay by political scientist Paul E. Sigmund, written more than four decades later, in 1987. He begins by exploring the "doctrinal neutrality" of the early church on forms of government. Because the church viewed itself as a spiritual community concerned with a kingdom not of this world, it was neutral between forms of government as long as they did not interfere with her mission and were responsive to and protective of the common good of citizens. During the Middle Ages, ambiguities arose, as some theologians and churchmen gave preference to monarchical forms of government, modeled on God's governance of the cosmos. To many, the advantages to the church of a throne-and-altar union were clear.

It was partly this theoretical legacy that made the church slow to embrace modern democracy, but Sigmund suggests that the lag had more to do with faulty liberal theories of man and state, along with violence propagated by liberals. As Sigmund notes, the "French Revolution swept away the privileges of the church, and forced its priests to swear to a *Civil Constitution of the Clergy*." If democracy meant, as the philosopher Denis Diderot once said, that "man will never be free till the last king is strangled with the entrails of the last priest," it would be hard for the church to embrace it. Sigmund walks readers through a history of nineteenth- and twentieth-century Catholic engagements with modernity, and the crucial role that the American Catholic experience played in showing an alternative way of coexisting with democracy. Of central importance in his history are several contributors to this volume, including Jacques Maritain and Yves Simon. As Sigmund puts it:

> Maritain was responsible for a new development in Catholic political thought that had been anticipated but never articulated in terms of the Catholic tradition by earlier French and Italian writers—the argument that democracy was not simply one of several forms of government, all of which were acceptable provided that they promoted "the common good," but was the one form that was most in keeping with the nature of man, and with Christian values. The traditional concern with justice had been expanded to give a religious justification for freedom, and the Christian belief in equality before God was now interpreted to include political and juridical equality as well.

Maritain's achievement in this respect lay in showing an alternative theoretical grounding for liberal institutions. As democracy became more appealing to Catholics in both theory and practice, they reevaluated its merits. Sigmund concludes that in the twentieth century the church came to support "democracy as morally superior and philosophically preferable" to all other forms of government.

In an essay published the following year, 1988, political scientist David C. Leege assumes the complementarity of Catholicism and liberal institutions and explores the behavior of Catholics within American democracy. His methods are empirical, including survey analysis.

Leege begins with a historical narrative of an evolution of American Catholics from being deferential to church authority and strongly affiliated with community to being much more independent in their voting and political behavior. The turning point was the election of President John F. Kennedy, who "proclaimed the political liberty of American Catholics." In contemporary America, Leege argues, Catholics are willing to take guidance from church authority, especially when the issues are complex, such as poverty and world peace, and when the spokesman is primarily the pope. When an issue is one that an American Catholic believes is within grasp, he or she is much more likely to label it a matter of individual conscience. Birth control, he argues, most fits this description, and women's rights, sex and violence on television, and racial integration come next. Leege's findings suggest a movement among American Catholics away from Catholic political liberalism, as defined in this introduction, and toward a liberalism of autonomy and individualism—a movement predicted by Tocqueville in the nineteenth century.

Religious Liberty

Religious liberty is arguably the most important issue at stake in the development of Catholic political liberalism. The church's failure to endorse this principle over centuries provoked the greatest criticism by liberals around the world and by Protestants and others in the United States. The Second Vatican Council's embrace of this principle in *Dignitatis Humanae* is what has most enabled the church to support and promote liberal democracy around the world.[9]

Remarkably prescient in this regard is a 1950 essay, "Church and State," by political philosopher Heinrich Rommen, which presents a case for religious liberty fully grounded in Catholic thought and tradition. Although Rommen is not nearly as well known as Murray for his early defense of religious freedom, his essay arguably anticipates the arguments of *Dignitatis Humanae* at least as well as Murray's arguments did. This essay from the *Review of Politics* deserves to be far better known.

Like Maritain, Rommen was a European Catholic émigré. He had fled to the United States in 1938 from Nazi Germany, where for a short time he was imprisoned by the Gestapo. Rommen came to admire American institutions of governance and to defend them on Catholic grounds.

Like other Catholic political liberals, Rommen regards the modern state, rooted in Enlightenment secularism, as a threat to the church. He begins his essay by warning of a secularist outlook—what Pope Benedict XVI would later call "negative secularism"—that would privatize the church and sharply control it. He defends the Catholic Church and argues that its visible, public form requires legal protection. He links his arguments with Catholic liberals who thought along similar lines, including Newman, Ketteler, and Murray.

Yet Rommen's essay is primarily devoted to defending a modern political arrangement that involves the separation of church and state and guarantees religious freedom for everyone. Such an arrangement corresponds to what Benedict XVI calls "positive secularism." Echoing Murray's contemporary arguments, Rommen worries that the Catholic Church's failure to embrace religious freedom alienates it from Protestants and erodes the church's credibility, and he calls for a decisive "renunciation of compulsion." Rommen rejects a view that had been espoused by the magisterium as the thesis/hypothesis doctrine, which he captures through a quotation ascribed—though wrongly, Rommen points out—to nineteenth-century French intellectual Louis Veuillot: "When you are the majority, we demand our liberty on the basis of your principles (the so-called Protestant principle or liberalist principle, of indifferentism). When we are the majority, we will refuse you your liberty on the basis of our principles." The church's thesis was that it ideally ought to enjoy established status and to deny religious liberty to others. Its hypothesis was that when it was in a minority or otherwise could not secure this status, it would demand religious liberty.

Rommen calls instead for religious liberty that is principled, not merely pragmatic—a right to be enjoyed by everyone, everywhere. He anticipates *Dignitatis Humanae* by defending individual religious freedom on the basis of conscience, the psychological conditions of embracing faith, and the contrariety of coercion to the gospel.

A famous contemporary of Rommen who is far more closely associated with *Dignitatis Humanae* is John Courtney Murray, S.J. Murray appears in the *Review of Politics* through a 1950 memorandum discovered by historian Joseph Komonchak and published in the *Review* in 1999, along with responses to Murray written by two of his contemporaries, Samuel Cardinal Stritch, archbishop of Chicago, and Fr. Francis J. Connell, dean of the School of Sacred Theology at the Catholic University of America. Murray wrote his memorandum for the use of Monsignor Giovanni Battista Montini of the Vatican Secretary of State, later to become Pope Paul VI, and it was distributed to the Holy Office at the Vatican and to the two American churchmen. In 1954 the Holy Office judged Murray's writings to contain serious errors and forbade him from writing on religious freedom. He regained the favor of the hierarchy when he was invited to the second session of the Second Vatican Council, where he contributed to the writing of *Dignitatis Humanae*.

Murray's memo and the two responses are a gold mine for understanding Murray's case for religious freedom and its differences from the prevailing views in the Vatican. Far from being a move toward secularism, Murray's argument in his memo is motivated by his worry about a growth in secularism in America, particularly through the doctrines of naturalism and positivism. He worried, too, about the totalitarian threat posed by Soviet and Chinese Communism. Murray hoped that the Catholic Church would respond to these threats by making common cause with American society and with Protestants in particular. This would benefit both the United States and the church, which, he thought, could evangelize more effectively if it could iron out its differences with the rest of America. The chief obstacle to this cooperation, in Murray's analysis, was the church's own doctrine of religious freedom, which ran contrary to the First Amendment to the U.S. Constitution and to the deeply held convictions of most Americans. Murray's intent, therefore, was to convince the church to embrace religious freedom and to find a genuinely Catholic foundation for the principle.

Echoing Catholic political liberalism, Murray stressed that the American experience of a secular state is very different from the European Jacobin one. Liberal institutions could be placed on a foundation distinct from that of the European Enlightenment. Murray also articulated a separate but related argument that came to fruition in the Second Vatican Council's seminal document, *Gaudium et Spes*—namely, that the differentiation in the roles and functions of church and state ought to be widened in the modern world. Properly configured, these roles and functions are complementary, compatible, and mutually under the law of God. Still, they are different, and they ought to be kept more separate and distinct than the church has allowed in the past. The state should concern itself with temporal matters, whose criterion is the natural law, and the church with spiritual matters, governable by divine law. The state, Murray argued, steps outside of its proper sphere when it suppresses religion by the force of law. Like Rommen, Murray called for an abandonment of the thesis/hypothesis doctrine and for a principled embrace of religious freedom.

Stritch and Connell each responded by defending the teaching of the church at that time. Attacks on the church in the modern world are nothing new, argued Stritch, and should not lead the church to change its doctrines. He quotes a statement of the thesis/hypothesis doctrine in Leo XIII's *Longinqua Oceani*, argues that the modern separation of church and state is not ideal even if it is necessary, and holds that the state should establish and uphold the rights of the church, including aspects of divine law. Connell agreed with Murray that the church in America was facing attacks but opposed the solution of making common cause with secular and Protestant America. While Catholics ought to be loyal American citizens, they should not compromise their claim to belong to the one true church. These responses to Murray found sympathy in the Vatican, which had not yet reached the stage at which it would develop its doctrine on religious freedom.

By the turn of the century, the debate over religious liberty and its relationship to Catholicism and liberalism in the United States had changed dramatically. A generation earlier, the church had adopted the liberal political principle of religious freedom but given it a Catholic foundation. Now, religious liberty was being threatened by a hostile secularism—much as the U.S. bishops would diagnose in 2012. Political scientists Gary D. Glenn and John Stack document and assess this new threat in an essay published in 2000, "Is American Democracy Safe for Catholicism?"

Glenn and Stack begin with a quotation from Murray, which can be paraphrased as follows: the pertinent question is not whether Catholicism is compatible with American democracy but whether American democracy is compatible with Catholicism. For a Catholic, in other words, the church's relationship with America must be judged by the criteria of the church. The authors document incompatibilities between American liberalism and Catholicism dating back to America's founding, but they also believe that before World War II there was room for pragmatic accommodation of the church under the rubric of a liberal constitution—what they call "civil liberty." The tensions became more ominous after World War II, however, when liberalism housed the concept of "civil liberties" in a doctrine of secularism, according to which religion should be privatized and subordinated to the individual conscience.

When such liberalism was deployed to interpret the Constitution, it amounted to an established relativism. Glenn and Stack trace the rise of this doctrine's influence from the Supreme Court's *Everson* and *McCollum* decisions of the late 1940s, through decisions on school prayer and abortion in the 1960s and 1970s, to cases on euthanasia. They also find the doctrine manifested in the thought and words of Catholic politicians such as John F. Kennedy and Mario Cuomo. In short, they find Catholic political liberalism challenged by secular liberalism.

In publishing Glenn and Stack's essay as part of a 2000 symposium on Christianity and Politics, the *Review of Politics* asked three commentators to respond to their argument. The critics recognize the problem that Glenn and Stack diagnose, and each takes up, in one way or another, the question whether the danger to Catholicism is different today than it has been in other times and places and even whether Catholics ought to expect a regime that comports with their convictions. Political scientist Clark Cochrane, for instance, argues that tensions between the teaching and doctrine of the church and certain American values are nothing new and are hardly surprising. Catholicism never was nor should be at home with America. In a similar spirit, political philosopher Glenn Tinder holds that Christians should not have high expectations about any state and should be grateful that their freedom to worship is secure under democracy, in comparison to a totalitarian state. He also argues that Christianity upholds a certain doctrine of individualism that should not be shunned. Michael Novak also adopts a historical perspective in asking whether a regime has ever existed that was "safe" in every sense for Catholics. The world, the flesh, and the devil have posed threats to the church in every political setting. Still, the American experiment in ordered liberty has proved, from the perspective of history, to be a salubrious arrangement for the church. Novak worries that Glenn and Stack are too pessimistic; the liberal elite, he argues, is disappearing, and the American experiment is intact.

Glenn and Stack respond to their interlocutors by arguing that some regimes are more dangerous than others and that a particular kind of danger has now arisen because Catholics are denied the opportunity to act publicly on their ideas of the good. Catholicism is a holistic, engaged faith, not one that is limited to worship and private acts.

As the U.S. bishops' 2012 statement suggests, this debate has not died down. Religious liberty remains at the center of the question of Catholic liberalism in the United States.

Faith and Reason, Ancient and Modern

In a sense, contributions by Catholics to the development of political liberalism are not distinctively Catholic insights or contributions. Critiques of Enlightenment liberalism and the buttressing of liberal institutions on more solid philosophical foundations draw from common sources of human rationality, which are available to all. It is the church's commitment to reason that enables such contributions. On the other hand, it is precisely the church's openness to revelation and its theological insights into the human condition that have allowed it to see further than unaided human reason alone. All of the writers discussed above are asking what kind of philosophical and theological foundations political liberalism requires to flourish. All of them hold that Enlightenment liberalism is problematic, and, in a variety of different ways, all draw from the premodern philosophical and theological traditions of the church and bring them to bear on today's challenges.

James Schall echoes many of these themes in his essay "*Fides et Ratio*: Approaches to a Roman Catholic Political Philosophy." Schall, a Jesuit priest and political philosopher, plumbs Pope John Paul II's 1998 encyclical letter *Fides et Ratio* for its political meaning. The encyclical itself dealt with the much broader crisis of rationality in metaphysics and ethics.

Schall places John Paul II in conversation with a range of political philosophers, including Leo Strauss in his famous essay "On the Mutual Influence of Theology and Philosophy." Whereas Strauss had argued that there was a fundamental disjunction between revelation and philosophy, Schall points out that the best Catholic thinking does not divide theology and philosophy quite so starkly. Although theology and philosophy are distinct disciplines, with their own starting points and subject matter, Schall insists that they "indicate different ways of seeking the truth, but they do not find different, unrelated truths." As a result, Catholics must be just as concerned with reason as they are with faith, and just as concerned with philosophy as with theology. Any authentically Catholic approach to seeking the truth needs to be concerned about the integrity of philosophy, for philosophy well done will point to the need for revelation and theology. Philosophy will lead people to seek answers to real questions that reason alone cannot adequately address. As Schall puts it, "Philosophy has to be proper philosophy to hear revelation. An inadequate philosophy is deaf to the voice of revelation. Revelation, rather frequently, has to defend philosophy itself from itself."

What does this mean—to defend philosophy itself from itself? A major thesis of *Fides et Ratio*, Schall argues, is that modern man has lost confidence in the ability of reason to discern truth. Skepticism has led not to man's liberation and flourishing but to his enslavement and debasement. In support, Schall quotes John Paul II: "At the deepest level, the autonomy which philosophy enjoys is rooted in the fact that reason is by its nature oriented to truth and is equipped moreover with the means necessary to arrive at truth." Certain strands of the later Enlightenment and postmodern era denied the existence of truth or questioned man's ability to discover it. Without a firm foundation in truth, however, little in political life—especially the protection of rights—can be secure for long. Only a political philosophy grounded in truth can provide a defense of a principled pluralism, one that can protect legitimate diversity and human rights and justice. Here, John Paul's thought, as conveyed by Schall, is linked to the pope's broader view of democracy, namely, that it can only be justified as a reflection and embodiment of truth and goodness and that it cannot be grounded on the idea that the popular vote determines truth and goodness. Here, too, John Paul II and Schall take their place in the tradition of Catholic political liberalism.

If the first step is defending philosophy from itself and restoring it to its ennobled position as capable of seeking—and attaining—truth, then the second step is for us to grasp that reason itself leads to a recognition of the need to take account of revelation. As Schall writes, "Political philosophy, for its part, cannot, without bad will, refuse to consider revelation's insight into political things when politics does not solve its own problems in its own terms about its own subject matter." This is true regardless of whether any given thinker accepts any given purported revelation to be truly revelatory. Part of a sound philosophy must include a willingness to consider what revelation has to say: "even the nonbeliever, genuinely aware of unanswered questions he shares with others, including believers, can appreciate that revelational arguments and positions can be seen as responses to genuine philosophic questions and enigmas. Even though such revelational responses can be rejected, it cannot be denied in some uncanny sense that they do present answers to philosophic questions as asked."

Schall concludes, as does John Paul II in *Fides and Ratio*, that both faith and reason are necessary for an adequate grasp of the fullness of truth, and that either in isolation can become dangerous and fanatical. Schall writes: "Reason and faith are everywhere directed at each other in such a way that they correct or better illuminate each other, without ceasing to be themselves. The biblical scholar who knows no philosophy is a dangerous man. The scientist who is unaware of the higher dimensions of philosophy locks himself into an autonomous ideology."

If the relation of faith and reason is one abiding theme in political philosophy, especially in Catholic contributions to political philosophy, so too is the relation of ancients and moderns. Is the concern for virtue in classical sources incompatible with the focus of Enlightenment and modern thinkers on rights? Was the natural law doctrine of the medieval schoolmen fundamentally rejected by Enlightenment thinkers in a way that renders modern political communities incapable of grasping natural law truths? Indeed, are modern political regimes that embrace liberal institutions and use the language of rights fundamentally flawed and hopelessly irredeemable? These are some of the debates that have animated Catholic contributions to political philosophy for the past several decades. And these themes come admirably to the fore in comparing Fr. Ernest Fortin's essay and the response by John Finnis, specially written for the current volume.[10]

Fortin's essay, "The New Rights Theory and the Natural Law," is a 1982 review of Finnis's influential 1980 book *Natural Law and Natural Rights*. Fortin argues that, for all of its undeniable merits, Finnis's book is fundamentally flawed because it attempts to reconcile two irreconcilable theories: that of natural law and that of natural rights. Finnis shares a weakness, Fortin believes, with numerous modern Catholic thinkers in this respect. The reason these theories are irreconcilable, according to Fortin, is that natural law theory is based on ancient and medieval thinking, while the idea of natural rights is a creation of Enlightenment thought, which explicitly rejected the idea of natural law. Fortin thus suggests that Catholic political liberals, for example, Maritain, Simon, and Murray, followed by Richard John Neuhaus, George Weigel, Michael Novak, and in his own way John Finnis, have set themselves an impossible task.

Fortin illustrates the problem through debates over abortion. He asserts that the modern Catholic approach to condemning abortion is "by means of a distinctively new argument based on natural or human rights rather than on the natural law." Although the ultimate conclusion—no intentional killing of the unborn—may be the same, "the reasoning behind it is obviously different." Fortin explains: "The old argument was mainly concerned with what abortion does to the person who performs it or allows it to be performed; the new one, with what it does to the aborted fetus. One argument emphasizes duties; the other emphasizes rights." According to Fortin, this is not merely a matter of emphasis or rhetoric. It also raises a deeper question of "whether the two approaches are fully compatible with each other or whether at a deeper level the tension between them is not such as to caution against any hasty substitution of one for the other." Fortin faults Finnis for uncritically attempting to make them compatible and substitute one for the other.

The heart of Fortin's critique is that the doctrine of natural rights rests on a fundamentally different foundation than that of natural law. Whereas classical natural law theory viewed human beings as naturally social and political,

> the natural rights theory proceeds on the assumption that these same human beings exist first of all as complete and independent wholes, endowed with prepolitical rights for the protection of which they "enter" into a society that is entirely of their own making. All rules governing their relations with one another and all principles of justice are ultimately rooted in rights and derive their efficacy from them.

These Enlightenment liberal principles, Fortin argues, are based not on considerations of the good—of human flourishing in its various aspects—but on calculations of utility: "the products of a calculus of means to a desired end in which discursive reason is called upon to play the leading role." Fortin concludes that it "would be surprising if, on the basis of such radically different premises, one were to come in all cases to identical or roughly similar results." So, while Fortin offers great praise for Finnis's work, he ultimately concludes that more work remains to be done if an attempted merger of natural *law* and natural *rights*, of ancient and modern political theory, is to be successful.

Finnis, in his essay for this volume, responds that Fortin fundamentally misread *Natural Law and Natural Rights*. His book was not an attempt to merge two opposing doctrines but rather a thoroughgoing critique of modern Enlightenment natural rights thinkers, such as Hobbes. Finnis argues that we should not jettison the concept of natural rights simply because Hobbesian natural rights theorists got them—and their foundations, scope, and justifications—wrong. The natural law tradition has its own theory of rights, a theory that the late scholastics had misunderstood and obscured. A central aim of *Natural Law and Natural Rights* (*NLNR*) was to set forth an understanding of natural law free from late scholastic distortions—distortions, Finnis argues, that have been carried over by Fortin and falsely attributed to Thomas Aquinas. As Finnis puts it:

> Anyone embarking on a project such as *NLNR* needed to investigate, as a top priority, whether Aquinas and Aristotle were guilty of the fallacies and elisions of neo-Thomism, and if they were not, whether a philosophically critical and free-standing exposition of the foundations of ethics and political philosophy would show that, in their main lines, Aquinas and Aristotle had *got there first*, so to speak, and can, now too, be philosophically helpful.

Finnis concludes that the theories of Aquinas and Aristotle, freed of later distortions, are not vulnerable to modernist attacks. Rather, both arrived at almost everything admirable in modern political theory before the moderns did—and with better theoretical foundations. With this argument, Finnis joins the tradition of Catholic political liberalism. He seeks to ground the central feature of modern liberal political institutions, namely, rights, on reasons that predate modernity.

Toward the start of his essay, "Grounding Human Rights in Natural Law," Finnis points out that when he wrote *NLNR* in 1980, he did not "envisage that scholars who thought of themselves as sensitive to 'the art of writing'"—including Fortin—"would turn out to be inattentive to the book's rhetorical and structural precautions for disarming or circumventing the hostility with which many modern readers approach anything associated by them with the past, especially the past of Christianity." As he puts it, "these are the readers whom the book seeks to meet where they are." But, Finnis notes, "few indeed, however, were the reviewers who noticed, or made even the slightest allowance for, the book's genre, its rhetorical predicament, and its strategies, its 'art of writing.'"

This being said, rights, Finnis points out, are not the foundation of his argument. He notes that it is only in the eighth of thirteen chapters of his book that rights even enter his discussion. And they enter as conclusions—not, as with the modern rights theorists, as starting points. Rights are the conclusions of the entire theory of natural law that Finnis presents before discussing them. As Finnis explains, "they are shown to be simply the entailments of the virtue of justice, the correlatives of duties of justice—not as mere shadows of those duties but as, in a way, their point." But the logic of his argument was lost on readers: "I hoped that, for example, my giving common good and justice priority over rights would signal to thinkers interested in and aware of the tradition of political thought that the book and its author stood in opposition to some main prejudices of modernity." Finnis laments that this hope was disappointed.

Finnis does not reply directly to Fortin's illustration on abortion, but his response is clear: There has been no fundamental change in how Catholics think about abortion. The good of human life always drove the argument, and it was for that reason that people had a duty not to kill—because, conversely, unborn children had a right not to be killed. The killing of unborn children corrupted the character of the abortionist precisely because the unborn child's life was of intrinsic worth, and thus had a right to life that the abortionist had a duty to respect.

None of this is new, Finnis suggests: "For it is as true now as it was in Aristotle's time or Gaius's or Aquinas's or Pius VI's, Leo XIII's, or John XXIII's that the philosophically or theologically defensible doctrine of virtue *includes* a doctrine of justice that in turn, given the resources of modern European languages, can most authentically be set out in terms of rights (which entail their correlative duties)." As Finnis points out, "Justice *always* concerns what I owe *to another*—what that other has the right to, from, or as against me. Everything *NLNR* says about rights has as its basis the virtue of justice, which is why its chapter on justice (as Fortin fails to note) *precedes* the chapter on rights." Finnis concludes that "[Fortin] was fundamentally mistaken, I believe, in his tying of *rights* to *freedom*—worse, to Hobbesian freedom from duty—and fundamentally mistaken in contrasting respect for rights (and claims of rights) with virtue, character-formation, the common good, and natural law (or natural *right*). One can, and every society and social, political, or moral theory should, marry both, for love." In other words, one can have both natural law and natural rights.

Finnis's essay contributes nicely to what Schall described as the Catholic contribution to political philosophy. Finnis lists some of his own conclusions:

> When writing *NLNR*, as now, I judged that the divine revelation constitutive of Christianity—the central form of which (as the book's index discreetly indicates) must be Catholicism—is the central event of human history and became the bearer of what is sound in the philosophical tradition of moral and political (and therefore legal) philosophy inaugurated, masterfully, by Plato and Aristotle. And I thought also that the moral and political philosophy shaped by Hobbes, Locke, Hume, Bentham, and their successors down to today is a series of blunders and oversights, partly but inadequately identified, and then inadequately resisted, by Kant and his successors, and partly prepared for by deficiencies in the (neo)scholasticism of Aquinas's sixteenth-century and later successors.

Finnis's overarching argument, then, is and was "to give an account of natural law that is philosophically sound, untouched by Humeian and all subsequent philosophical and cultural objections, and at the same time—to the extent permitted by philosophically critical criteria—is more authentically in line with St Thomas's thought than were his most influential sixteenth-century commentators and followers." For Finnis, the intellectual prejudices of his day, including a refusal to consider that Thomism might be true, shaped every step of his argument in trying to reach and persuade his readers.

Finnis, like Schall, also suggests that reason alone proves ultimately insufficient in dealing with ultimate issues:

> The real bearing of Christian revelation on these matters is richer and more extensive than any traditional concepts of the ultimate last things, proposing as it does, a kind of continuity—intelligible though entirely dependent on miraculous divine action, gratuitous but promised in revelation—between the building up of persons and their communities in morally good choices (and "works") and eternal life in the completed Kingdom. *NLNR* attempted no more than to open a pathway towards a point—call it a way-station—from which a reader might trek on, by another way and not without labor or grace,

to the vantage point of true revelation, from which point concepts or realities such as the Kingdom of God and its completion and its conditions of citizenship can become visible, and enticing. A political theory worthy of the name of philosophy has to venture towards that way-station and be able to indicate how it can reasonably be judged to be only a way-station and starting point for something more and, in its own way, better.

Finnis's essay, in addition to being a careful response to the misreadings and thus misplaced criticisms of Fortin, is also a tour-de-force defense of his theory of natural law. Whereas Fr. Schall's essay can be profitably read as a response to the view that reason and revelation are incompatible, Finnis's essay can be read as a response to the view that ancient and modern thought on natural law and natural rights are incompatible.

The Common Good

A central idea in Catholic political liberalism is the common good. In the Catholic tradition, the common good is the justification for both political action and authority, and it forms the core of a distinctively Catholic justification for liberal institutions. The common good is the explicit focus of several essays in this volume. A 1960 essay by political philosopher Yves Simon, "Common Good and Common Action," seeks to refute misguided liberal theories that understand authority—be it familial, commercial, or political—as a result of deficiency. Simon responds to the argument that if people were perfectly virtuous, intelligent, and well-informed, there would be no need for the exercise of authority because everyone would recognize and do the right things, and thus authority exists only to make up for a defect.

According to Simon, this argument gets the idea of human good—the common good—wrong and thus fails to appreciate the essential role that authority *must* play in helping people realize common goods. Simon argues instead that "authority, in certain cases and domains, is made necessary not by human deficiencies but by the very nature of man and society." This is because the nature of man is to live in society and seek the common good—that is, the well-being of himself and his neighbors. But a virtuous person who is seeking to pursue the common good—even with perfect human knowledge—will not know how to act for the common good because of the inherit pluralism of human nature. Human goodness is not monolithic, and expert knowledge—as those of a scientific bent might suppose—does not settle important choices. Genuine *choices* must be made, including choices of options that are all equally good but cannot be realized all at once. This reality gives rise to the need for authority: "The existence of a plurality of genuine means in the pursuit of the common good excludes unanimity as a sufficient method of steadily procuring unity of action."

Authority also may be necessary because of deficiencies in virtue or knowledge, but that should not hinder people from grasping the essence of authority: coordination in the service of common action in pursuit of the common good. Or, as Simon puts it, "*The most essential function of authority is the issuance and carrying out of rules expressing the requirements of the common good considered materially*" (emphasis in original). Simon is a crucial figure in twentieth-century Catholic thinking about politics because he helped provide a framework for thinking about political liberalism that was based not on skepticism about the human good, but on a principled pluralism of the human good that provides the justification for political authority.

Simon's ideas were taken up again in the pages of the *Review of Politics* more than three decades later in a 1996 debate between Thomas R. Rourke and Michael Novak. Novak is a prominent American Catholic neoconservative writer, famous for defending democratic capitalism. Rourke, a Catholic political scientist, argues in his essay "Michael Novak and Yves R. Simon on the Common Good and Capitalism" that Novak's account of the common good, inspired by faulty modernist liberal theories, is too thin. Simon, in contrast, offers a more authentic theory that captures the complexity of thinking about the common good. Novak's neoconservative preference for economic freedom, Rourke charges, also ignores essential aspects of the need for authority. Although, in a formal sense, a will open to the well-being of oneself and one's neighbors says something about the common good, Simon held that authority is required to help settle choices and direct that will toward the common good in a material sense as well—an idea, Rourke claims, that Novak rejects.

Rourke opens his essay by highlighting the historical tensions between Catholicism and political liberalism:

> The contradiction between the Catholic and liberal approaches to the organization of society has traditionally been perceived by both sides as fundamental. Catholic thought, grounded in Saint Thomas and expressed in numerous encyclicals, defined itself in opposition to liberalism on the

grounds that the latter rejected the Catholic concept of the common good in favor of a relatively unrestricted pursuit of individual goods.

Novak's work, Rourke suggests, has "attempted to close the gap" between Catholicism and liberalism. Simon, in contrast, criticized liberalism on Catholic grounds. The difference between the two approaches is best seen in their accounts of the common good.

Novak's emphasis on freedom and on the pluralism of a free people pursuing what they take to be the common good has limited the role that political authority should rightly play in fostering the common good. Rourke argues that Novak has reduced the common good to the collection of individual goods, with the state merely providing the rules of the road for each member of society to do as he or she pleases as long as others are not harmed. Novak thus uses the indeterminancy of the common good as the reason to *limit* political authority, rather than as its justifying point.

Novak's approach, Rourke concludes, leads him to an embrace of free markets as a means to the common good that is far too favorable: "The distancing of political authority from the realization of the common good materially considered largely determines Novak's approach to the economic system." This is problematic for Rourke because the common good is important and is the justifying point of political authority. The problem is that "Novak's new concept of the common good does not adequately address the problems of exclusion and isolation from the common good so prevalent in modern liberal societies." Rourke characterizes Novak's theory as a "partnership in mutual self-interest" and concludes, in objection, that "partnerships inherently exclude those who are not party to them."

In his response essay, "A 'Catholic Whig' Replies," Novak argues that Rourke has fundamentally misread him and therefore misevaluated his project for three reasons: "First, he interprets Catholic social doctrine as though it were the ideology of social democracy. Second, he cannot seem to understand other points of view. Third, he systematically misstates my views by reading into them secular liberal philosophical commitments that I have long written against." Novak argues that much hinges on the word "liberalism"—as in Rourke's statement, quoted above, that there is a contradiction between it and Catholicism. According to Novak, he is in a long line of Catholic thinkers who argue that secular liberal *philosophical* theories are not required to embrace liberal political institutions— precisely the Catholic political liberalism discussed here. Novak explains:

The *institutions* that have been developed in countries sometimes described as liberal are one thing; *doctrines* put forth by liberal philosophers to defend them are another. Often, liberal institutions embody elements derived from the dynamism of earlier Jewish and Christian cultures. Thus, Jacques Maritain saw in democratic institutions under the rule of law, constituted by limited government, and protecting the rights of individuals and minorities, the slow working out in history of the yeast of the Gospels. Maritain and Simon taught two generations (including Paul VI) that, while liberal doctrines are insufficient to explain or to defend democratic institutions, the latter merit a profound philosophical and theological defense by Christian thinkers and activists. Even earlier, at the Third Plenary Council of Baltimore in 1884, the U.S. Catholic bishops noted that, under Providence, the U.S. Founders had built "better than they knew."

Novak then offers point-by-point responses to what he regards as misreadings by Rourke. This exchange is brought to a conclusion with a brief retort from Rourke.

The debate between Rourke and Novak is ultimately one about the nature of the distinctively political common good and the role of political authority in realizing common good writ large. Novak's theory, while he never quite states it in the following way, limits the role of the state precisely because it treats the political common good as itself limited in order to create space for other institutions to freely pursue their common goods. In talking about the common good, neither Rourke nor Novak fully accounts for the fact that there are many common goods of many societies. In order to achieve the common good of the society as a whole, it is crucial that political authority seek to promote the political common good, allowing other authorities the ability to promote their distinctive common goods.

The distinction between the political common good and the common good of other associations is also apparent when considering the common good of different *political* communities. What is the nature of the *international* political common good, for instance? What does it imply for international political authority? These questions are taken up by political philosopher William A. Barbieri, Jr., in his 2001 essay "Beyond the Nations: The Expansion of the Common Good in Catholic Social Thought." The concept of an international common good, as Barbieri defends it, overlaps strongly with liberal ideas and institutions, especially human rights, but is arguably thicker than that allowed by liberal philosophy. Barbieri traces the application of the concept of a common good to the international realm in Catholic social thought, citing the work of several thinkers who appear in these pages, including Maritain, Simon, and Murray, as well as a succession of magisterial teachings, including *Mater et Magistra* (1961), *Pacem in Terris* (1963), *Gaudium et Spes* (1965), *Solicitudo Rei Socialis* (1987), and *Centesimus Annus* (1991). For Barbieri, Maritain is especially important given his enthusiasm for federalism at both the global and the European level.

Barbieri examines problems of scope, organization, and authority and argues that the idea of an international common good can be built around a discourse of rights and duties found in international human rights documents; the requirements of social agency for all persons; and the amelioration of conflict. What does he propose in terms of institutions? Shunning the idea of a single global government that would promulgate a particular tradition of thought, Barbieri appeals to the Catholic idea of subsidiarity, or respect for the local, in proposing a pluralism of polities and overlapping institutions.

What happens when the common good becomes privatized and thus is no longer truly common? Even worse, what happens when *good* becomes privatized? How can a community of people live together and flourish when they have no shared conception of human goodness? These have been central themes in Alasdair MacIntyre's critique of Enlightenment liberal moral philosophy, his defense of virtue ethics, and his proposal for a politics of local communities of virtue. These ideas are taken up by Thomas S. Hibbs in his 2004 essay, "MacIntyre, Aquinas, and Politics."

MacIntyre's thesis is that we can only understand what it is right to do in light of what is good for human beings to be. The moral principles, rules, and virtues that constitute a society's moral code only make sense in terms of the human goods they seek to protect and promote. But the characteristic move of liberal philosophy was to privatize the good and speak solely of "rights." Without being educated and habituated into a theory of the good, however, people will neither understand nor live out moral norms.

If modern liberal political societies are devoid of any shared, rationally justifiable conception of human good, then perhaps, MacIntyre proposes, smaller communities of virtue and shared human good are possible that can foster human flourishing in modernity. This is the famous appeal to a new St. Benedict made at the end of MacIntyre's *After Virtue*. Such solutions that ignore politics, however, are inadequate, according to Hibbs. Arguing from a Catholic liberal standpoint—one that seeks to ground liberal institutions in virtue and the common good—Hibbs suggests that in many of his writings MacIntyre plays down politics in a distinctly un-Aristotelian, as well as un-Thomistic, fashion. As Hibbs puts it, "In his account of the virtues, MacIntyre regularly refers to Aristotle; yet MacIntyre almost wholly neglects Aristotle's politics, in spite of the fact that Aristotle offers a politics of the common good." Aristotle offered a rich analysis of types of political regimes, based on who ruled—the one, the few, or the many— and whether or not they ruled for the sake of a common good. What has MacIntyre offered instead? According to Hibbs, "he wants Aristotle's ethics without his politics, in spite of the fact that Aristotle presents them as complementary."

The heart of Hibbs's critique is that virtue theory cannot rest content as a virtue ethics. A virtue politics must also be developed, and thus no virtue theorist can ignore political theory or the political realities of modernity. Any adequate focus on the common good requires a focus on politics—on political forms and political authority—and not merely subpolitical groupings of virtue. And such a focus needs to be more capacious than MacIntyre's denunciation of modern democratic capitalism: "If Aristotle shares MacIntyre's exalted conception of politics as the pursuit of the common good of virtuous living, he appears more willing to countenance imperfect realizations, even distortions, of this ideal." Indeed, politics is, as the saying goes, the art of the possible.

This sort of careful prudential analysis is key for contemporary Catholic debates about government in the United States, for instance. As Hibbs notes: "The prudential assessment of what is given in actually existing regimes, of their complexities and internal conflicts, and of the forces that provide for their amelioration and longevity—these are the central preoccupations of Aristotle's politics. Yet these have little or no place in MacIntyre's political thought." This is sadly true of much contemporary criticism of American government and society from political philosophers. The need, as Hibbs points out, is to be attentive to various conflicts in less than ideal political realities:

> Yet, MacIntyre ignores regimes entirely, focusing instead on local communities, communities even smaller than that of the ancient *polis*. By contrast, Aristotle and Aquinas describe the political order as a "composite," a complex mixture not just of goods but of levels and parts. The defense of a mixed, constitutional regime requires careful analysis of conflicts of goods and interests and of the levels of participation and degrees of allegiance.

This attentiveness to the particularities of specific, concrete political communities reminds us that theoretical critiques alone will never provide remedies: "It is certainly not the case that Aristotle or Aquinas thinks that the theoretical exposing of incoherence or contradiction in an existing regime will resolve anything at the level of practice. Nor do they suppose that the political theorist can operate as a social engineer." So while political theorists can point out a variety of ways in which any given political regime fails to be ideal—"exposing incoherence or contradiction"—this alone does not help political leaders or reformers in their work.

Liberalism and Virtue

It would not be suprising for a political theorist to point out that modern liberal democracy threatens certain virtues that are endemic to the human good and needed for a healthy polis. Two essays in this collection argue much along these lines. The first, from 1950, is by the German Catholic philosopher Josef Pieper, the second by contemporary political philosopher Carson Holloway. Although neither of them articulates precisely the thesis of Catholic political liberalism, each reasons in a similar spirit. Neither rejects modern liberal institutions, but each argues that these institutions are weakened, impoverished, and detrimental to human flourishing unless they are complemented by virtues that come from the ancients (for instance, Aristotle's focus on leisure) and Christianity (for instance, its focus on humility and magnanimity).

In his essay "The Social Meaning of Leisure in the Modern World," Pieper argues that modern society has eclipsed the importance of and opportunities for leisure. Not only have planned economies and totalitarian regimes so controlled people's lives that they have no time for leisure, and not only do certain expressions of modern capitalism leave wage earners with little time apart from work, but also liberal societies shape people so that they choose to leave no time for leisure and are instead preoccupied with busyness and productive activity. Pieper focuses on this spiritual form of poverty. He contrasts the *artes serviles*, which have value through serving other human goods, with the *artes liberales*, which have an intrinsic rather than instrumental value:

> [The liberal] arts and activities are internally legitimized *not* because they serve the necessities of life, or because of their contribution to the public need, or because of any usefulness; the liberal arts derive their character from

this: they do *not* belong to the process of using and working; they have their dignity in themselves; they do not need to receive their *raison d'être* from their usefulness, from their relation to an aim outside themselves. The liberal arts signify the central sphere of culture—if one considers culture to be something which *exceeds* all that is merely useful or even necessary with regard to the immediate aims of practical life.

Leisure, then, is about cultivating the liberal arts: "Leisure is a certain condition of mind, a certain state of soul; leisure is not given merely with the external fact of spare time. Man has to become able to realize leisure in itself, to fill up the room which is no longer occupied by the process of work." It is with this analysis in mind that he defines *proletarian*: "A proletarian is one whose space of existence is completely filled up by being fettered to the process of working, because this space of existence of itself has become narrow by reason of an inner shrinkage, because man is no longer able to realize that there is possible a reasonable, sensible doing, which is *not* work and *not* just nothing else." Pieper does not limit his analysis to the so-called working class but extends it to all people in modern societies: "The psychic inner condition of proletarity is a very common fact—not at all limited to the sphere of what usually is called the proletariat. It is a very common fact that people simply do not know what to do in their spare time, what to do on Sunday: to do something which is *neither* simply rest *nor* simply entertainment, play, amusement." Pieper argues for a recovery of the liberal arts, of the forms of study and play that truly liberate the human spirit. Too much of modernity is focused merely on the servile, or useful, arts. As Pieper notes, "Leisure is the origin of culture (if we understand culture as all those values which exceed immediate need and utility)." The restoration of leisure to modern society is Pieper's defining ambition.

For political scientist Carson Holloway, magnanimity is the virtue of which modern society needs to be reminded. Though written in 1999, nearly fifty years after Pieper's essay, Holloway's essay "Christianity, Magnanimity, and Statesmanship" shares Pieper's concern for the virtues that modern societies—including liberal political orders—threaten and yet depend upon for their health. After a careful analysis of the Aristotelian and Christian understandings of magnanimity, Holloway applies it to the modern context. He argues "that in the modern world Christianity alone can make magnanimous statesmanship possible."

Holloway responds to the political theorist Larry Arnhart, who "contends that the lack of great statesmanship in the modern world is due to the 'political influence of Christianity,' which condemns the magnanimous man as 'too proud, too preoccupied with human glory, to be truly virtuous.'" Arnhart, according to Holloway, argues that "Christianity makes magnanimity impossible. The magnanimous man exalts himself, claiming for himself the greatest honors. In contrast, Christian morality appears as one of self-abasement rather than self-exaltation." In reality, Holloway argues, the opposite is the case: "I contend that Christianity is the cure for the abject vulgarity of democratic peoples and that the application of this cure requires magnanimous statesmanship.... Christianity provides the only hope in a democratic world that such statesmanship will be forthcoming, that those capable of it will enter political life." For the magnanimous Christian "may claim the honors those virtues merit, including great honors if one's virtues are great, so long as one recognizes that ultimately those virtues are from God and thus that ultimately those honors belong to Him."

Holloway echoes a theme of the founders of the United States and of Tocqueville: democracy needs magnanimous people—public-spirited and virtuous souls to stand against mob rule and help elevate politics to its higher ends. But where are such people to be found or formed? For Holloway, the answer is in "Christianity, which provides the magnanimous man with the motive he needs to lower himself by entering democratic politics. That motive is charity, or love of the people." Holloway's argument is that a liberal politics requires *pre*-political values—namely, virtues. And Christianity provides the best foundation for those virtues:

> The love that he owes his neighbor and the possibility of the great good that might be achieved through his statesmanship—the possibility that it might help some to avoid endless damnation and to achieve endless glory—provide the Christian great-souled man sufficient motive to endure the mortification he necessarily feels at lowering himself to participate in democratic politics.

Whereas some have argued that truly enlightened persons would avoid any participation in politics, Holloway suggests that Christianity can inspire them to subject themselves to the annoyances of political life in order to serve the common good, while also recognizing that their virtue is ultimately from God and for God. In arguing for the dependence of liberal institutions on Christianity, Holloway joins the tradition of Catholic political liberalism.

RADICAL CRITICISM

As we have seen, some Catholic intellectuals are skeptical of Catholic liberalism. They question its robustness and staying power. Glenn and Stack, for instance, see it sharply challenged by secular liberalism. They, like the U.S. bishops in their 2012 "Statement of Religious Liberty," believe that a robust Catholic liberal synthesis once existed but is now endangered.

Other skeptics take a far more radical position and question whether such a synthesis was a good idea in the first place. For them, liberalism fundamentally corrupts Catholicism. Free market capitalism shapes people in the direction of greed and exploitation and corrodes communal ties, family, and local ownership. Liberal political institutions shape people toward individualism and self-defining autonomy rather than toward virtue, faithfulness, and interdependence. Most of all, liberalism does little to mitigate and in its own way fosters militarism, wars, and other forms of violence. Whereas the Catholic political liberal tradition holds that liberal rights and institutions can be grounded on traditional Catholic principles and indeed that Catholicism offers a uniquely strong grounding for these rights and institutions, such critics hold that in becoming a partner to liberal institutions, Catholicism itself becomes reshaped—that is, secularized—by these institutions. Nor is it easy, they argue, to separate adherence to liberal institutions from adherence to secular Enlightenment philosophy, which is deeply inimical to Catholicism.

Protestant thinkers writing from the early 1970s, including the Mennonite pacifist theologian John Howard Yoder and one of his disciples, the theologian Stanley Hauerwas, have played a central role in developing and making prominent this type of critique regarding Christianity and liberalism. Hauerwas, in turn, influenced the thought of younger radical Catholics, including Michael J. Baxter and William T. Cavanaugh, two of whose essays are included here. Another important influence on Hauerwas and on his Catholic students was Alasdair MacIntyre, a strong critic of liberal modernity who himself became a Catholic in the early 1980s.

Though not of this intellectual lineage, theologian David L. Schindler shares many of these commitments. His intellectual provenance is the *Communio* school of theology, which was formed around the thought of theologian Hans Urs von Balthasar. One of its most prominent members was Joseph Ratzinger, who became Pope Benedict XVI. Schindler too is a strong critic of liberalism—both liberal thought and liberal institutions, which he does not believe can be easily separated. He is particularly critical of John Courtney Murray, one of the pioneers of the Catholic liberal synthesis.

Schindler's signature book is *Heart of the World, Center of the Church: Ecclesiology, Liberalism, and Liberation*, appearing in 1996. In 1998 the *Review of Politics* published a symposium on the book, featuring a review by Baxter and responses to this review from Schindler and Michael Novak. In choosing Baxter, the *Review* awarded Schindler a sympathetic critic. Not only was Baxter a student of Hauerwas and a follower of MacIntyre and Yoder, but he was also shaped strongly by the Catholic Worker movement, whose founder, Dorothy Day, was an outspoken pacifist and critic of the American liberal state. Baxter begins his review with the assertion, "It is a commonplace among Catholic social ethicists in the United States that the Church has finally made its peace with liberalism in the postconciliar era," and then makes it clear that "*Heart of the World, Center of the Church* challenges this account."

As Baxter explains, Schindler rejects models of church engagement with the world that mistakenly take on the terms of the world, understood as pre–Vatican II integralism, involving close partnership with the state; liberationism, which purports to replace unjust structures with a secularized vision of justice; and neoconservatism, which uncritically celebrates the free market and free political institutions. Schindler proposes instead to reason about the church and society through ecclesiology, namely, an "intrinsicist" vision through which the church shapes the world by being what it most truly is: Trinitarian life in communion. He views the fiat of Mary, through which she received God and brought him into the world, as the church's basic mode of being and acting.

Liberalism for Schindler is a threat to the church's authentic life and influence because it purports to be neutral with respect to conceptions of the good but in fact is not. Hence, it plays a "con game." In reality, liberalism creates a world built on self-interest, rights claims, and power that is detached from the work of grace through the church. Schindler pursues his critique of liberalism in the spheres of politics, economics, and the university. In all of these realms, he argues, liberalism purports to create an autonomous sphere that is delinked from the life of grace and prone to totalitarianism. Although liberals may not wish to admit it, they too espouse a theology—a view of the human person and of the human good in relationship to God—just as all ideologies do.

In the realm of politics, Schindler's critique of liberalism is a critique of Murray, which Baxter describes and extends in his review. Whereas Murray defended liberalism as a neutral, nonideological structure in which the Catholic Church could operate freely, according to its commitments, Schindler argues that Murray ended up advancing a form of liberalism that entails a "subtle and irresistible secularism." Although thinkers such as Komonchak have sought to show that Murray's view has deep theological roots, in fact, according to Schindler, Murray leaves theology behind when he treats the public realm. Murray accepts a series of dualisms: the state should be kept separate from the church, the secular should be kept separate from the sacred, and nature should be kept separate from grace.

Baxter admires Schindler's efforts but closes his review by criticizing Schindler for failing to explain how his ethic applies to public institutions. How does Schindler avoid returning to the pre–Vatican II integralism of coercion without also falling into the dualisms ascribed to Murray? Schindler has all too little to say about any substantive area of politics that is constructive, Baxter charges. In his response essay, Schindler carefully addresses Baxter's criticisms, thus deepening the introduction to Schindler's thought that readers will acquire through Baxter's review. Although Schindler professes not to reject engagement with the state, his priorities are to identify, expose, and challenge the pervasive influence of liberalism on culture, the family, the economy, the university, and other spheres of life.

In Michael Novak's response to Baxter's review of Schindler, "Liberal Ideology, an Eternal No; Liberal Institutions, A Temporal Yes?," Novak comes to the defense of Murray against Schindler. Arguing squarely in the tradition of Catholic liberalism, Novak repeats the kind of argument he made against Rourke, described above—that is, he defends liberal institutions provisionally while rejecting liberal ideology. He argues that we should not interpret the United States and its founding in light of contemporary liberal philosophy, which is secular and individualistic, and that the American experiment is far more religious than Schindler allows, combining charity and prudence. Espousing quintessential Catholic liberalism, Novak appeals to the fact that "both Orestes Brownson and Alexis de Tocqueville held that one day Catholics might be the Americans best placed to offer a profound and coherent defense of the American achievement, and to prevent it from eroding, crumbling and losing its intellectual footing. Furthermore, Catholics might also supply (one day) a philosophical defense of the Constitution." Still, Catholics should not interpret the Constitution in an exclusively Catholic fashion or assert the Catholic faith as the basis of public discussion. Rather, they should look to their own tradition for resources, such as the concept of natural law, that encourage debate across religious lines, an insight that Novak believes Murray understood.

The other major articulation of radical Catholicism in the *Review of Politics* also takes the form of a review essay, though not a review of a single book but rather of an author's entire corpus. In 2009, political scientist Paul Rowe wrote an essay on the thought of Cavanaugh that the *Review* paired with a response by Cavanaugh. Like Baxter, Cavanaugh was a student of Hauerwas and was influenced by the Catholic Worker movement; he has also drawn from the Radical Orthodoxy movement in theology, associated with theologian John Milbank and others. Since the appearance in 1998 of Cavanaugh's first book, *Torture and Eucharist*, he has produced a succession of writings that offer a thorough and incisive critique of liberal thought, politics, economics, and culture.

As Rowe explains in his essay, Cavanaugh presents himself as a Christian theologian writing to other Christians out of concern that their loyalties have been redirected too far toward the modern liberal state and capitalist economy. A phrase that Cavanaugh uses for this redirection in other writings of his is "migration of the holy," which he borrows from the theologian Henri de Lubac's reflections on the evolving meaning of the Body of Christ in the Middle Ages. For Christians this transfer of loyalty, categories of thought, and social identification from the church to the state becomes idolatry. Cavanaugh, Rowe explains, holds that this shift in loyalties took place in early modern Europe, when, for modernist interpreters, the wars of religion of the 1500s and early 1600s yielded the secular modern state as a realm of truce. The lesson drawn from this history by Enlightenment liberals was that religion is inherently violent, while secularism brings peace and stability. In fact, Cavanaugh argues, these wars of religion were not really about religion but rather about the violence associated with the rise of modern state institutions and their usurpation of the church's power. Today, the church has been relegated to being one more actor in civil society, one of many lobbyists, and has been consigned to "spiritual" matters. The latter are subordinate to politics and economics, which are the affairs of the "body," the state. Such a critique of the dualism of the spiritual and the political echoes Baxter's and Schindler's critique of Murray.

Rowe's response is that Cavanaugh is too hard on the modern state. What Cavanaugh describes and criticizes, Rowe argues, is the early modern absolutist state, but this state has been improved upon by the modern liberal state, which is limited in its powers, is often committed to the welfare of its citizens, and, in some areas of the world, has constructed a zone of peace with other liberal states.

The modern liberal state, Rowe contends, is not merely a coercive apparatus but also promotes the common good. Cavanaugh fails to acknowledge that the modern liberal state allows substantial freedom for nonstate actors and their claims to legitimacy. Cavanaugh also overexalts the church without acknowledging its own tendencies to division, violence, and disrespect toward nonmembers.

Cavanaugh responds by reasserting his standpoint as a theologian writing for other Christians about the tendency to idolize the state. He stresses the violent character of the nation state and its tendency to occupy more and more of civil society's space. Rather than acquiesce in becoming one more political actor among many, the church should create alternative spheres to the state and become a community of witness. Cavanaugh claims that he does not directly, explicitly, and totally reject the modern liberal state. Still, his criticism of it is so strong, his sympathy so sparse and weak, and his proposals so directed away from the state that he can be placed among the radical critics of Catholic liberalism.

The debate over Catholic liberalism will not abate any time soon. The worries expressed by the United States bishops in 2012 have only deepened with the 2015 decision of the U.S. Supreme Court in *Obergefell v. Hodges* that redefined marriage throughout the United States to eliminate the norm of sexual complementarity.[11] Not only does this decision render as the law of the land an understanding of marriage that contradicts the church's understanding based on both reason and revelation, but it will also likely lead to numerous legal challenges to religious liberty. Some Catholics will claim that this renewed and deepened tension between the church and the liberal state is an inevitable working out of liberalism, and that Catholics were naive ever to join with it as a partner. Others will say that the Catholic liberal synthesis remains defensible but is being challenged more sharply than ever by a rival secular liberalism. Still others may remain optimistic and confident that the Catholic liberal synthesis remains alive and well. Wherever one's sympathies lie, one can find the history and deep logic of this debate traced out in the essays that follow—and, if the past is prologue, in the pages of the *Review of Politics* in the years ahead.

Notes

1. United States Conference of Catholic Bishops, Ad Hoc Committee on Religious Liberty, "Our First, Most Cherished Liberty: A Statement on Religious Liberty," April 12, 2012. http://www.usccb.org/issues-and-action/religious-liberty/our-first-most-cherished-liberty.cfm.

2. See Leo XIII's encyclicals *Immortale Dei* (1885) and *On the Nature of Human Liberty* (1888).

3. See John Rawls, *Political Liberalism* (New York: Columbia University Press, 1993), xxii–xxvii; John Rawls, *The Law of Peoples* (Cambridge, MA: Harvard University Press, 1999), 19–23; John Rawls, "On My Religion," in *A Brief Inquiry into the Meaning of Sin and Faith*, ed. Thomas Nagel (Cambridge, MA: Harvard University Press, 2009); Mark Lilla, *The Stillborn God: Religion, Politics, and the Modern West* (New York: Alfred A. Knopf, 2007), 52–53, 73–74; and Pierre Manent, *An Intellectual History of Liberalism*, trans. Rebecca Balinski (Princeton, NJ: Princeton University Press, 1995), 115.

4. See Philip Jenkins, *The New Anti-Catholicism: The Last Acceptable Prejudice* (Oxford: Oxford University Press, 2003).

5. Bernard M. G. Reardon, *Liberalism and Tradition: Aspects of Catholic Thought in Nineteenth-Century France* (Cambridge: Cambridge University Press, 1975), 94–95.

6. Emile Perreau-Saussine, *Catholicism and Democracy: An Essay in the History of Political Thought* (Princeton, NJ: Princeton University Press, 2012), 57–58.

7. Quotation from Arline Boucher and John Tehan, *Prince of Democracy: James Cardinal Gibbons* (Garden City, NJ: Image, 1962), 158.

8. For an argument along these lines, see Martin Rhonheimer, "Benedict XVI's 'Hermeneutic of Reform' and Religious Freedom," *Nova et Vetera* 9, no. 4 (2011): 1029–54.

9. On this global promotion of democracy, see Daniel Philpott, "The Catholic Wave," *Journal of Democracy* 15, no. 2 (April 2004): 32–47.

10. The Finnis response, commissioned for this volume, did not appear in the *Review of Politics*, but a shorter version was published in the *American Journal of Jurisprudence* in 2015.

11. See Ryan T. Anderson, *Truth Overruled: The Future of Marriage and Religious Freedom* (Washington, DC: Regnery, 2015).

CHAPTER 1

The End of Machiavellianism

JACQUES MARITAIN

Jacques Maritain (1882–1973) was born in Paris and studied philosophy at the Sorbonne and the University of Heidelberg. His thinking was heavily influenced by his conversion to Catholicism. Before World War II, he moved to America, where he taught philosophy and Catholic theology at Columbia and Princeton and frequently lectured at other universities, such as the University of Chicago and the University of Notre Dame. Maritain understood himself to be a "critical realist," emphasizing metaphysics over epistemology and rejecting rationalist and positivist accounts of knowledge. As a so-called neo-Thomist, he argued against a rigid and unreflective understanding of scholasticism. But, like Aquinas, he maintained that reason and revelation are not fundamentally in opposition and that philosophy can demonstrate the truth of certain religious beliefs, for example, the existence of God. Maritain sought to ground human rights and duties in a conception of natural law that derived its purpose from the divine. At the same time, he held that Catholic teachings were fully compatible with science and democracy.

I

My purpose is to consider Machiavellianism.[1] Regarding Machiavelli himself, some preliminary observations seem necessary.

Innumerable studies, some of them very good, have been dedicated to Machiavelli. Jean Bodin, in the sixteenth century, criticized *The Prince* in a profound and wise manner. Later on Frederick the Great of Prussia was to write a refutation of Machiavelli in order to exercise his own hypocrisy in a hyper-Machiavellian fashion, and to shelter cynicism in virtue. During the nineteenth century, the leaders of the bourgeoisie, for instance the French political writer Charles Benoist, were thoroughly, naively, and stupidly fascinated by the clever Florentine.

As regards modern scholarship, I should like to note that the best historical commentary on Machiavelli has been written by an American scholar, Professor Allan H. Gilbert.[2] As regards more popular presentations, a remarkable edition of *The Prince* and the *Discourses* was recently issued by the Modern Library.

Max Lerner, in the stimulating, yet somewhat ambiguous introduction he wrote for this edition of *The Prince* and *The Discourses*, rightly observes that Machiavelli was expressing the actual ethos of his time, and that "power politics existed before Machiavelli was ever heard of, it will exist long after his name is only a faint memory."[3] This is perfectly obvious. But what matters, in this connection, is just that Machiavelli *lifted into consciousness* this ethos of his time and this common practice of the power politicians of all times. Here we are confronted with the fundamental importance, which I have often emphasized, of the phenomenon of "prise de conscience," and with the risks of perversion which this phenomenon involves.

Before Machiavelli, princes and conquerors did not hesitate to apply on many occasions bad faith, perfidy, falsehood, cruelty, assassination, every kind of crime of which the flesh and blood man is capable, to the attainment of power and success and to the satisfaction of their greed and ambition. But in so doing they felt guilty, they had a bad conscience—to the extent that they had a conscience. Therefore a specific kind of unconscious and unhappy hypocrisy—that is, the shame of appearing to oneself such as one is—a certain amount of self restraint, and that deep and deeply human uneasiness which we experience in doing what we do not want to do and what is forbidden by a law that we know to be true, prevented the crimes in question from becoming a rule, and provided governed peoples with a limping accommodation between good and evil which, in broad outline, made their oppressed lives, after all, livable.

After Machiavelli, not only the princes and conquerors of the *cinquecento*, but the great leaders and makers of modern states and modern history, in employing injustice for establishing order, and every kind of useful evil for satisfying their will to power, will have a clear conscience and feel that they accomplish their duty as political heads. Suppose they are not merely skeptical in moral matters, and have some religious and ethical convictions in connection with man's personal behavior, then they will be obliged, in connection with the field of politics, to put aside these convictions, or to place them in a parenthesis, they will stoically immolate their personal morality on the altar of the political good. What was a simple matter of fact, with all the weaknesses and inconsistencies pertaining, even in the evil, to accidental and contingent things, has become, after Machiavelli, a matter of right, with all the firmness and steadiness proper to necessary things. A plain disregard of good and evil has been considered the rule, not of human morality—Machiavelli never pretended to be a moral philosopher—but of human politics.

For not only do we owe to Machiavelli our having become aware and conscious of the immorality displayed, in fact, by the mass of political men, but by the same stroke he taught us that this very immorality is the very law of politics. Here is that Machiavellian perversion of politics which was linked, in fact, with the Machiavellian "prise de conscience" of average political behavior in mankind. The historic responsibility of Machiavelli consists in having *accepted*, recognized, endorsed as a rule the fact of political immorality, and in having stated that good politics, politics conformable to its true nature and to its genuine aims, is by essence non-moral politics.

Machiavelli belongs to that series of minds, and some of them much greater than himself, which all through modern times have endeavored to unmask the human being. To have been the first in this lineage is the greatness of the narrow thinker eager to serve the Medici as well as the popular party in Florence, and deceived on both sides. Yet in unmasking the human being he maimed its very flesh, and wounded its eyes. To have thoroughly rejected ethics, metaphysics and theology from the realm of political knowledge and political prudence is his very own achievement, and it is also the most violent mutilation suffered by the human practical intellect and the organism of practical wisdom.

Radical pessimism regarding human nature is the basis of Machiavelli's thought. After having stated that "a prudent ruler ought not to keep faith when by so doing it would be against his interest, and when the reasons which made him bind himself no longer exist," he writes: "If men were all good, this precept would not be a good one; but *as they are bad*, and would not observe their faith with you, so you are not bound to keep faith with them." Machiavelli knows that they are bad. He does not know that this badness is not radical, that this leprosy cannot destroy man's original grandeur, that human nature remains good in its very essence and its root- tendencies, and that such a basic goodness joined to a swarming multiplication of particular evils is the very mystery and the very motive of struggle and progression in mankind. Just as his horizon is merely terrestrial, just as his crude empiricism cancels for him the indirect ordainment of political life toward the life of souls and immortality, so his concept of man is merely animal, and his crude empiricism cancels for him the image of God in man—a cancellation which is the metaphysical root of every power politics and every political totalitarianism. As to their common and most frequent behavior, Machiavelli thinks, men are beasts, guided by covetousness and fear. But the prince is a man, that is, an animal of prey endowed with intelligence and calculation. In order to govern men, that is, to enjoy power, the prince must be taught by Chiron the centaur, and learn to become both a fox and a lion. Fear, animal fear, and animal prudence translated into human art and awareness, are accordingly the supreme rulers of the political realm.

Yet the pessimism of Machiavelli is extremely removed from any heroic pessimism. To the evil that he sees everywhere, or believes he sees everywhere, he gives his consent. He consents, he aspires to become a clearsighted composite of fox and lion. "For how we live," he says, "is so far removed from how we ought to live, that he who abandons what is done for what ought to be done, will rather learn to bring about his own ruin than his preservation." Therefore we have to abandon what *ought to be done* for *what is done*, and it is necessary for the prince, he also says, "to learn how not to be good, and to use this knowledge and not use it, according to the necessity of the case." And this is perfectly logical if the end of ends is only present success. Yet such an abandonment, such a resignation would be logical also, not only for political life, but for the entire field of human life. Descartes, in the provisory rules of morality which he gave himself in the *Discours de la Méthode*, made up his mind to imitate the actual customs and doings of his fellow-men, instead of practicing what they say we ought to do. He did not perceive that this was a good precept of immorality: for, as a matter of fact, men live more often by senses than by reason. It is easy to observe with Max Lerner that many Church princes, like the secular princes, and above all that Alexander VI whom Machiavelli gives often in example, were among the principal followers of Machiavelli's precepts. But never has any catechism taught that we must imitate the Church princes in our conduct, it is Christ that religion teaches us to imitate. The first step to be taken by everyone who wishes to act morally is to decide not to act according to the general customs and doings of his fellow men. This is a precept of the Gospel: "Do not ye after their works; for they say, and do not...."[4]

The practical result of Machiavelli's teachings has been, for modern conscience, a profound split, an incurable division between politics and morality, and consequently an illusory but deadly antinomy between what they call *idealism* (wrongly confused with ethics) and what they call *realism* (wrongly confused with politics). Henceforth, as Max Lerner puts it, "the polar conflict between the ethical and the ruthlessly realistic." I shall come back to this point. For the present I wish to note two kinds of complications which arise in this connection in the case of Machiavelli himself.

The first complication comes from the fact that Machiavelli, like many great pessimists, had a somewhat rough and elementary idea of moral science, plainly disregarding its realist, experiential, and existential character, and lifting up to heaven, or rather up to the clouds, an altogether naive morality which obviously cannot be practiced by the sad yet really living and laboring inhabitants of this earth. The man of ethics appears to him as a feeble-minded and disarmed victim, occasionally noxious, of the beautiful rules of some Platonist and separate world of perfection. On the other hand, and because such a morality is essentially a self-satisfying show of pure and lofty shapes—that is, a dreamed-up compensation for our muddy state—Machiavelli constantly slips from the idea of well-doing to the idea of what men admire as well-doing, from moral virtue to appearing and apparent moral virtue: his virtue is a virtue of opinion, self-satisfaction and glory. Accordingly, what he calls vice and evil, and considers to be contrary to virtue and morality, may sometimes be only the authentically moral behavior of a just man engaged in the complexities of human life and of true ethics: for instance, justice itself may call for relentless energy—which is neither vengeance nor cruelty—against wicked and false-hearted enemies. Or the toleration of some existing evil—if there is no furthering of or cooperating with the same—may be required for avoiding a greater evil or for slowing down and progressively reducing this very evil. Or even dissimulation is not always bad faith or knavery. It would not be moral, but foolish, to open up one's heart and inner thoughts to whatsoever dull or mischievous fellow. Stupidity is never moral, it is a vice. No doubt it is difficult to mark exactly the limits between cunning and lying, and even some great saints of the Old Testament—I am thinking of Abraham—did not take great care of this distinction. This was a consequence of what may be called the twilight status of moral conscience in the dawn-ages of mankind.[5] Yet a certain amount of cunning, if it is intended to deceive evil-disposed persons, must not be considered fox's wiles, but intellect's legitimate weapon. Oriental peoples know that very well, and even evangelical candor has to use the prudence of the serpent, as well as the simplicity of the dove (the dove tames the serpent, but the lion does not tame the fox). The question is to use such cunning without the smallest bit of falsehood or imposture: this is exactly the affair of intelligence; and the use of lying—namely the large-scale industrialisation of lying, of which contemporary dictatorships offer us the spectacle—appears from this point of view, not only as moral baseness, but also as vulgarity of mind and thorough degradation of intelligence.

The second complication arises from the fact that Machiavelli was a cynic operating on the given moral basis of civilized tradition, and whose cruel work of exposure took for granted the coherence and density of this deep-rooted tradition. Clear-sighted and intelligent as he was, he was perfectly aware of that fact; that is why he would pale at the sight of modern Machiavellianism. This commentator of Titus Livius was instructed by Latin tradition, he was a partaker as well as a squanderer of humanist learning, an inheritor as well as an opponent of the manifold treasure of knowledge prepared by Christian centuries, and degenerating in his day. He never negates the values of morality, he knows them and recognizes them as they have been established by ancient wisdom, he occasionally praises virtuous leaders (that is, whose virtues were made successful by circumstances), he knows that cruelty and faithlessness are shameful, he never calls evil good or good evil. He simply denies to moral values—and this is largely sufficient to corrupt politics—any application in the political field. He teaches his prince to be cruel and faithless, according to the case, that is, to be evil according to the case, and when he writes that the prince must learn how not to be good, he is perfectly aware that not to be good is to be bad. Hence his difference from many of his disciples, and the special savor, the special power of intellectual stimulation of his cynicism. But hence also his special sophistry, and the mantle of civilized intelligence with which he unintentionally covered and veiled for a time the deepest meaning, the wild meaning, of his message.

Finally, the "*grammar of power*" and the recipes of success written by Machiavelli are the work of a pure artist, and of a pure artist of that Italian Renaissance where the great heritage of the antique and Christian mind, falling in jeopardy, blossomed into the most beautiful, delightful, and poisonous flowers. What makes the study of Machiavelli extremely instructive for a philosopher, is the fact that nowhere is it possible to find a more purely artistic conception of politics.[6] And here is his chief philosophical fault, if it is true that politics belongs to the field of the "praktikon" (to do), not of the "poietikon" (to make), and is by essence a branch—the principal branch, according to Aristotle—of ethics. Politics is distinct from individual ethics as a branch from another branch on the same tree, it is a special and specific part of ethics, and it carries within itself an enormous amount of art and technique. It is organically, vitally and intrinsically subordinated to the molding intelligence, and imagination is much greater in political than in individual or even familial ethics. But all this amount of art and technique is organically vitally and intrinsically subordinated to the ethical energies which constitute politics, that is to say, art is there in no manner autonomous, art is there embodied in and encompassed with and lifted up by ethics, as the physico-chemical activities in our body are insubstantiated in our living substance and superelevated by our vital energies. When these merely physico-chemical activities are liberated and become autonomous, there is no longer a living organism, but a corpse. Thus, merely artistic politics, liberated from ethics, that is, from the practical knowledge of man, from the science of human acts, from truly human finalities and truly human doings, is a corpse of political wisdom and political prudence.

Indeed, Machiavelli's very own genius has been to disentangle as perfectly as possible all the content of art carried along by politics from the ethical substance thereof. His position therefore is that of a separate artistic spirit contemplating from without the vast matter of human affairs, with all the ethical cargo, all the intercrossings of good and evil they involve, and to teach his disciple how to conquer and maintain power in handling this matter as a sculptor handles clay or marble. Ethics is here present, but in the matter to be shaped and dominated. We understand from this point of view how *The Prince* as well as *The Discourses* are rich in true observations and sometimes in true precepts, but perceived and stated in a false light and in a reversed or perverted perspective. For Machiavelli makes use of good as well as of evil, and is ready to succeed with virtue as well as with vice. That specific concept of *virtù*, that is, of brilliant, well-balanced and skilled strength, which was at the core of the morality of his time, as an aesthetic and artistic transposition of the Aristotelian concept of virtue, is always present in his work.[7] He knows that no political achievement is lasting if the prince has not the friendship of the people, but it is not the good of the people, it is only the power of the prince which matters to him in this truth perversely taught. *The Discourses*[8] eloquently emphasize the fundamental importance of religion in the state, but the truth or falsity of any religion whatsoever is here perfectly immaterial, even religion is offered as the best means of cheating the people, and what Machiavelli teaches is "the use of a national religion for state purposes," by virtue of "its power as a myth in unifying the masses and cementing their morale"[9]: a perversion of religion which is surely worse and more atheistic than crude atheism—and the devastating effects of which the world may see and enjoy in the totalitarian plagues of today.

Here we are confronted with the paradox and the internal principle of instability of Machiavelli's Machiavellianism. It essentially supposes the complete eradication of moral values in the brain of the political artist as such, yet at the same time it also supposes the actual existence and actual vitality of moral values and moral beliefs in all others, in all the human matter that the prince is to handle and dominate. But it is impossible that the use of a supramoral, that is, a thoroughly immoral art of politics should not produce a progressive lowering and degeneration of moral values and moral beliefs in the common human life, a progressive disintegration of the inherited stock of stable structures and customs linked with these beliefs, and finally a progressive corruption of the ethical and social matter itself with which this supramoral politics deals. Thus, such an art wears away and destroys its very matter, and, by the same token, will degenerate itself. Hence Machiavelli could only have rare authentic disciples; during the classical centuries of Henry VIII and Elizabeth, Mazarin and Richelieu, Frederick, Catherine of Russia and Talleyrand, the latter was perhaps the only perfect pupil of Machiavelli; finally Machiavelli's teachings, which imply an essentially rational and well-measured, that is, an artistic use of evil, were to give place to that use of every kind of seemingly useful evil by great irrational and demonic forces and by an intelligence no longer artistic but vulgar and brutal and wild, and to that immersion of the rulers as well as of the ruled in a rotted ethics, calling good evil and evil good, which constitute the common Machiavellianism of today.

II

But so much for Machiavelli. It is this common Machiavellianism that I wish now to consider. In so doing, I should like briefly to touch the three following points: first, the notion of common good and the factual triumph of Machiavellianism; second, the crucial conflict which here constitutes the main problem, and the resolution thereof; third, the roots and the more subtle implications of this resolution, which concern the specific structure of politics in its relationship with morality.

Now for my first point. For Machiavelli the end of politics is power's conquest and maintenance, which is a work of art to be performed. On the contrary, according to the nature of things, the end of politics is the common good of a united people; which end is essentially something concretely human, therefore something ethical. This common good consists of the good life—that is, a life conformable to the essential exigencies and the essential dignity of human nature, a life both morally straight and happy—of the social whole as such, of the gathered multitude, in such a way that the increasing treasure and heritage of communicable good things involved in this good life of the whole be in some way spilled over and redistributed to each individual part of the community. This common good is at once material, intellectual, and moral, and principally moral, as man himself is; it is a common good of human persons. Therefore, it is not only something useful, an ensemble of advantages and profits, it is essentially something good in itself—what the Ancients termed *bonum honestum*. Justice and civic friendship are its cement. Bad faith, perfidy, lying, cruelty, assassination, and all other procedures of this kind which may occasionally appear *useful* to the power of the ruling clique or to the prosperity of the state, are in themselves—insofar as political deeds, that is, deeds involving in some degree the common conduct—injurious to the common good and tend by themselves toward its corruption. Finally, because good life on earth is not the absolute ultimate end of man, and because the human person has a destiny superior to time, political common good involves an intrinsic though indirect reference to the absolutely ultimate end of the human members of society, which is eternal life, in such a way that the political community should temporally, and from below, help each human person in his human task of conquering his final freedom and fulfilling his final destiny.

Such is the basic political concept which Machiavellianism broke down and destroyed. If the aim of politics is common good, peace—a constructive peace struggling through time toward man's emancipation from any form of enslavement—is the health of the state; and the organs of justice, above all of distributive justice, are the chief power in the state. If the aim of politics is power, war is the health of the state, as Machiavelli put it, and military strength is the chief power in the state. If the aim of politics is common good, the ruler, having to take care of the temporal end of a community of human persons, and having to avoid in this task any lack of clear-sightedness and any slip of will, must learn to be, as St. Thomas taught, a man good in every respect, *bonus vir simpliciter*. If the aim of politics is power, the ruler must learn not to be good, as Machiavelli said.

The great rulers of modern times have well understood and conscientiously learned this lesson. Lord Acton was right in stating that "the authentic interpreter of Machiavelli is the whole of later history."[10] We have to distinguish, however, two kinds of common Machiavellianism. There was a kind of more or less attenuated, dignified, conservative Machiavellianism, using injustice within "reasonable" limits, if I may put it so. In the minds of its followers, what is called *Realpolitik* was obfuscated and more or less paralyzed, either by a personal pattern of moral scruples and moral rules, which they owed to the common heritage of our civilization, or by traditions of diplomatic good form and respectability, or even, in certain instances, by lack of imagination, of boldness, and of inclination to take risks. If I try to characterize more precisely these moderate Machiavellians, I should say that they preserved in some way, or believed they preserved, regarding the *end* of politics, the concept of common good—they were unfaithful to their master in this regard; and that they frankly used Machiavellianism regarding the means of procuring this common good. Such an unnatural split and disproportion between means and ends was, moreover, inevitably to lead to a perversion of the idea of common good itself, which became more and more a set of material advantages and profits for the state, or territorial conquests, or prestige and glory. The greatest representative of moderate Machiavellianism was, in my opinion, Richelieu. Bismarck was a transition from this first form of Machiavellianism to the second one, of which I shall now speak.

This second form of Machiavellianism is absolute Machiavellianism. It was intellectually prepared, during the nineteenth century, by the Positivist trend of mind, which considered politics to be, not a mere art, but a mere natural science, like astronomy or chemistry, and a mere application of so-called "scientific laws" to the struggle for life of human societies—a concept much less intelligent and still more inhuman than that of Machiavelli himself. Absolute Machiavellianism was also and principally prepared by the Romanticist German philosophy of Fichte and Hegel. It is well known that Fichte made an analysis of Machiavelli part of his *Address to the German Nation*: as to the Hegelian cult of the state, it is a metaphysical sublimation of Machiavelli's principles. Now the turn has been completed, ethics itself has been swallowed up into the political denial of ethics, power and success have become supreme moral criteria, "the course of world history stands apart from virtue, blame and justice," as Hegel put it, and at the same time "human history," he also said, "is God's judgment." Machiavellianism is no longer politics, it is metaphysics, it is a religion, a prophetical and mystical enthusiasm.

It sufficed for such an enthusiasm to enter into some desperados who were empty, as it were, of the usual characters of rational personality, but open to the great collective forces of instinct, resentment, and tellurian inspiration; it sufficed for such leaders to give a full practical significance to the old infernal discovery of the endless reserves of evil when thoroughly accepted and utilized, and of the seemingly infinite power of that which negates, of the dissolving forces and of the corruption of human consciences—in order for absolute Machiavellianism to arise in the world, and in order for the unmasking Centaur to be unmasked in its turn.[11] Here we are confronted with that impetuous, irrational, revolutionary, wild, and demoniacal Machiavellianism, for which *boundless* injustice, *boundless* violence, *boundless* lying and immorality, are normal political means, and which draws from this very boundlessness of evil an abominable strength. And we may experience what kind of common good a power which knows perfectly how not to be good, and whose hypocrisy is a conscious and happy, ostentatious and gloriously promulgated hypocrisy, and whose cruelty wants to destroy souls as well as bodies, and whose lying is a thorough perversion of the very function of language, what kind of common good such a power is able to bring to mankind. Absolute Machiavellianism causes politics to be the art of bringing about the misfortune of men.

That's how it is. But absolute Machiavellianism succeeds, does it not? At least it has succeeded for many years. How could it not succeed, when everything has been sacrificed to the aim of success? Here is the ordeal and the scandal of contemporary conscience. Moreover it would be astonishing if a timid and limited Machiavellianism were not overcome and thrown away by a boundless and cynical Machiavellianism, stopping at nothing. If there is an answer to the deadly question which we are asked by the Sphinx of history, it can only lie in a thorough reversal of a century-old political thought. In the meantime, the peoples which stand against absolute Machiavellianism will be able to stop its triumphs and to overcome its standard-bearers only in wasting and sacrificing in this struggle their blood and their wealth and their dearest treasures of peaceful civilization, and in turning against this Machiavellianism its own material weapon, material techniques and gigantic means of destruction. But will they be obliged, in order to conquer it and to maintain themselves, to adopt not only its material weapons, but also its own spirit and philosophy? Will they yield to the temptation of losing for the sake of life their very reason for living and existing?

III

Here we arrive at the crucial conflict which I intend to discuss as my second point.

Confronted with any temptation of Machiavellianism, that is, of gaining success and power by means of evil, moral conscience answers and cannot keep from answering, just as when it is tempted by any profitable fault: it is never allowed to do evil for any good whatsoever. And Christian conscience in this case is strengthened by the very word of the Gospel. When the devil tempted Jesus by showing him all the kingdoms of the world, and the glory of them, and telling him: "All these things will I give thee, if thou wilt fall down and worship me," Jesus answered, "Get thee hence, Satan. For it is written, Thou shalt worship the Lord thy God, and him only shalt thou serve."[12]

Such is the answer that the human person, looking up to his own destiny as a person, to his immortal soul, his ultimate end and everlasting life, to his God, gives to politics when politics offers him the kingdoms of the world at the price of his soul. This answer, and the personage to whom it was given, show us the root significance of politics making itself absolutely autonomous, and claiming to be man's absolutely ultimate end. It shows us the transcendent meaning of the pagan empire, and of any paganized empire, and of any self-styled holy empire if its Caesar—be he a Christian emperor or a socialist dictator, or any kind of Great Inquisitor in the sense of Dostoyevsky's famous legend—wills to settle and manage on earth the final kingdom of God or the final kingdom of man, which is the same final kingdom. "Get thee hence, Satan," answers Christ. State and politics, when truly separated from ethics are the realm of those demoniacal principalities which St. Paul spoke of. The pagan empire is the empire of man making himself God, the diametrical opposite of the kingdom of redemptive incarnation.

Yet the answer we are considering does not solve our conflict. On the contrary, it increases this conflict, it widens the tear to the infinite, it clamps down on the Machiavellian temptation without appeasing the anguish and scandal of our intellect. For it is an answer given by personal ethics to a question asked by political ethics; it transcends the question, as the person, with regard to his eternal destiny, transcends the state; it cuts short the question, it does not resolve it. Obviously no assertion of the individual ethics of the person, as absolutely true, absolutely decisive as it may be, can constitute a sufficiently adequate and relevant answer to a problem stated by the ethics of the state. Exactly because it is a transcendent answer, it is not a proper one. Machiavellianism succeeds, does it not? Absolute Machiavellianism triumphs on earth, as our eyes have seen it for years. Is morality willing, is Christianity willing, is God willing that, of necessity, all our freedoms be conquered, our civilization destroyed, the very hope annihilated of seeing a little justice and brotherly amity raise our earthly life—willing that, of necessity, our lives be enslaved, our temples and institutions broken down, our brethren persecuted and crushed, our children corrupted, our very souls and intelligence delivered over to perversion by the great imperial standard-bearers of Machiavellianism, because of the very fact that we adhere to justice and refuse the devil, while they dare to use injustice and evil and accede to the devil up to the end?

It is the true goal of the *person* which is eternal, not that of the *state*. If a man suffers martyrdom and enters paradise, his own soul enjoys bliss. But suppose all the citizens of a tributary state of some Nero suffer martyrdom and enter paradise, it is not the soul of this state which will enjoy bliss; moreover, this state no longer exists. The state has no immortal soul, nor has a nation, unless perhaps as concerns a merely spiritual survival of its common moral heritage in the memory of men or in the virtues of the immortal souls which animated its members long ago, at the time when it existed. It is a joke to console Frenchmen and ask them to accept the destruction or the enslavement of France in speaking to them of *la France éternelle*. The soul of a nation is not immortal. The direct and specifying end, the common good of a nation is something temporal and terrestrial, something which can and should be superelevated by Gospel virtues in its own order, but whose own order is natural, not supernatural, and belongs to the realm of time. Therefore the very existence, temporal and terrestrial, the very improvement, temporal and terrestrial, the very prosperity of a nation, and that amount of happiness and glory which arises from the crises themselves and from the ordeals of history, really and essentially pertain to the common good of this nation.

No doubt—to imagine a thoroughly extreme example—a nation or a state could and should accept destruction, as did the legion of Mauritius, if its citizens were summoned to choose between martyrdom and apostasy; but such a case would not be a political case, it would be a case of sacrifice of political life itself to divine life, and a witnessing, in some way miraculous, of the superiority of the order of grace over the order of nature. But in political life itself, in the order of nature, in the framework of the temporal laws of human existence, is it not impossible that the first of the normal means of providing the common good of a state, that is, justice and political morality, should lead to the ruin and disaster of this state? Is it not impossible that the first of the means of corrupting the common good of a state, that is, injustice and political treachery, should lead to the triumph and prosperity of this state?

Yes, this is impossible.

Yet Machiavellianism succeeds in political history? Evil succeeds?

What is then the answer?

The answer is that evil *does not* succeed. In reality Machiavellianism does not succeed. To destroy is not to succeed. Machiavellianism succeeds in bringing about the misfortune of man, which is the exact opposite of any genuinely political end. More or less bad Machiavellians have succeeded for centuries against other more or less bad Machiavellians, this is mere exchange of counterfeit coin. Absolute Machiavellianism succeeds against moderate or weak Machiavellianism, this also is normal. But if absolute Machiavellianism were to succeed absolutely and definitely in the world, this would simply mean that political life would have disappeared from the face of the earth, giving place to an entanglement and commixture of the life of the animals and the slaves, and of the life of the saints.

But in saying that evil and injustice do not succeed in politics, I mean a more profound philosophical truth. The endless reserves of evil, the seemingly infinite power of evil of which I spoke a moment ago, are only, in reality, the power of corruption—the squandering and dissipation of the substance and energy of Being and of Good. Such a power destroys itself in destroying that good which is its subject. The inner dialectic of the successes of evil condemn them not to be lasting. The true philosophical answer consists therefore in taking into account the dimension of time, the duration proper to the historical turns of nations and states, which considerably exceeds the duration of a man's life. According to this *political duration* of vital maturations and fructifications, I do not say that a just politics will, even in a distant future, always actually succeed, nor that Machiavellianism will, even in a distant future, always actually fail. For, with nations and states and civilizations we are in the order of nature, where mortality is natural and where life and death depend on physical as well as moral causes. I say that justice works through its own causality toward welfare and success in the future, as a healthy sap works toward the perfect fruit, and that Machiavellianism works through its own causality for ruin and bankruptcy, as poison in the sap works for the illness and death of the tree.

Now, what is the illusion proper to Machiavellianism? It is the illusion *of immediate success*. The duration of the life of a man, or rather the duration of the activity of the prince, of the political man, circumscribes the maximum length of time required by what I call *immediate success*, for immediate success is a success that our eyes may see. But what we are speaking of, what Machiavelli is speaking of, in saying that evil and injustice succeed in politics, is in reality *immediate success*, as I have defined it. Now immediate success is success for a man, it is not success for a state or a nation. It may be—it is, in the case of Machiavellian successes considered as to their inner causal law, a disaster according to the duration proper to state-vicissitudes and nation-vicissitudes. It is with regard to immediate success that evil and injustice enjoy a seemingly infinite power: a power which can be met and overcome only by a heroic tension of the antagonistic powers. But the more dreadful in intensity such a power of evil appears, the weaker in historic duration are the internal improvements, and the vigor of life, which have been gained by a state using this power.

As I have already put it in other studies, the good in which the state's justice bears fruit, the misfortune in which the state's injustice bears fruit, have nothing to do with the immediate and visible results; historic *duration* must be taken into account; the temporal good in which the state's justice fructifies, the temporal evil in which its iniquity bears its fruit, may be and are in fact quite different from the immediate results which the human mind might have expected and which the human eyes contemplate. It is as easy to disentangle these remote causations as to tell at a river's mouth which waters come from which glaciers and which tributaries. The achievements of the great Machiavellians seem durable to us, because our scale of duration-measurements is an exceedingly small one, with regard to the time proper to nations and human communities. We do not understand the fair play of God, who gives those who have freely chosen injustice the time to exhaust the benefits of it and the fullness of its energies. When disaster comes to these victors the eyes of the righteous who cried against them to God will have long putrefied under the earth, and men will not know the distant source of the catastrophe.

Thus it is true that politics being something intrinsically moral, the first political condition of good politics is that it be just. And it is true at the same time that justice and virtue do not, as a rule, lead us to success in this world. But the antinomy is solved, because on the one hand success in politics is not material power nor material wealth nor world-domination, but the achievement of the common good, with the conditions of material prosperity which it involves. And because, on the other hand, these very conditions of material prosperity, as terrible as the ordeals may be which the requirements of justice impose on a people, are not and cannot be put in jeopardy or to destruction by the use of justice itself, if historical duration is taken into account and if the specific effect of this use of justice is considered in itself, apart from the effect of the other factors at play.

I do not mean that God recompenses the just peoples by the blessings of military triumphs, territorial aggrandizements, accumulation of wealth, or infinite profit in business: such values are but secondary, sometimes even injurious to the political common good. Moreover, if it is true that the political life of peoples may be enveloped in its own order by Christian influences, it may be that a Christian nation has to undergo in a measure the very law of evangelical trials, and to pay for a certain abundance of spiritual or cultural improvements at the price of certain weaknesses and infirmities in worldly values. Such was the case of Italy in the Middle Ages and the Renaissance. Never did Italy know a more splendid civilization, than in those times when the power of the Popes brought her, as Machiavelli points out, weakness and pain regarding her political unity. Nor do I mean that a state using political justice is by this fact alone protected against ruin or destruction. What I mean is that in such a misfortune the very cause of ruin or destruction is never the use of justice. What I mean is that the very order of nature and of natural laws in moral matters, which is the natural justice of God, makes justice and political righteousness work towards fructifying, in the long run, as regards their own law of action, into an improvement of the true common good and the real values of civilization. Such was the case for the policy of St. Louis, although he was beaten in all his enterprises of crusade. Political injustices, on the other hand, political treacheries, political greed, selfishness or cowardice, exploitation of the poor and the weak, intoxication with power or glory or self-interest—or that kind of political cleverness which consists, as a professor in international policy told me candidly some years ago, in using flattery and leniency toward our enemy, because he is an enemy, and therefore is to be feared, and in forsaking our friend, because he is a friend, and therefore is not to be feared—or that kind of political firmness which consists in denouncing some predatory state which is attacking a weak nation, and in selling weapons and supplies to the same aggressor, because business must keep going—all this is always dearly paid for in the end. Wars, even just wars which must be waged against iniquitous aggressors, are often the payment thus exacted from a civilization.[13] Then war must be waged with unshaken resolution. But victory will be fruitful only on the condition of casting away the wrongdoings of the past, and of decidedly converting oneself toward justice and political righteousness.

The more I think of these things, the more I am convinced that the observations I proposed a moment ago on the dimension of time are the core of the question. To be lasting is an essential characteristic of the common good. A forester who would seek immediate visible success in planting plenty of big old trees in his forest, instead of preparing young saplings, would use a foolish forester policy. Machiavelli's prince is a bad political man, he perverts politics, because his chief aim is his own personal power and the satisfaction of his own personal ambition. But, in a much more profound and radical sense, the ruler who sacrifices everything to the desire of his own eyes to see the triumph of his policy is a bad ruler and perverts politics, even if he lacks personal ambition and loves his country disinterestedly: because he measures the time of maturation of the political good according to the short years of his own personal time of activity.

As regards the great representatives of contemporary Machiavellianism, with their mad lust for personal power, nothing is more instructive in this connection than the ferocious impatience of their general policy. They apply the law of war, which requires a series of immediate striking successes, but which is a supreme and abnormal crisis in the life of human societies, to the very development of the normal life of the state. In so doing, they appear, not as empire-builders, but as mere squanderers of the heritage of their nations.

Yet a fructification which will come into existence in a distant future but which we do not see, is for us as immaterial as a fructification which would never exist on earth. To act with justice, without picking any fruit of justice, but only fruits of bitterness and sorrow and defeat, is difficult for a man. It is still more difficult for a man of politics, even for a just and wise one—who works at an earthly work that is the most arduous and the highest among temporal works—the common good of the multitude—and whose failures are the failures of an entire people and of a dear country. He must live on hope. Is it possible to live on hope without living on faith? Is it possible to rely on the unseen without relying on faith?

I do not believe that men in politics can escape the temptation of Machiavellianism, if they do not believe that there exists a supreme government of the universe, which is, properly speaking, divine, for God—the head of the cosmos—is also the head of this particular order which is that of ethics. [They also cannot avoid this temptation][14] if they do not entrust the providence of God, by faith, with the care of all that supra-empirical, dark and mysterious disentanglement of the fructifications of good and evil which no human eye can perceive—thus closing their eyes, by faith, as regards the factual achievements in the distant future, while they open their eyes and display, by knowledge and prudence, more watchfulness than any fox or lion, as regards the preparations of these achievements and the seeds to be presently put into the earth.

A merely natural political morality is not enough to provide us with the means of putting its own rules into practice. Moral conscience does not suffice, if it is not at the same time religious conscience. What is able to face Machiavellianism, moderate Machiavellianism and absolute Machiavellianism, is not merely natural, as it were, just politics, it is Christian politics. For, in the existential context of the life of mankind, politics, because it belongs by its very essence to the ethical realm, demands consequently to be helped and strengthened, in order not to deviate and in order to attain a sufficiently perfect point of maturation, by everything man receives, in his social life itself, from religious belief and from the word of God working within him. This is what the authors of the Declaration of Independence and of the Constitution of this country understood and expressed in a form adapted to the philosophy of their time, and what makes their accomplishment so outstanding to the mind of everyone who believes Christianity to be efficacious not only for heaven but also for earth: among modern states, there is one state to whose political instinct and understanding Machiavellianism is basically repugnant, this one is the United States. Christian politics is neither theocratic nor clerical, nor yet a politics of pseudo-evangelical weakness and non-resistance to evil, but a genuinely political politics, ever aware that it is situated in the order of nature and must put into practice natural virtues; that it must be armed with real and concrete justice, with force, perspicacity and prudence; a politics which would hold the sword that is the attribute of the state, but which would also realize that peace is the work not only of justice but of love, and that love is also an essential part of political virtue. For it is never excess of love that fools political men, but without love and generosity there is regularly blindness and miscalculation. Such a politics would be mindful of the eternal destiny of man and of the truths of the Gospel, knowing in its proper order—in a measure adapted to its temporal ends—something of the spirits of love, and of forgiveness.

IV

We arrive now at the third consideration I indicated at the beginning, in which I should like to make clearer certain particular points concerning the relationship between politics and morality.

As I have previously pointed out, political reality, though principally moral, is by essence both moral and physical, as man himself, but in a different manner from man, because it does not have any substantial immortal soul. Societies are like ever-growing organisms, immense and long-living trees, or coral-flowers, which would lead at the same time a moral and human life. And in the order to which they belong, which is that of Time and Becoming, death is natural; human communities, nations, states and civilizations naturally die, and die for all time, as would these morally-living coral-flowers of which I just spoke. Their birth, growth and decay, their health, their diseases, their death, depend on basic physical conditions, in which the specific qualities of moral behavior are intermingled and play an essential part, but which are more primitive than these qualities. Similarly, imprudence or intemperance may hasten the death of a man, self-control may defer this death, yet in any case this man will die.

Justice and moral virtues do not prevent the natural laws of senescence of human societies. They do not prevent physical catastrophes from destroying them. In what sense are they the chief forces of the preservation and duration of societies? In the sense that they compose the very soul of society, its internal and spiritual force of life. Such a force does not secure immortality to the society, no more than my immortal soul protects me from death. Such a force is not an immortal entelechy, because it is not substantial; yet, insofar as it is spiritual, it is by itself indestructible. Corrupt this force, and an internal principle of death is introduced into the core of the society. Maintain and improve this force, and the internal principle of life is strengthened in the society. Suppose a human community is hammered, crushed, overwhelmed by some natural calamity or some powerful enemy: as long as it still exists—if it preserves within itself justice and civic friendship and faith, there is actual hope of resurging within itself, there is a force within itself which tends by itself to make it live and get the upper hand and avail itself of disaster; because no hammer can destroy this immaterial force. If a human community loses these virtues, its internal principle of life is invaded by death.

What therefore must be said, is that justice and righteousness *tend by themselves* to the preservation of states, and to that real *success* at long range of which I spoke a moment ago. And that injustice and evil *tend by themselves* to the destruction of states, and to that real *failure* at long range of which I also spoke.

Such is the law of the fructification of human actions which is inscribed in the nature of things and which is but the natural justice of God in human history.

But if the normal fruit of success and prosperity called for by political justice and wisdom does not come into actual existence because the tree is too old or because some storm has broken its branches; or if the normal fruit of failure and destruction, called for by political wickedness and madness, does not come into actual existence because the physical conditions in the sap or in the environment have counterbalanced the internal principle of death—such an accident does not suppress that regularity inherent in the law which I emphasized in the previous part of this essay, and only bears witness to the fact that nations and civilizations are naturally mortal. As I pointed out some moments ago, justice may sometimes, even in a distant future, not actually succeed in preserving a state from ruin and destruction. But justice tends by itself to this preservation; and it is not by virtue of justice, it is by virtue of physical conditions counterbalancing from without the very effects of justice that misfortune will then occur. Machiavellianism and political perversion may sometimes, even in a distant future, not actually break, they may triumph decisively over weak and innocent peoples. But they tend by themselves to self destruction; and it is not by virtue of Machiavellianism and political perversion, it is by virtue of other conditions counterbalancing from without the very effects of these, that success will then occur.

If a weak state is surrounded and threatened by Machiavellian enemies, it must desperately increase its physical power, but also its moral virtues. Suppose it delivers its own soul to Machiavellianism—then it only adds a principle of death to its already existing weaknesses. If a civilization grown old and naturally bound to die, as the Roman Empire was at the time of St. Augustine, if a political state artificially and violently built up, and naturally bound to fail, as was the German Reich of Bismarck and Wilhelm, wished none the less to escape either death or failure by letting loose evil and perversion, then it would only poison centuries and prepare for itself a historical hell worse than death.

It seems not irrelevant to add the two following observations. First: innumerable are, in the history of mankind, the cases where the strong have triumphed over the weak; yet this was not always a triumph of strength over right, for most often right's sanctity was as immaterial to the conquered weak as it was to the conquering strong. Greece was conquered by Rome (and was to conquer intellectually Roman civilization): at that time Greece had lost its political soul.

Second: As to the lasting or seemingly lasting triumphs of political injustice over innocent people, they also are not rare, at least at first glance. They concern most often, however, the enslavement, sometimes the destruction, of populations or human groups not yet arrived at a truly political status by nations enjoying this very status—of such a fact the most striking instance is to be found in the history of modern colonization. But it seems that in proportion as peoples arrive at a truly political status, and really constitute a *civitas*, a political house and community, in this proportion the immaterial internal force which abides in them and is made up of long-lived justice and love and moral energies, and of deep-rooted memories, and of a specific spiritual heritage, becomes a more and more *formed* and cohesive soul; and in this very proportion this soul takes precedence over the merely physical conditions of existence and tends to render such peoples unconquerable. If they are conquered and oppressed, they remain alive and keep on struggling under oppression. Then an instinct of prophecy develops among them, as in Poland at the time of Mickiewicz,[15] and their hopes naturally lift up toward the supernatural example of any historical perennity in the midst of oppression, the example of the house of Israel, whose internal immaterial force and principle of communion is of a supra-political and supra-temporal order.

Yet a final question arises now, which is of a rather metaphysical nature. I have said that the natural laws, according to which political justice fructifies by itself into the good and the preservation of a given human community, evil and political injustice into its destruction, are to be identified with the natural justice of God in human history. But is not an essential tendency only connoted here? Did I not emphasize the fact that even at long range such normal fructifications may fail, that the fruit of evil for the unjust state, the fruit of good for the just one, may be marred, because of the physical factors and particularly because of the physical laws of senescence and death which interfere here with the moral factors? If this is the case, where is the natural justice of God? Justice does not deal with tendencies, as essential as they may be, whose factual result may fail to appear, it deals with sanctions which never fail.

The question we are facing here transcends the field of moral philosophy and historical experience, and deals with the knowledge we are able to stammer of the divine government of created things. The first answer which comes to the mind of a Christian metaphysician consists in affirming a priori that the natural fructifications of good and evil never fail, the fruit of justice and the fruit of injustice are never marred: which seems self-evident, since the justice of God cannot be deceived. Because states and nations have no immortal destiny, not only must the sanctions deserved by their deeds reach men within time and upon the earth, but they must do so in an absolutely infallible manner.

In considering the problem more attentively, I believe, however, that this answer results from a kind of undue reverberation of considerations pertaining to theology upon metaphysical matters, which causes things which belong to time and history to be endowed with that absolute firmness which is proper to things relating to eternity.

It is perfectly true that God's justice cannot fail as regards the immortal destiny of each human person, which is accomplished in fact, according to Christianity's teachings, in the supernatural order. Yet it would be too hasty a procedure simply to conceive the divine justice which rules the historical fate of human societies, according to the pattern of that divine justice which rules the suprahistorical destiny of the human person. In these two cases justice applies to its subject-matter in an analogical fashion. The supra-historical justice cannot fail, because it reaches moral agents—the human persons—who attain their final state, above time. But the historical justice, dealing with human societies, reaches moral agents who do not attain any final state: there is no final sanction for them, sanctions are spread out for them all along time, and intermingled at each moment with their continuing and changing activity; often the fruit of ancient injustice starts up into existence at the very moment when a revival of justice occurs in a given society. Moreover, and by the same token, it appears that these sanctions *in the making* do not enjoy that absolute necessity which is linked with the immutability of some ultimate, eternal accomplishment. What seemed to us, a moment ago, to be self-evident, is not self-evident. It is possible that in the case of human societies the natural fructifications of good and evil be sometimes marred. The sanctions deserved by the deeds of nations and states must reach men within time and upon the earth, yet it is not necessary that they do so in a manner absolutely infallible and always realized.

Consider the civilization of the peoples which lived on legendary Atlantis. The good and bad political deeds of these peoples tended by themselves to bear fruit and to engender their natural sanctions. Yes, but when Atlantis was engulfed by the Ocean, all these fruits to come were cancelled from being as well as the peoples and the civilization from which they were to spring forth. The natural justice of God, as regards human societies, that is, moral agents immerged in time, may fail just as nature may fail in its physical fructifications. Because this natural historical justice of God is nothing else than nature itself in its not physical, but moral fructifications. God's justice is at work in time and history, it reigns only in heaven and in hell. The concept of perfect and infallible retribution for human deeds, with its absolute adamantine strength, is a religious concept relating to the eternal destiny of human persons; it is not the ethical-philosophical concept which has to be shaped relating to the destiny of human communities in time and history.

Such is the answer which appears to me the true answer to be made to the question we are considering. But we must immediately add that these failures of historical justice are to occur in the fewest number of cases, just as do the failures of nature in the physical order, because they are accidents, in which the very laws of essences do not reach their own effect. There is, indeed, in nature an immense squandering of seeds in order that a few may have the chance of springing up, and still fewer the chance of bearing fruit. Even if the failures of natural historical justice were *abnormities as regards individual accomplishment*, as frequent as the failures of so many wasted seeds, the truth that I am pointing out throughout this essay would none the less remain unshaken: namely, that justice tends by itself toward the welfare and survival of the community, injustice toward its damage and dissolution, and that any long-range success of Machiavellianism is never due to Machiavellianism itself, but to other historical factors at play. Yet the abnormities which really occur *ut in paucioribus* in physical nature are *abnormities as regards specific accomplishment*—as is the production of something deviating from the very essence of the species, the production of "freaks." And it is with such physical abnormities as regards specific accomplishment that the failures of the natural fructifications of good and evil, the failures in the accomplishment of the specific laws of moral essences, must rather be compared. We must therefore emphasize more strongly than ever the fact—which I have already stressed in a previous section—that the sanctions of historical justice fail much more rarely than our short-sighted experience might induce us to believe.

Here a new observation seems to me particularly noticeable. These sanctions, which have been deserved by the deeds of the social or political whole, must not necessarily reverberate on this political whole as such, on the state itself in its existence and power. They may concern the common cultural condition of men considered apart from the actual framework of this whole, yet in some kind of solidarity with the latter: because the political whole is not a substantial or personal subject, but a community of human persons, and a community related to other communities through vital exchanges. Thus, during the life of a state the fruit of its just or perverted deeds may appear only in some particular improvement or plague of its internal strata; but still more, when a state, a nation, a civilization dies, it is normal that the fructifications of good and evil which its deeds had prepared pass over—in the cultural order and as regards such or such a feature of the common social or cultural status—to its remnants, to the scattered human elements which had been contained in its unity and to their descendants, or to the human communities which are its successors and inheritors.

Then a state or a civilization dissolves, but its good or bad works continue to bear fruit, not strictly political (for the word political, in its strictest sense, connotes the common life of a given state), yet political in a broader and still genuine sense, which relates to the cultural life and to the common cultural heritage of mankind. For there exists a genuine temporal community of mankind—a deep intersolidarity, from generation to generation, linking together the peoples of the earth—a common heritage and a common fate, which does not concern the building of a particular *civil society*, but of a *civilization*, not the prince, but the culture, not the perfect *civitas* in the Aristotelian sense, but that kind of *civitas*, in the Augustinian sense, which is imperfect and incomplete, made up of a fluid network of human communications, and more existential than formally organized, but all the more real and living and basically important. To ignore this non-political *civitas humani generis* is to atomize the basis of political reality, to fail in the very roots of political philosophy, as well as to disregard the progressive trend which naturally tends toward a more organic international structure of peoples.

Thus another fundamental consideration must be added to that of *historic duration*, which I emphasized some time ago: namely the consideration of the *human extension*, down through generations, of the fructifications of political deeds. Then we see in a complete manner the law which binds Machiavellianism to failure, as a rule and as regards the essential tendencies inscribed in nature. If, even at long range, political justice and political injustice do not ever fructify into the political success or disaster of the state itself which has practiced them, they may still produce their fruit according to the laws of human solidarity. By the same stroke we perceive Machiavellianism's mischievousness, weakness and absurdity in their full implications. It is not only for particular states that it prepares misfortune and scourges—first the victims of Machiavellian states, then the Machiavellian states themselves—it is also for the human race in general. It burdens mankind with an ever-growing burden of evil, unhappiness and disaster. By its own weight and its own internal law it brings about failure, not only with reference to given nations, but with reference to our common kind, with reference to the root community of nations. Just as every other sort of selfishness, this divinized selfishness is essentially blind.

To sum up all that I have stated, I would say first: It suffices to be just in order to gain eternal life; this does not suffice in order to gain battles or immediate political successes.

Second: In order to gain battles or immediate political successes, it is not necessary to be just, it may occasionally be more advantageous to be unjust.

Third: It is necessary, although it is not sufficient, to be just, in order to procure and further the political common good, and the lasting welfare of earthly communities.

The considerations I have developed in my essay are founded on the basic fact that politics is a branch of ethics but a branch specifically distinct from the other branches of the same generic stock. One decisive sign of this specificity of political ethics in contradistinction to personal ethics is that earthly communities are mortal as regards their very being and belong entirely to time. Another sign is that political virtues tend to a relatively ultimate end which is the earthly common good, and are only indirectly related to the absolutely ultimate end of man. Hence many features of political ethics which I can only allude to here, and which secure its truly realist quality; in such a way that many rules of political life, which the pessimists of Machiavellianism usurp to the benefit of immorality, like the political toleration of certain evils and the recognition of the *fait accompli* (the so-called "statute of limitations") which permits the retention of long ago ill-gotten gains, because new human ties and vital relationships have infused them with new-born rights, are in reality ethically grounded; and in such a way that political ethics is able to absorb and digest all the elements of truth contained in Machiavelli, namely, to the extent that power and immediate success are part of politics, but a subordinate part, not the principal part.

May I repeat that a certain hypermoralism, causing political ethics to be something impracticable and merely ideal, is as contrary to this very ethics as Machiavellianism is, and finally plays the game of Machiavellianism, as conscientious objectors play the game of the conquerors. The purity of means consists in not using means morally bad in themselves, it does not consist in refusing pharisaically any exterior contact with the mud of human life, and it does not consist in waiting for a morally aseptic world before consenting to work in the world, nor does it consist in waiting, before saving one's neighbor, who is drowning, to become a saint, so as to escape any risk of false pride in such a generous act.

If this were the time to present a complete analysis of the particular causes of lasting success and welfare in politics, I should add two observations here. First: While political justice—which is destroyed both by the perversion, that is, by Machiavellianism, and by the distraction of ethics, that is, by hypermoralism—is the prime spiritual condition of lasting success and welfare for a nation as well as for a civilization, the prime *material* condition of this lasting success and welfare is on the one hand that heritage of accepted and unquestionable structures, fixed customs and deep-rooted common feelings which bring into social life itself something of the determined physical data of nature,[16] and of the vital unconscious strength proper to vegetative organisms; and on the other hand that common inherited experience and that set of moral and intellectual instincts which constitute a kind of empirical practical wisdom, much deeper and denser and much nearer the hidden complex dynamism of human life than any artificial construction of reason. And both this somewhat physical heritage and this inherited practical wisdom are intrinsically and essentially bound to and dependent upon moral and religious beliefs. As regards political ethics and political common good, the preservation of these common structures of life and of this common moral dynamism is more fundamental than any particular action of the prince, however serious and decisive this may be in itself. And the workings of such a vast, deep-seated physical-moral energy are more basic and more important to the life of human societies than particular political good or bad calculations. They are for states the prime cause of historic success and welfare. The Roman Empire did not succeed by virtue of the stains, injustices, and cruelties, which were intermingled in its policy, but by virtue of this internal physical-moral strength.

Now, and this is my second observation: what is in itself, even in the order of material causality, primarily and basically destructive of lasting historic success and welfare for a nation as well as for a civilization, is that which is destructive of the common stock and heritage I just described: that is, Machiavellianism on the one hand and hypermoralism on the other. Both destroy, as do gnawing worms, the inner social and ethical living substance upon which depends any lasting success and welfare, of the commonwealth, as well as that political justice which constitutes the moral righteousness, the chief moral virtue and the very "soul" of human societies.

Thus the split, the deadly division created between ethics and politics both by Machiavellians and by hypermoralists is overcome. Because politics is essentially ethical, and because ethics is essentially realistic, not in the sense of any *Realpolitik*, but in the sense of a real common good.

I am aware that if this antinomy which has been the scourge of modern history, is to be practically, not only theoretically, overcome, it will be only on condition that a kind of revolution take place in our conscience. Machiavelli has made us conscious of what is in fact the average behavior of politics in mankind. In this he was right. It is a natural incline that the man who endeavors to overcome dissociation, the man of unity, has to climb up again. But inclines are made to be climbed. As Bergson pointed out, a genuine democracy, by the very fact that it proceeds from an evangelical motive power, works against the grain of nature and therefore needs some heroical inspiration.

With whatever deficiencies human weakness may encumber the practical issue, the fact remains, in any case, that such an effort must be made, and the knowledge of what is true in these matters is of first and foremost importance. To keep Machiavelli's awareness, with reference to the factual conduct of most of the princes, and to know that this conduct is bad politics, and to clear our conscience from Machiavelli's rules, precepts and philosophy—this is the very end of Machiavellianism.

Here I emphasize anew what I pointed out at the beginning of this essay. Machiavellianism does not consist of this unhappy lot of particular evil and unjust political deeds which are taking place in fact by virtue of human weakness or wickedness. Machiavellianism is a philosophy of politics, stating that by rights good politics is supra-moral or immoral politics and by essence must make use of evil. What I have discussed is this political philosophy. There will be no end to the occurrence of misdeeds and mistakes as long as humanity endures. To Machiavellianism there can and must be an end.

Let us conclude. Machiavellianism is an illusion, because it rests upon the power of evil, and because, metaphysically, evil as such has no power as a cause of being; practically, evil has no power as a cause of any lasting achievement. As to moral entities like peoples, states, and nations, which do not have any supra-temporal destiny, it is within time that their deeds are sanctioned, it is upon earth that the entire charge of failure and nothingness with which is charged every evil action committed by the whole or by its heads, will normally be exhausted. This is a natural, a somewhat physical law in the moral order, although thwarted in some cases by the interference of the manifold other factors at play in human history: as a rule Machiavellianism and political injustice, if they gain immediate success, lead states and nations to misfortune or catastrophe in the long run; in cases where they seem to succeed even in the long run, this is not by virtue of evil and political injustice, but by virtue of some inner principle of misfortune already binding their victim to submission, even if the latter did not have to face such iniquitous enemies. Either the victims of power politics are primitive tribes which had been in a state of inexistence as to political life and therefore as to political justice: and their unjustly-suffered misfortune, which cries out against heaven and makes God's justice more implacable with regard to the personal destiny of their executioners, does not reverberate upon the unjustly conquering state unless in the form of some hidden and insidious, not openly political, self-poisoning process. Or else the victims of power politics are states and nations which were already condemned to death or enslavement by the natural laws of senescence of human societies or by their own internal corruption. And here also the very effect of the injustice which has been used against them is to introduce a hidden principle of self-destruction into the inner substance of their conquerors.

In truth the dialectic of injustice is unconquerable. Machiavellianism devours itself. Common Machiavellianism has devoured and annihilated Machiavelli's Machiavellianism; absolute Machiavellianism devours and annihilates moderate Machiavellianism. Weak or attenuated Machiavellianism is fatally destined to be vanquished by absolute and virulent Machiavellianism.

If some day absolute Machiavellianism triumphs over mankind, this will only be because all kinds of accepted iniquity, moral weakness, and consent to evil, operating within a degenerating civilization, will previously have corrupted it, and prepared ready-made slaves for the lawless man. But if for the time being absolute Machiavellianism is to be crushed, and I hope so, it will only be because what remains of Christian civilization will have been able to oppose it with the principle of political justice integrally recognized, and to proclaim to the world the very end of Machiavellianism.

There is only one determining principle before which the principle of Machiavellianism finds itself spiritually reduced to impotence: that is the principle of real and absolutely unwavering political justice, as St. Louis understood it. Men will have to spring up to array against the knighthood of human degradation the true knighthood of justice.

The justice of which I speak is not an unarmed justice. It uses force when force is necessary. I believe in the effectiveness of the methods of Gandhi, but I think that they are suitable only in certain limited fields of political activity. Especially in the case of war, other means must be used. And when one considers the course of the wars waged by total Machiavellianism, one can but wonder to what extent aggressors, who respect nothing, force the rest of mankind to have recourse to the terrible law of just reprisals, or to put aside momentarily, if a superior concept of justice necessitates our doing so, certain juridical rules which the barbarous action of the adversary has rendered inefficacious in justice.

But the more forceful and even horrible the means required by justice, the more perfect should be the men who use them. The world requires, for the affirmation to the end, and the application without fear, of the terrible powers of justice, men truly resolved to suffer everything for justice, truly understanding the part to be played by the State as judge, the part which according to the great theologian Francisco de Vitoria, belligerent States assume in the absence of any international entity endowed with universal jurisdiction. Men truly certain of preserving within themselves, in the midst of the scourges of the Apocalypse, a flame of love stronger than death.

In his introduction to Machiavelli, Max Lerner emphasizes the dilemma which democracies are now confronted with. This dilemma seems to me perfectly clear: Either to perish by continuing to accept, more or less willingly, the principle of Machiavellianism, or to regenerate by consciously and decidedly rejecting this principle. For what we call democracy or the commonwealth of free men is by definition a political regime of men the spiritual basis of which is uniquely and exclusively law and right. Such a regime is by essence opposed to Machiavellianism and incompatible with it. Totalitarianism lives by Machiavellianism, freedom dies by it. The only Machiavellianism of which any democracy as such is capable is the attenuated and weak Machiavellianism. Facing absolute Machiavellianism, the democratic state inheritors of the *ancien régime* and of its old Machiavellian policy will therefore keep on using weak Machiavellianism and be destroyed from without, or they will decide to have recourse to absolute Machiavellianism, which is only possible with totalitarian rule and totalitarian spirit; and thus they will destroy themselves from within. They will survive and take the upper hand only on condition that they break with every kind of Machiavellianism.

The end of Machiavellianism, that is the aim, that is the moral revolution to which, in the depth of human history, amidst savage wars which must be waged with inflexible determination, free men are now summoned.

NOTES

Reprinted from *The Review of Politics* 4, no. 1 (January 1942): 1–33. Thanks are due to A. James McAdams for several of the editor notes.

1. This lecture was delivered in an abbreviated form at the symposium on "The Place of Ethics in Social Science," held in connection with the 50th Anniversary celebration at the University of Chicago, September 26th, 1941. John U. Nef chaired the session, which included three other speakers, the university's president, R. M. Hutchins, R. H. Tawney, and C. H. McIlwain.

2. See Allan H. Gilbert, *Machiavelli's Prince and Its Forerunners*: The Prince *as a Typical Book* De Regimine Principum (Durham, NC: Duke University Press, 1938). I think that Professor Gilbert is right in locating the *Prince* in the series of the classical treatises *De Regimine Principum*. Yet the *Prince* marks the end of this series, not only because of the political changes in society, but because its inspiration utterly reverses and corrupts the medieval notion of government. It is a typical book *De Regimine Principum*, but which typically puts the series of these books to death.

3. Max Lerner, Introduction to *The Prince and the Discourses* by Niccolò Machiavelli (New York: Modern Library, 1950), xxi and xlii.

4. Matt. 23:3.

5. Cf. Raïssa Maritain, "Histoire d'Abraham ou la Sainteté dans l'etat de nature," *Nova et Vetera*, no. 3 (1935).

6. "In these things lie the true originality of Machiavelli; all may be summed up in his conviction that government is an independent art in an imperfect world." Gilbert, *Machiavelli's* Prince *and Its Forerunners*, 235.

7. According to a very just remark by Friedrich Meinecke, the two concepts of *fortune* and *necessity* complete the trilogy of the leading ideas of Machiavelli: *virtù, fortuna, necessità*. Cf. Meinecke, *Die Idee der Staatsräson* (Munich and Berlin: Oldenbourg, 1924), chapter 1.

8. Some authors magnify the divergences between *The Prince* and the *Discourses*. In my opinion these divergences, which are real, relate above all to the literary genus of the two works, and remain quite secondary. The *Discourses on the First Ten Books of Titus Livius* owed it to their own rhetorical and academic mood as well as to Roman antiquity to emphasize the republican spirit and some classical aspects of political virtue. In reality neither this virtue (in the sense of the Ancients) nor this spirit ever mattered to Machiavelli, and his own personal inspiration, his quite amoral art of using *virtù* to master for-

tune by means of occasion and necessity, are as recognizable in the *Discourses* as in *The Prince*.

9. Lerner, Introduction, xxxvii.

10. [Acton's quote is to be found in *The History of Freedom, and Other Essays*, ed. John Neville Figgis and Reginald Vere Laurence (London: Macmillan and Co., 1922). Ed.]

11. "Hitler told me he had read and reread the *Prince* of the Great Florentine. To his mind, this book is indispensable to every political man. For a long time it did not leave Hitler's side. The reading of these unequalled pages, he said, was like a cleansing of the mind. It had disencumbered him from plenty of false ideas and prejudices. It is only after having read the *Prince* that Hitler understood what politics truly is." Hermann Rauschning, *Hitler m'a dit* (Paris: Coopération, 1939). [In 1985, Rudolf Haenel, a Swiss schoolteacher, demonstrated that Rauschning's book was merely a compendium of others' accounts and not to be taken seriously. See *Der Spiegel* 37 (1985): 92–99. However, Maritain's point seems perfectly defensible. Ed.]

12. Matt. 4:10.

13. What Sir Norman Angell said in Boston in April, 1941, is true for all contemporary democracies. "If we applied," he said with great force,

> ten years ago resolutely the policy of aiding the victim of aggression to defend himself, we should not now be at war at all.
>
> It is a simple truth to say that because we in Britain were deaf to the cries rising from the homes of China smashed by the invader, we now have to witness the ruthless destruction by invaders of ancient English shrines.
>
> Because we would not listen to the cries of Chinese children massacred by the invader we have now, overnight, to listen to the cries of English children, victims of that same invader's ally.
>
> Because we were indifferent when Italian submarines sank the ships of republican Spain we must now listen to the cries of children from the torpedoed refugee ship going down in the tempest 600 miles from land.

But the remote responsibilities thus alluded to by Sir Norman Angell go back much farther than ten years. Western civilization is now paying a bill prepared by the faults of all modern history. [Angell, an economist and Member of the British Parliament, was awarded the Nobel Peace Prize in 1933. Ed.]

14. [A. James McAdams added these six words to make the sentence comprehensible. Ed.]

15. [Adam Mickiewicz was a Polish romantic poet and playwright who protested against Russian control of Poland and was arrested and exiled in 1823. Ed.]

16. See my "The Political Ideas of Pascal," in *Ransoming the Time* (New York: Charles Scribner's, 1941).

CHAPTER 2

The Development of Newman's Political Thought

ALVAN S. RYAN

Alvan S. Ryan (1912–1996) was a scholar of English literature who held numerous academic positions. He received his B.S. from the University of Massachusetts in 1934, an A.M. from Harvard in 1938, and his Ph.D. in English from the University of Iowa in 1940. His dissertation, "Newman's Conception of Literature," was published by the University of Iowa in 1941. After holding positions at several universities, he was named chair of the English Department at the University of Notre Dame in 1962. In 1965 he moved to the University of Massachusetts (UMass) system as chairman of Humanities and founding professor of English at the newly-established University of Massachusetts Boston. He was named the university's first emeritus professor and was honored in 1985 with an honorary doctorate in Humane Letters from UMass Boston. He was a specialist in nineteenth-century English literature and English criticism. His scholarship included subjects ranging from treatments on Frost and Emerson to analyses of Catholic social thought.

I

An account of Newman's political thought must explain a paradox. Newman declared that the principal aim of his life was to combat religious liberalism; and however novel may have been his approach to many problems, no charge against the orthodoxy of his theological writings has ever been sustained. Yet Newman was considered dangerously liberal by many. A few years after Newman had been made a Cardinal, Lord Selborne, during an audience with Pope Leo XIII, chanced to mention the name of Newman. The Pope's face brightened. "It was not easy; no, it was not easy. They said he was too liberal; but I was determined to honor the Church by honoring Newman. I have always felt a deep veneration for him. I am proud that it has been given me to honor such a man."[1] In what sense could it be said of Newman that he was too liberal? A study of his political thinking will, I think, take one far toward an answer to the question.

On first consideration, it might seem that Newman's political thought is of scant significance. For it must be admitted at once that unlike such other representative English prose writers of the Victorian Age as Mill, Ruskin, Carlyle, and Arnold, Newman rarely addressed himself to the "Condition-of-England question." Social questions were not his primary concern, and in fact occupy but little space in his collected writings. So it has come to be the conventional practice to contrast him with Cardinal Manning,[2] whose efforts in behalf of the working classes, and whose settling of the London Dock Strike are well known. Such comparisons, however, fail to do justice to Newman's mind. For if it is true that Newman conceived his work to be in quite other lines than those followed by Cardinal Manning, it is also true that it was never indifference to social problems, but rather a different way of approaching them, that marks the history of his opinions. There is, in fact, implicit in Newman's books and correspondence a very definite political thought which, because it was never articulated fully in any of his better-known works, is largely ignored. I have tried to trace out the significant features of Newman's political thought, and to show that while before his conversion in 1845, and afterward, he was occupied with adjusting the respective claims of church and state, a highly important development occurs in Newman's thinking on this subject before he arrives at his mature views.

II

The occasion of Newman's first extensive development of his political consciousness is, of course, the Oxford Movement.[3] It is no exaggeration to say that the Movement was as much concerned with politics as with religion, for from its inception the central question was that of the relation between church and state. And Newman more than any other individual shaped the course the Movement took.

Although the Movement did not begin until 1833, the alignment of forces began earlier. It is therefore important to point out how vehement was the protest of Newman and his friends at some of the reform bills of the twenties. Such reforms as the repeal, in 1828, of the Test and Corporation Acts and then the Roman Catholic Emancipation in 1829 were to Newman manifestations of indifference rather than tolerance. With the Reform Bill of 1832, as Laski says, "it must have seemed to indignant Tories that the flood gates of democracy had been opened."[4] For Newman, Froude and Keble had already come to see the rising tide of liberalism as the chief danger to the Anglican Church and to Christianity. It is true that by liberalism they meant chiefly religious liberalism, what Newman called the anti-dogmatic principle. But political liberalism was no less the enemy, since it early became clear that the reforming spirit would not stop with political and social changes, but would lay hands on the Church as well.

Of this period, Newman says in the *Apologia*: "While I was engaged in writing my work upon the Arians, great events were happening at home and abroad, which brought out into form and passionate expression the various beliefs which had so gradually been winning their way into my mind. Shortly before, there had been a Revolution in France; the Bourbons had been dismissed: and I held that it was unchristian for nations to cast off their governors, and, much more, sovereigns who had the divine right of inheritance. Again, the great Reform Agitation was going on around me as I wrote. The Whigs had come into power; Lord Grey had told the Bishops to set their house in order, and some of the Prelates had been insulted and threatened in the streets of London. The vital question was, how were we to keep the Church from being liberalized?"[5]

It was, in fact, only a year after the passing of the Reform Bill that the Ministry of Lord Grey moved to reform the Anglican Church in Ireland. State support was continued, but ten bishoprics were suppressed. At the time when the action on the Bill was pending, Newman was in the Mediterranean with Richard Hurrell Froude. He writes in the *Apologia*: "The Bill for the Suppression of the Irish Sees was in progress, and filled my mind. I had fierce thoughts against the Liberals."[6] Newman continues: "It was the success of the Liberal cause which fretted me inwardly. I became fierce against its instruments and its manifestations. A French vessel was at Algiers; I would not even look at the tricolour. On my return, though forced to stop twenty-four hours at Paris, I kept indoors the whole time, and all that I saw of that beautiful city was what I saw from the Diligence."[7]

Delayed many weeks by illness, Newman did not return to England until July 9, 1833, and five days later Keble, protesting against the suppression of the bishoprics but even more against the principle it invoked, preached the Sermon on "National Apostasy," which marked the start of the Oxford Movement. In condemning the interference of Parliament in the case of the bishoprics, Keble declared at the outset what was to be one of the basic principles of the Movement, for it can only be understood as an attempt to ascertain the exact nature of the English Church and its relation to the state. To ask such questions was to raise many others of an historical, doctrinal, and political nature. Newman, standing with Keble and Froude at the center of the Movement, himself the sole author of many of the tracts and a collaborator in the writing of others, worked out his answers to these questions over a period of twelve years. In these answers we find the fullest expression of Newman's political thinking up to his entrance into the Catholic Church.

To Newman, the Erastian view of church and state, recognizing as it does state supremacy, robbed the Church of the independence that was essential to her dignity and the performance of her spiritual mission. It was in the Apostolic Church, in the Church of England as she continued the tradition of the Early Church, not in the Establishment, that Newman found his ideal, and the tracts emphasized from the beginning an essentially Catholic conception of the church. Thus they flew in the face of the generally accepted view of the Church of England as the creation of the State. "The Church of England," said John Cam Hobhouse in the House of Commons, "is emphatically the offspring and child of the law, and the parent may deal with the child."[8] This, of course, was the very claim that Newman denied; and it was his attempt to justify historically his position that led him first to his theory of the *Via Media* and finally to his assertion in Tract 90 that the Thirty-nine Articles would bear a Catholic interpretation.

The irony inherent in the inception of the Oxford Movement as a protest against suppressing Anglican Bishoprics in Catholic Ireland has often been emphasized. What is less frequently noticed is that during the thirties Newman's suspicions of Rome were increased because, so he thought, she was allied with the very forces of liberalism which were to him anathema. Thus Newman writes in the *Apologia*, that though after 1839 he had a growing dislike "to speak against the Roman Church herself or her formal doctrines"[9] yet he felt he "could not be wrong in striking at her political and social line of action. The alliance of a dogmatic religion with liberals, high or low, seemed to me a providential direction against moving towards Rome...." "I had," continues Newman, "an unspeakable aversion to the policy and acts of Mr. O'Connell, because as I thought, he associated himself with men of all religions and no religion against the Anglican Church, and advanced Catholicism by violence and intrigue."[10]

Even more significant is Newman's attitude toward the dominant continental movements of this period, and especially toward such French Catholics as Lamennais, Montalembert, and Lacordaire. Their influence on the Oxford Movement is not generally recognized, and it is one of the great merits of Christopher Dawson's study[11] that it emphasizes this fact, and gives special attention to Richard Hurrell Froude's role as spokesman for certain ideas of these French writers.

In Dawson's words, the Oxford Movement "brought the English tradition out of its spiritual isolation into contact with the main currents of western culture, with Catholicism and Liberalism."[12] The Mediterranean voyage of Froude and Newman in 1832 was instrumental in achieving this wider perspective not particularly because of their visit to Rome; rather, it was Froude's return through France, while Newman remained in Sicily, that was important. For in France Froude first learned of the religious movement led by Lamennais, and recognized in the issue between the ultramontanism of Lamennais and the Gallican party the same struggle that was being waged in England between liberalism and traditionalism. But in France the foe, as Dawson remarks, "was not the watered-down Liberalism of the English reformers and their Whig allies, but the party of revolution who marched under the banner of Voltaire and Rousseau."[13] And unlike the "shy and diffident scholar" Keble, whose whole career centered in Oxford and his parish in the Cotswolds, Lamennais "descended into the arena and fought with all the weapons of the journalist and the popular agitator."[14] It was his conviction "that the new social order that was arising in Europe demanded a spiritual principle and that it could only find this principle in Catholicism."[15] If the Church were to assume the leadership in the great changes taking place in European society, "she would recover civilization for Christ and once more, as in the Middle Ages, become the mistress of the spirit of the age."[16]

But since Froude was, like Newman at that time, a Tory in his political views, it is therefore likely that, as Dawson suggests, he was repelled by the democratic element in Lamennais' programme and by his sympathy with the revolutionary movements in Ireland and on the Continent. What did attract Froude was the ultramontane ideal of the spiritual sovereignty of the Church and its complete independence of the state. It is not surprising, then, that Froude so vehemently denounced the Erastianism of the Anglican establishment, and that he did so "with the same arguments and sometimes with the same words with which Gallicanism was attacked in the pages of *L'Avenir*."[17]

It was chiefly owing to the influence of Froude, the "radical" and the enthusiast of the early stages of the movement, that the Tractarian Party was so early distinguishable from the old High Church Party. Froude's scorn for "pampered aristocrats" and "resident gentlemen" was limitless, nor did he believe in moderating his expressions of scorn in the interest of expediency. Froude's influence was no doubt decisive in attracting such disciples as W. G. Ward from the Liberal camp, and despite Newman's assertion to the contrary,[18] Dawson conjectures that "the idea of the Tracts themselves which, if we may believe the testimony of Isaac Williams, was first suggested by Froude at Oxford before Newman's return, owed something to the influence of *L'Avenir*."[19]

The most definite evidence of the influence of Lamennais, Lacordaire, and *L'Avenir*, however, is to be found in the articles by Froude that appeared first in the *British Magazine* and after Froude's death in the *Remains*, in the section entitled "Remarks on State Interference in Matters Spiritual."[20] Often the articles are virtually a paraphrase of pages from *L'Avenir*, and quotations are frequent. Most significant of all, Froude concludes with a quotation from Lacordaire's stirring challenge to the French bishops:

> *Que craignez vous! N'etes vous pas eveques?* Bishops of Christ's holy everlasting Church: who shall interfere with the free exercise of your indelible prerogative? Consecrate or refuse to consecrate: who shall reverse your decree? You can bind, and who shall loose? *Une seule chose leur est possible; le retranchement de notre budget.* Eveques de France! nous ne vous en disons pas d'avantage; c'est à vous de voir lequel vous préférez laisser sur vos sièges en mourant, ou un Episcopat riche et corrupteur, ou un Episcopat pauvre et digne de vous succéder.[21]

That Newman was also following the French movement during these years is apparent in his essay "The Fall of De La Mennais," which first appeared in the British *Critic* in 1837. Newman, having actively opposed the Erastian element in the Church of England for four years, takes comfort from his conviction that "the poor Gallican Church is in a captivity, not only doctrinal, which we all know, but ecclesiastical, far greater than ours."[22] He then reviews examples cited by Lamennais in his *Affaires de Rome*, the book written by Lamennais after he decided to live outside the Church. The cause of this condition, says Newman, is "the working, not of infidelity, but of Gallicanism; . . . the Gallican principle is the vindication of the Church, not into independence, but into State patronage. The liberties of the Gallican Church are its *establishment*, its becoming, in Scripture language 'the servant of men.'"[23] Newman outlines Lamennais' argument further, stating that according to him the cause of the "enslavement" of the Church is the temporal power and possessions of the Pope.

Newman is in essential agreement with Lamennais on these two points. But when he turns to the democratic elements in Lamennais' program he concludes that Lamennais' desire that the Church "throw herself upon the onward course of democracy," and "lead a revolutionary movement, which in her first ages she had created"[24] is his basic error. "Liberty," writes Newman, summarizing Lamennais' thought, "is the cry of the day; Christian liberty is the idea which the Church must develop, and on which the society which lies before us is to be built."[25] But, says Newman, he "does not seem to recognize, nay, to contemplate the idea, that rebellion is a sin."[26] "He seems to believe in the existence of certain indefeasible rights of man, which certain forms of government encroach upon, and against which a rising is any time justifiable.... Hence he is able to draw close to the democratical party of the day, in that very point in which they most resemble antichrist; and by a strange combination takes for the motto of his *L'Avenir*, 'Dieu et la Liberte.'"[27] "It is not wonderful that, with these principles, he cordially approves of what the Roman Church and Mr. O'Connell are doing in Ireland, sympathizes in their struggle, and holds them up for the edification of the Pope and Papal world."[28] Lamennais, in short, ought, so Newman argues, to profess "utilitarianism to be the true philosophy of political action."[29] Yet false as Lamennais' views are, they faithfully represent, says Newman, the nature of the Catholic Church, for "while its carriage is aristocratic, the true basis of its power is the multitude; and de la Mennais, like a keen sighted man, has discovered and zealously inculcates this truth."[30]

Newman, it can be seen, was far more critical of Lamennais in 1837 than Froude had been at any time up to his death in 1836. While it remains true that Froude's convictions weighed heavily with Newman especially in the early stages of the Movement, Newman did in fact act as a brake upon the enthusiasm of Froude, who made judgments hastily and forthwith acted upon them. Yet allowing for this fact, it remains true that during the Oxford Movement Newman, like Froude, saw in the ultramontanism of his French contemporaries many of the principles for which he fought. Moreover, it is evident that the provincialism of Newman's early attitude toward the French—"the French are an awful people"[31]—gave way to growing admiration for the spirit of such men as Lacordaire, Montalembert, and Dupanloup, who, though of liberal mind, did not share Lamennais' political views. The development of their whole conception of the relation of church and state closely paralleled the changes Newman's thought is destined to undergo. Without anticipating here questions that will be discussed farther on, it is worth noting that twenty-seven years after his Lamennais essay, Newman will emphasize in his *Apologia* his concurrence with the main line of thought of Montalembert and Lacordaire. It is also clear, however, that neither at the time when he wrote this essay, nor at any later date, did Newman accept Lamennais' interpretation of democracy. Newman concludes his essay by saying of Lamennais: ". . . there is just that ill flavour in his doctrine, which, in spite of all that is excellent in it, reminds one that it is drugged and unwholesome; and the conviction of this makes one tremble lest the same spirit, which would lead him to throw off civil authority, may urge him under disappointment to deny the authority of Religion itself."[32]

III

Newman's first important work after he became a Catholic was, characteristically, concerned with education. The story of the seven years during which, as Rector of the newly-founded Dublin University, he attempted to establish a Catholic University in the face of insurmountable difficulties, has been told many times. The "Campaign in Ireland," as Newman referred to this period, is important, however, not only because it gave us Newman's *Idea of a University*, but also for its political and social implications. From the outset differences with Bishop Cullen, who invited Newman to the Rectorship, hampered Newman's work. Even a few words concerning Dr. Cullen's outlook go far to make these differences comprehensible.

Dr. Cullen had received his early theological training, and had given his public disputation for the doctor's degree, in the Rome of Pope Leo XII.[33] It was, however, the Pope who came to the throne in 1830—Gregory XVI—that aroused Dr. Cullen's enthusiasm. Gregory it was who condemned the ideas of Lamennais' *L'Avenir* in the famous Encyclical *Mirari Vos*, and Lamennais' *Paroles d'un Croyant* in *Singulari Nos*. Pope Gregory's attitude "embodied that ideal of the Church as being in a state of siege which has so largely prevailed since the Reformation,"[34] and Dr. Cullen adopted the same attitude in Ireland. To quote Newman himself, "Dr. Cullen always compared Young Ireland to Young Italy, and with the most intense expression of words and countenance assured me they never came right—never—he knew them from his experience of Rome."[35]

One of the chief causes of friction between Newman and Dr. Cullen was the fact that while Newman insisted that laymen should have a real share in the administration and faculty of the University, Dr. Cullen was suspicious of any such lay influence. He wanted neither Irish nor English laymen to have a substantial place. Newman, however, wanted to develop a tone similar to that in the continental universities. The issue was as much political as educational, for it happened that the ablest lay professors were Englishmen or Young Irelanders[36] and Dr. Cullen, a staunch conservative, was jealous of the influence of both. "The Young Irelanders had swept the country ten years before, in a revulsion of feeling against Daniel O'Connell after his failure to achieve repeal by his monster meetings. They had come forward with a new programme, much as Sinn Fein came forward in recent years, refusing to submit to the mechanical party discipline of the older Nationalist agitation, and concentrating largely upon economic questions and a cultural revival."[37] Though most of the Young Ireland leaders were imprisoned after the abortive rebellion of 1848, their influence still lived and "while Dr. Cullen disapproved intensely of their new spirit of adventure and revolt, Newman was very soon attracted by the sincerity and the idealism of the younger men. They were just the type of active and generous minds whom he desired to attract to the University; and their devotion to the revival of Celtic studies and national tradition had created something like the atmosphere in which he had hoped to conduct his faculty of Celtic research."[38]

The conflict with Cullen was to have a lasting effect upon Newman's attitude towards the laity in later years. "On both sides the Channel," said Newman in a letter to his friend Robert Ornsby, "the deep difficulty is the jealousy and fear which is entertained in high quarters of the laity. Dr. Cullen seems to think that 'Young Irelandism' is the natural product of the lay mind everywhere, if let to grow freely; and I wish I could believe that he is singular in his view. Nothing great or living can be done except when men are self-governed and independent; this is quite consistent with a full maintenance of ecclesiastical supremacy."[39] Many similar remarks are to be found in Newman's letters of this period, and in his Retrospective Notes. Their cumulative effect leads one to recognize Newman as a champion of the Catholic laity, and as anticipating the modern emphasis on the lay apostolate.

The change that took place in Newman's attitude during this period needs to be emphasized. As Gwynn has pointed out, while Manning "was becoming more and more involved in policies which aroused opposition among the laity,"[40] Newman advanced to a position strangely remote from his earlier attitude in the days of the Tractarian Movement. Then liberalism had been the foe; while his dislike of O'Connell and his belief that Catholics made common cause with liberalism kept him, as I have already pointed out, from an understanding of the true position of the Catholic Church. "Yet now, after his three years in Ireland, he had returned from Dublin with a real sympathy towards the Irish Catholic democracy; and his conflicts with the Irish bishops over the claims of the laity to representation in the University had made him so far an upholder of the rights of the laity that, within a few years, he was to be denounced in Rome, and even delated to the Holy See, as the most formidable agent of Catholic Liberalism in England."[41]

The importance of the "Irish Campaign," then, is that it represents Newman's first significant work as a Catholic, and unquestionably the experience did much to modify the somewhat uncritical enthusiasm of his first years in the Church. Wilfred Ward speaks quite justly of the period from 1853 to 1858 as "a landmark in Newman's history."[42] Newman puts the matter boldly in his Retrospective Notes. He had believed, he says, that over and above the attribute of infallibility "a gift of sagacity" had in every age characterized the Holy See, so that we might be sure that "what the Pope determined was the very measure, or the very policy, expedient for the Church at the time when he determined. . . . I am obliged to say," Newman continues, "that a sentiment which history has impressed upon me, and impresses still, has been very considerably weakened as far as the present Pope, Pius IX, is concerned. . . . I was a poor innocent as regards the state of things in Ireland when I went there, and did not care to think about it, for I relied on the word of the Pope, but from the event I am led to think it not rash to say that I knew as much about Ireland as he did."[43]

Furthermore, one needs to keep in mind Newman's experience in Ireland in order to understand his later attitude on such issues as the temporal power and the definition of infallibility. For as Ward writes in his comment on the passage by Newman just quoted, "The failure of a scheme in which rigid principles had been enforced and acted upon, in defiance of what common sense and experience warranted as practicable, seems to have sunk deep into his mind."[44]

IV

The fullest and most direct statement of Newman's political thinking appears in a little known essay, entitled "Who's To Blame." It consists of a series of letters addressed in 1855 to the editor of *The Catholic Standard*, and was occasioned by the public clamor over the early disasters of the Crimean War. Newman answers his question, "Who's to blame for the untoward events in the Crimea?" in what he admits is a circuitous manner, for it is only in the last paragraph that he concludes that "they are to blame, the ignorant, intemperate public, who clamour for an unwise war. . . ." But however circuitous the essay, it is valuable to us as an exposition of the kind of conservatism Newman adhered to in the political order.

Newman's thesis is that the British Constitution "is admirably adapted for peace, but not for war"; and that consequently "the sooner we know our capabilities and our true mission among the nations of the earth, and get back into a state of peace, in which we are really and truly great, the better for us."[45] He argues further, that England is great not so much as a State but rather as a people or nation.[46] It is, so he holds, one of the classical problems in any society to see that "the State is kept *in statu* and its ruler is ruled" in order that the people or the nation may have the maximum of liberty and independence compatible with that power which is necessary for protection.[47] The British Constitution is an instrument admirably fitted to accomplish this purpose. By the term "Constitution" Newman does not mean Magna Carta or the Bill of Rights alone, but the character of the English race; and "a certain assemblage of beliefs, convictions, rules, usages, traditions, proverbs, and principles. . . ."[48] This complex of tradition he holds to be the creative and conservative influence in a society.[49]

The British are, says Newman, like the Athenians, lovers of personal freedom and independence, and as it was personal enterprise and daring that distinguished the Athenians from the rest of Greece, so the Englishman "likes to take his own matters into his own hands. . . . He can join too with others, and has a turn for organizing, but he insists on its being voluntary."[50] In foreign trade or colonizing, the Englishman has shown his genius for private enterprise; but the very independence that makes him so successful here, becomes, in time of war, a hindrance to effective action.

There is another reason why the English have been able to enjoy so much independence: they have been protected by the sea from external danger. Thus they "have been able to carry out self-government to its limits."[51] To the English "a government is their natural foe; they cannot do without it altogether, but they will have of it as little as they can. They will forbid the concentration of power . . . and make it safe by making it inefficient . . . a free people will maim and cripple their government lest it should tyrannize."[52] The English prefer "the system of checks and counter-checks, the division of power, the imperative concurrence of disconnected officials,"[53] and as a result "England, surely, is the paradise of little men, and the purgatory of great ones."[54] The insults aimed at military and government leaders for their errors Newman calls "doubly deplorable, as being unjust and unpolitic," but adds that "perhaps they must ever more or less exist, except where a despotism, by simply extinguishing liberty, effectually prevents its abuse."[55]

This characteristic jealousy of too much power appears also in the attitude of the nation to its law courts. The courts do not, says Newman, dispense justice in any abstract sense; rather they seek "such a justice ... as may not be inconsistent with the interests of large conservatism."[56] For "it is the Nation's right to impose upon the Judges the duty of expounding certain points of law in a sense agreeable to its high and mighty self."[57]

Finally, the Englishman's desire to preserve his independence from encroachments is shown in his attitude toward the army. Three precautions have been taken in England in dealing with the soldier—"precautions borrowed from the necessary treatment of wild animals—(1) to tie him up, (2) to pare his claws, and (3) to keep him low."[58] "Material force," says Newman, "is the *ultima ratio* of political society everywhere"[59] and therefore a standing army is a necessity. But England has always feared an *imperium in imperio* and hence has surrounded her military with precautionary devices aimed to restrict its power.

The conclusion of Newman is that this state of affairs makes for the safeguarding of English liberty, but weakens the state in time of war. It is a necessary weakness, he says, which cannot be set right without "dangerous innovations."[60] For "after all, reforms are but the first steps in revolution, as medicine is often a diluted poison."[61] There is a touch of irony here, for Newman illustrates this remark by citing Dr. Whately's claim in 1826 that the Anglican Church ought to throw off state control as an example of revolutionary doctrine. By this test Newman himself had been an arch revolutionary.

This essay is, in many ways, extremely difficult to interpret. It is journalistic and informal in manner, and filled with the repetitions Newman felt necessary in a series of letters published at intervals. One should, perhaps, guard against giving it too much weight in proportion to Newman's other writings. Yet it is, I believe, meant seriously, and its paradoxes, its irony, its devastating exposals of the weakness of the British system in the very act of praising its virtues, all make it at once puzzling and revealing. Newman can say, on the one hand, that the English "make government safe by making it inefficient";[62] that her leaders continually find themselves "in the fetters of Constitutional red tape";[63] that whereas "some States are cemented by loyalty, others by religion," England is held together "by self-interest, in a large sense of the word";[64] that "wealth does not indeed purchase the higher appointments in the Law, but it can purchase situations, not only in the clerical, but in the military and civil services, and in the legislature";[65] that, furthermore, "from the time of Sir Robert Walpole, bribes, to use an uncivil word, have been necessary to our Constitutional *regime*";[66] and for all that, Newman can say that "England is, in a political and national point of view, the best country to live in in the world."[67] Yet Newman disavows the charge of satire; he merely wants "to look facts in the face."[68] "Such is self-government. Ideal standards, generous motives, pure principles, precise aims, scientific methods, must be excluded, and national utility must be the rule of administration. It is not a high system, but no human system is such."[69]

The true antecedents of Newman's view of the constitution are in Edmund Burke and to a lesser degree in Coleridge. The parallels are striking, but not surprising when one recalls how great was Newman's debt to Burke especially. The distinction between the nation and the state, which lies at the center of Newman's whole discussion, had been made familiar by Burke and continued by Coleridge. The community or nation, acquiring its character over a long period and embodying its experience in laws and customs, is, according to this view, something quite different from the state, which is primarily the nation under the single aspect of power and organization. It has been said of Burke that "The British Constitution is the solid foundation on which all his theorizing is built, and the ark of his adoration."[70] The same may be said of Newman so far as his thought finds expression in the essay under discussion. Newman's very words and the turn of his sentences are reminiscent of Burke. Compare, for example, Newman's definition of the constitution with this from Burke: "It is a Constitution made by what is ten thousand times better than choice, it is made by the peculiar circumstances, occasions, tempers, dispositions, and moral, civil and social habitudes of the people, which disclose themselves only in a long space of time."[71]

To be adequately appreciated, Newman's essay needs, furthermore, to be viewed in relation to his own religious history. As an Anglican he had protested against the Erastian principle and had defended the spiritual prerogatives of the Anglican Church. Now, as a Catholic, he found himself among a minority group in religion; and it was only four years earlier that Newman, in his *Present Position of Catholics*, had successfully appealed to the English nation to respect the right of conscience of himself and his fellow Catholics. Newman says, therefore, that he "is thankful that he is born under the British Constitution," that "any Catholic who dreads the knout and the tar-barrel, will, for that very reason, look with great jealousy on a state of things which not only doubles prices and taxes, but which may bring about a sudden infringement and an irreparable injury of that remarkable polity, which the world never saw before, or elsewhere, and which it is so pleasant to live under."[72]

Insofar as Newman is defending a kind of pluralism in the political order, one can accept the general conclusions of the essay. Like Acton he sees the constitution as balancing powers so that abuses are difficult. But Newman seems to be somewhat out of touch, in his essay, with the social and political problem of the period. Brinton puts his finger on the weakness of Newman's position when he writes: "So little did he trust the State to provide a full sanction for moral conduct, that . . . he was willing enough to let the State proceed, within definite limits, along Liberal lines."[73] "Newman is willing to admit a great deal of *laissez-faire* in politics."[74] Concerned as he is to safeguard the individual against the tyranny of the state, he seems almost to acquiesce in the abuses of an industrial society as inevitable. It would be unjust to draw from his views conclusions which he himself would be the first to repudiate; on the other hand, it is hard to deny that the conservatism of "Who's To Blame" is almost an anachronism in 1855. It is an effective defense of the constitutional principle to be sure; but it also furnishes arguments for preserving the *status quo*. In the words of a contemporary critic: "The principle of the political equality of man, the justification of free activity, the doctrine of self-development through effort and struggle—these fair doctrines were used by a class which called itself a 'rising' middle class but which was already entrenched. Individualism meant ruthless self-seeking; *laissez faire* was the letting-alone not of useful personal energies but of a man's illegitimate power over his fellow men, the letting-alone of 'the iron law of wages.'"[75] If Newman did not condone such conditions, neither did he adequately treat them either here or elsewhere in his writings.

V

The years between 1858, when Newman delivered his last address as Rector of Dublin University, and 1864, when the *Apologia* appeared, were chiefly filled with the protracted controversy over two Catholic reviews, the *Rambler*, and the *Home and Foreign Review*. Since the controversy continually touched upon political questions, it has special interest for us here.

In 1857, before Newman left Dublin, he had encouraged the launching of the *Atlantis* magazine as part of the program of Dublin University. It was at first intended to encourage scientific studies, and though its scope was later widened somewhat to include articles of an historical and literary nature, it did not deal with controversial subjects in such a way as to invite censure.

The case of the *Rambler* was different. Its career was a stormy one. The *Rambler* started in 1848 as a weekly addressed primarily to English Catholics and became a monthly in the fall of the same year. It was successful from the first. Treating philosophical and social problems, as Wilfrid Ward says, "on markedly Liberal principles,"[76] its editors stated in one number: "Modern society has developed no security for freedom, no instrument of progress, no means of arriving at truth, which we look upon with indifference or suspicion."[77]

Newman's connection with the *Rambler* was at first entirely informal, and did not commence, apparently, until 1857 or thereabouts.[78] At this time Newman was in "constant correspondence" with Frederick Capes, the editor of the *Rambler*. Newman encouraged Capes in his work, for he felt that such a review as the *Rambler*, addressing itself to the philosophical, social, and political problems which critical minds were bound to consider, could be of inestimable value. But complaints were made by many Catholic readers at the often vehement tone of the *Rambler*, and Newman himself thought "there was something defiant and ill-considered and unsettling in some of the *Rambler* articles."[79]

Capes resigned the editorship in 1858, and was succeeded by Mr. Richard Simpson. More important than this change, however, was the fact that Sir John Acton, then a young man of twenty-six, began to collaborate with Simpson and to use the *Rambler* as the chief mouthpiece for his philosophy. Acton and Newman had met in 1857 and several visits took place in 1858, but it was Acton's intimate association with Döllinger at Munich that constituted the decisive experience of his early life.[80] His admiration for Döllinger was great, for "he saw in the school of German savants, of whom Döllinger was the chief, the harbingers of a great movement, of which the characteristics should be a thorough independence and frankness in critical and historical and scientific investigation, a broader theology, and union of the progressive creed of the nineteenth century with acceptance of the Church's defined dogma."[81] Acton was eager to find an outlet in England for his writing and the *Rambler* seemed exactly suited to his purpose.

Newman had already been "dismayed" by some of Capes' articles. Acton, however, went further. He invited Döllinger and Montalembert to contribute to the review, and Döllinger's speculations soon brought the *Rambler* into trouble. "A statement by Döllinger to the effect that St. Augustine was 'the father of Jansenism' resulted in his articles being delated to Rome."[82] Without at any time committing himself to the extreme or erroneous statements of certain of the contributors, Newman had done his best to encourage the *Rambler* in its main program; so on hearing that it was to be denounced in the bishops' Lenten pastorals, he assented to Cardinal Wiseman's request that he should accept the editorship himself. Yet even the May number which he edited was severely criticized, whereupon Newman asked for a theological censor for the review. Since this was not feasible, Newman resigned the editorship after the July number. During the next year Newman contributed to the *Rambler*, but tried to make clear the fact that he no longer had any official connection with it.

Finally an issue rose that spelled the end of the *Rambler*. Cavour's spoliation of the papal territories in 1860 brought the subject of the temporal power to the fore. At the time of the Revolution of 1848 sympathy with the Pope was widespread; now the case was different. In England this was especially true, and it created a crisis among Catholics. Manning and W. G. Ward began an enthusiastic campaign among English Catholics in support of the temporal power. The *Rambler*, on the other hand, adopted the tone of indifference that characterized most English thinking on the subject at that time. The position of the *Rambler* was further complicated by the fact that Sir John Acton, still its leading spirit, sat on the Liberal side in Parliament, and the Liberal Government was considered to be against the Pope's claims to the territory that had been taken from him.[83] Finally Manning informed Acton that Cardinal Antonelli had written a letter "with the Pope's cognizance, connecting the support given to Government by Catholic Members with things that have appeared in the *Rambler*."[84] A censure of the *Rambler* was to be expected, and Acton was advised to wash his hands of the review.

Newman followed the whole controversy with mixed feelings, and when Acton turned to him for advice, Newman unfortunately offended him by seeming to withdraw the support he had given him earlier. Newman, to be sure, thought Cardinal Antonelli was interfering; and even though he was to speak later of the followers of Victor Emmanuel as "sacrilegious robbers," he considered the temporal power an extremely complex question, and resented the implications of certain of its defenders that "its necessity was a dogma obligatory on Catholic belief."[85] But Newman also felt that Simpson's editorship of the *Rambler* was indefensible, and that Acton should let it go out of existence. His advice was not followed, however, and when in November the *Rambler* ran an article challenging Manning's extreme views of the temporal power, condemnation was inevitable. Whereupon, in 1862, the monthly was turned into a Quarterly, to be called *The Home and Foreign Review*, with Sir John Acton as editor, and the rest of the staff carried over from the *Rambler*.

The *Home and Foreign Review* was unable to dispel the suspicions already aroused by the tone of the *Rambler*; and after two years, during which it was in some ways one of the most distinguished reviews of the century, it was discontinued. In supporting with enthusiasm the program of Döllinger for treating dogmatic questions in a manner removed from traditional scholastic theology, *The Home and Foreign Review* brought itself under the papal censure that followed Döllinger's address at the famous Munich Conference of 1863. Acton decided to suspend publication, and *The Home and Foreign Review* appeared for the last time in April, 1864.

Newman found himself caught in the cross-fire of this series of battles over the Catholic reviews. During this time, of course, the *Dublin Review*, under W. G. Ward's editorship, represented just that position the *Rambler* and *The Home and Foreign Review* were most fond of attacking. Newman did not wish to become embroiled in such debates; he agreed with extremists on neither side. As he characteristically expressed it, anyone who had been involved, as he had, with both Simpson and W. G. Ward, would need a volume to state precisely his own view on all the issues between them. It is significant, too, that after the experience with the *Rambler*, Newman refused to write for *The Home and Foreign Review*. Neither would he accept Ward's invitation that he contribute to the *Dublin*. His reply to Ward's invitation is suggestive both of his disapproval of the *Dublin Review* policies and the "interest and disappointment" he felt with regard to *The Home and Foreign Review*: "I could not write for the *Dublin* without writing also for the *Home and Foreign*, and I mean to keep myself, if I can, from these public collisions, not that in that way I can escape the evil tongues of men great and small, but reports die away and acts remain."[86]

In the phrase "interest and disappointment," Newman sums up his attitude toward the Liberal Catholic reviews. They were needed, and there was an important work that they might have done. But the recklessness of their spirit, the unwillingness of their editors to use moderation in treating delicate questions, and other like deficiencies, were as clear to Newman as were the opposite faults of the ultra-conservative publications.

VI

Newman's difficulties with the Catholic reviews were but part of the whole struggle between liberal and conservative forces that took place within the Church during the papacy of Pius IX. It is not surprising, therefore, that soon after Newman severed connections with *The Home and Foreign Review*, he should become involved in other equally heated controversies.

In December 1864 Pius IX issued the famous Encyclical *Quanta Cura*, and the *Syllabus of Errors*. Their publication created a tremendous sensation, and the cry was raised that the Pope had declared war against modern civilization.[87] Among Catholics the *Syllabus* was received with sharply divergent sentiments, and it is important to understand exactly Newman's reaction. He sided with such moderates as Bishop Dupanloup against the extremists represented on the Continent by Louis Veuillot, editor of the French publication *Univers*, and by such English Catholics as W. G. Ward. Newman's attitude directly after the publication of the *Syllabus* is made clear in his letters, especially one written to Ambrose St. John:

> I am glad you are seeing the Puseyites. I suppose they will be asking you questions about the Encyclical. There are some very curious peculiarities about it, which make it difficult to speak about it, till one hears what theologians say ... it is difficult to know *what he means* by his condemnation. The words 'myth,' 'non-interference,' 'progress,' 'toleration,' 'new civilization,' are undefined. If taken from a book, the book interprets them, but what interpretation is there of popular slang terms? 'Progress,' e.g., is a slang term. Now you must not say all this to your good friends, but I think you will like to know what seems to be the state of the case. First, so much they ought to know, that we are bound to receive what the Pope says, and not to speak about it. Secondly, there is little that he says but would have been said by all high churchmen thirty years ago, or by the *Record* or by Keble now. These two points your friends ought to take and digest. For the rest, all I can say (*entre nous*) is that the advisers of the Holy Father seem determined to make our position in England as difficult as ever they can. I see *this* issue of the Encyclical, —others I am not in a position to see. If, in addition to this, the matter and form of it are unprecedented, I do not know how we can rejoice in its publication.[88]

W. G. Ward, however, did rejoice at the unprecedented frequency of papal encyclicals, allocutions, and briefs, during Pius IX's regime, and claimed that Pius IX spoke infallibly far oftener than previous Pontiffs;[89] whereas Newman, as he says in his letter, felt that Ward's extravagant claims only made difficulties for many Catholics where none existed before. For example, a few months after the publication of the *Syllabus*, W. G. Ward wrote to the *Weekly Register* stating that the Encyclical and *Syllabus* were unquestionably the Church's infallible utterances. It was just such views that Newman deplored, and he was gratified to learn that theologians in Rome did not countenance these interpretations of the *Syllabus*.

If we compare Newman's attitude toward the *Syllabus of Errors* with his denunciation of liberalism during the Oxford Movement, we face once again the paradoxical fact that he seems less vehement in his criticisms of liberalism after entering the Church than he was before. The well-known note on liberalism at the end of the *Apologia* makes this clear. It will be remembered that Newman commences the Note by saying that an explanation of what he meant during the Oxford Movement by the term liberalism "is the more necessary, because such good Catholics and distinguished writers as Count Montalembert and Father Lacordaire use the term in a favorable sense, and claim to be Liberals themselves...." He continues:

> I do not believe that it is possible for me to differ in any important matter from two men whom I so highly admire. In their general line of thought and conduct I enthusiastically concur, and consider them to be before their age.... If I hesitate to adopt their language about Liberalism, I impute the necessity of such hesitation to some differences between us in the use of words or in the circumstances of country....
>
> If I might presume to contrast Lacordaire and myself, I should say, that we had been both of us inconsistent; —he, a Catholic, in calling himself a Liberal; I, a Protestant, in being an Anti-Liberal ... we were both of us such good conservatives, as to take up with what we happened to find established in our respective countries, at the time when we came into active life. Toryism was the creed of Oxford; he inherited, and made the best of, the French Revolution.[90]

Newman concludes his note with a series of eighteen propositions which, at the time of the Oxford Movement, he "earnestly denounced and abjured." It is interesting to compare the propositions with the eighty condemned theses of the *Syllabus of Errors*. The two documents are in essential agreement, though Newman's statements are for the most part less specific. His propositions 14 to 17, those most pertinent to the present discussion, are as follows:

> 14. The Civil Power may dispose of Church property without sacrilege.
> Therefore, e.g. Henry VIII committed no sin in his spoliations.
> 15. The Civil Power has the right of ecclesiastical jurisdiction and administration.
> Therefore, e.g. Parliament may impose articles of faith on the Church or suppress Dioceses.
> 16. It is lawful to rise in arms against legitimate princes.
> Therefore, e.g. the Puritans in the 17th century, and the French in the 18th, were justifiable in their Rebellion and Revolution respectively.
> 17. The people are the legitimate source of power.
> Therefore, e.g. Universal Suffrage is among the natural rights of man.[91]

After listing the propositions, Newman writes: "How far the Liberal party of 1830–40 really held the above eighteen Theses, which I attributed to them, and how far and in what sense I should oppose those Theses, now, could scarcely be explained without a separate Dissertation."[92] Though Newman never wrote such a dissertation, his attitude toward the *Syllabus of Errors* reveals that he considered a purely negative attitude insufficient. He returns to the whole subject of the *Syllabus* in the *Letter to the Duke of Norfolk*, and since the view he presents there is his considered judgment, ten years after the *Syllabus* appeared, one must turn to the *Letter* for the best statement of Newman's attitude.

The Gladstone Controversy[93] and Newman's famous *Letter to the Duke of Norfolk* (Dec. 27, 1874) arose directly from the Vatican decree of 1870. For that reason it is necessary to deal with a subject—papal infallibility—which at first seems to have no bearing on Newman's political thought.

Gladstone,[94] irked no doubt at the defeat of his Irish University Bill of 1873 by the Irish bishops, and inspired also by his interest in his friend Döllinger's resistance to the "decree of 1870," published an article in which he declared that since the events of 1870, "No one can become her convert [a convert to the Roman Catholic Church] without renouncing his mental and moral freedom, and placing his civil loyalty and duty at the mercy of another."[95] In November, 1874, he published a 'political expostulation' entitled "The Vatican Decrees in Their Bearing on Civil Allegiance."

Gladstone took Cardinal Manning's recently published lecture "Caesarism and Ultramontanism" as the outcome of the Vatican decrees as "understood by the most favored ecclesiastics."[96] Manning had contended in his lecture that "Ultramontanism and Catholicism are identical" and had quite justly condemned the Falk Laws and Bismarck's campaign against the Catholic Church as modern Caesarism. But he had overstated the supremacy of the Church, in failing to emphasize that this supremacy, like that of the civil power, had definite bounds and limitations. Reading the lecture today one is impressed by the accuracy with which Manning anticipates the course of Caesarism in our own day. Yet one can also understand that its tone would inevitably irritate Englishmen. England during the twenty-odd years since the re-establishment of the hierarchy, had certainly not been moving toward such usurpations of the spiritual power.

To strengthen his own case Gladstone treated the definition as identifying the Catholic Church forever with the policy and spirit of such men as Manning, W. G. Ward, and Louis Veuillot.[97] Thus in replying to Gladstone, Newman was also able to protest against the very exaggerations and extravagances on the part of these men that he had long deplored.

The lucidity, the subtlety, and the eloquence of the *Letter* make it one of Newman's masterpieces. Although he was seventy-three when he wrote it and his "old fingers," as he said, "did not move quick," no lessening of his powers is anywhere evident. Laski, whose judgment could hardly be discounted as being biased in Newman's favor, has said of it : "It remains with some remarks of Sir Henry Maine and a few brilliant dicta of F. W. Maitland as perhaps the profoundest discussion of the nature of obedience and of sovereignty to be found in the English language. In the reply to his critics which Mr. Gladstone published it is clear that of his argument alone did he take serious account. For Newman, even apart from his theology, was an able political thinker.... The pamphlet, in a sense, was the summation of his life's work." [98]

In answering the charge of divided allegiance, Newman defines carefully the nature of obedience and authority as he understands them. He shows that though the jurisdiction which the civil law exercises over Englishmen is extensive, "affecting our actions in various ways, and circumscribing our liberties,"[99] yet "the thraldom and irksomeness is nothing compared with the great blessings which the Constitution and Legislature secure to us."[100] Then turning to the charges that "the Pontiff declares to belong to him the *supreme direction* of Catholics in respect to all duty,"[101] Newman shows how in the realm of morals Catholics are guided by moral theology, and asserts that: "So little does the Pope come into this whole system of moral theology by which (as by our conscience) our lives are regulated, that the weight of his hand upon us, as private men, is absolutely unappreciable."[102] And when Newman develops the justly famous passage on "Conscience" he declares that "did the Pope speak against Conscience in the true sense of the word, he would commit a suicidal act," and concludes with his well known sentence: "Certainly, if I am obliged to bring religion into after-dinner toasts, (which indeed does not seem quite the thing) I shall drink,—to the Pope, if you please—still, to Conscience first, and to the Pope afterwards."[103]

Of special importance are Newman's comments in the *Letter* on the Encyclical of 1864 and the *Syllabus of Errors*, for in a sense they recapitulate his earlier opinions and state his mature views. First, as to the Encyclical *Quanta Cura*, which was, as Newman says, "one of the special objects of Mr. Gladstone's attack." Newman contrasts the England of 1870 with the England he knew as a young man, and points out that then "the old idea of a Christian Polity was still in force. . . Men of the present generation, born in the new civilization, are shocked to witness in the abiding Papal system the words, ways, and works of their grandfathers. In my own lifetime has that old world been alive, and gone its way."[104] Newman then cites the Corporation and Test Acts, the fines imposed for non-attendance at religious services,[105] and other restrictions, to show that only a generation earlier England herself had recognized and accepted that principle, calling it Toryism, which it now "called Popery and reviled."[106] But all this is now changed, says Newman, and he proceeds to make clear his attitude toward the revolution that has occurred within his own lifetime.

> The cause of this great revolution is obvious, and its effect inevitable. Though I profess to be an admirer of the principles now superseded, in themselves, mixed up as they were with the imperfections and evils incident to everything human, nevertheless I say frankly I do not see how they could possibly be maintained in the ascendant. . . . During the last seventy years, first one class of the community, then another, has awakened up to thought and opinion. Their multiform views on sacred subjects necessarily affected and found expression in the governing order. . . . The State ought to have a conscience; but what if it happen to have half-a-dozen, or a score, or a hundred, in religious matters, each different from each? I think Mr. Gladstone has brought out the difficulties of the situation himself in his Autobiography. No government

could be formed, if religious unanimity was a *sina qua non*. What then was to be done? As a necessary consequence, the whole theory of Toryism, hitherto acted on, came to pieces and went the way of all flesh. This was in the nature of things. Not a hundred Popes could have hindered it, unless Providence interposed by an effusion of divine grace on the hearts of men, which would amount to a miracle, and perhaps would interfere with human responsibility. The Pope has denounced the sentiment that he ought to come to terms with 'progress, liberalism, and the new civilization.' I have no thought at all of disputing his words. I leave the great problem to the future. God will guide other Popes to act when Pius goes, as He has guided him. No one can dislike the democratic principle more than I do. No one mourns, for instance, more than I, over the state of Oxford, given up, alas! to 'liberalism and progress,' to the forfeiture of her great medieval motto, 'Dominus illuminatio mea,' and with a consequent call on her to go to Parliament or the Heralds College for a new one; but what can we do? All I know is that Toryism, that is, loyalty to persons, 'springs immortal in the human breast;' that Religion is a spiritual loyalty; and that Catholicity is the only divine form of Religion. And thus, in centuries to come, there may be found out some way of uniting what is free in the new structure of society with what is authoritative in the old, without any base compromise with 'Progress' and 'Liberalism.'[107]

In the next section of the *Letter*, Newman reiterates his earlier attitude toward the *Syllabus*, and insists on the untenability of Gladstone's assumption that the *Syllabus* and the Encyclical with which it was issued must both be looked on by Catholics as infallible. Of the *Syllabus*, Newman writes: "There is not a word in it of the Pope's own writing."[108] "Moreover," says Newman, "if the Pope drew up that catalogue, as it may be called, he would discriminate the errors one from another, for they differ greatly in gravity, and he would guard against seeming to say that all intellectual faults are equal."[109] The *Syllabus*, in short, must be looked on as an index, and its value "lies in its references." Newman tests several of the theses by referring to the allocution or Encyclical which treats the particular error condemned, and shows how unfounded are Gladstone's assumptions as to the meaning of the *Syllabus*.

As for Thesis No. 80[110] Newman says "I turn to the Allocution of March 18, 1861, and find there is no formal condemnation of this Proposition at all. The Allocution is a long *argument* to the effect that the moving parties in that Progress, Liberalism, and new Civilization, make use of it so seriously to the injury of the Faith and the Church, that it is both out of the power, and contrary to the duty, of the Pope to come to terms with them. Nor would those prime movers themselves differ from him here; certainly in this country it is the common cry that Liberalism is and will be the Pope's destruction, and they wish and mean it so to be."[111]

This passage is representative of the whole spirit of Newman's *Letter*. He answers Gladstone by replacing inaccurate paraphrases and unexamined assumptions with precise and discriminating definitions. Likewise, when Newman discusses the Vatican definition of infallibility, he suggests the drift of all he has to say on it in these words: "so difficult a virtue is faith, even with the special grace of God, in proportion as the reason is exercised, so difficult is it to assent inwardly to propositions, verified to us neither by reason nor experience, but depending for their reception on the word of the Church as God's oracle, that she has ever shown the utmost care to contract, as far as possible, the range of truths and the sense of propositions, of which she demands this absolute reception."[112] Here, of course, is an attitude directly opposed to that of W. G. Ward; and it is clear Newman had him in mind when in the same paragraph he recalls that those who conformed to this rule of the Church were "a few years ago" called "Minimizers."

The *Letter to the Duke of Norfolk* was Newman's last important work. In 1878, three years after it appeared, Pius IX died and Leo XIII commenced his reign. It must be said that despite his affection for Pius IX, and despite his loyalty to the Holy See, Newman had had little enthusiasm for the policies of Rome during these thirty years. Just as Newman considered Pius IX's liberal policy in the years preceding the Revolution of 1848 as ill-advised, so he considered the reversal of policy and the *non possumus* of the later years as equally ill-adapted to the situation in England. And it is also clear that Newman had been, as Ward said, under a cloud in the official Roman world almost from his conversion.[113] But from the beginning of Leo XIII's reign it was apparent that a change had taken place in ecclesiastical policy. "It seemed that a new spirit had penetrated into the Vatican, and that what had been impossible with Pius IX was no longer so with his successor."[114] Accordingly, English Catholics made the representations to the Vatican that issued in Newman's elevation to the Cardinalate in 1879. Thureau-Dangin's comments are revealing:

> Leo XIII received the petition of the English Catholics all the more favourably as it appears that of his own accord he had had the same desire from the very

beginning. Being asked by Monsieur de Rossi soon after his election, 'What would be his policy as Pope?' he had answered, 'Wait till you see my first Cardinal; that will show you what will be typical of my reign:' It was believed that in these words he was referring to Newman. . . .[115]

VII

Certain conclusions follow from the foregoing remarks. First, it is clear that there is an unmistakable development in Newman's political thinking, a development that parallels the history of his religious opinions, as well as the changes that occur in his thinking on many other subjects. As Newman remarked in his note on liberalism in the *Apologia*, since "Toryism was the creed of Oxford," in his earlier period he took up with what he happened to find established there. His alliance with John Keble in launching the Oxford Movement, his refusal even to look at the tricolour at Algiers harbor, his violent dislike of Daniel O'Connell, were in keeping with his Tory views.

The progress of Newman's thought during the Oxford Movement leads him to a defense of the Anglican Church against the state and ultimately to embrace a religion that places him among a religious minority in the State. His clear sense of the implications in his own spiritual journeyings accounts for Newman's later position, when as a Catholic he opposes the ultramontanism of Ward and Manning, even though as an Anglican he could endorse the ultramontanism of Lamennais. Is there not a great inconsistency, then, between his Anglican and his Catholic periods? An answer becomes the easier if we recall that Montalembert and Lacordaire, who with Lamennais, upheld the ultramontane position in the thirties, later were considered the leaders in France of the liberal group, which was opposed to the ultramontanism of Veuillot's *Univers*. Newman's attitude upon nearly all the questions that were so keenly debated after he became a Catholic—the *Syllabus of Errors*, the temporal power, the definition of infallibility—shows him to be aligned with the moderate policy of Montalembert and Lacordaire.

In terms of his political thought, Newman's attitude involves no diminution of loyalty to the Church, though such was the charge of those who called him a minimizer.[116] Instead, it signifies Newman's recognition that any practical solution of the problem of church and state in England, at least, involves an acceptance as he says of "liberal principles," or a principle of pluralism.[117] It is well to emphasize, however, that Newman does not make a universal of this solution, nor does he call for a "Free Church in a Free State" as did Montalembert in his address of 1863 that was delated to Rome. But when Newman says apropos of the *Syllabus of Errors* that "the advisers of the Holy Father seem determined to make our position in England as difficult as ever they can";[118] when he emphasizes in "Who's To Blame" the advantages to Catholics of living under a Constitution such as the English; and when in both the "Letter to the Duke of Norfolk" and the "Biglietto Speech" he stresses the problem raised by the numerous religious sects in England, Newman is simply indicating that the position of the Catholic in the modern State makes the acceptance of "liberal principles" inevitable. It was an alternative to the simple declaration of a *non possumus* against the modern State, and the conflict between these views is at the root of many of Newman's difficulties as a Catholic.[119]

It is clear, then, that the importance of Newman's political thought lies in his life-long concern with the problem not only of church and state, but more accurately, of the church, the state and the human person in their mutual relations. "The very same persons and the very same things belong to two supreme jurisdictions at once, so that the Church cannot issue any order, but it affects the persons and the things of the State; nor can the State issue any order, without its affecting the persons and things of the Church."[120] When the state respects "the things of the Church" and the church respects "the things of the State" all goes well; but as Newman knew, the struggle and martyrdom of St. Thomas à Becket was the symbol of what has gone on throughout nineteen centuries.[121]

If one were to summarize Newman's thought, it might be said that it has four phases: (1) the denial of the excessive claims of the state against the church; (2) the de facto recognition of cultural and national traditions as determining the mode of operation of the church in each state; (3) the affirmation of the rights of the person against the state, which leads Newman to his distinction between nation and state, and explains his distrust not only of the tyranny of unregulated State power, but his dislike for radical democracy; (4) the affirmation of the dignity of the person, and the appeal to the dictates of conscience against the extreme advocates of papal supremacy, whose views, by the way, cannot be identified with those of the Church. Only by recognizing such a complex of relationships, so Newman held, could just and lasting solutions of political problems be achieved.

If we compare Newman's political thought with that of such modern Catholic writers as Maritain, or Don Luigi Sturzo, we see not only that Newman was keenly alive to one of the major problems of our time, but that even his conclusions have a real pertinence and validity today. Like these thinkers, and like Christopher Dawson, Newman saw that beyond the political problem is the problem of a deep-seated social regeneration. Newman saw the danger of "the absorption of the supernatural in the natural and the Church in the totalitarian State."[122] He realized, too, that history is irreversible, and hence he did not recommend in an unreal fashion a solution that would have been feasible perhaps only in the medieval period. Instead, even though he did not develop his ideas fully, Newman was working toward such a solution as Maritain has propounded in works like *True Humanism*. There might even be some parallel to be seen between Newman's development and the course of Maritain's thought from the *Anti-moderne* (1922), and *Three Reformers* (1925) to *Christianity and Democracy* (1944). It is true, on the one hand, that Newman never expressed the idea of a dynamic Christian democracy in the clear constructive fashion of Maritain; in fact, his "Who's To Blame" is, as I have said, in many respects unsatisfactory; but it is no less true that Newman's thought moved toward a Christian conception of human freedom akin to Maritain's and in nowise toward that authoritarianism and contempt for "ballot-boxes and Parliaments" that vitiates much of the later work of Carlyle and Ruskin.

A quotation from an analysis of Maritain's political philosophy must suffice to suggest certain parallels with what has gone before: "This New Christendom, the soul and heart of the true humanism, will recognize the existence of different religious beliefs and corresponding religious groups as a fact which has to be accepted. That, of course, does not mean a dogmatic toleration in which no dogma matters, because all can be true or all can be wrong. But the civil toleration does not exclude the orientation of all communities towards the temporal common good. Maritain believes that only the Christians who are citizens of the one *supratemporal* polis, the Church, know about the deepest foundation and ultimate finality of this common good, but it remains given to all groups, though in a more or less imperfect way, and not as an expression of a minimum of theoretical philosophical agreement, but as a common duty and work."[123] It is hardly necessary to point out that in this passage we have a statement of the position Newman maintains in his remarks on religious sects in England already quoted.

To return to the question with which I commenced my essay: Was Newman "too liberal" in his political thinking? My answer is emphatically "no." In the strictly political order, he is in one sense a conservative of the school of Edmund Burke, but with one important difference. Newman sees the movement of history sweeping away the very basis of the earlier English conservatism, and he recognizes the necessity of meeting the new situation, "of uniting what is free in the new structure of society with what is authoritative in the old." Newman's whole work as a Catholic was an attempt to complete the appeal to authority, to tradition, to the essentially conservative forces in both Church and civil society, by a fearless confronting of the manifold problems raised by modern scientific thought, modern religious developments, and modern philosophical speculations. It is clear that this attempt to approach such questions courageously carries over into his political thought. Newman's work inevitably aroused hostility, and hostility in turn led to the unfounded charge that he was "too liberal."

Notes

Reprinted from *The Review of Politics* 7, no. 2 (April 1945): 210–40.

This essay was originally published in the centenary year of Newman's conversion to Catholicism, on October 9, 1845.

1. Paul Thureau-Dangin, *English Catholic Revival in the Nineteenth Century*, 2 vols., translated by Wilfred Wilberforce (New York: E. P. Dutton & Co., 1899), 2:362.

2. [Henry Edward Manning (1808–1892) was the Roman Catholic archbishop of Westminster as of 1865 and became a cardinal in 1875. Ed.]

3. [The Oxford Movement was a coalition of Anglican intellectuals who advocated for a retrieval of ancient Christian traditions in liturgy and theology and opposed an increase of state control over the Anglican Church. They published their ideas in *Tracts for the Times* between 1833 and 1841. Ed.]

4. H. J. Laski, *Studies in the Problem of Sovereignty* (New Haven, CT: Yale University Press, 1917), 70.

5. John Henry Newman, *Apologia Pro Vita Sua: Being A History of His Religious Opinions* (London: Longmans and Green, 1934), 30.

6. Ibid., 31.

7. Ibid., 33.

8. Laski, *Studies in the Problem of Sovereignty*, 76.

9. Newman, *Apologia*, 121.

10. Ibid., 123. See also 125, where Newman writes, "[b]reak off, I would say, with Mr. O'Connell in Ireland and the liberal party in England. . . ."

11. Christopher Dawson, *The Spirit of the Oxford Movement* (New York: Sheed & Ward, 1934).

12. Ibid., 3–4.

13. Dawson, *Spirit of the Oxford Movement*, 64. There are few studies on Lamennais available in English. H. J. Laski's *Authority in the Modern State* (New Haven, CT: Yale

University Press, 1919), and E. L. Woodward's *Three Studies in European Conservatism* (London: Constable & Co., 1929), are both important.

14. Dawson, *Spirit of the Oxford Movement*, 64.

15. Ibid.

16. Ibid., 65.

17. Ibid., 67.

18. "'I . . . had out of my own head begun the Tracts," wrote Newman in *Apologia Pro Vita Sua*, 40.

19. Dawson, *Spirit of the Oxford Movement*, 68.

20. R. H. Froude, *The Remains of the Late Reverend Richard Hurrell Froude*, ed. John Henry Newman and John Keble (London: J. G. and F. Rivington, 1838), 4 vols. The publication by Newman and others of the *Remains* was, as is well known, considered one of the blunders of the movement. It is not surprising, for the uncompromising tone of volume 3, especially, shows that Froude was running out far ahead not merely of such moderates as Keble, but even of Newman himself.

21. Froude, *Remains*, 3:194–95. Quoted by Dawson, *Spirit of the Oxford Movement*, 70. [The French translates to: "What do you fear? Are you not bishops? There is only one thing they could do: the curtailment of our budget. Bishops of France! We will not tell you any further; it is up to you to decide what you prefer to leave on your seats at your death: either a rich and corrupt Episcopate or an Episcopate that is poor and worthy of succeeding you." Ed.]

22. John Henry Cardinal Newman, *Essays Critical and Historical*, vol. 1 (London: Longmans, Green, and Co., 1890), 140.

23. Ibid., 145.

24. Ibid., 156.

25. Ibid., 157.

26. Ibid.

27. Ibid., 157–8.

28. Ibid., 160.

29. Ibid.

30. Ibid., 162.

31. *Letters and Correspondence of John Henry Newman*, ed. Anne Mozley (London: Longman, 1891), 1:233.

32. Newman, *Essays Critical and Historical*, 1:172.

33. Wilfrid Ward, *The Life of John Henry Cardinal Newman, Based on His Private Journals and Correspondence* (London, UK: Longmans, Green, and Co., 1912), 1:365.

34. Ibid., 1:365.

35. Ibid., 1:382.

36. Ibid., 1:361.

37. Denis Gwynn, *A Hundred Years of Catholic Emancipation (1829–1929)* (London, UK: Longmans, Green, 1929), 164.

38. Ibid., 164–65.

39. Ward, *The Life of Newman*, 1:367.
40. Gwynn, *Hundred Years of Catholic Emancipation*, 169.
41. Ibid., 169–70.
42. Ward, *The Life of Newman*, 1:389.
43. Ibid., 1:388.
44. Ibid.
45. John Henry Newman, "Who's To Blame," in *Discussions and Arguments on Various Subjects* (London: Longmans, Green, and Co., 1924), 307.
46. Ibid., 311.
47. Ibid., 317.
48. Ibid., 315.
49. Ibid., 316.
50. Ibid., 336.
51. Ibid., 339.
52. Ibid., 341–42.
53. Ibid., 342.
54. Ibid., 343.
55. Ibid., 344.
56. Ibid., 350.
57. Ibid., 350–51.
58. Ibid., 357.
59. Ibid., 355.
60. Ibid., 360.
61. Ibid.
62. Ibid., 342.
63. Ibid., 343.
64. Ibid., 348.
65. Ibid., 351.
66. Ibid., 351–52.
67. Ibid., 353.
68. Ibid., 360.
69. Ibid., 352.
70. Alfred Cobban, *Edmund Burke* (New York: Macmillan Co., 1929), 58.
71. Edmund Burke, *Works* (London: Henry G. Bohn, 1873), 6:147.
72. Newman, *Discussions and Arguments*, 309–10.
73. Crane Brinton, *English Political Thought in the Nineteenth Century* (London: Ernest Benn, 1933), 154.
74. Ibid., 158.
75. Lionel Trilling, *Matthew Arnold* (New York: Norton, 1939), 181.
76. Wilfrid Ward, *William George Ward and The Catholic Revival* (London: Macmillan, 1893), 139.
77. Ibid.

78. Ward, *The Life of Newman*, 1:416ff.
79. Ibid., 1:440.
80. [Ignaz von Döllinger (1799–1890) was a German Catholic priest and theologian who held liberal theological views, rejecting, for instance, the dogma of papal infallibility that the first Vatican Council declared in 1870. Ed.]
81. Ward, *Catholic Revival*, 143.
82. Gwynn, *Hundred Years of Catholic Emancipation*, 175.
83. Ward, *The Life of Newman*, 1:520ff.
84. Ibid., 1:522. Acton's words in a letter written to Newman.
85. Ibid., 1:520.
86. Ward, *Catholic Revival*, facsimile letter, opposite p. vi.
87. Ward, *The Life of Newman*, 2:79.
88. Ibid., 2:80.
89. Ibid., 2:83.
90. Newman, *Apologia*, Note A, 286.
91. Ibid., 296.
92. Ibid., 297.
93. Ward, *The Life of Newman*, 2:397ff.
94. [William Ewart Gladstone (1809–1898) was prime minister of the United Kingdom in 1868–74, 1880–85, February–July 1886, and 1892–94. Ed.]
95. Ward, *The Life of Newman*, 2:40.
96. Ibid., 2:401.
97. Ibid., 2:402.
98. Laski, *Studies in the Problem of Sovereignty*, 202.
99. Newman, *A Letter Addressed To His Grace The Duke of Norfolk on Occasion of Mr. Gladstone's Recent Expostulation* (London: Pickering, 1875), 41.
100. Ibid., 42.
101. Ibid., 41.
102. Ibid., 43.
103. Ibid., 66.
104. Ibid., 67.
105. Ibid., 69.
106. Ibid., 68.
107. Ibid., 70–72.
108. Ibid., 78–79.
109. Ibid., 80.
110. "The Roman Pontiff can and ought to reconcile himself to, and agree with progress, liberalism, and civilization as lately introduced." From *Allocution Jamdudum cernimus*.
111. Newman, *Letter to The Duke of Norfolk*, 85.
112. Ibid., 111.
113. Ward, *The Life of Newman*, 2:435.

114. Thureau-Dangin, *English Catholic Revival*, 2:359.

115. Ibid., 2:361–62.

116. Newman jokingly speaks of his moderation on the subject of the temporal power as his "supposed complicity with Garibaldi." Ward, *The Life of Newman*, 1:585.

117. See Luigi Sturzo, *Church and State*, trans. Barbara Barclay (New York: Longmans, Green, & Co., 1939), 432. Sturzo points out that Msgr. Dupanloup, Bishop of Orleans, in his pamphlet on the Syllabus "concluded that it was the duty of Catholics, taking their stand on the *de facto* situation, to adapt themselves to the conditions of the moment and to fight with the modern arms of freedom of conscience, of the press and of the vote." This interpretation was in accordance with Newman's own thinking on the subject.

118. Ward, *The Life of Newman*, 2:81.

119. Even as late as 1882 he speaks in a letter of "what may be called Nihilism in the Catholic Body and in its rulers. They forbid, but they do not direct or create." Ibid., 2:486.

120. Newman, *Certain Difficulties Felt by Anglicans in Catholic Teaching Considered* (London: Longmans, Green, 1891), 1:173. These lectures were delivered in 1850.

121. Ibid., 1:184.

122. Sturzo, *Church and State*, 558.

123. Waldemar Gurian, "On Maritain's Political Philosophy," in *The Maritain Volume of "The Thomist"* (vol. 5 of *The Thomist*) (New York: Sheed and Ward, 1943), 16–17.

CHAPTER 3

Church and State

Heinrich Rommen

Heinrich Albert Rommen (1897–1967) was a prominent political philosopher who brought his Catholic commitments to the subjects of natural law, the state, and democratic politics. He earned degrees from the University of Münster and the University of Bonn in the 1920s. In 1933 the Nazi government closed the school that Rommen directed, the Franz-Hitze-Schule, and had the Gestapo arrest Rommen, who spent six weeks in jail for his anti-Nazi writings and his involvement with the "Circle Königswinter," a group of German Catholic intellectuals that included the theologian Oswald von Nell-Breuning. In 1938, Rommen emigrated to the United States, where he pursued a productive academic career through a series of university posts, culminating in an appointment at Georgetown University in 1953. Among the highlights of his scholarship are writings on the natural law thought of Francisco Suárez, his 1945 book, The State in Catholic Thought, *and his book of 1936,* The Natural Law. *Rommen is known for the phrase "the eternal return of natural law."*

I

The problem of Church-state relations—if under "Church" is understood the church universal in its Catholic form—may be answered without too much difficulty on a high abstract level. But on the contingent level of concrete historical development the problem becomes not only highly involved, but almost inexhaustible. For every growth in the Church's doctrine (for example, the decrees of the Vatican Council and every deeper-going change in the other partner's constitutional forms or in its philosophical and ethical justification or a change in its aims to greater comprehensive competencies) poses a new problem. No wonder, therefore, that in our era of restlessness, of dynamic social changes, of conflicting ideologies fighting for the baffled minds of the masses, of wavering traditions decomposed by the acid of nihilist skepticism, the Church-state problem arises in a new intensity and urgency. The external signs are there for everyone to see: the fury of a Hitler against the "Black International," the violent persecution of the Church in the satellite countries of the Russian orbit, and the complete subjugation of the Orthodox Church not to a "Christian" Czar but to the confessedly atheistic Politburo. In minor degree the problem is also bothering the people of the United States. A secularist outlook, indeed, may slur over the reality and intensity of the true problem. For the secularized outlook the Church in her essence—and even more so the churches and the sects—is not different in genre from other numerous private organizations for the furtherance of more or less rational aims and longings in a constitutionally pluralist society. The secularist will, therefore, recognize only one pragmatic rule: tolerance unless the public order and the competency of the police power is directly concerned. Public order includes all too often for the secularist his reform ideas and his social ideals based on a relativist pragmatism in ethics and thus makes him highly sensitive to the criticism by a Church which bases ethics on revelation and on competencies which the secularist can only consider as unfounded and arrogant. Only if the Church remains in the private sphere of private individuals and stays in this "free" sphere where the secularist will tolerate any mass idiosyncrasies, only thus will he condescendingly tolerate the Church. His attitude may be explained to a degree by the fact of an exceedingly strong religious individualism and a subjective and emotional spiritualism, inimical to form and tradition (indigenous to this country and resulting in the easy dissolution of doctrinal unity into a multiplicity of sects). This spiritualist "formlessness" of religion, here, makes the emphasis on organically grown and established forms and on the objective institutions of religious life, so characteristic of the Catholic Church, a somewhat strange and suspicious thing. Yet there is no avoiding the nature and self-understanding of the Church, if the problem of Church and state should be approached. Otherwise the term "Church" would stand only for utterly private opinions by very private individuals in that sphere of irrational feeling and unscientific imagination which for the secularist agnostic is religion. And it is clear that upon such suppositions it would follow that the political authority has exclusive and plenary competency to judge about the compatibility of such a religion with the policy and the public order of the state. The consequence of such thinking is the abolition of the Church-state problem by the complete elimination of the Church.

The term "Church," then, as used here means and must mean the church universal, the divine institution with the constitution and divine positive law of a supernatural society, with a claim and a competency established directly by God, and not by the collective will of the faithful. The Church is "founded" by Christ; therefore it is juridically a "foundation," not a corporation, and its constitution, its fundamental law, is given directly by God and not ordained by the people. The Church, though she may participate in certain measures in the essentials of all societies, is nevertheless, a society *sui generis*—so much that she is necessarily *una sancta*, in essence and in history. The philosopher has to accept this theological essence of the Church as an established fact. That is the reason, in the last analysis, why the problem of Church-and-state has always been and will always be primarily and paradigmatically the problem of the Roman Catholic Church and the temporal states in their historical varieties. It is this Church alone that stands in perpetual identity through history and history's many contingent creations—civilizations, cultures, nations, economic systems—and will so stand to the end of history, the final realization of the Kingdom of God. All history of mankind since the Epiphany is necessarily also the history of the Church. The philosopher, consequently, has to adopt the theological doctrine *De Ecclesia*. This strict obligation is limited, of course, to the acceptance only of that which is truly authoritative doctrine and *sententia communis*; he need not heed that which is historically conditioned, that which is the great process of development of doctrine or that which through the testing disputes of the theological schools, has been modified or abandoned. This does not mean that the philosopher is wholly prohibited from applying his methods and the principles of his social philosophy to matters concerning or involving the Church.

As canon law comprises not only positive divine law but natural and positive human law as well, so does the active work of the Church include that which is human and historically changing. The Church's end and constitution are absolute, always the same, above civilizations and historical periods. The Church's activity extends into the "World"; the Church as the *populus christianus* lives in the "World." The Church as an institution will develop methods and accommodations, policies and genuine compromises of *modi vivendi* about means and proximate aims in meeting the World and challenging its undue claims. In each civilization and era of history the "idea" of "the" state finds expression in concrete form, for example, monarchy or democracy, with a Bill of Rights. Thus there is produced beyond the abstract Church-state relationship on the abstract-general level a particular concrete Church-state problem which requires its own concrete answer without the sacrifice of the perennial principles governing Church-state relationships. The state is concretely a changing institution and, though based upon and ruled directly by the natural law, changes in its historical form. Thus, the Church has experienced the pagan state in the form of imperial Rome; the medieval Christian empire in the form of the feudal law; the Gallican nation-state and the confessional state of the "divine right" theory; the Christian state of the parity of religious groups; and, finally, the modern secular state, be it of the religiously neutral form based on the natural law without a positive acceptance of the positive divine law, or be it in the form of the intensely laicist and violently anti-clerical state. In this perennial dispute, the *"Aus-einandersetzung"* between the Church and the various types of concrete states, the doctrine of Church-state relations is constantly being tested and clarified, not in the unchanging essentials, but in the remoter conclusions developed therefrom. Bellarmine's and Vittoria's treatises, *De Summo Pontifice* and *De Potestate Ecclesiae*, were put on the Index in 1590 because they rejected the doctrine that the Pope had *jure divino* a direct power in *temporalibus*. After the death of Sixtus V the treatises were removed from the Index. Yet today, theologians still criticize Bellarmine's *potestas indirecta* theory and often regard as being in grave error his thesis that heretics may be persecuted by the secular power even to the imposition of the death penalty.[1] Here, if anywhere, delicacy and circumspection are required and due consideration must be given to all the fine nuances in the doctrinal documents. In the following discussion the Catholic doctrine of the nature, constitution, and authority of the Church is presupposed as thesis.

II

Before we go into one of the concrete problems of the "secular" neutral state to be defined later and into the problem of the Bill of Rights and its relation to the Church-state problem, a few brief remarks are necessary concerning the principle of homogeneity as the concrete basis of the state as a *unitas ordinis*, that is, as a *unitas* and as an *ordo*. Societies are distinguished primarily by their objective ends, by their common goods as *causae finales*, and secondarily by the subjective social acts through which the members integrate themselves or are directly and coercively integrated to the realization of the common good. In the natural societies, such as the family or the state, this objective end, that is the common good, is predesigned in human nature, and is beyond the free and the arbitrary will of the members. Every society as such is based upon a homogeneity of purpose among the members, and upon their actual consent to a set of rules determined by the common end or good. This homogeneity is then, not physical or biological but, rather, moral and cultural and may, depending on circumstances, be broad or narrow. If we speak of a "Catholic" state, then we mean that the people as the ruled and the rulers are "Catholic" and that, consequently, their religious homogeneity expresses itself necessarily and quite naturally also in the state as the political form of this Catholic people. For instance, they accept the rule of canon law in the matter of the bond of matrimony, and protect the Church against slander and libel directed against Catholic doctrine and Church institutions; the state, represented by its rulers or representatives, worships God in the Catholic religion publicly. Even here, however, Church and state are still distinguished and are both in *suo ordine* sovereign and do not form a union, complete and strict, but are ordained to cooperate and help one another. Meanwhile the *potestas indirecta* of the Church as a superior *potestas circa temporalia non per se* and *propter se* but by reason of its superior end teaches, admonishes, and—under circumstances to be determined by the spiritual power—corrects the secular power of the Catholic ruler and invalidates laws which are unjust according to natural and divine positive law.

Under such conditions, where religious unanimity forms the basis of political homogeneity, there often arises the danger that religious conformity is considered the basis of political loyalty. As a consequence the religious heretic or nonconformist is considered to be politically disloyal. History teaches us that it was the Catholic princes and rulers who stressed this, for instance, in their repression of the Jews and also in their suppression of heretics, like the Albigensians, who all too often endangered that which was then considered by almost all to be the public order, the public safety of a Christian state. An impartial study of the Inquisition shows that it was often necessary for the Popes to admonish the rulers, who sought all too frequently to use that institution for political purposes, that they should strictly observe canon law, which was, it should be said to its honor, more humane than the criminal law and procedure of the state. Nevertheless, the Inquisition is and remains a "dark historical event" and nobody wishes its return.[2] Rightly Vacandard says: "The repression of heresy has had forever deplorable consequences and raised terrible hatred against the Church. Violent measures it is conceded are obsolete."[3] Vacandard says further that such measures have been disastrous and are never to be revived. Furthermore, in this matter we are today not speaking of the situation that often was presupposed in the Middle

Ages, of one empire, one great *Republica Christiana*, one *orbis christianus* under two powers; we are speaking of two perfect societies, each truly sovereign in *suo ordine*, each having its own objective end and corresponding order of law. An interference of the one, the superior power objectively speaking, with the other is extraordinary, strictly circumscribed, and may not be arbitrary, however much the question *quis judicabit* about the circumstances may be—and ought to be— determined in favor of the spiritual power which has, of course, in justice and before conscience the burden of proof.

III

But all this is not a problem of our times. For historical contingent reasons and because of the mistakes of ecclesiastics, we live today in the religiously neutral state, that is, a state which through a Bill of Rights (be it positively formulated or merely implied as a part of modern civilization) declares the freedom of worship or the free exercise of cults, freedom of conscience, freedom from state interference in the religious life of the citizens, and the equality of all before the strictly secular, though not necessarily "secularized" law, without regard for religious affiliation. Yet this state is not wholly "neutral"; for it still claims the right to demand of its citizens that their religious practices as external acts do not disturb the public order, meaning those ethical values which it considers the basis of its own existence. Examples of this are the insistence upon monogamy as against the polygamy of the Mormons, or the various techniques employed in dealing with the radical pacifism of the religiously motivated conscientious objector.

Different difficulties arise from our dual role as Catholics and citizens in the modern state, either the neutral state or the "Christian" state, which also, nowadays, recognizes in its Bill of Rights the freedom of conscience and, almost always, the freedom of religious cults (though it may as a "Catholic" state, like Spain, not grant equality of cults but reserve for Catholicism only the right to a *public* form of worship). We may dispute about the rise of this neutral state; it is the reality in our day. We should be aware that it is beyond the realm of possibility to return to such Church-state relationships as prevailed in the medieval empire, or in the confessional state of the counter-reformation with its faults— (the liberties of the Gallican Church are its servitudes to the King, said Fénélon). Also, the whole discussion concerning the *jus gladi*, a topic that still appears rather frequently in the books of some scholars of the *jus publicum ecclesiasticum*, seems to be more of historical interest, as Father Capello, S.J., implies when he says that the dispute is rather speculative because in practice one must say that the use of the *jus gladi* is foreign to the Church.[4] It is likely that, as Vermeersch and many others suggest, the argument for the *jus gladi*, which has never found general acceptance in the history of the Church and which is foreign to the common law, is based on the overstressing of the *societas perfecta* concept of the Church in a sense similar to the state.[5] Though it may have been true historically that the methods of the Inquisition had the initial effect of preserving certain countries for the Catholic Church, on the other hand, the violation of consciences, the abuse of force in religious matters, and the almost inevitable political abuse of what was originally an ecclesiastical institution served ultimately to produce such evil after-effects in some of these countries that only recently, that is during the last century, have we come to understand the true extent of the harm done.

Before we go on to discuss the relationships between the Church and the modern, that is, neutral, state, two points should be clarified. First, the authority of the Church is wielded primarily over its members, that is, validly baptized Christians. The *potestas indirecta* can, therefore, reach first the Christian ruler and citizens in their secular political life, that is the state as a natural law institution for Christians (the term "Christians" here, means validly baptized persons); secondly, it can reach, though obviously to a minor degree, non-Christians in the Christian state, such as the Jews or the Saracens in the mediaeval cities, and, lastly, it can reach out to the rulers of the states of infidels. Here the spiritual right of the Church to send out missionaries to preach the Gospel issues into a *potestas indirecta* of the Church to summon the help of Christian rulers for the protection of the missionaries against the resistance of the infidel rulers, especially since the latter in their resistance also violate a rule of the *jus gentium*, namely that of free international intercourse. This was the general doctrine of the theologians in dealing with the question of Iberian colonialism; but they also stressed the fact that, beyond insisting upon the admission of the missionaries, the Pope has no *potestas indirecta* over the infidels. They cannot, for instance, be bereft of their political power because they indulge in unnatural vices, or because as idolators they blaspheme God, or because they are generally "barbarian." This brief mention of the states of the infidels and their rights based on the natural law and the *jus gentium* leads to the second point which must be made. When the Schoolmen up to the eighteenth century speak of a Christian state they mean a Catholic state; indeed, at Bellarmine's time even the states of heretics were still juridically Catholic states because the theologians could not yet accept the idea that the Reformation had definitely rent asunder the *una sancta*. If, therefore, we look for a paradigm of the modern neutral state in the theories of the earlier theologians, their idea of the pure natural law state of the infidels, of course, *mutatis mutandis*, comes nearest to the pattern of the modern secular state, over which the Church can claim only a very tenuous *potestas indirecta*. And this natural law state was actually conceived of by St. Thomas when he substituted it for the Augustinian idea of the *Civitas Dei* which had so powerful an influence over medieval thought from Charlemagne to Dante. But in the natural law state the more fruitful and appropriate doctrines may be that of the Church as a spiritual *societas perfecta* and of the *libertas ecclesiae* and less that of the *potestas indirecta*.

The term "neutral" secular state is chosen because it implies the Bill of Rights with its civil tolerance, freedom of religion and worship, freedom of consciences (plural!) and, through these, equality before the law. It does not mean the absence of concordats and cooperation, as is proved, for instance, by the constitutional provisions of the separation of Church and state in the (defunct) Constitution of Prussia of 1920 and in the Concordat of 1929. "Neutral," furthermore, is opposed to the quasi-religious totalitarian state as represented by the national-socialist and the communist states and as is implied in Rousseau's state with its intolerant *religion civile*. Nor does neutrality necessarily mean accepting a philosophy of laicism as was the case in the French Third Republic; for here the fight for religious freedom turned—as it was intended to turn by the exponents of violent anti-clericalism, or, better, anti-religious rationalism—into a fight for freedom from all religion and especially against the Catholic Church in her essence. The neutral secular state is simply a state in which the necessary moral homogeneity is based purely on natural values as they are declared or recognized in the preambles of the modern constitutions and especially in their Bills of Rights. These, together with the preambles, form the substance and values that constitute democracy and which are more important than the mere techniques of democratic government. Thus, "neutral" means merely that the state and the law must serve all citizens on the basis of the fundamental rights and, therefore, as a practical political maxim, must not infringe on or judge the religious beliefs of the citizens—not because all religions are equally right or wrong (which would constitute theological or philosophical *indifferentism*), but because the *unitas* and the *ordo* must be based on secular, yet on nonetheless commonly accepted values, irrespective of the fact that theologically or philosophically these values may be *per accidens* wrongly motivated. The neutral state is not primarily interested in whether a citizen accepts the freedom of worship because he is, like

Jefferson, a deist or whether another accepts that freedom because he abhors any political compulsion in this most sacred sphere of the person. The community refuses to use the power of the law so long as the exercise of the right of the one does not lead to the violation of the rights of others, so long as the particular wrong motivation does not result in such external acts as would violate the public order. It is not necessary to be convinced that all religions are equally true and good in order to be able to honor the genuine convictions of one's fellow citizens, however erroneous they may seem to be or are. In respecting the convictions of others we do not honor the "error," but instead, we give honor to the *bona fide* conscience and the person of our fellow-citizen, his freedom and his sincerity, without regard for the objective error. We recognize the fact that, according to our own doctrine, he is obliged to follow his conscience even though that conscience may be erroneous.

And "secular," or perhaps better "temporal," state need not mean the "secularized" state such as the laicists in France want any more than natural law means the denial of the *status gratiae* however much the rationalist philosophy of the eighteenth-century "jusnaturalism" (Don Sturzo's good expression)[6] may have thought. Secular means a clear distinction from the spiritual and includes a separation of Church and state which need not be hostile. The Cardinal Patriarch of Lisbon expressed it neatly when he said: "The Portuguese state is essentially a secular state by constitutional act; the separation between Church and state (since 1911) defines the relations between them. . . ."[7] A policy of religious tolerance has been adopted since 1918 and since then has become accentuated, the *Estado Novo* (Salazar)[8] developing after 1928 this policy through the Concordat of 1940. It should be clear that the state cannot be "secularized" so easily; first the ruling classes or the majority of the people are "secularized," as in the Third Republic, and then the laicist laws are introduced, and thus the state is secularized as a reflex, so to speak.

IV

Among non-Catholic citizens, be they believing Protestants or secularist liberals, there prevails a thesis about the Catholic doctrine on Church and state that, in the last analysis, is equivalent to the famous dictum ascribed to Veuillot[9] (though he never said it). "When you are the majority, we demand our liberty on the basis of your principles (the so-called Protestant principle or liberalist principle of indifferentism). When we are the majority, we will refuse you your liberty on the basis of our principles." Consequently, these citizens do not trust our sincere belief in and acceptance of the Bill of Rights and of the practical maxim of religious and political tolerance. They quote *Mirari vos arbitramur* and *Quanta cura*; they quote c. 2198 of the *Codex Juris Canonici*, according to which if it is opportune, the Church may in the case of an ecclesiastical delict request the help of the *brachium saeculare*. They point out that the theory of the *potestas indirecta* (which it may be conceded is often taught without the necessary qualifications) must necessarily lead to making the Bill of Rights impotent should Catholics become an overwhelming majority in a state, despite the solemn assurances of a Cardinal Manning and many other dignitaries.

It follows first, that we must show how sincerely we accept the values which the Bill of Rights protects; freedom of worship and of religion; freedom of speech and press; freedom of religious affiliation—and this involves the sincerity of our concern for the protection of religious non-conformists in predominantly "Catholic" states. For the Church executes her missionary work not only in countries with Catholic majorities but even more so in states with overwhelming Protestant, Mohammedan, or Confucianist majorities, and her work is very dependent on the recognition of the principles of freedom of religion, of conscience, of speech and of teaching. Consequently the Church sincerely favors an international Bill of Rights, as Pius XII recently declared. She, furthermore, cannot insist upon a Bill of Rights in the one "non-Catholic" state and refuse to recognize it in the other according to whether Catholics are a minority or a majority in a particular state. Father Pribilla quotes in this connection, in his excellent article "Dogmatical Intolerance and Civil Tolerance," the Bulla of Gregory IX of April 6, 1233 to the Bishops of France concerning the protection of Jews: "The Jew is to be shown that benignity which the Christians living in pagan countries wish to experience for themselves."[10] Certainly this is a principle of general application.

Secondly, in the matter of the general doctrine of Church and state relations we must distinguish as clearly as possible between the purely historically-determined, contingent legal systems and theories and opinions on the one hand, and the essential, superhistorical core of what is true dogmatically and *fide catholica* on the other. Finally, we must make due allowance for the fact that we often use terms which are meaningful in an earlier historical period, but which have today lost much of their former meaning; we must further recognize that the Curia uses a certain style peculiar to itself just as theology has its own style and that this style requires translation into modern language, for example, the term "heretic" when used in connection with *bona-fide* non-Catholic Christians, etc.

We may and must sincerely accept the practical and constitutional meaning of the Bill of Rights. We should stress the fact that freedom of the press and of conscience and of science (philosophy) was condemned only insofar as it was demanded on the basis of theological indifferentism or philosophical relativism. We should stress, furthermore, that however much these rights were demanded historically on the basis of a wrong philosophy, such as rationalism and deism (for example, Jefferson), this historical origin does not imply a kind of original sin with which the rights themselves are contaminated. We should go on to show that, on the contrary, these rights are not matters of theological or metaphysical truth but practical political maxims, that the rights of the person, of the parent, are based on the natural law which is not abolished by faith. We must give proper emphasis to the fact that the validity of the thesis "truth only has rights; falsehood (error) has no rights," does not abolish the rights of those who are *per accidens* and without *male fide* in error and do not disturb the public order, if this thesis is at all meaningful; for abstraction or relations—and truth and error are such, if they do not stand for Christ and Satan—have no rights: only persons and organized groups of persons have rights, either as natural or moral-legal persons. Furthermore, we have recently gained a greater awareness of the "psychological" conditions of the Faith, and of the search for and the acquisition of truth than was possessed by the more homogeneous and more ontologically and metaphysically orientated Middle Ages. A non-conformist—ecclesiastical as well as political and sociological—was then virtually *prima facie* "guilty." That is the reason for the quick and to us, often violent reaction of the tight and rather "static" and at the same time much less individualist-personalist community, against the nonconformist. This reaction, having little regard for the sincerity of the offender's nonconformism, often involved the use of force upon occasions where even the most "orthodox" of today would hesitate to employ it. We are aware of the apostasy of whole classes, such as the intellectuals and, later, the proletarian masses, the great scandal of our times; in both instances it would be difficult to speak of personal guilt, as Newman demonstrates in connection with his friend Froude, and Bishop Ketteler as regards the proletarians.[11] We are, furthermore, and rightfully, aware today of the great danger of civil and social intolerance and recognize the right of persons to be respected in the sincerity of their consciences, just as we are aware of the intrinsic freedom of the act of faith and of the obligation binding on everyone to obey his subjectively clear conscience. For a Protestant has subjectively the duty (from which follows the obligation of the community to recognize his right to be undisturbed in the fulfillment of that duty) to adhere to his church and its teachings as long as he is subjectively convinced of its truth; nay, as long as he is not subject to the pressure of urgent and serious doubts, he may not even give up his faith.[12] The sincerity of the erroneous conscience demands reverence and has the right of being free from violent intervention, provided, of course, that the erroneous conscience does not lead to external acts that are in obvious contradiction with that basic area of agreement or assent which makes the community a *unitas ordinis*, that is, its "public order." Not only the right conscience has rights; the sincere though erroneous conscience has rights, too, rights limited only by what we call the "public order," that is, the essential conditions of socio-political life, strictly understood.

Today we are not bound by what theologians who were too much affected by their time and its circumstances taught concerning the personal rights. I fully agree with Father Courtney Murray's statement in his Bellarmine article about a "new Christendom" in 2045,[13] after having studied the opinions of the Doctors from Vittoria to Bellarmine and the excellent work of Professor Joseph Höffner (at the Seminar at Trier) in his *Christianity and Human Dignity, The Colonial Ethics of the Spanish Theologians in the Golden Era*.[14] In such matters there occurs a development of doctrine, as we might say, with all appropriate qualifications, a development that purifies, enlightens, makes explicit what was earlier imperfectly thought out, what was too quickly accepted or only implicitly held and thus in its complexity not fully comprehended.

V

Let us consider several pertinent problems. First: let us consider the rights of parents, to which Father Joseph Schröteler has devoted a volume of 400 pages.[15] He is concerned with the dispute of the Thomists and the Scotists over the compulsory baptism of Jewish children before they reach the full use of reason and against the will of their parents. Father Schröteler also discusses the still earlier custom of child-oblates, and the more recent practice of compelling Jews in the papal states to attend sermons of instruction. This last practice was often defended in the missionary theory for the pagans though both Las Casas and Salmeron severely criticized the practice. Father Schröteler continues the discussion of parental rights, treating, among others, the famous Mortara case and various provisions concerning parental rights in modern constitutions.

If one thing is clear then it is this: the Scotist view was already given up by the sixteenth century. The Thomist doctrine that such a compulsory baptism is a grave and ordinarily indefensible violation of the parental rights is authoritatively established in the famous *Postremo Mense* of Benedict XIV, the great canonist on the papal throne. In 1848, Emmanuel von Ketteler, then the deputy at the Frankfort Parliament and later the Bishop of Mainz, stated in the deliberation of the Bill of Rights: "I demand for Catholics and believing Protestants, the right to have their children educated in the Catholic or Protestant Faith just as I will acknowledge the terrible right of the unbeliever to have his poor children educated in unbelief." That is the same doctrine which the U. S. Supreme Court accepts in the famous Oregon cases of 1925 and which the Encyclical *Divini illius Magistri* by Pius XI quotes as an example of the natural law. Concerning the compulsory attendance at sermons, Schröteler comes to the conclusion that the theologians would very likely have refused to approve of this practice if it had not been used in the papal states. He finishes this interesting chapter by saying that such compulsion is a useless means anyway and would cause the opposite of what is intended; furthermore the use of such compulsion would easily lead to a similar coercion of Christian minorities in a non-Christian country (such as the compulsory attendance of indoctrination-courses in the Hitler Youth and especially in communist countries). If we vehemently condemn this last not only because what is indoctrinated is atheistic but also because it violates freedom of consciences, then the second point applies also in the case discussed above. "We are coming nearer a time," says Father Pribilla, "in which all civilized mankind principally rejects compulsion in spiritual (*geistigen*) and especially in religious matters and regards the use of force in such matters as a form of barbarism against which the nations of Western civilization gather all their powers. It can only be a blessing for the Church if she recognizes the freedom of conscience and of religion and renounces voluntarily, all means of compulsion, offered by the state, even where they still might be tendered."

Father Pribilla also points out that the Church would lose all respect and in addition would not be successful, if each act of tolerance were considered by her as a mere concession, only reluctantly granted and revocable at any time. It may be remarked here that Pius IX blamed rather severely some Catholic states of Latin-America because they admitted non-Catholics as immigrants, but in 1899, the well known professor of dogmatic theology, Joseph Pohle, writing for the semi-authoritative Wetzer's and Welte's church-encyclopedia, stated that in general, most states recognized the principle of freedom of immigration and emigration, that the legal grant of the free exercise of religion and worship in Catholic countries does not endanger the internal peace. On the contrary, a refusal of such a freedom would very likely threaten the internal peace for these states: the trend and the need of the time are once and for all more towards freedom of religion than towards compulsion and restriction in the exercise of religion. This thought is based obviously on Leo XIII's *Immortale Dei* (on the Christian constitution of states, not only the Natural Law constitution): there may arise social conditions in which a government, remaining wholly Christian and Catholic, may and ought to use tolerance in what concerns the general direction of the state. We might add that today the freedom of missionary activity on the basis of freedom of religion and worship has become a generally accepted rule of international law.[16]

What is expressed, then, even in international law is a consequence of a doctrinal development. Since the Middle Ages our sense of the importance and the rights of consciences, especially of the erroneous conscience, has been much refined. Whatever one may think of the development of philosophy from Kant through romanticism and to Kierkegaard and the Existentialists, one positive feature stands out: an increasingly higher evaluation of freedom and of personal dignity as against the impersonal powers and the intolerant trends of tight and restrictive collectives which again arise in modern totalitarianism in a diabolical measure. Along with this personalism increases also the respect of the innermost sacred sphere of the person where in *ultima solitudine* the individual conscience rules. Consequently a non-conformist conscience is not, as it was rather customary to explain in the Middle Ages (and quite often well-founded) an intentional and guilty one, as of *mala fide*. By reason of our greater knowledge of psychology and of the acts of conscience, especially of the acts of faith and of the loss of faith, and considering the facts that the process of civilization has built up generally acknowledged minimal norms of external behavior, our reaction against the non-conformist takes more into account the possible, nay probable, *bona fides*, the sincerity of the objectively erroneous conscience and shies away from means which by reason of our respect for conscience seem inappropriate. Against Karl Jaspers' fear, that if Catholicism should become influential again, heretics would once more burn at the stake, Father Brunner, S.J., affirms that the respect for conscience demands that the religious error of a person be enlightened by appropriate, that is, spiritual means, by means which do not violate his freedom and personal dignity, not by force.[17] It need not be stressed that the non-conformist cannot himself deduce from this an uncontrolled right of aggressive action against the equally-to-be-respected consciences of the conformists. We may conclude that there is to be recognized a right of sincerity. For it seems illogical to declare, on the one hand, a right to respect the erroneous conscience and, on the other, to enforce an external conformity which the erroneous conscience feels gravely sinful. Professor Jacques Leclercq says, therefore, rightly, "A society in which the only chance to make a career is by being Catholic would be a society where that right of sincerity would be violated. Such a condition would lead to a forced conversion with a consequential poisoning of the Church of God. Out of love for the Church and of respect for human dignity we do not want any such conversions under force or pressure by social conditions."[18]

VI

Parallel to this development runs the other one which stresses not only the *societas perfecta* character of the Church as an institutional juridical framework, as a *Heils-anstalt* which some canonists seem to overstress perhaps, but the character as the Church as a *Heils-gemeinschaft*, as the *populus christianus* and as the *mater ecclesia*. In this problem Father Congar, O.P., states: "We have not yet a satisfactory theology of the laymen in the Church. If we do not get it [he says] we shall have in the face of a laicised (secularized) world only a clerical Church, which can not in the strict sense be 'the people of God'."[19] Reading this thought-provoking essay, one perceives that today our problems are not covered either by the two-powers theory of the Middle Ages or by the later theory of the Church and state in the strict sense, but that the new point of view embraces the idea of the Church also as the people of God, sent to witness for God in the secular society, culture, civilization as the grown sons of the *mater ecclesia*. But then the Bill of Rights becomes of paramount importance. For by it is staked out that field of private and communal activity and initiative with which the state has no right to interfere. The Bill of Rights, of the personal rights, separates the state from "society" and its innumerable free organizations of the "*saeculum*." Then the Church-state relation shifts to a degree. Not only, or even primarily, does it become a question of *potestas*; no, the *libertas ecclesia* as *Anstalt* and as the people of God moves into the foreground.

For this development—and it is such—we have an excellent example in a country where this Christian cultural and social movement as the expression of the Church and as an impression on society has flourished and still flourishes: Belgium. The first claim of the Church as against the state, society, and nation, is the *libertas ecclesia*. God loves above all to have His Church free (Anselm). In order to fulfill its supernatural mission the Church needs the *libertas*. Even in those ages when the *potestas* concept seems to prevail it is actually, if we look deeper, the *libertas ecclesia* which is truly meant, as becomes rather clear if one reads the documents of Gregory VII or of Boniface VIII. The superiority of the Church, her end, her constitution are the ultimate basis for this liberty, though in our times the *libertas ecclesia* is often indirectly based, so to speak, on the personal rights of her children. Belgium was the first state to establish popular sovereignty with a Bill of Rights in the Charter of 1830, following years of political reaction and a revival of jurisdictionalism and the quasi-divine rights theory of the *ancien régime*. Some traditionalists and conservatives attacked the positive attitude of the Belgian Catholic episcopate towards the Charter. But the latter insisted: religion needs liberty and liberty needs religion. In our age we need no other guarantees for the fulfillment of our religious duties except liberty itself. The Church needs nothing more than her liberty in order to maintain herself in her doctrinal purity and in her plenitude (Mérode). The Catholic in Belgium cannot be alone free; the liberty of all has become the condition of their liberty.[20] The Archbishop of Malines wrote to the National Congress: "We do not want privileges, we want a perfect liberty with all its consequences."[21] Gregory XVI, author of *Mirari vos arbitramur*, declared that he had no inquietude concerning the Belgian Constitution, and Adolphe Deschamp could challenge in 1856 the anti-clerical Left to cite one papal word about the alleged incompatibility between the Constitution of Belgium and Catholic doctrine.[22]

VII

On the school question, too, we find the Belgian example instructive. It is against the principle of justice, once the parental rights in the matter of education are recognized, for the state to refuse to permit parents to use the schools according to those rights. It is against justice that parents should be taxed for the maintenance of the public schools and still be compelled to sacrifice income to make use of their rights. In Belgium (of course, Belgium does not know 230 different Protestant sects) the state, represented by the town, has to establish public schools of Catholic character if Catholic parents of a minimum number of children so demand; in addition, the state pays the University of Louvain a certain amount per student to compensate for the savings to the state universities through the work of Louvain. Even in certain parts of France, towns have lately distributed a subsidy to parents of children in the parochial schools with the stipulation that the money be devoted wholly to defray the costs of the parochial, so-called free schools. This seems to me to be an application of a good principle, one that is also used in our country in relation to the educational privileges offered under the Veteran's Bill of Rights. It is, after all, the child as a future active citizen, represented by his parents, who has the right to an education, a right corresponding to the demand of the state that its future active citizens be educated and well-informed. These inter-relations are not given their proper considerations in the United States, possibly because, due to a lack of discretion, it was too often contended that the Churches as such had the superior right to determine the education. Instead, as the *Codex Juris Canonici* clearly proclaims, that right belongs primarily to the parent and, consequently, it becomes his strict duty to exercise it.

It would seem that in modern times the "rival" of the Church is not so much the modern democratic state with its regard for personal dignity and freedom, but rather the totalitarian pagan movements, like Nazism and communism. They are not "states"; they are impersonal forces possessed of evil. What Mirabeau said of Prussia, namely that while states ordinarily have an army, Prussia is an army that has a state, can just as truly be said of these terrible movements; they are ruthless groups who control and employ the states for their inhuman purposes.

VIII

Let us summarize our rather sketchy thoughts. For the Church, liberty is no danger; for a sect, it may be. The difference between them, in the sociological sense, is that the Church has a body of doctrine, a *depositum fidei*, an untouchable treasury of objective truth containing also a minimum of organization which is independent of the "will" of the Church as a corporate body. The sect is wholly spiritualist; its organization is accidental; it has no objective *depositum fidei*; instead, it has only a chance agreement of individual minds. Consequently a Church is internally dogmatically intolerant.[23] This is *a fortiori* true for the Catholic Church. The first claim of the Church is, therefore, the *libertas ecclesiae*, that is, its free corporate life, unhindered by any human intervention in her government, in her cult, worship or her teaching. The positive guarantee of this freedom against such interference or hindrance by the secular government, whether based on the Bill of Rights (that is, the religious freedom of its members as citizens) and the *jus commune*, or on the formal provisions of a concordat or on a constitutional provision, is more a matter of historical development conditioned by circumstances. In order that the Church may grow and fulfill its supernatural function, let us repeat, it needs only her *libertas* based at the minimum on the religious freedom of the Bill of Rights and the *jus commune* (U.S.A.), based, in the ideal, on the full recognition of canon law and of the Church as a *societas perfecta*, as is the case in Belgium, where the Church is recognized as a public corporation.

A last remark: we must since Leo XIII be careful with our application of the thesis that because politics concerns morality and consists of moral acts, it therefore is subject *simpliciter* to the authority of the Church. We must always distinguish clearly in the sphere of morality between the fields of religious and ecclesiastical activity, the field of political, economic, scientific, and artistic activity, and that field of intimate personal activity in which the person has to reach his decision wholly on his own responsibility. The principle of "metaphysical hierarchy of values" does not abolish the equally important principle of autonomy.

It is true that the state has a duty under divine and natural law to acknowledge its Creator and to worship Him. Yet the state is not a substantial being, not a person in the strict sense; it has no *in se et per se esse*. The state acts only through the acts of persons; and, although the common good is related to religion and morality in that it is part of the cosmos of ends *in ordine* to the *summum bonum*, and although the postulate that the state ought to worship God in the way that God has Himself revealed is true, it still remains equally true that, in this worship and in the state's positive relation to religion, the state cannot act immediately but only through the mediation of the persons who constitute its members, those in authority and the citizens. If all—or practically all—of these are Catholic, then, necessarily, worship and religion become a public duty. But if the *materia* of the state, the people whose *forma* the state is, are religiously not homogeneous at all, then the "state" cannot treat as *res publica* that which is not *res publica*. Since the state can only worship through its citizens, if the citizens are in wide disagreement about worship and religion in the sense of revealed theology, to require them to worship in a religion over and above one based on natural theology would only lead to insincerity and the inevitable violation of consciences. A "neutrality" of the state in religious matters, not as a metaphysical principle but as a political maxim, would be the means by which the *libertas ecclesiae* would be best guaranteed.

The temporal *bonum commune* is the proper end of the state according to natural law. Thus, even in the case of the Christian prince, if he restricts himself to this end without putting any difficulties in the way of the freedom of the Church to realize its end, he would still fulfill his strict duty. And to the content of this *bonum commune* belongs the shaping of the public order and the public institution in such fashion that there exist the optimal chances for the citizen to find the truth, natural and supernatural. This seems to be the meaning for us today of the sentence that the state should give preference and favor to the truth as against error.

Notes

Reprinted from *The Review of Politics* 12, no. 3 (July 1950): 321–40.

1. Cf. Father Broderick, "Letter to the Editor," *The Tablet*, no. 5589 (5 July 1947), 10.
2. O. Pfülf, S.J., "Ein parteilos Wort über die Inquisition," *Stimmen der Zeit* 77 (1909): 290, 422.
3. Vacandard, *Dictionnaire de Théologie Catholique*, 7:2066.
4. Capello, *Summa jus publ. eccl.*, 270.
5. Arthur Vermeersch, S.J., *Tolerance*, trans. W. Humphrey Page (London: R & T Washbourne, 1913), 85.
6. [Fr. Luigi Sturzo (1871–1959) was an Italian Catholic priest and politician, one of the founders of the Partito Popolare Italiano in 1919, and a key figure in the history of Christian Democracy. Ed.]
7. "The Church in Portugal: An Interview with the Cardinal Patriarch of Lisbon from a Correspondent," *The Tablet*, no. 5654 (2 October 1948), 215.
8. [António de Oliveira Salazar (1889–1970) was prime minister of Portugal from 1932 to 1968. Ed.]
9. [Louis Veuillot (1813–1883) was a French journalist and author known for his advocacy of ultramontanism (supporting strong papal authority). Ed.]
10. Max Pribilla, S.J., "Dogmatische Intoleranz und bürgerliche Toleranz," *Stimmen der Zeit* 144 (1948/49): 27.
11. [In addition to John Henry Cardinal Newman, Rommen refers here to James Anthony Froude (1818–1894), an English historian, novelist, biographer, and editor of *Fraser's Magazine*, and Wilhelm Emmanuel von Ketteler (1811–1877), a German

theologian and politician who served as bishop of Mainz and wrote on church-state issues. Ed.]

12. Augustin Lehmkul, *Theologia Moralis* (Friburgi Brisgoviae: Herder, 1914), 1:415.

13. [The year 2045 is a hypothetical future date chosen by Murray. Ed.]

14. [The article to which Rommen refers is John Courtney Murray, "St. Robert Bellarmine on the Indirect Power," *Theological Studies* 9 (December 1948): 491–535. Joseph Höffner's work is *Christentum und Menschenwürde, das Anliegen der spanischen Kolonialethik im Goldenen Zeitalter* (Trier: Paulinus Verlag, 1947). On the Jesuit theologian Murray, see also chapter 16 in this collection: Joseph Komonchak et al., "'The Crisis in Church-State Relationships in the U.S.A.' A Recently Discovered Text by John Courtney Murray." Ed.]

15. Joseph Schröteler, *Das Elternrecht in der katholisch-theologischen Auseinandersetzung* (Munich: Neuer Filser Verlag, 1936).

16. Kongo-acts, 1895; Acts of Antislavery Congress, Brussels, 1890; Art. 22 of the League of Nations Covenant, and now the already mentioned international Bill of Rights and the Four Freedoms.

17. See Karl Jaspers, *Der philosophische Glaube angesichts der Offenbarung* (Munich: R. Piper & Co. Verlag, 1947), 73; August Brunner, "Das Weltgefühl des Menschen von heute," *Stimmen der Zeit* 143 (1948/49): 438.

18. Jacques Leclercq, "État chrétien et liberté de l'Église," *La Vie Intellectuelle* (January 1949): 109.

19. Yves M. J. Congar, *Jalons pour une théologie du laïcat* (Paris: Éditions du Cerf, 1948), 42.

20. Georges Goyau, *Catholicisme et politique* (Paris: Éditions de la Revue des Jeunes, 1923), 112.

21. Ibid., 117.

22. Ibid., 120.

23. Cf. the Protestant theologian H. Liermann, *Deutsche Beiträge zu Amsterdam*, 1949, p. 191.

CHAPTER 4

The Social Meaning of Leisure in the Modern World

JOSEF PIEPER

Josef Pieper (1904–1997) was a German Catholic philosopher who focused on the revival of the thought of Thomas Aquinas. He was a professor at the University of Münster from 1950 to 1976, and continued teaching there until 1996, a year before his death. His best-known books include The Four Cardinal Virtues, The Philosophical Act, *and an outgrowth of this essay titled* Leisure: The Basis of Culture, *for which T. S. Eliot wrote the original introduction.*

My intention is to try to face a certain central social problem in its connection with the concept of leisure. And I hope that a solution of that problem, or at least some ways towards a solution, may become more clear and visible. This is a rather modest purpose (because problems are still not solved when a solution has become visible or even when some ways of a solution have become more clear than before).

I shall not consider the social problem from a formally sociological point of view or from a formally political point of view, but from a philosophical point of view. It shall *not* be spoken of in such a way that the field of vision is completely filled with it. The point of view does not lie so close to the concrete phenomena that our attention is occupied and consumed by their immediate impact. Philosophical consideration means that a certain subject is considered within the horizon of the total and universal reality; it belongs to the essence and nature of a really philosophical question, that not only this question itself comes into play, but that——considering, meditating this question—one is obliged to bring into play the totality of the world, even God and the world. In such a view the discussion loses perhaps some actual interest for the politician or for an immediately involved man. But on the other hand, it might be that deeper possibilities of a solution become perceivable, just because the totality of the real world, especially the totality of human nature, comes into the range of vision. It might be, too, that there are social and political problems which, from the mere viewpoint of sociology and politics, cannot be solved. And perhaps this possibility is relevant to our present case. I would like to formulate the claim very modestly. In question is a sort of attempt, a proposal, to view the problem from a new and familiar standpoint. There may result an insight into the social problem—which possibly can become useful within the sphere of politics.

The problem which I would like to consider is the problem of *proletariat*. The encyclical *Quadragesimo Anno* calls this problem, or better the problem of *deproletarianization* (*redemptio proletari*), one of *the* central problems of our time.[1]

Now, first of all, it is necessary to formulate as exactly as possible, what this problem means, and what our formal subject will be. I think it will be good to begin by asking what these concepts—"proletariat," "proletarian," "proletarity," "proletarianization," "deproletarianization"—mean exactly. The central concept is, of course, the concept of *proletarity*. This means the concept of that condition which is characteristic of the proletariat and of the social group as proletariat, which becomes real by the process of proletarianization, and which has to be overcome by the opposite process of deproletarianization. What does proletarity mean? Under what circumstances does a man become a proletarian? One cannot say in which way proletarity will and has to be overcome, if he does not know what proletarity means—what the special distinguishing existential condition means which makes the proletariat proletariat. A first step towards an answer would be: proletarity is not the same thing as poverty. A poor man is not necessarily a proletarian, and a proletarian is not necessarily poor. The beggar within the mediaeval society is not exactly a proletarian. (However, in our epoch a poor, propertyless man normally will become a proletarian.) But the second part of this point seems to be more important: one might be not at all poor, or propertyless, but nevertheless he might be a proletarian. Surely, this condition is valid today. An engineer in Soviet Russia, or a scientific "specialist" undoubtedly is not a poor man; but without any doubt he is a proletarian. The official doctrine of Lenin and Stalin does not misunderstand the structure of Soviet reality, which is called a proletarian state and a people of proletarians.

That distinction between proletarity and poverty is rather important; and consequently it is rather important to distinguish measures for overcoming poverty and emergency (for instance among the refugees) from the necessary realization of a social order; the essential feature of this realization has to be the overcoming of proletarity. A second point, also a negative one, might be phrased as follows: the essential feature of proletarity does not lie in its class-character; that is to say, the negativity of proletarity does *not* consist in its limitation to a certain social group—so that the negativity would be removed if the limitation should disappear. In other words, one cannot say that proletarity would not be so bad if *all* people were proletarians. This is nonsense, of course. But this nonsense is the basis of the ideal: proletarianization of *all*. Yet, it is impossible, of course, to overcome proletarity by the proletarianization of all. The evil in proletarity would just become a universal one.

But now, once again, what does proletarity really mean? The social and economic sciences have given quite a number of answers. If we try to concentrate all those definitions, we may be allowed to conclude: proletarity means to be fettered to the process of working; a proletarian is a man who is fettered to the process of working; deproletarianization would mean to overcome this condition of being fettered.

In order to be exact we must explain what the process of working means, and what it means to be fettered to it. Working is understood in a special limited sense; it does not mean *all* kinds of human activity. It means *useful* activity, activity in so far as it is useful for the necessities of life (as Aristotle says); work here means activity which aims at the realization of a *bonum utile*, of public need. The process of working is the process of the realization of public need, in so far as public need is something different from the concept "commonweal," or better in so far as public need means only a certain part of the commonweal (the latter concept is a much more extensive one—including much more than what is needed, what is 'of use' in the strict sense; contemplation, philosophy, the arts certainly belong to the commonweal, but they do *not* belong to the public need, and so they do not belong to the process of working). The process of working is, in general, the process of production, of using the powers of nature; it is the process of appeasing hunger and all the other necessities of man—a very necessary process manifestly, which never has been and never will be interrupted.

Now, just what does "to be fettered to that process" mean? To be fettered means to be bound, but bound to such a degree that there is no more room for anything else, anything which does not belong to the process of working. To be fettered to the process of work means that one's range of life is consumed and completely occupied by the process of production of, say, the realization of the Five-Year Plan by this social process of using. It means that there is, within the existence of man, no remaining spare time and room, which could be occupied by something which is *not* work and production and Five-Year Plans.

It gradually comes to light that proletarity is a phenomenon very closely connected to economics, but not at all a merely economic fact. One takes the concept of proletarity much too narrowly, if one defines it as a merely (or even as a mainly) economic concept. To be sure, it is not mere chance that the social and economic sciences developed the concepts proletariat and proletarity. But even if we concede that a certain economic condition is the main source and root of proletarity, even then it has to be perceived that the full existential phenomenon of proletarity stretches out beyond the sphere of economics; it is a very anthropological phenomenon, transgressing the region of property-conditions and industrial labor-conditions. Proletarity is a phenomenon, which cannot be sufficiently described or even understood by the notional means of the economic and social sciences. It has to be viewed from a properly philosophical standpoint. It escapes all merely scientific attempts at definition. And all efforts towards a deproletarianization which exclusively or predominantly aim at a mere change and improvement of economic conditions are fruitless from the beginning.

Such theoretical and practical efforts overlook the fact that a lack of property is not at all the only reason for proletarity; it is perhaps *one* main reason. It is, in our modern world, poverty (propertylessness) by which a man is forced to put his own working-power, and that means to put himself, again and again on the labor market and to sell his working-power anew, the working-power which is his only and inclusive property. Thus Goetz Briefs defines proletarity as the obligation (compulsion) to reproduce always the condition of a paid workman.[2] Likewise *Quadragesimo Anno* defines the proletarian as the paid workman without property who possesses nothing else than his own working power, and who *therefore* is fettered to the process of working.

But this is not the only root of proletarity. The condition of being fettered to the process of working can be caused by the dictum of a totalitarian working-state. So the following definition would be valid, too: a proletarian is anyone (whether he possesses private property or not) who, by order of other people (say by order of the political power), is bound to the process of production, of the realization of a plan (the process of using) to such a degree that no room for personal existence remains. *Quadragesimo Anno* speaks of the total and inconsiderate subordination of man to the objective necessities of absolutely expedient and efficient production. This is the precise situation of the engineer and specialist in the totalitarian working-state. He is completely fettered to the process of working, to the fulfillment of the plan.

But there is conceivable a third root of man's being fettered: the inner impoverishment of man. This phrase is not offered as a vague complaint about the intellectual and spiritual condition of modern people. It means exactly the fact that the modern working man is not able to realize (neither by thinking nor by doing) a sphere of human life which could be filled up by something which is not useful work (something which is not only amusement, play, or relaxation and recreation—from work and for new work!). Thus it can be asked: who is a proletarian? A proletarian is one whose space of existence is completely filled up by being fettered to the process of working, because this space of existence of itself has become narrow by reason of an inner shrinkage, because man is no longer able to realize that there is possible a reasonable, sensible doing, which is *not* work and *not* just nothing else. Of course, there exists rest and recreation too, and a refreshing pause or interval. At bottom, there exists only work and man may do many things in such intervals. But all this has no dignity in itself; it is legitimized since it makes possible the process of working and using—legitimized only by reference to public need.

The psychic inner condition of proletarity is a very common fact—not at all limited to the sphere of what usually is called the proletariat. It is a very common fact that people simply do not know what to do in their spare time, what to do on Sunday: to do something which is *neither* simply rest *nor* simply entertainment, play, amusement. This consequently would mean that proletarity is a very common fact—even where the objective facts of proletarian economic conditions do not actually exist. And perhaps all of us are on the way to becoming proletarians—in the meaning of inner impoverishment.

By the way, all the roots of proletarity are essentially connected with each other, in particular both the latter ones—compulsion by the dictate of a working-state and inner impoverishment—are very closely connected to each other and evoke and confirm each other. The totalitarian working-state needs exactly this kind of human "material"; it needs impoverished souls, the ideal substance out of which it can secure enthusiastic or at least non-resistant functionaries. On the other hand, such human beings, such "heroic functionaries" by their own will are inclined to consider and to acknowledge the life of "service," a life with the duties of the functionary, as the only truly accomplished human life.

One may be allowed to ask the question: whether modern people—to the degree of their inner impoverishment—are altogether in danger of becoming functioning parts of a social machinery, of becoming functionaries at the disposal of a totalitarian work-world and of a collectivistic despotism.

Here lies, it seems to me, the deeper historical actuality of the problem "proletariat" and "deproletarianization"—an actuality which stretches out beyond what we are used to call the social problem (in the sense that there would be primarily in question the respective relations of social groups and classes). And it appears that in the exclusively political sphere, it will be impossible to immunize the mind and the thinking of man against the tempting and seductive power of totalitarian ideals and of real totalitarian structures. There is necessary a deep conversion and a new orientation (or better, a return) to the *old* truth. The truth concerning the ultimate meaning of human existence. In this field lies an educational task of extreme importance.

It is in connection with this that a very old and seemingly antiquated, old-fashioned distinction acquires a new importance and a new face. It is the distinction between liberal arts and servile arts. This distinction seems to be a very typical one. *Artes liberales*: these arts and activities are internally legitimized *not* because they serve the necessities of life, or because of their contribution to the public need, or because of any usefulness; the liberal arts derive their character from this: they do *not* belong to the process of using and working; they have their dignity in themselves; they do not need to receive their *raison d'être* from their usefulness, from their relation to an aim outside themselves. The liberal arts signify the central sphere of culture—if one considers culture to be something which *exceeds* all that is merely useful or even necessary with regard to the immediate aims of practical life.

Artes serviles are defined (for instance, by St. Thomas) thus: they are directed towards "utility which is realizable by activity." So it is peculiar to the servile arts that they receive their *raison d'être* from an aim outside themselves. The fruit of the servile arts is only a *bonum utile*. They serve the needs and necessities of life. In this is *their* dignity (which perhaps at first sight seems to be denied by the name "servile arts"); nobody would dare to say that the Church, which speaks explicitly of servile activities and forbids them on Sundays and feast days, condemns these activities or considers them to be something not really human—not at all.

But there is a true difference of ranks and a true order of rank. For the Ancient Greek it was quite easy to understand this difference, because it was based on (or corresponded with) the difference between free men and slaves; liberal arts were the activities of the free, servile arts were the activities of the slaves. Cardinal Newman tried to translate this difference into the modern way of thinking and speaking; he called the liberal arts *gentleman*-activities, and he opposed to them the useful activities of functionaries. Of course, he did not understand this difference between gentleman and functionary as a difference between social groups, and even less as a *rank*-difference between social groups. He thought of a general anthropological difference between two different aspects of human existence; and he did consider this difference as a *rank*-difference (as the Church does too!).

This rank-difference means: the true richness of man does *not* consist in the satisfying of the necessities of life (in spite of the fact that this appeasing is something altogether necessary!); it means that the true richness of man does not even consist in his mastery of the powers of nature, not in his being or becoming the owner and master of nature (*maître et possesseur de la nature*), in which Descartes and Bacon and most of the founders of modern philosophy saw the task of philosophy. The rank-difference between liberal and servile arts is something higher and greater than the production of the useful; it is something which cannot be immediately of use but which nevertheless cannot be missing in a truly human life; something which is necessary for the perfection of human society (as St. Thomas says of contemplative life) and nevertheless quite unable to become a part of a Five-Year Plan. We must certainly not forget that man first of all needs the mere means of subsistence, and that food is more necessary than philosophy and all other liberal arts. But we will not forget either that it was a hungry man who said "Man cannot live by bread alone" (Luke 4:4)—which means, to be sure, at the same time, that man cannot live either if he would have, in addition to bread, only liberal arts and philosophy.

How and why can this distinction between liberal arts and servile arts have any importance and meaning for our question: what does proletarity mean? It is certainly possible to understand proletarity as the limitation and restriction of man to the sphere of servile arts. A proletarian is one who is limited in his existence to the kind of activities which serve the needs of mankind. *Limited* means that the entire space of life is filled up and completely occupied by those servile activities. Once again, this fact of being limited and occupied can be caused by propertylessness, and by the compulsion of a totalitarian working-state, which allows exclusively servile activities (more concretely and more modernly but very exactly spoken: which declares undesirable all activities which have no connection with a Five-Year Plan); and last but not least, that limitation to and imprisonment within the sphere of servile activities can be caused by the inner poverty of man.

To this meaning of proletarity there corresponds, of course, the meaning of deproletarianization (*redemptio proletariorum*). Deproletarianization means to overcome and to remove the state of being fettered to the process of working and of being restricted to the sphere of servile activities. This overcoming has to be realized by removal of the causes, first by developing and making possible private property for the working-man, and second by excluding or removing any collective totalitarian power (which is not necessarily limited to totalitarian regimes), and third, by conquering the internal impoverishment of modern mankind. This threefold aspect of deproletarianization seems to be rather important. It means above all that deproletarianization cannot be realized merely through economic and social (or socialistic) policy. It is thinkable that all things done in the economic and social field may have been done because politicians forgot to overcome and even to fight the internal roots of the state of being fettered to the work-process, forgot to make people internally able to transgress the frontier of that blocked area of servile activities.

The educational task, implied in deproletarianization, comes to light here. One has to enable the proletarians (but in this special aspect perhaps all of us proletarians, as I have already said) to enter the sphere of liberal activities, the region of activities which are neither "work" (in the meaning of immediate utility) nor simply play, recreation, amusement—activities which are not needed but which nevertheless cannot be missing in a fully-realized human life. It belongs to a truly human life to be able to transgress the sphere of need, of utility, of work, and to enter the sphere of leisure. Of course, with regard to this aim, it is not enough to give people more spare time, not enough simply to give them the opportunity to have their own house. (I do not say that those things would not be important or even necessary steps of deproletarianization; I only maintain that these steps are not enough, and that even if they were realized, a decisive problem would be still unsolved). Leisure is a certain condition of mind, a certain state of soul; leisure is not given merely with the external fact of spare time. Man has to become able to realize leisure in itself, to fill up the room which is no longer occupied by the process of work. "This is the main question: what activity will fill up leisure time?" Aristotle wrote this, in his *Politics* (which seems to show that Aristotle saw very clearly the social and even political meaning and importance of the concept "leisure"—or shall I say that Aristotle was convinced that within the region of policy and politics merely political categories are not sufficient?).

Thus proletarity, in its deepest negativity, can only be perceived, and accordingly deproletarianization as a legitimate and genuine aim can only be understood, and of course will only then be realized, if the difference between *artes liberales* and *artes serviles* is understood and acknowledged as a rank-difference. Of course the terminology does not matter. The decisive point is to acknowledge a rank-difference (or at least simply a difference) between merely useful activities which serve a need, and another kind of activities which are not of immediate use, but are nevertheless valuable in themselves. Whenever this difference is denied, the aim "deproletarianization" cannot be affirmed, it cannot even be thought. And as a matter of fact the defenders of a universal proletarianization really do explicitly deny that distinction; they explicitly say that such a difference does not exist and cannot be maintained. It is not only the defenders of an extreme Marxism who say so; it seems to be a very common modern opinion altogether. For instance, Jean Paul Sartre, the French existentialist, proclaimed very explicitly in an important essay (in the first issue of his periodical *Les Temps modernes*) that literature (including poetry and philosophy) must be regarded as a mere social function, as "work" ("intellectual work") and the writer as a workman who gets with his "honorarium" simply the pay for his labor (whereas the ancient concept of honorarium, the recompense appropriate to the liberal arts, is not just identical with a payment but includes the idea of an essential incommensurability between a certain performance and its recompense in money). If we apply the old formulation, Sartre's statement means that there exist only servile activities!

Once again, it is simply impossible to understand from this point of view the meaning of deproletarianization. For this idea involves the overcoming of the limitation and restriction to the sphere of servile activities; the widening of the space of existence beyond this sphere of utility, need and labor; the enabling of people to enter the realm of liberal activities, in which man is internally free from the chains of the necessities of life. In other words, deproletarianization means (or at least includes) that people become competent in leisure. Leisure is the origin of culture (if we understand culture as all those values which exceed immediate need and utility). Leisure is, as Aristotle says (in the same chapter of his *Politics*, 8.3), "the cardinal point around which everything turns." And in the same chapter he says that education to a right realization of leisure has its dignity in itself and exists for its own sake, whereas whatever is learned for professional work serves a need and is therefore only a means but not aim in itself (in which formulation, by the way, deproletarianization once again appears as an immense task of education).

With this high valuation of leisure, the importance of the following fact becomes visible in a new way: there exists one institution in the world (whilst the totalitarian work-world declares undesirable or even illicit all activities which are not referable to the public need, all activities not "of use," even the spare time is from this viewpoint) which declares undesirable on certain days just useful activities, those which serve for profit and for need. The Church knows that on Sundays and feast days there is procured forever a space of leisure, of freedom, of a non-proletarian existence.

One of the earliest European socialists, Pierre Joseph Proudhon—whom, it is true, Karl Marx dismissed as a *petit bourgeois*—seems not to have been so wrong when he began, one hundred years ago, with a booklet on the *celebration du dimanche* (the celebration of Sunday), the social meaning of which he formulates in the following way: "During this one day the servants got back their dignity as men and placed themselves again on the same level with their masters." This terminology became in the meantime obsolete and to some even unbearable. But what is meant is something quite true, namely, that the sphere within which social peace and alliance are to be expected, is not the sphere of a common and mutual proletarity, rather the sphere in which man is not a functionary but a human being. Social peace cannot be established on the basis of proletarianization of all, but only on the basis of deproletarianization! The following sentence from Proudhon gets to the heart of the problem: "Considering all questions of labor and wages, of the organization of industry and national plants which involve the public, I thought it might be sensible to make a study of legislation, the basis of which is a theory of rest." Proudhon has in mind the Old Testament laws on the Sabbath. To be sure it is impossible to get any sight of the ultimate depth of this "theory of rest" if one considers it (as Proudhon does) only from the viewpoint of "public health, morality, family and civil conditions."

Proudhon did not become aware of the main point. Proudhon did not perceive, and he was not able to perceive, what Plato—the old Plato of the *Laws*—very clearly saw and understood and formulated, namely, that the deepest root of a feast day is the divine cult, and that it is the cult which primarily sets man free and makes possible the freedom in which man ceases to be a mere functionary. Plato saw that the festive intercourse with the gods makes man able to overcome the menial labor of work and to win back his original uprightness. Plato says: "The Gods, in pity for the human race, thus born to labor, have ordained the feasts as periods of respite from their painful work; and they have granted them as companions in their feasts the Muses and Apollo the Master of Muses and Dionysius—that they, nourished by the festive intercourse with the Gods, may win back their upright shape" (*Laws* II, 653c–d).

This is another idea and a new viewpoint: deproletarianization in its deepest and radical meaning hardly seems to be possible without a *religious* renewal and revival, and more exactly, without a new living understanding of cult. It is one of the highest tasks of philosophy, to make possible and even unavoidable penetrations into the sphere of theology and cult. But to speak more explicitly of that religious revival stretches out beyond a philosophical meditation on the social meaning of leisure.

NOTES

Reprinted from *The Review of Politics* 12, no. 4 (October 1950): 411–21.

1. [*Quadragesimo Anno* is a papal encyclical issued in 1931 by Pope Pius XI on the occasion of the 40th anniversary of Leo XIII's *Rerum Novarum*. Both encyclicals deal with the social doctrine of the church, particularly the conditions of workers after the industrial revolution and the rise of both capitalism and totalitarianism. Ed.]

2. [Goetz Briefs (1889–1974) was a German Catholic social thinker who influenced Pope Pius XI. Some scholars speculate that he helped draft *Quadragesimo Anno*. Ed.]

CHAPTER 5

Common Good and Common Action

YVES R. SIMON

Yves Simon (1903–1961) was a French Catholic political philosopher who studied under Jacques Maritain, earning degrees at the Sorbonne and the Institut Catholique. He wrote extensively on Thomism and political liberalism. His writings have helped the Catholic Church come to embrace—and also criticize—democracy on the basis of Thomistic thought. Among his best-known works are A General Theory of Authority, Philosophy of Democratic Government *(Charles R. Walgreen Foundation Lectures)*, The Tradition of Natural Law: A Philosopher's Reflections, *and* Work, Society, and Culture. *In the United States he taught at the University of Notre Dame (1938–1948) and the University of Chicago's Committee on Social Thought (1948–1961).*

Anarchy is rarely or never upheld with consistency. In the pedagogy of Rousseau, there is a set purpose to let the child be guided by natural necessity rather than by human command, and to let him learn from the experience of physical facts rather than by obedience. "Keep the child solely dependent on things; you will have followed the order of Nature in the process of his upbringing. Never oppose to his unreasonable wishes any but physical obstacles or punishments resulting from the actions themselves—he will remember these punishments in similar situations. It is enough to prevent him from doing evil without forbidding him to do it. . . ." (*Emile*, II). Remarkably, the theory that the method of authority is a poor substitute for the pedagogical power of nature has been accepted, in varying degree of enthusiasm or reluctance, by most schools of pedagogy and has demonstrated lasting power. Yet the authority of parents and tutors is present throughout pedagogical theories, even when it is passed over in silence.

Childhood is the domain where the suppression of all authority is obviously impossible. The most radical constructs of anarchy, as soon as they rise above the level of idle rhetoric, admit of qualifications so far at least as the immature part of mankind is concerned. Anti-authoritarian theorists, with few exceptions if any, do not mean that authority should disappear or that it can ever cease to be a factor of major importance in human affairs. What thinkers opposed to authority generally mean is that authority can never be vindicated except by such *deficiencies* as are found in children, in the feeble-minded, the emotionally unstable, the criminally inclined, the illiterate, and the historically primitive.

The real problem is not whether authority must wither away: no doubt, it will continue to play an all-important part in human affairs. The problem is whether deficiencies alone cause authority to be necessary. It is obvious, indeed, that in many cases the need for authority originates in some defect and disappears when sufficiency is attained. But the commonly associated negation, that authority never originates in the positive qualities of man and society, is by no means obvious and should not be received uncritically. The supposition that authority, in certain cases and domains, is made necessary not by human deficiencies but by the very nature of man and society—this supposition is not evidently absurd. To hold, in some *a priori* way, that it does not deserve examination would merely evince wishful thinking of the least scientific kind. The truth may well be that authority has several functions, some of which would be relative to deficient states of affairs and others to such features of perfection as the existence of human communities, their actions, and their achievements.

If any functions of authority originate in nature and plenitude rather than in deficiency, it can be reasonably conjectured that they are relative to common existence and common action. Granted that in many cases authority merely substitutes for self-government, the theory that it also has essential functions must be tested first in the field of community life. But the definition of this field presupposes an inquiry, no matter how brief, into human sociability.

Grounds and Forms of Sociability

The Needs of the Individual

It is perfectly obvious that the needs of the individual call for the association of men; yet significant implications of this proposition are commonly ignored. For one thing, the notion of individual need is often restricted, in most arbitrary fashion, to needs of a biological, physical, material character. The necessity of mutual assistance and division of labor in the fight against hunger and thirst, cold, wild beasts, and disease is more commonly expressed than the immense and almost constantly increased service that society renders to individuals in intellectual, aesthetic, moral, and spiritual life. Any improper emphasis on the physical needs served by society suggests that the purposes and the requirements of social life are contained within a sphere of material goods. Concomitantly, it is often taken for granted that the goods of the spirit are altogether individual and that their pursuit is an entirely individualistic concern. Thus, human life would be split into a part socialized by material needs and a nobler part distinguished both by spirituality and individual independence. To dispose of this construct, just think of what a beginner in the sciences owes to the daily assistance of society. A comparison between a student in our universities and a man self-educated in the wilderness would involve a good deal of fiction, but we have all the data needed to compare, with regard to proficiency, students separated by a few generations. In the fields where the social life of the understanding is most successful—mathematics, physics—the men of the younger generation can solve with the resources of ordinary intelligence problems which were hardly treatable for geniuses of earlier ages.

By another unwarranted restriction of meaning, it is often held that a need is necessarily self-centered. In fact, the notion of need expresses merely the state of a tendency not yet satisfied with ultimate accomplishment. Among the tendencies which make up the dynamism of a rational being, some are self-centered and some are generous; all admit of a state of need, and the need to give is no less real than the need to take. Consider the grounds of friendship and the ways in which a man is related to his friends. A young fellow, uncertain about what he is and what he wants to be, with little background, no estate, no steady position, with much anxiety, will be looking for friends in a context of self-centered needs. No ethically unfavorable connotation attaches to the notion of a need centered about the self. Whether the center of a need is within the self or beyond it depends upon the nature of the tendency involved and is antecedent to moral use. Needs relative to such goods as food and shelter are self-centered by nature and remain self-centered in the most disinterested man despite all the generosity which enters into his way of satisfying his needs and of relating their satisfaction to further ends.

But some needs have their center beyond the self; a man whose personality features contrast with those of the young fellow described just above still needs friends. He does not depend on the help of friends for food or shelter, for his fortune is already made; he is not in the least motivated by the expectation of physical care in case of disease, for he is in good health and anyway has little fear of disease and death; neither does it occur to him that he may need friendly attention to soothe him in case of emotional disaster, for his nervous balance is well assured; and he does not feel that the company of friends is necessary to him as protection against boredom, for he does so well in the company of his ideas, his memories, his books, and familiar belongings that the threat of boredom is not felt. We are describing a distinguished instance of mature development, strength of character, soundness, dominating indifference, freedom. Yet this accomplished person needs the company of loved ones, inasmuch as his very state of accomplishment intensifies in him every generous trait and every tendency to act by way of superabundance. He needs to give. True, the center of the act of giving is found in the beneficiary of the gift, and the gift is primarily designed to satisfy a need in the receiver. Yet the gift satisfies also a need in the giver. Such a non-self-centered need may attain a high degree of intensity. The accomplished person whom we are considering would be unhappy if he knew no children to please with Christmas presents, and his homecoming from happy journeys would be gloomy if no one expected him to bring jewelry or dresses from the remote land. His knowledge would give him little joy if he had no chance to impart it to eager intellects, and the very firmness of his character would seem to him a tedious advantage if it should never result in a friend's achieving greater mastery over himself.

For the sake of clarity, we have used the example of a firm and accomplished person to describe other-centered needs. In such persons generosity is most obviously noticeable. However, other-centered needs exist in all; they secretly move the last of men. To appreciate the power and the social significance of other-centered needs in everyone, it suffices to remark that in case of frustration the tendency to act generously becomes the most redoubtable of antisocial drives. Men would rather stand physical destitution than be denied opportunity for disinterested love and sacrifice.

The Common Good

The question now arises whether the needs of the individual are the only cause of human association and whether, correspondingly, society has no purpose beyond the satisfaction of individual needs. The word "individualism," which so often is made worthless by confusion, admits of a precise sense insofar as it designates the theory that the single purpose of society is the service of the individual. The individualistic interpretation of sociability appeals to souls trained in humane disciplines and possessed of an exacting sense for the human character of everything that pertains to society. As soon as it is suggested that the purpose of human effort lies in an achievement placed beyond the individual's good, a suspicion arises that human substance may be ultimately dedicated to things as external to man as the pyramids of Egypt. In all periods of history, voluminous facts signify that under the name of common good, republic, fatherland, empire, what is actually pursued may not be a good state of human affairs but a work of art designed to provide its creator with the inebriating experience of creation. The joy of the creator assumes unique intensity when the thing out of which the work of art is made is human flesh and soul. The artist's rapture is greatest when he uses as matter of his own creation not marble and brass but beings made after the image of God. "The finest clay, the most precious marble—man—is here kneaded and hewn...."[1] True, the common good conceived as a work of art and a thing external to man is merely a corruption of the genuine common good. In this world of contingency, every form or process admits of imitation; in human affairs, the most dreadful counterfeit is often so related to the genuine form that it appears, with disquieting frequency, precisely where the genuine form is most earnestly sought. An inquiry into the common good must involve constant awareness that its object may, at any time, be displaced by deadly counterfeit.

To answer the question of whether the association of men is designed to serve not only the needs of the individual but also goods situated beyond individual achievement, we should turn our attention, first, to the limitations of individual plenitude; then we may be able to understand, just by glancing at the daily life of human communities, how these limitations are transcended.

Individuals are narrowly restricted with regard to diversity, and inevitable circumstances hold in check the desire for totality which belongs to rational nature. In terms of essential causality, there is no reason why one and the same man should not be painter, musician, philosopher, captain of industry, and statesman. In fact, personalities developed excellently on more than a very few lines are extremely rare, and significant limitations can easily be found in Leonardo da Vinci and Goethe. The rule to which all men are subjected in varying degree is one of specialization for the sake of proficiency. This rule entails heavy sacrifices even in the most gifted. A man highly successful in his calling accomplishes little in comparison with the ample virtualities of man. He has failed in a hundred respects. Only the union of many can remedy the failure of each. But of all the restrictions inflicted upon the boundless ambition of our rational nature, the most painful concerns the duration of individual achievements. Within the temporal order we would feel hopeless if the virtually immortal life of the community did not compensate for the brevity of individual existence. Death is known to be particularly hard and surrounded with anxiety for those who end their days in individualistic loneliness.

These are the familiar facts referred to by a well-known text of Aristotle, ordinarily summed up in the following words, "The common good is greater and more divine than the private good."[2] "Greater" expresses a higher degree of perfection with regard both to duration and to diversity. "Divine," as translating the Greek *theion*, does not designate so much a godlike essence as a participation in the privilege of imperishability. In this world of change, individuals come and go. The law of generation and corruption covers the whole universe of nature. This law is transcended in a very proper sense by the incorruptibility of the species and the immortality of human association. The masterpiece of the natural world cannot be found in the transient individual. Nor can it be found in the species, which is not imperishable except in the state of universality; but in this state it is no longer unqualifiedly real. Human communities are the highest attainments of nature, for they are virtually unlimited with regard to diversity of perfections, and virtually immortal. Beyond the satisfaction of individual needs the association of men serves a good unique in plenitude and duration, the common good of the human community.

Partnership and Community

To state the problem of authority, we still need an inquiry into the basic forms of association. The main patterns of human societies are the mere partnership and the community. Of course, these two types may combine, but the obscurity of mixed realizations just renders more valuable the understanding of typical forms. Let us first consider familiar examples. A merchant succeeds in convincing an owner of capital that money invested in his business would bring nice dividends. By the terms of their contract, any profits will be divided according to a definite ratio. Then the merchant goes to the market, and the money-lender sits back and awaits the event. Their "common interest" was celebrated in expectant toasts, but they are not engaged in any common action designed to promote any "common interest." The merchant works by himself or with his employees; he does not work with the money-lender, who remains a silent partner. Where there is no common action, there is no common good. These two men do not make up a community. What they call their "common interest" is in fact a sum of private interests that happen[3] to be interdependent.

In contradistinction to mere partners, the members of a community—family, factory, football team, army, state, church—are engaged in a common action whose object is qualitatively different from a sum of interdependent goods. Whereas the contractual relation is normally the sufficient rule of the mere partnership, our problem is precisely to decide whether the community normally calls for the kind of rule known as authority.

To conclude this preliminary inquiry, let us remark that contract and community can be related in diverse ways. (1) The association established by contract may be of such nature that the relation between the associates remains exclusively contractual. The money-lender and the merchant exemplify such a case. (2) The association founded by contract may be of such nature as to involve a common action. When they sign a contract, partners may be entering into a society which is not a mere partnership. Such is the case, for instance, in the hiring of labor. Production demands that manager and laborer act together, and neither has the character of a silent partner. However, communities of this type can, in most instances, be dissolved at will, or according to terms specified by the initial contract. (3) The community founded by contract may not be dissoluble at will. It may even be of such nature as not to be dissoluble at all. Because the contract is the only rule of the mere partnership, it is commonly assumed, by unwarranted inference, that persons associated by contract necessarily remain mere partners and can dissolve their association. The relation between man and wife involves a character of stability determined by the very nature of the man-and-wife community. Yet this community was founded by contract.

If nothing abnormal occurs, the need for authority is never felt in a relation of mere partnership. The contractual arrangement which, as such, is absolutely equalitarian, suffices. A decision by authority will be necessary only if the working of the contract is impeded by such accidents as misunderstanding, bad faith, or unforeseen conjuncture. Thus, if all human societies were mere partnerships, authority would never be needed except on account of some fault or accident. The deficiency theory of authority would be entirely vindicated.[4]

The Unity of Common Action

Assuming now the features proper to the kind of association described as community, let us state the problem of united action. Every community is relative to a good to be sought and enjoyed in common. But, by the very fact that a community comprises a number of individuals, the unity of its action cannot be taken for granted: it has to be caused. Further, if the community is to endure, the cause of its united action must be firm and stable. Since rational agents are guided by judgment, the problem of bringing about unity in the action of men resolves into the problem of insuring the unity of their practical judgment. For example, the family community would cease to exist if each member did not judge—for one reason or another—that he ought to reside in this particular locality and in this particular house. A farm would soon be ruined if those engaged in the production of wheat did not all judge—again, for one reason or another—that these fields ought to be put into wheat this year. A factory could not operate if the members of its personnel did not all judge that a definite schedule ought to be observed. A deliberating assembly is indeed a community designed to stand disagreement, yet in order that it should exist at all, there must be some agreement regarding the place and time of its meetings, regarding the rules of procedure, and regarding some principles. In these and all similar cases, unity of judgment cannot be procured by rational communication. The believers in a social science which would, under circumstances of perfect enlightenment, eliminate the decisions of authority—and those of freedom as well—assume that the kind of necessity which makes demonstration possible extends to the particulars of social practice. But, clearly, such propositions as "It is good for us to live in this house," and "It is proper that our assembly should meet at noon," admit of no demonstration. Philosophical prejudice alone may cause failure to perceive the contingency in which such propositions are engaged. United action demands a principle that works steadily amidst the overwhelming contingencies of perishable existence. Rational communication, which is bound up with essential necessities, is not such a principle.

Does it follow that unanimity is under all circumstances an uncertain and precarious principle of unity in action? This question requires that we consider a community whose members are, without exception, ideally virtuous and enlightened persons. Unanimity is well known to be a most precarious achievement in communities afflicted by such common deficiencies as ignorance, prejudice, selfish interest, and the like, but our purpose is to decide whether authority is ever needed independently of deficiencies. We must bear in mind, accordingly, a group free from stupidity and ill-will. If such a group were a Utopian fiction, it still could play a part in the understanding of society. In fact, there exist groups whose members are all intelligent and morally excellent; that these groups are very small makes no difference for the purposes of rational analysis.

Rational Communication and Affective Communion

Since unanimity cannot be established in these practical matters by the power of demonstration, the ideally clever and virtuous members of a community cannot be unanimous in more than fortuitous fashion unless a determined course of action is demanded by the virtuous inclination of their hearts. Whenever wisdom has to find its way in the midst of circumstances contingent and possibly unique, the certainty of its judgment results from its agreement with honest inclination. An ethical issue universal in character—say, a general problem of justice—can be answered, as St. Thomas puts it, in either of two ways, the way of cognition and the way of inclination. In the way of cognition, the answer proceeds from principles by logical connections. This is how the moral philosopher is supposed to answer questions, and no other method is acceptable in philosophy, because no other method procures certainty in knowledge as knowledge.[5] But an honest man unacquainted with deductive processes may find the answer intuitively and in incommunicable fashion by feeling that such and such a way of doing things pleases or revolts his sentiment of justice.[6] Provided his is a genuine virtue—as distinct from emotional counterfeits—and is sufficiently developed, the judgment dictated by such a sentiment of agreement or aversion is certain. By love for what justice demands, the heart of the just is shaped after the pattern of justice, and his inclination is one with the requirement of his virtue. To say that a will is virtuous is to say that its movements coincide with the demands and aversions of virtue itself. Between the ethically good appetite and ethical goodness there exists a unity of nature, a con-naturality, which constitutes a dependable source of practical truth. Because the just will corresponds in all its movements to the object of justice, the inclinations experienced by the just are like statements uttered by the object of justice. Here, according to the words of John of St. Thomas, "Love takes on the role of the object."

It is entirely by accident that we can demonstrate so little about the requirements of justice or chastity, considered in their intelligible universality, but it is not by accident that nobody can demonstrate what the rule of justice consists in under individual, historically-conditioned, absolutely concrete, and possibly unprecedented and unrenewable circumstances. Here the rule of justice is not uttered by an essence and cannot be grasped by the demonstrative power of the intellect. It is uttered by the love which is the soul of the just and it can be learned only by listening to the teaching of love. Take for instance the problem of ownership in case of extreme necessity. Our sense of justice acknowledges that a starving person, without money and without liberal friends, has a right to save his life with food that he cannot pay for. No doubt, such a proposition can be demonstrated, and St. Thomas successfully designated the middle term of its demonstration when he remarked that in case of necessity all things become common.[7] But argumentation will never establish a logical connection between the theory of property and the answer that *I* am looking for when, already weakened by hunger, I wonder whether my case is actually one of extreme necessity. A man in need will know for sure whether his necessity is extreme or not if and only if he is so just as to feel how far the right of his neighbor and his own right go, so temperate as not to mistake an accidental urge for a real need, and so strong as to fear neither the sufferings of hunger nor the resentment of his illiberal neighbors.

Thus, whereas a question relative to an ethical essence can be answered both by way of cognition and by way of inclination, the way of inclination alone can procure an answer when a question of human conduct involves contingency. This holds for the rules of common action as well as for those of individual conduct. Political prudence is no less dependent upon the obscure forces of the appetite than prudence in the government of individual life. However, with regard to unity of judgment among men, there is a significant difference between individual prudence and any prudence concerned with the conduct of a community. The prudence of the individual normally involves something singular and peculiar—it would almost be appropriate to say "eccentric." In their hopeless search for guidance amidst the obscurities of action, men easily assume that problems of individual conduct are the same for all, or at least for many, and that the rule which led one to a happy solution can be confidently followed by others. This assumption works sometimes, when problems are not significantly modified by individual circumstances; yet it is false, and may at any time bring about disastrous effects, for, in the broad field that lies beyond determination by ethical essences, it never can be said *a priori* that individual features are irrelevant. A life of moderate work and strict parsimony may be precisely what a certain family needs, but misfortune may befall a neighboring home unless the line followed is one of rather lavish expenditure at the cost of strenuous work, and in still another case real wisdom may paradoxically require liberal spending, an abundance of leisure, and willingness to go into debt. Of such contrasting rules of action, some may prove sound in a great number of cases and some may prove harmful save for rare exceptions. Yet it is never possible to know in advance—prior to an investigation of whatever unique features a case may comprise—that the rule required in this individual case is not precisely the one which would prove unsuited to nearly all other cases. Because of the possible relevance of unique features in the determination of individual prudence, each man is threatened with the contingency of having to make his decisions in utter solitude and to act like no one else. The anguish of such solitude is more than most men can stand, hence the tendency to take refuge in uniformity and conformity, even though precious features of individual destiny may be destroyed by adherence to common practice.

When the prudence of men is concerned with the welfare of one and the same community—their community—individual features have, in principle,[8] nothing to do with the making of a wise decision. Among the most significant data, some are, indeed, strictly unique, but they pertain to the community's unique history and thus tend to cause agreement rather than diversity of judgment. Any common pursuit, on no matter how humble a level, is a welcome remedy to the anguished solitude of individual prudence. To be sure, science is a factor of human unity, but it is in a world of abstraction that it causes men to elicit identical judgments. In common action alone does concrete existence, with all its determinateness, with its character of totality, its location in time, and its contingency, tend to procure unity among men. Assuming that our community is made entirely of clever and well-intentioned persons, whatever is needed for its welfare is the object of unanimous assent. Affective communion achieves what cannot be expected of rational communication: it brings about unanimity of judgment in the life of action. Again, every certain judgment concerning what we have to do under concrete circumstances is dictated by an affective motion and owes its certain truth to its agreement with dependable inclination. But when the pursuit is that of a common good, the part played by affective and secret determinants is no longer an obstacle to unity of judgment among men. Wills properly inclined toward the same common good cannot but react in the same way to the same proposition, if what this proposition expresses is definitely what the common good demands. In groups small enough not to involve much error and bad will, the adherence of all to decisions that are necessary though indemonstrable brings about marvels of united action. As to larger communities—say, cities or nations—where all sorts of evils and deficiencies are inevitable, situations resembling unanimity and entailing most of the effects that unanimity would entail are a comparatively frequent occurrence. Consider the case of a nation attacked by a neighbor eager for territorial expansion. That resistance is better than appeasement cannot be demonstrated, and many citizens do not have the civic virtue which would procure indefectible adherence to what common salvation demands. Yet history shows that spontaneous unity often characterizes the reaction of peoples in this predicament. If there were a question of polling opinion, it would be impossible to speak of unanimity. There are traitors, collaborationists, neutralists, abstentionists, honest men deceived by overwhelming illusions, and passive citizens without an answer to a question that never actually reached their minds. But these disrupters of unanimity are comparatively few, and they carry so little weight as to make little difference. Practically and for all significant purposes, the situation is about what it would be if unanimity were realized.

But after having recognized the marvels that unanimity, or quasi-unanimity can work, let it be remarked that *unanimity is a precarious principle of united action whenever the common good can be attained in more than one way*. All that has been said in the foregoing about the power of unanimity simply makes no sense except when the way to the common good is uniquely determined. If the common good can be attained in more than one way, neither enlightenment nor virtue, but only chance, can bring about unanimity. Accordingly, if unity of action is guaranteed by no other principle than that of unanimous agreement, it becomes an entirely casual affair, the result being either stalemate or divided and destructive action. Circumstances may be such that the happy life of a man-and-wife community can be easily attained either in Washington or in New York, but if one member of the community prefers, with the best of intentions, Washington, and the other, with an equally virtuous disposition, New York, the principle of action by unanimous agreement determines the separation of these well-meaning spouses.

There is nothing wrong with a man who, so far as he is concerned, likes to drive on the right-hand side of the road, and nothing wrong with the fellow who, if he had his own choice, would drive on the left. Thus traffic rules cannot be decided by the unanimous consent of enlightened and virtuous drivers. Assuming that all good citizens are agreed that the public budget cannot be cut below such and such an amount, it is obvious that the money needed for public purposes can be gathered, without injustice or particular harm, in a diversity of ways. Citizens may, without there being anything wrong with their intelligence or intention, take diverse stands with regard to such methods of taxation as sales tax, gross income tax, or a combination of both. In military operations, either of two plans of attack may provide a reasonable chance of victory, but defeat is certain if the attacker's power is split between the two plans. Among the most experienced and dependable leaders, some prefer one plan and some the other. There is no reason why they should be unanimous, since each plan, insofar as those things fall under human providence, is a way to victory. Among the many ways of playing a concerto of Bach, several satisfy the requirements of great music, and highly qualified musicians will clash as to how the fourth Brandenburg Concerto should be played. Yet the members of an orchestra cannot be allowed conflicting interpretations of a concerto. In fact, any conceivable instance of common action, if considered in all its modes and particulars, admits of being carried out according to one or another of several methods, all leading to the common good.

Knowledge and Freedom

To the proposition that authority, as the cause of united action, exercises an essential function, a function made necessary not by any evil or deficiency but by the nature of common action, it is currently objected that any multiplicity of ways leading to a common purpose is an illusion that social science, if better developed, would dismiss. The problem involved here is that of choice, and it pertains to the subject of liberty more directly than to the subject of authority.

When the theory of liberty is not enlivened by some sort of ethical enthusiasm, it often is surrounded by a cloud of misgivings, as if liberty could be preserved only by cherished ignorance and should yield to unique determination as soon as the truth is known about the proper way to our end. Indeed, everyone's experience tells of deliberations that bear on illusory as well as genuine means. If proper information comes before decision is made, and excludes the illusory means—the lines of action which, in spite of appearances, do not lead to the end but to failure and perhaps disaster—everything is better in all conceivable respects. Considering that a wholesome simplification takes place whenever an illusory means is ruled out, we sometimes dream of carrying simplification down to the state of unique determinateness, and we like to imagine that in perfect acquaintance with the real state of affairs the lines of action originally listed as means would, with but one exception, be identified as so many illusions. It is easy to see that this postulate expresses aversion to the mystery involved in free choice as well as to the darkness of contingency. Relations characterized by sheer determinateness, without contingency and without freedom, offer an average type of intelligibility which has been constantly preferred by rationalism. Indeed, any feature of contingency is a restriction on intelligibility, but the world of reality may be such as not to be intelligible in all respects. It is, after all, a question of fact, and we must be ready to accept whatever conclusion is reached by the scientific and philosophic description of the world. Freedom, on the other hand, if there is such a thing, would involve extraordinary plenitude of being, causality and intelligibility. But the more intelligible is not always the more easy to understand. In all scientific disciplines there are admirably simple views and methods which remain inaccessible to all but a very few scholars. Why are these things so hard to grasp? Not because they lack intelligibility, but rather because they are so excellently intelligible that only the best intellects are proportioned to them. With a mind open both to the restricted intelligibility of things contingent and to the secrecy of freedom, it is possible to inquire into the meaning of choice without begging any question. Let the problem be stated in these simple words: Is choice necessarily narrowed down to one genuine and one (or several) ungenuine means? Is choice necessarily between one good and one (or several) evils? *Is there such a thing as a choice among goods?* Can there conceivably be several means to an end? In a comparison of agents, should it be said that some are restricted to one or few means and that others have a wide variety of means at their disposal?

As soon as these questions are posed without any prejudice relative to the intelligibility of things, experience supplies the basic answers. Several diets can maintain the health of a healthy man, but a diseased organism may need, as a *sine qua non* of survival, what everyone calls a strict, uniquely determined, diet. An ordinary student, to attain proficiency in mathematics, needs all the complex system worked out by academic societies—teachers, textbooks, treatises, discussions, tutorials—but in the case of genius alternative means make it possible to dispense with much of the academic apparatus. It has been remarked that when a new pedagogical method is tested by a born teacher, success proves nothing, for born teachers are known to achieve success with almost any method; in order to know how good a method is, it is better to have it tested by an undistinguished teacher who depends heavily on the quality of the method used.

A man trained in one craft and unable to do any other job has to work in uncongenial conditions; the man with many skills can afford to be more particular about the circumstances of his employment. No one would say that the broader choice open to the man with many skills originates in ignorance and illusion;

clearly, it results from a greater power and presupposes more and better knowledge. An industrial enterprise with little capital must produce only that which will surely bring immediate returns; the privilege of contributing extensively to diversity and novelty in the market belongs to firms better financed. It is a commonplace of American history that waste of natural resources was determined initially by an acute shortage of manpower. The only ways of development open to a young community placed in natural abundance were the wasteful ones. We judge more severely the habits of waste in those later generations which, owing to great numbers, firmer establishment, more advanced techniques, and many other forms of increased power, have choices that the early settlers did not have. A nation with no navy, a very small army, no financial stature, and declining population, if offered the alliance of a powerful neighbor, has to accept it albeit at the cost of heavy sacrifices and historical resentments; but given great bargaining power, a nation can choose its allies. In all conceivable circumstances, power increases choice. The proper effect of enlightenment, accordingly, is twofold: improved knowledge rules out illusory means and, insofar as it entails greater power, multiplies the genuine ones. To destroy the illusion of a means is not to cut the amplitude of choice, for, insofar as it extends to illusory means, choice itself is but an illusion. In an ideally enlightened community, authority would be spared the unhappy task of directing the common effort, in the darkness of illusion, along a possibly disastrous line. But, inasmuch as an excellent condition of knowledge implies greatly increased power, social science at its perfection would multiply genuine means and broaden real choice. *It would, consequently, increase the need for authority as a factor of united action in the cases where the plurality of the genuine means renders unanimity fortuitous.*

Strikingly, it is a better understanding of freedom which first discloses the essential character of the need for authority in common action. But why is it that whenever we think of diverse ways leading to the common good we are so strongly tempted to attribute their diversity, and the corresponding variety of preferences, to our ignorance of some relevant features or circumstances? A stubborn objection holds that if men were omniscient, unanimous adherence to the end would necessarily entail unanimity regarding the means. Let us briefly inquire into the cause of this belief.

In all domains of understanding and interpretation, whether trivial or lofty and subtle, we are inclined to transfer the properties of the better known subjects to subjects that are not so well known. This is why Aristotle—or some follower of his—says that it is unreasonable to seek at the same time the science of a subject and the method of this science:[9] unless the method is known in advance—albeit in the most rudimentary fashion—we shall inevitably force upon the new study dispositions acquired in previous studies, for example, apply to medicine dispositions which proved excellent in mechanics, or consider ethics with the bias of a mind trained in theoretical science.

Notice, at this point, that the things pertaining to cognition are better known than the things pertaining to appetition and volition. Every time we turn to some aspect of appetitive and volitional life, we carry with us frames of mind and schemes of interpretation developed in our endeavor to understand cognitive life. We are inclined to reconstruct appetition after the pattern of cognition. But cognition is not free from deficiency unless it is strictly determinate. If the problem is to know what the things are, nothing is worse than perfect indifference, the state in which a proposition appears just as plausible as its contradictory. Things are somewhat better if one part of the alternative is more probable than the other, but so long as one of the two is not excluded by unqualified necessity, cognition remains defective. With regard to facts and to essences as well, the faculty of choosing, at will, between assent and dissent is not an asset but expresses an entirely negative state of affairs. Accordingly, the understanding of cognition results in a pattern where perfection strictly coincides with uniqueness. But appetition is, in a way, the opposite of cognition, for, whereas the known is attracted into the knower, the lover is attracted toward the beloved, and whereas the true exists in the mind, the good exists in the things.[10] This basic contrast reverses the meaning of uniqueness, plurality and indifference, when inquiry moves from cognition to appetition. A plurality of possible assents with regard to one and the same subject evidences failure to attain truth with certainty; the indifference of the uncertain mind is made of inachievement, indetermination, potentiality, passivity. On the contrary, a plurality of means with regard to one and the same end evidences mastery, domination, actuality, activity, superdetermination. The myth of a perfect knowledge which would eliminate authority and liberty rests upon a crude confusion of two kinds of indifference: the passive one, which results from potency and inachievement, and the dominating one, which results from excellence.

An Essential Function of Authority

The existence of a plurality of genuine means in the pursuit of the common good excludes unanimity as a *sufficient* method of steadily procuring unity of action.

To achieve indispensable unity in common action, one method is left, which can be described as follows: whether we prefer to live in Washington or in New York, whether we prefer to drive on the right or on the left side of the road, whether we prefer sales tax, gross income tax, or their combination, whether we prefer a richer or a more austere orchestration of Bach, every one of us, insofar as he is engaged in the common action, will accept and follow, as rule of his own action, one judgment thus constituted into rule for all. This rule of common action may coincide with my own preference, but this is of no significance, for the common rule might just as well be at variance with my liking, and I would be equally bound to follow it out of dedication to the common good, which cannot be attained except through united action. *The power in charge of unifying common action through rules binding for all is what everyone calls authority.*[11] It may be a distinct person designated by nature, as in the couple and in the family. It may be a distinct person designated by God, as in the cases of Saul and Peter. It may be a distinct person designated by the people, as in the case of David. It may be a distinct person designated by birth and accepted by the people. It may be a distinct group of persons designated by heredity or by election or by lot. And it may be no distinct person or group of persons, but the community itself proceeding by majority vote. The problem of the need for authority and the problem of the need for a distinct governing personnel have often been confused: at this point, it is already clear that they are distinct and that the argumentation which establishes the need for authority, even in a society made of ideally enlightened and well-intentioned persons, leaves open the question of whether some communities may be provided with all the authority they need without there being among them any distinct group of governing persons.

Thus, authority does not have only substitutional functions; in other words, it is not made necessary by deficiencies alone. We know, by now, that in one case at least the need for authority derives not from any lack or privation but from the sound nature of things. Given a community on its way to its common good, and given, on the part of this community, the degree of excellence which entails the possibility of attaining the good in a diversity of ways, authority has an indispensable role to play, and this role originates entirely in plenitude and accomplishment. The deficiency theory of authority is given the lie. An ideally enlightened and virtuous community needs authority to unify its action. By accident, it may need it less than a community which, as a result of ignorance, is often confronted by illusory means. But by essence it is more powerful than any community afflicted with vice and ignorance, and as a result of its greater power it controls choices involving new problems of unity which cannot be solved by way of unanimity but only by way of authority.

The Form and the Matter of the Common Good

Engaged in the pursuit of a common end, we deliberate about ways of insuring the unity of our action. These may be the steady ways of authority or, should it prove impossible to embody the principle of authority in an appropriate agency, the precarious ways of unanimity. But the problem would not arise if we were not already intending in common a certain end. Underlying any problem relative to the unity of common action, there exist problems relative to the end of the action to be united. The next step in the theory of authority concerns the end willed in common, as presupposed by the question of the way to unify action toward this end. Let this problem be posed as follows: granted that authority has an essential part to play in the unifying of action toward the common end, does it have any essential part to play with regard to the common end itself?

The precise vocabulary worked out by Aristotle (*Nic. Ethics* 3) and improved by Aquinas (*S.T.*, I-II.6ff.) can supply much valuable clarity. In perfect accord with the best usage of common language, philosophers describe "volition" as the act by which the will adheres to its end. If the end is considered, not absolutely as a thing good to attain, but more precisely in terms of a means or series of means, the act of the will is called "intention." "Choice" deals with a diversity of means relative to the thing intended and willed. Thus, after having established that authority has an essential function in the order of choice and means, we are asking whether it has, by reason of the nature of things and not merely by accident, anything to do with the volition and the intention of the common good explicitly considered as an end.

To say the least, appearances strongly suggest that any function of authority concerned with the end is merely substitutional. It looks very much as if, in a community made exclusively of enlightened and virtuous persons, the volition and intention of the common good should be fully insured by the qualities of the persons. Whoever disregards the common good is not virtuous but selfish, and whoever is dedicated to genuine virtue is, by the very efficacy of his virtue, ready for any sacrifice that the common good demands. It seems that ideally enlightened and virtuous persons would be adequately related to the good of their community by their enlightened virtue. In societies such as the cities and states of our experience, where selfishness and ignorance prevail, persons have to be constantly directed and often coerced toward the common good. Men of ill will seek their own advantage and ignore the good of all, and many whose will is honest and even generous happen to place the character of common good where it does not belong. But suppose that both ill will and error are removed: the need for authority, insofar as the common good itself is concerned, seems to disappear. Authority, in an ideal community, would have no essential function, except with regard to the unity of common action when there exists a plurality of genuine means.

It sometimes happens that a very simple analysis suffices to bring into focus difficulties hidden by familiar appearances. In a discussion of authority with regard to the *end* of common action, it is decisively important to bear in mind the meaning of the polar opposition between form and content within the object of volition and intention. Consider this object, the end willed (as a thing absolutely good) and intended (as a term of means). It can be willed and intended in two ways. I may will and intend what is good without knowing *what the thing is* that is good. The daily life of a man of good will is made of problems of content stated on the basis of a satisfactory answer to a problem of form. The man of good will, by definition and hypothesis, wills that which is good, and firmly adheres to the form of goodness. If only he knew *what the thing is* in which the form of goodness resides, he would do the good thing and all would be perfect. There is an evil harmony in the sinful will which adheres to evil things known to be evil—known to bear the form of evil[12]—and there is a blessed harmony in the good will which, for the sake of goodness, adheres to things that are actually good. And between these two harmonies there is the daily problem of the man of good will who indeed adheres to the form of the good but feels uncertain about the thing in which this form resides, in other words, the matter or content of this form.

So far as community life is concerned, the problem of matter and form within the end can be posed as follows: Is it desirable that the common good be willed and intended, both with regard to matter and with regard to form, by private persons acting in a private capacity? In order to be sure that we reach the root of the issue, let us consider the case of a society with no distinct governing personnel. Here are a few hundred farmers who gather periodically into a people's assembly, and this assembly is the only government of their community. Assuming that the order of virtuous intentions obtains, I recognize in each farmer a dual capacity. Between the sessions of the assembly, he is Philip or Bartholomew, a private person, the husband of Ruth or Patricia, the father of these children, and the owner of this particular land unmistakably distinguished by a fence from the rest of the world. His duties are unique. A good neighbor and companion, he wants all fields to bear abundantly; yet he is responsible, in a unique way, for the plowing of the field described as his. A good-hearted man, he is ready to help any child that God places in his path, yet there would be dire subversion of order if he did not show special dedication to the children who are his, and prefer them, in intention and in action, to other children who, though equally lovely, are not in equal degree entrusted to his love.[13] In the relation of man and wife, a dedication unique in all respects is the essence of indissoluble marriage.

When the assembly meets, every citizen is expected to assume a new capacity. A man who yesterday was admired for his industry on his family farm would today be blamed if his devotion did not belong entirely to the community. Between the private and the common welfare, the relation is often one of harmony. But conflicts may arise at any time and a public person, say, a member of the people's assembly, is bound to uphold the public welfare, regardless of how his private interest is affected. For instance, a certain method of taxation, plainly beneficial to the community as a whole, may cause serious difficulty to the kind of enterprise that he is managing. If a member of a popular assembly is known to have opposed a taxation law for no other reason than the threat of increased difficulty for his own enterprise, we consider him, according to the seriousness of the circumstances, either a weak person or a despicably bad citizen. At any rate, this accident of private interest interfering with public service in the discharge of a public function is inconceivable in the community of virtuous and enlightened persons which remains the principal subject of our inquiry. Considering, thus, the citizen of a direct democracy who, by the very fact that there is no distinct governing personnel, is the bearer of two capacities—the public and the private, according as the people's assembly is or is not in session—and assuming, further, that this person acts blamelessly in each capacity, I recognize in him two relations to the common good, and I wonder precisely what difference there is between these two relations.

The problem would certainly be overlooked if we were satisfied with the contrast between the private and the common. Again, this virtuous citizen is dedicated to the common good at all times, whether or not the assembly is in session, and, unmistakably, the difference that we are trying to express concerns, not the common good and its opposite, but two relations to the common good. The private person, inasmuch as he is morally excellent, wills and intends the common good, and subordinates his private wishes to it. He may not know what action the common good demands, but he adheres to the common good formally understood, to the form of the common good, whatever may be the matter in which this form resides; as far as content or matter is concerned, it is his business to will and intend private goods. But the public person is defined by the duty of willing and intending the common good considered both in its form and in its matter. And because the service of the common good normally involves an arrangement of things private, and sometimes requires the sacrifice of private interests, the subject of the public capacity exercises authority over the private person, whose business it is to look after particular matters.

In spite of appearances, the essence of authority and that of obedience are integrally preserved in a community practicing government by majority vote without any distinct governing personnel. The decisive question is not whether the content or matter of the common good is entrusted to distinct persons; it rather is whether, by reason of the common good's primacy, the volition and intention of *that in which* the common good resides must be expressed by a rule of action binding on all. The citizens of a direct democracy are inclined to boast of having no other masters than themselves.[14] This attitude may mean merely that they like to do without a distinct governing personnel. But the same boastful words may express the will to eliminate, through constitutional contrivance, the essence of authority and that of obedience. The soul of the system is revealed by the interpretation of majority, minority, and opposition. A citizen who, whenever the assembly meets, finds himself in the majority, may believe that he obeys only himself. But how is he going to feel when the majority votes against his preference? If he considers that the law he voted against is just as obligatory, and for the same reasons, as any law that he voted for, he is a law-abiding and obedient citizen for whom personal preference is altogether accidental. But if a person considers himself free from obligation to a law which he opposed, we understand that he has always been a rebel. True, he gave no signs of rebellion so long as the law was to his liking; but his later attitude discloses that having his own way has always been for him the thing essential, and obedience to the law a mere appearance.

The Most Essential Function of Authority

Thus, bringing about unity in common action is not, among the functions of authority, the only one which should be described as essential. Again, the problem of how to unify action—whether by unanimity or by authority—arises only on the ground of an already determinate volition and intention of the common good. Such volition and intention involve an antecedent function of authority, and this function, inasmuch as it is relative to the very end of common action, is more essential than anything pertaining to means. *The most essential function of authority is the issuance and carrying out of rules expressing the requirements of the common good considered materially.*

This theory implies that two capacities are normally and desirably distinguished in every community. With reference to the best known case, that is, that of the body politic versus its components—individuals, families, and the like—these capacities have been called public and private. But in the present inquiry they should rather, by the rule of strict appropriateness, be designated as common and particular. Indeed, the capacity thus far called public exists in all communities, whether actually public, like a township, a county, and a state, or private, like a family. On the other hand, we shall soon see that the basic opposition is not between the common and the private but, more precisely, between the common and the particular: for privateness is but one mode of particularity. *The common capacity is defined by a relation to the common good considered not only in its form but also in its matter or content.* As to the particular capacity, it involves a relation to the form of the common good but not to its matter. Clearly, if the particular capacity were related to both the form and the matter of the common good, it would cease to be particular; the problem of authority would disappear, as far at least as the volition and intention of the common good are concerned. The whole theory truly stands or falls upon the answer to this simple question: Is it desirable that there should exist, in every community, persons whose business it is, within the order of material consideration, to look after goods particular rather than after the common good?[15] It almost irresistibly seems that a disposition concerned with the form of the common good but not with its matter is just about half of a virtue. A person determined to serve the common good but unconcerned with the matter of its requirements seems to stop halfway, and it looks very much as if a "full measure of devotion" would extend to the matter of the common good as well as to its form.

Let us refer, once more, to a community governed by a majority vote. According to a project under deliberation, a certain road, so far a very quiet one, would be paved and opened to fast-moving traffic. Large families live on this road, and the parents are worried about increased danger to their children. But, in spite of the risk involved, the good of the community demands that the road should be paved, and worried fathers, acting as members of the people's assembly, support the project. By the terms of the preceding description, these good citizens, exercising the capacity of particular persons between the session of the assembly, should oppose the project as dangerous to their children, with a firm determination, however, to abide by the decision of the majority. Here, the twofold capacity described in the foregoing seems irrelevant. These citizens, though lovingly concerned with danger to their children, will and intend the form of the common good. Consequently, they refrain from any rebellious act against the decision to pave the road, although they do their best under all circumstances to reduce the danger. *If these good people can do so much, why should they not do a little more* and, without waiting for the emergence of a new capacity at the assembly's session, confess that the road should be paved? The construct of a community made of ideally enlightened and virtuous persons seems to imply, over and above adherence to the common good formally considered, the determinate volition of the things that the common good actually requires or contains. But then, the volition and intention of the common good, both with regard to form and with regard to matter, are adequately guaranteed by enlightened virtue. As far, at least, as the volition and intention of the common good are concerned, an ideally perfect community seems able to do without authority.

Thus, according to a plausible hypothesis, the perfection of virtue causes the capacity described as particular to disappear into the common capacity. A single capacity is left, which is altogether relative to the common good. *The particular capacity, by taking in hand the matter of the common good, has indeed become common.* Such transmutation is precisely what was suggested when we voiced the conjecture that excellent citizens, fully prepared to make all sacrifices required by the common good, should take one more step and, without assuming any new capacity, should will and intend the common good materially considered. *It remains to be decided how the common good itself is affected by the disappearance or impairment of the particular capacity.*

The Function and the Subject

But let us first analyze particularity into its main types. Every community exercises several functions—in the case of the state, justice, defense, diplomacy, public works, and the like—and in relation to the whole life of the community each function obviously has the character of a part. But in what specific sense does the notion of particularity apply here? Take, for instance, national defense. It is aimed at protecting all the national territory, all its wealth, all its counties, townships, families, and citizens. This function is altogether relative to the common good, yet it retains the character of a part inasmuch as its object is not the total good of the community but only one aspect of it. The object of a function is a certain aspect of a whole, and this is what defines particularity in the case of the function. The subject whose good is sought may be an individual organism—indeed the concept of function is basic in biology; it may be a person, and it may just as well be a community of any rank and description. Whether the subject considered is an organism, a person or a community, the successful exercise of one function is only an aspect and a part of its good condition; if other functions are defective, disaster is not ruled out. A function may be public in an unqualified sense, as in the case of the functions pertaining exclusively to the body politic, without ceasing to be particular, inasmuch as its object is but one aspect of a complex good.

In sharp contrast to the particularity of the function, a good may be particular by reason of its subject. Consider the activities involved in the upbringing of a child: taken together, they intend the whole good of the child, not one aspect of it. But because the child is part of the community, his is a particular good. Private communities, as the family, and such public communities as the township, the county, and the units of a federal organization are also related to the larger communities of which they are members as particular subjects. The state is the community which is so complete and self-sufficient that its good is not that of a particular subject—individual, family, township, and the like—but, unqualifiedly, the common good of men assembled for the sake of noble life.

Let us now examine the question of the excellence of the particular in the two ways of particularity just defined. Familiar experiences suffice to show how desirable it is that functions should be clearly distinguished, and that each of them should be exercised with a special eagerness for what is unique about it. It is good for the community that military men be devoted with a passion to national defense, bridge builders to the building of bridges, foresters to the preservation of forests, physicians to public health, and classicists to the study of the classics. The particularity of the function removes confusion and opens the way to the advantages of specialization. It is hardly possible that both the task of building bridges and that of conserving forests should be successfully fulfilled by the same persons; but even if a team happened to be expert both in bridge building and in forestry, a division of social labor would still be necessary with regard to place and time. One reason why we keep re-reading the *Republic* of Plato is that it expresses better than any other book the ideal of a community from which confusion is removed, and in which justice is achieved, through wise division of labor and dedication to specific tasks. A most enjoyable clarity pertains to the distinctness of the function, for every function is relative to an object, and, in human affairs at least, every object is definable. When the object of a social function no longer can be defined, the function itself becomes meaningless: this is when reformers step in. The administration of justice, the conduct of foreign relations, the management of public finances, and the like, are so many functions defined by perfectly intelligible objects.

Since functions are concerned with distinct aspects of the common good, functional diversity causes a need for an agency relative to the common good as a whole. Bringing about order among functions is the job of this central agency. What ratio of public funds can be allocated to agricultural projects without jeopardizing national defense or public health? This is an issue on which the function of promoting agriculture, the function of defending the national territory and the function of procuring good health conditions have nothing to say, except in purely preparatory and indecisive fashion. Decision pertains to a power which, inasmuch as it is responsible for order among the functions, necessarily controls all of them and commands all the functionaries.

The particularity of the function, as ground of authority, has a negative feature of major significance: it does not, in any essential manner, set limits to the authority that it grounds. In fact, authority is commonly restricted, and often crippled, by the resistance of its functionaries: but this is an entirely accidental occurrence. Such resistance is foreign and opposed to the concept of function. True, it may be held desirable that functionaries be possessed of some autonomy, and it may be a matter of fact that they always are. But their autonomy is caused by a particularity which is not that of the function. This simple remark sums up many products of political theory as well as many facts pertaining to the history of government. Because the functionary, as such, is an instrument, the particularity of the function is a thing that despots do not dread. They know that, all other things being equal, the clear division of social labor into functions increases the efficacy of their power.

Let us now ask whether the particularity of the subject possesses an excellence of its own. No doubt, it helps to remove confusion. A good way to make sure that every farmer knows what piece of land he is supposed to till is to divide the land into homesteads. This is indeed a result of considerable value, and it may constitute an everlasting argument in favor of private ownership. However, the power of removing confusion does not belong to the particularity of the subject in strict appropriateness, since it also belongs to the particularity of the function. A factory where rigorous discipline obtains and whose workers, for the most part, can be easily replaced, has but minimum recourse to the particularity of the subject. The feats of order accomplished by the modern organization of industry have given a new appeal to the old ideal of a state which would keep free from confusion without releasing the suspicious energies of such powers as privately owned land, privately conducted schools, strongly organized families, and citizens protected by inalienable rights.

The decisive fact is that the particularity of the subject, in all its forms and degrees, involves autonomy. To use a simple example, let us imagine that all the parts of a vast plain, by reason of homogeneity in all relevant respects, produce the same crops. Within such functional unity, farming can be administered according to the diversity of the tasks (plowing, fertilizing, sowing); then it is a public affair, entrusted, say, to a branch of the Department of Agriculture. But the cultivation of this plain can also be entrusted to a multiplicity of farms each of which is governed by its individual proprietor. For the comparison to be meaningful, we must, of course, assume that other things are equal. Under definite circumstances, one system of management may insure a much higher yield than the other. On the assumption that the production is about the same in either system, let us ask whether it is better that the job be done by a multitude of self-ruling agents or by mere instruments of a central agency.

To ask this question is like asking whether there is more perfection in life than in lifelessness, in activity than in mere instrumentality, in plenitude than in emptiness. Clearly, a whole is better off if its parts are full of initiative than if they are merely traversed by an energy which never becomes their own. Much can be learned from the fact that social thinkers and metaphysicians conduct, on the subject of plenitude versus vacuum, parallel dialogues. The book of William James, *A Pluralistic Universe*, forcefully expresses the metaphysical sentiment that genuine plurality, in the world of our experience, is the condition of meaning and plenitude. A totality which does not admit of autonomous parts disappears into the vacuum caused by its imperialistic arrogance. But the particularity of the subject, in the social as well as in the metaphysical world, harbors mysteries that are extremely uncongenial to the rationalistic mind. Whenever it has its own way in social affairs, rationalism exalts the clarity of the function and crushes the particularity of the subject.

To be sure, contingency often makes it impossible to vindicate in an entirely rational fashion the distinction between communities of the same functional type. What reasons could we bring forth if we had to explain why two states or nations remain separated by a borderline instead of merging into one unit? The notion of natural boundary is not absurd, and sometimes a fence built by nature serves quite reasonably to distinguish one community from another. Spain is south of the Pyrenees Range and France north of it. But in many other cases, the most famous of which is the great East European plain, nations remain stubbornly distinct although they cannot claim any natural boundary. Sometimes language supplies reasonable principles of unity and diversity, but it also happens that people refuse to merge in spite of linguistic unity (the French-speaking Swiss and Belgians do not want to be one nation with the French) and it also happens that the unity of a nation (Switzerland) is in no way jeopardized by diversity of language. After having probed all such causes of unity and diversity let us yield to the accidents of history: for theirs is the final power of decision. Whatever is accidental is, as such, unexplainable, but in the world of action a thing can be significant, worthy, treasurable, without having any character of essentiality or intelligibility: it just is, it has been, it tends to keep being, and this is why it is significant, without any further explanation. The precise location of the borderline between Canada and the United States is, in a number of places, entirely conventional, but, by the decision of history the community centered about Ottawa is something else than the community centered about Washington, D.C. Again, there may be no good reason why the borderline between Colorado and New Mexico should be where it is rather than a few miles farther north or south. Yet it is hardly questionable that the community whose main centers are Colorado Springs and Denver is, by the decisions of history, different from the community whose main centers are Santa Fe and Albuquerque. Any rationalist, if in the position of philosopher-king, would erase the borderline between Colorado and New Mexico and reduce the fifty States to a smaller number of more rational units. Such operations, which would sweep away a great deal of mystery, would also destroy much historical substance and, in a number of cases, leave only deceptive clarity where there used to be historical plenitude. No doubt, existent particularities may be dead remnants and their suppression may prove beneficial. But it also happens that the works of the past, no matter how contingent, are so full of life that their disappearance would involve great destruction. In a profound sense a "survival" is a thing which maintains in the present some of the life which was that of the past. Such life is not clearly intelligible, for an important part of it results from the successful management of contingent occurrences over a long time.

The Person

It is in the individual subject of human existence that we can best observe the relation between the mysteries of contingency and those of free choice. As a member of a species, distinguished within the species by the material components of his being, a human subject is more properly designated as an individual. Considered as a complete substance which owes to its rationality a unique way of being a whole and of facing the rest of the universe, he is more properly designated as a person. The fortune of "personalism" in the ideologies of our time is clearly traceable to the promises held by the notion of person, as distinct from that of individual, in the working out of difficulties which, though of all times, have assumed extraordinary significance in the last generations. Indeed, the word personalism often stood for doctrines and attitudes that "individualism" would designate with equal or greater accuracy. Such a confusing change in expression bears witness to the power that the idea of the person came to possess in minds confronted by problems which, sometime before, were not held so obvious and momentous. Many, who would have been satisfied with the language of individualism half a century ago, were necessitated by the spirit of the age to speak a personalistic language. But what is it that caused, in such a large variety of doctrinal contexts, the decline of individualistic rhetoric, and a new attention to the meaning of the person? With due allowance for profound diversities among the so-called personalistic schools of thought, it can be said that the displacement of "individualism" by "personalism" generally expressed the following insights:

(1) As recalled in the foregoing, the philosophy of individualism implies that whatever is called common good is merely useful, that things common are but means, and that the character of end belongs exclusively to the individual. "Means" and "end" must be understood here rigorously: a mere means is a thing which has no desirability of its own and which would not be desired at all if it did not lead to a thing desirable in its own right. The mere means, in other words, the thing that is merely useful, is just traversed by the goodness of the end. To treat the common good as a thing merely useful becomes the *critical* periods, but as soon as the possibility of a new *organic* period[16] is strongly felt, to repre-

sent the common good as sheer utility without any dignity of its own is unbearably paradoxical. Only the pressures and appeals of a critical period can make men blind to the character of the common good as autonomous good, *bonum honestum*, and to the primacy that it enjoys as long as the common and the particular are contained within the same order. When such pressures and appeals have become things of the past, the sense for the eternal worth of the human individual is not necessarily weakened, but why should we keep the language and the ways of a philosophy committed to treating the common good as a thing with no excellence of its own?

(2) Another aspect of classical individualism concerns the role of material causality in human affairs. The features involved belong both to economic and political theory. The individualism of the economists proceeds, in part, from the stubborn belief that the best state of affairs is brought about by the independent operation of ultimate units, the independent money-maker, the individual supplier of labor-force, the individual consumer, the individual organizer, and the like, all moved by the power of individual well-being. Likewise, some democratic polities embody the postulate that what is best for the state is steadily brought about by the solitary determination of its individual components. These polities, famously associated with the teaching of Rousseau and with Jacobinism, strive to maintain the isolation of the citizen. The best state would emerge from the sheer multitude of its citizens and be confronted by nothing but such a multitude.[17] Again, we are dealing here with a disposition marked by the characteristics of the critical periods.

The use of the word *organic*, as in "organic period," suffices to conjure up the danger of attributing to society a unity of *primary* character. Likening society to an organism may be useful as long as we remain in control of our analogies and understand that society is not one after the fashion of an organic body. Its individual members are not organs or cells but primary subjects of human existence. What we need is a concept expressive of the unique way in which an individual exercises membership in a set when the set is a community of intelligent beings. This concept is that of person rather than that of individual. True, the person is sociable by essence and it is capable of playing the role of part (the persons who make up the Senate are parts of the Senate), and the individual, inasmuch as it is a thing "undivided in itself and divided from all the rest,"[18] implies a character of wholeness and separation. But when the being which is an individual and a person is considered *as member of a set* (and this is the relevant way of considering it in the theory of society, for the unity of society is that of an ordered set), the concept of person restricts the character of part whereas the concept of individual expresses no such restriction. *As member of a set* the individual is purely and simply a part. But because personality, in every possible connection, expresses a universe of reason and freedom, emphasis on the person implies emphasis on the privileges of this universe. In its most intelligent forms at least, personalism, with all its ambiguities, had the merit of tracing to the unique kind of totality which results from rationality and liberty effects that the individualism of the critical period used to trace to the spontaneity of the part. If atoms were persons, their arrangements would account for many wonders that Epicurean imagination leaves unaccounted for.

(3) Above all, the autonomy of the individual man, as fact of nature and as moral requirement, is incomparably better expressed by the notion of person than by that of individual.[19] Just as it is desirable, in all respects and most precisely in relation to the common good, that the affairs of the state be not managed by the federal power but by the state itself, and the affairs of the county by the county, and the affairs of the township by the township, and the affairs of the family by the family, so it is ultimately desirable that the affairs of the individual man, as long as he is free from important deficiency, be managed by himself. But when the individual man is precisely considered as a being possessed of integrity and rationality, when he is considered as an agent in control of his destiny, when he is considered as an agent which contains its own law not merely by way of natural constitution, but also and principally by way of understanding, voluntariness and freedom, the aspect brought forth is that of personality. On the level of individual existence, autonomy belongs to the person more properly than to the individual. Such greater propriety makes much difference both in terms of explanation and in terms of appeal. The most valuable contribution of personalism is the general theory that the particularity of the human individual, in ultimate contradistinction to that of the function, is a privilege of personality.

Indeed, it is historically absurd to speak of personalism in the singular, as if the various personalistic movements were possessed of doctrinal unity. Endless variety is found in the positive content of their programs, and, whereas each of them is marked by sharp opposition to some general feature of the modern world, the objects of their oppositions may not coincide and may even contrast with each other. Yet there is more unity in the aversions of the personalists than in their assertions, and of all their aversions the most constant concerns the predominance of function in the order of society. If the use of one word to designate such a variety of doctrines, attitudes, inspirations and moods can be justified at all, it should be justified by the central significance, in all personalistic movements, of the conflict between person and function.

The Subject and the Person

Thus, in terms of most essential necessity, authority is needed because it is desirable that particular goods should be taken care of by particular agencies. Some of these agencies are defined by their functions, others are constituted by subjects of various kinds. Along the line which goes from the broader to the more narrow, a particular subject may be a state in a federal union, a county in a state, a township in a county, a family in a township. The ultimateness of the individual is accompanied by the emergence of significant features: this whole, the individual man, is possessed of substantial unity, whereas the other subjects, state, township, family, are not. And by reason of its rational nature, this whole, the individual man, is, in a way, all things, adheres to the absoluteness of the good, and thereby achieves mastery over its own acts. Extreme amplitude arises just when the most narrow unit is attained, for it is not in a merely metaphorical sense that a complete substance of rational nature is said to be a universe. As soon as this is understood, a new light is shed on the particularity of the antecedent subjects. A family, for instance, is not just a smaller group within a township: each of its members is, all things; a family is a whole made of universes, each of which is in control of its own operations—a perfection that no solar system can achieve. Owing to the unique character of totality which belongs to the individual substance of rational nature, the whole system of the subjects is transfigured: a family, a township, a county are particular subjects, they are particular after the fashion of the subject, they are parts indeed, but of these parts the ultimate components are wholes which in a way comprehend all things. At all levels of human association the presence of the person causes the energies of totality, rationality, and liberty to be present.

Looking again at the series of the particular subjects, but from the opposite standpoint, let us now remark that the most particular of them, the person, comes to exist, by virtue of its own sociability, in subjects that are less and less particular, up to the level of a community describable as complete.[20] With regard to the social character of the person, much confusion would be spared if some attention were given to the difference between (1) sociability as such and (2) the tendency to exist in a society as a part in a whole. To be sure, the notion of person expresses wholeness and opposes the character of part, just as the notion of freedom expresses dominating indifference and opposes contingency, and just as the notion of being expresses actuality and opposes potency. But just as finite being cannot exist without an admixture of potency, and just as our freedom cannot exist without harboring a passive indifference, so the person of man, by reason of all the limitations which place it at an infinite distance from absolute personality, demands to exist in a community as a part in a whole. Yet, certain features of sociability belong to the human person *qua* person, and in all the system of human relations, nothing is more determining, more decisive, more distinguishing, and more final than the acts traceable to the sociability of the person considered as such. In the small area of concentrated energy where these acts take place, the disinterestedness of tendencies and the other-centeredness of needs are more than facts of nature: they involve a commitment of the self in its distinct existence. No doubt, disinterested tendencies and other-centered needs are present in animals, but so long as the reason is not at work the individual agent contributes only a tendency toward its own satisfaction. Disinterestedness and other-centeredness are contributed by nature; in other words, they are caused by a dynamism antecedent to individual activity. The experience of human disorder shows that a tendency which, by nature, is disinterested and which, in fact, serves another subject, may involve no generosity on the part of the agent. Thus, some mothers love their children in a selfish way; out of selfish love they would do many things beneficial to the child, expose themselves to great dangers and inflict upon themselves great sacrifices. Here, other-centered needs are satisfied and some acts demanded by disinterested tendencies are elicited. But the way of acting remains interested and self-centered. Effects of generous love are brought into existence without generosity. Much is given, and yet action does not *proceed by way of gift*. When the devotion of a mother to her child bears these characteristics, it is commonly interpreted as an animal passion, and thereby we mean that it is nature—that is, a dynamism antecedent to reason and voluntariness—which places the effect of love in another rather than in the acting self. It is only where reason, voluntariness, and free choice are at work that the subject takes care of transcending its subjectivity: then actions that are gifts also *proceed by way of gift*. Such disinterestedness, which concerns both the content and the ways of action, originates in rationality, but inasmuch as it implies the actual transcending of the self by itself, it is traceable, in strict appropriateness, to the way of subsisting and to the way of acting which belong to a complete substance of rational nature. In short, it is traceable to personality. Qualities are transcended and the relation of friendship is established on its true basis. As long as it is directed to qualities, friendship remains uncertain: it achieves complete genuineness only when it exists between person and person, regardless of what happens to the qualities of the beloved. Then, the question *why* one loves is best answered—if this can be called an answer—by pointing to what is unique and unutterable about a person. This state of affairs is powerfully described in a celebrated essay of Montaigne. "If I am entreated to say why I loved him, I feel that this cannot be expressed except by answering 'Because it was he, because it was I.' Beyond all my discourse and whatever I can say distinctly about it, I do not know what unexplainable and overwhelming force is instrumental in such a union."[21] In all likelihood Pascal was commenting on Montaigne when he wrote these words:

> But if one loves another one because of his beauty, does he love him? No: for smallpox, which kills the beauty without killing the person, will put an end to love. And if one loves me for my judgment, for my memory, does one love me? No, for I can lose these qualities without losing myself. But where is this self, if it is neither in the body, nor in the soul? and how would it be possible to love the body and the soul, except for these qualities, which do not constitute the self, since they are perishable? should one love the substance of the soul of a person abstractly, and regardless of the qualities in it? that cannot be, and that would be unfair. Thus, one never loves any person, but only qualities.[22]

The last sentence will be misunderstood unless it is held to express the sorrowful perplexity of a man who does not see the answer to a question that he has stated with extreme keenness. Pascal knows that the object of genuine love cannot be anything else than the self. Then, perhaps with some bitterness, he turns to the fact that people are liked and loved because of their qualities, which seems to imply that they never are loved genuinely and that they are bound to remain unhappy. Both in terms of natural possibility and in terms of justice, he sees no way out of this fateful state of affairs. Apparently, he is not unaware of the difference between "being an object of love," and "being a ground of love"; on the one hand, he speaks of loving a person *because* of his beauty, *for* his judgment, *for* his memory; on the other hand, he speaks of loving qualities, not persons. To get more out of the distinction between ground and object of love, let us see in what sense friendship can make itself independent of its own grounds. Indeed, the only thing that human love cannot do is to create out of nothing the goodness, the desirability of its object. Divine love alone causes the beloved to be good, independently of any goodness antecedent to love. In order to be an object for the love of a creature, a thing must already be good: in that sense it is true that no one is loved or liked by his fellow man except for his qualities. But, although many of these qualities are subject to destruction—the first example of Pascal is beauty—a human being will never be totally devoid of qualities. There will always be in him a ground, or a multiplicity of grounds, for disinterested love. Even though a lady has been loved for her beauty, smallpox does not necessarily cause her to be neglected. Under the worst of circumstances, the excellence of human nature, considered in actual existence and in relation to its end, would still be a perfect ground for loving a person without measure. And this excellence of man becomes an infinitely more powerful ground of love when man is considered in the mystery of his supernatural relation to God. Pascal seems to have missed, at least in the present fragment, this ability of love to transcend qualities and be concerned with persons. But without such ability, the other-centered needs which bind men together would be sheer facts of nature and in no way pertain to reason and freedom. Friendship would be impossible. And civic virtue would be impossible.

To sum all up, let us imagine, again, that the members of a community, in a supreme act of boundless dedication, resolve to will and intend, under all circumstances, the matter of the common good as well as its form. By this resolution the particular capacity is abolished: from now on, it will be up to the common capacity to take care of the most particular business.

As far as the function is concerned, the disappearance of the particular capacity results in a loss of order, and among the forms which make up order those are more directly and seriously damaged which are rational in character. As far as the subject is concerned, the disappearance of the particular capacity entails also a loss of order, and this damage is greater where order is mostly made of historical settlement. If the particularity of the subject alone were impaired, and its ordering power transferred to the function, as in the *Republic* of Plato, whatever is historical in the arrangement of the state would be replaced by a rational disposition, and this would make a great deal of difference, for any impairment of particularity, in the case of the subject, entails a loss of autonomy.

It is the excellence of autonomy which vindicates the particularity of the subject and whatever forms of authority are needed for the preservation of this particularity. Familiar contrasts are transcended, authority and autonomy do not conflict with each other and do not restrict each other. They cause and guarantee one another. But no rebel perceives the great unity, the great peace which obtains at this very deep level. Autonomy implies the interiority of the law, a condition which, for human agents at least, is not native, but has to be achieved through arduous progress. Rebels hate the sacrifices that the interiorization of the law requires. It is bad enough for them that the law should exist outside man, and hover around after the fashion of a threat. Autonomy will never lead them to the understanding of authority, for their notion of autonomy is itself a counterfeit.

NOTES

Reprinted from *The Review of Politics* 22, no. 2 (April 1960): 202–44.

In drafting this paper I have been helped by two friends who were kind enough to act as my secretaries, Professor Robert Bunker of Highland University, New Mexico, and Mrs. Pauline Ryan. Let this be an expression of my gratitude.

1. Friedrich Nietzsche, *The Birth of Tragedy* (Garden City, NY: Doubleday Anchor, 1956), 24.
2. Aristotle, *Nicomachean Ethics* 1.2.1094b7.
3. The notion of contingency conveyed by "happen" is understood here with strict propriety. The fact that the capital of the enterprise, or part of it, is owned by a lender, is accidental to the commercial operations: these would not be essentially different if the merchant had inherited all the capital he needs. Consider, on the other hand, the cooperation of the surgeon, his assistant, the anesthetist, and the nurses in the treatment of a surgical case: it would not occur to anybody to say that the purposes of these persons just "happen" to be interdependent. Their unity is not a sheer happening.
4. In fact, when the theory of anarchy took hold of a thinker free from any connection with the spirit of individualistic revolt and possessed with a strong sense for order and the excellence of the human association, this theory assumed the form of a contractual system—supplemented, however, with an authoritarian treatment of the relations involving significant deficiency. The social philosophy of Proudhon owes nothing to the romantic exaltation of primitiveness, cosmic emotion, infrarational life, individualistic solitude, and rebellion against society. The work of a mind intensely dedicated to "the creation of order in mankind" (the title of a book of Proudhon, 1843) and convinced that the masterpiece of the universe is human society, the Proudhonian theory of anarchy consists in an ambitious plan for the extension of contract to many relations traditionally settled by way of authority. For some time Proudhon recommended and promised the withering away of the state. Yet, a day came when he realized that every step in the conquering of the state was accompanied by a residual assertion of political authority, which thus proved irreducible and perennial. Proudhon's anarchism finally matures into a theory of federation, and there is no longer any question of eliminating the state. Rather, the state itself is forced into a contractual relation. In this reconsidered theory of anarchy, the general endeavor to substitute equilibrium for subordination, and contract for authority, does not spare the state; but instead of being, in Utopian fashion, driven out of

existence, the archetype of authority, the state, is treated as the perennial partner of liberty. Insofar as authority itself enters into a contractual arrangement, the ideal of anarchy is not given up.

To the indignation of many, this unyielding anarchist, Proudhon, abides by the most uncompromising standards of traditional authoritarianism with regard to the family community. The inexperience of the child vindicates, with no need for elaboration, authority in the paternal relation. The case of the woman is not so obvious, and the intuitive genius of Proudhon, always somewhat awkward when there is a question of dissociating the components of an historical trend, never succeeded in avoiding misinterpretations. Proudhon did not explain quite convincingly in what respects the woman is equal to man and in what respects she is not. On his deepest level of thought, he believes that she is incomparably more subject than man to those irrational drives which originate in the cosmic part of human nature and in which he sees the worst enemies of justice and freedom. The deepest reason of Proudhon's aversion to Rousseau is that, in his interpretation, the philosophy of Rousseau delivers man and society to the infrahuman powers of emotions, passions, natural spontaneity, and cosmic drives, and that Rousseau calls freedom precisely this submission to the infrahuman. Because of this greater subjection to cosmic nature, the woman is a permanent minor and needs to be guided by father, husband, brother, or son. At times Proudhon reveals that authority, which he generally seems to confine within the family, has a part to play whenever a deficient state of affairs makes it impossible for men to do by themselves the things that mature people are supposed to accomplish without guidance. In his remarks on the American Civil War in *La guerre et la paix*, first published in 1861, ed. Célestin Bouglé and Henri Moysset (Paris: Marcel Rivière, 1927), 176–80, he goes so far as to write, by one of those paradoxes which cast obscurity on the best parts of his work, that Southern slavery supplied the proper circumstances for the training of primitives who had somehow to acquire the discipline of labor. Thus, the social philosophy of Proudhon is a theory of order through a system of contractual anarchy supplemented with a deficiency theory of authority.

5. The words "is supposed to" are not used casually. Moral philosophy is still in a rather primitive stage, and moral philosophers commonly fail to render obvious the deductive connection of their answers with the self-evident principles of the moral order. Their answers may still be true and good and worth adhering to: but the cause of their certainty is an inclination, not a deduction, and for a conclusion so attained to be safe, the philosopher's—or the theologian's—inclination must be sound, which is the same as to say that the fellow must be possessed, first, of genuine virtue and, second, of all the conditions and instruments required for the regular functioning of virtuous inclination as cause of true practical judgment. Of course whoever writes a book of ethics, whether philosophical or theological, likes the reader to believe that every bit of it is scientifically established: in case it were not, the only guaranty of his statements would be the perfection of his virtue: a thing that moralists, understandably, do not like the public to inquire into.

6. Such words as "heart," "sentiment," etc., must not be allowed to convey the belief that the determination of the right and the wrong ever is entrusted to *emotional* reactions. Let it be said that there exist inclinations of a purely intellectual character, the best example of which is the familiarity of a man of science with his own scientific field; thus, he is able to put his finger on the true statement a long time—a few years or a few centuries—before this statement is demonstrated. The inclinations which assure the determination of the right and the wrong in contingency are not of purely intellectual nature. They pertain to the appetite and can be termed *affective* with propriety provided it is understood that the appetite of man comprises, as its principal part, the systems of desires and aversions born of rational apprehension, that is, the will. The affective inclination which alone can determine the right and the wrong when demonstration is powerless is *principally* the inclination of the will, an inclination born of intelligent apprehension, and constantly strengthened by dedication to truth. Inclinations of an emotional character are by no means excluded, but they are subordinated. It often is a *feeling* of charm or disgust which notifies us that—perhaps in spite of appearances—there is something definitely right or wrong about a situation; but if such a feeling were let loose, and allowed to work outside an integrated system whose principal part is the will, we would run into all the absurdities of the doctrines, so popular at the end of the eighteenth century and in the Romantic period, which give infrarational sentiment ultimate control over the determination of the right and the wrong and the utterances of reason. The "conscience" of the Savoy Vicar (J. J. Rousseau, *Emile*, Amsterdam: Jean Neaulme, 1762, III, 114) would not perform any of the wonders that Rousseau describes if it were not precisely this: an inclination antecedent to reason, more *native* than anything born of understanding, closer to cosmical energies, closer to animals and plants and other things of nature, and closer to sheer existence.

7. Thomas Aquinas, *Summa Theologiae*, II-II, 32, vii, ad. 3.

8. To see why the qualification "in principle," is necessary, consider the case of a leader who knows that, under the circumstances, he cannot resign, and that it is he, and no one else, who has to guide the community toward a certain goal. Two ways, *a* and *b*, are open; *a* would be preferable if it were not for a feature pertaining to the individual history of this leader, who cannot resign, but, his individual history being what it is, *b* ought to be preferred. In fact, whenever an individual feature modifies the ability of a leader to carry out a certain policy, this feature belongs to the system of data that *public* prudence is confronted by and has to reckon with.

9. Aristotle, *Metaphysics* 2.3.995a13. That the treatise classified as Bk. 2, (a) of *Metaphysics* was written by Aristotle himself is questioned by some.

10. Ibid., 6.4.1027b25.

11. Between the concept of authority and that of law there exist enlightening relations. It is, indeed, perfectly proper to speak of the authority of the legislator, and nothing would warrant the identification of authority with executive power. Many acts of authority assume the form of laws passed by assemblies. However, authority and law

evidence opposite intelligible tendencies inasmuch as the more a proposition is expressive of necessity, the more it participates—other things being equal—in the character of law, whereas there is nothing, in the concept of authority, that expresses aversion to contingency. A law rules human acts in the capacity of premise, not of conclusion; now, the more a premise is independent of contingency, the more of a premise it is. The first or absolute premises regulating human actions express the absolute necessities intelligibly following upon the rational nature. But authority is perfectly at home in the management of contingency and in the uttering of practical conclusions. A decree which applies a law to a particular and unique situation is no less an act of authority than a law passed by an assembly to establish a principle that can be applied to indefinitely many particular situations. No doubt, this law is already so particularized, and so engaged in contingency as not to be a sheer expression of natural necessity. Yet it retains the character of premise, and calls for further determination in terms of adjustment to contingencies that an assembly cannot deal with. Common usage contrasts government by law and authoritarian government. Both of these expressions are objectionable, and their meaning has to be carefully specified. In a way every government is authoritarian. On the other hand, "government by law" conveys the suggestion that propositions retaining the character of premises may suffice to guide a community in entirely concrete and perhaps unique situations, and this involves the nonsense of a premise which is also an ultimate conclusion. Provided these abusive interpretations are definitely ruled out, it is perfectly correct to use the expression "government by law" when a political system depends as much as possible on premises established by the wisdom of the legislator, and to call "authoritarian" the system of government which gives the few men in the executive power the greatest possible liberty to manage the concrete circumstances by connecting the conclusions of their choice with premises that have no other source than their pleasure, since no positive enactment ever gave these premises any juridical existence.

12. Evil is a privation, not a form, but this privation is understood after the pattern of a form and cannot be understood otherwise.

13. According to a well-known remark of Aristotle, the natural order of excellence may be reversed by a condition of emergency. To philosophize is, absolutely speaking, better than to make money; but for the fellow who is in dire poverty, to get money is better than to philosophize. Likewise, the order of love which requires that, under ordinary circumstances, I should provide my own children with advantages that many other children do not have, also requires that in an emergency—flood, epidemic, war, revolution—I should deprive my own people of goods that are not needed for their survival in order to insure the survival of children who are not mine.

14. There are, in the history of mankind, only a few communities governed exclusively by the methods of direct democracy. But every democracy, no matter how important the part that a distinct personnel plays in its operation, embodies direct democracy in some of its political processes. These processes may either pertain to the written constitution, for example, a plebiscite, or to the unwritten one—the influence of public opinion. In all cases the citizens of a democracy are tempted to boast of having no masters except themselves, for they truly exercise much political power besides the electing of

their leaders. The United States Constitution mentions two assemblies: the House and the Senate. There is a third one which does not need to be mentioned because its existence is obvious and which could hardly be mentioned in a written document, because of the indefiniteness of its role and power: it is the People of the United States.

15. Once more, we are not asking whether society necessarily ought to be divided into a distinct governing personnel, and the governed. When we speak of "persons whose business it is . . . to look after particular goods . . . ," we do not exclude the possibility that all these persons should, in another capacity, constitute the agency in charge of looking after the common good.

16. These Saint-Simonian expressions (*Exposition de la doctrine de Saint-Simon*, ed. Elie Halévy and Célestin Bouglé [Paris: Marcel Rivière, 1924], 127) are used here without the connotations implied by the Saint-Simonian philosophy of historical causality. For the Saint-Simonists, the great facts of change as well as the great facts of permanence in human history are determined by ideas, and especially by religious beliefs. Accordingly an organic period is defined as one "in which all the facts of human activity are classified, foreseen, and set in order by a general theory, and in which the goal of social action is clearly defined." A critical period is one "in which all communion of thought, all common action, all coordination have ceased to exist, and in which society has become nothing else than an aggregation of isolated individuals fighting against each other." The distinction between organic and critical periods remains meaningful without deciding whether the organic and the critical characters are due to beliefs or to factors of another kind, or to a diversity of factors including beliefs.

17. Proudhon was a firm opponent of democracy so understood. (He called it "democracy" with no further specification.) In his 1848 pamphlet *Solution of the Social Problem*, a subtitle attracts the attention of the philosophers: *Democracy is materialistic and atheistic*. In Jacobin democracy he recognized the traditional picture of the Epicurean universe where all things result from the encounters of particles, without patterns of wholes, without plans and without final causes: "Universal suffrage is a kind of atomism by which the legislator, being unable to make the people speak in the unity of its essence, invites the citizens to express their opinion by heads, *viritim*, just as the Epicurean philosopher explains thought, will, understanding, by arrangements of atoms. This is political atheism in the worst sense of this expression. How could a general thought ever result from the addition of any number of votes?" (A. Lacroix, ed., 62–63.)

A brief elaboration on the concept of materialism will help to understand these confused, but challenging remarks. Let it be said, in general terms, that a materialistic explanation is one which forcibly traces to material causes effects belonging to causes of another description. This is the case whenever the material cause needs to assume the character of a thing in act. What is material is, as such, potential; if, in order to play the explanatory role that it is expected to play, it has to be credited with actuality, explanation is materialistic in a proper sense. Since the parts are the matter of the whole, explanation forcibly follows the line of the material cause whenever effects belonging to the power of the whole are traced to the part. What the words of Proudhon mean is that individualistic democracy, as well as Epicurean physics, credits things considered in the capacity of parts with the ability to bring about the perfections of the whole. Individualism, in its use of material causality as well as in its interpretation of means and ends, pertains to the spirit of the critical periods: when the question is to dispose of the old order, to dissolve traditional setups, to destroy crippling structures, the theory that the greatest good results from the nonintegrated operation of the parts looks congenial enough. But as soon as the possibility of a new organic period is perceived, minds no longer expect so confidently that the perfection of the whole will steadily proceed from the sheer operation of the parts.

18. *S.T.*, I, 29, iv.

19. When individuation originates in matter, as it does in all composite substances, man included, to speak of the "autonomy of the individual" involves a degree of inappropriateness. To be sure, individuals are possessed of autonomy, but the principle of their autonomy is not the same as the principle of their individuality. Matter is that which has no law of its own. In a composite substance all that has the character of a law comes from the form. But the form is specific and consequently all the law of the material individual is the law of its species. In order to reach the principle of a norm concerned with what is unique in the individual substance, we have to turn to the concept which results from tile union of *completeness* in substantial constitution and *rationality* in specific nature: this is, by the celebrated definition of Boethius, the concept of person. Among the many writings of Professor Maritain on the person, see, in particular, *The Person and the Common Good* (New York: Scribner's, 1947).

20. It is obvious that no human community is unqualifiedly complete, but insofar as the most comprehensive of our communities remains incomplete, we keep struggling toward something beyond the least incomplete of the existent communities.

21. Michel de Montaigne, *Essays*, Bk. I, ch. 27.

22. Blaise Pascal, *Pensées: The Provincial Letters* (New York: Modern Library, 1941), 109.

CHAPTER 6

The New Rights Theory and the Natural Law

ERNEST L. FORTIN

Ernest Fortin, A.A. (1923–2002), was a professor of theology at Boston College and a Roman Catholic priest in the order of Augustinians of the Assumption (Assumptionists). Fr. Fortin joined the Assumptionists in 1944, graduated from Assumption College in 1946, and earned his licentiate in theology from the Angelicum in Rome in 1950 and his doctorate from the Sorbonne in 1955. Fortin taught at Assumption College from 1959 to 1971, and at Boston College from 1971 to 1997, when he suffered a stroke. Though housed in the theology department, Fortin's scholarly work focused on political philosophy. His work explored the intersection of Christian thought and political theory as well as the history of political thought. Through a friendship with Allan Bloom while studying in Paris for his doctorate, Fortin was introduced to the work of Leo Strauss and became one of the more prominent Catholic Straussians. His collected essays are published in four volumes: The Birth of Philosophic Christianity: Studies in Early Christian and Medieval Thought; Classical Christianity and the Political Order: Reflections on the Theologico-Political Problem; Human Rights, Virtue, and the Common Good: Untimely Meditations on Religion and Politics; *and* Ever Ancient, Ever New: Ruminations on the City, the Soul, and the Church.

> I love Carolina,
> I love Angelina, too,
> I can't marry both,
> So what I gonna do?

Judging by the number of books and articles that have lately been devoted to it, one has the impression that the much maligned natural law doctrine is due for yet another of its periodic revivals. The new syndrome, which seems to have taken some of our contemporaries by surprise, was not totally unpredictable. As far back as 1929, even as staunch an advocate of legal positivism as the late Hans Kelsen was forced to admit that "before we had reason to expect it, a reaction (had) set in which (augured) a renaissance of metaphysics, and, thereby, of natural-law theory."[1] The reaction, he thought, was prompted by other than purely theoretical reasons. It was part of an "eternal undular movement" by which the human spirit is carried "from pessimism or optimism to the ideal of objectivity" or "from metaphysics to the critique of knowledge and back again."[2] Its immediate cause was the shaking of the social foundations brought about by World War I and the ensuing conflict among a variety of "interest groups" who naively sought to justify their claims by appealing to an illusory notion of "right."

If the shattering events of those and more recent years have taught us anything, it is indeed that human beings cannot easily dispense with objective principles of justice and right, whether they be enunciated in the form of a "transcendent law of nature and of nature's God,"[3] or for that matter in any other form. But while few thoughtful people would deny that such principles are eminently desirable, there is still considerable disagreement as to how or how well they can be established. One of the major difficulties facing the natural law theorist is that his understanding of human nature was originally bound up with a teleological view of the universe that has seemingly been destroyed by modern science. Quite apart from that, however, one does well to bear in mind that the natural law has always been in some sort of trouble, as is evident from the numerous debates it has sparked and the frequent revisions to which it has been subjected in the course of its long history.[4] In view of this situation, it is understandable that it should continue to pose a problem, not for its opponents—they have long since abandoned it as a myth-eaten anachronism—but for its own defenders.

One gathers as much from the heated discussions surrounding the abortion issue at the present moment. Although the Roman Catholic Church has not altered its official stand on this matter and gives no indication of wanting to do so, it now supports it by means of a distinctively new argument based on natural or human rights rather than on the natural law. The bottom line may be the same in both instances, but the reasoning behind it is obviously different. The old argument was mainly concerned with what abortion does to the person who performs it or allows it to be performed; the new one, with what it does to the aborted fetus. One argument emphasizes duties; the other emphasizes rights. The question, bluntly stated, is whether the two approaches are fully compatible with each other or whether at a deeper level the tension between them is not such as to caution against any hasty substitution of one for the other.

The prevailing view among Catholic scholars is that they are in fact compatible and that the modern rights doctrine is simply a perfected version of the old natural law doctrine. Such was the position taken by Jacques Maritain in a number of works, including *The Rights of Man and Natural Law* and *The Person and the Common Good*, which exerted considerable influence in the forties and fifties; and such also is the position taken, independently of Maritain and from a different perspective, by John Finnis in a recent book entitled *Natural Law and Natural Rights*,[5] which has already attracted widespread attention in Catholic as well as non-Catholic circles and which affords an excellent opportunity to explore some of the issues implied in the problem at hand.

Like Maritain, Finnis is persuaded that, properly interpreted and whatever one may think of its tainted origins (cf. *Natural Law and Natural Rights*, 221), the rights theory is nothing other than a more supple and differentiated way of articulating the essential demands of justice and of a just social order. His own method of procedure is largely deductive in character and resembles that of Rawls and H. L. A. Hart more than it does that of Thomas Aquinas, despite numerous references to him in the text. It consists in laying down as self-evident a number of premoral "basic values" from which by way of entailment human reason is able to fix the universal norms of private and public morality. These values represent the goals or ends to which all human activity is directed. Unlike Rawls's "primary goods," they are desired for their own sakes and not merely as a necessary means to some unspecified and freely chosen end, as would be, for example, liberty or wealth in the Rawlsian scheme (cf. 82). Whereas Hart, on the other hand, speaks only of one such value, namely, survival or life, Finnis singles out six others for special consideration: knowledge, play, aesthetic experience, sociability or friendship, practical reasonableness, and religion. All seven values are to be regarded as "equally fundamental" (92–95) and none deserves to be privileged above any of the others. To pursue them in any of their various forms and combinations corresponds to what has always been understood by human fulfillment or "flourishing," Finnis's word for "happiness."

The analysis of these basic values leads in due course to the identification of the nine principles of "practical reasonableness" (originally Joseph Raz's term)[6] in which for Finnis the whole of morality is summed up. Included in the list are such items as the need to form a "coherent plan of life" (shades of Rawls again), to avoid arbitrary preferences among values or persons, to refrain from actions directly opposed to any of the basic values, to behave rationally and in accordance with the requirements of practical reasonableness, to foster the common good, and to follow one's conscience at all times. The rest of the book is in large part an attempt to show how the observance of these principles conforms in all essentials to the traditional understanding of justice, both general and particular, and insures that the demands of the common good will be met. The final chapter ("Nature, Reason, and God") broadens the scope of the inquiry by placing it within the cosmic setting from which human activity draws its ultimate significance.

No brief summary will ever succeed in conveying a sense of the richness of this complex work, of the acuteness of its analyses, of its attention to detail, and of its willingness to come to grips with concrete moral and legal issues. Seldom in our time have such vast stores of historical, philosophic, and juridical information been brought to bear on the problems with which it deals, and seldom have they been deployed with such obvious mastery. Not the least of the book's many advantages is that its approach is not tied to a teleological conception of nature and is thus immune to the objections that might otherwise be leveled at it on modern scientific grounds. What we are given or promised instead is a view of justice that retains its validity even on the assumption of the nonexistence of God (49). Another feature that deserves to be singled out is the able defense of the objectivity of moral standards against "skepticism" or scientific value relativism, which is shown to be self-defeating inasmuch as the skeptic's belief in the value of science is undermined by his denial of the scientific character of all value judgments (cf. 74–75). Furthermore, the morality in behalf of which the book speaks is a noble or dignified morality, as opposed to the low-minded morality of utilitarianism (since Elizabeth Anscombe, "consequentialism"),[7] which, as the analysis demonstrates, is impracticable anyway for the simple reason that the utilitarian has no reliable criterion by which to decide whether a particular action is or is not conducive to the greatest good of the greatest number (111ff.).

Finnis's theory can likewise claim the merit of ascertaining with quasi-mathematical rigor and determinateness the specific norms by which human choices are to be guided. In that respect, it overcomes one of the conspicuous deficiencies or would-be deficiencies of the Thomistic teaching, which leaves it at saying that all such norms are derived from the common principles of the natural law without stipulating any rule or method by which the process of derivation might be carried out (cf. 34). It should be noted in passing that the discussion of Thomas's position on this as well as on other matters has a freshness that is often lacking among present-day theorists, many if not most of whom tend to read Thomas as an intruder from the past rather than as a contemporary. As a scholar trained in the best tradition of analytical jurisprudence, Finnis is noticeably unhampered by the typical historicist preoccupation with the sense of "alienness" supposedly engendered by the temporal distance that separates Thomas's century from ours. The focus of attention remains squarely on substantive moral issues, which are never allowed to disappear beneath a rubble of exegetical or methodological commentary.

The whole achievement is by any standard an impressive one, combining as it does the best of many worlds. For that reason it is sure to appeal to a broad spectrum of readers: to liberals, who generally feel at home with the language of universal human rights, but also to conservatives, for whom the best way to serve the needs of the present is to show a greater respect for the legacy of the past. Given the looseness, not to say the emptiness, of so much of the current talk about rights, one cannot imagine a more timely and challenging book.

Where there is so much to praise, one hesitates to enter even a slight demurrer. Still, in the interest of clarity, it may be worth our while to take a closer look at the other side of the picture, and all the more so as Finnis himself is the first to concede that "few problems are ever solved once for all" (233). The reader is informed early on that what he has before him is a book on "natural law" (25) and, some time later, that almost everything in it is about "natural rights" (198). Defending the synonymity or the fundamental harmony of these two originally antithetical doctrines is unfortunately not always as easy as one would like it to be. According to the original natural law theory, human beings are social and political by nature.[8] They form part of a larger whole to which they owe their primary allegiance and outside of which for the most part they are nothing. As physical beings they may be unified and self-subsisting wholes, but wholes which are nonetheless intrinsically ordered to a determinate end or ends that cannot be actualized without the collaboration of others. They do not have from the start all that they require for their well-being and attain their full development only by engaging in activities that involve them in a web of reciprocal relationships typically structured within the context of civil society—ideally the *polis*—the comprehensive and truly self-sufficient human association and hence the only one capable of satisfying their longing for completion or wholeness. Any life other than the political life is either subhuman or superhuman.[9] Thus understood, civil society is natural, not in the sense that it is supplied by nature, but in the sense that it corresponds to the natural needs and aspirations of its members and that human nature itself inclines to it.

In contrast to the natural law theory, the natural rights theory proceeds on the assumption that these same human beings exist first of all as complete and independent wholes, endowed with prepolitical rights for the protection of which they "enter" into a society that is entirely of their own making. All rules governing their relations with one another and all principles of justice are ultimately rooted in rights and derive their efficacy from them. These principles are not indemonstrable or self-evident principles, intimated to us through the natural inclination toward the good that the individual experiences within himself,[10] but the products of a calculus of means to a desired end in which discursive reason is called upon to play the leading role. Any knowledge that one may have of them presupposes that one's intellectual capacity is sufficiently developed to engage in this kind of calculus.[11] In Hobbes's version of that theory, the one right on which everything else depends is the right of self-preservation, which alone constitutes the low but solid foundation on which the whole of the social life is made to rest.[12] The original Hobbesian view underwent a series of improvements as time went on, especially at the hands of Rousseau and Kant, but it still provided the model from which all of the most influential political thinkers of the modern period would henceforth work.

It would be surprising if, on the basis of such radically different premises, one were to come in all cases to identical or roughly similar results. By grounding the modern rights doctrine in the intrinsic dignity and worth of the human person, Finnis has unquestionably succeeded in infusing it with a properly moral content. His own view of morality would thus appear to be as far removed from contemporary utilitarianism as is Kant's moral philosophy from Hobbesian or Lockean utilitarianism. Therein lies its greatest strength. Yet the break with the utilitarian tradition is not nearly as deep or as complete as it is presumed to be. What we actually witness could more aptly be described as a simple transformation of the older rights theory, a transformation accomplished less by eliminating any element of personal advantage or expediency from the determination of the rules of morality than by prescinding altogether, as Kant had done, from the distinction between base or selfish and noble or unselfish impulses.

Accordingly, the rights whose defense the book takes up are still perceived as absolute or unconditional rights, circumscribed only by the derivative requirements of practical reasonableness and a proper respect for the rights of others (cf. 218, 225). This horizontal limitation guarantees that my own rights will not be infringed and for that reason I have no choice but to accept it. To do otherwise would be both immoral and foolish. On that level of generality, what is good for me is good for everyone else, but I shall not have it unless they have it too. Self-interest and public interest coalesce into a harmonious whole which does not depend for its coming into being on the conversion from a selfish concern for worldly goods to a concern for the good of the soul or the transformation of the individual into a citizen through the mediating agency of virtue. To be sure, moral virtue is not excluded, but neither is it indispensable. Courage, moderation, generosity, and the other moral virtues are not themselves basic or non-negotiable values; they are ways or modes "deemed" by some people to fit them for the attainment of the basic values (cf. 90–91). One need not acquire them in order to enjoy their benefits. Justice is always to my immediate or long-range advantage and the just life is the most pleasant life. At the extreme limit, no one has to worry about ever having to sacrifice himself for the common good.

Concrete situations are obviously not always that simple, for there are times when rights or "opportunities" come into conflict with each other, as they do, for example, when my friend's well-being "can only be secured by my ruin or destruction" (372). Self-sacrifice is too much a part of human life to be ruled out a priori. It, too, must somehow be "rational," although its "reasonableness," the defense of which is relegated to the last and most tentative chapter, is never made completely clear.[13] If virtue is not choiceworthy for its own sake, one is hard-pressed to say why anybody would want to sacrifice himself for others, save for personal or subjective reasons.

This explains why there is in fact so little talk about virtue in the book. The closest thing to it is not justice, which is not treated as a disposition of the soul (161–97), but practical reasonableness, which bears a superficial resemblance to Aristotle's and Thomas's prudence and which could conceivably stand for the whole of virtue (cf. 102). But practical reasonableness, as distinguished from prudence, does not appear to be connected in any way with the inclinations of the appetite or dependent on them for the rectitude of its judgment.[14] It functions exclusively as an intellectual capacity whose role, as was mentioned earlier, is to deduce from the postulated basic values the best and possibly the only decent set of rules governing human conduct. The soul, its passions, and the reordering of those passions do not enter into account. Human beings may remain as they are as long as the institutions under which they live are as they ought to be. The whole scheme, needless to say, is admirably suited to the conditions that prevail in modern liberal society, which it regards as normative and to which it lends theoretical support. How such a society came into being in the first place, and whether even it could endure without some dedication to virtue on the part of its citizens, are questions that are never envisaged or fully elucidated.

The foregoing remarks are only apparently belied by the rare emphasis that is laid on the common good not only in the chapter that is expressly devoted to it (134–60) but throughout the book. As is his wont, Finnis has again carefully distinguished the different meanings of this tricky notion. The one for which he settles is given as an improvement on Aristotle, who allegedly lacked a "technical notion" of the common good and was therefore unable to supply any "distinct and enumerable" requirements of practical reasonableness (165). It might be observed that Aristotle was not unaware of this difficulty but thought that one merely distorted moral phenomena by treating them with greater exactness than their extreme variability allowed. For him, the acme of precision (*akribeia*) was not necessarily mathematical precision but the highest degree of precision attainable in any given case.[15]

Be that as it may, Finnis's own preferred definition is more specific, though considerably weaker. It sees the common good as constituted by an ensemble of "conditions" that makes it possible for the members of a community to collaborate with one another "positively and/or negatively" in the pursuit of the basic values in terms of which human flourishing has been described (155). Human beings are not united in a common dedication to a common goal. They are not "parts," as Thomas Aquinas still taught,[16] but atomic wholes, open to others and often in need of them, but nonetheless free to organize their lives or devise their "life-plans" as they see fit, provided they do not interfere with the freedom of others. No one has any real duties other than those entailed by the requirements of practical reasonableness or the need to protect the rights with which he was already gifted prior to his incorporation into civil society. At most, the central issue of the relation of rights to duties remains blurred and the section that deals with it thematically (205–10) does little to remove the ambiguity. Rights and duties are said to be correlative, as indeed they are—if I have a duty to do something I also have the right to do it, although the converse is not always true—but this still leaves open the question as to which of the two is the fundamental moral fact. Did Socrates have a right to defend himself or was it above all his duty to do so? The query may not admit of any clear-cut answer, especially since it was never formulated in those specific terms by the ancients and since their own notion of the good as something to be pursued was free of any connotation of duty in the modern or Kantian sense. Allowing for such differences of meaning, however, the likely supposition is that they would have come out on the side of duty. They took it as a matter of course that what the law did not expressly permit it forbade and never doubted that one's first responsibility was to the common good.[17] The same holds for the Bible, which does not promulgate a bill of rights but issues a set of commandments, duly situated within the context of a covenant of love. In both cases, duties and not rights was the principal "moral counter" (221). The individual who voluntarily harms himself or permits others to harm him commits an injustice not toward himself but toward the community by depriving it of the services that he owes to it.[18] For Socrates, to philosophize was a duty; for Spinoza, it was a right. The opposition between the two views is not reduced but merely concealed by the assertion that "human rights are not subject to the common good" if only because they are themselves an "aspect" of the common good (218). One regrets in a way that the interesting remarks about certain African dialects in which duties are given the edge over rights were not followed up to better advantage (cf. 209–10).

The usual objection to this argument is that it does not sufficiently take into account Thomas's qualification to the effect that, although the individual human being is essentially a part of the political community to which he belongs, "he is not ordered to it with regard to the whole of himself and to all that he has."[19] At first glance, this could be taken to mean that there is an important segment of human life in which the individual remains supreme and is thereby absolved from some of the obligations that the community might wish to impose on him in virtue of his participation in it. Yet Thomas also says that "each human being, in all that he is and has, belongs to the community, just as the part, in all that it is, belongs to the whole."[20] Just how these two apparently conflicting statements can be reconciled is a problem that has long divided Thomistic scholars and which would require a much fuller discussion than any that can be entered into here. According to one interpretation, the solution lies in Thomas's distinction between the human being as an "individual" and the human being as a "person."[21] By reason of their material individuality, human beings are ordered to the good of the society of which they form a part. As persons, on the other hand, they are themselves autonomous wholes, existing within society and bound to it only insofar as their own good is served by it.[22] The difficulty with this answer is that in none of the pertinent texts does Thomas invoke the distinction between individuality and personality or speak even of the "person" as superior to the common good. Rather, his point seems to be that civil society is not the sole society to which human beings are ordered. The individual person does indeed transcend civil society, but only as a member or a part of a universal community, ruled by God, whose common good is *eo facto* preferable to that of any particular society.[23] The good in which human beings find their perfection is never a "private good" but a good that is shared or capable of being shared by others and which for that reason takes precedence over any good that they could claim as theirs alone.[24] For the same reason there is no talk anywhere in Thomas of such primordial rights as would not be subordinated to the common good or contingent on the fulfillment of antecedent duties.

On this score, one is entitled to ask whether the "shift of perspective" that Finnis detects in the Thomistic commentators of the sixteenth and early seventeenth centuries is as "drastic" as it is made out to be (207). It is true that the characterization of *ius* or "right" as a "faculty" appears for the first time in the writers of that period, most notably in Suarez and Grotius;[25] and it is also true that prior to that time people spoke of the rightness of things rather than of the rights of persons. The significant fact, however, is that the rights to which Suarez and Grotius refer are still defined and hence limited by law. Moreover, they have to do less with universal human rights than with the specific rights of rulers and subjects, parents and children, masters and slaves, property owners and workers, and the like. Contrary to what is suggested, the real "watershed" in the history of the rights doctrine is not to be located somewhere between Thomas and Suarez; it occurs with Hobbes, who set the stage for all subsequent discussions of this matter by denying that human beings are political by nature (something that Suarez and Grotius never did) and by proclaiming the absolute priority of rights to duties.[26]

All of the points alluded to thus far are of more than purely speculative interest. They are fraught with definite practical implications, which come to the fore when one considers, for example, Finnis's pivotal thesis concerning the fundamental equality of all basic values. His is the neutral perspective of the detached observer who surveys the world of values from an Archimedean point outside of it and is able to disregard the claims to superiority raised on behalf of these values by their adherents. Even knowledge, through which the proposed scheme is devised and which is treated extensively in a separate chapter (59–80), is not objectively higher than, say, aesthetic experience, sociability, or play. It is simply "*made*" so by an individual's choice of it rather than of some other value as the one that is more important or fundamental "*for him*" (93, Finnis's emphasis). It follows that the life of a great scholar, statesman, or religious leader is not intrinsically superior to that of a music buff, a valetudinarian, or a ski bum. In the absence of any natural hierarchy of ends, it becomes impossible to rank people on the basis of the choice that they make of this or that particular value. Human beings are equal not only before God, or before the law, or in regard to self-preservation, but by the mere fact that they have the capacity to "realize" or, better, "participate in" any or all of the aforesaid basic values. It is entirely up to them to set their own priorities or change them if they have any reason to do so, preferring one value to another at different times and under a different set of circumstances. Thus, "if one is drowning, one is inclined to shift one's focus to the value of life as such" (92)—again a sign that the values in question cannot be ordered hierarchically.

The argument does not prove very much, however, for it suggests only that there are moments when more important things have to be set aside temporarily for the sake of more urgent ones. I may be planning to study philosophy or legal theory, but if I am suddenly stricken with appendicitis, the surgical operation will have to come first. Nor is the example of the drowning person always as unambiguous as it sounds. Suppose that *two* persons, a father and his son, are drowning and that only one of them can be saved. Would we still venture to say that the father's willingness to give up his own life is reducible to such incidental factors as "one's temperament, upbringing, capacities, and opportunities"? In all such cases, the tendency to favor the young over the old may be more than either a generally accepted convention or a matter of personal preference. It has something to do with the good of the species, which hinges on the survival of those who are most likely to propagate it. If so, does it not in point of fact direct our attention to "differences of rank of intrinsic value between the basic values" (94)? And, while we are on the subject, does not Socrates' resolve to accept death rather than stop philosophizing become trivial when viewed apart from any consideration of the hierarchy of values implied in such a choice?

Finnis's solution has neatness in its favor, but it can hardly be said to account for all the facts of experience. It is not easily reconcilable with the universal phenomenon of admiration and is bound to work to the detriment of the rarer forms of human "flourishing" to which that phenomenon points. Its spirit is that of democratic liberalism, whose leveling tendencies it reflects without much concern for the deprivations imposed on certain higher types of human beings, to say nothing of the community as a whole. It is doubtful whether anyone who subscribes to it will be inspired to make the almost superhuman effort required to attain the lofty goals of wisdom, prudence, or piety that an older tradition of ethical thought sought to promote. The new program serves everybody equally well, but this is as much as to say that it does not serve anybody particularly well. It can make light of the distinction between the wise few and the unwise many because, even though it can be comprehensively elaborated only by a theoretical person, it does not rely on wisdom, any more than it does on moral virtue, for its successful implementation. Trustworthy institutions, geared to the achievement of modest goals, will give us what we could never be sure of having otherwise, at the risk of making us forget that human beings once thought it possible to aspire to something higher.

Further complications arise when one ponders some of the consequences of Finnis's teaching regarding the absolute inviolability of all basic human rights, none of which, we are told, can ever be infringed, be it only for the sake of averting a catastrophe (cf. 119–20, 224–26). Take, for instance, the principle that prohibits the recourse to torture under any circumstances (164, 213). Well and good, if one thinks only of the frightening abuses to which such a practice lends itself. But how "practically reasonable" is it to refrain from torturing a known criminal if this should prove to be the only way of securing the information that will save the lives of his innocent victims? A world in which terrorism of the most brutal sort has become an almost daily fact of life may not always be able to afford the luxury of showing the same respect for assassins as for anyone else; and, besides, a morally sensitive person might have some qualms about signing away the lives of others or indulging in what from another point of view could just as easily be interpreted as heroism by proxy. Finnis's principle, noble as it may be, is more readily applicable to normal than to emergency situations. It owes much of its attractiveness to the fact that individuals are thereby spared the necessity of engaging in an always precarious "casuistry of duties" (225) or of wrestling with excruciatingly difficult prudential decisions of the kind over which Augustine agonizes in book 19, chapter 6, of the *City of God*. Whether this is enough to validate it is another matter, the laudable concern to steer clear of the pitfalls of utilitarianism notwithstanding.

Surprisingly little thought seems to have been given to the intellectual pedigree of many of these motifs. The overriding and somewhat insular preoccupation with utilitarianism and moral skepticism has resulted in a peculiar blindness to other powerful currents of thought whose language the book often speaks, as is abundantly attested to by the constant recurrence of such characteristic expressions as "personal authenticity," "commitment," "self-realization," "individual autonomy," "creativity," "values," and "lifestyles," the modern substitute for what used to be called the "good life" (cf. 129–30). Serious reflection on this state of affairs might have alerted the author to the enormous difficulties involved in any attempt to recapture the spirit of the natural law tradition and revealed the degree to which his own thinking remains in thrall to the dominant spiritual and political consciousness of the times. One is reminded by contrast of de Tocqueville, who also thought it necessary to go along with the new trend but was much more keenly aware of the price that human beings would have to pay for acquiescing in it. De Tocqueville knew from experience that the modern principles would produce a different type of human being and one which was not in every way superior to the type it was destined to replace. Because he had an alternative, dead as it may have been in his own eyes, he was able to illuminate the present situation and, in its own interest, warn of the dangers that threatened it from within. It would never have occurred to him to say that the new ideal was just like the old one, only better.

Finnis's endeavor to moralize the modern rights doctrine goes *pari passu* with a no less concerted effort to rationalize or demythologize Thomas's natural law doctrine by stripping it of any element of coercion. On his reading, the natural law as Thomas understands it is nothing more than an attempt (admittedly "undeveloped") to spell out what it means to live as a fully rational being. It is only "analogically law" (280) and does not impose any type of behavior under pain of sanction. It merely points to what one must do or avoid in order to fulfill oneself and hence would be just as valid even if there were no God to enforce it. The sole obligation that it carries with it is a "rational necessity of certain sorts of means to certain sorts of ends."[27] The same is also evident from an analysis of the notion of *imperium* or "command," which Thomas defines as an act of the intellect rather than of the will.[28] The very term "natural law" is a "rather unhappy" one (374) for which other expressions, such as "natural right," "intrinsic morality," or "right reason" could be substituted without any loss of meaning (281). Its association with the notion of compulsion or obligatoriness, so prevalent today, is traceable to a misunderstanding perpetrated by Vasquez and Suarez, both of whom dismissed Thomas's concept of *imperium* as "unnecessary," "inept," or "fictitious" (339).

Finnis's interpretation is not his alone since it is already found in a number of late medieval writers from Gregory of Rimini onward,[29] and since it figures prominently in the Prolegomena to Grotius's *Law of War and Peace*; but never has it been defended so forcefully. If it were to be followed, it would go a long way toward resolving the famous dilemma of Plato's *Republic* concerning the goodness of justice in the absence of a legislating God. Yet it was always rejected by the mainstream of the Thomistic tradition and with good reason. For all his insistence on the role of reason in matters of legislation, Thomas does not neglect to draw attention to the fact that a law or command owes its moving power to the will of the legislator.[30] The general principle that one ought to do good and avoid evil, and the more specific principles to the effect that one should not lie, steal, or commit adultery, are not or not yet moral *precepts*. They become precepts only when intimated in the form of an imperative: *Fac hoc*.[31] It is at this point that they cease to be simple rules of rational or sensible behavior and acquire the force of law.

That all of this applies to the natural law does not appear to be open to question. Thomas makes it plain that, insofar as it concerns human beings (as opposed to brutes), the natural law is a law in the proper sense of the word: *proprie lex uocatur*.[32] He also makes it plain that the notion of law includes two elements: first, it is a "rule of human acts" and, secondly, it has "coercive power."[33] Granted, sanctions are not explicitly mentioned in the definition of law with which the treatise opens (I-II, 90), but they are mentioned in connection with the effects of the law in Question 92. The missing reference to them in the formal definition proves no more than that, following the rules of Aristotelian logic, Thomas regarded them as a "property" of the law rather than as part of its essence. There is thus ample reason to think that in his view the natural law is not a mere *lex indicans*, as Finnis would have it, but a *lex praecipiens*, enjoining or forbidding certain actions not only as intrinsically good or bad but as meritorious or demeritorious.[34]

If the thematic account of the *Summa Theologiae* leaves little doubt about the strictly *legal* character of the natural law, it does raise some interesting questions about its *natural* character. One of the peculiarities of that account is that, while it often alludes directly or indirectly to the punishments to which acts contrary to the natural law are subject, it fails to specify the nature of those punishments.

The lacuna is remedied to some extent by the parallel treatment of the *Summa contra Gentiles*, which spells out in great detail the various penalties attached to the transgressions of the law, namely, in order of importance, the forfeiture of eternal bliss, the deprivation of virtue, the disorder of the natural powers of the soul, bodily pain, and the loss of external goods.[35] The oddity in this instance is that, although Thomas appears to have the natural law in view, he never refers to it by name, in all likelihood because his work was primarily intended as a Christian reply to the objections of the Arabic philosophers, in whose thought the natural law plays no role whatever. It is safe to assume that what is said here about sanctions applies preeminently to the natural law, since the acts which they cover are not specifically those prescribed by the divinely revealed law or by the human law, but one still finds it strange that the application is not expressly made by Thomas himself and especially that it is not made in the *Summa Theologiae*, where it would most normally be expected to occur.

One possible reason for the omission is hinted at in his discussion of the relationship between the natural law and the precepts of the Decalogue.[36] The position set forth at the outset is that the entire moral legislation of the Old Law, as distinguished from its ceremonial and judicial legislation, is encapsulated in the Ten Commandments and forms part and parcel of the natural law. Having conceded this much, Thomas immediately introduces a restriction with regard to the precepts of the First Table, enjoining the love and worship of God, the knowledge of which, he says, is not simply natural but requires "divine instruction."[37] The restriction is presumably dictated by the need to account for the prevalence of polytheism among the ancients, a practice that could not have met with universal approval if the cult of the one true God were manifestly prescribed by the natural law. As for the precepts of the Second Table, they are said to pertain to the natural law "absolutely speaking" and are thus held to be self-evident to all human beings.[38] One need not quarrel with this line of reasoning as long as one takes it that the two Tables bear no intrinsic relation to each other. Not so, however, if it can be shown that they are inseparable and, furthermore, that the First Table serves as the mandatory ground of the Second. That this is in fact the case may be illustrated from the following consideration.

What the Thomistic theory essentially requires is not only that the content of the natural law be naturally known to all human beings but that it be known precisely as belonging to the natural law, that is to say, to a law which is both promulgated and enforced by God as the author of nature and hence indispensably binding on everyone. Since all laws draw their effective power from the will of the lawgiver, such a view clearly presupposes that the divine nature is characterized by will no less than by intellect. It becomes intelligible only within the framework of a providential order in which the thoughts, words, and deeds of individual human beings fall under God's supervision and are duly rewarded or punished by him. Here precisely is the difficulty to which on its own ground the argument is exposed; for, the truth of the proposition that the God of nature is a solicitous God, entitled to and demanding the love and worship of all rational creatures, would appear to be secured only through the precepts of the First Table, which, by Thomas's own admission, are not universally accessible without the aid of divine revelation. It goes without saying that the evidence of a conclusion cannot exceed that of its premises or, to use an old Scholastic adage, that a river never rises above the level of its source. If the precepts of the First Table are not naturally known in the strictest sense of the word, one is at a loss to explain how the precepts of the Second Table, which depend on them for their effectiveness, can be regarded as fully natural.

In view of the circumspection with which Thomas chose to deal with this issue, one is tempted to think that he had some reservations about the demonstrably lawful character of the moral order and that, in his mind, the status of the natural law as a philosophical concept was at best problematic. The same conclusion is borne out by what he says elsewhere about sin, which is viewed by theologians principally as a (punishable) offense against God, but by philosophers only as something that is contrary to reason.[39] Suarez, who grapples with the problem, probably comes close to Thomas's position when he argues that natural reason knows only that sins against the natural law deserve to be punished; it knows nothing about the quantity or the mode of the punishment.[40] As far as that goes, it may not even be able to tell whether in every single instance they are punished at all.[41]

Assuming that there is something to be said for this interpretation, the term "natural law" could well be a misnomer of sorts, introduced into the tradition in somewhat accidental fashion by Cicero and later enshrined in innumerable theological and legal texts to which it is indebted for the enormous prestige that it acquired over the centuries.[42] To put the matter in more concrete terms, human reason, left to itself, cannot be absolutely certain that crime never pays and that in the end the only people who are happy are the ones who deserve to be happy. There is ample evidence that a life of crime is not a pleasant one—nobody in his right mind envies Al Capone—and it is equally evident that some actions bear their punishments with them: if I eat or drink to excess, I will suffer the consequences.⁴³ But this still leaves the possibility that some lucky person might commit a single undetected crime by means of which he obtains the fortune or the position on which his heart is set and then, without repenting or surrendering any of his ill-gotten gains, live "honestly" and happily thereafter. Short of appealing to retributions in an afterlife, on which the unaided human reason is unable to pronounce itself, the strict natural law theorist has no option but to deny that such a person can ever be at peace with himself. As that great twentieth-century authority on the natural law, Hercule Poirot, says to the villain of *Death on the Nile*, "Mademoiselle, if you but once allow evil into your heart, it will make a home for itself there." The advice is practically sound, but this is not the same as to contend that it is demonstrably true or empirically verifiable. We sometimes hear of criminals who spontaneously turn themselves in simply because they can no longer live with themselves. There may be others who would never dream of doing as much and show no signs of being similarly afflicted by the pangs of a guilty conscience. The happy crook, if such there be, is not likely to brag about his success since it is in the nature of the case that he cannot do so without jeopardizing his situation. Nietzsche was right when he remarked that this is a species which moralists are only too eager to bury in silence.⁴⁴ The problem, as far as I can tell, remains unsolved and may not admit of any completely satisfactory solution.

All of the preceding comments were intended less as a criticism of Finnis than as a first feeble attempt to highlight but a few of the questions that his book raises or invites us to consider. In fairness, it should be promptly added that his is a philosophic work, which makes no claim to following Thomas to the letter and which will ultimately have to be judged on its merits (cf. p. v). Digesting its contents and coming to terms with its leading assumptions promises to be a long and arduous task. Suffice it to say for the time being that in scope and depth it surpasses anything that has yet been produced by a Roman Catholic scholar in our generation. In an age that has virtually given up on the possibility of establishing any kind of moral standard, let alone the highest, it fully deserves the enthusiasm with which it has been greeted, and more. The basic question is whether its dazzling amalgamation of the old and the new has eluded the danger of eclecticism and yielded the theoretically viable synthesis that we so badly need. We should have every reason to rejoice if, without further surgery, the two theories under consideration, natural law and natural rights, could be made to sit together as comfortably as we are given to understand. Even if they cannot, we may still be grateful that the groundwork has at last been laid for a fruitful comparison of their respective merits. Fortunately, the reader is not obliged to agree with everything Finnis says in order to appreciate the magnitude and quality of his effort. Critical as he may be of the central thesis, the reader will soon discover that he stands to learn more from Finnis than from most of the authors with whom he might agree.

NOTES

Reprinted from *The Review of Politics* 44, no. 4 (October 1982): 590–612.

1. Hans Kelsen, "Natural Law Doctrine and Legal Positivism," trans. Wolfgang Herbert Kraus, in Kelsen, *General Theory of Law and State* (Cambridge, MA: Harvard University Press, 1949), 446.

2. Ibid., 445.

3. James Madison, "Federalist, No. 43," in *The Federalist Papers*, ed. Clinton Rossiter (New York: Signet Classics, 2003), 247.

4. For a recent and reasonably complete survey of these avatars, cf. Michael Bertram Crowe, *The Changing Profile of the Natural Law* (The Hague: Martinus Nijhoff, 1977).

5. John Finnis, *Natural Law and Natural Rights*, Clarendon Law Series, ed. H. L. A. Hart (Oxford: Oxford University Press, 1980), xv, 425. Subsequent parenthetical page references are to this edition.

6. [Joseph Raz, a professor of philosophy of law, was a colleague of John Finnis's at Oxford, and both were doctoral students of H. L. A. Hart. Ed.]

7. [Anscombe was a mid-twentieth-century philosopher who revitalized virtue ethics. See, for example, G. E. M. Anscombe, "Modern Moral Philosophy," *Philosophy* 33, no. 124 (January 1958): 1–19. Ed.]

8. E.g., Thomas Aquinas, *Summa Theologiae*, I, 96, 4; I-II, 72, 4; 95, 4; II-II, 109, 3, ad 1m; 114, 2, ad 1m; 129, 6 ad 1m; *De Regno*, I, 1; *In decem libros Ethicorum expositio* (hereafter, *In Ethic.*), IX, lect. 10, no. 1891; *In libros Politicorum expositio* (hereafter, *In Polit.*), I, lect. 1, etc.

9. Cf. Th. Aq., *Quaestio disputata de virtutibus cardinalibus*, a. 1, c; *In Polit.*, I, lect. 1, no. 39.

10. Th. Aq., *S.T.*, I-II, 94, 2; cf. *Quodlibetum* 1, 4, 8: "Inclinationes naturales maxime cognosci possunt in his quae naturaliter aguntur *absque rationis deliberatione*; sic enim agit unumquodque in natura sicut aptum natum est agi." Also *S.T.*, I, 60, 5.

11. As Locke puts it, the natural law is "intelligible and plain" only to the "studier of that law," *Second Treatise of Civil Government*, II, 12; cf. ibid., IX, 124: "For though the law of nature be plain and intelligible to all rational creatures, yet men, being biased in their

interest as well as ignorant *for want of studying it*, are not apt to allow of it as a law binding to them in the application of it to their particular cases" (emphasis mine). See the discussion of this early modern view by Rousseau, who points out that "it is impossible to understand the law of nature and consequently to obey it without being a great reasoner and a profound metaphysician" (*Discourse on the Origin and Foundations of Inequality among Men*, trans. R. Masters [New York, 1964], 94).

12. E.g., Hobbes, *De Ciue*, 1.1, 7: "Therefore the first foundation of natural right is this, that every man as much as in him lies endeavor to protect his life and members." *Leviathan*, I, 13–14.

13. Finnis readily admits that, when it comes to that, the believer in divine revelation has an easier time of it since his faith tells him that the hoped-for convergence of the common good and the well-being of persons is insured by an all-knowing and loving God, albeit "in ways often unintelligible to us" (*Natural Law and Natural Rights*, 406). He can thus love the common good "for a new reason," namely, because God loves it. The position of the philosopher is not as enviable, but neither is it altogether hopeless. The solution to the problem, if any exists, is to be found, not in Stoic or Kantian moralism (373–78), but in Plato's concept of *logismos* (which again translates into "practical reasonableness," [408]). The person who allows himself to be guided by reason need not view life as tragic. He can refuse to take success or failure too seriously and see himself as participating in a kind of cosmic game which, unlike practical reasonableness, has no point beyond itself, as Plato would have taught in Book VII of the *Laws*. The explanation has its obvious limitations, however, and Finnis himself recognizes that the "structure of practical reasonableness" remains "finally unproved." The only reason for not discarding it is that it is still "more reasonable than any logically possible alternative structures" (405). Whether it is or not is the question by which his book may be thought to stand or fall. For a slightly different and perhaps more faithful interpretation of *Laws*, VII, 803b–c, see Thomas L. Pangle, *The Laws of Plato* (New York: Basic Books, 1980), 484f.

14. Cf. Th. Aq., *S.T.*, I-II, 56, 3; 57, 4; 57, 5, ad 3m; 64, 3; II-II, 47, 4; 47, 13, ad 2m; *In Ethic.*, VI, lect. 7, no. 1200.

15. Aristotle, *Ethicorum Nicomacheorum* (hereafter, *Ethic. Nic.*), I, 3, 1094b20f.; 7, 1098a20f.; II, 2, 1104 a1f. *Metaphysics*, II, 3, 995a6f.

16. See, among innumerable references, *S.T.*, I, 60, 5; I-II, 21, 3–4; 90, 2; 92, 1, ad 3m; 96, 4; II-II, 58, 5; 61, 1; 64, 5; 65, 1.

17. Aristotle, *Ethic. Nic.*, V, 11, 1138a4f.

18. Ibid., 1138a10f. Cf. Th. Aq., *S.T.*, II-II, 59, 3, ad 2m; 64, 5.

19. *S.T.*, I-II, 21, 4, ad 3m: "Homo non ordinatur ad communitatem politicam secundum se totum et secundum omnia sua."

20. *S.T.*, I-II, 96, 4: "Cum enim unus homo sit pars multitudinis, quilibet homo, hoc ipsum quod est et quod habet, est multitudinis."

21. E.g., *S.T.*, I, 29, 4; 30, 4; *De Potentia*, 9, 2. Cf. Jacques Maritain, *The Person and the Common Good* (Notre Dame, IN: University of Notre Dame Press, 1966), 73–74.

22. Maritain, *Person and Common Good*, 61.

23. Cf. *S.T.*, I-II, 109, 3: "Manifestum est autem quod bonum partis est propter bonum totius. Unde etiam naturali appetitu uel amore unaquaeque res particularis amat bonum suum proprium propter bonum commune totius uniuersi." Also I-II, 21, 4; II-II, 26, 3; *Quaestiones Disputatae de Caritate*, 2, c.

24. Thomas's remarks on this controversial subject are obviously not meant to be interpreted in any collectivist or totalitarian sense. Civil society is not itself a person, even though it is often compared to one. Its unity is only a "unity of order" (*unitas ordinis*), as distinguished from the substantial unity of the individual person (cf. *In Ethic.*, I, lect. 1, no. 5). Its function is to enable its citizens to attain their full development and it deserves its name only to the extent to which it promotes the ends to which human nature is ordered. The human beings who compose it are not destroyed by it, as they would be if they were parts of a substantial whole. The perfection that they reach through it remains intrinsic to them. Differently stated, the common good is not an alien good but the "proper good" (*bonum proprium*) of those who share in it (cf. *Summa contra Gentiles*, III, 24). If the common good were not distributed among the members of the community, it would not be truly common. Only on this condition can it be an object of desire. The good sought by any being is necessarily its own good (*bonum suum*), whether it be a particular good or the common good, for which it has an even greater natural love (*S.T.*, I, 60, 5, c. and ad 1m). The need for justice and civic virtue is rooted in the potential conflict between these two types of good or the tendency of the part to set itself up as the whole. Were it not for this conflict, moral virtue would be expendable. Indeed, according to Aristotle, the perfect man stands in relation to others as the whole in relation to the part (*In Polit.*, III, 17, 1288a27). Having no desire for goods that cannot be shared, he appears as a god among human beings (*In Polit.*, III, 13, 1284a10; see also, on the absence of moral virtue among the gods, *Ethic. Nic.*, X, 8, 1178b10f.). He is not subject to the common good because he is himself, so to speak, the common good and hence the source of everyone else's perfection. Only in this ideal case is the good of the individual commensurable with the common good. It matters little whether such a perfect being ever existed or can exist since the purpose of Aristotle's observation is merely to bring to light the problem inherent in any form of political rule. —On Thomas's understanding of the common good, see Charles De Koninck, *De la primauté du bien commun contre les personnalistes* (Quebec and Montreal: Éditions de l'Université Laval, 1943), 7–79. De Koninck's essay was widely interpreted at the time as a silent attack on Maritain and was so interpreted by Maritain himself in his restatement of the problem, *Person and Common Good*, 16, n. 6. See also Ignatius Theodore Eschmann, "In Defense of Jacques Maritain," *Modern Schoolman* 22, no. 4 (1945): 183–208; Charles De Koninck, "In Defense of Saint Thomas: A Reply to Father Eschmann's Attack on the Primacy of the Common Good," *Laval théologique et philosophique* 1, no. 2 (1945): 9–109; Yves Simon, "On the Common Good," *Review of Politics* 6, no. 4 (1944), 530–33. Simon, who professes to be in general agreement with De Koninck's views, denies that they were directed against Maritain, with whom he also agrees.

25. Francisco Suarez, *De Legibus*, I.2, 5. Hugo Grotius, *De Iure Belli et Pacis*, I.1, 4. The transition to the new understanding of "right" (*ius*) as a "faculty" (*facultas*) appears to have been facilitated to some extent by the frequent appearance of the word *ius* in the Vulgate. Suarez, ibid., refers to Genesis 23:4, where Abraham is shown negotiating with the Hittites for the purchase of a grave in which to bury Sarah. The text reads: "Give me property among you for a burying place (ªhuzzat- queber; Sept.: *ktêsin taphou*) that I may bury my dead out of my sight." The Latin version, *da mihi ius sepeliendi*, could easily suggest that Abraham was demanding, not a plot of land (the first to be acquired by a member of the Chosen Race in Canaan), but the right to bury his dead. Suarez takes *ius sepeliendi* to mean *facultas sepeliendi*. Cf. also Genesis 1:19–21: Jacob, who has finally outwitted Laban, flees "with all that he had," which in the Latin text is rendered by "everything to which he had a right": *omnia quae iuris sui erant*. For an account of the historical evolution of the notion of right as a faculty, cf. Richard Tuck, *Natural Rights Theories; Their Origin and Development* (Cambridge: Cambridge University Press, 1979).

26. E.g., *De Ciue* I.1, 2: "The greatest part of those men who have written aught concerning commonwealths, either suppose, or require us, or beg of us to believe that man is a creature born fit for society. The Greeks call him *zôon politikon*; and on this foundation they so build up the doctrine of civil society as if for the preservation of peace and the government of mankind there were nothing else necessary than that men should agree to make certain covenants and conditions together, which themselves should then call laws. Which axiom, though received by most, is yet certainly false and an error proceeding from our too slight contemplation of human nature."

27. Finnis, *Natural Law and Natural Rights*, 341, n. 42, with references to *S.T.*, I-II, 100, 1 and II-II, 58, 3, ad 2m.

28. Cf. *S.T.*, I-II, 17, 1.

29. Gregory of Rimini, *In Librum Secundum Sententiarum.*, dist. 34, qu. 1, art. 2; Gabriel Biel, *In Secundum Lib. Sent.*, dist. 35, qu. 1, art. 1, and the other references cited by Suarez, *De Legibus*, II.6, 3.

30. *S.T.*, I-II, 17, 1: "Primum autem mouens in uiribus animae ad exercitum actus est uoluntas. . . . Cum ergo secundum mouens non moueat nisi in uirtute primi mouentis, sequitur quod hoc ipsum quod ratio moueat imperando sit ei ex uirtute uoluntatis." Cf. I-II, 90, 1, ad 3m.

31. Ibid., I-II, 17, 1.

32. Ibid., I-II, 91, 2, ad 2m. As regards irrational creatures, the natural law is said to be a law only *per similitudinem*, i.e., by analogy or by reason of a certain resemblance with the manner in which it applies to human beings. See also I-II, 93, 5, c. and ad 1m.

33. I-II, 96, 5: "Lex de sui ratione duo habet: prima quidem quod est regula humanorum actuum; secunda, quod hab et uim coactiuam." Cf. I-II, 90, 3, ad 2m.

34. Cf. I-II, 18, 5, ad 3m; 92, 2; 93, 6, ad 2m; 100, 9. The principles of the natural law are generally referred to as "precepts," e.g., I-II, 94, 1, 2, and 6. But precepts, as distinguished from simple rules or principles, are binding under pain of sanction. Cf. I-II, 99, 5:

"Quaedam moralium praecise praecipiuntur uel prohibentur in lege, sicut Non occides, Non furtum facies. Et haec proprie dicuntur praecepta." I-II, 100, 9: "Praeceptum legis habet uim coactiuam. Illud erge directe cadit sub praecepto legis ad quod lex cogit. Coactio autem legis est per modum poenae." Finnis notes perceptively that for Plato "obligatum ... is not the framework or final authoritative category of 'moral' thought" (409). But Plato was not a natural law thinker. He spoke only of natural "right," which is not quite the same thing, however frequently the two expressions may be confused, as they are, for example, in the article by Joseph P. Maguire, "Plato's Theory of Natural Law," *Yale Classical Studies* 10 (1947), cited on 413.

35. *Summa contra Gentiles*, III, 141, 3.

36. This paragraph and the next one reproduce with minor additions and modifications an argument previously developed in Ernest Fortin, "Augustine, Thomas Aquinas, and the Problem of Natural Law," *Mediaevalia* 4 (1978): 197–98.

37. *S.T.*, I-II, 100, 1; 104, 1, ad 3m: "Ad tertium dicendum quod etiam in his quae ordinant ad Deum quaedam sunt moralia quae *ratio fide informata* dictat, sicut Deum esse amandum et colendum."

38. Ibid., I-II, 100, 1: "Quaedam enim (praecepta moralia) sunt quae statim per se ratio naturalis cuiuslibet hominis diiudicat esse facienda vel non facienda, sicut Honora patrem tuum et matrem tuam, et Non occides, Non furtum facies. Et huiusmodi sunt absolute de lege naturae."

39. Ibid., I-II, 71, 6, ad 5m: "A theologis consideratur peccatum praecipue secundum quod est offensa contra Deum; a philosopho au tern morali, secundum quod contrariatur rationi."

40. Suarez, *De Legibus*, I.15, 13: "Nam lex, imponendo necessitatem uirtutis seu honestatis, consequenter facit ut transgressor legis sit dignus poena saltern apud Deum, quia suam obligationem lege impositam non obseruat. Quod locu habet tam in lege naturali quam in positiua, diuina, uel humana, quia supposita lege actus est inordinatus, et ilia dignitas poenae intrinsece sequitur ex militia actus, etiamsi malitia fortasse fuerit ex occasione legis positiuae. Est tamen differentia in hoc inter legem naturalem et positiuam, quod lex naturalis, licet faciat uel ostendat actum esse malum, tamen ut est mere naturalis non taxat modum uel quantitatem poenae. Nulla enim ratione intelligi potest hoc fieri sine decreta alicuius liberae uoluntatis." Cf. *S.T.*, I-II, 95, 2: "Lex naturae habet quod ille qui peccat puniatur; sed quod tali poena puniatur, hoc est quaedam determinatio legis naturae."

41. Thomas's muted reservations about the complete naturalness of the natural law come out in other ways as well. One of them is hinted at in his treatment of suicide, which is said to be contrary to the natural law and which is "always" a grievous sin. By taking his own life, the suicide commits an injustice toward the city and he commits an injustice toward God, in whose image he was created; cf. *S.T.*, I-II, 59, 3, ad 2m; 64, 5. That such an act should be unjust from the point of view of the city is obvious enough, since the city is thereby robbed of the services of one of its members. That it should likewise be unjust from God's point of view is obvious only to someone who accepts the biblical teaching

regarding man's creation in the image of God. The more delicate problem, however, is that the city is not necessarily hurt and might even be helped by the loss of an unproductive member, especially if it should be stricken with famine and unable to support its population. What reason sanctions in such unusual circumstances could conceivably differ from what divine revelation imposes as a universal duty. Suicide is also ruled out on religious grounds by Cebes and Simmias in the *Phaedo*, 61a–62a. Socrates does not object to the argument, although it is not completely clear whether it reflects his own thinking on the matter. Much depends on what one makes of the ensuing discussion, in which Socrates defends his resolve to die as both "wise" and "just," i.e., as something good for himself as well as for his friends.

42. The origin of the natural law doctrine is unfortunately shrouded in mystery. Scholars have generally traced it back to the Stoics, but Helmut Koester has shown that the expression itself does not occur in any of the surviving fragments from the early Stoa. It is attributed to Zeno of Cittium by Cicero in one and only one text whose authenticity is not corroborated by independent evidence; *De Natura Deorum* I.14, 36: "Zeno . . . naturalem legem diuinam esse censet, eamque uim obtinentem recta imperantem prohibentemque contraria." The term reappears a hundred years later in Philo, who does not seem to have been influenced by Cicero. Cf. H. Koester, "*NOMOS PHUSEÔS*: The Concept of Natural Law in Greek Thought," in *Religions in Antiquity: Essays in Honor of E. R. Goodenough*, ed. J. Neusner (Leiden: E. J. Brill, 1968), 521–41. The close textual parallels between Philo and Cicero nevertheless point to a common source which, according to one hypothesis, could be Antiochus of Ascalon; cf. Richard A. Horsley, "The Law of Nature in Philo and Cicero," *Harvard Theological Review* 71 (1978): 35–59.

43. On the general unpleasantness of the nonvirtuous life, cf. Aristotle, *Politics* VII, 1, 1323a27–34: "No one would maintain that he is happy who has not in him a particle of courage or temperance or justice or prudence, who is afraid of every insect that flutters past him, and will commit any crime, however great, in order to gratify his lust for meat or drink, who will sacrifice his dearest friend for the sake of a farthing, and is as feeble and false in mind as a child or a madman."

44. Friedrich Nietzsche, *Beyond Good and Evil*, aph. 39 and 197. Thomas, who was not unaware of the problem, notes that the wicked are sometimes punished by being granted the prosperity that incites them to evil; *Summa contra Gentiles*, III, 141, 6.

CHAPTER 7

Grounding Human Rights in Natural Law

JOHN FINNIS

John Finnis was born in Adelaide, South Australia, in 1940. He studied law at the University of Adelaide and philosophy of law with H. L. A. Hart at Oxford, before teaching law and legal philosophy at the University of Oxford from 1966 to 2010. From 1995 to date he has taught jurisprudence and the moral, political, and legal theory of Aquinas at the University of Notre Dame Law School. Around the time he moved from Adelaide to Oxford, he abandoned the atheism of Hume and Russell for Catholic Christianity. Following Aquinas's teaching that metaphysics comes last in the order of learning, and that the features of human nature decisive for moral thought are discovered (and warranted philosophically) by attention to the objects of human deliberation, free choice, and action, Finnis rearticulated the moral, political, and legal theories generally called "natural law theory," mainly in his Natural Law and Natural Rights *(1980, 2nd ed. 2011),* Fundamentals of Ethics *(1983),* Moral Absolutes *(1991),* Aquinas: Moral, Political and Legal Theory *(1998), and the five volumes of* Collected Essays of John Finnis *(2011). He has collaborated with Germain Grisez in much published and unpublished work in moral philosophy and theology, largely sharing Grisez's adversely critical view both of neo-scholasticism and of much neo-Thomism (including Maritain's), considering them philosophically unfaithful in some foundational respects to Aquinas, reality, and reason's practical insights. He was a member of the International Theological Commission (chaired by Cardinal Ratzinger) from 1986 to 1991.*

I. Purposes, Predicament, Method, and the "Art of Writing"

My work *Natural Law and Natural Rights*[1] (hereafter *NLNR*) says nothing about rights until the eighth of its thirteen chapters. By then, it has taken up (i) the methodology of social (including political) science and (ii) the errors of many early modern and contemporary thinkers about natural law theory and about their own traditions. It has (iii) teased out and (iv) elaborated the first principles of practical thinking and deliberating, and then (v) the foundational moral principles that resolve, in principle, the problem that our choices must be made— and should be made *reasonably*—among multiple intrinsically valuable and intelligible goods all actualizable in the lives of many human persons. The book then considers (vi) the fundamental types of human association and community, and the intelligibility, goodness, and centrality of *common* good in family, voluntary and civic associations, and political communities. It reviews (vii) the forms of *justice*, the principles that give that supreme inter-personal virtue specificity by identifying how the demands of the supreme moral virtue—practical reasonableness or *prudentia*—bear on chosen conduct or inaction that affects other persons. Only after all this does *NLNR* consider (viii) rights. They are shown to be simply the entailments of the virtue of justice, the correlatives of duties of justice—not as mere shadows of those duties but as, in a way, their point. There follow chapters on (ix) authority, on (x) law as the politically desirable standard form of authority, on (xi) obligations in morality and law as the requirements of acting for common good, on (xii) the reality and nullity of unjust laws, and on (xiii) the need for, and availability of, a meaningful philosophical response to questions about the ultimate origins and sense of all these intelligibilities.

Each of the thirteen chapters, like the whole venture of displaying their mutually supportive explanatory and practical force in personal and political life, has the purpose of making available to young, secular students the main *truths* of the classical tradition in political philosophy. The principal bearers of that tradition, for many centuries, have been thinkers who also accepted the truth of Christian revelation as transmitted in Catholic doctrine and theological reflection. Most of the book's readers could be expected to approach it with assumptions widely and deeply opposed to that doctrine and theology. Every part of *NLNR* is shaped and marked by consciousness of that challenging fact.

It was written during the very years of what Ernest Fortin justly called "the pseudomorphic collapse of Neo-Thomism in the wake of Vatican II."[2] I shared

Fortin's judgment that the neo-Thomism current in manuals and textbooks in the decades before 1965 was philosophically inauthentic. Anyone embarking on a project such as *NLNR* needed to investigate, as a top priority, whether Aquinas and Aristotle were guilty of the fallacies and elisions of neo-Thomism, and if they were not, whether a philosophically critical and free-standing exposition of the foundations of ethics and political philosophy would show that, in their main lines, Aquinas and Aristotle had *got there first*, so to speak, and can, now too, be philosophically helpful. The work of recovering the real theses and argumentation of, particularly, Aquinas had been pursued in the late 1950s and the 1960s by French-speaking Dominicans such as P. M. Van Overbeke and P.-D. Dognin,[3] and then, with decisive clarity, by Germain Grisez.[4] The testing of Aquinas's theses in dialectic with Hume and with the main academic British moral philosophers of the twentieth century, during the gestation of *NLNR*, can in part be traced in essays of the 1970s published first or republished in *Collected Essays of John Finnis* (2011).[5]

NLNR is written primarily for law students, undergraduate and graduate,[6] and for lecturers and other teachers many of whom have little acquaintance with, and no predisposition to favor, the philosophical and theological tradition in which the term "natural law" finds its origins and its home. These are the readers whom the book seeks to meet where they are. Few indeed, however, were the reviewers who noticed, or made even the slightest allowance for, the book's genre, its rhetorical predicament, and its strategies, its "art of writing."

I hoped that, for example, my giving common good and justice priority over rights would signal to thinkers interested in and aware of the tradition of political thought that the book and its author stood in opposition to some main prejudices of modernity. That scholars who thought of themselves as guardians of *the* tradition, or of classical wisdom, would turn out to be readers whose comprehension was blocked by questionable presuppositions—as far-reaching, or nearly so, as the errors and oversights of those who think of themselves as moderns—was something I did not really envisage. Nor did I really envisage that scholars who thought of themselves as sensitive to "the art of writing" in oppressive circumstances would turn out to be inattentive to the book's rhetorical and structural precautions for disarming or circumventing the hostility with which many modern readers approach anything associated by them with the past, especially the past of Christianity and of all that ante-dates the secular "liberalisms" and conventional radicalisms of 1980 and today.

The long review of *NLNR* by Ernest Fortin in 1982 showed up these mistaken hopes of mine, and my failures of foresight, with special clarity. The review has had considerable influence over the subsequent thirty-some years, and the present essay is a belated but still perhaps timely response.

When writing *NLNR*, as now, I judged that the divine revelation constitutive of Christianity—the central form of which (as the book's index discreetly indicates) must be Catholicism—is the central event of human history and became the bearer of what is sound in the philosophical tradition of moral and political (and therefore legal) philosophy inaugurated, masterfully, by Plato and Aristotle.[7] And I thought also that the moral and political philosophy shaped by Hobbes, Locke, Hume, Bentham, and their successors down to today is a series of blunders and oversights, partly but inadequately identified, and then inadequately resisted, by Kant and his successors, and partly prepared for by deficiencies in the (neo-)scholasticism of Aquinas's sixteenth-century and later successors.

Fortin seems not to have noticed the book's own statement of its program. As the preliminary Part I of *NLNR* draws towards its close, and after more than a page expounding the errors of Gabriel Vazquez, Francisco Suarez and later neo-scholastics about obligation, errors occasioned by their departures from Aquinas's thought, and by neglect of *ends* and *goods*, *NLNR* states:

> The reader will ask how Aquinas explained the difference between moral thinking and merely prudential reasoning (in the modern sense of 'prudential'), and how he accounted for the peculiarly conclusory sense of the moral 'ought'. The answer must be that Aquinas's account of these matters is, at best, highly elliptical, scattered, and difficult to grasp, and at worst, seriously underdeveloped; and that these deficiencies occasioned the unsatisfactory responses of those who professed to follow him in the later history of philosophical theology. But to this I must add that the materials for a *satisfactory development of the sort of position espoused by Aquinas* are available, and that the attempt to put these materials to use is encouraged by the impasse in which the sixteenth- and seventeenth-century theories of natural law manifestly found themselves. *The subsequent chapters of this book incorporate such an attempt.*
>
> ... the reason for making the attempt is that a theory of practical reasonableness, of basic forms of human good, and of practical principles, such as

the theory Aquinas adumbrated but left insufficiently elaborated, *is untouched by the objections which Hume (and after him the whole Enlightenment and post-Enlightenment current of ethics) was able to raise* against the tradition of rationalism eked out by voluntarism.[8]

NLNR thus defined itself as an attempt to *develop* Aquinas's theory, so as to give an account of natural law that is philosophically sound, untouched by Humean and all subsequent philosophical and cultural objections, and at the same time—to the extent permitted by philosophically critical criteria—is more authentically in line with St. Thomas's thought than were his most influential sixteenth-century commentators and followers.

The book's prominent statements[9] that it is not deferring to the authority of Aquinas, or proceeding out of reverence for him (or for Catholic doctrine), are sincere and true. They are also rhetorically strategic, because countless readers will approach the book with the Protestant and secularist assumption that a Roman Catholic is a mental slave, and a Thomist abjectly so. The assumption is fallacious, a *petitio principii*, a vicious circle, insofar as it covertly or overtly assumes that Catholicism and Thomism are false or substantially erroneous. For that is the very question in issue in the work of Thomists.[10] If Thomism turns out to be substantially correct by the autonomous criteria of critical, free-thinking philosophy, a good working method in philosophizing is to start with Thomas's positions and test them as rigorously as one can against those autonomous criteria and against the most careful and stringent criticisms that one can find in the literature or devise in one's reflection.[11] If the assumption of Thomists' mental servitude is to be held non-fallaciously, it must be accompanied by a willingness to consider the possibility that Thomist positions in philosophy are true, and are reachable by autonomous critical reflection; testing that possibility will then be a kind of joining in the enterprise of Thomists, albeit without the *initial* presumption that this investigation will be fruitful in attaining substantive philosophical truths about reality and value. Then, as investigation confirms the plausibility of Thomist positions, especially when considered not one by one but as a network, though always also in light of the evidence of experience, history, and logic, one's initial presumption of Thomism's falsehood withers away and one can start to hold the contrary presumption that it is a generally sound guide to truth-attaining positions in philosophy. So none of this need proceed *from* reverence for Aquinas, or *out of* deference to his (or the Catholic Church's) authority. Hence the book's disclaimers, which are fully compatible with its method.

What is that method? As is easily noticed by careful readers, especially if they attend to the argument of chapter II and the endnotes to chapters III and IV (or subsequent chapters), the book treats its own theses as also Aquinas's (and vice versa) except when it specifically asserts some deficiency in the latter—a deficiency or flaw that almost invariably is not error on his part but unclarity or some other form of incompleteness in the provision of premises. Such readers—especially those properly attentive to "the art of writing"—soon judge that the book is treating Aquinas's views as warranted (and true) save when it specifically says otherwise. Fortin's reading is faulty exegesis insofar as it sees only "numerous references to [Aquinas] in the text" (173). Indeed, the lead-up to that remark is severely mistaken about all the four authors mentioned: "[Finnis's] own method of procedure is largely deductive in character and resembles that of Rawls and H. L. A. Hart more than it does that of Thomas Aquinas, despite numerous references to him in the text" (173). In truth, the book scorns Rawls's[12] and Hart's[13] methods (widely different from each other!) of dealing with the foundations of ethics (and thus of political and legal theory), especially their theories about human good(s). It equally disdains the foundationless and unwarranted character of their principal theses in ethics, politics, and jurisprudence.

Nor can the book's method of identifying basic human goods and the main requirements of practical reason be reasonably said to be deductive. It does not "lay down as self-evident" the basic premoral values (basic human goods), but resorts to a variety of encouragements to readers to reenact for themselves, reflectively, the process—called by Aristotle, Aquinas, and thus by the book *inductive*[14]—by which they attained some insight into those basic goods. Every reader, Fortin included, certainly did once (good by good), when young, attain such insights, and also began to deploy them with more, or less, adequate coherence and integrity as—when taken thus in combination with each other and as goods realizable in the lives of others as well as oneself—morally as well as pragmatically significant guides to decision making. No one who seriously reflects upon the lines of thought developed at chapter length (chap. III) about the good of knowledge, and upon the argumentation (III.6) on the dialectical defensibility but radically basic character of our knowledge of that good's goodness, will call this a "laying down" of anything. The same goes for chapter IV's identification of other basic goods/values. And chapter V, like the rest of the book, plainly denies Fortin's claim that *NLNR* presents "the universal norms of private and public morality" as reached "by way of entailment" from the premoral basic values/goods.[15] For between the basic goods and any norms of morality stand, as new premises, the "methodological requirements of practical reasonableness," attained by another but quite different kind of *induction* (or abduction).[16] No deduction or entailments here, nor indeed much "quasi-mathematical rigor" (174), meritorious or otherwise. Instead, an itemization of aspects of deliberation and choice that philosophers have reflectively identified as preeminently important elements of reasonableness in action.

II. The Governing Natural Virtues: Practical Reasonableness and Justice

As *NLNR* repeatedly indicates, its key term "practical reasonableness" is intended to be understood as the precise counterpart and translation of *phronēsis* as that word appears in Plato and Aristotle, and of *prudentia* as used by Aquinas. Fortin claims (173) that the term was first used by Joseph Raz, with whom I conducted seminars in Oxford for a quarter-century and more; I doubt the claim, and reject Fortin's assertion (177) that practical reasonableness bears only "a superficial resemblance to Aristotle's and Thomas's prudence." As for the word or phrase, I came up with it (so far as I remember) in reflection upon the common law concept of the reasonable man, and upon the excessive grandeur of the common translators' term "practical wisdom" (for, say, Aristotle's *phronēsis*). Be that as it may, this is *NLNR*'s pivotal concept, and Fortin's misunderstandings of it pervade his review.

In the book, practical reasonableness is introduced as "the integrating good," the basic human good whose subject matter or content is precisely the integration of the pursuit of any and all of the basic goods and corresponding practical principles. In the same breath, "the moral principles" are introduced as what are "involved in the pursuit" of this good of practical reasonableness.[17] This is the basic human good that makes nonsense of Fortin's claims that the book's "pivotal thesis concern[s] the fundamental equality of all basic values." Having misunderstood the book's thesis that the basic goods are "all equally fundamental," Fortin converts it into a denial that there is "any natural hierarchy of ends," and concludes: "It follows that the life of a great scholar, statesman, or religious leader is not intrinsically superior to that of a music buff, a valetudinarian, or a ski bum" (181).[18] But valetudinarians, by definition, are unreasonably concerned about their own health, and necessarily neglect the good of practical reasonableness. Ski bums are bums because, for the good of play, they shamefully neglect all other basic human goods, instrumentalizing the good of association to their self-centered purpose, and in constant violation, therefore, of the good of practical reasonableness too.[19] Fortin's interpretation of chapter IV.4's remarks about the senses in which there is no single hierarchy *of value* among the basic goods simply sets aside the truly "pivotal thesis" on the opening page of chapter V. Headed "*The good of practical reasonableness structures our pursuit of goods*," that page states first that the multiplicity of basic goods, none instrumental or simply subordinate to the others *in value*, leaves us all with the questions "What is to be done? What may be done? What is not to be done?" It states next that to be free *and responsible* is to have choices, such as between concentrating on (say) one value and commitment to others. And then it explains this responsibility:

> For among the basic forms of good that we have no reason to leave out of account is *the good of practical reasonableness*, which is participated in precisely by *shaping one's participation in the other basic goods*, by guiding one's commitments, one's selection of projects, and what one does in carrying them out.[20]

And this is the point at which the book reaches, and reaches into, morality:

> The principles that express the general ends of human life do not acquire what would nowadays be called a "moral" force until they are brought to bear upon definite ranges of project, disposition, or action, or upon particular projects, dispositions, or actions. How they are thus to be brought to bear *is* the problem for practical reasonableness. "Ethics," as classically conceived, is simply a recollectively and/or prospectively reflective expression of this problem and of the general lines of solutions which have been thought reasonable.
>
> How does one tell that a decision is practically reasonable? This question is the subject-matter of the present chapter.[21]

Manifestly, then, the book treats the good of practical reasonableness as standing in a hierarchical relationship to all the other basic human goods.[22] The book denies that the hierarchy is one of *value*. It impliedly asserts that the hierarchy is one of *significance for*, that is, *importance in*, making choices and commitments of every kind of generality, specificity, or particularity.

Fortin seems not to have noticed that moral significance or importance might derive from something other than *simple superiority* in *premoral value*.[23] That that importance *is* derived from something other is one of the book's most pivotal theses. The deeper understanding of Aquinas's ethics that I gained in writing *Aquinas: Moral, Political, and Legal Theory* (1998) only confirmed that for Aquinas, too, the *bonum rationis*, the good of practical reasonableness, is pivotal.[24] This architectonic good is decisively important not because it ranks higher *in goodness* than life, knowledge, friendship, or love of God, but because of its inherent content: the goodness of pursuing intrinsic human goods in a reasonable way. And the classical synonym for that "in a reasonable way" is *virtuously*.

NLNR abstains, just as Fortin notices, from the classics' *talk* of virtue, virtues, and so forth. What he fails to notice is that the abstention is largely rhetorical, and that *virtue dominates the book* under another name, or pair of names. The first name is practical reasonableness. The equivalence of that with *prudentia* and *phronēsis* is absolutely explicit,[25] and as Fortin well knew, *prudentia* is the supreme natural moral virtue that settles the shape and content of all other natural moral virtues,[26] and is the only virtue that is both an intellectual and a moral virtue.

The other moral virtue to which the book gives elaborate attention (again, without using the word "virtue" or its cognates) is, of course, justice. In the classical schema of the cardinal virtues, it is next in strategic importance to *prudentia*. Fortin claimed that the book does not present justice as a virtue, that is, "as a disposition of the soul" (177). But he was again entirely mistaken. According to *NLNR* (not to mention Aquinas),[27] all aspects of justice are particularizations of General Justice, and General Justice is defined as precisely a disposition of the soul; in the concluding, summarizing words of chapter VII.2:

> Justice, as a *quality of character*, is in its general sense always *a practical willingness* to favour and foster the common good of one's communities, and the theory of justice is in all its parts, the theory of what in outline is required for that common good.[28]

The next section of chapter VII proceeds to show that realizing the common good involves (i) problems of distributing resources, opportunities, burdens of cooperation, etc., to particular individuals, and (ii) a range of other problems *not* involving common enterprises and dangers but responsibilities of one individual to another, such as duties of carefulness, duties of performing undertakings, and duties of compensation, etc. The guiding thought is that mere disposition to favor common good, in any of these ways, is not enough. Justice, as Aquinas observes, is not like courage and temperance, cardinal virtues measured by practical reasonableness's constitutional rule over *passions* of aversion and desire.[29] Justice is about the right *external* action (or forbearance) in relation to *other* people, and justice is done even when it is done without good dispositions. So the measure of the virtue of justice is the right *proportionality* between one's actions (or abstentions) and the rights of the other; dispositions (the material of virtues) take second place in working out the theory of justice, and rightly make no further appearance in *NLNR*'s chapter on justice after the definition quoted above.

Quite generally, the problems of individual and communal moral life are not solved by talk about virtues. *NLNR*'s terse explanation of its abstention from talk about virtue and virtues is on the page immediately following the page (just quoted from above) defining "Ethics" and the "'moral' force" of the basic goods or general ends of human life. The explanation is implicit in the following:

> How does one tell that a decision is practically reasonable? This question is the subject-matter of the present chapter. The classical exponents of ethics (and of theories of natural law) were well aware of this problem of criteria and standards of judgment. They emphasize that an adequate response to that problem can be made only by one who has experience (both of human wants and passions and of the conditions of human life) and intelligence and a desire for reasonableness stronger than the desires that might overwhelm it.[30]

I interrupt to note Fortin's assertion that in *NLNR* "practical reasonableness . . . does not appear to be connected in any way with the inclinations of the appetite or dependent on them for the rectitude of its judgment" (177). The lines just quoted contradict him, as is confirmed a few lines later when I say (about two specifically Aristotelean and Thomist articulations of the general interrelationship between right judgment and good character) "Such assertions can scarcely be denied."[31] But, as I go on to state,

> they are scarcely helpful to those who are wondering whether their own view of what is to be done is a reasonable view or not. The notion of "the mean" . . . seems likewise to be accurate but not very helpful. . . . For what is "*the mean and best, which is characteristic of virtue*"? It is "to feel [anger, pity, appetite, etc.] when one ought to, and in relation to the objects and persons one ought to, and with the motives and in the manner that one ought to. . . ." Have we no more determinate guide than this?

In the two millennia since Plato and Aristotle initiated formal inquiry into the content of practical reasonableness, philosophical reflection has identified a considerable number of requirements of method in practical reasoning. Each of these requirements has, indeed, been treated by some philosophers with exaggerated respect, as if it were the exclusive controlling and shaping requirement. For, as with the basic forms of good, each of these requirements is fundamental, underived, irreducible, and hence is capable when focused upon of seeming the most important.

Each of these requirements concerns what one must do, or think, or be if one is to participate in the basic value of practical reasonableness. Someone who lives up to these requirements is thus[32] Aristotle's *phronimos* and has Aquinas's *prudentia*; they are requirements of reasonableness or practical wisdom, and to fail to live up to them is irrational....[33]

The paragraph and section proceed for another couple of dozen lines, explaining why the resultant of these requirements is *eudaimonia*, that is, flourishing, and why these requirements of moral goodness are thus also requirements for fulfilling one's nature and of "natural law." *NLNR*'s undertaking to its readers, in short, is to provide something more helpful as a guide to conscientious decision-making in individual and social life than a mere naming of relevant virtues and counseling a life of virtue, with reason ruling the passions but (as Fortin would have it) with rectitude of rational judgment dependent on "the inclinations of the appetite"[34]—advice easy enough to give but not much help to anyone, above all in the fields of social life and thus of justice (the book's fields).

In my 2011 postscript to *NLNR*, there is a short preliminary section headed "Virtues and Principles":

The book says little about virtue(s). That was deliberate, but it would have been appropriate to explain both the decision and the intrinsic relationship between virtues and principles, the priority of the latter, and the bearing of free choices' intransitive aspects (their lasting in the dispositions of the chooser) on the formation of virtues and vices. *Aquinas*, 124, explains why principles, propositional practical truths, are more fundamental than virtues, even than the master virtue of practical reasonableness (*prudentia*): 'for virtues are the various aspects of a stable and ready willingness to make good choices, and like everything in the will, are a response to reasons, and reasons are propositional'.³⁵ And the relevant propositions are the first principles of practical reason(ing) (Chapters III and IV above) and the requirements of practical reasonableness (Chapter V), together with the more specific moral norms which result from bringing these two levels of principle to bear on one another. Some of this is hinted at in the paragraph on p. 102 above concerning Aristotle's idea of the 'mean' (virtue's mean between the vices of 'too much' and 'too little'—where reasons are the measure of the excessive and the fitting). But spelling out the inherent connection between principles and virtue(s), the logical and rational primacy of the former (a primacy acknowledged by Aquinas),³⁶ and the grounds on which, nonetheless, Aquinas could judge it reasonable to arrange his largest discussion of morality under the various cardinal virtues, would have helped avoid the suspicion that 'virtue ethics' was or is an unexamined alternative to the kind of moral theory deployed in this book. It is not.³⁷

That was said at large. But let me address one of Fortin's main criticisms: that in *NLNR* "the soul, its passions, and the reordering of those passions do not enter into account. Human beings may remain as they are as long as the institutions under which they live are as they ought to be" (178). The claim is contradicted by many passages,³⁸ among them one that various readers have found pungent, pertinent, and suggestive of wider issues touching the soul and the ordering of its passions:

> The fact is that human rights can only be securely enjoyed in certain sorts of milieu—a context or framework of mutual respect and trust and common understanding.... Consider, now, the concept of public morality, in its oddly restricted [conventional], sexual sense.... If it is the case that sexuality is *a powerful force which only with some difficulty, and always precariously, can be integrated with other aspects of human personality* and well-being—so that it enhances rather destroys friendship and the care of children, for example; and if it is further the case that *human sexual psychology has a bias* towards regarding other persons as bodily objects of desire and potential sexual release and gratification ... then there is reason for fostering a milieu in which children can be brought up (and parents assisted rather than hindered in bringing them up) so that they are relatively free from *inward subjection to an egoistic, impulsive, or depersonalized sexuality*. Just what such a milieu concretely

amounts to and requires for its maintenance is something that is matter for discussion and decision, elsewhere. But that this is an aspect of the common good, and fit matter for laws which limit the boundless exercise of certain rights, can hardly be doubted by anyone who *attends to the facts of human psychology as they bear on the realization of basic human goods.*[39]

The passage makes clear that the "milieu" or matrix in which human goods can be realized, harmed, or destroyed includes the inner life, "psychology" in the sense that it can be affected for good or ill by cultural/educational encouragement to or discouragement from the self-discipline and virtue needed to integrate passions with reason and reasonable relationships, and so forth.

Fortin says that, in *NLNR*, "human beings may remain as they are. . . ." But the book's central section, on the specification of rights (to which I shall return below), states that

> there is, I think, no alternative but to hold in one's mind's eye some pattern, or range of patterns, of human character . . . and then to choose such specification of rights as tends to favour that. . . . One attends not merely to character types desirable in the abstract. . . . So one will bear in mind . . . that . . . friendship and respect for human personality really are threatened by hatred, group bias, and anarchic sexuality . . . that servility, infantilism, and hypocrisy really are evils . . . that where 'paternalism' on the part of the political community is justified it is . . . to be no more than a help to *self-correction*. . . .[40]

The passage, which in the temper of the age is *much* more noticeable to the book's average and likely readers than to Fr. Fortin,[41] shows how questionable not only is his remark about people remaining as they are, but also another set of assessments he makes, presenting the book as "prescinding altogether, as Kant had done, from the distinction between base or selfish and noble or unselfish impulses," and as treating moral virtue as dispensable (176–77). In the end, Fortin's presentation of my position ascends to fantasy:

> One need not acquire [courage, moderation, and the other moral virtues] in order to enjoy their benefits. Justice is always to my immediate or long-range advantage and the just life is the most pleasant life. At the extreme limit, no one has to worry about ever having to sacrifice himself for the common good. (177)

The real-world *NLNR*, however, begins and ends its long discussion of the common good with prominent reminders of the moral necessity, sometimes ineluctable, of self-sacrifice:

> Does not the analysis of morality as reasonableness in self-constitution overlook the fact that moral responsibilities can require one to sacrifice not merely one's selfishness, and one's self-interest, but even, on occasion, *oneself*?
>
> This chapter undertakes a fuller analysis of the proper relationship between one's own well-being and the well-being of others. It does not complete that analysis. . . . The question just raised, about the reasonableness of self-sacrifice, and the related question whether the effort to be reasonable is in the end just a pursuit of self-perfection, are questions to be tackled and resolved only in Chapter XIII.[42]

When the issue is resumed, as promised, at the outset of chapter XIII, it is framed as arising both in the context of friendship, when my friend's well-being "can be secured only by my ruin or destruction," and in the context of responsibilities to family or political community, responsibilities which "*reasonably may require self-sacrifice*."[43] The question is kept in view.[44] The curious inadequacy of Aristotle's attempt to "explain the reasonableness of self-sacrifice for one's friend" is recalled.[45] The book's explanation "in principle" of "how self-sacrifice in friendship can make sense," along with "our obligation to favour the common good," is finally pointed to in a (very reserved) discussion of divine revelation, first as holding out a divine friend whose favor for the good of one's friends and neighbors "is given knowing fully the true worth and all-explaining point of everything, of the existence of every person, and of the history of every community."[46] On this basis "we would have a new and pertinent reason for loving [the] common good [of human persons], pertinent even though we could not see how that love would work out in the perspective of all times and places."[47] But the explanation only concludes on the book's original final page of text, with the conclusions drawn from the evocation, via Plato's *Laws*, of participation in the divine play—in accordance with the divinely-sourced pull of the law (*nomos*) of practical reasonableness (*logismos*)—that "in the last analysis . . . is the *only* really serious matter."

> In such a "final analysis," in which we seek an understanding going beyond our feelings, the "serious things of life," even atrocious miseries, are really

serious only to the extent that they contribute to or are caught up into a good play of the game of the God who creates and favors human good.[48]

Fortin like everyone else would be fully entitled to say that the book's attempt to make full sense of self-sacrifice is of very limited success—or even to try to argue that it simply fails. He was not entitled to suggest that the book in any way teaches that "the just life is the most pleasant life.... no one has to worry about ever having to sacrifice himself for the common good."[49]

III. Rights, Their Logic, and Virtue

The main thesis of Fortin's review is articulated in its motto, the "little ditty my gang used to sing when I was a kid":

I love Carolina,
I love Angelina, too,
I can't marry both,
So what I gonna do?

His point: one "can't marry both" "rights or freedom on the one hand, and ... virtue, character formation, and the common good on the other."[50] He was fundamentally mistaken, I believe, in his tying of *rights* to *freedom*—worse, to Hobbesian freedom from duty—and fundamentally mistaken in contrasting respect for rights (and claims of rights) with virtue, character-formation, the common good, and natural law (or natural *right*). One can, and every society and social, political, or moral theory should, marry both, for love. And this is not polygamy, for they are not two distinct realities but two aspects of—two ways of talking about—one and the same fruitful object of reasonable love and devotion.

The corresponding Straussian bifurcation of history, too, is mistaken, and it pervades Fortin's review.[51] *NLNR* rejects the mistake, but not clearly enough. Its discussion should have attended more closely to the Roman-law definition of justice that St. Thomas adopted for his vast treatise on justice,[52] and to his decision to head up that treatise with a whole article on *ius*.[53] For the most correct English translation of that article's subject matter (*ius*) is "rights," plural (even though the Latin word is singular). The object of the virtue of justice, and of acts of justice, is *rights*—in the central sense of that English term, the sense in which its correlative is *duties*, that is, duties of justice resulting from the directives of natural and, where pertinent, just positive law. These facts, which I believe to be beyond dispute, render the contrasts alleged (albeit variously) by Leo Strauss, Michel Villey, and Ernest Fortin simply untenable, both historically and philosophically. It is deeply regrettable that so much scholarly time has been diverted to tracing differences that are in the last analysis almost imaginary.

The mistake takes a particularly muddled form in Fortin's review, because it misunderstands the basic logic of the correlativity of rights (to be treated justly) and duties (of justice)—a correlativity with which Aquinas was working throughout his treatise on justice, and which I spell out in a formally complete way at the beginning of *NLNR*'s chapter on rights. Here is Fortin on that correlativity:

> No one [according to *NLNR*] has any real duties other than those entailed by the requirements of practical reasonableness[54] *or the need to protect the rights with which he was already gifted prior to his incorporation into civil society.*[55] At most, the central issue of the relation of rights to duties remains blurred [in *NLNR*] and the section that deals with it thematically (pp. 205–10) does little to remove the ambiguity. *Rights and duties are said to be correlative, as indeed they are—if I have a duty to do something I also have the right to do it,* although the converse is not always true—but this still leaves open the question as to which of the two is the fundamental moral fact. (178–79)

The blurring, like the "leaving open the question," is in Fortin's eye, and has as its direct cause his misunderstanding of the correlativity of rights and duties.[56] The true correlative of A's duty to B is *B's right*,[57] not, as Fortin asserts, A's liberty-right to do his duty. And *that* liberty of A is so trivial—so merely tautologically entailed by A's duty—as to be of no interest to Aquinas, lawyers ancient or modern, or *NLNR*.[58] The true correlative of a one person's duty is *another person's* right, and vice versa. Justice *always* concerns what I owe *to another*—what that other has the right to, from, or as against me.[59] Everything *NLNR* says about rights has as its basis the virtue of justice, which is why its chapter on justice (as Fortin fails to note) *precedes* the chapter on rights.

This makes *NLNR*'s treatment of the "fundamental moral fact" question (rights? or duties?) not blurred but rather transparent:

> In short, the modern vocabulary and grammar of rights is a many-faceted instrument for reporting and asserting the requirements or other implications

of a relationship of justice from the point of view of the person(s) who benefit(s) from that relationship. It provides a way of talking about "what is just" from a special angle: the viewpoint of the "other(s)" to whom something (including, inter alia, freedom of choice) is owed or due, and who would be wronged if denied that something. And the contemporary debate shows that there is a strong though not irresistible tendency to specialize that viewpoint still further, so that the peculiar advantage implied (on any view) by any ascription of rights is taken to be the advantage of freedom of action, and/or power to affect the freedom of action of others. . . .

. . . there is no cause to take sides as between the older and the newer usages, as ways of expressing the implications of justice in a given context. Still less is it appropriate to argue that "as a matter of juristic logic" duty is logically prior to right (or vice versa). But when we come to explain the requirements of justice, which we do by referring to the needs of the common good at its various levels, then we find that there is reason for treating the concept of duty, obligation, or requirement as having a more strategic explanatory role than the concept of rights. The concept of rights is not on that account of less importance or dignity: for the common good is precisely the good of the individuals whose benefit, from fulfillment of duty by others, is their right because required in justice of those others.

As I put it, more tersely but to the same effect, in my *Aquinas*:

In Aquinas' understanding of justice, rights are as fundamental as duties, and duties as fundamental as rights. We have duties which are not duties of justice, so *duty* is the wider concept. But when a duty is to another human person, it is a duty of justice, and that other person's right is its very object or point.[60]

Fortin's blunder about the elementary logic of rights and duties is surely a prime source of his mistakes about the history of the rights tradition. For he sees the origin of that tradition in Hobbes.[61] I'm sorry to say that he omits even a hint about the existence of *NLNR*'s exposé, or demolition, of Hobbes's theory of rights:

This [Hobbes's] shift of perspective [towards the perspective of the beneficiary] could be so drastic as to carry right-holders, and their rights, altogether outside the juridical relationship which is fixed by law (moral or posited) and which establishes *jus* in Aquinas's sense: "that which is just."[62] For within a few years Hobbes is writing:

> ...*jus*, and *lex*, right and law... ought to be distinguished; because right, consisteth in liberty to do, or to forbear; whereas law, determineth and bindeth to one of them: so that law, and right, differ as much, as obligation, and liberty; which in one and the same matter are inconsistent.[63]

Pushed as far as Hobbes's purposes, this contrast between law and rights deprives the notion of rights of virtually all its normative significance. Hobbes wishes to say that one has most rights when one is in the "state of nature," i.e. a vacuum of law and obligation, since "in such a condition, every man has a right to everything; even to one another's body."[64] But we could just as well say that in such a condition of things, where no persons have any duty not to take anything they want, *no one has any rights*.[65]

In other words, Hobbes's theory of rights is rationally ineligible, an outrageous muddle: the state of nature is a condition in which there are not only no legal rights but also *no human or natural rights*. Hobbes's confused prioritizing of bare liberty, unprotected by any claim-rights, had some influence on other voluntarist thinkers such as Locke and Pufendorf. But their deployment of a partially Hobbesian, liberty-prioritizing logic of rights was watered down by their simultaneous, partly incoherent, but real adherence to main elements of the classical and Christian conception of rights: as correlatives of duties defined by the same natural law as provides the propositional content of the arduous virtues of *prudentia* and justice. Hobbes cannot conceivably be the originator of the modern sense of rights, as one finds them stated in the Universal Declaration of Human Rights 1948 or any of its countless derivatives and antecedents.

Since the matter is so important for an understanding of political thought, old and current—not least Catholic political thought—it is worth going through Fortin's summary of his position,[66] commenting briefly by interjection into the continuous passage setting it out:

> It is significant that the notion of universal human rights, understood as rights that inhere in each human being by reason of the fact that he or she is a human being, does not occur anywhere in premodern thought and, until very recent times, only sparingly in Roman Catholic thought.

Not so. Just as a notion of the Trinity occurs in the New Testament[67] without the term "Trinity" or any verbal equivalent, so the notion of universal human rights has been present in "premodern" and "Roman Catholic" thought, expressed in statements to the effect that all human beings are protected by the duties of justice, duties that are owed to, for example, the newborn child who might by custom be left to die on the mountainside, or the servant-girl or -boy who might by custom be taken for sex, or the passing stranger who might by some custom be robbed at least of his luxury goods.[68]

> The Bible itself, which shares to some degree the perspective of classical philosophy on this point, does not promulgate a Bill of Rights, of which it knows nothing; instead, it issues a set of commandments.

Yes, and these are the precepts of which Aquinas says (i) that they apply to every human being alike (*communiter omnibus* and *indifferenter*[69] or *inquantum est homo*[70]), and (ii) that, being precepts of justice, they have as their very object the rights of those—everyone—to whom justice is owed.[71]

> For centuries, the corner-stone of Catholic moral theology was not the natural or human rights doctrine but something quite different, called the natural law.

No: natural law, like the set of duties it picks out and directs us to—not least but not exclusively duties to others with corresponding rights—remains the corner-stone of Catholic moral theology. The fact that that theology is now *articulated* in terms of rights as well as duties changes its propositional content not at all, but (when rightly understood) clarifies both its bases and its implications. Natural law stands to natural rights, not as something "quite different," but as premises stand to entailments.

> Rights, to the extent that they were mentioned at least by implication, were contingent on the fulfillment of prior duties.

Not true. It is the repeated teaching of St. Thomas, with no sense of innovation, that children incapable of fulfilling prior duties had rights, including rights against their parents, who wronged them—implicitly, violated their rights—

when they violated parental duties of care and respect, and the child's entitlement not to be obliged to do wicked things and to make his or her own choice of life-vocation and spouse.[72]

> Far from being absolute or inalienable, they could be forfeited and were so forfeited by the individual who failed to abide by the law that guaranteed them.

The rights that are truly absolute today were absolute, and for the most part clearly recognised as absolute, in classical Christian doctrine and theology. Fortin errs fundamentally when he says that "the rights whose defense [*NLNR*] takes up are still perceived as absolute or unconditional rights" (177) and speaks of "Finnis's teaching regarding the absolute inviolability of all basic human rights" (182).[73] The term "basic rights" did not appear in the book Fortin was reviewing, and the rights which *NLNR* defends as natural include many that cannot sensibly be called absolute but rather are contingent, for their specification (their specific application), on other changeable aspects of the common good of the communities in which respect for them comes in issue.[74] The absolute rights that *NLNR* proposes and defends in the short section entitled "Absolute Human Rights," at the end of the chapter on rights, are few in number (though of strategic significance for law, politics and individual life).

Finally, then, the passage I have been quoting from Fortin concludes:

> Simply stated, what the church taught and tried to inculcate was an ethic of virtue as distinct from an ethic of rights.

But although the Church was not unreasonably hesitant to adopt an idiom that had been so prominently abused by bitterly anti-Catholic and philosophically (and theologically) very confused thinkers, such as Hobbes and Locke and the swarm of revolutionary propagandists who promulgated the "rights of man and citizen," it was never the case that an ethic of virtue need be in any way, even slightly, opposed to a reasonable ethic of rights. For it is as true now as it was in Aristotle's time[75] or Gaius's[76] or Aquinas's or Pius VI's, Leo XIII's, or John XXIII's that the philosophically or theologically defensible doctrine of virtue *includes* a doctrine of justice that in turn, given the resources of modern European languages, can most authentically be set out in terms of rights (which entail their correlative duties).[77]

IV. Rights and Modernity

The more or less Straussian view of political history that Fortin seems to have accepted[78] is, I believe, historically very flawed insofar as it views political or political-theoretical history as divided—by a caesura, if not a watershed—between a premodern age, innocent of rights (or at least of human rights), and a modern age, insistent on rights (and *pro tanto* careless of virtue and common good). For such matters do not turn on a word or a concept. To go no further than Aristotle's *Politics*:

> In democracies of . . . the type which is regarded as being peculiarly democratic . . . [there is] a false conception of liberty . . . of individuals. The democrat starts by assuming that justice consists in equality . . . he ends with the view that "liberty and equality" consist in "doing what one likes "— . . . for any end one chances to desire.[79]

A more real caesura or watershed is the emergence and working through of the Christian conception of radical equality of all human beings, in humanity and destiny. This would have worked its leaven or ferment regardless of the emergence of a vocabulary of rights.

Conversely, the irresponsibility of many revolutionary proclamations of rights, and today the injustice and destructiveness of "the woman's right to choose [to kill her child]" or the follies and injustice of "gay rights," "the right to private life," or "the right to migrate," could and I believe would have emerged when they did, regardless of theories of rights. The premodern vocabulary of *liberty* and *equality* available to the sophists and demagogues known to Plato, Thucydides, and Aristotle could today as then—and just by itself—serve as matrix for demands promoting the vices of lust, cowardice and injustice (and for sophisms rationalizing these violations of *prudentia*) just as well as any modern idiom of rights can serve.

V. "Only analogically law"

Fortin's review most particularly obscured potential readers' view of the book with his claim that for *NLNR*, "the natural law as Thomas understands it . . . is only 'analogically law' (p. 280)" (183).[80] Fortin links this with claims about *NLNR* having a purpose of "stripping" natural law doctrine of any element of coercion or sanction. I will take the two issues separately.

Fortin's purported quotation from page 280 of *NLNR* is highly misleading, and has misled a good many. The sentence from which he quoted the two words "analogically law" states, "'Natural law' . . . is only analogically law, *in relation to my present focal use of the term*: that is why the term has been avoided *in this chapter*"—the chapter on law as it is found in "the central case of law and legal system . . . of a complete community purporting to have authority to provide comprehensive and supreme direction for human behavior in that community, and to grant legal validity to all other normative arrangements affecting the members of that community" (*NLNR*, 260, opening words of the chapter). The section from which Fortin was quoting is entitled "A Definition of Law," and begins with the book's notorious sixteen-line definition, which includes, as one element among many, "buttressed by sanctions in accordance with the rule-guided stipulations of adjudicative institutions."[81] That element is only one of a number that make the definition inapplicable, in any non-analogical way, to natural law. And the snippet quoted by Fortin comes near the end of a paragraph the whole burden of which is that what is central, and what analogical, depends on one's theoretical purposes. What is centrally law for physicists is only analogically or metaphorically law for jurists. Ignoring this, Fortin eventually has me saying that "the natural law is. . . a mere *lex indicans*," not "a *lex praecipiens*, enjoining or forbidding certain actions not only as intrinsically good or bad but as meritorious or demeritorious" (184).

Once again, Fortin treats "meritorious and demeritorious" as if these predicates turned on sanctions, and I will return to this in a moment. The point to make just now is that throughout *NLNR*, natural law is treated as genuine law, not merely "indicating" what is "intrinsically good or bad," but rather *requiring* conduct as *obligatory*,[82] such that noncompliance is not merely bad but *wrongful* and *culpable* and in many cases *deserving* or *meriting* of punishment for the sake of retributive justice. For *NLNR*, natural law, both in itself and for Aquinas, is *praecipiens*, imperative, though not by reason of a superior's command, still less by reason of sanctions imposed by a commander.[83] (*Pace* Fortin, *NLNR* does clearly affirm the existence of "natural sanctions" [*poena naturae*].)[84] No, the reason why natural law has law's quality of being preceptive, imperative or mandatory, *obligatory*, compelling in conscience, and so forth, is because it rationally picks out and directs us to *common* good in the measure prescribed by the requirements of practical reasonableness. Following the precepts of the natural law is what it takes to be practically reasonable, whatever the personal cost of doing so and being so.

And that is not a matter of subjection to divine sanctions. Fortin tries to make St. Thomas hold that natural law is law, obligatory, because of divine "enforcement," God's threatened sanctions. But the texts he cites[85] relate—quite plainly, when they are read through beyond the snippets he selects from them—to human law or revealed divine law, each of which Aquinas clearly distinguishes from natural law, notwithstanding that the content of human and divine law, respectively, should and does overlap substantially with the content of natural law. Coerciveness is simply no part of Aquinas's careful definition[86] of *law*, a defining precisely for the purpose of showing how and why natural law, divine revealed positive law, and human positive law (not to mention the eternal law of Providence) are, each in its own significantly differing way, law. No need to dwell on this part of Fortin's review, which runs into the sands, as he virtually admits when trying to account for the absence of natural law from the *Summa contra Gentiles*. St. Thomas holds what St. Paul holds in Romans 2:12–16: that even those human beings who have never heard, or heard of, the divine law, or of God, can know "by nature" what the divine law requires; what they know is precisely the natural law, which accuses them in their consciences when they violate it, even though they are unaware that God too will in due time accuse them of such violations. Yes, revelation discloses that the natural law is upheld by divine sanctions (and corresponds in its content to much of the divine law), but *the sanctions (and the overlap with divine law) are not what make it law or binding*.[87]

In a curious aftermath of the review of *NLNR*, Fortin and Edward Goerner engaged in an exchange "on the naturalness and lawfulness of the natural law." Goerner's views on Aquinas were even more skewed than Fortin's were by Straussian misreadings: he saw Aquinas as a practicer of veiled, esoteric writing to conceal and convey an elitist conception of morality as comprising unnuanced norms (of law, *lex*) for the many but nuanced, equitable norms (of right, *ius*) for the few—so that "Thomas's moral and political doctrine is not fundamentally a natural law teaching at all, and that in his teaching the morality of natural law is crucially different from (and subordinate to) the morality of natural virtue."[88] He also shared Fortin's mistakes[89] about the necessarily sanctioned character of (Aquinas's) natural law, which according to him "leads men to obedience by fear of punishment."[90] But the point is that the debate between them elicited from Fortin the statement or admission that he himself had *no natural law theory*.[91]

This helps explain his somewhat shaky grip on issues such as obligation, and his collapse of Aquinas's resolutely reason-, good-, and end-centered account of law, natural law, and much else, into voluntarism, primacy of will, and even dependence on sanctions, to explain what makes law law. *NLNR* is from beginning to end a critique of such a flight from the normativity, the imperative preceptiveness, of reasons.

VI. Exceptionless Moral Norms: For and (Fortin) Against

Fortin's remarks (182) in (not quite fully assertive) defense of the use of torture (with no suggestion of inherent limits)[92] in exceptional, emergency circumstances constitute his response to a theme that in *NLNR* goes wider and includes other kinds of cases, notably (so far as concerns the book's rhetorical energy), the killing of innocent, noncombatant hostages in war, and the deterrent threat to do so maintained by "every government that has the physical capacity to make its threats credible."[93] *NLNR* carries through its defense of exceptionless moral norms, commenced in chapter IV.7 and crystallised in chapter VIII.7's discussion and list of half-a-dozen absolute human rights. The tone and content of Fr. Fortin's comment are strongly reminiscent of the pungent passage in the exact center of Strauss, *Natural Right and History*, pages 160 to 162 of that 323-page book, in the core of his discussion of the central type among the "three types of classic natural right teachings." As I say in my 1990 essay on it:

> This passage of Strauss's is to be taken as a studied defense of the "total war" policy of the Allies in the war which ended only four years before Strauss's lectures—a policy extended into western post-war security policy. Nuclear deterrence treats the "extreme situation" as, in a decisive aspect, the simply "normal."[94]

That last sentence is my comment, not Strauss's admission. As I also note there, Strauss's discussion (of which I quoted a substantial central part with which readers could profitably compare Fortin's paragraph on torture)

> anticipated, remarkably, the main themes of the critique which, in the following forty years, was to be directed by certain Catholics[95] against the Christian moral teachings which Aquinas helped transmit. These themes: Moral

judgment has its truth only in and for "particular situations;" in situations of "conflict" one should decide by reference to a particular "common good" which relativizes the principles of justice and suspends certain "rules of natural right;" "there is not a single [moral] rule ... which is not subject to exception;" and what ultimately matters, in the exceptional situations, is not what one does but that one does it with an *attitude*, for example of "reluctance." Whatever Strauss's success in articulating the spirit of "the classics," he certainly conveyed some characteristic elements of the spirit of the mid- and late twentieth century.

But even if one frees oneself as best one can from the spirit of the age,[96] and from the spirit of ancient paganisms, philosophical or otherwise, and from every illusion about our ability to assess and evaluate *by reason* the overall likely consequences of alternative options available to us (including, not least, the reflexive consequences for the character of all who choose or approve an option), it remains that agonizing predicaments—of the kind Fortin gestures towards as emergencies, and as potentially tragic—are real, and really test every philosophical moral judgment that seeks to be principled, truly reasonable, more than a sophisticated rationalization. I think Fortin was fair to imply that *NLNR* takes too few brushstrokes to paint this predicament in all its darkness, and in hinting at heaven as resolution of the divine game[97] should also have hinted at hell—as *Fundamentals of Ethics*'s last chapter was soon to do (with more than hints). But the real bearing of Christian revelation on these matters is richer and more extensive than any traditional concepts of the ultimate last things, proposing as it does, a kind of continuity—intelligible though entirely dependent on miraculous divine action, gratuitous but promised in revelation—between the building up of persons and their communities in morally good choices (and "works") and eternal life in the completed Kingdom.[98] *NLNR* attempted no more than to open a pathway towards a point—call it a way-station—from which a reader might trek on, by another way and not without labor or grace, to the vantage point of true revelation, from which point concepts or realities such as the Kingdom of God and its completion and its conditions of citizenship can become visible, and enticing. A political theory worthy of the name of philosophy has to venture towards that way-station and be able to indicate how it can reasonably be judged to be only a way-station and starting point for something more and, in its own way, better.[99]

Notes

After writing this response in 2014–15 to Ernest Fortin's original 1982 review essay (reprinted as chapter 6 in this anthology) of my *Natural Law and Natural Rights*, at the generous invitation of the editors of this volume, I unearthed a manuscript the contents of which I had forgotten, titled "Comments on Ernest Fortin's 'The New Rights Theory and the Natural Law,'" written in 1984 evidently for a seminar (quite possibly at Notre Dame in March of that year). Its running header summary of its topics was: (i) obligatoriness of natural law; (ii) virtue and soul; (iii) rights; (iv) torture; and (v) basic goods; a final section discussed and illustrated "a pervasive weakness of Straussian methodology: that it looks to words rather than meanings and propositions." Where my thoughts of more than thirty years ago may perhaps be still of interest, I have added them in the following notes. Fortin's 1982 review essay in the *Review of Politics* was also republished in J. Brian Benestad, ed., *Ernest Fortin: Collected Essays*, vol. 2, *Classical Christianity and the Political Order: Reflections on the Theologico-Political Problem* (Lanham, MD: Rowman & Littlefield, 1996), 265–86.

The parenthetical page references to Fortin's review in this essay and its notes are to the pages of the reprinted version in the current volume, rather than those in the original *Review of Politics* version.

A similar version of this response essay (with page references to the original *Review* version of Fortin) has appeared in *The American Journal of Jurisprudence* 60, no. 2 (2015): 199–225.

    1. John Finnis, *Natural Law and Natural Rights*, Clarendon Law Series (Oxford: Oxford University Press, 1980); 2nd edition, with identical pagination and a 65-page postscript, 2011.

    2. Ernest Fortin, "The Trouble with Catholic Social Thought" (1988), reprinted in J. Brian Benestad, ed. *Ernest Fortin: Collected Essays*, vol. 3, *Human Rights, Virtue, and the Common Good: Untimely Meditations on Religion and Politics* (Lanham, MD: Rowman & Littlefield, 1996), 303–13, at 311. A pseudomorphic crystalline is one that assumes the shape of another mineral that it has replaced; I take it that Fortin's phrase predicates (by hysteron proteron) pseudomorphism of Neo-Thomism rather than of its collapse (which was real enough, sociologically speaking). On the inauthenticity (pseudomorphism) of the "neo-Suarezian theory . . . widespread in Catholic seminaries until the 1960s," see *NLNR*, 49; also 47.

    3. See *NLNR*, 228.

    4. Germain Grisez, *Contraception and the Natural Law* (Milwaukee: Bruce, 1964), and "The First Principle of Practical Reason: A Commentary on the *Summa Theologiae*, 1-2, Question 94, Article 2," *Natural Law Forum* 10 (1965): 168–96.

    5. *Collected Essays of John Finnis*, 5 vols. (Oxford: Oxford University Press, 2011); hereafter *CEJF*. See especially *CEJF* I (*Reason in Action*), essays 6 (1970), 7 (1971), 8 (1975);

CEJF III (*Human Rights and Common Good*), essays 3 (1973), 11 (1972), 18 (1973); *CEJF* IV (*Philosophy of Law*), essay 18 (1972); and *CEJF* V (*Religion and Public Reasons*), essay 7 (1973). There were also others, notably, John Finnis, "Natural Law in *Humanae vitae*," *Law Quarterly Review* 84 (1968): 465–71, and "Natural Law and Unnatural Acts," *Heythrop Journal* 11 (1970): 365–87.

6. But H. L. A. Hart, who had commissioned it and specified its title, said, a touch gloomily, after a first reading of the typescript, that it would appeal more to philosophers.

7. See, e.g., my "Catholic Positions in Liberal Debates" (1999), essay 6 in *CEJF* V, *Religion and Public Reasons*, 113–26, at 118. It is widely assumed that to hold such an opinion is to render oneself unfit for genuine philosophical enquiry and argument, and is to make one little more than an apologist for doctrine and theology. But the assumption cannot be explicated or defended without resort, covert if not overt, to the premise that Catholicism is false. For if Catholicism is substantially true, then a Catholic scholar can pursue philosophical, scientific, or historical inquiries and discussions with full freedom of mind—as many have done and do—confident that when pursued with such resolute freedom and diligence their findings and results will not conflict with Catholic doctrine and, where their subject matter overlaps with Catholic doctrine, will turn out to be clarified and, if possible, made more certain by the additional information conveyed by the divine revelation embodied in that doctrine. *NLNR* does not proclaim this, but tacitly proceeds on this basis.

8. *NLNR*, 46–47 (emphases added). The passage continues:

> That tradition presented itself as the classical or central tradition of natural law theorizing, but in truth it was peculiar to late scholasticism. It was attractive to non-Catholics (like Grotius, Culverwel, and Clarke) who adopted its major concepts not least because of its strong verbal and conceptual resemblances to the Stoicism (XIII.1) so much admired in European culture from the Renaissance to the end of the eighteenth century. The substantive differences between the theory of natural law espoused by Vazquez and Suarez (and most Catholic manuals until the other day) and the theory espoused by Aquinas are scarcely less significant and extensive than the better-known differences between Aristotelian and Stoic ethics.

The section ends with a series of far-reaching critical remarks about ethical and metaethical positions characteristic of the period from 1630 to today, in which Aquinas is presented as the primary critic, and as one who quite obviously speaks for the book's author.

9. See *NLNR*, vi, 46.

10. I call persons "Thomists" if they regularly agree with positions of St. Thomas himself, and work with a presumption that Aquinas is much more likely to be sound than mistaken. Such a person would be well advised not to accord the same presumption to the works of other Thomists, still less to the works of neo-scholastics, many of whom adopted, consciously or not, philosophical positions at odds with Aquinas. I call positions "Thomist" if they are positions of Aquinas himself, taken as a coherent whole, not simply statement by statement; such a whole I call "Thomism."

11. The testing should not take positions in isolation, but as parts of a much wider network of Thomist positions, all of which are implicitly in issue in the testing of any one of them—for similarly, critical objections, though they sincerely and reasonably present themselves as particular, in fact presuppose a network of supportive presuppositions, all of which are thus implicitly in issue.

12. Against Rawls's method and theory, see *NLNR*, 76 (the first sentence quotes Rawls, the second is a root-and-branch rejection of his foundational assumption and method); 82 (Rawls's "primary goods" are *not* basic human goods); 106 (we *must not* use Rawls's theory of "thin theory of the good" or his would-be "democratic" but in fact *arbitrary* "impartiality between differing conceptions of human good," his "radical emaciation of human good"); 109 (Rawls disregards the second requirement of practical reasonableness, and his basic position about selection of principles in the Original Position is made worthless by an elementary logical fallacy); 130 (ditto); 157 (Rawls's view of the "shared final end" of members of a society is mistaken); 163 (a theory of justice should not be restricted, as Rawls's is, to the basic institutions of society); 164 (nor should a theory of justice be restricted, as Rawls's is, to a society whose members are fully compliant with the principles of justice); 293 (erroneous social engineering and social control theories of law are in the spirit of Rawls's "thin theory of the good"); and now 453 (the critiques on 108–9 go to the heart of *A Theory of Justice* and should be extended to his *Political Liberalism*). Alongside these multiple rejections of Rawls's main views are three or four favorable references to quite minor aspects of his theory and method. For my very considered but dismissive 1973 review of *A Theory of Justice*, see *CEJF* III, essay 3 (pp. 72–75).

13. Against Hart's ethical method and theory of "the minimum content of natural law," see *NLNR*, 30–31 (against Hart's claim that "the good for man" is all debatable); 52–53 (against Hart's depiction of the teleological view of nature); 82 (against Hart's confusion between basic values and the material conditions for pursuing them, and against his reduction of basic goods to one, survival [and whose? of what?]); 163 (against Hart's restriction of the principles of justice to "treat like cases alike, different cases differently'); 227 (against Hart's preference for a "choice" theory of rights).

14. *NLNR*, 77 (commenting on the character of the book's account of first principles of practical reason):

> Aquinas followed Aristotle's theory of 'induction' of indemonstrable first principles by insight working on observation, memory, and experience, but extended the account to a parallel 'induction' of indemonstrable first principles of practical reason (i.e. of natural law) by insight working on felt inclinations and a knowledge of possibilities: *S.T.* I-II q. 94 a. 2 (first principles, naturally known, of natural law) . . . I-II q. 10 a. 1c; II-II q. 47 a. 6c; II-II q. 79 a. 2 ad 2; *In 2 Sent.* d. 24, q. 2 a. 3 (for any definite knowledge of first principles we need both sense-experience and memory).

15. The only talk of entailment in the book's presentation of basic moral theory is at *NLNR*, 225, where it is said that the absolute human rights (*pace* Fortin [177], a small

subset of human rights) are correlative to "the exceptionless duties entailed by [the seventh] requirement [of practical reasonableness] . . . that it is always unreasonable to choose directly against any basic value, whether in oneself or in one's fellow human beings." Two entailments are mentioned here: the rights entailed by the duties and the duties by the seventh requirement. In the book's account of natural law, natural rights, and moral and political theory, these—the only entailments asserted—occupy only a small part (albeit a very important one).

16. A year or two after *NLNR*—belatedly!—I reconceptualized these as implications of a master principle of openness to integral human fulfillment: Finnis, *Fundamentals of Ethics* (Oxford and Washington, DC: Clarendon Press and Georgetown University Press, 1983), 76. Behind this, again, was work by Grisez, and our joint work yielded Germain Grisez, Joseph Boyle, and John Finnis, "Practical Principles, Moral Truth, and Ultimate Ends," *American Journal of Jurisprudence* 32 (1987): 99–151, at 109, 112, 125–26, etc. See now *NLNR*, 419–20 (postscript); Joseph Boyle, "On the Most Fundamental Principle of Morality," in *Reason, Morality, and Law: The Philosophy of John Finnis*, ed. John Keown and Robert P. George (Oxford: Oxford University Press, 2013), 56–72, and my response at 473–75.

17. *NLNR*, 49. The book's first reference to it is at p. 23 (emphasis added):

What are principles of natural law? The sense that the phrase 'natural law' has in this book can be indicated in the following rather bald assertions, formulations which will seem perhaps empty or question-begging until explicated in Part Two. There is (i) a set of basic practical principles which indicate the basic forms of human flourishing as goods to be pursued and realized, and which are in one way or another used by everyone who considers what to do, however unsound his conclusions; and (ii) a set of basic methodological requirements of *practical reasonableness (itself one of the basic forms of human flourishing)* which distinguish sound from unsound practical thinking and which, when all brought to bear, provide the criteria for distinguishing between acts that (always or in particular circumstances) are reasonable-all-things-considered (and not merely relative-to-a-particular purpose) and acts that are unreasonable-all-things-considered, i.e. between ways of acting that are morally right or morally wrong—thus enabling one to formulate (iii) a set of general moral standards.

18. In my 1984 paper I wrote the following: What I object to is the construction of this paragraph so as to suggest that *I think* it "follows" that "the life of a great scholar or statesman is not intrinsically superior to that of a music buff, a valetudinarian [someone who chooses to live as an invalid], or a ski bum."

19. In 1984 I wrote: The true comparison with a great scholar or statesman is, of course, a great composer, a great conductor, or a great actor. The life of the ski bum is inferior to all these lives precisely because it does not live up to the requirements of practical reasonableness, requirements such as respect for *common* good, sense of vocation, constancy of commitment to that vocation, and so on. And these last requirements show how utterly contrary to my theory is the view attributed to me that "it is entirely up to

[human beings] to . . . change their own priorities if they have *any* reason to do so."
(Today, I would qualify the second sentence's assumption that all great scholars, conductors and actors respect the common good more than any ski bums do.)

20. *NLNR*, 100 (emphases added).

21. *NLNR*, 101.

22. See also *NLNR*, 450:

> "[T]here is no objective hierarchy amongst them" (p. 92). This proposition . . . would better have been: there is "no single, objective hierarchy" [thus *Fundamentals of Ethics* (1983), 51]. There are various hierarchies. Life is most necessary, as precondition for the others; transmission of life shares in that kind of necessity. As for practical reasonableness, its very intelligibility as a good is as being *in charge of* (and in that sense, above) the pursuit and realization of all the other basic goods.]

23. In 1984 I wrote: Fortin has just failed to grasp the fact that one of basic goods, the one whose pursuit *structures* the pursuit of all the others and is never optional, is practical reasonableness. He says (181):

> Suppose that *two* persons, a father and his son, are drowning and that only one of them can be saved. Would we still venture to say that the father's willingness to give up his own life is reducible to such incidental factors as "one's temperament, upbringing, capacities, and opportunities"? In all such cases, the tendency to favor the young over the old may be more than either a generally accepted convention or a matter of personal preference. It has something to do with the good of the species, which hinges on the survival of those who are most likely to propagate it. If so, does it not in point of fact direct our attention to "differences of rank of intrinsic value between the basic values" ([*NLNR*,] p. 94)?

The answer to that question is No—and Fortin does not even suggest what the basic values at stake might be; on each side is *life*, his, his son's, and his son's possible sons and daughters. What makes sense of the father's self-sacrifice is not some higher value, but rather the practical reasonableness of impartial concern for the realization of the good of life in other human beings, not to mention the friendship involved.

24. John Finnis, *Aquinas: Moral, Political, and Legal Theory* (Oxford: Oxford University Press, 1998) [hereafter *Aquinas*], 83–85, 93, 98–99, 107–8, 119, 140, 225n. Most of these passages also state and verify its essential equivalence to the *bonum virtutis*, the good of virtue. See also *CEJF* I, 34, 176–77, 182–83.

25. *NLNR*, 128: "the person who has *phronēsis*, practical wisdom, full reasonableness (in the Latin writings, *prudentia*)"; see also:

> Aquinas, *S.T.* I-II q. 58 a. 4c, is very clear: no one can be morally upright without (a) an understanding of the first principles of practical reasoning and (b) the practicalreasonableness (*prudentia*) which brings those principles to bear, reasonably, on particular commitments, projects, actions . . . (*NLNR*, 52)

Each of these requirements concerns what one must do, or think, or be if one is to participate in the basic value of practical reasonableness. Someone who lives up to these requirements is thus Aristotle's *phronimos* and has Aquinas's *prudentia*; they are requirements of reasonableness or practical wisdom... (*NLNR*, 102)

And *NLNR*, 398: "Aquinas's account of *prudentia*, practical reasonableness..."; see also 51, second note.

26. See *Aquinas*, 84: "As Aquinas says, 'all moral virtues involve a sharing in the good of practical reasonableness {bonum prudentiae}' [fn. II-II q. 53 a. 5 ad 1...; III *Sent.*. d. 36 a. 1c...; I-II q. 61 a. 3c... etc., etc.]." Also *Aquinas*, 104, 107n16, 108n18, 119, 123–24, and texts of Aquinas there cited.

27. *Summa Theologiae* [*S.T.*] II-II q. 58 a. 7; q. 61 a. 1; *Aquinas*, 133.

28. *NLNR*, 165; *S.T.* II-II q. 58 a. 6c; *Aquinas*, 133.

29. *S.T.* II-II q. 58 a. 10.

30. *NLNR*, 101.

31. *NLNR*, 102. That the book associates itself with "the classical exponents of ethics" in their concern about experience of passions (and an inclination to practical reasonableness stronger than competing passions) is clear also from the endnote to that passage, at p. 128:

> *Elaboration of moral principles, and particular moral decisions, both require wisdom that is far from universal* ... see, e.g., *S.T.* I-II q. 100 aa. 1, 3, 11; this wisdom is *prudentia* (*S.T.* II-II q. 47 a. 2c ad 1; aa. 6, 15; and notes to II.3 above). On the folly of the many see *S.T.* I-II q. 9 a. 5 ad 3; q. 14 a. 1 ad 3. On the corruption of practical reasonableness in various cultures and people(s), see *S.T.* I q. 113 a. 1; I-II q. 58 a. 5; q. 94 a. 4; q. 99 a. 2 ad 2; and II.3 above, and 225 n. 28 below.

32. Note the equivalence indicated between the three terms by this "thus."

33. *NLNR*, 102, emphases adjusted.

34. Fortin, at 177.

35. Finnis, *Aquinas*, 124; see also ibid., 187–88.

36. *Aquinas*, 124 nn. 103, 104.

37. *NLNR*, 421–22.

38. In 1984 I wrote: I need only refer to *NLNR*, 85, 90, 91, 101, and 125; and 127 (where the book explains moral diversity by biases introduced by "uncritical, unintelligent spontaneity," "conventions of language, social structure, and social practice," and most radically "by the bias of self-love or of other emotions and inclinations that resist the concern to be simply reasonable"). On p. 51 of *NLNR* I point out that for Aquinas, *prudentia* is necessarily connected with the inclinations and (in Fortin's words) "dependent on them for the rectitude of its judgment": I say there that "a man cannot reason rightly in matters of practice, i.e., cannot have *prudentia*, unless he is well-disposed towards [the] ultimate ends [(*fines*) of human action]." I repeat this view of Aquinas on p. 52. On p. 128, I point out both the need for wisdom and the prevalence of folly and corruption; and that *prudentia* is a *virtue*, the virtue that makes the other virtues possible....

And . . . on p. 127, I expressed the dependence of practical reasonableness on right appetite in my own words.

39. *NLNR*, 216–17 (emphases added).

40. *NLNR*, 219–20 (emphasis added).

41. The paragraph begins with overt challenges to the demotic egalitarianism and vulgar disdain for nobility and virtue that Fortin finds pervasive in the book: "So one will bear in mind, on the one hand, that art . . . really is better than trash, that culture really is better than ignorance, that . . . children really do benefit from a formation that defines paths as well as illuminating horizons" (*NLNR*, 220). This for many readers will have recalled the provocation and ironizing offered at the outset of the book's discussion of distributive justice:

> the objective of justice is not equality but the common good, the flourishing of all members of the community, and there is no reason to suppose that this flourishing of all is enhanced by treating everyone identically when distributing roles, opportunities, and resources. Thus . . . what is unjust about large disparities of wealth in a community is not the inequality as such but the fact that (as the inequality suggests) the rich have failed to redistribute that portion of their wealth which could be better used by others for the realization of basic values in their own lives. If redistribution means no more than that more beer is going to be consumed morosely before television sets by the relatively many, and less fine wine consumed by the relatively few at salon concerts by select musicians, then it can scarcely be said to be a demand of justice. But if redistribution means that, at the expense of the wine, etc., more people can be preserved from (non-self-inflicted) illness, educated to the point where genuine self-direction becomes possible for them, defended against the enemies of justice, etc., then such redistribution is a requirement of justice. (*NLNR*, 174)

42. *NLNR*, 134–35.

43. *NLNR*, 372.

44. *NLNR*, 378.

45. *NLNR*, 397–98, citing *Nicomachean Ethics* IX.8: 1169a18–26.

46. *NLNR*, 406.

47. *NLNR*, 407.

48. *NLNR*, 410.

49. Having made the suggestion (177), Fortin then quotes (177) from some of the passages that refute it. But he leaves the suggestion in place and compounds it by insinuating that, in *NLNR*, "virtue is not choiceworthy for its own sake" (177). But of course, practical reasonableness, the very source and form of virtue, is a basic human good, choiceworthy for its own sake like all basic human goods and unlike the others in that it has all of them, and one's participation in them, as precisely its subject matter. Still, footnote 11 shows Fortin worrying away at the matter, as one should.

In 1984 I wrote: Why "so little talk about virtue in the book" (177)? Because everything in the book is about virtue; but one teaches virtue not by talking about it but by trying to show its intelligible attractiveness. Similarly, one "reorders" the human passions not by describing and talking about them, but by presenting the intelligible goods to which they can be attracted.

50. The description of the motto, and the statement of its meaning, are from Fortin, "The Trouble with Catholic Social Thought," 311.

51. See Leo Strauss, *Natural Right and History* (Chicago: University of Chicago Press, 1953). Nonetheless, I profited from the book, especially its chapter IV, "Classic Natural Right," as the markings and annotations to my 1969 copy of it indicate. To take just one example: on p. 127, I marked the passage beginning: "the proper work of man consists in living thoughtfully, in understanding, and in thoughtful action." But *NLNR* accepts that it cannot *presume* that human beings have a "proper work," but rather *shows* this by displaying the good of practical reasonableness, and its intrinsic subject matter, i.e., the direction of action as a pursuit of this and other basic goods realizable in the life of the acting person and of others—and so forth.

52. *S.T.* II-II q. 58 a. 1c (justice's fitting definition: "the lasting and steady willingness to give to each his/her right(s)").

53. *S.T.* II-II q. 57 a. 1 (justice's object: *ius*). On all this, see my *Aquinas*, 133–34.

54. Quite so; practical reasonableness is nothing other than my translation of *prudentia*, the master moral and intellectual virtue, which cannot be found independently of justice (not to mention courage and temperance). It is inconceivable, for St. Thomas as for *NLNR*, that there could be moral or legal duties not required by the virtue and insights of *prudentia*.

55. Aquinas's way of referring to duties owed to—and therefore, by entailment, rights possessed by—persons whether or not they have the benefit of living in civil society is to say that there are important respects in which justice is *owed* to everyone alike (*indifferenter*) rather than to particular persons or classes of person for reasons particular to them (*ex aliqua speciali ratione*): see *Aquinas*, 136.

56. He never noticed or shook free from this large mistake. Thus in a posthumously published essay (ca. 1992) that is, I think, his most thorough treatment of the issue and the scholarly literature (especially Michel Villey, Richard Tuck, and Brian Tierney), Fortin says:

> Granted, one cannot conclude from the absence of any explicit distinction between objective and subjective right in their works that the classical philosophers and their medieval disciples would have objected to the notion of subjective rights. . . . Since rights are already implied in the notion of duty—*anyone who has a duty to do something must have the right to do it*—there appears to be no reason to dichotomize them. What they represent would be nothing more than two sides of a single coin. If, as was generally assumed in the Middle Ages, there is such a thing as the natural law, one has every reason to speak of the rights to which it gives rise as being themselves natural. (emphasis added)

Fortin, "On the Presumed Medieval Origin of Individual Rights," in *Classical Christianity and the Political Order*, 247. In Fortin, "The Trouble with Catholic Social Thought," 304, likewise:

What once presented itself as first and foremost a doctrine of duties and hence of virtue or dedication to the common good of one's society now takes its bearings, not from what human beings owe to their fellow human beings, but from what they can claim for themselves. . . . duties are [in modern ethical theory] rooted in pre-existing rights which everyone is obliged in conscience to honor and which must, therefore, be regarded as the primary moral phenomenon.

At first glance, the difference between the two views might be looked upon as one of approach rather than of genuine substance, and the more so as *rights and duties are to some extent correlative. If I have a duty to do something, I must also have the right to do it*, though the converse need not be true. (emphasis added)

57. In the Hohfeldian terminology adopted and explained carefully on *NLNR*, 199–200, this kind of right—the most fundamental kind—is a claim right: a claim on A that he shall do or forbear in relation to B in some specific respect.

58. The confused interest in this trivial liberty is not original to Fortin; it is to be found in a continental neo-scholastic tradition.

59. *S.T.* II-II q. 57 a. 1c, q. 58 aa. 1c, 2c, q. 80 a. un. c.; *NLNR*, 161–62.

60. *Aquinas*, 170. That rights are the point or object of justice and its duties (what it owes): *Summa Theologiae* II-II q. 57 a. 1c, q. 58 a. 1c, q. 60 a. 1c; *Aquinas*, 133; and see generally ibid., 133–38.

61. Fortin, "The Trouble with Catholic Social Thought," 305:

To the best of my knowledge, the true originator of the rights doctrine is Hobbes, from whom it was taken over by virtually all of the great early modern thinkers, Spinoza, Locke, and Rousseau foremost among them. That doctrine emerged by way of a reaction against premodern thought and signals a radical departure from it. . . . Its underlying premise is that, contrary to what had been previously assumed, human beings are not intrinsically ordered to a natural end, in the attainment of which they find their happiness or perfection. In Hobbes' own words, "there is no such *finis ultimus*, utmost aim, nor *summum bonum*, greatest good, as is spoken of in the books of the old moral philosophers." *Human beings are universally actuated, not by a desire for the good of reason*, but by an amoral passion, and not the most noble one at that; to wit, the fear of violent death, which constitutes the sole foundation on which a viable theory of justice can be erected. (emphasis added)

In *NLNR*, and for St. Thomas, human beings naturally understand the "good of reason," that is, the good of practical reasonableness, and beyond the fear of violent death they naturally understand the *intelligible* good of life, in themselves and their fellows; and likewise the other basic intelligible human goods (including friendship). Hence the book's first proposition about Hobbes: "In short, analysis of political community should not be based on a view of what would be reasonable in Hobbes's 'state of nature'" (*NLNR*, 160).

62. By "Aquinas's sense," *NLNR* meant the sense primary in Aquinas's official list of meanings of "*ius*": see *NLNR*, 206 and 207. It is in relation to this that *NLNR*, 206–8

talks about a "shift of perspective" and a watershed." On all this, the postscript to *NLNR* (2nd ed.) now comments (465):

> The discussion of the history of the word 'jus' in the present section fails to notice how Aquinas's definition of justice, and his prior identification of *jus* as the very object (proximate goal and rationale) of justice, entail that—though it does not clearly appear from his formal account of the senses of '*jus*'—in his view, *jus* (a right) is something that belongs to the subjects of law or moral relationships, and therefore has the essential characteristic of a subjective right. This being so, the 'watershed' spoken of in the first full paragraph on p. 206 must be regarded as much more a matter of appearance and idiom than of conceptual, let alone political or philosophical, substance. Evidence for this conclusion is in *Aquinas* 133–8; and [in Finnis, "Aquinas on *jus* and Hart on Rights: A Response" (to Tierney), *Review of Politics* 64 (2002): 407–10], (to which Tierney's reply, in the same issue of the *Review of Politics*, seems ineffective, because he misunderstands the modern concept of rights). As to the meaning of '*jus*' in Roman and mediaeval canon law (see the second endnote on [*NLNR*] 228), Tierney's rapprochement with Villey in 2002 is the more surprising in light of his refutation of Villey, in Tierney, 'Villey, Ockham and the Origin of Individual Rights', J. Witte and F. Alexander (eds), *The Weightier Matters of* the Law (Atlanta, Scholars Press: 1988), 1–31. The willingness of a scholar as historically informed and linguistically sensitive as Honoré to attribute thoughts about human rights to classical Roman jurists such as Ulpian is important evidence against the strong watershed theory.

63. *Leviathan* (1651) ch. xiv. Thus for Hobbes, as for Hohfeld, liberty is simply the negation of duty, and this "liberty-right" is the only right Hobbes has in mind.

64. *Leviathan* (1651) ch. xiv.

65. *NLNR*, 208 (emphasis in the original), which adds:

> The fact that we could well say this shows that the ordinary modern idiom of 'rights' does not follow Hobbes all the way to his contrast between law and rights. Nor did Locke or Pufendorf; yet they did adopt his stipulation that 'a right' (jus) is paradigmatically a liberty.

66. Fortin, "The Trouble with Catholic Social Thought," 304–5. My criticisms of this passage do not detract from my agreement with a number of the severe criticisms Fortin in that paper makes of the methodology of various episcopal (not to mention papal) "social teaching" documents.

67. E.g., Matthew 28:19.

68. See, e.g., from the first century AD, the *Didache* II.2, and the *Epistle of Barnabas* XIX.4 and 5. Each presents the negative duty (not to choose such types of act) within the positive duty to follow the Way of life and light.

69. *S.T.* II-II q. 122 a. 6, "to everyone in common," "without distinction"; *Aquinas*, 136–37.

70. *S.T.* II-II q. 57 a. 4 ad 2; *Aquinas*, 171.

71. *S.T.* II-II q. 57 a 1c; q. 58 a. 1c; q. 60 a. 1c; *Aquinas*, 133.

72. See *Aquinas*, 11, 18, 169, 171, 172n, 174–75, and the texts of St. Thomas there cited.

73. The same astonishing mistake is made by Edward Goerner in his extensive remarks about *NLNR* in "Letter and Spirit: The Political Ethics of the Rule of Law versus the Political Ethics of the Rule of the Virtuous," *Review of Politics* 45 (1983): 553–75, at 561:

> [According to *NLNR*] questions about what is just or right are always and only to be answered by showing that a proposed course of action is logically consistent with the body of propositions stating the universally applicable rules or laws concerning rights. . . . the rights which are thus laid down and their correlative duties are, and must be, to use Finnis's terms, "exceptionless" and "absolute."

74. See *NLNR*, ch. VIII.4 (Rights and the Common Good) and VIII.5 (The Specification of Rights). The key passage regarding specification is quoted above in main text, at n. 40.

75. See Fred. D. Miller, *Nature, Justice and Rights in Aristotle's* Politics (New York: Oxford University Press, 1995), just insofar as it argues that Aristotle had "locutions for rights" (93) even though "no single Greek word corresponds to the single modern term 'right'" (196).

76. Gaius in the second century AD taught that neither state law nor communal convention can do away with natural rights. See *Digest* 43.18.2: *civilis ratio corrumpere naturalia iura non potest.* Likewise Gaius, *Institutes* II.65.

77. Curiously, perhaps, Fortin's 1988 article "The Trouble with Catholic Social Thought" concludes:

> My point, and it is the only one I have tried to make, is that the bishops may have confused some of their readers by using language that looks in two different directions at once: that of rights or freedom on the one hand, and of virtue, character formation, and the common good on the other. *They would certainly be ill-advised to give up their vigorous defense of rights,* especially since the pseudomorphic collapse of Neo-Thomism in the wake of Vatican II *has left them without any alternative on which to fall back*; but they have yet to tell us, or tell us more clearly, how the two ends are supposed to meet. Reading their letters reminded me of a little ditty my gang used to sing when I was a kid:
> I love Carolina . . .

78. The schedule and reading list for Fortin's graduate/undergraduate course "Natural Law" (Th. 580) at Boston College in Spring 1978 assigned Strauss's *Natural Right and History* for eight of the fourteen classes, in six of these as the sole "recommended" secondary source.

In 1984 I wrote the following: It is a pervasive weakness of (quasi-)Straussian interpretative methodology that it looks to words rather than meanings and propositions. Often enough this leads to huge mistakes even about the words: E. A. Goerner recently claimed, in "Thomistic Natural Right: The Good Man's View of Thomistic Natural Law," *Political Theory* 11 (1983): 393, that there is silence about natural *law* (as distinct from natural *right*) in the *Secunda Secundae* [IIa-IIae of the *Summa Theologiae*]. . . . it turns out that in the very portions of the IIa-IIae mentioned by Goerner there are just as many references to "natural law" as to "natural right" (8 references to each). Again, Goerner says that "Thomas never mentions 'natural law' when speaking of natural right"—and again, in those portions alone, Aquinas does just that, twice (II-II q. 85 a. 1, q. 187 a. 3 ad 1), together and interchangeably—as someone who has followed Aquinas's *meaning* would readily predict. So too, Fortin says that Plato is not a natural law thinker; "He spoke only of 'natural right' [607 n. 32]." This will seem very questionable to one who reflects on the meaning of a passage such as *Laws* IV, 715c–716d, quoted at *NLNR*, p. 396. . . . Again, in his footnote on the origins of the natural law doctrine [610 n. 40] . . . he focuses on "the expression itself" and so does not see the relevance of a text such as *NLNR* quotes on p. 411 [as ascribed to Zeno of Citium in Cyprus], which does not use the phrase "natural law" but affirms the existence of such a law with unmistakable clarity ["the end (of man) may be defined as life in accordance with nature, i.e. in accordance with our human nature as well as with that of the universe—a life in which we refrain from every action forbidden by the law common to all things. But this law is nothing other than right reason"]. The reason why I am not too happy with the term "natural law doctrine" is that it really is appropriately used as a generic description of such a doctrine as Zeno's, which is very different from Plato's, or Aristotle's, or Aquinas's, or, on a less sublime plane, my own.

79. *Politics* V.ix sec. 16:1310a (trans. Barker). *Pol.* VI.ii secs. 2–4:1317b explains that equality in the "democratic" conception of it is arithmetical, not proportionate to desert or merit—though *restricted to citizens*, not slaves—and on that understanding is "a general system of liberty based on equality."

80. In 1984 I wrote: Fortin's sentence ends "and does not impose any type of behavior under pain of sanctions." No reference is or could be given; I never assert that the natural law is unsanctioned. I affirm the existence of "natural sanctions" or *poena naturae* or "self-avenging laws of conduct" in blunt terms on [*NLNR*] pp. 380 and 411; and I fail to affirm divine sanctions in my own voice only because of the nature of my book; however, I quote with manifest approval Plato's affirmation: *NLNR*, 396. But of course, like Aquinas, I want to see how far one can get without appeal to the revelation of divine sanctions, which are not the principal ground of obligation.

81. *NLNR*, 276–77.

82. And this includes obligations in respect of one's own self-regarding conduct: *NLNR*, 298. But it is a devastating error for Fortin to think that, for *NLNR*, natural law "merely points to what one must do or avoid in order to fulfill oneself" (183). The fulfilment to which natural law points is, as I make clearer from 1983 onwards, *integral human fulfilment*—that is, the fulfilment of all human persons and communities, in which one's own fulfilment has no priority of value but only of responsibility: *NLNR*, 419–20. Equally devastating as a misreading is Fortin's claim that, according to *NLNR*, the term "natural law" is associated with the notion of obligatoriness only by a misunderstanding perpe-

trated by Vazquez and Suarez and prevalent today (183–84). This ignores wide tracts of the book, for example, the formal treatment of obligation in chapter XI, which identifies (*NLNR*, 303) the key move in explaining obligation (e.g., the moral obligation of promises) as the ascent to the level at which the explanation incorporates

> what we have previously laboured to explain: that one (everyone) has reason to value the common good—the well-being alike of oneself and of one's associates and potential associates in community, and the ensemble of conditions and ways of effecting that well-being—whether out of friendship as such, or out of an impartial recognition that human goods are as much realized by the participation in them of other persons as by one's own (see VI.4, VI.6, VII.2).

And it is this connection to *common good* that can, and often does, make moral obligations burdensome for the one who has them (see 307) or even (as Fortin remembers elsewhere in the review but not here) catastrophically burdensome (224–26) and in need of some further explanation (see at nn. 38–41 above).

83. *NLNR*, 44–46, 54, 122, 259, 338–42, 425, etc.

84. *NLNR*, 380, 411.

85. *S.T.* I-II q. 96 a. 5 entirely concerns human (positive) law, not natural law as such; the ad 3m, for example, holds that the ruler who is not subject to the law's *vis coactiva* is nonetheless subject to its *vis directiva* (which is far more than mere *lex indicans*, and *ought* to be obeyed by the ruler unless he happens to have power to dispense from it); I-II q. 100 a. 9c repeatedly says it concerns *lex divina et lex humana*.

86. *ST* I-II q. 90 a. 4c: an ordinance (prescription) of reason for the common good of a community, promulgated by the person or body responsible for looking after that community. *Aquinas*, 256, commenting on this, says:

> Aquinas takes an early opportunity to supplement his definition by stating that it is characteristic of law {de ratione legis} that it be coercive (threatening force against violators). [fn. I-II q. 90 a. 3 ad 3, q. 96 a. 5c. Both passages also link law's coerciveness with its public character.]

Here, as generally though not universally, throughout qq. 90–105, Aquinas quietly treats human positive law as the central case of law and focal meaning of *lex* and (in one of its two main senses) *ius*.

87. Fortin had worked intensively on natural law theory not many years before his review of *NLNR*, and had concluded to—or perhaps started from—the position that natural law, as distinct from (or contrasted with) natural right, is "a legally sanctioned order extending to the whole of human life," a "universal law whose injunctions can never be infringed with impunity"; to believe in natural law is to believe "that crime never pays and that in the end the only people who are happy are the ones who deserve to be happy," by virtue of "a law of the cosmos certifying that justice will necessarily prevail in human affairs," in "a morally lawful universe in which all evils are eventually set straight": Ernest Fortin, "Augustine, Thomas Aquinas, and the Problem of Natural Law,"

in *Classical Christianity and the Political Order*, 199–222, at 201. Having invented this idea of natural law, Fortin of course had difficulty finding anyone, ever, who has defended a natural law theory; I know of no one.

88. See Goerner, "Thomistic Natural Right," 393–94; see also his "On Thomistic Natural Law: The Bad Man's View of Thomistic Natural Right," *Political Theory* 7 (1979): 101–22. For a brief refutation of the main thesis, see my *Aquinas*, 134. Some passages where Aquinas uses *ius* and *lex* together and interchangeably are *S.T.* II-II q. 85 a. 1, and q. 187, a. 3 ad 1. Edward A. Goerner was a professor of political theory at the University of Notre Dame for more than fifty years, beginning in 1960.

89. Goerner, "Thomistic Natural Right," cited other texts, however, though no more relevantly than Fortin: in *S.T.* I-II q. 92 a. 2c and ad 3 & 4 and q. 100 a. 1c, not to mention q. 90 a. 3 ad 2, natural law is not under consideration when Aquinas is speaking of *vis coactiva* (coercive force) or *metus poenae* (fear of penalty).

90. Goerner, "Thomistic Natural Right," 395 (in the course of expounding "the conventional view"); his "Thomistic Natural Law," 111, states:

> The natural law, like all law (cf., I-II q. 92, art. 2, ad 3), is an external constraint effective through fear of punishment whereas natural virtue is an internal principle effective by love of the good.... That is to say, a full understanding of Thomas's natural ethics must rest on his teaching about natural virtue rather than about natural law.

91. "He [Goerner] may even wish to develop his own natural law theory, as I hope he will. Having no such theory myself, I was merely content with trying to make sense of Thomas's statements on the subject." Fortin, "On the Naturalness and Lawfulness of the Natural Law: A Few Remarks on Ernest Fortin's Doubts: Response," *Review of Politics* 45 (1983): 446–49, at 448–49.

92. On what really is torture, exceptionlessly excluded from conscientious choice by natural law, see Patrick Lee, "Interrogational Torture," *American Journal of Jurisprudence* 51 (2006): 131–47; and my *CEJF* I, at 102. Lee's conclusions, although significantly more exact, are similar to what I wrote in my 1984 essay, as follows: Notice that my list [of absolute rights, *NLNR*, 225] does not include torture; the page references given by Fortin for my references to torture should have shown him that I was referring, without comment, to the modern opinion that torture is absolutely prohibited even in emergency situations. I neither affirmed nor denied that position. My opinion is that, since pain is not *per se* the denial of any basic good, not every form of torture is excluded—but only those forms that damage health or bodily integrity.

93. *NLNR*, 224, where both the content of the threat and the motivations for making it are said to be the same (albeit not yet executed) "as old-fashioned torturers seeking to change their victim's mind or the minds of those next in line for the torture."

94. *CEJF* I, essay 12 ("Moral Absolutes in Aristotle and Aquinas"), 187–98, at 188. Cf. Fortin's *NLNR* review essay (182): "Finnis's principle [prohibiting recourse to torture under any circumstances], noble as it may be, is more readily applicable to normal than to emergency situations."

95. Notably, those currents of proportionalist and other thought identified more or less adequately in the encyclical of John Paul II, *Veritatis Splendor* (1993), currents opposed to the doctrine (upheld in that encyclical) that there are moral truths of moral law that exceptionlessly exclude certain types of act as intrinsically wrong and never to be chosen, whatever the circumstances: for the exact formulation of the doctrine, see secs. 76, 78, 80. On the origins of this movement of thought among Catholic theologians, see Finnis, *Moral Absolutes: Tradition, Revision, and Truth* (Washington, DC: Catholic University of America Press, 1991), ch. 4.

96. In 1984 I wrote the following: How much Fortin's own thinking remains in thrall to the dominant political consciousness of our times is clear from (182): "A world in which terrorism of the most brutal sort has become an almost daily fact of life *may not always be able to afford the luxury* of showing the same respect for assassins as for anyone else . . . or indulging in what *from another point of view* could *just as easily* be interpreted as heroism by proxy" (emphases added). The central message of my book—clear from the beginning of the chapter on community and from the last chapter—is that no adequate sense can be made of self-sacrifice—e.g. of abstaining from murder of hostages even when the abstention results in destruction of oneself and one's community—except in the perspective of a revelation of a wider and more lasting community: the Kingdom of God that is present now only in mystery but which will be found at the end of our time. The critique of consequentialism—a critique which Fortin does not challenge—established that what is claimed to be "necessary" cannot be rationally affirmed to be unconditionally necessary; for no attainable end or purpose can be rationally identified as the overall net best situation or greatest good. On the other hand, without the information given by faith about the attainability of a transcendent Kingdom by faithfulness in doing good and refusing to do moral evil in this life, decent people will inevitably treat their own civil community as a practical absolute, and will thus embrace Caiaphas's principle that it is better that one innocent man be murdered than that the people should perish. (Notice the intellectual superiority of Caiaphas's language: "it is better that . . ." compared with the twentieth-century cant: "we are not able to afford the luxury . . . .")

My view could be summarized like this: just as Aquinas teaches that man has a natural last end but that it cannot be identified without revelation or attained without supernatural grace, so too moral reason discloses that Caiaphas's absolutizing of the civil community does not give sound moral guidance, but natural reason cannot show the sense of the alternative option in a rationally satisfying light without the revealed information about the more basic, embracing and lasting community of God's realm.

97. *NLNR*, 410.

98. *CEJF* V, 119, 228, 254, 366, 371.

99. But that is not to say that every book that takes its place among ventures both philosophical and Catholic needs to attempt to give such an indication, let alone an explanation of the indication. And *NLNR*, even in its postscript, abstains—for the reasons suggested in part I above—from such an attempt, leaving that to other works such as, *inter alia*, my 1999 essay "Catholic Positions in Liberal Debates."

CHAPTER 8

The Catholic Tradition and Modern Democracy

Paul E. Sigmund

Paul E. Sigmund (1929–2014) was a distinguished professor of politics at Princeton University for over forty years. Sigmund focused on both political theory and Latin American politics and was one of the first Catholic professors at Princeton. His books include Nicholas of Cusa and Medieval Political Thought; The Overthrow of Allende and the Politics of Chile, 1964–1976; *and* Liberation Theology at the Crossroads: Democracy or Revolution? *He is the editor of the Norton Critical Editions of both Thomas Aquinas and John Locke's political writings.*

"Catholicism is the oldest and greatest totalitarian movement in history."
—Sidney Hook, *Reason, Social Myths, and Democracy*

"You cannot find in the entire literature of Catholicism a single unequivocal endorsement by any Pope of democracy as a superior form of government."
—Paul Blanshard, *American Freedom and Catholic Power*

"It is in full accord with human nature that juridical-political structures should, with ever better success and without discrimination, afford all their citizens the chance to participate freely and actively in establishing the constitutional bases of a political community, governing the state, determining the scope and purpose of various institutions, and choosing leaders."
—Second Vatican Council, *Pastoral Constitution on the Church in the Modern World (Gaudium et Spes)*

It would seem to be an impossible task to relate a tradition that is nearly 2,000 years old to a set of political theories and institutions that only emerged in the late eighteenth century. Yet this is done all the time, both by the spokesmen for that tradition and by politicians and statesmen who are influenced by it. In this article I will attempt to evaluate four basic responses to the question of the relation of the Catholic tradition and democracy. The first argues that the Catholic tradition is unconcerned with forms of government, provided only that they promote the general welfare ("the common good") of the people. The second and more critical view maintains that the primary concern of the leadership and spokesmen of the church is the protection of the institutional interests of the church and that any political order that respects those interests, however manifestly unjust, will receive the cooperation, and often the support of the church. A third critical response holds that a church that is hierarchical and quasi-monarchic in structure is likely to promote—and has done so historically—attitudes and practices on the part of its adherents that favor authoritarianism in government. Finally, there is a fourth position that argues that the basic values of Christianity that have been taught by the church are such as to lead over time to a recognition of the moral and religious superiority of democratic government. The following discussion will attempt to evaluate these positions, and if I can communicate my own view at the outset, it will argue that all four have some historical basis but that the official teaching of the Catholic Church has moved from the first to the fourth positions—that is, from indifference among forms of government that promote the common good, to support for democracy as morally superior and philosophically preferable.

Modern liberal constitutional democracy as we know it involving the actual or potential exercise of universal suffrage in periodic contested elections, the rule of law, and guarantees of individual rights only emerged in the late eighteenth century. It was especially associated with the American and French revolutions, although the earlier English constitutional experience exercised an important influence upon it. Forms of direct democracy had developed in Athens of the fifth century B.C., in the medieval communes and Italian city-states, and in the Swiss cantons, but "modern" democracy with its representative institutions, constitutional guarantees, and independent judiciaries was a relatively late development. In its Anglo-American form that development took place under primarily Protestant auspices, and did not require a response on the part of the Catholic Church other than the hope for religious toleration. (I am aware that there was a short-lived Catholic experiment in Maryland, but its general significance was limited.) It was only when the democratic wave affected countries that were basically Catholic that the institutional church was required to make a doctrinal response. The nature and circumstances of that response fundamentally affected the relationship between Catholicism and democracy for a century and a half, and provided empirical evidence for those who maintain the first three theses listed above. Yet throughout the period of what was an essentially negative or at least neutral attitude toward modern democracy there were those who argued the fourth position and they were ultimately triumphant in the Second Vatican Council.

In doing so, they were able to point to certain elements in the Catholic tradition which were congruent with, indeed contributory to, the development of democratic values and institutions. These were important arguments in a church in which tradition was one of the bases for doctrine, and that tradition contained not one, but a number of different implications for political practice. I would like to summarize the components of that tradition as they developed in three different historical periods that antedated the emergence of modern democracy and provided elements for the Catholic response.

The Bible and the Experience of the Early Church

The historical debate on the political meaning of the New Testament has focused on a number of biblical passages. Christ's response to the question of the legitimacy of the payment of taxes to Rome, "Render to Caesar, the things that are Caesar's, and to God, the things that are God's" (Matthew 22:21), has been the source of a considerable literature on the relations of the spiritual and the temporal. It introduced an element of dualism into Christian political thinking which in its Catholic institutional expression led to the establishment of a separate institutional structure, the church, that was not, as nearly all earlier religious institutions had been, a part of the ethnic or political structure of existing communities. That separate structure soon felt the need for authoritative definition of dogma and membership, but the evidence seems to indicate the structure of church authority involved several different forms of church government. Peter and his successors were understood to have received a special commission from

Christ, "Thou art Peter and upon this rock I will build my church" (Matthew 16:18), but the apostles and their successors, the bishops, were also given a universal mission by Christ ("Going therefore teach ye all nations" Matthew 28:19), and the early Christian communities were also seen as recipients of divine grace and inspiration ("Where two or three are gathered together in My name there am I in the midst of them" Matthew 18:20) and acted as communities to make decisions about common affairs, becoming almost independent self-governing entities in periods of persecution.[1] Thus the government of the early church partook of elements of all three of the classic forms, monarchy, aristocracy, and democracy, and when later Christians looked back to it as a model they could find all three elements within it.

A similar ambiguity could be found in two New Testament texts concerned with political obligation. Paul's Letter to the Romans advises, "Let every soul be subject to higher powers. For there is no power but of God. The powers that be are ordained of God. Whosoever resisteth the power, resisteth the ordinance of God" (Romans 13:1–2), but when Peter was called before the Sanhedrin and forbidden to preach, he replied, "We must obey God rather than men" (Acts 5:29). Political obligation was religiously based, but it was limited by a higher religious duty. The appropriate Christian response in cases of conflict between the two was to be a continuing subject of controversy.

Medieval Theory and Practice

When the Christian message was expressed in philosophical terms by the Fathers of the Church the fusion of Christianity and classical culture included the adoption by many Christian writers of the neo-Platonic hierarchical models, especially as mediated through the writings of Dionysius the Areopagite.[2] Hierarchy in theory was reinforced by hierarchy in practice as the Western Church was organized in a centralized hierarchical way under the papacy in the later Middle Ages, and feudal theory and practice conceived of medieval political and social life in terms of ranks and orders. Theorists such as John of Salisbury (1120–1180) employed classical organic analogies to describe the organization of society along lines that paralleled the structure of the human body, and medieval lawyers used such analogies to describe the organization and legal status of the emerging "corporate" groups, guilds, religious orders, etc.

On the other hand there were also more democratic elements in the medieval tradition. Law and government were seen as emerging from the people and justified by their consent (in the sense of *consensus*). Authority was limited by customary and natural law, as well as by a confused network of judicial bodies and authorities. In the church-state conflicts between the spiritual and temporal powers, each side appealed to the role of people to weaken the claims of the other side, and in the constitutional crises of the church associated with the Conciliar Movement conciliar writers used both aristocratic ("episcopalist") and democratic (the tradition of election of bishops and of the pope) arguments to limit papalist claims.[3]

The combination of hierarchical (in Walter Ullmann's terms, "descending") and democratic ("ascending") elements in medieval political thought is illustrated in the political writings of Thomas Aquinas. On the one hand, law is made by "the whole community or the person who represents it" (*S.T.* I-II q. 90 art. 3) and the best form of government is one in which "all participate in the election of those who rule" (*S.T.* I-II q. 105), but on the other, government by a monarch is best because it promotes unity and follows the pattern of divine monarchical government of the universe (*De Regimine Principum*, chap. 3). The pope leads the church to a higher spiritual goal of man, but (at least in one interpretation of Aquinas) can only intervene in temporal affairs "with respect to those things in which the temporal power is subject to him" (*S.T.* II-II q. 60 art. 6). Law is morally obligatory and reflects the divine purposes in the world, but an unjust law that violates natural or divine law is no law at all, but an act of violence (*S.T* I-II q. 96 art. 2). All men are equal in the sight of God and even slaves have rights, but "there is an order to be found among men" according to which even before the Fall the more intelligent are to lead the less intelligent (*Summa Contra Gentiles*, 4. 81; and *S.T* I q. 92 arts. 3–4).[4] Authoritarian, constitutionalist (St. Thomas as "the first Whig"), and democratic conclusions can be drawn from Aquinas's writings.

The Protestant Reformation and the Rise of the Modern State

The ambiguities of medieval thought were made less ambiguous by the reaction of the papacy in the early modern period to the Reformation and the rise of the absolute monarchs. While religious pluralism and the claims of conscience led Protestant writers such as Milton and Locke to argue for religious toleration, the popes preferred to centralize dogma and discipline and to deal with the absolute monarchs through concordats (i.e., treaties), that guaranteed the rights of the church, including religious uniformity and financial support, and special rights in the areas of education and marriage. The "descending" thesis was applied unambiguously to the papacy, but its temporal counterpart, the "divine right of kings" as enunciated by James I, was rejected in favor of "ascending" theories put forward by Jesuit writers such as Robert Bellarmine and Francisco Suarez on the derivation of political authority from God through the people. There were debates as to whether the transfer of authority from the people to the ruler was an irrevocable one, and those who argued for a conditional transfer made important contributions to the constitutional tradition that was later developed by the Puritans and Locke. However, while there were moral and constitutional limits on his rule, the Catholic writers endorsed the rule of the monarch, who, while he did not rule by unlimited divine right, received his authority through an implicit or explicit grant from the people ultimately from God.

Thus by the beginning of the eighteenth century, the Catholic Church in Western Europe was the state church in the principalities and kingdoms of southern and central Europe and Protestantism had a similar position in northern Europe. The union of throne and altar allied the interests of Catholicism closely to those of the absolute monarchs, and gave them considerable control over the churches in their territories, especially through the right of "patronage," naming bishops in cooperation with the Vatican either directly, or by selecting a candidate from a list, or at least vetoing unacceptable nominees.

This comfortable but corrupting arrangement was threatened in both theory and practice by the philosophies and political movements of the Enlightenment. "Ecrazez l'infame," exclaimed Voltaire, and Rousseau's *Social Contract* proposed a compulsory civil religion according to which loyalty to the General Will was to replace a Catholicism that divided the allegiances of its adherents. The French Revolution swept away the privileges of the church, and forced its priests to swear to a *Civil Constitution of the Clergy* (1792). In the early nineteenth century Napoleon and later the restored Bourbons reestablished the alliance of the church with the forces of order, authority, and dynastic legitimacy. In France two great spiritual political families, monarchists and republicans, entered into a struggle for power that dominated nineteenth-century French politics, and the church was clearly identified with the monarchy. Similarly in Italy and in Spain the liberal movement attacked the privileges of the church, and in Italy the Papal States that divided Italy diagonally from just north of Naples to just south of

Venice provided a ready target for Italian nationalists. The church was placed in a defensive position against a rising tide of liberalism, nationalism, and revolution, and all three were linked to popular sovereignty.

A combination of territorial and institutional interests and a concern to defend the spiritual values represented by the church led the nineteenth-century popes to issue the famous denunciations of liberal democracy which were later so frequently quoted by Paul Blanshard and others who viewed the rising influence of Catholicism in the twentieth century as a threat to American freedom. Among those popes were:

(a) *Gregory XVI* (1831–1846). When efforts were made in France under the leadership of the Abbé Felicité de Lamennais through his journal, *L'Avenir*, to persuade the church to align itself with democracy and popular sovereignty, Gregory reacted with *Mirari Vos* (1832), a strongly worded encyclical that condemned the "absurd and erroneous proposition which claims that liberty of conscience must be maintained for everyone," along with "that harmful and never sufficiently denounced freedom to publish any writings whatsoever and disseminate them to the people." The pope called for "action to destroy the plague of bad books" and recommended "trust and submission to princes," denouncing those who, "consumed with the unbridled lust for freedom, are entirely devoted to impairing and destroying all rights of dominion while bringing servitude to the people under the slogan of liberty" and attempting "to separate the Church from the state and to break the mutual concord between temporal authority and the priesthood."

Gregory's intemperate words were written in reaction to a revolution in the Papal States which he had suppressed with the help of Austrian troops, but it set the tone for papal statements for much of the rest of the century. Those who attempted to derive democratic conclusions from the Catholic tradition were to be fighting an uphill battle for the rest of the century, and indeed into the early twentieth century.[5]

(b) *Pius IX (1846–1878)*. As is well known, Pius began his pontificate with considerable sympathy for the liberal movement, but the revolution that drove him out of Rome from 1848 until 1850 changed his attitude. In 1864 he published two important documents relating to liberalism and democracy. His encyclical, *Quanta Cura*, condemned those who assert that "that is the best condition of civil society in which no duty is recognized as attached to the civil power, of restraining, by enacting penalties, offenders against the Catholic religion." He quoted Gregory XVI who had described liberty of conscience as "an insanity" and freedom of speech as "injurious babbling." The encyclical was accompanied by *The Syllabus of Errors*, a compilation of past papal statements on related topics. Included among the errors listed were the belief "that every man is free to embrace the religion he shall believe true by the light of reason; . . . that the eternal salvation may at least be hoped for, of all those who are not at all in the Church of Christ; . . . that it is no longer necessary that the Catholic religion be held as the only religion of the state," and (the most famous error) "that the Roman pontiff can and ought to, reconcile himself to, and agree with, progress, liberalism, and modern civilization."

(c) *Leo XIII (1878–1903)*. In the next pontificate the papacy initiated attempts to find a more positive response to democracy. Leo encouraged an effort by French Catholics to come to terms with the French Third Republic in the so-called *ralliement* policy. In Italy, however, he did not lift the ban on Catholic participation in Italian politics that had been imposed by his predecessor in 1867 following the seizure of the Papal States. The famous labor encyclical, *Rerum Novarum* (1891), called attention to the plight of the working classes and encouraged the formation of (Catholic) trade unions. Despite the pressures of Catholic monarchists, Leo argued in his encyclical, *On the Christian Constitution of States (Immortale Dei)*, issued in 1885, that "no one of the several forms of government is itself condemned. . . . Neither is it blameworthy in itself in any manner, for the people to have a share, greater or less, in the government; for at certain times and under certain laws, such participation may not only be of benefit to the citizens, but may even be of obligation."[6] However, in both this encyclical and in *Human Liberty (Libertas Humana)* issued in 1888, he reaffirmed Gregory's denunciations of freedom of worship, of expression, and of teaching, accusing the liberals of making "the state absolute and omnipotent" and of proclaiming "that man should live altogether independently of God." Indeed the whole liberal project was described as "the sullied product of a revolutionary age of man's unbounded urge for innovation." Following this denunciation, however, Leo qualified it by stating that the church "does not forbid public authority to tolerate what is at variance with truth and justice, for the sake of avoiding some greater evil or preserving some greater good." (This passage gave rise to the distinction by Catholic theologians between the "thesis" of Catholicism as the established church, and the "hypothesis" of religious toleration in a situation of religious pluralism.)

Leo was thus demonstrating greater flexibility toward liberal democracy but he was still suspicious of what he saw as its anticlerical tendencies currently being illustrated in France in the effort of the Third Republic to separate church and state in the areas of education and of public support of the Catholic religion. He also viewed as dangerous the development of cooperation with other religions such as the Parliament of Religions at the Chicago World's Fair in 1892 in which Cardinal Gibbons shared the platform with Protestant dignitaries. Late in the nineties the Vatican discovered a new heresy, "Americanism," which was the subject of a letter from the pope to Cardinal Gibbons which drew attention to the errors "called by some, Americanism" which maintained that the church should adapt itself to the modern age and promote the active virtues rather than those of contemplation and penitence. The Apostolic Delegate to the United States when he returned to Rome in 1895 saw to it that the rector of Catholic University was removed, and that the "naturalism" of the American church and its tendency to minimize its differences from Protestants were officially condemned.

(d) *Pius X (1903–1914)*. Leo's effort to encourage a reconciliation between French Catholics and the Third Republic had fallen afoul of the polarization of France into two camps as a result of the Dreyfus affair at the end of the century, but not before it had produced an effort by a French Catholic leader, Marc Sangnier, to establish Le Sillon, a movement to encourage Catholic participation in French political life. His organization fell victim to the increased conservatism of the Vatican that followed the election of Pius X in 1903 and the formal separation of church and state in France in 1905. In 1907 Pius issued a decree and an encyclical against the heresy of "Modernism" which was accused of "proposing a reform of church government to bring it into harmony with men's conscience which is turning towards democracy." Three years later Le Sillon was condemned by the pope because "in order to justify their social dreams they appeal to the Gospel, interpolated in their own manner, and what is still more grave to a disfigured and diminished Christ,"[7] and this incipient movement towards Christian democracy was destroyed. Another small party of Christian Democratic inspiration, the Popular Democratic Party, was established in the 1930s, but it was not until after World War II that a large Catholic-based party committed to democracy emerged in France. Similarly in Italy the boycott by Catholics of the republic was only finally lifted in 1919, and the Popular Party founded by Don Luigi Sturzo after spectacular initial electoral success was in effect dissolved by the Vatican after the triumph of Mussolini, and Sturzo went into exile.

(e) *Pius XI (1922–1939)*. Despite these actions, which were more related to French and Italian politics than to the general political thought of the church, one began to see the beginnings of an attempt by Catholic leaders in a number of

European countries to reexamine the question of the relation of Catholicism and democracy. It is true that the papacy under Pius XI seemed willing to enter into agreements with the fascist dictators. Pius XI signed the Lateran Treaty with Mussolini in 1929. In 1933 the votes of the Catholic Center party gave Hitler absolute power through the Enabling Act which was followed by the signing of a Concordat between the Vatican and the Hitler government. There seemed to be some not-accidental resemblances between the quasi-corporatist structures of cooperation between labor and business recommended in Pius XI's encyclical, *Quadragesimo Anno* (1931), and the corporatism adopted by authoritarian regimes in Portugal, Austria, and Italy in the twenties and thirties. However by the mid-1930s the totalitarian character of the Italian and German regimes had become evident, and in 1937 Pius XI issued two denunciatory encyclicals, *Mit Brennender Sorge* and *Abbiamo Bisogno*. However, the important developments were not so much in the area of international politics but in that of Catholic philosophy.

One of Leo XIII's many accomplishments was to promote the revival of the study of St. Thomas Aquinas in Catholic seminaries and institutions of higher learning through his encyclical, *Aeterni Patris* (1879). The study of Thomism led theologians such as John A. Ryan in America and Jacques Maritain in France to return to the sources in St. Thomas, Suarez, and Bellarmine to find the doctrine of the popular origin of political authority and to apply it to argue that government must be based on the explicit or implicit consent of the people. They accepted the traditional Catholic doctrine that the origin of all authority is from God, but argued that the Catholic tradition also provided for its mediation through the people. Although Maritain was converted to Catholicism in 1906 and to Thomism in 1912, he only began to write about politics in the late 1920s following the 1926 condemnation by Pius XI of the right-wing French movement, Action Francaise, with which Maritain had been sympathetic. From that time until the 1950s Maritain wrote many books about the application of Thomist principles to democracy. The best known of those books, *Integral Humanism* (originally published in French in 1936), *Scholasticism and Politics* (New York, 1940), *The Rights of Man and the Natural Law* (New York, 1943), and *Man and the State* (lectures delivered in English at the University of Chicago in 1950 and published in the following year), argued that "integral" or "personalist" and "communitarian" democracy was the best application of Christian and Thomist political principles and that the modern democratic state was the result of the "leavening" influence of the Gospels in human history.[8] Maritain distinguished his religiously based personalism from what he considered to be the egoistic individualism of "bourgeois liberalism" and the collectivism of Marxism, but he argued, on religious and philosophical grounds, for a religiously pluralist and socially concerned democratic state. In *The Rights of Man and the Natural Law*, he developed a list of basic human rights that anticipated the listing in the United Nations Universal Declaration of Rights, basing it on a reinterpretation of Aquinas's discussions of natural law in the *Summa Theologiae* (I-II q. 94). Along with others such as Yves Simon (*Philosophy of Democratic Government*)[9] and Heinrich Rommen (*The State in Catholic Thought*)[10] as well as non-Catholic neo-Thomists such as Mortimer Adler of the University of Chicago,[11] Maritain was responsible for a new development in Catholic political thought that had been anticipated but never articulated in terms of the Catholic tradition by earlier French and Italian writers—the argument that democracy was not simply one of several forms of government, all of which were acceptable provided that they promoted "the common good," but was the one form that was most in keeping with the nature of man, and with Christian values.[12] The traditional concern with justice had been expanded to give a religious justification for freedom, and the Christian belief in equality before God was now interpreted to include political and juridical equality as well.

Christian Democracy

Maritain's writings on democracy were directly adopted, read, and commented upon by leaders of the Christian Democratic movement in Europe and Latin America. Indeed, in the latter case my own research on the origins of the Christian Democratic party in Chile has revealed a direct connection between a visit to Argentina by Maritain in the late 1930s and the foundations of the predecessor party to the Christian Democrats as a result of the breakaway of the youth section of the church-influenced Conservative party. The publication in Chile of Maritain's *Letter on Independence* at the time of his visit to Argentina led to his discovery by the founders of the new party. Two of its leaders, Jaime Castillo (currently Chairman of the Chilean Human Rights Commission) and the late Eduardo Frei, the future president of Chile (1964–1970), wrote books and pamphlets about his work. In other countries research institutes on Catholic social and political thought used his works, and they became a major source of democratic theory in Latin America.

The same thing occurred in Europe after World War II with the emergence of large Christian Democratic parties in France (the MRP), Germany (CDU-CSU), and Italy (DCI) that became bulwarks of postwar European democracy. For all of these parties, as their names indicate, Christianity implies democracy, and Maritain's personalism and communitarianism provided a theoretical justification that drew on Catholic and Thomist conceptions of human nature to argue for free institutions, the welfare state, and political democracy.

The conservative and integralist resistance to democracy that had had such a powerful influence over the Vatican in earlier decades was now largely discredited, and beginning with the Christmas messages of Pope Pius XII during World War II, the official statements of the papacy began to draw direct links between freedom, democracy, and the Christian message. The clearest example of this new attitude is Pius XII's Christmas message of 1944. Yet even when he praises democracy, the pope warns of possible abuses. In his message, he distinguishes between "the people" and "the mass," describing the latter as "the main enemy of true democracy and of its ideal of liberty and equality." "A democratic state left to the arbitrary will of the mass . . . becomes a pure and simple system of absolutism. State absolutism consists as a matter of fact, in the wrong principle that the authority of the state is unlimited . . . and there is not left any appeal whatever to a superior and morally binding law."[13] Pius seems to have been thinking of the Communist invocation of the name of the people to justify its oppression, but there is also an effort to maintain continuity with the criticisms of liberal democracy made by his predecessors.

In Latin America Catholic conservatives still resisted the message of Maritain. An Argentine theologian, Julio Meinvielle, published a number of attacks on Maritain, the best known of which is *De Lamennais à Maritain* which quoted from the nineteenth-century papal condemnations to argue for the heterodoxy of Maritain.[14] Yet it was a losing battle for the Latin American conservatives and the Latin American church in the postwar period began to undergo a rapid political transformation from the role of a principal supporter of the traditional order to that of a defender of democracy and human rights. Particularly significant was the conduct of the hierarchy in most Latin American countries (Argentina would be the exception) in explicitly defending human rights and democracy against the military rulers who seized power in most of the countries in the area in the 1960s and 1970s.

It was ironic therefore that just as Catholic Europe and Latin America were finally opting for democracy, bitter debate broke out in the United States over the relation of Catholicism and democracy. That debate was prompted by the appearance of Paul Blanshard's *American Freedom and Catholic Power* in 1948 but it extended into areas of public policy, especially the question of public aid for parochial schools. For a time in the late 1940s the editorial and letter columns of the *Washington Post* were full of references to nineteenth-century papal statements, and American liberals worried publicly about the possible threat to the American tradition posed by increasing Catholic political influence.

Blanshard quoted from a standard, if at that time somewhat dated, source, *The State and the Church*, by John A. Ryan and Moorhouse F. X. Millar,[15] a sentence that terrified his liberal Protestant and Jewish readers: "If there is only one true religion and if its possession is the most important good in life for the State as for individuals, then the public profession, protection, and promotion of this religion and the legal prohibition of all direct assaults upon it, becomes one of the obvious and fundamental duties of the state" (p. 35). Less threatening but still disturbing was the discussion in the more recent version of that work, retitled *Catholic Principles of Politics*, written by Msgr. Ryan and Francis J. Boland.[16] Ryan had long argued for the Catholic and scholastic roots of democracy (*Catholic Doctrine on the Right of Self-Government*)[17] citing Aquinas, Suarez, and Bellarmine among others on the people's role as the mediator of political authority which although it originates with God is transmitted by the consent of the people, and can be limited by that same people. Yet Ryan had to admit that earlier Catholic writers had not in fact concluded that representative democracy was the logical application of the popular origin of political authority and that more recent Catholic writers had cast doubt on the popular role. However, he argued that "many Catholic writers of the nineteenth century" had departed from the doctrine of Bellarmine and Suarez because of "the superficial resemblance between this doctrine and the theories of popular sovereignty associated with the French Revolution and subsequent revolutionary movements," and thus had "turned their backs on the traditional teaching" (p. 80). Yet even mainstream Catholic writers, Ryan and Boland wrote, held that once the people had transferred their authority to the monarch, it was almost impossible for them to recover it, even when there was "profound determination" on the part of the people to establish a republican form of government.

As late as the 1940s, the official Vatican position on politics was still that enunciated in *Immortale Dei* in 1885, and Ryan and Boland felt compelled to print extracts from that encyclical and to follow it with a somewhat lame defense of Leo XIII's teaching there that the state should formally recognize the true religion and limit freedom of expression by other religious groups. They argued that while "error has not the same rights as truth," "the foregoing propositions have application only in the completely Catholic state" (pp. 318–19). In a situation of mixed religions, "even Spain and the South American republics," interference with "established religious groups" would "do more harm than good," and in many cases would violate the governing constitution to which the people had consented. Yet in the 1940s there were still restrictions on the rights of Protestants to proselytize in Catholic countries such as Spain and Colombia and American critics worried that something similar might be imposed if Catholics gained power. American Catholic spokesmen insisted that there was no danger that a Catholic majority would repeal the First Amendment, but Blanshard could respond by recalling the thesis-hypothesis distinction of the time of Leo XIII to prove that the hypothesis of religious toleration would be converted into the thesis of state support for Catholicism if American Catholics were ever able to exercise sufficient political power. To militant liberals for whom "anti-Catholicism is the anti-Semitism of the intellectuals,"[18] the whole debate was not reassuring.

What was more reassuring and Blanshard in the 1958 edition of his book felt it necessary to warn Americans not to be deceived by its "jesuitical" character (p. 346) was a series of articles in *The Proceedings of the Catholic Theological Society* (1948) and in *Theological Studies* (June–September 1949) that argued on the basis of medieval sources, especially the thirteenth-century theologian, John of Paris, that the authentic Catholic tradition does not necessarily imply that the Catholic ideal is the establishment of a state church, and that indeed the United States was closer to that ideal than was Franco Spain. The Vatican, in the person of Cardinal Ottaviani, head of the Holy Office, was not sympathetic to [John Courtney] Murray's argument (see his statement in *New York Times*, 23 July 1953), and his arguments were extensively debated in *The American Ecclesiastical Review* over the next several years. Murray's writings, however, were widely influential both in the United States and in Europe, and as a *peritus* at the Second Vatican Council Murray exerted significant influence over the preparation of *The Declaration on Religious Freedom* (1965).

A combination of developments in theory and in practice in Europe, Latin America, and the United States thus combined to produce the setting for a significant modification of the Vatican position on democracy, as well as to render moot the earlier liberal suspicions in the United States. In the United States the whole issue was aired at length during the presidential campaign of John

Kennedy in 1960. His own statements as well as his conduct of the presidency seem to have laid to rest permanently the fear that Catholics in American politics are likely to threaten American freedoms. The saliency of Catholic opposition to abortion, the one major religio-political issue that could have been a source of difficulties with regard to the imposition of Catholic moral standards upon the rest of the country, has been softened by the significant involvement of conservative Protestants and Jews in the anti-abortion movement, as well as by public dissent on the part of some Catholic politicians (e.g., Geraldine Ferraro and Mario Cuomo) from the hierarchy's position favoring a legislative or constitutional prohibition.

The change in the Vatican position on religious freedom dates not from 1965, the date of the Vatican II decree, but from 1963 with the publication of Pope John XXIII's encyclical *Pacem in Terris*.[19] The encyclical begins in what appears to be a classically conservative fashion with a discussion of "order between men." After stating that every human being is a person by virtue of which "he has rights and duties of his own, flowing directly and simultaneously from his very nature," the encyclical then moves immediately into a discussion of human rights (followed later by discussion of duties, a reversal of the usual order in earlier Catholic statements on the subject).

The third right that is discussed is "the right to worship God according to one's conscience" and this is described as follows: "Every human being has the right to honor God according to the dictates of an upright conscience, and therefore to worship God privately and publicly." The reference to the right to public worship was the first indication of a change in the official position which in places like Spain had tolerated non-Catholic worship only in private, a policy which as recently as 1953 had been defended by Cardinal Ottaviani. Two pages later, the encyclical seems to endorse liberal democracy stating that "the dignity of the human person involves the right to take an active part in public affairs and to contribute one's part to the common good of the citizens" and adding, "The human person is also entitled to the juridical protection of his rights." In the next section, the encyclical states that "it is impossible to determine, once and for all, the most suitable form of government," but it reasserts the advantages of participation and alludes to the need for ministers of government to hold office only for a limited time, thus apparently arguing for a system of periodic elections. It was left, however, to the Second Vatican Council to commit the church fully to democracy, when it stated in *Gaudium et Spes* that "it is in full accord with human nature" that all should "participate freely and actively in establishing the constitutional bases of a political community, governing the state, determining the scope and purpose of various institutions, and choosing leaders." The paragraph had footnotes to the 1942 and 1944 Christmas messages of Pope Pius XII and to *Pacem in Terris*, but it clearly marked a much more complete commitment to democracy than heretofore.

The council also moved toward a partial decentralization of the internal structure of the church in the *Dogmatic Constitution on the Church* (*Lumen Gentium*) which defined the church as "the people of God" (chap. II), and stated that "the order of bishops is the successor to the college of the apostles in teaching authority.... Together with its head, the Roman Pontiff and never without this head the episcopal order is the subject of supreme and full power over the universal church" (chap. III). There is a footnote reference to a report to the First Vatican Council which was never acted upon because of the breakup of the meeting due to foreign occupation of Rome, but it is very doubtful that the statement quoted above would ever have been adopted in 1870–71. The document also included a lengthy discussion of the role of the laity emphasizing their duty to sanctify the world and stating that "The laity are gathered together in the People of God and make up the body of Christ under one Head" (chap. IV).

The subsequent effects of these important changes are well known. Synods of bishops meet regularly in ordinary or extraordinary (as on the twentieth anniversary of the Council in late 1985) session. The laity has been more deeply involved, and new theologies have been developed which emphasize the importance of the involvement of the laity, especially the poor. The church itself has not become a democracy, and those who have argued too strongly for an increase in internal democratization have sometimes had difficulties with the Vatican.[20] It has, however, moved away from the nineteenth-century monarchical model to a mixture of forms of authority that, I would argue, is closer to its original structure.

Conclusion

What are we to conclude, then, from our discussion of the relation of the Catholic tradition and modern democracy? The pattern that emerges from the above review is a complex one, but it is not impossible to summarize. Elements of community participation in church affairs have been present in Catholicism from the beginning, but they have always combined with more hierarchical elements, both in order to safeguard the deposit of the faith and to continue the Apostolic Succession to the apostles and St. Peter. The early church tolerated the empire, only to be embraced (some say co-opted) by it. The medieval church however managed to maintain independence from, and even at times preeminence over, the temporal power, but in both church and state the tradition of a mixture of forms of government prevailed. With the Reformation, the more democratic and aristocratic forms of church constitution were embodied in the various forms of Protestantism, while Catholic controversialists argued for papal monarchy but continued to insist on the popular origins of political authority against the claims of the absolute monarchs of the day. In the early modern period the populist elements in the Catholic tradition were deemphasized, as church teaching tended to support monarchy in church and state. When the French Revolution took an anticlerical turn, and nineteenth-century democratic and liberal movements pressed for the separation of church and state, attempted to wrest control over education from the church, and annexed the Papal States as part of the struggle for Italian unification, the papacy responded with a series of condemnations of an exaggerated and stereotyped liberalism both because it threatened its institutional privileges and because it appeared to be inspired by an anti-Christian naturalism and rationalism. Efforts in France and Italy to relate liberal democracy to Catholicism met with repeated papal condemnations, or, later in the century, reluctant toleration. It was only in the middle third of the twentieth century that the ancient religious roots of popular participation were rediscovered in Europe and Latin America and in the postwar period what had been an embattled Christian Democratic philosophy became the dominant Catholic political theory in Europe and Latin America. At last these developments which had always been supported by Catholics in England and the United States were given formal expression and approval in the Second Vatican Council, which also acted to reverse the tendency to ecclesiastical centralization and authoritarianism which had been dominant since the Counter Reformation.

We return then to the four positions outlined at the beginning of this paper. As this outline has indicated indifference as to the various forms of government that promote the common good has finally yielded to the recognition of the moral superiority of democratic government and guarantees of human rights. The hierarchic and centralized structure of the church has been modified, and with it the associated fear of democracy that seems to have motivated the nineteenth-century popes. Those who argue that the movement to democracy and human rights by Catholicism is only a maneuver to maintain its institutional interests may not be convinced, but I hope that this review will indicate that the shift that I have described is something more than tactical, that it is deeply rooted in the Christian tradition, and that (as the heroic actions of many Catholics in Latin America during the last two decades in defense of human rights have demonstrated) it has profound implications for the future of democracy and freedom in the world today.

NOTES

Reprinted from *The Review of Politics* 49, no. 4 (Autumn 1987): 530–48.

1. On the political structure of the early church, see the documents assembled in James T. Shotwell, ed., *The See of Peter* (New York: Columbia University Press, 1940).

2. Especially *The Celestial Hierarchy* and the *Ecclesiastical Hierarchy*. Dionysius was a fifth-century neo-Platonist Syrian monk, who was believed to be the "Dionysius the Areopagite" converted in Athens by St. Paul after his speech on the Unknown God (Acts 17:34). See my discussion in *Nicholas of Cusa and Medieval Political Thought* (Cambridge, MA: Harvard University Press, 1963), chap. 3.

3. See the documents in Brian Tierney, ed., *The Crisis of Church and State, 1050–1300* (Englewood Cliffs, NJ: Prentice-Hall, 1964). On the Conciliar Movement see Brian Tierney, *Foundations of the Conciliar Theory* (Cambridge, MA: Cambridge University Press, 1955); Francis Oakley, *The Political Thought of Pierre d'Ailly* (New Haven: Yale University Press, 1964); and Sigmund, *Nicholas of Cusa*, chap. 4.

4. See Walter Ullmann, *A History of Medieval Political Thought* (New York: Penguin Books, 1975); and Paul E. Sigmund, ed. and trans., *St. Thomas Aquinas, On Ethics and Politics* (New York: W. W. Norton, 1988).

5. The encyclicals of Gregory XVI and Pius IX are quoted from the English translations collected in Claudia Carlen, ed., *The Papal Encyclicals*, vol. 1, *1740–1878* (Raleigh, NC: McGrath Publishers, 1981). For background reading, the best sources are the writings of E. E. Y. Hales, especially *Pio Nono* (London: Eyre and Spottiswood, 1954) and *The Catholic Church in the Modern World* (Garden City, NY: Hanover House, 1958); and H. Daniel-Rops, *The Church in an Age of Revolution, 1789–1870* (New York: E. P. Dutton, 1965). Excerpts from *The Syllabus of Errors* (1864) of Pius IX appear in Henry Bettenson, ed., *Documents of the Christian Church* (New York: Oxford University Press, 1947).

6. Leo XIII's encyclicals are translated in Joseph Husslein, S.J., ed., vol. 1 of *Social Wellsprings* (Milwaukee: Bruce Publishers, 1940).

7. Quoted in Alec R. Vidler, *A Century of Social Catholicism* (London: SPCK, 1964), 138.

8. By 1958 Maritain's American experience had led him to extol the most bourgeois liberal of all modern states as the best application of Christian principles; see his *Reflections on America* (New York: Scribner's, 1958).

9. Yves R. Simon, *Philosophy of Democratic Government* (Chicago: University of Chicago Press, 1951).

10. Heinrich Albert Rommen, *The State in Catholic Thought* (St. Louis: Herder, 1945).

11. Mortimer J. Adler and Walter Farrell, O.P., "The Theory of Democracy," *The Thomist* 3 (July 1941): 397–449.

12. On the development of Maritain's political theory see my article "Maritain on Politics," in *Understanding Maritain*, ed. Deal Hudson and Matthew Mancini (Atlanta: Mercer University Press, 1987). The best introduction to his political thought is *Man and the State* (Chicago: University of Chicago Press, 1951). See also the selections in Joseph W. Evans and Leo R. Ward, eds., *The Social and Political Philosophy of Jacques Maritain* (New York: Scribner's, 1955; paperback ed., Garden City, NY: Doubleday Image, 1965). Like Maritain, Rommen believes that democracy is the product of "Christian ideas matured to their full meaning" (*State in Catholic Thought*, 485), but he is more willing to take account of the papacy's hostile attitude toward democracy, which he attributes to its concern to defend the Papal States and opposition to internal democratization in the church (489). Thinking apparently of Alexis de Tocqueville and Lord Acton, Rommen also notes that "a great many nineteenth-century (Catholic) writers of influence (understand) that freedom and democracy must be valued positively, and can be valued so especially well from the principles ever present in Catholic thought" (492).

13. Quoted in Oscar Halecki, *Pius XII* (London: Weidenfeld, 1954), 152.

14. Julio Meinvielle, *De Lamennais à Maritain* (Buenos Aires: Nuestro Tiempo, 1945; French translation, Paris: La Cité Catholique, 1953; rev. ed., Buenos Aires: Ediciones Teoria, 1967).

15. John A. Ryan and Moorhouse F. X. Millar, *The State and the Church* (New York: Macmillan, 1920).

16. John A. Ryan and Francis J. Boland, *Catholic Principles of Politics* (New York: Macmillan, 1940).

17. John A. Ryan, *Catholic Doctrine on the Right of Self-Government* (New York: Macmillan, 1919).

18. [This often-repeated quote is attributed to the writer Peter Viereck. Ed.]

19. Pope John XXIII, *Peace on Earth (Pacem in Terris)* (Huntington, IN: Our Sunday Visitor Press, 1963). All quotations are taken from this translation.

20. Cf. the 1984 summons to Rome of Frei Leonardo Boff because of statements made in his book, *Church, Charism, and Power* (New York: Crossroad, 1985) regarding the "expropriation of the spiritual means of production by the hierarchy." It is noteworthy that he was accompanied to Rome by two Brazilian cardinals and (fellow-Franciscans). For a discussion of this and related post-conciliar developments, see my forthcoming study, *Liberation Theology at the Crossroads: Democracy or Revolution?*

CHAPTER 9

Catholics and the Civic Order

Parish Participation, Polities, and Civic Participation

DAVID C. LEEGE

David C. Leege (1939–) is Professor Emeritus in the Department of Political Science at the University of Notre Dame. He received his B.A. at Valparaiso University in 1959 and his Ph.D. at Indiana University in 1965. His scholarship has focused on American voting behavior, religion, and the politics of cultural differences. He is a co-editor of the book series Cambridge Studies in Social Theory, Religion, and Politics and co-author of The Politics of Cultural Differences: Social Change and Voter Mobilization Strategies in the Post-New Deal Period. *He is author or co-author of numerous other books and articles, including several on American Catholics and politics. Among his many professional honors, Leege chaired the Board of Overseers of the American National Election Studies and remains associated with its development of measures of religiosity.*

CHANGING VIEWS ON CATHOLICS AND POLITICS

Historians and pundits have treated the political behavior of American Catholics with great relish. Textbooks and newspaper morgues are replete with colorful descriptions of urban party machines. From the chronicles of Tammany Hall to the malaprops of Mayor Daley, some have come to think of Catholics and politics through terms like ethnic coalitions, slating, spoils, and corruption.[1]

Another term from these accounts stands out—deliverable. If the ward committeeman could not deliver the vote the parish priest could. Behind the instructions from the pulpit, in the jaundiced eyes of many, were the manipulations of Rome.[2]

Such mind-pictures may have described some cities and some parishes in some time periods. Recently, scholars have suggested that the picture is badly overdrawn, that there were differing experiences from locale to locale, from one ethnic group to another.[3] Church leaders were often reluctant to speak or act politically for fear of arousing anti-Catholic hostility and suspicion. For theological reasons, some priests deliberately limited their efforts to the "spiritual," not the secular domain. And the Catholic laity were hardly sheep. In some ethnic groups, for example Italians, males retained anticlerical attitudes from the old country and would have treated clerical attempts to lead them politically with derision—especially if the clerics were Irish. Regardless of the inaccuracies of newspaper and historical accounts of the earlier years, such portraits certainly were far from the demographic realities of American Catholics by the eve of the election of John Fitzgerald Kennedy to the presidency.

Today a quite different picture of the political behavior of Catholics is being drawn. Social theorists are beginning to see Catholic parishes and American Catholic bishops as a source of hope. In a society of rampant individualism—where what *I* want, what *I* feel, and what are *my* rights forms the basis for the common good; where, in the words of Robert Bellah, and associates,[4] "the nature of success, the meaning of freedom, and the requirements of justice" are devoid of a transcendent referent outside oneself—in such a society social theorists look for institutions that can recapture a sense of community and commitment. Catholic parishes, as well as some Protestant congregations and Jewish synagogues, are thought to be such "communities of memory" that bond us to the values of the past and include the hopes of the future in the way *we*, not I, judge the present. The pastoral statements of American bishops on peace and the economy are seen as serious attempts to initiate dialogue along the moral dimensions of public policy.

Somewhere within but beyond the "private-regardingness" of the spoils politician, the "kept" flock of the parish priest, and the search for the common good and transcendent standards of the social theorist, there is an important contemporary story about Catholics and the American civic order. We hope to unravel at least a small part of it in this article. We begin with a short history of change in the civic participation of American Catholics and then interpret questionnaire data from the Notre Dame Study of Catholic Parish Life to address three questions: (1) Do parish participation and civic participation overlap?

(2) Are the religious values of Catholic parishioners connected in any noticeable ways to their political values? (3) Do parishioners feel it appropriate for their church leaders to offer teachings on personal morality and social and political questions?

Linking Parish Life, Political Values, and Civic Life

From Immigrant Communities to World War II

In his pathbreaking book *The American Catholic: A Social Portrait,* Andrew Greeley argues that the dominant reality for American Catholics is the recency of the immigrant experience. Even in the decade after President Kennedy's election, 40 percent of adult American Catholics were either immigrants or children of immigrants.[5]

Historian Jay Dolan tells us much about the immigrant church.[6] It was ethnic. Ironically, although the Mass was celebrated in Latin, a universal language which some wag says was "read only by priests and understood only by God," nevertheless, the basis of the parish was the ethnic group, its native tongue, and its cultural traditions. A clarion call of the times was "he who loses his language loses his faith." A Polish parish church might be located less than fifty yards from an Irish parish church, but Mass should not be celebrated jointly. The arrangement of many parishes by ethnic enclaves both reflected and reinforced social and political differences among Catholic immigrant groups.

One thing these ethnic groups had in common was the search for opportunity, but they often found an inhospitable environment. They faced economic and social discrimination and sometimes religious persecution. Many, not far removed from the serfdom of eastern, central, and southern Europe, were now huddled in the squalor of industrial cities. They had little facility with the English language.

According to historians, the immigrant parish experience was custom-made for leaders who would act as brokers. Some parish communities had left the old country and arrived under the leadership of a priest; he was already a dominant force in their religious, social, and political lives.[7] In other situations, people of common ethnic background would find each other, petition mission societies in the home country to send a priest, then organize a proto-parish awaiting his leadership. In some of these parishes, authority remained with the people through a trusteeship system, but that did not set well with the emerging American hierarchy who wanted parish authority lodged in the priest, as the local representative of the bishop.[8]

Finally, there seemed to be a ready supply of Irish priests who were often assigned to parishes of other ethnicity. While people grumbled about the situation, they had to recognize that the Irish priest's facility with English helped in temporal affairs, and his contact with Irish politicians would open opportunities for jobs, city services, and staying on the right side of the law.

Regardless of the ethnic parish's experience in acquiring priestly leadership, there were some pressures to look to the priest for political leadership. Whether he could offer it from the pulpit, in the newsletter, and in conversation at wakes, devotional societies, and fraternal halls depended in part on ethnic values brought from the old country, in part on the extent to which parishioners already had a sense of "ownership" over their parish, and in part on the hierarchy's sense that it was either "un-American" or theologically inappropriate to extend spiritual leadership to temporal matters.

The immigrant parish experience was also custom-made for acting in concert and instilling a sense of *community* interest. Seldom did community interest extend beyond opportunity for members of one's ethnic tribe, but at least it did offer a frame of reference for involvement in civic affairs that was beyond the individual. Some nowadays complain that the emphasis on social justice in the contemporary American Catholic Church deviates from the church's historic focus on spiritual concerns. In reality, it perpetuates an ethnic parish tradition of social involvement, but in a different and broader context.

The parish benevolence societies and the ethnic betterment societies, always with the counsel of a priest, offered charity to those less fortunate in the parish; more important, these societies worked to improve economic and political opportunity and social acceptance for their kind of people in the larger community. The precursors of the social justice emphasis are not solely Dorothy Day or Daniel Berrigan, but the Italian American Relief Association or the Polish Roman Catholic Union, the German bunds or the Flemish krings. The difference is that those Catholics who now "have" are asked to advocate the same opportunities for "have-nots" outside the tribe. Whether this expansion of community-mindedness will succeed in the future may depend in part on the extent to which the stories of community concern from the past are retained and applied anew.

The immigrant community, then, provided three staples linking parish life and the civic order: (1) the sense of the underdog who hopes dearly to "make it" in the face of persecution, (2) community identity and action as avenues to betterment, and (3) where conditions permitted such clerical leadership, some deference to clergy not only on spiritual matters but also on temporal affairs.

The GI Bill and JFK

In the three decades following the Second World War, however, a lot was changing in the life of Catholics that would change forever the mixture of these elements linking religion and politics. American Catholics became educated, mobile, pragmatic, and free. In retrospect, it appears that two watershed events shifted the relationship between parish life and civic life: the GI Bill and the election of President Kennedy. The American parish's later application of the goals and principles of the Second Vatican Council must be interpreted against the backdrop of these social and political changes.

The GI Bill and its permanent democratizing effect on educational opportunity enabled not only the earlier-assimilated, English-speaking Irish Catholics to pursue higher education, but for young people (then, mostly men) of *all* Catholic ethnic backgrounds to pursue higher education. Greeley documents the time-point when each ethnic group overtook the educational achievement norm for the rest of American society.[9] Nowadays, people in most Catholic ethnic groups have educations that nearly match those of Jews. Their education rivals those of "silk-stocking" mainline Protestants such as Presbyterians, Episcopalians, and Congregationalists (UCC), and considerably exceeds Methodists, Lutherans, Baptists, and Pentecostals.

Just as important as the level of attainment is the location of study. Increasingly the bachelor's degree was completed at national rather than local Catholic institutions, at state universities, and at the elite private colleges. Loyalties were instilled toward a non-Catholic alma mater. Now it is commonplace to find Catholics establishing endowed chairs in Catholic studies at, for example, Florida or Cornell, rather than for programs at Benedictine or St. Joseph's, Notre Dame or Georgetown.

Just as the war had taken them to Dunkirk or Guadalcanal, so the GI Bill and its aftermath moved them from the old neighborhood to the suburb. Fewer returned to the ancestral parishes and the neighborhood communities with ties that bind and priests who direct. More Catholics settled in subdivisions that came to be served by very new, very active suburban churches. Much as they shopped for suburban housing and commuted long distances to work in jobs of their choosing, a growing number shopped for a church that "met their current needs," and sometimes passed by the local parish church on their commute to the Catholic church of their choice. In time, a decline in vocations to the priesthood and to women's religious orders meant that the many parish programs and ministries that "served their needs" would have to be led by the laity themselves. Laypersons not only shouldered responsibility for parish ministry, but became increasingly involved in parish administration and governance. Canon law changed, partly in recognition that the church is "the *people* of God," but also in recognition that parishes are better served by consultative and enabling leadership than by authoritarian direction. We are now on the threshold of the third generation of post–GI Bill families—a laity educated, mobile, pragmatic, and free.

The nature of the temporal authority of the clergy was also greatly affected by the election of John Fitzgerald Kennedy. Lacking authentic American Catholic heroes, the upwardly mobile GI-Bill generation and their children were captivated by this young prince. What he did on the road to the presidency was not only to embrace the religious pluralism of America, but to proclaim the political liberty of any Catholic. Kennedy's dramatic address to the Houston Ministerial Alliance during the 1960 campaign was based on the American experience; the roots of his argument tapped not the syllabus of errors, the First Vatican Council, or the papal denunciation of Americanism in 1899, but the Catholic Maryland colony's declaration of religious liberty and John Courtney Murray's writings which put Murray on the Index. (Historian Martin Marty, political scientist Mary Hanna, and Mr. Kennedy's wife have all observed that Kennedy himself was not steeped in Catholic intellectual traditions and was perhaps not so sensitive as others to church-state issues. Thus, to rely on the American experience came quite naturally for him.) A few years later, the Second Vatican Council embraced similar positions in its teaching on religious freedom and ecumenism. These themes, which have come to be normative not only for the American church but for the worldwide church, were advocated at the Council sessions especially by the American cardinals, Spellman and Dearden.

For many Catholics in that day, this Catholic in the White House symbolized the inappropriateness of religious bases for political judgments. For Catholic Republicans (of whom there were many among Italians, Germans, and earlier-assimilated generations), subtle appeals to cross over and vote for a fellow Catholic were taken as an insult to their political freedom. In our day, the notion that a priest or a bishop with less education than many parishioners and certainly less schooling in the ways of economic and political institutions should attempt to instruct parishioners in how to vote is usually regarded with annoyance or amusement. For some in the present generation, even reminders of the social teachings of the church through bishops' pastoral letters have become a call to action—in opposition. Thus, the recent draft pastoral on the American economy was met with a counter-pastoral, even before its final adoption.[10] The connections between parish life and civic life have become increasingly nuanced.

Today American Catholics are in the cultural mainstream of the nation. The nature of the Catholic community and its institutions has changed—some say for the better, some say for the worse. For example, George Gallup, Jr., and Jim Castelli, reviewing Gallup religious surveys of recent years, note, but do not bemoan, the Americanization of Catholics.[11] Instead, they celebrate the Catholicization of America. Gallup and Castelli suggest that Catholic experience and action have made unique and positive contributions to American cultural norms and political discourse regarding: (1) tolerance, (2) women's rights, (3) the communal dimension of society, (4) presidential politics, and (5) peace. That is why social theorists are again paying attention to American Catholics. Relationships between church life and civic life that were relatively stable in the immigrant church appear to have changed. Social theorists anticipate that there will be significant changes in civic values, as well.

Religion in Social Theory

Social theorists have long argued that religion is the glue that holds the social, economic, and political orders together. To know what a people values religiously is to know what they expect of their political order. And to observe how they interact in their religious institutions is to presage how they will behave in the civic order.

In the 1830s, Alexis de Tocqueville claimed that religion in America was a "doers" matter.[12] How one lived his life in the community was the test of whether a person was a Christian and could be trusted in matters political and economic. In contrast to Europe where religion was sacramentally based and offered an otherworldly salvation to the Catholic, Anglican, or Lutheran communities, in the United States, religion was individualistic and worn in public; it called for "decisions for Christ" (not Tocqueville's words) and testimony within this world. It created a tradition of political discourse laced with morality and organized as a crusade, a tradition that carries to our day: abolition, civil war, manifest destiny, temperance, women's suffrage, white man's burden, make the world safe for democracy, civil rights and racial integration, war on poverty, right to life, evil empire, and so on.

In the early 1900s, sociologists of religion, Max Weber and Ernst Troeltsch, referred to this phenomenon as "sect-type" religiosity rather than "church-type" religiosity.[13] In *church-type religiosity*, one is born into the religious community and attains salvation through the church's sacramental acts; in large part, the religious community and all God-ordained social institutions are prior to the individual. In *sect-type religiosity*, however, it is the individual who comes to embrace Christ, who understands God's will through personal study of the Scriptures, who communicates directly with God in prayer, and who shows the in-dwelling of God through public conduct. The individual chooses which church he will join, just as he gives or withholds support for public institutions based on his perception of how they conform to God's laws. Weber and Troeltsch's sect-type religious culture described well Tocqueville's "doers" religion and helps to explain the extraordinary mingling of religion and politics in America. It also helps to explain the moral crusades of American politics, as well as the volatility of support for political leaders and the skepticism about governmental institutions. In the American way, no institution has prior claim to legitimacy; it must prove itself in the court of individual choice.

Tocqueville paid special attention to Catholics in America, who in the 1830s were not a large segment of the population. He noted that American Catholics seemed more communal and less individualistic in orientation. He traced that to a church-type religious culture in the mother countries. Yet the host culture of America was sect-type and individualistic. Tocqueville was uncertain whether Catholics would transform the culture or the culture would transform Catholics. Some charge that the massive entry of Catholics into the American mainstream has been accompanied with the embrace of individualism. We will explore that contention shortly through our data.

Another theme of Tocqueville appears in more recent social theory: the best protection against the tyranny of the state is a civil society organized into many institutions which compete with each other, while reflecting transcendent values. The specter of totalitarianism, whether in fascist or communist form, has caused many social theorists to fear both liberal individualism and the homogenization of mass society. Peter Berger and Richard Neuhaus, among others, have looked to mediating institutions as forces that protect the individual from an all-powerful state, that become centers for identity rivaling the attraction of the nation-state, that provide services so that the individual does not become totally dependent on the state, and that offer moral criteria for judging the performance of the state.[14] Religious communities are thought to be particularly well suited as mediating institutions.

Kenneth Wald, developing this argument from the perspective of a political scientist, argues that church members derive four essential political skills from their parish or congregational involvements: (1) they acquire social skills in listening, mediating, and leading, (2) they learn about public issues from a religious perspective, (3) they receive encouragement to join in civic and community activities, and (4) they come to see a sacred character in those social obligations that transcend selfish interests.[15]

The link any given individual may make between religious beliefs, political values, and civic participation may take a variety of forms. Parish members are already "joiners," and numerous sociological studies have documented that church "joiners" are more likely than nonjoiners to belong to other voluntary associations.[16] The transference of political skills from the church setting to other civic and public settings is also reasonably well documented, although it varies in strength.[17]

What is a matter of much more dispute among sociologists and psychologists of religion is the manner in which specific religious beliefs get translated into public policy positions. Studies by Charles Glock and Rodney Stark and by others have indicated that orthodox and, to some extent, fundamentalistic beliefs about God and the Scriptures are associated with the support of conservative, status quo–oriented, and anti–civil libertarian public policies.[18] Milton Rokeach offered a similar finding for those who value salvation more highly than a variety of other goals in life.[19] Yet, Dean Hoge and others have shown that the saliency of religion in one's life predicts well to attitudes on family and sexuality issues but not very well to other major public policy matters.[20]

Leege, Welch, and Trozzolo have shown that, among Catholics who marry a Catholic spouse, there is greater consistency with church teachings on family and sexuality but less consistency with church statements on justice, peace, the economy, and equal opportunity, than is found among Catholics with a non-Catholic spouse.[21] The lesson from such studies is that the linkage between religion and political questions depends both on what is taken as evidence of religiosity and what is the specific public policy.

In studies that move beyond the level of the individual to the activities of the parish or congregation, there are many ways the religious institution may manifest its presence in the community. A recent work by David Roozen and his collaborators has suggested four ways that the local religious institution may choose to organize its people toward the outside community: (1) in an *activist* orientation, where it takes corporate social, economic, or political action to overcome an injustice in the community; (2) in a *civic* orientation, where it informs individual members about social problems and encourages their participation, but as individuals, not as members of the parish; (3) in a *sanctuary* (i.e., withdrawal) orientation, where members can retreat from the ills of the world and join in common rituals and readings, in anticipation of the afterlife; and (4) in an *evangelistic* orientation, where members are expected to witness their hopes of salvation in an evil world and thus to transform the hearts of fallen people.[22] Just as we can expect Catholics, the products of church-type religiosity in a sect-type religious culture, to embrace a wide variety of political views, so we can expect that their parishes may take any one of these stances toward civil society, depending on their locale, their traditions, and their local leadership.

Topics and Sources and Data

This article will examine many of these concerns about the linkage among parish life, political values, and civic life. The data are examined in three parts. First, we will see to what extent there is an overlap between parish participation and civic participation, whether the same kinds of people participate in each, and whether specialization in some field of parish activity is accompanied by involvements in similar civic organizations. Secondly, we will summarize a program of research undertaken by Leege and Welch to examine what political values active Catholic parishioners have, to see what kinds of religious values best predict political orientations, and to assess whether social characteristics or religious values offer stronger explanations for Catholic parishioners' political views. Thirdly, we will explore what Catholic parishioners feel are the appropriate political roles of their priestly leadership, and the areas where it is acceptable for the hierarchy to offer social teachings.

Our primary data base is the 2,667 parish-connected Catholics who responded to the Notre Dame Study of Catholic Parish Life. We remind readers to exercise caution in generalizing from our findings. We should expect differences between our findings and general population surveys of Catholics of the kind done by the Gallup organization, the National Opinion Research Center, or the Institute for Social Research. Our data include Catholics with parish connections, who were carried on the rolls of the 36 non-Hispanic parishes selected through a mixed probability design as representative of American parishes, and who were sufficiently interested to respond to a long questionnaire. Earlier reports and methodological papers have identified the strengths and biases of such a sample.[23]

Parish Participation and Civic Participation

Early in the questionnaire, we asked respondents to list all the parish activities, programs, or ministries in which they had participated during the last year, to estimate the number of hours per month spent in each, and to indicate what kind of leadership position, if any, they held. Later in the questionnaire we asked a similar question about their participation, hours, and leadership in various civic organizations outside the parish community, ranging through fraternal or sorority, service, veterans, political, labor, recreational, youth, school service, hobby or social, nationality, farm, literary, professional, or neighborhood, as well as similar extra-parish church-related organizations. Table 1 shows the proportion of the respondents participating in parish and in extra-parish or civic activities.

The table offers several lessons. The percent of respondents who participate in no civic or extra-parish organizations is slightly higher (56.7%) than those who participate in no parish activities besides Mass and devotional rituals (50.9%). However, only a little over one-third (34.9%) participate in neither. That is to be expected, given the nature of our parish-connected respondents. They are "joiners" by definition.

Table 1. Comparison of Parish Participation with Civic Participation, 2,667 Parishioners

Civic or Extra-Parish Participation	Parish Participation				
	None	One Activity	Two Activities	Three or More	Total
None	34.9%	10.8%	6.4%	4.6%	56.7%
One organization	7.8	4.3	2.4	2.7	17.2
Two organizations	3.9	3.1	2.5	2.4	11.9
Three or more	4.3	3.1	3.3	3.3	14.0
Total	50.9%	21.3%	14.6%	13.0%	99.8%*

*Error due to rounding

Of greater interest is the question of whether parish joiners are civic joiners, and vice versa. If one adds along the first row (10.8 + 6.4 + 4.6), it can be seen that 21.8 percent of the respondents engage in one or more parish activities but no civic activities, while if one adds the first column (7.8 + 3.9 + 4.3), it can be seen that 16.0 percent of the respondents engage in no parish activities, but do participate in one or more civic organizations. Finally, if one adds all the remaining cells together, it can be seen that 27.1 percent of the parish-connected Catholic respondents are at least minimally active in both parish and community, that is, they participate in one or more activity of each.

In sum, among Catholics who appear on parish membership lists and respond to surveys of this kind, nearly two-thirds are "active" in either their faith community or their civic community and over one-fourth of them (27.1%) are active in both. Further, when specialization occurs, a higher proportion of parishioners limit their participation to parish affairs (21.8%) than to civic affairs (16.0%).

Joiners and Leadership

If joining is a reasonable indicator, there is active participation in both the church and civic sectors by a sizeable proportion of the parishioners. Thus, it can be argued that the Catholic parishioners in this sample show at least the first condition for linking parish life and civic life: they join both. At the same time, over 50 percent (56.7%) "belong" to nothing outside their parish and over one-third (34.9%) engage in neither nonliturgical activities within the parish nor civic activities. Whether the joiners are linking parish activity to civic activity, we cannot say. At least some overlap exists.

To measure the overlap more precisely we decided to see whether the specific kinds of things one does in the parish are paralleled by the specific kinds of things one does in the civic community. To examine this issue we have classified parish involvements into the following categories: (1) governance (e.g., parish council, finance committee), (2) liturgical leadership (e.g.; lector, Eucharistic minister, cantor, musician), (3) education or evangelism (e.g., religious education teacher, discussion group leader, RCIA sponsor), (4) devotional or renewal (e.g., prayer group, RENEW team), (5) social or recreational (e.g., church dinners, social clubs, athletic teams), and (6) welfare or social justice (e.g., visits to sick, soup kitchen, social issues). Then we used correlation measures between participation in such parish activities and in the civic organization enumerated earlier.

Parishioners who participate in governance, liturgical leadership, or education or evangelism activities are the ones most likely to engage in many kinds of extra-parish civic activities. That is no surprise. All involve leadership, that is, sufficient education, self-confidence in front of groups, and a track record of responsible action. The latter two can be learned either in parish settings or civic settings, and all three are valued both by church and civic organizations. Those in parish governance are more likely to be involved in civic service organizations, in political organizations, and in extra-parish programs aimed at religious study and leadership development. Those involved in parish liturgical leadership roles are also quite likely to join civic service organizations and social or hobby groups. Those involved in parish education and evangelism tend to be highly specialized, with extra-parish involvements in school service activities and youth groups. Those involved in devotional and renewal activities are likely to have an extra-parish frame of reference but it is with church service, political, and discussion groups rather than nonchurch civic organizations. Finally, those involved in parish-based welfare and social justice activities are the most specialized of all in their civic activities, devoting a great deal of effort to political organizations.

Given the degree of civic specialization in some of these categories of parish activists, it is worth examining whether parish joiners and civic joiners seem to be responding to the same stimuli. For this purpose we have used two statistical techniques: *multiple regression* analysis and *logistic regression*. We have looked at the degree of parish involvement, the degree of civic involvement, and the overlap between the two, as a function of such social characteristics as age, stage in the family life-cycle, education, income, ethnicity, urban-rural locale, and region; such political characteristics as party preference and liberalism-conservatism; and such religious "intensity" measures as frequency of Mass attendance, frequency of Bible reading, and proportion of education completed in Catholic schools. The resulting tables are too technical and lengthy to include as appendices, but they can be made available to scholars interested in them. Here we will summarize the key findings.

Gender, Culture, and Education

The greatest differences between parish participation and civic participation among Catholic parishioners involve gender: the parish is mainly the domain of women, and civic life is mainly the domain of men. To be sure, many men and women are found in both parish activities and civic organizations, but where there is specialization it most clearly relates to gender.

Many social theorists would interpret gender differences by the church's function as the extension of home and hearth, and by the roles of women as nurturers and preservers of values. Men, by contrast, are seen as the traditional material providers; the civic involvements of men are seen as extensions of their economic interests. If these notions are accurate, however, there is a paradox with Catholic women and men.

While it is true that many of the parish involvements of Catholic women involve nurture and value-conservation (e.g., religious education) and extensions of the hearth (e.g., dinners, bake sales, altar care), nevertheless, earlier reports in the *Report* series have shown that women are now as deeply involved as men in parish governance and liturgical leadership roles.[24] Furthermore, to focus on the parish-hearth activities of Catholic women and to suggest that these involve few civic skills is to overlook the large numbers of Catholic men engaged in parish fraternal and recreational activities which, for many, involve little exercise of civic skills. Finally, women who have organized a parish bake sale or tried to move things along in the parish kitchen know the complex range of political skills that must be exercised in that process. Thus, for women, not only social participation but leadership skills are honed in the parish.

The paradox comes with the transference of those skills to extra-parish civic organizations. Outside the parish it is the Catholic men who are more likely to participate and lead. Yet, the women also have the skills. It is not that Catholic women lack economic interests. Examination of recent national surveys shows a slightly higher proportion of two-earner families among Catholics than among Protestants. Catholic women have been employed outside the home for years. We hypothesize, however, that their jobs lack the status and the earning power of their husbands' jobs, and that their jobs are less likely to involve them in the web of community organizations. We also suspect, but cannot document from available data, that Catholic women have retained primary, if not sole, responsibility for the hearth, and have less disposable time for civic affairs.

Although family and economic realities change, cultural patterns that reinforce role specialization linger longer. Scholars have argued that the Protestant women long active in the reform movements of this country—abolition, child labor, temperance, suffrage, etc.—often had supportive husbands or were the daughters of clergymen who encouraged their daughters to "transform the world in the name of God." They have noted that Catholic women were disproportionately absent from such movements, they obviously did not have clergy fathers, and they had to fight male definitions of their roles as confined to the hearth.[25]

(It should also be remembered that during the great reform years of 1840 to 1920, most Catholics were living in immigrant ghettos, were not yet awakened to "national" issues, and were often unwelcome if they did care about these issues.) Under the circumstances, some historians have argued the best opportunities to join in social reform and exercise "civic" leadership were through women's orders; thus, a religious sister might become a hospital administrator or operate a settlement house.

If these arguments are correct they may shed light on the current paradox of Catholic women as leaders in the parish but as less involved than Catholic men in civic organizations. We would anticipate that the increasing parity of education between Catholic men and women, the massive entry of young Catholic women into business and professional occupations, the later age of marriage and smaller families, stronger expectations of household roles for men, along with the increasing incidence of divorce and its attendant economic pressures, particularly on those Catholic women who are less educated—all will contribute toward greater balance between the sexes in their parish involvements and civic involvements. For now, however, both lingering cultural norms and economic structures may inhibit the transference of civic skills from parish to civic organizations.

Putting gender differences aside, the best overall predictor of both parish participation and civic participation is education. Education is a much stronger predictor of civic involvement than of parish involvement, but in both, the higher the education, the more one will participate. Education raises sights and raises the sense of responsibility. Education develops skills and the most important attribute of leadership—self-confidence. The interplay of all these traits is seen in the data. In the civic arena, education is a slightly better predictor of the participation of Catholic women; in the parish, education is a slightly better predictor of the participation of Catholic men.

Bible Reading and Devotions

Another vitally important predictor of parish involvement is one of the religious intensity measures—frequency of Bible reading. Although Bible reading does not rival education as a predictor of both parish and civic involvements, it far exceeds education in its effects on parish involvement. And it is far more important in understanding women's parish participation than men's.

There appears to be a renewed gift of the Spirit operating in Catholic circles nowadays. Vatican II encouraged greater devotion to the Holy Scriptures, and much ceremony attends the public reading of the lessons from The Book. Furthermore, the first two lessons are typically read by the *laity*, not the clergy. But Vatican II also encouraged growth in the *individual's* understanding of the Christian faith. Compared with historians' estimates of the past, there appears to be an increase in private devotions involving Bible reading. Our data show that while one-third of the sample never read the Bible privately, nearly one-fourth are fairly regular readers (several times a month up to daily).

We have much data on Catholic devotional practices. The fascinating conclusion is that no other private or public devotional practice does a better job of predicting parish involvement than does the frequency of Bible reading. Recall earlier in our discussion of sect-type religious culture, that social theorists drew a link between biblical devotional styles, civic participation, and civic responsibility. We can certainly draw that link for *parish* participation among Catholics, and a bit later we will show some of its relationship to political values. We cannot say that Bible reading *causes* involvement; perhaps involvement causes Bible reading. What we can say is that the two are part of the same complex and that they have positive effects on each other. In a church defined as "the *people* of God," Bible reading and parish involvement are hard to separate.

This linkage can be seen especially when we examine our parish-connected samples regionally. According to most of the measures used in previous issues of the *Report* series, Catholic parishes in the Northeast have been slower to adapt to the reforms advocated by Vatican II than parishes elsewhere in the country. It is precisely in the Northeast where frequent Bible reading is the strongest predictor of parish participation. Thus, where other forms of encouragement for lay growth and responsibility are limited, it appears that Bible reading is extraordinarily strongly related to participation in parish programs and ministries. In theological terms, the power of both components of the equation—*Word* and Sacraments—can be seen.

Life-Cycle and Social Status

Some other predictors are important either in parish life or civic life. Stage in the life-cycle is not far behind education in predicting the parish participation of both men and women. As people get married, have children, and the children grow into their teens and leave the nest, parish participation increases. But civic participation is not geared so closely to stages in the life-cycle.

Civic participation, however, is quite responsive to social status as measured by a family's income level. The higher the income, the greater the participation.

Income level is more important for women than for men, and it is somewhat important for women in their church participation as well. We suspect that these findings index the amount of available time that women have. Where family income is higher, often women have more discretionary time to devote to both civic life and church life. (The absence of discretionary time also helps to explain why Catholic women were sparse in the great reform movements of the 1840s to the 1920s.)

None of the other factors matter a great deal in predicting parish involvements or civic involvements.

Catholics' civic involvements are more responsive than parish involvements to the class basis of American society. Additional analyses must be completed before we can say whether civic skills learned in the more "class-blind" parish situation help to overcome the class basis of American civic life. At this point we know that some involvements and skills carry from church to society, but we also have good hints about the cultural and economic factors that limit the transfer of skills.

SOCIAL BACKGROUNDS, RELIGIOUS VALUES, AND POLITICAL VALUES

Much has been written by social scientists contrasting the political values of different religious bodies. For the most part Catholics are more Democratic, more liberal on welfare issues, more tolerant on intergroup relations, and less hawkish on national defense than are members of other Christian bodies, but are less so than Jews or those with no religious identity.[26] An increase in Republican identity and political conservatism of Catholics as a result of their enormous upward social mobility has not materialized to the degree most theorists would have expected, although there is some movement along both dimensions.[27]

Not all Catholics agree, of course, in their political values. Our data are useful for clarifying two questions. First, are parish-connected Catholics different in political values from all self-identified Catholics in national polls? Second, what factors influence Catholics in forming their political values? We look at each in turn.

Party Affiliation and Issue Positions

Table 2 offers a comparison of the party identifications of Catholics in our parish sample and self-identified Catholics in general population surveys of the National Opinion Research Center. Because of the Notre Dame group's decision to

Table 2. Party Affiliation of Non-Hispanic Catholics, Comparison between Parish-Connected Sample and General Population Samples*

Category	Notre Dame's Parish Sample '83–'84	NORC's Gen. Pop. Samples '82–'84
No Preference**	21%	1%
Independent	12	35
Republican	19	18
Democrat	48	46
	100%	100%
	(2667)	(1213)

* For purposes of comparison, Hispanic Catholics are excluded from this table.
** Not asked on NORC studies; appears only as a residual category.

limit this initial study to non-Hispanic surnamed parishioners, we have also excluded self-identified Hispanics from the NORC/GSS data reported in this table. (In its phrasing of the question, NORC does not separate "no preference" from "Independents.")

The Notre Dame Study, a sample of "churched" Catholics who are slightly older, and the NORC/GSS studies, samples including both "churched" and "unchurched" Catholics who are slightly younger, look rather similar. Jim Castelli, comparing the Notre Dame data with Gallup data for the same period, finds that 50 percent of all self-identified Catholics call themselves Democrats, 19 percent Republicans, and 33 percent Independents.[28] Thus, on the dimension of party identification, parish-connected Catholics are not notably different from self-identified Catholics.

Nor are there many major differences in their political viewpoints. Castelli has also compared the Notre Dame sample with the Gallup data along a variety of issues.[29] The combination of churched and unchurched Catholics in the Gallup data are notably more likely to permit abortion in all or most circumstances than are the churched Catholics in the Notre Dame sample (22% to 6%). The majority of both (57% and 69%) express support for abortion only in "extreme circumstances" such as rape, incest, or threat to the life of the mother. Finally, 19 percent of the former and 26 percent of the latter express support for the official church position which bans all abortions. On the Equal Rights Amendment, Castelli finds that 69 percent of each sample expresses support.

Churched Catholics are more supportive than the combined population of churched and unchurched Catholics on two issues identified as part of the "seamless garment" of human life: a bilateral nuclear freeze and opposition to capital punishment. According to Castelli, 92 percent of the Notre Dame sample supports the bilateral freeze as opposed to 70 to 84 percent of the Catholics in Gallup's samples of the same period. Further, about one-third of the Notre Dame sample opposes capital punishment but only one-sixth of Gallup's Catholics oppose it. Both are issue areas where the American bishops have offered public teaching and, as might be expected, the churched Catholics' position is closer to that of the teaching. Greeley has documented a remarkable movement in the polls toward the nuclear freeze position, once the bishops' statement worked its way into the public sphere.[30] About three-quarters of both samples favor gun control through registration of firearms.

The responses of the Catholic parishioners in our Notre Dame Study to a variety of public issues are shown in Table 3. Generally only 3–5 percent of the respondents offered no opinion and are excluded from the table.

Many political scientists have noted the difficulty of characterizing people as "liberal" or "conservative" by their issue positions.[31] A person may be liberal on one matter but conservative on another matter which seems to the experts to be related to the first. And so it is with Catholic parishioners. Large majorities support gun control, ERA, and the bilateral nuclear freeze. But substantial majorities support the death penalty, boycotts of TV sponsors of morally objectionable shows, prayer in public schools, and equal time for teaching of creationism; similarly, they oppose allowing homosexuals to teach in public schools, school busing for racial integration, and a unilateral nuclear freeze. There is overwhelming support for tuition tax credits and about a fifty-fifty split on defense spending.

One of the reasons for both the consistencies and inconsistencies is that people have little information about public issues and are simply responding to "catchwords." Thus, the raw figures presented in tables such as Table 3 have to be taken with a grain of salt. Nevertheless, slogans are the stuff of the political agenda and few people understand in depth any public issue.

What factors help to explain differences in political orientations among Catholic parishioners? In dealing with this question, it is appropriate to recall the findings of Greeley, Wald, and Castelli: on most public issues Catholics are slightly more liberal than others who have Christian church affiliations. But what seems to make some more liberal or more conservative? In a series of scholarly papers and journal articles, we have been untangling these questions through complex models. Here we will summarize the findings.[32]

Table 3. Parishioners' Opinions on Selected Public Issues (N=2667)

Issue	Strongly Favor	Favor	Oppose	Strongly Oppose
Registration of all firearms	42%	32%	15%	11%
Death penalty for persons convicted of murder	22	43	27	7
The Equal Rights Amendment (ERA)	21	48	22	9
Requiring prayer in public schools	23	46	26	5
Requiring public schools to give equal time for the teaching of creation theory and evolution theory about man's origins	16	51	26	7
Allowing homosexuals to teach in public schools	3	32	40	25
Busing to achieve racial integration in public schools	4	22	44	30
Increased spending for national defense	8	41	36	15
Boycotting or not buying the products of those companies who sponsor television shows in which there is morally objectionable content	22	50	23	6
Urging our own government to "freeze" the development of nuclear weapons regardless of what the Soviet Union does	11	24	44	21
Urging both the United States and the Soviet Union to "freeze" the development of nuclear weapons	53	39	5	3
The government should let parents deduct some of the costs of sending their children to parochial schools	38	45	12	5

Social scientists have traced differences in political orientations to a variety of factors such as social class, degree of ethnic assimilation, degree of communalism (i.e., exclusive involvement with people of one's own kind), differences in political generations or age cohorts, differences in regional political cultures (e.g., tolerance of public corruption is different between Wisconsin and Louisiana, and attitudes toward governmental spending are different between Iowa and

New Hampshire), and gender roles. Different groups have different histories along these dimensions. The same is thought to be true *among* Catholics. Therefore, Leege and Welch tested the impact of these factors on parishioners' party identification, political ideology, and issue positions. The models isolate the *unique* impact of each factor.

Social Structure and Party Identification

Leege and Welch have found that differences in party identification among Catholic parishioners are primarily the result of ethnic assimilation, income, and political generation. Catholics from the earlier, more assimilated, and higher income ethnic groups (such as English, Scandinavian, German, and Irish) are somewhat more likely to be Republican than Catholics in later, somewhat lower income, or less assimilated Catholic groups (such as Poles, Upper New England French, Hispanics, or Blacks). Furthermore, younger Catholics are far less likely to have a party affiliation at all than are older Catholics.

Leege and Welch contend that party affiliation is primarily responsive to social structural features and less responsive to deeper religious beliefs and social values. But that creates conflict with the other political orientations of Catholics, because political ideology and issue positions are sometimes more sensitive to religious beliefs and social values than to social structure.

Religious Individualism and Communitarianism

One of the strongest predictors of Catholic parishioners' sense of whether they are political liberals or conservatives is our measure of religious individualism and communitarianism. This may come as a surprise to those who think political ideology is solely a function of one's income, social class, or party affiliation. In fact, it is a rather important finding of the entire Notre Dame Study and especially germane to the arguments of social theorists such as Tocqueville, Bellah, or Berger. *How* a person is religious does matter politically.

To capture the degree of religious individualism or communitarianism, we asked respondents to select from a list or write in their own words: (1) what the fundamental problem of human existence is, (2) how religion responds to that problem, and (3) what the outcome of that solution is. They then drew lines connecting the responses from each of these questions so that a problem-process-outcome sequence was mapped. Those for whom the sequence clearly used *me*, *my* problems, *my* salvation as the frame of reference were classified as *religious individualists*. Those for whom *relationships, inter-group* conflict, and *community* concerns were clearly the frame of reference were classified as *religious communitarians*. Those who mixed elements of both in their sequences were classified as *integrated*.[33] Our current work with these measures classifies 38 percent of the parishioners as individualists, 29 percent as integrated, 18 percent as communitarian, and 15 percent as anomalous, not fitting any pattern.

The utility of this measure of "deep" personal religious orientation can be seen especially in the relationship to political ideology but also to some social issue positions. The more a Catholic is religiously individualistic, the more he or she is likely to be a social issue conservative; the more a Catholic is religiously communitarian, the more he or she is likely to be a social issue liberal. There are also consistent patterns on women's rights, male-female family roles, the threat of secular humanism, and sexuality—with the religious individualists taking more conservative (traditional) positions and the religious communitarians taking more liberal (change-oriented) positions. Interestingly, the religious individualists are more likely than the communitarians to claim that their religious values will influence their voting behavior. This measure of "deep" religious orientation does not predict other public policy positions as well, however, as do some other factors in the backgrounds of Catholic parishioners.

Income, Generations, and Region

A Catholic's income level and social class are also strong predictors of political ideology and positions on defense and disarmament issues: the higher the income, the more conservative, the more supportive of defense spending, and the more opposed to disarmament.

To no one's surprise, there are very large conflicts among Catholic political generations or age cohorts. These show especially on perceptions of the threats of communism and secular humanism, changing family roles, sexuality, and women's rights and gay rights. The younger generations are more liberal; their elders, more conservative.

Regional differences, however, are the best predictors of all for Catholics' viewpoints on racial matters, law-and-order issues, school-related issues, and the defense-disarmament complex. While there are consistent issue differences by degree of assimilation and by gender, these are not so strong when the other factors are considered.

To summarize, then, social structure (especially ethnic assimilation, social class, and political generation) is important in understanding differences in the party identification of Catholics, but their political ideology and issue positions are responsive to a mixture of these factors as well as others.

Imagery of God and Devotional Style

Differences in Catholics' political orientations can be traced to several other "deeper" measures of *how* they are religious. Welch and Leege have formulated measures of *imagery of God, devotional style,* and *closeness to God,* in addition to religious *individualism-communitarianism*. The first two are especially useful. The former is a measure of what Catholics think about God while the latter is a measure of what Catholics *do* in their religious practices.

Imagery of God was developed by presenting the respondents with a list of twenty-seven adjectives or descriptive phrases and asking how accurately each characterizes their picture of God. Responses were factor analyzed to identify which images are coherent with other images. Although our current work isolates four sets of images (companion, father, judge, savior), one in particular predicts political orientations well: images of God as *judgelike*. Those who think of God primarily as strict and judgmental, rather than in other ways, are considerably more likely to be self-classified as political conservatives and to take consistently conservative positions across the whole range of public policies and social issues. They also are more likely than others to feel that their religious values affect their voting behavior.

It appears as though those Catholics who picture God primarily as a judge would like to order the world in a predictable way through tradition and a strong, status quo–oriented government. In still another question, we asked respondents whether the best way to deal with injustice and social problems was to change the social and political structures or to change the hearts of people. Those who imagined God as a judge were far more likely to choose the latter.

Devotional style was constructed by factor analyzing a list of twenty-one items that indicated how frequently respondents participated in a wide variety of public devotional rituals and private devotional practices. This time, five coherent patterns emerged and one was especially useful in predicting differences in Catholics' political orientations. This factor we called *evangelical-style devotionalism*. It consists of frequent Bible reading alone or with friends, sharing religious beliefs, private prayer, and prayer in small groups of family and friends. It is much less likely to include more traditional devotional practices such as novenas, public rosary, benediction, stations of the cross, fasting, or confession.

Those Catholics who score high on evangelical-style devotionalism are much more likely to feel that their religious values affect their voting behavior. Their issue positions are an interesting composite. They are consistent on many of the "seamless garment" issues, opposing abortion and capital punishment and calling for reduced defense spending and the bilateral freeze. They support, as expected, school prayer. They oppose ERA and affirm the male breadwinner role, but are surprisingly less judgmental about premarital sexual behavior. Just as we noted earlier the linkage between Bible-reading devotionalism and parish participation, so we note the distinctiveness of this type in their political orientations. Ideologically they are neither predictably liberal nor conservative; in fact, on the self-classification measure, they do not choose one over the other. But the fact that this group consciously relates religious values to voting, even more so than those consistent political conservatives who view God as judgelike, suggests not only an important measure of religiosity but also perhaps a new political sector among the Catholic population.

No other pattern of devotional style was found effective in predicting political orientations. The measures of closeness to God, captured horizontally through a social connection or vertically through a spiritual connection, were interesting theoretically but did not differentiate political orientations well.

To summarize again, there are political differences among Catholics that are based not only on their social backgrounds but especially on how they conceive of their faith. Images of God, devotional styles, and foundational beliefs all have a differential impact on political values. And since these elements of both social background and religiosity vary among Catholics, there are major political differences. Religious differences survive in importance even when differences in social backgrounds have been considered. While there is one Catholic faith, there are many religious and political manifestations of it in America. Then how can the pope, American bishops, and priests hope to offer social teachings that will apply the church's moral values to contemporary issues? To that matter we now turn.

Should Church Leaders Speak Out on Issues?

When contrasted with countries like, for example, Poland or the Philippines, American Catholics become quite edgy about "directions" from bishops or priests on "political" matters. Perhaps it betrays their long period as an underdog, when others regarded Catholic clergy as "un-American" if they made pronouncements on social issues or encouraged support for a candidate. Perhaps it reflects a pervasive American cultural value of skepticism or even distrust toward anyone in authority. Americans give and withdraw popular consent quickly from our administrations—witness the roller coasters of the Johnson, Nixon, and Reagan presidencies. Perhaps it results from the self-confidence of an educated, economically achieving, politically secure Catholic population. Whatever its source, polls continually document that American Catholics hold the "political" pronouncements of their leaders at arms' length. Reporting on the Gallup data, Castelli notes that 55 percent of Catholics reject the proposition that bishops should speak out on "political issues like the war and the economy."[34]

Yet when the question is phrased in such a way that the word *political* is not so apparent, American Catholics are more likely to accept guidance from church leaders on "moral issues in the political realm." It is, after all, a church with a century of social encyclicals, a church with a social philosophy that finds *virtue* in public service, and a church with nearly two millennia of dealings with the state.

We phrased our question in such a way that it omitted the word *politics*. It spoke not of hypotheticals, but of a reality, that church leaders do "offer guidance and teaching on current matters in a number of different ways." We then listed several issue areas and asked the respondent to check "which level of authority, if any, ought to speak on that matter," or "whether this is a moral judgment that should be made only by the individual Catholic." Respondents were free to check several levels of church leadership (e.g., pope, bishops, parish priests) as well as "individual conscience" simultaneously. As Table 4 indicates, some of them did so.

Levels of Church Voice on Seven Issues

Table 4 shows the proportion of respondents (1) who limited their checkmarks to some level(s) of the hierarchy (Column 1), (2) who checked some level(s) of the hierarchy but also checked individual moral judgement (Column 2), or (3) who felt it was a matter for individual conscience alone with no moral guidance from church leaders (Column 3). The final column shows which level of authority—pope, bishops, priests, individual Catholic—received the most mentions on each issue. The table presents the issues in order, from the most emphasis on church leaders to the most emphasis on individual judgment.

Table 4. Church Voices on Public Issues: Who Should Speak, in the Viewpoints of American Parishioners

Issue	Some Levels of the Hierarchy Should Speak	Combination of Hierarchy Speaking and Individual Deciding	A Matter of Individual Conscience Alone	Primary Level of Church That Should Speak
Aid to poor countries	83%	7%	10%	Pope (70%)
Eliminating poverty from this country	83	8	9	Bishops (67)
Action for world disarmament	75	9	16	Pope (74)
Racial integration	64	10	26	Bishops (46) Priests (45)
Sex and violence on TV	61	11	27	Priests (52)
Equal opportunities for advancement regardless of workers' sex	56	7	38	Individ (43) Priests (38) Bishops (38)
Birth control	45	8	47	Individ (54)

Some readers may be puzzled in contrasting our findings with those of earlier Gallup polls or some questions on the recent *National Catholic Reporter*-Gallup poll, where seemingly very little role was accorded church leaders.[35] In part, that is because of sample differences: Gallup addresses self-identified Catholics, both churched and unchurched, while the Notre Dame Study focuses on active parishioners. More importantly, the differences result from question wording. In American culture, language that includes "politics" or asks "who should have the final say"—"church leaders" or "individuals"—and defines "individuals" to mean "persons taking church leaders into account and then deciding for themselves" will generate responses favorable to "individuals." Americans do not like to give up their ultimate ("final") moral autonomy, although they might allow church teachings some role. In contrast, our wording implies that since such teaching is offered, it may be appropriate for church leaders to do so. In Gallup's question wording, it is easy for the Catholic to choose the individual, while still respecting church teachings. In our wording, it would take a much stronger revulsion toward the role of the church leaders as social teachers to select "individual moral judgment." Thus we might consider the NCR-Gallup findings as tracing the lower boundary on church leaders' moral authority, whereas our findings might set the upper boundary.

The data sustain a strong generalization with several ramifications: Catholic parishioners are generally not averse to the pope, bishops, or their priests offering moral guidance on public issues. Nevertheless, on some issues fairly large proportions of parishioners feel that church leaders should not speak out. Parishioners are most willing to accord a role to church leaders on complex matters of world poverty and peace, and the spokesman is primarily the pope. When poverty in the United States is at issue, two-thirds of the parishioners view it as proper for bishops to speak out. When the issue gets closer to something the individual parishioner perceives is within grasp, he or she is more likely to label it a matter of individual conscience. Birth control is the most obvious of these; the church's leadership is accorded far less authority to guide its people here than on other issues. Women's rights, sex and violence on TV, and racial integration, in that order, are the issues on this list next most likely to be perceived as matters for individual conscience alone. Even then, parishioners grant that the more local leaders (e.g., priests or bishops) might have some moral authority on such issues.

Patterns of Differences in Parishioners' Views

Do parishioners take a consistent position about the moral authority of church leaders, or do they change their position depending on the issue? For example, would a person who rejects the authority of *Humanae Vitae* over birth control also reject papal teaching on disarmament? And would a person who accepts papal authority over birth control also accept church leaders' pronouncements on world hunger? We suspected that the coalitions would change from issue to issue. Therefore, we first designed cluster analyses that found whether any patterns from the issues in Table 4 showed coherence, making sense both statistically and substantively; then we used *discriminant function analysis* to identify what kinds of Catholics were found in each of the patterns.

Cluster analysis is a complex trial-and-error procedure, but the best fit of data and substantive interpretability yielded four patterns. We employed twenty-two variables as predictors, including all of the social background, political party and ideology, and religious practice variables used to explain political orientations in the previous section. To these we added the respondent's *own* issue position on the topic under consideration. The four patterns and the kinds of Catholics who fit each pattern are as follows:

1. *Church leaders may speak out on all the issues.* Of the parishioners, 36 percent approximate this pattern. Besides their general willingness to accept the church leaders' teaching on birth control, the most distinctive things about these parishioners is that they are older, less educated, and quite likely to be opposed to ERA. They tend to be moderately conservative politically, but their issue positions are not consistently conservative. They feel religious organizations should lobby on policy questions and that their religious values affect their voting behavior.

2. *Church leaders may speak on all issues except birth control, where the individual alone must make moral judgments.* This group includes 34 percent of the parishioners. It is composed especially of better educated, younger parishioners who are politically moderate to liberal, who support the freeze and ERA, oppose defense spending, are willing to accept busing for desegregation, who feel their religious values affect their voting behavior, and are willing to have church leaders lobby on issues. But they are both strongly opposed to the church leadership's position on birth control and feel that church leaders have no authority to offer it.

3. *Church leaders should not speak out on issues, although it is somewhat more legitimate to do so on international poverty issues than on other matters.* This pattern is approximated by 20 percent of the parishioners. These Catholics are conservative ideologically and consistently conservative on their issue positions, ranging from peace through social justice and racial discrimination, but curiously they support ERA. They do not feel their religious values affect their voting behavior, and they are opposed to church leaders' lobbying. They are slightly younger, are a bit better educated and better off financially, and are strongly opposed to the church leadership's position on birth control.

4. *Church leaders should speak out on matters of sexual morality, but the individual conscience is the sole basis for judgment on matters of justice and peace.* This small group, only 2 percent of the parishioners, is older, very conservative, likely to be men from less assimilated ethnic groups, and strongly opposed to church leaders' lobbying.

(An additional 8 percent of the parishioners could not be classified into any of the four patterns that were reasonably well predicted by these political, social, and religious characteristics.)

Surprisingly absent or infrequent from the characteristics that predict well these patterns toward church teaching authority are gender, political party identification, frequency and kinds of religious practices, and proportion of education that was completed in Catholic schools. More important are the amount of education completed, age cohort, political ideology, and specific issue positions.

These data suggest, then, that when church leaders exercise their teaching authority on political or social questions, they will often receive a polite reception from American Catholic parishioners. Nevertheless, the closer the teaching gets to personal morality, the less authority the people accord to it. The teaching will have to contend with the parishioners' existing political predispositions. Except for perhaps a quarter of the parishioners who routinely consider church teaching highly suspect, the pronouncements of church leaders may help shape the dialogue along with other political forces. Sometimes, it seems, church leaders will cross a threshold, where the statement is perceived as blatantly "political" or is thinly disguised so as to make only one choice possible. As the Gallup data attest, American Catholics do not take well to such efforts.

In the American context, the moral authority of the Catholic Church's leaders is held in delicate balance by parishioners who are educated, mobile, pragmatic, and free. There is some evidence that parish participation and civic responsibility reinforce each other among Catholics. There is further evidence of considerable variability in political views. These can be traced not alone to different social backgrounds but also to different ways of thinking about God, of ways in which they feel religion responds to fundamental human problems, and of their preferred patterns for communicating or learning about religious values.

If historical accounts are credible, major changes in the authority of the church over temporal affairs have occurred. To be sure, over two-thirds of the parishioners in our sample feel it is appropriate for religious organizations to try to influence legislation, and slightly under one half of them feel that their voting is guided in large part by their religious values. Furthermore, parishioners often expect statements from church leaders as part of their moral calculus. But it is that—a calculus, a mix of elements. In the 1980s, "deliverable" would clearly be the wrong word to describe American Catholic parishioners, pulpits, and politics.

What American experience, the GI Bill and the election of JFK hath wrought, Vatican II doth seek to sanctify. Therein lies an opportunity and a challenge for the Catholic church in American culture.

NOTES

Reprinted from *The Review of Politics* 50, no. 4 (Autumn 1988): 704–36.

An earlier version of this paper by the same title appeared as Report 11 in the *Notre Dame Study of Catholic Parish Life Report Series* (Notre Dame, October 1987). The author is indebted to his collaborator, Prof. Michael R. Welch, and four graduate students, Thomas Trozzolo, Edwin Hernandez, William Demars, and Nancy Powers, for computing assistance or ideas incorporated into the original draft report. The report also received critical suggestions from Prof. Mary Hanna of Whitman College, Prof. Dean Hoge of Catholic University, and collaborator Msgr. Joseph Gremillion. Finally, we acknowledge use of General Social Survey data for one of our tables and several comparisons. The author alone is responsible for positions taken in this paper and for interpretations of data.

1. See for example, Richard Hofstadter, *The Age of Reform* (New York: Alfred A. Knopf, 1955); Edward C. Banfield and James Q. Wilson, *City Politics* (Cambridge, MA: Harvard University Press, 1963); W. L. Riordan, *Plunkitt of Tammany Hall* (New York: McClure, Phillips, 1905); Mike Royko, *Boss: Richard J. Daley of Chicago* (New York: Signet, 1971); Milton Rakove, *Don't Make No Waves, Don't Back No Losers* (Bloomington: Indiana University Press, 1975).

2. A. James Reichley offers a useful summary of such sources in *Religion in America Public Life* (Washington, DC: Brookings Institution, 1985), 182–88. Similar arguments are found from Walt Whitman to the columns of Muckraker journalists during the Progressive Era. For representative quotations see Robert C. Brooks, *Political Parties and Electoral Problems* (New York: Harper and Brothers, 1933).

3. Harold J. Abramson, *Ethnic Diversity in Religious America* (New York: Wiley, 1973), especially 125–46; Philip E. Hammond and Benton Johnson, eds., *America Mosaic: Social Patterns of Religion in America* (New York: Random House, 1970); Mary Hanna, *Catholics and American Politics* (Cambridge, MA: Harvard University Press, 1979); Kenneth D. Wald, *Religion and Politics in the United States* (New York: St. Martin's, 1987), especially 223; Jay P. Dolan, *The American Catholic Experience* (Garden City, NY: Doubleday, 1985).

4. Robert N. Bellah et al., *Habits of the Heart: Individualism and Commitment in American Life* (Berkeley: University of California Press, 1985), especially 22–26, 152–65. Although he has differences with the content of recent bishops' statements, Richard John Neuhaus can also be included in this camp; see Neuhaus, *The Naked Public Square* (Grand Rapids: Eerdmans, 1984) and *The Catholic Moment* (San Francisco: Harper & Row, 1987).

5. Andrew M. Greeley, *The American Catholic: A Social Portrait* (New York: Basic Books, 1977), 38.

6. Dolan, *American Catholic Experience*, 127–57.

7. A particularly engaging case history of the religious, social, and political life of German Catholics in Dubois County, Indiana, is offered in Frank J. Munger, "Two-Party Politics in the State of Indiana" (Ph.D. diss., Harvard University, 1955).

8. Dolan has a particularly useful summary of the "republican period" of the Church and of trusteeism, *American Catholic Experience*, 101–24.

9. Greeley, *American Catholic*, 39–47.

10. The initial counter-pastoral was *Toward the Future: Catholic Social Thought and the U.S. Economy: A Lay Letter* (Washington, DC: Lay Commission on Catholic Social Teaching and the U.S. Economy, November 1984); the final version following the promulgation of the bishops' pastoral was William E. Simon and Michael Novak, *Liberty and Justice for All: Report on the Final Draft (June 1986) of the U.S. Catholic Bishops' Pastoral Letter "Economic Justice for All"* (Washington, DC: Lay Commission on Catholic Social Teaching and the U.S. Economy, December 1986).

11. George Gallup, Jr., and Jim Castelli, *The American Catholic People: Their Beliefs, Practices, and Values* (Garden City, NY: Doubleday, 1987), especially 188–91.

12. Alexis de Tocqueville, *Democracy in America*, two volumes (Mayer edition) (Garden City, NY: Doubleday, 1969); see especially vol. 1, chap. 17; vol. 2, bk. 1, chaps. 5 and 6; bk. 2, chaps. 2, 4, 5, 7–9; bk. 3, chap. 18.

13. Ernst Troeltsch, *The Social Teachings of the Christian Churches* (London: George Allen, 1931), translated by Olive Wyon from original ed. of 1911, especially 993–1002; Max Weber, writing in 1906, as translated in H. H. Gerth and C. Wright Mills, eds., *From Max Weber, Essays in Sociology* (New York: Oxford University Press), chaps. 12, 13.

14. Peter Berger and Richard John Neuhaus, *To Empower People* (Washington, DC: American Enterprise Institute, 1977).

15. Wald, *Religion and Politics*, 29–32.

16. See, for example, M. Hausknecht, *The Joiners* (New York: Bedminster, 1962).

17. Wald, *Religion and Politics*.

18. Illustrative of this genre of research is Charles Y. Glock and Rodney Stark, *Christian Beliefs and Anti-Semitism* (New York: Harper and Row, 1966).

19. Milton Rokeach, "The Paul H. Douglass Lectures for 1969: Part I, Value Systems in Religion," and "Part II, Religious Values and Social Compassion," *Review of Religious Research* 11, no. 1 (Autumn 1969): 3–23 and 24–39, respectively.

20. Dean R. Hoge and Ernesto de Zulueta, "Salience as a Condition for Various Social Consequences of Religious Commitment," *Journal for the Scientific Study of Religion* 24 (1985): 21–37.

21. David C. Leege, Michael R. Welch, and Thomas A. Trozzolo, "Religiosity, Church Social Teaching, and Sociopolitical Attitudes," *Review of Religious Research* 28 (1986): 118–28.

22. David A. Roozen, William McKinney, and Jackson W. Carroll, *Varieties of Religious Presence: Mission in Public Life* (New York: Pilgrim Press, 1984).

23. Drawn from a methodological paper first presented to the American Political Science Association in 1985 and later expanded, the following source presents our most complete critique of the study design: David C. Leege and Michael R. Welch, "Catholics in Context: Theoretical and Methodological Issues in Studying American Catholic Parishioners," *Review of Religious Research* 31 (forthcoming). More succinct assessments are also found in Reports 1 and 4 of the *Report* series.). [The article "Catholics in Context" appeared in vol. 31, no. 2 (December 1989). Ed.]

24. See, for example, Reports #3 and #9, where leadership roles are analyzed at length.

25. Eleanor Flexner, *Century of Struggle: The Woman's Rights Movement in the United States*, rev. ed. (Cambridge, MA: Harvard University Press, 1975), 309.

26. See, for example, Greeley, *American Catholic*; Gallup and Castelli, *American Catholic People*; Wald, *Religion and Politics*.

27. See, for example, James M. Penning, "Changing Partisanship and Issue Stands among American Catholics," *Sociological Analysis* 47 (1986): 29–49.

28. Jim Castelli, "A Tale of Two Cultures," *Notre Dame Magazine* 15 (1987): 33–34.

29. Ibid.

30. Andrew M. Greeley, *American Catholics Since the Council: An Unauthorized Report* (Chicago: Thomas More Press, 1985), 42ff. The dramatic change was first chronicled by Greeley in an article in the *National Catholic Reporter*.

31. The most comprehensive study is by Pamela Johnston Conover and Stanley Feldman, "The Origins and Meaning of Liberal/Conservative Self-Identifications," *American Journal of Political Science* 25 (1981): 617–45.

32. Representative of the papers and articles are David C. Leege, "Toward a Mental Measure of Religiosity in Research on Religion and Politics," in *Religion and American Political Behavior*, ed. Ted G. Jelen (New York: Praeger, forthcoming, 1989); David C. Leege and Michael R. Welch, "Religious Roots of Political Orientations: Variations among American Catholic Parishioners," *Journal of Politics* 51 (February 1989, forthcoming); Michael R. Welch and David C. Leege, "Religious Predictors of Catholic Parishioners' Sociopolitical Attitudes: Devotional Style, Closeness to God, Imagery, and Agentic/Communal Religious Identity," *Journal for the Scientific Study of Religion* 27 (December 1988): 536–52.

33. This measure is inspired by the approach to measurement of religiosity reported in Peter L. Benson and Dorothy L. Williams, *Religion on Capitol Hill* (San Francisco: Harper & Row, 1982).

34. Castelli, "Tale of Two Cultures."

35. Reported and analyzed in a special section of the *National Catholic Reporter*, 11 September 1987.

CHAPTER 10

Michael Novak and Yves R. Simon on the Common Good and Capitalism

THOMAS R. ROURKE

Thomas R. Rourke is professor of political science at Clarion University of Pennsylvania. He is author of The Social and Political Thought of Benedict XVI *and* A Conscience as Large as the World: Yves R. Simon versus the Catholic Neoconservatives, *and co-author of* A Theory of Personalism.

The contradiction between the Catholic and liberal approaches to the organization of society has traditionally been perceived by both sides as fundamental. Catholic thought, grounded in Saint Thomas and expressed in numerous encyclicals, defined itself in opposition to liberalism on the grounds that the latter rejected the Catholic concept of the common good in favor of a relatively unrestricted pursuit of individual goods. Nevertheless, in recent years, Michael Novak has painstakingly attempted to bridge the gap between the Catholic and liberal traditions, arguing that the Catholic tradition will best be extended by incorporating heretofore unrecognized liberal insights into both the theory and the practice of the common good. By way of contrast, the late Yves R. Simon, in his attempt to articulate the meaning of the common good in the latter half of the twentieth century, rejected constitutive features of liberalism. Despite the impressive achievements of modern liberal societies, Simon continued to see moral problems in the theory and practice of liberalism that liberal democracy had failed to address adequately.

As Novak's influence grows, and as debates over liberalism within the Catholic tradition continue to rage, it is timely to consider Novak's "new concept" of the common good in light of Simon as a distinguished expositor of the traditional concept. Both writers are within the Catholic tradition; both address the common good extensively; both are familiar with the theory and practice of the modern liberal society. The clear contrasts between the two will hopefully shed some light on contemporary debates over both Novak's attempts to redefine the Catholic tradition and, more broadly, the relationship between liberalism and the Thomist tradition.

Novak on the Common Good

Novak's central argument is twofold: first, liberalism has an insufficiently recognized concept of the common good; second, the Catholic common good tradition can and must benefit from incorporating the insights of the liberal tradition. What is necessary is to "work out the liberal conception of the common good in a Catholic context."[1] Although Novak believes that the older Catholic concept is in need of revision, he credits the tradition for revealing some fundamental truths. From Aristotle, we learned to distinguish the individual good from the common good, and to perceive the moral primacy of the latter.[2] Second, the biblical tradition taught us to emphasize the role of the will in the realization of the human good.[3] The unruly human will so often chooses actions that reason has judged to be wrong that we do not know the extent to which people will be willing to act on behalf of the common good, even when they know in what such a good consists. Moreover, the propensity to sin ensures that the common good is never to be realized fully in this world. Third, Novak contends that Aquinas exercised a singular influence through his incorporation of the dignity of the person into the common good tradition.[4] This is crucial to the revival of the theory of the common good in the contemporary world because such theory must be open to new insights by reflective persons, fully historical, and appropriate to persons fundamentally free.

Despite the merits of the common good tradition, Novak argues that it suffered some serious flaws later rectified by the liberal tradition. The greatest contributions of the latter are in the field of practical wisdom. The classical liberals had "insight," that is, the capacity to go beyond general rules of action based on abstract and universal concepts to the practical ability to identify which rules and concepts apply to particular situations and, most importantly, *how* to apply them. True, the importance of this virtue had been recognized by Aristotle.[5] However, it was left to the liberal tradition to discover the particular insights most conducive to achieving the common good. In the contemporary world, the realization of the common good depends upon grasping this interrelated series of insights into how societies function best. Such a grasp is best attained, not by the study of theory, but through practical experience. The lack of practical insight explains the failures of the common good tradition to achieve its noble intentions. For its shortcomings in this area, the common good tradition coexisted with a tribal mentality wherein creativity and initiative were stifled by authority. Moreover, insufficient attention was paid to the propensity of political authority to lord it over its subjects; little was done in practice to protect the common good against abuses by authority. The common good tradition awaited classical liberalism to develop its theory and better its practice.

Three features of the liberal American experiment are crucial to Novak's new concept of the common good: the distinction between the state and society, the need to restrict political authority, and the realization that the modern social order is ideally tripartite, consisting of economic, political, and moral-cultural systems.[6] According to the first of these principles, the people themselves are the primary agent of the common good. In what the common good will consist is determined by the consent of persons who have the capacity to reflect and to choose freely. Such people voluntarily form a variety of groupings, such as labor unions, trade, professional, cultural, and religious associations, all of which extend beyond mere individual concerns.[7] If the primary agent of the common good is a free people who form a multitude of associations, then political authority must be strictly limited so as not to supersede this primacy of the people. To define the state as the principal agent of the common good is an authoritarian notion incompatible with a society of free persons. Therefore, the liberal tradition found it prudent to limit the extension of the political system, to preserve a free economy of private owners and workers as well as an independent moral-cultural system wherein churches, universities, and the press would have the role of promoting and preserving culture and morals while also serving as a check on the activities of government.

Perhaps nothing is more crucial to the grasp of the new concept of the common good than the insight that its achievement takes place in societies fundamentally free and pluralistic. According to Novak, the free society is characterized by people who decide for themselves in what "the good life" consists. This autonomous pursuit of the good life is not limited to the pursuit of individual goods. Free persons are also entitled to pursue their own versions of the common good. Novak writes:

> The free persons of modern societies are expected to form their own judgments about the good, not only about their own personal and familial good but also about the common good. . . . [Therefore,] the common good of a modern society must respect the pluralism of free persons . . . [by leaving] space for the *personal definitions of the good cherished by free persons.*[8]

By respecting the freedom of the person, new thinking about the common good can shed the remnants of tribalism which beset the older tradition.[9] In static, simple societies, it is possible to speak of the common good as a particular, concrete state of affairs. If a tribe has no source of food, it makes sense that tribal leaders make the determination that the tribe move elsewhere for the good of all its members. The more complex society becomes, however, the more difficult it becomes to speak of the common good in definitive material terms. Modern societies are enormously complex, resulting in a genuine ignorance on the part of the citizen of all of the conditions attached to the lives of fellow citizens. In addition, even if all citizens agreed on the ends to be pursued, we can hardly predict the results of particular policy choices; unforeseen consequences always abound. Finally, agreement on the ends to be pursued in common is not a part of the conditions of life for free persons. Therefore, Novak concludes that "a veil of ignorance" surrounds any contemporary attempt to bring about the common good; no one can really claim to know the material content of such a good.

A crucial conclusion of the "veil of ignorance" which surrounds any attempt to conceptualize and to achieve the common good in the contemporary world is that political authority must not attempt to realize the material common good. Political authority cannot, first of all, genuinely claim to know in what such a good consists. Second, authority must acknowledge that people are rightfully originating sources of insight, free to pursue the good life as they determine it to be. It is inappropriate for authority to attempt to achieve the common good in ways that run roughshod over personal conscience. Third, as the liberal tradition has demonstrated, the social order is best conceived as three orders, not one. Therefore, political authority is not primarily responsible for bringing about the common good in the economic and moral-cultural spheres.

Novak expresses his new concept of the common good in traditional Thomistic language.[10] Following Yves R. Simon, Novak is aware of the distinction between the form and the matter of the common good. Unlike Simon, he speaks of a "formal concept" and a "material concept" of the common good, as though somehow form and matter do not coexist.[11] According to Novak, the formal concept points to the full development of the potentialities of every person and of the entire community as well. Thus, the formal concept stands as a never realized, transcendent standard, pointing to ever further stages of development. On the other hand, the material concept is always characterized by unrealized potentiality. Its existing condition is always directed to the next highest step on the ladder. The distinction is further clarified when we consider the responsibilities of the citizen with respect to each. The virtuous citizen will always will the common good formally. He will always desire an ever fuller development of the potentials of his fellow citizens and of the community at large. However, his attempts to contribute to the common good materially will always be limited by both the "veil of ignorance" and the necessary pluralism of the free society. He therefore does not intend the common good materially.

Novak's view of the relationship between the formal and material concepts of the common good is perhaps best illustrated in his treatment of the Thomistic themes of private property and common use, where Saint Thomas postulates that it is morally acceptable to possess goods as one's own, though the use of goods should be common. In the case of serious need, common use would have precedence over private ownership. Novak characterizes this doctrine as saying that private property is the means and common use is the end.[12] Common use would then be an economic component of the form of the common good; we desire it and aim toward it as a benchmark. Moreover, any attempt to bring it about is fraught with unresolvable difficulties resulting from the differences that arise with respect to the means by which to achieve it. Novak's solution is to suggest that the market system is the best means to promote the end of common use. Hence, he interprets the Thomistic doctrine to say that the end to be striven for (formal common good) in an economic system is common use; the means (material common good) is the free market.

The distancing of political authority from the realization of the common good materially considered largely determines Novak's approach to the economic system. Attempts made on the part of political authority to regulate economic results confront the inherent difficulty of the "veil of ignorance." Not even the

Nobel laureates can tell us with certainty how attempts to advance the material common good will actually turn out. At any given point in time, claims are made for such diverse policies as raising interest rates, lowering interest rates, raising taxes, lowering taxes, securing free trade agreements, and passing protectionist legislation. Second, and even more problematic, is the fact that demands for various components of the material common good conflict with one another.[13] Spending more money to repair our infrastructure may drive up inflation. Spending less money to lower inflation may cost people their jobs.

Whatever the difficulties of discerning the material common good, Novak is confident that history has demonstrated the perennial viability of certain approaches. First and foremost, he is convinced that private ownership must be the basis for any successful economy. As important as private property is, however, Novak notes that this institution long predated capitalism and is therefore not capitalism's distinguishing feature. In addition to the primacy of private property, Novak stresses the corresponding right of economic initiative.[14] Novak views this right as an important yet frequently neglected development in our thinking about rights. It is important to the common good because experience shows that individuals are far more apt than the state to know where their own economic good lies. Moreover, the right of economic initiative is the key to the creation of wealth that is so necessary for the common good.

Novak is well aware of the traditional criticism that capitalism, with its emphasis on private acquisition and individual initiative, encourages an ethos of competition as opposed to concern for the common good.[15] Nonetheless, he is convinced that the image of the autonomous individual seeking individual goods in isolation from others is a caricature that has all too often mistaken the absence of a centralized order for utter disorder. The truth of the matter, however, is that the absence of centralized economic planning reflects the real conditions under which any theory of the common good must operate in the modern world. Since no one can rightfully claim to know the best way to arrive at the material common good, and since no one knows in advance how all the components of the common good can be made to fit together, we allow individuals to choose freely. Although a "veil of ignorance" surrounds knowledge of the fullness of the common good, people have very adequate understandings of what their needs are and should therefore be allowed to pursue them as they see fit. The fundamental misconception of capitalism's critics is to assume that the result is some kind of Hobbesian world. In fact, in the absence of central planning, people voluntarily cooperate and organize to fulfill their needs. The marketplace, Novak insists, is a veritable miracle of order. In the absence of a centralizing orderer, rational human beings create their own spontaneous order.[16] The unprecedented levels of wealth produced in the brief history of capitalist development is the story of what an order based on voluntary cooperation can accomplish.

By realizing that the common good does not consist in common intentions and by abandoning the impossible task of willing the common good materially, we are better able to appreciate the common good not as some rigid, static conception, but as something which shares in the dynamism and growth of liberal societies by establishing a framework of laws to promote the benefits of cooperation. The common good demands the promotion of the habits, ideals and institutions which encourage this common pursuit. "In practice," Novak writes, *"the essence of the common good is to secure in social life the benefits of voluntary cooperation."*[17] When this is accomplished, we find that liberal, pluralist societies of free persons pursuing a variety of goods possess a material common good superior to the results brought about by the older common good thinking.

NOVAK AND SIMON ON THE COMMON GOOD: POINTS OF TENSION

When viewed in light of Yves Simon, Michael Novak's concept of the common good appears somewhat "thin." This is clearly seen in the distinction Simon makes between a partnership and a community. Partnerships are characterized by individuals who mutually pursue individual benefits in a relationship of voluntary cooperation. For example, a bank lending money to a business would constitute a partnership for Simon, but there would be no common good involved, as there would be in Novak's theory. Why? For Simon, an authentic common good does not exist whenever several people both know and desire the same object; in the case at hand, profit. The existence of a common good "implies, in addition to immanent acts relative to the same object, my knowing that the others know and desire the same object and want it to be effected by the action of our community."[18] The common good, therefore, is inherently incompatible with exclusion; it must be distributed among citizens.[19] Moreover, Simon believes that living in a society relative to a common good is normally the only means by which the person is freed from the anxiety of isolation.[20] Yet Novak's new concept of the common good does not adequately address the problems of exclusion and isolation from the common good so prevalent in modern liberal societies. His view of the common good as partnership in mutual self-interest overlooks the fact that partnerships inherently exclude those who are not party to them. Novak argues that the partnerships which pertain to the market economy are open to expansion and hence the inclusion of those who do not currently participate in the production and distribution of goods and services. Nonetheless, there is no inherent necessity for such an expansion. The new worker is not hired unless the manager(s) perceive that they stand to gain by employing him. Thus, Novak's new approach to the common good does not include the proposal of a sufficient cause to approximate the condition of full inclusion. Such a deficiency would prompt Simon to deny the presence of the common good.

Simon's argument against Novak would go deeper than the fact that partnerships do not necessarily expand. First, the common good of the civil society must be more than a series of partnerships. It requires communion of intention at two levels. First, at the level of civil society itself, or macro-level, it requires communion with respect to the common good formally considered.[21] Second, at the micro-level, the common good is enhanced by a proliferation of other communities wherein communion in intention would exist at the material level as well. Communion in intention is necessary to resolve the stickiest problems of liberal societies: genuine exclusion from economic, social, and cultural benefits of membership, and the heavy sense of isolation which afflicts so many. Simon writes:

> Communions in immanent actions make up the most profound part of social reality; . . . there alone the individual is freed from solitude and anxiety. Mere partnership, on the other hand, does not do anything to put an end to the solitude of the partners. They may be better off as a result of their contract, but their contract will not relieve their lonesomeness. It may be that in our time mere partnership plays too great a role in the life of men at work. . . . Members of a working group do not always understand very clearly what they are doing together and do not always desire ardently the effect of their common action.[22]

Novak bases much of his argument for a thinner concept of the common good on two propositions. First, the common good of the modern society is practically unknowable, that is, surrounded by a "veil of ignorance." Second, the practice of modern liberal societies has demonstrated that the common good, realistically considered, is best attained when no one intends it. At the root of these claims is an appeal to practical reason. As we will see, this appeal is problematic.

Both Simon and Novak concur on some important points concerning the role of practical reason in the attainment of moral ends such as the common good. Both are very much aware of the impossibility of arriving at necessary conclusions in practical moral matters. Both appreciate the function of practical reason to deliver the concrete and specialized knowledge of how to apply moral principles in the proper way under specific circumstances. Moreover, they both understand that the philosophical competence to grasp the concept of the common good does not translate into the practical capacity to achieve it. In the sense that there is no unique material solution to the question of how the common good can be achieved, a solution the necessity of which would flow from the dictates of deductive reasoning from known universal premises, both Simon and Novak agree that there is a "veil of ignorance" surrounding the attempt to achieve the common good materially.

Beyond these points of agreement, two points of divergence emerge. First, in Simon's eyes, the problem of acquiring precise knowledge of the material content of the common good is not really unique to the modern society, though admittedly the issue is surrounded by a significant increase in practical difficulties. This should initially caution us against the notion that a "new concept" of the common good is in fact what is needed. Second, and more fundamentally, Simon shows that it is unnecessary to conclude that the common good is so radically unknowable that it can no longer be an object of practical knowledge and intention. For Simon, practical knowledge is a knowledge of contingent matters where conclusions could be otherwise than they are.[23] It is certainly the case that judgments about the common good materially considered will inevitably be weak with respect to scientific knowledge.[24] Yet, although such judgments do not yield necessary and unique solutions, they are not merely arbitrary. Simon explains:

> [Practical] judgment ... is capable of another type of truth, of a practical truth, of a truth that becomes it properly as a practical judgment, of a truth that is one not of cognition but of direction, of a truth that consists ... in conformity to the demands of an honest will, in conformity to the inclination of a right desire.... For a judgment that is unqualifiedly practical, the proper way to be true is to be true in a practical sense; that is, to be true as a rule of action. The genuineness of a rule of action is its conformity to intention, provided, of course, that intention itself is genuine, that is, relative to the proper end. Posit the intention of the proper end and posit, in relation to the means,

a judgment in unqualified agreement with the genuine intention. This judgment is the true rule of action.[25]

What Simon is saying here is that, when confronted with a practical moral matter such as the determination of what economic policies are most conducive to the advancement of the common good, one must be aware from the beginning that the judgment rendered will not admit of necessary truth. Nonetheless, the common good can be known and advanced. Despite the "veil of ignorance" and the doctrine of unintended consequences, we can reasonably estimate the amount of food, clothing, and shelter people need to live. We know the overall state of relations between workers and managers with respect to collective bargaining and benefits. What Simon is saying is that we must take into account these and other requirements of the common good to the extent that we can reasonably know them. Then, it is necessary to consider the diversity of means by which the desired results might best be attained. Here other principles will come into play. For example, government spending not corresponding to production is likely to be inflationary. Moreover, rising interest rates will most likely slow down borrowing. All such factors must be considered to the extent possible in the stage of deliberation. In the final analysis, the practically true judgment about the common good consists of two parts: its genuine intention and the honest consideration of all of the factors relevant to its realization. Although experienced persons of practical wisdom may indeed arrive at different determinations, these determinations are far from arbitrary. Clearly, policies adopted simply according to what labor, big business, or any other *part* of society desires, are not for the common good. What Simon's theory of practical wisdom tells us is that we cannot leap from the truth that a "veil of ignorance" surrounds the achievement of the common good to Novak's false solution of allowing people to determine for themselves in what the common good consists, which encourages moral arbitrariness. Novak's understanding of practical reason operates without a clear sense of the moral ends to be achieved.

The problem of the absence of moral ends to guide practical reason shows up again in Novak's discussion of the material and formal concepts of the common good. Form and matter are metaphysical co-principles of being, which is to say that they always coexist. Form defines being as of a specific *kind* or *type*. Matter limits form as to a unique, specific material expression. The apple on my table shares the form of apple with all the other apples in the world. However, its matter determines it uniquely to be this one apple distinct from all the others.

Metaphysically, form is a principle of unity while matter is a principle of differentiation. In real beings, however, they always exist together. In order to be an apple, the matter of the apple must always exist in the form of an apple. Similarly, the common good must always have the form of the common good, which is to say that it must be a good in which all members participate and whose distribution to one does not exclude the participation of others. Of course, the form of the common good is compatible with a wide range of material possibilities. Moreover, the material common good is, as Novak argues, something always to be striven for, that is, open to new developments. What Simon's thought will not countenance, however, is Novak's proposal that instead of the form and the matter of the common good we can speak of two concepts of the common good, a formal and a material, wherein the formal provides the unrealizable exemplar toward which the latter strives.[26] In fact, more is required of the material common good than this. The matter of the common good must exist in the form of the common good. Yet, in Novak's theory, the form of the common good is reduced to a mere higher standard by which society is to be judged. Finally, the way Novak splits the form from the matter of the common good subtly denies the form of the common good its role as a moral principle by which society is to be judged. As this conclusion diverges from Novak's stated position that the form serves as a benchmark for the material common good, further elaboration is required.

Let us take Novak's own example that, with respect to the economic system, private property is the means and common use is the end. Normally, when one proposes that A is the means to B, we accept that the realization of B after A is implemented is the test of the original proposition. In the case at hand, if we propose that private ownership is the means by which to achieve common use, then we accept that the results of private ownership must indeed result in the universal destination of goods. If the results are otherwise, we would be forced to reconsider the original proposition. Yet it is precisely this kind of test which is absent in Novak. Again, because of the way the formal common good is separated from the material, the universal destination of goods no longer serves as a real, independent standard by which to evaluate the liberal economy. (At least, there is little politically relevant sense in which this principle serves as a standard.) As a result, the proposal that the liberal economy is the best means to provide for the needs of all has become transformed and hardened into a first principle of social morality no longer subject to evaluation by any independent ethical norm. Having stripped the common good of its role as normative standard, societies are now to be judged according to the extent to which they are liberal. Failures to achieve the universal destination of goods are simply assumed to be the failure to implement liberalism.[27] In all of this, practical reason has undergone a profound transformation. No longer guided by the imperative of achieving the common good, practical reason is left with no principles extrinsic to liberalism by which it might be guided. Practical reason must now build the democratic capitalist society which Novak has redefined as the common good.

Related to Novak's desire to move away from a substantive common good independent of liberalism is his crucial rejection of the role of public authority as the agent responsible for intending the common good materially considered. Novak criticizes such a role for authority as tribalism which would stifle individual autonomy and therefore be incompatible with the free society. The charge of tribalism, however, does not apply to the traditional concept of the common good. In order to see this clearly, however, we must proceed by steps.

According to Simon, the theory and practice of the common good accept the legitimacy of both interests which conflict with the common good and interests which conflict with one another. It is perfectly acceptable for individuals to will particular goods, even when those goods are not in conformity with the common good. What is required of all good citizens is that, in willing a particular good, they "refer it to the common good as an end."[28] In other words, when the realization of their particular desires would be detrimental to the common good, they agree to forego the legitimate goods attached to those desires. Saint Thomas completes the explanation as follows:

> Now it is the end that supplies the formal reason, as it were, of willing whatever is directed to the end. Consequently, in order that a man will some particular good with a right will, he must will that particular good materially, and the [common] good, formally. Therefore, the human will is bound to be conformed to the [common good], as to that which is willed formally, for it is bound to will the [common good]; but not as to that which is willed materially.[29]

In the case of the wife of the murderer condemned to death, Simon argues that, in willing her husband to live for the good of her family, she does exactly what the common good demands. Her disagreement with the common good is only under its material aspect. By submitting to its demands, she wills the common good under its formal aspect, which is all that is required of her.[30]

Beyond mere toleration of the desire for particular goods, Simon argues further, "*That particular goods be properly defended by particular persons matters greatly for the common good itself.*"[31] Simon writes:

> A society in which none intends ... a particular good is like a dead world.... Far from being genuinely exalted, the common good has become a mere appearance. Common good cannot exist unless it does exist as the good of a multitude; but there is no good "of a multitude" unless particular goods are intended by particular appetites and taken care of by particular agents.[32]

Clearly, then, the common good has no intrinsic link with a tribalism wherein all intend the same goods.

Novak and Simon agree that the common good demands a proliferation of individual goods and excellences. Where Simon departs from Novak is in the latter's unwarranted leap to the conclusion that no one need intend the common good materially, and that the intention of the material common good would necessarily threaten autonomy and the pursuit of excellence. Simon's response is that although the primary material concern of citizens *qua* citizens is to pursue particular goods, such pursuits, even when directed to genuinely good things, can and do conflict with one another and with the common good. Such conflicts cannot always be allowed to coexist; at times, definite resolution is needed. My pursuit of property and other forms of wealth may come to the point where they conflict with the common good. Therefore, Simon reasons that, over and above my willingness to limit my pursuit of individual goods on behalf of the common good, the latter requires that someone, or some institution(s), attend to the requirements of the common good materially considered. This is precisely where authority rightly and necessarily enters the picture. Moreover, with respect to public functions, that is, functions which are intrinsic *parts* of the common good, it is easy to see that the one-sided pursuit of any number of public functions would be destructive of the common good. What if, for example, in order to promote public health, the Surgeon General were to issue a decree that automobiles were to be completely eliminated from use? Here again, it is precisely the pursuit of a genuine, though particular good, which necessitates that some agent be responsible for the matter of the common good. In Simon's words, "*The most essential function of authority is the issuance and carrying out of rules expressing the requirements of the common good considered materially.*"[33] Far from limiting the pursuit of particular goods and excellences, it is precisely when authority fulfills its most essential function that it preserves their proper role. As Simon puts it:

> Let it be emphasized ... that the theory of authority as agency wholly concerned with the common good is connected with the excellence of particularity. Insofar as the particularity involved is that of the subject ... the theory of authority comprises a vindication of autonomy at all levels.[34]

Novak seeks nothing less than to deny authority its most essential function as the agent which intends the common good materially. Private actors are free to pursue their own particular goods as well as their own conception of the common good.[35] Novak overlooks the extent to which his theory contributes to a conflict of interests *which can only be resolved by private accumulations of political and economic power*. If each citizen intends, materially speaking, both his own individual good and the common good, how are conflicts among individuals to be resolved? Novak places hope in voluntary cooperation, but this is surely not the only way conflicts are resolved. Novak tends to play down the extent to which the private accumulation of economic power determines outcomes. Take, for example, a case where the managers of a company believe that lower wages and lower benefits are for the common good. According to Novak's theory, no one has the authority to tell them otherwise. If, however, managers and workers disagree over the contribution which lower wages and benefits will make to the common good, management is free to attempt to impose its own will. Workers are formally free to resist, but rarely are their resources equal to those of management. What Novak's theory actually does is to limit political authority in such a way as to permit private accumulations of economic, political, and cultural power to secure outcomes which may well not be in accord with the common good materially considered. This danger is heightened by the fact that, as Simon points out, private economic actors have no responsibility to intend the matter of the common good anyway.

The flaw in Novak's theory of the common good and authority seems to have two principal roots. First, he accepts too uncritically the liberal assumption that the pursuit of mutual self-interest suffices for the common good. A closer examination of his argument shows that he gives a very liberal twist to the following point made by Simon: "To the degree that a created person is a person there is a tendency toward a coincidence of personal good and common good."[36] Here

Simon was drawing on Jacques Maritain's crucial distinction between personal and individual. Maritain wrote: "Man will fully be a person . . . only in so far as the life of reason and liberty dominate that of the senses and passions in him; otherwise he will remain like an animal, a simple *individual,* the slave of events and circumstances, always led by something else, incapable of guiding himself."[37] Novak is too quick to identify Simon's conditional identification of personal good with common good with the liberal tradition's identification of "private rights and public happiness."[38] The lack of correspondence between the two is best seen when one considers economic goods. Once the satisfaction of human needs is fulfilled, further accumulations of material possessions and expenses on diversions have only a very tenuous relationship with personal good. Yet, as Simon and common sense witness, the accumulation of goods apart from needs is common in the liberal economy.[39]

The second source of Novak's problem is his concept of freedom. Although he carefully distances himself from libertarianism and nihilism, his suggestion that freedom is in conflict with authority, his notion of personal definitions of the common good, his rejection of a substantive common good in favor of pluralism, all point to the fact that the modern understanding of freedom is at the basis of his thought. Novak unfortunately misses the rich Thomistic understanding of freedom developed by Simon. For Simon, freedom has largely been misunderstood in the modern world as a form of indetermination, which is to say a condition where the acting person is not determined to act in any specific way; to be free is to be able to choose a variety of directions. In contrast, Simon found that freedom has an objective moral foundation. Freedom, he argued, is a form of *superdetermination,* that is, that particular kind of determination resulting from a sustained commitment to and maturity in attaining moral goodness, the directedness of the will to the good as such. It is precisely this transcendent commitment to the good beyond any particular goods which sets one free from being mastered by circumstances and a variety of inclinations. Simon writes:

> [F]reedom proceeds, not from any weakness, any imperfection, any feature of potentiality on the part of the agent but, on the contrary, from a particular excellence in power, from a plenitude of being and an abundance of determination, from an ability to achieve mastery over diverse possibilities, from a strength of constitution which makes it possible to attain one's end in a variety of ways.[40]

When the connection between freedom and its objective moral foundation is broken, as it is at times in Novak, freedom cannot escape being identified with arbitrariness in moral matters; if my freedom is not rooted in the desire for the good as such, then it is chimerical. I will in the final analysis be determined by circumstances, a complex of emotional drives, and egoism. This is the crux of Novak's problem. Unwilling to ground freedom in the commitment to the good, he does not give freedom a sure set of underpinnings. Although Novak himself laments the degeneration of freedom into nihilism, he is in his own way unwittingly contributing to the problem by siding too strongly with the modern understanding of freedom against the Thomistic.

Moral Problems of Capitalism

With respect to the economic ordering of society, Simon does not accept Novak's liberal argument that the market yields the best realistic approximation of the common good. Rather, Simon believed that serious issues of justice remained unresolved by the market system of exchanges. Moreover, he sees ways that the market economy is community eroding. In what follows, the argument will be made that Simon's critical perspective points to moral problems with capitalism that are still very much with us, yet played down or ignored by Novak.

The activities of the market economy are one area where the pursuit of particular goods frequently conflicts with the common good. Although Simon is by no means opposed to the market economy in principle, he does identify areas where the pursuit of profit regularly and systematically conflicts with the common good. As economies become more and more modernized, the direct association between production and use gets increasingly obscured by the tendency of production for use to be replaced by production for exchange. Whenever this occurs, "service and profit of work are separated."[41] Of course, Simon is aware that only the most primitive economy can function without commerce, and he certainly does not propose that we should try to go back in time. In fact, when the distance between service and profit of work is small, for example, "the case of a handicraftsman in a small town who keeps up daily relations of co-citizenship and neighborhood friendship with the beneficiaries of his services," there is a subordination of profit to service.[42] Problems emerge, however, when the distance between service and profit increases, as it has in the modern industrial economy. Simon quotes Thorstein Veblen[43] as follows:

The vital point of production with [the contemporary businessman] is the rendibility of the output, its convertibility into money values, not its serviceability for the needs of mankind. A modicum of serviceability, for some purpose or other, the output must have if it is to be salable. But it does not follow that the highest serviceability gives the largest gains to the business man in terms of money, nor does it follow that the output need in all cases have other than a fictitious serviceability.[44]

The moral problem occasioned by production for exchange is best seen when we consider the condition of the production and consumption of food in the world today. For thousands of years, land in the third world was used for subsistence farming. As capitalism expands into the third world, however, land is seen as too commercially viable to remain outside the cycle of exchange. Large food producers either buy up land directly or work in conjunction with local owners to convert land to the production of crops to be exchanged on the world market, such as flowers and coffee. Millions of former subsistent farmers no longer have access to land. Rather, they have become dependent on the money economy. Although some find employment, many more make their way to urban areas forming the basis for the ugly shantytowns that grow in and around major Latin American cities such as Mexico City, Rio de Janeiro, and Buenos Aires. As food becomes a commodity in the market, access to it depends on money. One of the great tragedies resulting from production for exchange instead of use is, along lines clearly stated by Yves Simon, the proliferation of dire need in the midst of plenty.[45] Food production is higher than ever in the world. Therefore, it is not accurate to say there is not enough food. The problem is that displaced farmers are either unemployed or earn insufficient money to purchase commercialized food products. Thus, it is clear that production for exchange on the market can be badly out of touch with even the most fundamental of human needs.

The increasing separation between service and profit causes confusion about the ends of both work and wealth.[46] While this is not a metaphysical necessity, Simon does see it as a strong and inevitable tendency under modern conditions of production. Moreover, it has two important consequences: "the lack of quantitative proportion between service and profit of work [and] the proliferation of illusory services."[47] With respect to the former, consider how poorly millions of workers are compensated in comparison with others who provide little service and receive enormous contributions. For example, plants licensed by Nike corporation, which manufacture athletic footwear, paid an average female worker in Indonesia approximately $.82 per day in 1991. The shoes cost less than six dollars to make and are sold at prices from $75 to $135. From the profits the company earned, it paid Michael Jordan $20,000,000. This figure was higher than the wages paid to all of the workers who produced the shoes in Indonesia.[48] With respect to illusory services, consider the considerable investment in advertising campaigns to sell nutritionally useless products to malnourished people in third world countries. Simon would want to know what genuinely human service such efforts provide.

With respect to distribution, Simon believes that an important principle governing the economic system, equality of exchange, is threatened under market conditions in the modern, industrialized economy. On this point, Simon was clearly influenced by the French philosopher Pierre Joseph Proudhon, who insisted that commutative justice demanded the strictest equality in the value of things exchanged.[49] Simon rejects the premise that it is necessarily true that the market system is the just way to determine prices.[50] He asks us to consider commercial activity in the sense employed by Aristotle and Saint Thomas, that is, as "operations consisting of purchase at a lower price followed by sale at a higher price, without any utility being produced in the meantime."[51] To make his point clear, Simon suggests that we consider only the merchant who has always been perfectly honest in all his dealings, that is, one who never tried to manipulate the market price or cheat others in any way. Simon contends that the wealth accumulated by such a merchant "is made up of values surrendered by his fellow men without their receiving any counterpart."[52] Independent of any dishonest dealings, when we consider the relationship between the merchant and society, there has been no real exchange of values. "In short," Simon writes, "*wealth has leaked out of society.*"[53] Simon is aware of the obvious objections that (a) there is in fact very little of what can properly be called purely commercial activities, and that (b) most merchants in fact do produce some utility. Simon's response is that the issue is not the extent to which commercial activities exist in pure form nor the number of people who gain all their income through speculative activities. With respect to the first objection, the relevant question is: "Over and above compensations obtained for services . . . is there such a thing as compensation corresponding to no production whatsoever but merely to an advantageous difference between price at the time of purchase and price at the time of sale?"[54] With respect to the second, Simon says that it matters not if wealth leaks out of society through agents who do nothing but commercial activities or through agents who derive income partially from changes in prices and partially from genuine services. The issue is that there is in fact a leak.[55]

For Simon, the problem of unequal exchanges is also relevant to the market for labor. Simon acknowledges that the modern wage-earner is equal to his employer from a legal standpoint. Nonetheless, Simon insists, exploitation does exist in the relationship whenever the compensation is below the value of the service rendered. Simon notes that it is still often the case that "a would-be wage-earner must simply accept whatever compensation is offered because he cannot afford to leave it."[56] Simon believes that such cases more often than not result in exploitation by unequal exchange and that the latter is "a species of servitude."[57]

Simon's objection to unequal exchanges in the market economy prompts him to make a most bold and striking claim with reference to the challenges they pose to democratic societies. He rejects the facile assumption that totalitarianism can be avoided without facing the issue of unequal exchange. Moreover, he rejects the assumption that the issue is no longer pressing when living standards are being raised. Despite the presence of a free market and growing living standards, "alienation through unequal exchange is the thing that democracy, in the second phase of its revolutionary development, has to deal with, just as alienation through institutional bondage was the thing that democracy had to deal with in its first revolutionary phase."[58]

The contemporary global market economy affords many examples of the phenomena to which Simon refers. Concerning unequal exchange, third world debt surely tops the list. Although the principle of repaying loans is surely not contrary to equality of exchange, the manner in which the crisis has been defused is. Beyond the mere fact that an impoverished region like Latin America became a net exporter of capital in the 1980s, it is those who received nothing from the original loans who bear the brunt of the deflationary measures—cuts in real wages and declining social spending—used to generate the savings to pay it back. Although one might argue that low wages in third world countries are due to lack of productivity, this is surely not always the case. Multinational firms deliberately pay workers in poor countries less to do the same work as their first world counterparts. To cite just one example, consider Green Giant corporation, which paid workers in California nine dollars an hour before transferring operations to Irapuato, Mexico, where it pays $4.28 per day.[59] A further example of unequal exchange is the phenomenon of "transfer pricing," an accounting practice which frequently takes place when a multinational firm transfers products from a subsidiary in one nation to a subsidiary in another. In such intra-firm transactions, prices are often adjusted for the purpose of declaring profits where taxes are low or are not well collected and avoiding the declaration of profits where conditions are the opposite. Transfer pricing is also implemented to escape restrictions placed on the transfer of profits by host-country governments.[60]

Another of Simon's concerns about market economies, speculative economic activities through which wealth "leaks out of society," has grown to proportions Simon could not have dreamed about in 1961. Speculation in foreign currency markets is one matter for grave public concern. According to the Bank of International Settlements, the figure is $640 billion a day. If this figure represented the purchase of goods and services, there would be no inherent difficulty. However, no more than 10 percent of this money has anything to do with the production and sale of goods and services. It is speculation pure and simple. The threat to the common good lies in the fact that large holders of a given currency can speculate against that currency so as to reduce very quickly the value of millions of people's savings. Speculation on foreign currency markets also makes it very difficult for any government to formulate economic policy, as large holders of any nation's currency can act in concert to undermine the value of the currency on the world market.

Though grave, the material problems of unequal exchange in capitalism are perhaps not the most serious. Simon argues that, when profit is the leading motive for production, workers tend to adopt the same mentality as owners.[61] This tends to erode another essential characteristic of a common good, namely, communion in desire. Workers who take up the profit motive as their central desire lose the sense of community in their work. According to Simon, under healthy circumstances, workers are aware that other workers desire that their common effort produce a genuine social good. In the modern market economy, however, where profit has an ambiguous relationship to service, and where workers may be unfairly compensated, the communion in desire gives way to individualistic loneliness, or alienation.

With respect to the role of authority in economic life, Novak and Simon share some common convictions. Both adhere to the traditional Catholic doctrine of subsidiarity.[62] Both see that the expansion of state ownership or management of economic enterprises will cause a decline in initiative and creativity on the part of the people. Nonetheless, both would, in principle, allow for some degree of government action to alleviate poverty and fulfill basic needs. Both speak sympathetically of employee stock ownership of enterprises as a way of expanding ownership of productive assets.[63] Finally, Novak favors an expansion of credit to the poor so that they can start their own enterprises, particularly in third world nations. Although Simon did not address this issue directly, it is so well in accord with his preference for an abundance of autonomic institutions, the proliferation of particular goods, and the preservation of self-employment, particularly in the form of the self-sufficient family farm, that we can at least say it is consistent with his views.

Despite these similarities, the diametrical opposition between Novak and Simon on the role of authority in procuring the common good materially considered prompts them to embrace the principle of subsidiarity in different ways. Novak has a strong tendency to interpret subsidiarity to mean the reduction of the role of the state, the privatization of publicly owned enterprises, and reliance on the market to solve the problem of poverty. By way of contrast, Simon has less faith in the invisible hand and sees the role of the state in economic matters in a more favorable light. More specifically, Simon diverges from Novak in the following four ways. First, Simon denies that wealth can be adequately distributed by the market. In his own words, "as a matter of fact, at all times and in all societies, a considerable amount of wealth has to be distributed by methods distinct from exchange."[64] Simon names the principles of distribution according to need and "free distribution" as two necessary supplements to the market.[65] Second, under most circumstances, Simon is convinced that political authority is likely to be necessary to maintain equality of exchange and to secure distribution according to need. In many instances historically, freedom from exploitation has also been secured by state intervention.[66] Third, political authority also functions so as to preserve autonomic institutions, including those of a wealth-producing nature. Simon gives the example of laws which protect a farmer's ownership of the land, defending him against both private and public powers.[67] Fourth, Simon believes that the destitute cannot be left to chance, which is to say that assistance should be institutionalized. Although not necessarily run directly by the state, all that goes under the name "welfare" cannot simply be left to "the fortuitousness of individual initiative."[68]

Simon's more circumspect view of the market and his insistence that political authority has an essential role to play in the determination of the requirements of the common good materially considered seem warranted by even a cursory examination of the market system as it exists in the world today. Just as capitalism has been necessary to increase the production of wealth, so regulation by authority has been necessary to secure adequate distribution, more equal exchanges, and in many cases a reasonably successful trajectory toward economic development.

The foregoing point is most clearly illustrated by considering the contrast between Latin America and South Korea. With respect to the former, Novak is well aware that these nations have been unable to "make their economies show steady, visible progress for the poor."[69] This prompts him to make the extraordinary oversimplification that Latin America is not capitalist.[70] Although reasonable people might debate over the degree to which Latin America is indeed capitalist, it is surely the case that Latin America has become far more capitalist in the last twenty years. This at times dramatic shift in the direction of liberalism has not improved the plight of the poor. The plight of the poor has worsened dramatically precisely in the nations most aggressively pursuing liberalization.[71] In Mexico, once a nation self-sufficient in food production, close to half of rural children now suffer from malnutrition.[72] Similarly, in Argentina, unemployed workers and young children begging for food have become a distressingly common sight. Throughout the region, informal and temporary labor became the norm for the region in the 1980s.[73] These results may well account for Novak's unwillingness to acknowledge just how liberal Latin American economies have become.

By way of contrast, South Korea has been able to achieve dramatic increases in wage levels, lower its level of unemployment, and better distribute wealth.[74] South Korean capitalism (and East Asian capitalism generally), however, has found no place for a negative attitude toward government intervention in economic matters. For example, the state worked very closely with heavily subsidized conglomerates to direct industrialization. Early on in the process, a highly authoritarian government nationalized the banking system. The export-oriented model pursued was funded and directed by the state. Far from eschewing protectionism, up until the mid-1980s, there was a fine of over one thousand dollars for smoking a foreign cigarette. They even resorted to that ultimate horror of the classical liberal: the Five Year Plan! Whatever South Korea had during its period of boom, it was not the "spirit of democratic capitalism."

CONCLUSION

This article has attempted to evaluate Michael Novak's "new concept of the common good" in light of the work of Yves R. Simon. Having reviewed the essential theoretical and practical issues involved, two conclusions emerge. First, a good deal of what Novak has to say in favor of the autonomy of the human person, liberty, economic initiative, and subsidiarity is not in fact in conflict with the "older concept," as Simon shows. Where Novak does genuinely diverge from Simon, in his reduction of the common good in economic matters to the opportunity to compete for individual goods, his rejection of the role of authority to express the requirements of the material common good, and his romanticized view of capitalism, Novak's argument falters in terms of theoretical coherence and its capacity to account for capitalism as it really exists in the world today. Thus, reconsideration of Simon's treatments of authority, the market, and human work seem most timely and needed as a sound corrective.

NOTES

Reprinted from *The Review of Politics* 58, no. 2 (Spring 1996): 229–58.

1. Michael Novak, *Free Persons and the Common Good* (New York: Madison Books, 1989), 1. This work is Novak's most developed expression of his thinking on the common good.
2. The following explication of Aristotle's role in the development of the common good tradition is taken from Novak, *Free Persons*, 22–26.
3. Ibid., 26–30.
4. Ibid., 28–29.
5. Ibid., 22–24.
6. Novak discusses the American contribution to the common good in ibid., 41–73.
7. Indeed, Novak believes that the capitalist society has contributed to the development of the "communitarian individual." See Michael Novak, *The Spirit of Democratic Capitalism* (New York: Simon and Schuster, 1982), 143–50.
8. Novak, *Free Persons*, 81–82. Emphasis mine.
9. The following discussion of tribalism, the "veil of ignorance," and authority is drawn from ibid., 78–95.
10. Novak discusses the formal and material concepts of the common good in ibid., 176–88. Here Novak also explicitly compares his work with Simon's.
11. Ibid., 177. The expressions "the material common good" (Novak) or "the common good materially considered" (Simon) do not refer simply to economic well-being. Everything specified by law and public policy would pertain to the material common good, and this clearly goes beyond economic matters. However, economic matters are, for both authors, a constitutive dimension of the material common good. Beyond an exploration of the different ways Novak and Simon explicate the theory of the common good (both materially and formally), this article intends to focus on the economic dimension.

12. Michael Novak, *The Catholic Ethic and the Spirit of Capitalism* (New York: The Free Press, 1993), 149–51.

13. Ibid., 180–81.

14. Michael Novak, *This Hemisphere of Liberty* (Washington, DC: American Enterprise Institute, 1990), 28–34.

15. The following observations on the communitarian and orderly nature of the market system is based on Novak, *Spirit of Democratic Capitalism*, 128–42.

16. Ibid., 104–16.

17. Novak, *Free Persons*, 80. Emphasis mine.

18. Yves R. Simon, *Philosophy of Democratic Government* (Notre Dame: University of Notre Dame Press, 1993), 65. Simon defines community as a society relative to a common good. A characteristic feature of such societies is "communion in immanent action," which Simon is explaining in the expression quoted here. Two other features of societies relative to a common good, collective causality and communion-causing communications, are mentioned by Simon but will not be discussed in this article. It is crucial to distinguish between a common good and *the* common good. There are any number of examples of common goods. Simon cites a team of workers, a football team, and the army as examples of societies pursuing common goods. *The* common good, however, refers to a comprehensive set of goods in which the entire civil society participates. Simon is not referring in this example to the material common good of an entire society, the requirements of which are normally expressed by the function of authority. Simon explains why the civil society is a society relative to a common good in *Philosophy of Democratic Government*, 63–68.

19. Yves R. Simon, *The Tradition of Natural Law* (New York: Fordham University Press, 1992), 98.

20. Simon, *Philosophy of Democratic Government*, 65.

21. This means that in the civil society the virtuous citizen genuinely desires and is willing to contribute to the common good. It does not mean that all citizens concretely will the same material state of affairs. The determination of the latter is the special function of authority.

22. Simon, *Philosophy of Democratic Government*, 64–65.

23. See Yves R. Simon, *The Definition of Moral Virtue* (New York: Fordham University Press, 1986), 61–67.

24. Here, scientific knowledge is understood in the Aristotelian sense as knowledge characterized by the strict, objective necessity of its conclusions.

25. Yves R. Simon, *Practical Knowledge* (New York: Fordham University Press, 1991), 13.

26. Novak's exact words are as follows: "The formal meaning points to the full (and future) conclusion of human development, both communal and personal. The material meaning points to the existing level of human development" (*Free Persons and the Common Good*, 177). Simon, on the other hand, speaks of a distinction between the form and the matter of the common good in the context of two ways of willing and intending the

common good, and not to suggest that the common good itself has two separable meanings or that the common good materially considered could somehow be present without the form.

27. This may well account for Novak's refusal to acknowledge the degree to which Latin American economies are already liberalized.

28. Thomas Aquinas, *Summa Theologiae* I-II, q. 19, a. 10, in *Introduction to Saint Thomas Aquinas*, ed. Anton C. Pegis (New York: Modern Library, 1948).

29. Ibid.

30. Simon, *Philosophy of Democratic Government*, 42.

31. Ibid., 41.

32. Ibid., 55.

33. Yves R. Simon, *A General Theory of Authority* (Notre Dame: University of Notre Dame Press, 1980), 29.

34. Ibid., 158.

35. Of course, Novak would demand a framework of laws in which the competition for particular goods takes place.

36. Simon, quoted in Novak, *Free Persons*, 32.

37. Maritain, quoted in Novak, *Free Persons*, 32–33.

38. James Madison, quoted in Novak, *Free Persons*, 32.

39. Simon writes: "What bears repeating is that the whole problem of the relationship between work and wealth depends on recognizing and admitting something that many economists want to leave out of the picture altogether, namely, the possibility of a discrepancy between human desires and genuine human needs" (*Work, Society, and Culture* [New York: Fordham University Press, 1971], 125).

40. Yves R. Simon, *Freedom of Choice* (New York: Fordham University Press, 1969), 153.

41. Simon, *Work, Society and Culture*, 120.

42. Ibid., 121.

43. [Thorstein Veblen (1857–1929) was a prominent American economist and sociologist, best known for his book *The Theory of the Leisure Class*, a book that introduced the phrase "conspicuous consumption." Ed.]

44. Thorstein Veblen, quoted in ibid.

45. Simon, *Work, Society, and Culture*, 139.

46. Ibid., 122.

47. Ibid.

48. Richard Barnet and John Cavanaugh, *Global Dreams: Imperial Corporations and the New World Order* (New York: Simon and Schuster, 1994), 326–28. While accepting inequalities in the recompense of human labor, Simon believes that there should be an upper limit, because "no aspect of the common good demands that any person should enjoy an income many times greater than his avowable needs" (*Philosophy of Democratic Government*, 250).

49. Simon considers Proudhon "an astonishingly perceptive observer of social life, with a special talent for identifying tendencies that remain constant in the play of social forces" (Yves R. Simon, "A Note on Simon's Federalism," trans. Vukan Kuic, *Publius* 3 [1973]: 19–30).

50. Yves R. Simon, *The Community of the Free* (Lanham, MD: University Press of America, 1984), 162.

51. Simon, *Work, Society, and Culture*, 35.

52. Simon, *Community of the Free*, 163.

53. Simon, *Philosophy of Democratic Government*, 240.

54. Simon, *Work, Society, and Culture*, 37.

55. Simon, *Community of the Free*, 163–64.

56. Simon, *Work, Society, and Culture*, 130.

57. Ibid.

58. Simon, *Philosophy of Democratic Government*, 248.

59. Barnet and Cavanaugh, *Global Dreams*, 254. Again, the issue for Simon here would not be simply to create equality of incomes. He is concerned, however, about wages of this kind which are not sufficient to maintain "common participation in the basic necessities of life" (*Community of the Free*, 172).

60. Thomas D. Lairson and David Skidmore, *International Political Economy: The Struggle for Power and Wealth* (Fort Worth: Harcourt Brace, 1993), 260.

61. Simon, *Work, Society, and Culture*, 122.

62. This doctrine was defined by Pius XI as follows: "Just as it is gravely wrong to take from individuals what they can accomplish by their own initiative . . . and give it to the community, so also it is an injustice and at the same time a grave evil . . . to assign to a greater and higher association what lesser and subordinate organizations can do" (encyclical letter *Quadragesimo Anno*, May 15, 1931, no. 79, at Vatican website).

63. For Novak's fears concerning the welfare state and its appropriate limits, see *The New Consensus on Family and Welfare* (Washington, DC: American Enterprise Institute, 1987). Novak mentions employee stock ownership in *This Hemisphere of Liberty*, 105. Simon mentions his fears of an excess of state management and his support of worker cooperatives in *Philosophy of Democratic Government*, 252.

64. Simon, *Work, Society, and Culture*, 140.

65. The former would insure that the needs of a worker's family would be considered in the determination of the wage. The latter would include all voluntary forms of distribution where recipients do not pay for what they receive.

66. Novak would not disagree, but he is far more concerned about exploitation by the state.

67. Simon, *Philosophy of Democratic Government*, 252–53.

68. Simon, *The Tradition of Natural Law*, 166. Of course, Novak does not argue directly that the poor should be left to chance. He argues, on the contrary, that the cycle of exchange be expanded to include the poor. But is this fundamentally different from leaving them to chance when there is no inherent necessity for the market to be inclusive?

Novak's theory suggests that all should take responsibility for the poor through voluntary institutions. However, if such institutions lack the people and the funds to deal with the problems, then it would seem that the reliance on private initiative would ultimately be indistinguishable from leaving the poor to chance.

69. Novak, *This Hemisphere of Liberty*, 101–2.

70. Ibid., 104.

71. I am not suggesting the simplistic and false argument that economic liberalism is the unique cause of Latin American poverty. I am suggesting that recent liberalization, particularly in the 1980s, has had a negative impact on the standard of living of the poor and does not show signs of reversing the problem.

72. For a discussion of contemporary Mexico, see Tom Barry, ed., *Mexico: A Country Guide* (Albuquerque: Inter-Hemispheric Education Resource Center, 1992).

73. Novak makes an astounding claim with reference to this phenomenon. He blames the proliferation of informal workers on the difficulties of obtaining legal incorporation for their efforts. Although I concur with the proposal to make incorporation easy, the absence of this factor cannot be said to account for the tremendous *proliferation* of informal workers. Liberal socioeconomic policies which prompted job loss and dramatically lower wages at the same time that social sector spending was being greatly reduced, surely played an important role in generating the millions of informal laborers in the 1980s.

74. The following is not intended as a simple endorsement of the South Korean model. The achievements of South Korea were related to a repressive political model. The following draws on Gary Dorrien, *The Neoconservative Mind* (Philadelphia: Temple University Press, 1993), 295–306.

CHAPTER 11

A "Catholic Whig" Replies

MICHAEL NOVAK

For several decades Michael Novak was the distinguished George Frederick Jewett Scholar in Religion, Philosophy, and Public Policy at the American Enterprise Institute. He is currently a trustee and visiting professor at Ave Maria University. From 1981 to 1982 he served as the United States Ambassador to the United Nations Commission on Human Rights, and in 1994 he was the winner of the one million dollar Templeton Prize for Progress in Religion. The author of over twenty-five books, Novak is best known for The Spirit of Democratic Capitalism *(1982),* Free Persons and the Common Good *(1988), and* The Catholic Ethic and the Spirit of Capitalism *(1993). He is credited for influencing the thought of Pope John Paul II, especially in his encyclical letter* Centesimus Annus *(1991).*

When the Whigs define themselves as the Party of Liberty, furthermore, they define liberty in a special way. They do not mean libertinism or any other disordered form of liberty, such as a supposed "liberty to do whatever one feels like doing." For them, a liberty undirected by reflection and choice is slavery. For them, liberty must be achieved through a self-mastery that nourishes reflection and choice. Such self-mastery is won by slowly gaining dominion over appetite, passion, ignorance, and whim. For them, the enabling agent and protector of liberty is virtue-indeed, a full quiver of virtues. (*This Hemisphere of Liberty*, 1992, pp. 9–10)

In his final sentences, after much smoke and fury, Professor Rourke makes quite modest (but still false) charges against my work. Were he to study this work more fairly, removing his ideological blinders provisionally, he might grasp at least its underlying intention, namely, to replace the unsustainable liberal argument for the free society with a Christian argument. Many people judge that I have achieved much of that. Even non-Christian thinkers are adopting parts of it.

Yet Rourke does not yet grasp my intention for three systemic reasons. First, he interprets Catholic social doctrine as though it were the ideology of social democracy. Second, he cannot seem to understand other points of view. Third, he systematically misstates my views by reading into them secular liberal philosophical commitments that I have long written against.

In addition, Rourke uses the term *liberalism* equivocally and nonhistorically, sweeping under one term a host of different positions taken by a host of diverse authors. In his book, *Liberalisms*, John Gray of Oxford shows greater wisdom. For the sense in which John Rawls speaks of liberalism is quite different from that often applied to Friedrich Hayek, and so forth. (Hayek, in fact, identifies himself with the "Whig" tradition, as embodied in St. Thomas Aquinas, Lord Acton, and Alexis de Tocqueville—as it happens, all Catholics.) Further, as E. E. Y. Hales, Etienne Gilson,[1] and other commentators on Catholic social thought have pointed out, the term liberalism means something very different in Italy, France, and Germany than in England, and something different again in the United States.

Having failed to sort out these equivocations in his use of a central term in his analysis, Rourke further fails to identify precisely what that great scholar Yves Simon meant by liberalism. Again, he disregards the crucial distinction between liberal *institutions* and liberal *doctrines* made on the first page of *Catholic Social Thought and Liberal Institutions*, the second volume of my trilogy on political economy. The thesis of this book, I wrote:

> may be simply stated: Although the Catholic Church during the nineteenth and early twentieth centuries set itself against liberalism *as an ideology*, it has slowly come to support the moral efficacy of liberal *institutions*. Most clearly, it has come to support institutions of human rights, but it has also—more slowly—come to support institutions of democracy and market-oriented economic development. (p. xiii)

This distinction is also the basic premise of my follow-up studies, *Free Persons and the Common Good* and *This Hemisphere of Liberty*. Unanchored without it, Rourke's argument is adrift on a sea of abstractions. If one lists the commitments that he attributes to "liberalism," one can immediately think of many liberals who do not share them, and will be hard pressed to think of anyone in the real world who holds all of them.

The *institutions* that have been developed in countries sometimes described as liberal are one thing; *doctrines* put forth by liberal philosophers to defend them are another. Often, liberal institutions embody elements derived from the dynamism of earlier Jewish and Christian cultures. Thus, Jacques Maritain saw in democratic institutions under the rule of law, constituted by limited government, and protecting the rights of individuals and minorities, the slow working out in history of the yeast of the Gospels. Maritain and Simon taught two generations (including Paul VI) that, while liberal doctrines are insufficient to explain or to defend democratic institutions, the latter merit a profound philosophical and theological defense by Christian thinkers and activists. Even earlier, at the Third Plenary Council of Baltimore in 1884, the U.S. Catholic bishops noted that, under Providence, the U.S. Founders had built "better than they knew."

An analogous shift occurred in Catholic social thought regarding the judgment to be rendered on institutions of religious liberty. Catholic thinkers have presented new philosophical, theological, and practical *grounds* for the defense of regimes of religious liberty, rejecting some of the doctrines put forward in this respect by various liberal theorists. As bishop of Krakow at the Second Vatican Council, Karol Wojtyla argued eloquently that the declaration *Dignitatis Humanae* was not only an issue for the United States, France, and other Western nations, but a universal issue rooted in the fundamental dignity of the human person. This argument is said to have been decisive for Paul VI, who sent the declaration forward for urgent action before the Council adjourned.

Regarding democracy and religious liberty, therefore, evidence is overwhelming that, having at first opposed institutions at first called "liberal," the Church has learned by experience to sift the wheat from the chaff—to accept certain institutions because of their proven fruits, while continuing to reject inadequate philosophies of human nature and destiny.

Today, the Church seems to be doing the same with regard to proven institutions in the economic field. For those, like Rourke, who have identified Catholic social thought with social democracy, this increasingly positive judgment on certain aspects of markets, incentives, enterprise, invention, and public choice economics, is obviously disturbing. The crucial prudential question they must face is which sort of economic system has historically proven better for the common good, and especially for the poor.

As of 1986, there had not been even one entry on the common good in *The Catholic Periodical and Literature Index* for nearly 20 years, and it was part of my purpose in *Free Persons and the Common Good* to remedy that neglect. Further, new definitions of the common good by Catholic scholars both just before and during the Second Vatican Council highlighted "the fulfillment of the *person*" as an essential aspect of the common good. This new stress on the person created certain strains in the definitions handed down by Aristotle and Aquinas. While the profound discussions of these matters by De Koninck,[2] Maritain, and Simon were available to guide my own argument for most of the way, they were pre-conciliar. My book was written for the fortieth anniversary of Maritain's. It would have been insufficient merely to parrot his views.

Besides, the minds of Maritain and Simon had been formed in Europe, and much of their writing during their most productive years was directed to the building of a new society in Europe on the ruins left by World War II. However, the political, cultural, and economic experience of the United States matters heavily for European reconstruction after 1945 and, further, offered new materials to universal reflection, with regard both to the person and to the common good. This is especially true regarding how the common good is actually achieved, and to a progressively higher level decade by decade. Maritain dared American Catholics to cease hiding under a bushel the light that flowed from our own distinctive traditions. For people born poor, he recognized, the level of opportunity was then, and is now, higher in America than in Europe. In many ways, the actual achievement of a higher level of the common good offers here more reasons for realistic hope. Why is that? What institutional design makes it so?

By my count, Rourke finds eight errors in my thought. At these points, he makes eight misstatements of my thought. A few examples may suffice. All his misstatements have a systematic source: he imputes to me liberal understandings that I do not share.

a. *That I deny the role of "authority as the agent which intends the common good materially"*: "Yet, precisely because not all citizens can know the full material content of the common good—what in particular needs to be done here and now—there emerges a natural need for organs of national decision-making; in short, for authorities of various types, responsible for exercises of expertise and power within a limited range. And, at some points, this veil of ignorance naturally requires the highest authority in the national community (executive or legislative or judicial, as appropriate) to make certain key decisions regarding next practical steps forward" (*Free Persons and the Common Good*, p. 184 and *passim*).

b. *That I have an individualist, and finally nihilist concept of freedom which breaks "the connection between freedom and its objective moral foundation."* Yet in *Catholic Social Thought and Liberal Institutions*, I wrote: "The Catholic tradition held that liberalism as a moral doctrine too lightly valued authority and tradition in religion, and yielded too much to individual conscience, which after all is prey to whim, the spirit of the age, and unreliable contrariety. Furthermore, excessive individualism destroys the family, as 'looking out for number one' destroys the national community. The distorting tendency of radical individualism is narcissism, which diminishes the moral stature of every person who yields to it" (p. 23).

In my Templeton address, "Awakening from Nihilism," I stressed that "There are two types of liberty: one pre-critical, emotive, whimsical, proper to children; the other critical, sober, deliberate, responsible, and proper to adults. Alexis de Tocqueville called attention to this alternative early in *Democracy in America*, and at Cambridge Lord Acton put it this way: Liberty is not the freedom to do what you wish; it is the freedom to do what you ought. Human beings are the only creatures on earth that do not blindly obey the laws of their nature, by instinct, but are free to choose to obey them with a loving will. Only humans enjoy the liberty to do what we ought to do—or alas, not to do it." I have written against the failures of liberal philosophies of liberty many times. Rourke attacks those I attack.

c. *That I deny the formal common good its role as a moral principle, splitting it from the material common good*: As Maritain used to say, *Distinguer pour unir*. (The distinction between the formal and the material common good is his.) "To exhort people to pursue the (formal) common good is easier than to figure out, in practice here and now, which of many material courses of action will best attain it" (*Free Persons and the Common Good*, p. 185). And again:

> Do the people of the United States will the common good—the good of the American experiment, the good of the nation? Many have willingly died for it. Lincoln led the nation through the bloodiest civil war until that time to preserve "the Union." And the will to pursue together the common good is fully implied within the much loved patriotic hymn:
>
> *God bless America! Land that I love.*
> *Stand beside her, and guide her,*
> *Through the night with the light from above.*

This stanza expresses almost perfectly the formal content of a properly formed commitment to the common good (the fidelity of the commonwealth to God's will). It evokes as well the veil of ignorance any people must face "through the night," in trying to discern which material content best achieves that formal intention in practice. (Ibid., pp. 187–88)

d. *That I deny the principle of the universal destination of material goods, by arguing that a regime of private property is the most practical way to attain it*: But so also argued Aristotle, Cicero, Aquinas, Leo XIII, and John Paul II—that experience shows in four or five different ways that a regime of private property is more likely than communal ownership to serve the universal destination of material goods. Rourke's hostility to a regime of private property is foreign to the Catholic tradition. In the United States, rights to private property may legally be overridden in certain circumstances and with due process; they are not absolute. In *Rerum Novarum*, however, Leo XIII, called them "sacred," perhaps to emphasize their importance at a time when socialism threatened to abolish them.

e. *That in my "enthusiasm" for capitalism I romanticize it, denying its many sins, faults, limitations, and omissions*: What I like about democracy and capitalism is that neither is romantic; both are poor systems, except that all known others are worse. Regarding these are two distinct objects of inquiry: the system's own ideals and its actual empirical record, flaws and all. Most leftists simply deny that democracy plus capitalism *has* any moral ideals, equivalent to socialist or social democratic ideals. This is false. It has such goals, and its goals are superior to, not equivalent to, those of social democracy and socialism.

On empirical matters, Rourke merely trots out a too-long series of charges from left-wing, anti-capitalist tracts with which all of us have been familiar for years (Barnet and Cavanagh, Lairson and Skidmore, Dorrien[3]). Most, if not all, are false. If we had space I would dispute them empirically. Yet, suppose that all of these charges *were* true. Suppose that serious reforms in capitalist practice are necessary, precisely in the light of democratic capitalist as well as Catholic ideals.

Does history show that the existing alternatives to democratic capitalism—a socialist regime, a traditional third world regime—better raise up the poor? A system of the democratic and capitalist type has systemic ways of prompting and executing reforms that its historical alternatives decidedly lack. That is why despite its faults it continues to prevail—and to be reformed.

f. *That I "reduce the common good in economic matters to the opportunity to compete for individual goods."* But capitalism cannot thrive without a constitutional political order and a moral order of a specific humanistic type; without rules, laws, common understandings, and common virtues; and without specific sets of institutions, practices, and tacit understandings. All these are crucial elements of the common good. So also are roads, bridges, harbors, airports, sewage systems, sources of pure drinking water, venture capital funds, cheap and easy access to institutions of credit, patent and copyright laws, and many other public goods. I suggest (*Free Persons and the Common Good*, p. 181) that the reader reflect on a long list of the public elements of the common good proposed by Maritain, and try to add to it. The view Rourke attributes to me is in fact repulsive to me.

In summary, throughout his discussion of my work, Rourke confuses my position with that of a laissez-faire, libertarian, secular nihilist. The shame is on him.

Both he and I have too much creative work to do. Where he finds I fall short, let him carry our mutual project further, and do it better.

NOTES

Reprinted from *The Review of Politics* 58, no. 2 (Spring 1996): 259–64.

1. [E. Y. Hales (1908–1986) was an English Catholic historian. Etienne Gilson (1984–1978) was a French Catholic philosopher, focusing on medieval philosophy, especially the thought of Thomas Aquinas. Ed.]

2. [Charles De Koninck (1906–1965), along with Maritain and Simon, was a Catholic philosopher working on Thomism and political liberalism. Ed.]

3. [Novak does not specify which works he has in mind, but he is likely referring to: Richard J. Barnet and John Cavanagh, *Global Dreams: Imperial Corporations and the New World Order* (New York: Simon & Schuster, 1994); Thomas D. Lairson and David Skidmore, *International Political Economy: The Struggle for Power and Wealth* (New York: Harcourt Brace, 1993); and Gary Dorrien, *The Neoconservative Mind: Politics, Culture, and the War of Ideology* (Philadelphia: Temple University Press, 1993). Ed.]

CHAPTER 12

Response to a "Catholic Whig"

Thomas R. Rourke

What is most striking about Michael Novak's response to my article is that he chooses for the most part to bypass the core of the argument. I compared Novak's and Simon's understandings of the common good and authority. In addition, rooted in Simon's work (which I find to be no less relevant today than forty years ago), I proceeded to critique Novak's understandings of the common good and what I find to be his unjustified conclusions about economic liberalism and the realization of the common good materially considered. (My use of Simon as a reference point is based on my judgment that he is the richest Catholic theorist on the subjects of the common good and authority.) I am trying to bring Simon's highly relevant work to bear upon the evaluation of Novak. Moreover, I try to show why Simon's criticisms of the market system are in fact more relevant now than when they were originally articulated by giving some contemporary examples. Novak elected not to engage these core points of my article, except for an outrageous statement, based on no evidence or argument (under point "f"), that most of the claims are false and are drawn from "left-wing, anti-capitalist tracts." Again, Novak cleverly bypasses the fact that the examples I give are simply contemporary manifestations of points raised long ago by Simon.

In the first half of what was supposed to be an engagement with my article, we find Novak *completely* bypassing the actual text of my article in favor of a largely irrelevant summary of his overall project. Since I never claimed to be doing an evaluation of his entire corpus, still less a systematic treatment of the varieties of liberalism, I see no need to respond to what Novak writes on these subjects here. (Those interested in a more extensive critique of Novak might wish to see my forthcoming book.)[1]

In the second half of his response, Novak finally gets around to addressing some of what I actually said in the article. Given the serious space limitations imposed, and the fact that most of what Novak writes here misrepresents me, I will respond to the two substantive criticisms I found here.

Under point "a," Novak claims that I misrepresent him when I say that he denies the role of authority as the agent which intends the common good materially. (The quote he provides in defense does not actually prove his point, since it merely acknowledges that there is a natural need for organs of decision-making, a point which I would not dispute.) Nevertheless, a reading of chapter three of his *Free Persons and the Common Good* confirms my interpretation. Here, Novak (a) equates authority's intention of the common good materially considered with tribalism, (b) argues that the understanding of the common good does not mean *any* conscious intentions, aims, or purposes, and (c) claims that the common good materially considered should not be intended, and can be achieved in the absence of such intentions. Moreover, above and beyond supporting a variety of rightly diverse personal contributions to the common good (which Simon would surely agree with), Novak proposes that individuals be allowed to pursue their own personal *judgments* concerning the content of the common good (pp. 81–82). Given these commitments, it is hard to see how Novak can now disagree with my conclusion that he denies to authority the role of intending the common good materially considered.

Concerning my claim that Novak in many respects romanticizes capitalism, what I mean to say is that Novak, while frequently repeating the disclaimer that the free economy permits a multitude of sins, actually pays little attention to the systematic nature of those sins, and generally ignores their severity. I cited some of the problems in the original article, limiting myself to examples which illustrated principles raised by Simon. There are in fact trends in contemporary global capitalism uglier than the ones I originally mention in the text. For example, there is the distressing proliferation of a problem once thought to have been largely overcome: the savage exploitation of women and children as laborers. American consumers wear articles of clothing made in places such as the Philippines and Guatemala, the production of which involves such violations of human dignity as seventy-seven hour workweeks for children of four to six years. How does Novak deal with such disturbing trends? He does so first of all by not mentioning them. But, more importantly, he has created an ideological construct to protect capitalism from such criticisms. When he does not deny or ignore the evils associated with capitalism as it exists, he prefers to interpret them as problems of personal character, unrelated to the good system. Here Novak is simply being arbitrary. Why are the evils of socialism and social democracy directly attributable to the system, while the sins of capitalism have nothing to do with the system, merely to individuals with bad characters? Novak would be wiser to concede the systemic flaws in capitalism as it exists. Another reason for my claim that Novak romanticizes capitalism is that, contrary to his stated conviction, his optimistic views of economic liberalism for the third world are not empirically sensitive. He ignores considerable evidence of the deterioration of living standards for the majority of people under economic liberalization programs.

Unlike my article, which grounds an interpretation of Novak in his texts, Novak attributes to me positions which I do not hold and for which he presents no basis in what I wrote. For the record, I have no *a priori* commitment to the social democratic ideology, although I would be willing to consider such measures subject to the constraints of the subsidiarity principle. Second, Novak says that I attribute to him a nihilistic concept of freedom, when in the last two paragraphs of the subsection, "Novak on the Common Good," I twice state the opposite. My real position is that there is a conflict between his non-nihilistic understanding of freedom in personal, moral matters, and his defense of liberalism in economic and political ones. Third, Novak claims that I am hostile to a regime of private property, when all I was doing was restating the traditional Thomist position that common use has a certain precedence over private ownership, particularly in cases where there is great need. Moreover, I was trying to show that Novak's subtle rewording of the argument in effect leaves out the priority of common use.

NOTES

Reprinted from *The Review of Politics* 58, no. 2 (Spring 1996): 254–67.

1. [Thomas R. Rourke, *A Conscience as Large as the World: Yves R. Simon versus the Catholic Neoconservatives* (Lanham, MD: Rowman & Littlefield, 1997). Ed.]

CHAPTER 13

Catholicism and Liberalism

Kudos and Questions for Communio *Ecclesiology*

MICHAEL J. BAXTER

Michael J. Baxter (1955–) teaches Religious Studies at Regis University in Denver. He received his Ph.D. in Theology and Ethics from Duke University in 1996 and taught theology at the University of Notre Dame from 1996 to 2011. Baxter is well known for his espousal of a radical Catholicism that is deeply influenced by Dorothy Day and the Catholic Worker Movement. Christian pacifism is a major theme of this thought. From this standpoint, he has frequently criticized the mainstream Catholic Church in the United States for being too accommodating of political and economic liberalism and too acquiescent in the U.S. government's use of military force. His articles have appeared in De Paul Law Review, Pro Ecclesia, Communio, The Thomist, *and* Modern Theology.

It is a commonplace among Catholic social ethicists in the United States that the Church has finally made its peace with liberalism in the post-conciliar era. The promulgation of *Gaudium et Spes* and *Dignitatis Humanae* at Vatican II is widely seen as an official endorsement of Western political liberalism, and the publication of *Centesimus Annus* by John Paul II in 1991 is interpreted by many as an endorsement of economic liberalism. These are hailed as monumental events by contemporary Catholic social theorists because for centuries the Church saw liberalism as a potential threat, if not indeed a direct challenge, to its authority in temporal affairs. Because it supported a secular (or lay) state and the free market, liberalism was thought to support a new political and economic order free of ecclesial oversight or intervention. As such it was met with official condemnation. The pastors of the Church, ever vigilant for the well-being of their flocks, warned Catholics against the subtle but wily claims of liberal freedom. Even after Leo XIII promulgated *Rerum Novarum* and inaugurated an apparently more positive approach to modern liberalism, the involvement of lay people in political parties, labor unions, and other temporal organizations was still to be carefully overseen by the hierarchy. Hence the so-called fortress mentality of the pre-conciliar era, which presupposed an opposition between the Church, which furnished the graces necessary for the attainment of eternal life, and the world, which was fraught with sin and thus had to be resisted. This opposition between a holy church and an evil world was overcome by Vatican II. Instructed in a new theology that held all persons and events to be intrinsically graced, the Council Fathers now assured Catholics that the modern secular world is a realm suffused with the supernatural, including modern secular politics and economics. Liberalism could finally be embraced as a salutary movement that would benefit both the Church and humanity as a whole. So goes the standard account of the Catholic Church's rapprochement with liberalism.

Heart of the World, Center of the Church challenges this account. According to David Schindler, professor of Fundamental Theology at the John Paul II Institute for Studies on Marriage and Family in Washington, D.C., and editor of the English-speaking edition of *Communio*, a theology in which the world is seen as intrinsically graced does not necessarily endorse liberalism, but in fact challenges liberalism and proposes an alternative to it.

Schindler stakes out his position in the introduction of the book by setting forth what he sees as the proper construal of the relation between the Church and the world. In keeping with the pronouncements of Vatican II, he repudiates any form of pre-conciliar integralism which would absorb the world into the Church by means of ecclesiastical governance of the affairs of secular life. But he also rejects two post-conciliar models of the church/world relation designed to guard against the threat of integralism. The first model Schindler calls "liberationist." Born out of a theological conviction that the secular realm is graced and that a commitment to social justice is indispensable, the liberationist model turns the Church radically toward the world, and insists that it is only there, in the world, that the Church can transform the institutions of oppression and alleviate the suffering of the poor. The problem with this model, Schindler contends, is that the Church empties out into the world while the world, so to speak, rushes in to fill the empty space left by the Church, so that ecclesial and worldly thought and institutional structures meld into one. The result is a post-conciliar form of integralism that mimics liberal democracy, a development evident in recent liberationist efforts to democratize church structures. The second church/world model rejected by Schindler is the "neo-conservative" or dualist model. In contrast to the liberationist melding of church and world, this dualist model divides the mission of the Church into two, a "heavenly" mission dealing with the spiritual life and an "earthly" or "worldly" mission that contributes to the common good by developing a theology, philosophy, and morality that is "public." The advantage of this division of labor, as neo-conservatives see it, is that the Church can preserve the integrity of its own doctrines and pastoral life and also devote itself to bettering life in the secular realm. But Schindler believes that this division allows the secular realm to become a realm unto itself, reproducing the pre-conciliar, two-tier conception of nature and grace, whereby the supernatural grace of Christ and the Church is added on to an already sufficient and autonomous "nature." Against the background of the problems with these three models of the relation between church and world—the integralist, liberationist, and neo-conservative—Schindler proposes an alternative model: "*communio* ecclesiology."

The crucial feature of *communio* ecclesiology is that it is "intrinsicist," that is, it views the Church as intrinsically turned towards the world as the object of its mission, and it views the world as marked by an intrinsic desire that is fulfilled in the life of Christ and the Church. The intrinsicist perspective dissolves the false opposition between a holy church and an evil secular world. Because it is grounded in the life of the Trinity as revealed by Christ, the *communio* of the Church is, Schindler admits, unworldly. "But here is the rub: the Church, *precisely in its 'unworldly' communio*, already itself bears an intrinsic dynamic for this-worldly transformation. The Church enters the world by being what it is, namely, *communio*; but it is of the very nature of *communio* to be missionary; *communio*'s 'being what it is' includes 'giving itself away'" (p. 10). With this notion of an "unworldly *communio*" producing "*this-worldly transformation*," Schindler is attempting to carve out a new ecclesiological vision. He rejects a liberationist collapse of the Church into the world, with its uncritical acceptance of worldly power. He rejects neo-conservativism's dualism, which also entails an uncritical acceptance of secular power. But because *communio* ecclesiology is intrinsicist in character, he also avoids the dangers of pre-concililar integralism. He insists that the Church's mission to the world be carried out not by political or juridical means, but by means of the Church's own life in communion with the Trinity, by means of attraction and invitation, not of violent imposition. It is a mission consistent with what John Paul II calls a "civilization of love."

Various aspects of *communio* ecclesiology are presented over the course of the forty-page introduction, ten chapters, lengthy footnotes, and brief conclusion that comprise this book. In the first half, entitled "Catholic Liberalism," Schindler argues against Catholic appropriations of liberal theory. The problem with liberalism is that it establishes institutional arrangements that purport to be neutral on matters of religion, assuming that a respectful silence avoids favoritism toward any particular religious group and thus provides for the freedom of all religious groups. But Schindler argues that liberalism's purportedly neutral institutional arrangements are anything but neutral when it comes to Christianity. This is because the very structure of liberalism's solution to religious pluralism excludes the Christian understanding of freedom, which is not doing what one prefers but acting in accord with one's destiny and final purpose—to see God. What can be done to resolve this conflict between Christianity and liberalism? Not much, as Schindler sees it, because liberalism creates a separate sphere, "the secular," where politics and economics are detached from the workings of grace and the Church; Christianity, by contrast, connects politics and economics with the redemptive action of Christ. Thus there is, as Schindler puts it time and again, an inner "logic" to liberalism, which opposes the inner "logic" of Christianity. By arguing for a purportedly neutral competition in a free market of religions, Catholic liberals ignore this opposition and draw the Church into what Schindler refers to at one point as liberalism's "con game" (p. 44).

This general critique of Catholic liberalism is elaborated in great detail in five successive chapters dealing with politics, economics, and academics. As regards politics (chapter one), Schindler advances his argument by means of an extended analysis of the rapprochement between Catholicism and liberalism attempted by John Courtney Murray. Murray was right, says Schindler, to insist on a Catholic affirmation of religious freedom, but he was wrong to define it solely in negative terms as freedom from coercion without also providing a positive account of the end to which freedom must be directed in order to be genuine freedom at all. This was no small omission, for the effect was to expel religious truth claims from public discourse and to consign them to a private sphere. As regards economics (chapters two and three), Schindler argues that the market in a capitalist economy is never neutral, as neo-liberal apologists such as Novak, Neuhaus, and Weigel assert, but rather always already embodies a notion of God, the self, and society. By elevating human creativity and initiative in economic activity above human receptivity, the capitalist market endorses selfishness over generosity. The cure is to recapture the kind of receptivity that comes with a contemplative regard for the other, a receptivity which remains the primordial disposition for the followers of Christ and which includes true creativity, as exemplified most clearly in the fiat of Mary. As regards academics (chapter four), Schindler once again attacks the liberal notion of neutrality, this time as it is manifested in the modern secular academy. The institutional arrangements of the modern academy, despite their claim of intellectual openness and diversity, are predicated on philosophical assumptions derived from naturalism and antirealism. This has been lost on most Catholic educators (special attention is given to Rev. Theodore Hesburgh, C.S.C., of Notre Dame) who, as part of their attempt to pattern their institutions after the best (read: Ivy League) schools, have uninhibitedly embraced a liberal understanding of academic freedom and institutional autonomy. In place of the secularizing logic of this position, Schindler calls for an alternative logic shaped by the doctrines of creation and redemption. In the conclusion to the first half of the book (chapter five), Schindler emphasizes the positive achievements of modernity, namely, a deeper appreciation of subjectivity and freedom, both personal and political, but he says that if liberalism remains our prevailing ideology, these achievements will be overshadowed by a "totalitarianism," so to speak, "of the strong over the weak" (the notion is taken from *Evangelium Vitae*, para. 20). Genuine subjectivity and freedom can be assured only by placing them within the context of a *communio* ecclesiology.

This constructive agenda is pursued in the second part of the book, where Schindler "attempts to describe some of the main presuppositions of a *communio* theology relative to our present cultural situation" (p. 38). Its implications for the modern and postmodern academy are explored in chapters six and seven. In chapter six, he credits Nietzsche and Derrida with unmasking the empty mechanistic worldview of modern liberalism, but complements their attack on a static, stable metaphysics with a relational metaphysics flowing out of the love of the Logos. This focus on the academy is extended in chapter seven. He says that "sanctity should provide the inner form of intellectual life, in a way that affects both the methods and the content of the modern academic curriculum" (p. 203), basing this proposal on the Christian doctrine of analogy, which asserts that all beings, including inanimate beings, are ordered from and toward Christ and thus have ontological and cosmological significance. All things are marked by an "inherent logic" (p. 205) intrinsically related to the Logos, thus bearing vestiges or images of the personal incarnate love of Christ. In chapter eight, Schindler offers a meditation on Eliot which shows that "liberal culture still leaves intact the opposition between contemplation and action characteristic of the Greek and Eastern views" (p. 222). By contrast, Christianity points to a unity which can be grasped not simply by contemplation alone, as held in the East, nor by action alone, as held in the technologically driven West, but by both fused together so that the opposition itself is dissolved in a relational being-for-others as exemplified in Christ. Chapter nine argues that the emphasis in modern liberal culture on making and doing has generated a false masculinization which has resulted in the description of homosexuality as an alternative lifestyle and the drift of feminist thought toward androgyny. What is needed, Schindler argues, is a retrieval of the meaning of the feminine as ontological perfection, and thus the theological meaning of love as *communio* or nuptiality. A premium would be placed on receptivity as exemplified in the relation between God and the world established in Christ through Mary-Church. In chapter ten, Schindler further explores this theme of receptivity, in terms of the fundamental structure of the human person. The leading emphasis is on the priority of contemplation over action and how this priority can be fully explicated on the basis of a theology, not just a philosophy, of the human person. This claim brings up the issue of the relation of philosophy and theology and Schindler stakes out his position clearly by locating it in the tradition of Augustinian Thomism, represented earlier in this century by Gilson and others. While some might claim that his work falls too squarely in line with a Bonaventurian emphasis on revelation at the expense of reason, Schindler notes that this depends on how one reads Aquinas, but declines to venture further into such complex matters in this book.

The five-page conclusion consists of a brief synopsis of the book, cast in the form of an explication of the leading emphases of the theology of Balthasar. As Schindler freely acknowledges throughout the book, Balthasar's theology is the shaping and driving force of his effort to articulate a "new understanding of the cosmos in the light of *communio*," one that "serves as the inner logic and dynamic of the Christian's mission to assist God in the liberation of the world" (p. 316). Here again, in the conclusion, he reiterates the central claim advanced throughout the book: only participation in the *communio* flowing from the life of the triune God can truly liberate the world.

Heart of the World, Center of the Church is one of the growing genre of books dedicated both to delivering a decisive critique of a Catholic accommodation to liberalism and to proffering an alternative to it, and like most books of this genre, it is at its most illuminating and trenchant in delivering the critique. The following remarks are directed to this critique as it pertains to the work of John Courtney Murray, for two reasons: one, because Schindler's analysis of Murray is the most well-developed and well-executed aspect of his critique of liberalism; and two, because this analysis shapes his reading of Novak, Neuhaus, Weigel, and Hesburgh, all of whom should be considered—and who indeed consider themselves—intellectual heirs to Murray and to the tradition of Catholic liberalism that Murray represented or, better yet, that he imagined into being.

Murray established the identity of this tradition of Catholic liberalism by aligning it with what he considered to be the broad liberal tradition of British and U.S. democracy (which he dubbed variously "the Great Tradition," "the ancient liberal tradition," or "the Western political tradition") and contrasting it with the doctrinaire liberalism of nineteenth-century continental Europe, particularly France. Setting these two traditions of liberalism in contradistinction to each other proved to be rhetorically very effective, for when those who were dubious of the very notion of a "Catholic liberalism" pointed out that the Church had consistently condemned liberalism since its inception, Murray was able to respond by noting confidently that the liberalism condemned thus far was that of the French variety and that British and U.S. liberalism had yet to be seriously examined and judged; once this occurs, it would be found that this liberalism can and should be embraced by the Church.

One way to establish the difference between these two traditions of liberalism is to posit a distinction between liberal structures and liberal ideology and to demonstrate that the French tradition of doctrinaire liberalism insists that all parties subscribe to liberal *ideology* whereas the British-U.S. tradition of broad liberalism merely provides a nonideological set of *structures* that make it possible for different groups in a pluralistic society to forge a common life. With this distinction at hand, it can be argued that structural liberalism in no way thwarts the mission of the Church, but rather facilitates it, by ensuring a level playing field in civil society wherein the Church may do its work without interference on the part of the state or those opposed to her mission. The precise terminology of this structures/ideology distinction comes not from Murray's writing, but from an essay defending Murray by Joseph Komonchak. The purpose of his essay is to point beyond facile declarations for and against liberalism to a more nuanced position that rejects ideological liberalism, yet embraces structural liberalism.[1] Taking up Komonchak's essay in his chapter on Murray, Schindler acknowledges the conceptual legitimacy of this structures/ideology distinction, but goes on to argue that while structural liberalism is not overtly ideological, it nevertheless undergoes a subtle, yet ineluctable transformation into what amounts to an ideology. In other words, the structures/ideology distinction implicit in Murray's work is a distinction without a difference.

This point has been convincingly made by a host of philosophers and political theorists, but rather than rehearse their arguments, Schindler analyzes Murray's reading of two texts crucial to his overall argument and reflective of its problems. The first text is the First Amendment, more specifically, the religion clauses of the First Amendment. Schindler maintains that Murray's reading of this text is ambiguous to the point of incoherence. On the one hand, Murray claimed that the First Amendment is predicated on the assumption that genuine civil discourse requires reason grounded in natural law and ultimately in the author of the natural law, God. Moreover, he also claimed that reasoned discourse presupposes a citizenry marked by prudence, self-discipline, and other minimal virtues. Thus Murray's account of reasoned discourse was by no means morally vacuous, nor even stripped of all religious reference to God; indeed, it was intended to oppose the moral and religious vacuity of the procedural liberalism of his day. On the other hand, Schindler points out, Murray claimed that the religion clauses of the First Amendment must be read as articles of peace, not articles of faith; as, in Murray's words, "'the work of lawyers, not of theologians or even of political theorists'" (p. 56). In this view, the First Amendment was the work of several different groups, Catholics, Protestants, Jews, and secularists, who joined hands to forge the law of the land in a religiously neutral fashion. Thus the First Amendment is not grounded in a particular faith (as Murray saw it, this was the erroneous view of sectarian Protestants), but rather in no faith whatsoever. Catholics can and should endorse the First Amendment because its religious neutrality provides the governmental protection needed for the profession and practice of the Catholic faith. What Schindler argues (with the help of Gerard Bradley)[2] is that Murray's articles-of-peace account of the First Amendment privatizes religion and works to undermine the kind of moral formation that, as Murray himself insisted, is necessary for sustaining reasoned civil discourse in a free society.

Schindler makes a similar point about Murray's reading of the Second Vatican Council's Declaration on Religious Freedom, *Dignitatis Humanae*. On the one hand, Murray reads *Dignitatis Humanae* as proffering a purely negative definition of religious freedom, "immunity from coercion in religious matters," a definition that "carries no ideological implications regarding the truth of religion."

Such a definition of religious freedom is, says Schindler, "identical in meaning with that of the First Amendment of the American Constitution" (p. 61). (Here it should be mentioned that this reading runs in deep tension with the leading emphasis of the second part of the document, on the moral obligation to search for the truth, the fullness of which is to be found in Jesus Christ; but as Schindler shows, Murray dismissed the second part as mere reassurance that the Council was not lapsing into indifferentism, which the Council Fathers were obliged to disavow; and this interpretation could certainly be squared with a negative definition of religious freedom as a formal-juridical immunity from governmental coercion.) And yet, on the other hand, Murray went beyond a purely negative definition of religious freedom by grounding it in the dignity of the human person as a free and intelligent moral subject, a dignity that, for him, reflected the ontological structure of the right to religious freedom and all human rights.

Murray's reading of both the First Amendment and *Dignitatis Humanae*, then, is conceptually ambiguous because of its competing understandings of religious freedom. According to Schindler, this ambiguity cannot be resolved within the liberal framework that Murray assumes. Thus while "Murray wants to affirm, and indeed in an important sense does affirm, that the human act is positively related to God, or at least must finally be so for its full integrity," he nevertheless "does not build this positive relation into the *first* meaning he accords the human act in his proposals for the public order" (p. 68). As a result, a discursive space is created wherein human action must be understood in a neutral or empty sense, which in effect tends "to disfavor those religions which understand the human act to be first 'full' of relation to God—to be positively *ordered* from the beginning, *in its very constitution as a creaturely act*, toward God" (p. 68). This empty space is a key ingredient for any action theory designed to accommodate a variety of views on the ultimate end of human life, but what it does not accommodate, and by its very structure cannot accommodate, is the view that all human action, including the many constituent parts of human action, intrinsically relates to its ultimate end in such a way that reference to this ultimate end must be included in all accounts of human activity—including political activity. In other words, Murray's conception of human action, tailored as it is to the strictures of liberal political order, contains an initial moment of silence about the ultimate purpose of human action; "this means that, when theists go on to fill this silence with speech, they must do so now precisely by way of *addition*" (p. 69); and this in turn means that "worldviews that favor silence about God in the affairs of the earthly or temporal order therefore always retain a[n *official-public*] theoretical advantage over worldviews that favor speech about God." In this sense, "Murray's project . . . seems to lead to a privatization of religion" (p. 69). On this score, Schindler notes that "in place of the overt and aggressive atheism of Europe, America in fact . . . officially affirms a covert and more passive a-theism, the peculiarity of which lies precisely in its ability to coexist with, indeed, to dwell within, a certain intention of theism" (p. 69). The upshot is that the distinction between the two types of liberalism—between a moderate theistic liberalism of the British and U.S. political traditions and an aggressively secular liberalism of the French political tradition—is rather blurry, so much so that what Komonchak calls "structural liberalism" metamorphoses into "ideological liberalism."

All of which is to say that Murray did not, despite his intentions and pronouncements to the contrary, propose a neutral, nonideological, merely structural form of liberalism, but rather a form of liberalism that advances a subtle and irresistible secularism. The only sure antidote to this secular drift, according to Schindler, is to place the Church's affirmation of religious freedom in the context of a broader and deeper affirmation of the need to order all freedom to the truth; or in other words, to dispense with the attempt to formulate a negative, neutral account of religious freedom and instead to assert a positive, theologically substantive account of religious freedom; or in still other words, to present the Church's endorsement of religious freedom not in terms of freedom *from*, but in terms of freedom *for*. This emphasis is central to the second part of *Dignitatis Humanae*, the part that Murray dismisses as dealing with pastoral rather than theological concerns. It is central to the first encyclical of John Paul II, *Redemptor Hominis*, which endorses the Council's affirmation of religious freedom, but also insists (unlike Murray) that it "not be separated from the fuller context of revelation which gives liberty its positive, and most proper, meaning" (p. 73). It is central to *Veritatis Splendor*, where John Paul II "places the question of freedom from the beginning in the context of the *sequela Christi*" (p. 74). But the passage that carries the most weight with Schindler, the one that John Paul II cites repeatedly in his many encyclicals, is found in *Gaudium et Spes*, n.22, to wit: "It is only in the mystery of the Word made flesh that the mystery of man truly becomes clear. . . . Christ . . . reveals man to himself." This passage is terribly important. It insists that intellectual inquiry springing from what might be termed Christian humanism, while it may possess a legitimate autonomy within its own limited sphere, must finally be seen as intrinsic to the mystery of Christian redemption.

The key word here, for Schindler, is "intrinsic," for it indicates that no sphere of knowledge can be rendered entirely independent of theology, that is to say, no sphere of knowledge can be considered entirely "secular."

But this independence is precisely what Murray allows. One reason he did so was because he assumed that a positive, substantive understanding of religious freedom—freedom *for*—was not useful for the project of refurbishing public discourse in a pluralistic society. Only a freedom intelligible apart from any claims about the ends to which that freedom is ordered, only a freedom defined negatively as freedom *from*, could serve as the basis for a public ethic in the United States. Reinforcing this pragmatic reason is what Schindler calls Murray's "theoretical dualism with respect to nature and grace" (p. 75). Here Schindler's analysis and critique of Murray becomes most incisive. He begins by citing an observation made by Yale theologian George Lindbeck in 1961 that is remarkable enough to reproduce here:

> The difficulty is not so much with the basic natural law position as with the unreconstructed and rationalistic traditionalism of Fr. Murray's version of it. He seems totally uninfluenced by the newer investigations into the meaning of "nature" and "natural" that are being carried out in Europe by such Catholic thinkers as K. Rahner, Siewerth, von Balthasar, Dondeyne and de Lubac.... One cannot help but suspect that the voice of natural law in America would be stronger if it learned the new accent. (p. 75)[3]

In order to underscore this contrast between Murray and these leading mid-twentieth-century European Catholic theologians, Schindler sets a passage by Murray on nature and grace alongside a passage by de Lubac, and then offers a summary of these contrasting views:

> For Murray, grace's influence on nature takes the form of assisting nature to realize its own finality; the ends proper to grace and nature remain each in its own sphere. For de Lubac, on the contrary, grace's influence takes the form of directing nature from within to serve the end given in grace; the ends proper to grace and nature remain distinct, even as the natural end is placed within, *internally* subordinated to, the supernatural end. For Murray, then, the result is an insistence on a dualism between citizen and believer, and on the sharpness of the distinction between eternal (ultimate) end and temporal

(penultimate) ends. For de Lubac, on the contrary, the call to sanctity "comprehends" the call to citizenship. The eternal end "comprehends" the temporal ends. (p. 79)

Schindler is careful to note that neither Murray nor de Lubac denies the distinctness of the goals of temporal existence in general and of citizenship in particular, but he maintains that the two conceptions are different, and that the difference is far-reaching, leading to "two different conceptions of the civilization toward which Christians should be working. One [de Lubac's] is a civilization wherein citizenship is to be suffused with sanctity; the other [Murray's], a civilization wherein sanctity is always something to be (privately, hiddenly) added to citizenship" (p. 80). Thus Schindler demonstrates that Murray's inadequate account of freedom—freedom *from*—stems from an overly dualistic understanding of nature and grace, an understanding that sees nature as autonomous and thus neutral toward God rather than as positively, dynamically oriented toward God.

Bringing de Lubac into the discussion is a splendid way to make this crucial point, for it brings to the fore the way in which Murray's political theory was deeply shaped by the standard, neo-scholastic, two-tier understanding of nature and grace. This is not to say that Murray was entirely unaware or unappreciative of arguments being put forth at mid-century by European theologians depicting humanity as having a single, supernatural end within which the ends of "natural" activities are enfolded. As Joseph Komonchak has shown in a relatively recent article, Murray was influenced early in his career by a host of scholars whose work made the Second Vatican Council possible, including proponents of the *nouvelle theologie*, and in particular de Lubac, whose *Catholicisme* (first published in French in 1937) figured heavily into lectures he delivered as early as 1942. Murray remained under this influence throughout his career, so that even *We Hold These Truths* (1960), a collection of essays intended to show both his Catholic and non-Catholic readers that natural law principles undergird the American Proposition, contains an entire essay comparing incarnational and eschatological humanism and also a brief explanation as to how natural law is not eradicated but perfected by the Christian vocation.[4] Komonchak's purpose in this article is to place Murray's political theory in the context of his vision of the role of the Church and Christians in the redemption of history and society and thus to refute the criticisms of Murray scholars—Schindler included—"that Murray ignored distinctively Catholic theological grounds for Christian discourse and action in the public arena."[5] After showing that Murray's project was formed by substantive theological concerns, he concludes that "it was in great part his *theology* that led Murray to opt for a public *philosophy*."[6] Komonchak's article is illuminating and his conclusion is certainly valid, but it must be noted that while Murray's work was shaped by a definite theology, it was nevertheless a theology that occupied a separate discursive space and performed a different function from philosophy—as is indicated in the wording Komonchak uses in his conclusion: theology with no adjective, in contrast to philosophy, with the adjective "public." For Murray, theology functions as an ecclesial discourse that (as Komonchak's article clearly shows) gives rise to a distinctly Christian anthropology grounded in claims about the incarnation, the cross and resurrection of Christ, the Holy Spirit, and baptism, among other things. Philosophy, by contrast, is a "public" discourse whose anthropology is grounded in natural law and apprehended by reason alone, and therefore bears no ecclesial references whatsoever, so that at one point in *We Hold These Truths* Murray could write, with remarkable bluntness, that "the doctrine of natural law has no Roman Catholic presuppositions."[7] As Murray turned his attention from the spiritual to the temporal order, he also turned from the discourse of theology to the discourse of philosophy where the substantive terms and categories of the *nouvelle theologie* lose their force and even disappear. In short, while Murray's public philosophy was indeed, as Komonchak shows, informed by a theology, it was a theology that effaced itself as Murray moved into the realm of public philosophy and politics. Therefore, even accounting for the qualifications that must be made in light of Komonchak's article, there is a basic validity to Schindler's characterization of Murray: that while clearly influenced by de Lubac and the *nouvelle theologie* in certain respects, Murray's thought as a whole was governed by a neo-scholastic paradigm that analytically separated the workings of grace from nature, confining the latter within a self-enclosed sphere with its own set of natural ends, the fulfillment of which is assisted by grace but not transformed by grace; and that this nature/grace dualism gave rise to a host of correlative dualisms—temporal/spiritual, secular/sacred, state/church, to name a few—that formed the conceptual core of his theory of liberal democracy.

This link between Murray's neo-scholastic description of nature and grace and his political theory has been noted by scholars in the past, but mainly as a prelude to arguing for a more theologically enriched vision of politics and public discourse than is provided by Murray, arguing, in other words, that Murray's call for a public philosophy should be reformulated into a call for a public theology.

Curiously, Schindler addresses the work of only one of these scholars, Leon Hooper, and then only very briefly (pp. 76–78).[8] The works of several noteworthy scholars among the public theologians (for example, David Hollenbach, John Coleman, or Kenneth and Michael Himes)[9] are not addressed. It is hard to understand why. After all, they, no less than Neuhaus, Novak, and Weigel, are intellectual heirs of Murray. And their work too can be shown to exhibit the secularizing tendencies that are endemic to the Murray legacy. Indeed, using the labels Schindler presents in his introduction, these public theologians would seem to fit the description "liberationist," but it is impossible to know for sure because neither group is analyzed.[10] This is especially unfortunate because, unlike the neo-conservatives, upon whom de Lubac et al. have had little impact, most public theologians claim to be working out of the tradition, or at least in the spirit of, the *nouvelle theologie* and thus would make an interesting object of Schindler's critique. Such a critique might focus on the way in which public theology insists that ecclesially specific beliefs and practices be translated into terms and categories acceptable to all groups within a religiously pluralistic society, in order to show that this kind of translation process amounts to little more than a minor adjustment that leaves the dualistic conceptual framework erected by Murray firmly intact.[11] In any case, Schindler neglects this avenue of critique, and in doing so, misses an opportunity to show that by endorsing liberal democratic theory in the tradition of Murray, the public theologians too, much like their neo-conservatives counterparts, fall heir to a conceptual framework in which politics must function as a secular discourse.

But how, it might be asked, could it be otherwise? For the protocols of modern liberal politics require of religious traditions the employment of some form of secular reason—that is, some form of reason not embedded in the beliefs and practices of a specific ecclesial body—and it is hard to imagine how Catholics could abide by these protocols without producing some variant of what Murray called "public discourse," whether a public philosophy or a public theology. This is not to say that Murray worked in bad faith; Schindler is very clear about this; the problem was not with Murray the thinker but with the categories that structured his thought. But it is to say that in seeking to refurbish public discourse in a pluralistic society, Murray was compelled to appeal to a reason independent of the elevating and perfecting corrections of faith. Thus the dualisms running through his thought—spiritual/temporal, religion/politics, church/state—should be seen as indispensable features of his project of infusing public discourse in the United States with the principles of natural law and right reason.

He could not have abandoned the dualisms without abandoning the project as well, an option that for Murray was simply unimaginable.

Then does Schindler want to abandon Murray's project? The answer seems to be yes and no; yes, in the sense that he wants to dispense with the neo-scholastic categories that enable Murray to put forth a public ethic on the basis of reason alone, without substantive reference to revelation; but no, in the sense that he does not want to abandon the project but rather reconceive it along the lines of de Lubac's understanding of freedom—freedom *for*. Here Schindler's argument turns from a critique of liberalism to a positive proposal and, as I indicated earlier, it is at this point, where he makes his positive proposal, that the argument falters.

In re-conceiving Murray's project along the lines of a positive understanding of freedom (which Schindler attributes to de Lubac),[12] the question arises, how can one avoid endorsing what Murray called "the confessional state," or what constitutional theorists call "an establishment of religion"? The answer Schindler provides is that one can avoid it by "recognizing that the order of grace is not first a juridical order" and thus "is not coextensive with the Church understood as a juridical-hierarchical entity. Rather, the meaning of grace is revealed above all in the divine trinitarian *communio*, and thus in the person and love of Jesus Christ." This *communio* entails an intrinsically juridical dimension in the Church, but not anywhere else, including the state; and yet it "*does* imply," Schindler insists, "that we seek to actualize the meaning of the state in terms of grace (or Church) now understood as *communio*. If the state and the Church are to remain ever distinct as juridical entities, they nonetheless maintain this distinctness now only from within nature's internal relation to grace" (p. 84). This is why de Lubac can call upon the Church to influence the state, and why John Paul II can refer to the Church as a *forma mundi*, without, in either case, endorsing theocracy. Rather, "what they both intend is simply that the whole world be inserted within the mission of Jesus Christ: that the whole world thus become a 'civilization of love'" (pp. 84–85). Schindler closes his essay on Murray by trying to explain how, in this "civilization of love," liberalism's purely formal account of religious freedom can be discarded without losing the positive value of religious freedom: "The point is not to deny freedom but to transform it with love: to seek to place freedom within the *communio* which alone finally frees and whose truth, as truth of love, remains ever and in principle—and not just for strategic reasons—committed to freedom" (p. 88). In this setting, a genuine freedom would be exercised, one that promotes "a truly ecumenical dialogue among all faiths—Jewish, Catholic, Protestant, Orthodox, secular, and all others, Eastern and Western." Here we would witness "the kind of pluralism which permits all parties to be open and honest about their deepest convictions, and in this to begin already to realize genuine community" (p. 88).

But this closing suggestion is problematic. It is not at all clear that "a truly ecumenical dialogue among all faiths" about their "deepest convictions" would facilitate the realization of "genuine community." After all, each faith group is sure to bring to such a dialogue a different understanding of "community," especially if they hold to the kind of tradition-specific, theologically shaped understanding of community recommended by Schindler. How can differences over the nature and purpose of community be adjudicated when those differences stem directly from theological convictions about God, creation, redemption, and so on? One strategy, of course, would be to set aside those convictions for the sake of concord within civic society, but this would be tantamount to Murray's articles-of-peace strategy of which Schindler is so critical. And yet Schindler's alternative proposal is cast purely in general terms—building a civilization of love, inserting the whole world into the mission of Jesus, actualizing the meaning of the state in terms of grace, and so on—terms that, without further specification, are bound to function much in the same way as public philosophy and theology in the Murray tradition. Therefore, it is incumbent upon Schindler to show how his "civilization of love" proposal translates into a public ethic that draws directly on substantive theological convictions without at the same time underwriting the kind of religious intolerance disavowed in *Dignitatis Humanae*. As Schindler's proposal is brought down to the concrete, I suspect that it will turn out not to be substantially different from what has already been proposed by Murray and his successors.[13]

The problem is that just when Schindler's proposal is getting interesting, it gets vague. A flurry of questions are left unanswered. What does a state under the sway of a "civilization of love" look like? Does it prohibit capital punishment? Does it follow Church teaching in its waging of wars, and in its military operations within wars? Do its people enjoy basic economic rights, such as the right to a living wage? Does it forbid abortions, and also provide young women with the means to deal with crisis pregnancies? It seems that the answer to these questions would have to be "yes," in which case another question arises: Where is this state? And if this state has no material existence, then it is as an ideal; and if it is an ideal, then we need know how this ideal is to be approximated; and if the task is to approximate this ideal, then we also need to know how this state can be established and sustained without employing the kind of brute force that is normally employed when moral ideals are incorporated into the workings of state politics. In short, Schindler does not explain how it is possible to bring the state under the sway of a civilization of love while escaping the problematics of modern statecraft. Of course, it may well be that it is *not* possible. It may well be, as Alasdair MacIntyre argues, that the modern state is incapable of embodying substantive practical agreement upon some strong conception of the human good. In this case, it may well be that in developing a politics in keeping with the papal vision of a civilization of love we must, as MacIntyre also suggests, turn from the modern state to small-scale, local forms of political association where friendship, the virtues, and a shared vision of the good serve as essential components to genuine community.[14] But none of these matters is addressed in any detail by Schindler.

This weakness also mars Schindler's constructive proposal for the academy. After showing that the modern university is not, as Catholic liberals assert, arranged in a theoretically neutral fashion, and then showing that its purportedly neutral approach to education opposes a Catholic vision of scholarship, Schindler argues that a Catholic intellectual vision is predicated, not on a fragmented vision of intellectual inquiry, but on a worldview in which inquiry in various disciplines is to be guided internally by a comprehensive, analogical vision, the full articulation of which is given by means of philosophical-theological discourse. In elaborating on this analogical vision, Schindler observes that "Christian faith requires an *a priori* anticipation that love is the truest and deepest meaning of both the methods and the context of the disciplines," but then he goes on to qualify this statement by noting that "it is essential that this anticipation not be construed such as to permit a direct interference or deduction from revelation regarding the precise meaning to be accorded order and love in any specific context of inquiry." So "the Catholic inquirer or researcher will be guided by a Catholic worldview, which nonetheless will not be allowed to function (except in theology) as an explicit premise for his or her argument" (p. 171).

"Guided by a Catholic worldview"—but guided how exactly? How would such guidance play out in, say, political science? Would departments of political science in Catholic schools operate as training centers for the future functionaries of the bureaucratic state? Would they appropriate more than they do presently from Marxist theory so as to indicate the proper Christian attitude toward politics in late-twentieth-century capitalist society?[15] Or would they wither away altogether? For in a "civilization of love" politics would surely not be studied in isolation, but would be examined in connection with economics, leading to the creation of departments of political economy. And of course all political phenomena would have to be studied in light of an Augustinian-Thomistic conception of the good. But Schindler offers few specifics on these matters. Surely it is difficult to envision a college, and especially a university, where inquiry is infused with "the sanctity proper to christology and liturgy" (206), but if Schindler is right about the formative role of a Catholic worldview on Catholic education—and I think he is—his proposal ought to be concrete and detailed enough to exert an impact on particular fields of inquiry. For now, we are left largely in the dark as to what a *communio*-type college or university looks like.

One way to think about *Heart of the World, Center of the Church* is that it is a book that calls for the writing of another book in which the political, economic, and academic implications of *communio* ecclesiology are spelled out in more detail. In this future book, Schindler will need to draw more deeply on the Scriptures than he has done thus far. He relies very heavily on the hymn to "the image of the invisible God" (Colossians 1:15ff.) and on passages in the Gospel of John where Jesus speaks in trinitarian themes about unity and love, but no parables are cited, nor any stories of Jesus healing the sick, casting out demons, raising the dead, and denouncing the Pharisees. Just as there is little about what Jesus actually did, so there is little about what his first followers actually did. That is why Schindler can give us only a thin account of what his followers are to do now.

What are the specific practices of *communio* ecclesiology? What does the Church's form of life look like? These are crucial questions precisely because the effects of liberalism *are* as corrosive as Schindler says they are, so much so that now we find the liberal state effecting, so to speak, the withering away of the Church. Murray, well aware of this, sought to rejuvenate public discourse through natural law. Schindler sees problems with Murray's project and seeks to rejuvenate it with a Balthasarian aesthetics rooted in the *forma christi*. But this requires further specification because the notion of *forma christi*, cast solely in terms of "love" and "unity," can too easily be associated with a wide variety of forms of life, from that of the Catholic Worker to St. Casimir's Parish in South Bend to the Legionaries of Christ. Let me sharpen the point a bit. I would argue that the *forma christi* commends to us the kind of life lived by Archbishop Romero, and not the kind of life lived by his current successor, Archbishop Saenz, a former chaplain in El Salvador's *Guardia Nacional* and known sympathizer to the political party (Arena) whose leadership has been clearly implicated in Romero's assassination. And I would advance this argument by showing that the life and death of Jesus Christ was dramatically reenacted in the life and death of Oscar Romero (d. 1980), as it must be in ours.

This line of argument would move from a theological aesthetics to a theological dramatics (a theo-drama), from an account of the beautiful to an account of the good, from the first part to the second part of Balthasar's monumental trilogy. Once this movement from aesthetics to dramatics is carried out more thoroughly by Schindler and others, we will discover, I think, that *communio* ecclesiology entails a genuinely radical form of Christian life, one that moves beyond pre-conciliar integralism, beyond post-conciliar liberalism in both its neo-conservative and neo-liberal manifestations, to arrive at a post-Constantinian vision in which the Church serves as, in the words of Gerhard Lohfink, "God's contrast society."[16] This might appear to involve an intolerable surrender of secular power on the part of the Church, but actually it means boldly redefining the Church's power in terms of Christ the King, whose reign makes folly of the rulers of this age even while his head is adorned with a crown of thorns.

NOTES

Reprinted from *The Review of Politics* 60, no. 4 (Autumn 1998): 743–64. This essay is a review of David L. Schindler's *Heart of the World, Center of the Church: Communio Ecclesiology, Liberalism, and Liberation* (1996).

1. Joseph Komonchak, "Vatican II and the Encounter between Catholicism and Liberalism," in *Catholicism and Liberalism*, ed. R. Bruce Douglas and David Hollenbach (Cambridge: Cambridge University Press, 1994), 76–99.

2. The article on which Schindler relies is Gerard V. Bradley, "Beyond Murray's Articles of Peace and Faith," in *John Courtney Murray and the American Civil Conversation*, ed. Robert P. Hunt and Kenneth L. Grasso (Grand Rapids: Eerdmans, 1992), 181–204.

3. The passage is from George Lindbeck, "John Courtney Murray, S.J.: An Evaluation," *Christianity and Crisis* 21 (November 27, 1961): 213–16.

4. Joseph Komonchak, "John Courtney Murray and the Redemption of History: Natural Law and Theology," in *John Courtney Murray and the Growth of Tradition*, ed. J. Leon Hooper, S.J., and Todd David Whitmore (Kansas City: Sheed and Ward, 1996), 60–81; see especially 67–68.

5. Ibid., 61.

6. Ibid., 79.

7. John Courtney Murray, *We Hold These Truths* (New York: Sheed and Ward, 1960), 109.

8. The work cited is J. Leon Hooper, S.J., introduction to *John Courtney Murray, S.J., Religious Liberty: Catholic Struggles with Pluralism*, ed. J. Leon Hooper (Louisville, KY: Westminster/John Knox, 1993), 11–48.

9. See for example, David Hollenbach, "Public Theology in America," *Theological Studies* 37 (1976): 290–303; John Coleman, "A Possible Role for Biblical Religion in Public Life," in "Theology and Philosophy in Public: A Symposium on John Courtney Murray's Unfinished Agenda," *Theological Studies* 40 (1979): 705; Michael J. Himes and Kenneth R. Himes, O.F.M., *Fullness of Faith: The Public Significance of Theology* (New York: Paulist, 1993), especially 8–20.

10. As regards the label "liberationist," it is misleading when attached to public theologians in the United States. Their positive assessment of the workings of liberal democracy in the United States puts them in stark contrast to most Latin American liberation theologians, whose general perspective on U.S. politics is not as positive, and rightly so.

11. This is the basic argument presented in my review of *Fullness of Faith* by Michael and Kenneth Himes. Michael J. Baxter, C.S.C., "Review Essay: The NonCatholic Character of the 'Public Church,'" *Modern Theology* 11 (April 1995): 243–58.

12. Whether or not one can legitimately attribute this understanding of freedom to de Lubac, at least in the context of these political questions, is a matter that is open to debate, but which will not be addressed here. For de Lubac's views on church and state, see Henri de Lubac, *Theological Fragments* (San Francisco: Ignatius Press, 1989), 199–286.

13. This is a point made in reference to the "public theologians" in Komonchak, "Murray and the Redemption of History," 80–81.

14. Alasdair MacIntyre, *After Virtue* (Notre Dame, IN: University of Notre Dame Press, 1984), and "A Partial Response to My Critics," in *After MacIntyre*, ed. John Horton and Susan Mendus (Notre Dame, IN: University of Notre Dame Press, 1994), 301–3.

15. Alasdair MacIntyre, *Marxism and Christianity*, 2nd ed. (London: Duckworth, 1995), vii.

16. Gerhard Lohfink, *Jesus and Community* (Philadelphia: Fortress, 1982), 157.

CHAPTER 14

Liberal Ideology, an Eternal No; Liberal Institutions, a Temporal Yes?

And Further Questions

MICHAEL NOVAK

Michael Novak (1933–) has been a major American Catholic public intellectual since the 1960s. He has worked as a journalist, served as a diplomat, authored or edited more than forty-five books, and held numerous academic positions. He was the George Frederick Jewett Chair in religion and public policy at the American Enterprise Institute from 1983 until his retirement in 2009. His thought migrated from that of progressivism in the 1960s, when he resisted the Vietnam War, to what became known as neo-conservativism in the mid-1970s and early 1980s, when he took up a defense of the family, anti-communism, nuclear deterrence and capitalism. He once described neo-conservatism as "a progressive with three teenage children." The book for which he is best known is The Spirit of Democratic Capitalism *(1982), which was read widely around the world, especially in Latin America, was distributed behind the Iron Curtain, and reportedly influenced the views of both Margaret Thatcher and Pope John Paul II. Novak has been awarded twenty-six honorary degrees and the prestigious Templeton Prize for Progress in Religion.*

Michael Baxter's long review provides an outline of David Schindler's useful first book; concentrates on its treatment of John Courtney Murray; gives a free pass to its lengthy ontological and theological speculations; and calls attention to its impracticality. Like Baxter, I share de Lubac's view of grace and nature (mediated to me by three Jesuits, Henry Bouillard, Juan Alfaro, and Bernard Lonergan), although I draw from it practical applications quite different from those of

Schindler and Baxter. Further, I agree with the main thrust of Baxter's criticism: just where one wants to test Schindler's grand hypotheses about how grace ought to work in a "civilization of love," particularly with regard to politics and economics, Schindler has almost nothing practical to say, and such few gestures as he offers seem lamely indistinguishable from those he criticizes, for example Murray (on the First Amendment) and Richard John Neuhaus (on the public square). His reading of my own work, too, is excessively polemical.

Three Disagreements

Before turning to properly political themes, I must flag without further comment my strong disagreement with three theological moves made by Schindler and apparently accepted by Baxter. First, it is not true that Vatican II canonized de Lubac's view of nature and grace. Equally, it is not true that Pope John Paul II's views of nature and grace are identical to, or even equivalent with, de Lubac's.

Second, Schindler's views of nature and grace are not precisely de Lubac's; they are an extreme radicalization of de Lubac's. De Lubac always insisted that God did not *owe* grace to nature. Thus, de Lubac's idea of a "unitary final end" is not collapsible into the proposition that grace is either in strict justice owed to nature or "intrinsic" to nature in the way Schindler says.

Third, contrary to Schindler, Murray's views of nature and grace were not only informed by de Lubac's work; they were also direct applications of it. As editor of *Theological Studies*, Murray published the most significant articles of our time on the history of the theory of nature and grace, the "*Gratia Operans*" articles of Bernard Lonergan, well-informed about the work of de Lubac and his colleagues. Schindler's extremism in theology and ontology tempts him to a kind of intellectual imperialism in other spheres, both in the academy and in politics. By contrast and following de Lubac, Murray was far more respectful of the limited but real autonomy of such disciplines as history, political philosophy, statesmanship, the philosophy of law, and jurisprudence, both in the academy and in the life of nations.

An Excursus on Nature and Grace

Although after Adam and Eve there has never been a time of "nature" without the Fall, and "nature" is therefore an abstraction not an historical reality, there *was* a time when Jesus had not yet come. Later, there were places where the grace of Jesus was not known. And there have been both times and places where many men knew of nothing more than reason and experience told them. In these cases, to speak of "nature" as distinct from "grace" seems not only just but illuminating.

To render judgment on the actions of good men and women, who to the best of their abilities pursued the good and the true, Thomas Aquinas, using Aristotle as a sort of numbered painting, filled in a picture of what "nature" *would have been* in these two cases: when persons did not know of the Fall and grace; and what is due to nature in itself, had the Fall and Redemption never happened. "Nature" is in this sense an abstraction, not a concrete reality. It is a theorem, devised as an aid to understanding. "Nature" in one of these two senses has been all that a great many human beings have known.

Yet this defense of "nature" as a theorem for understanding is important. It protects the limited yet real authority of those academic disciplines that prescind from revelation. It guards the arts of painting, sculpture, architecture in their proper respect for objects of nature in their naturalness (of form and matter), as well as literature, philosophy, and history. This theorem enabled Thomas Aquinas to write, against *The Sentences* of Peter Lombard, the classical textbook of the preceding century and a half, that men and women without grace, lacking faith, and ignorant of the Word of God, could in fact accomplish morally good deeds, pursue noble moral purposes, and build good cities ruled by good laws. Without grace, such deeds might not suffice for salvation, but in a plain moral sense they are good. Of course, such persons, too, suffered from the effects of the Fall. They, too, stood in need of the full healing and full sanctification effected by the grace of Jesus Christ. But they did not know this, except obscurely and by a kind of inexpressible longing.

This legitimate use of the abstract term *nature* to help distinguish among daily realities of our lives is of high utility. It prevents theological imperialism on the part of Christians. It teaches Christians to be as patient and respectful of the twisting paths of personal biographies as God is. More profoundly, this usage grounded the great flowering of Christian humanism in the three centuries following the death of Thomas Aquinas. The cathedral he built in his *Summa* was matched in poetry (Dante), architecture (Chartres and St. Peter's), painting (Fra Angelico to Michelangelo), and all the liberal arts and newly launched sciences of the many new universities of the West.

We should note, finally, that "grace" too is a theorem, worked out in technical language over many centuries to account for the complex data of revelation.

The merit of de Lubac was to remind us that these theorems of "nature" and "grace," so useful for theology as a science, do not alter the concrete facts of the current human condition: everything we see within us and around us is fallen, and everything has been redeemed. As the country priest of Georges Bernanos writes at the end of his *Diary*, "Everything is grace." If we distinguish, it must be in order to unite.

The Vocation of Lay Persons in the World

Nonetheless, having put that much on the record, it would be an error, in a review dedicated to politics, to dwell here mainly on ontology and theology. I appreciate for this reason Baxter's willingness to stick to one main issue, Murray on the First Amendment. Both Schindler and even more radically Baxter go wrong in their criticism of Murray. Political philosophy is a habit of mind, and not at all the same habit of mind as theology or ontology. More narrowly still, political statesmanship—in this case, the act of actually founding a new republic—is yet another habit. It was this last habit that led to the First Amendment to the U.S. Constitution, an amendment that had been promised, along with others, in the debates concerning ratification. (Constitutional scholar Robert Goldwin has collectively called these first ten amendments "the people's article" of the Constitution.)[1] The American people are a religious people, and they were not satisfied with the relative silence about religion in the body of the Constitution. Many of the ratifying states had established churches, and some required that public officers be believing and observant Protestant Christians. Cumulatively, the states wanted to be certain that the new federal government did not force any one religion upon the people, and did not inhibit the free exercise of religion that the people already cherished.

James Madison was the particular person in whom this habit of statesmanship lived, in him a habit of a very high order. Practically single-handedly he put the Bill of Rights on the agenda of the First Congress, drafted it, and shepherded it through a largely unwilling and otherwise preoccupied Congress, believing that without it the Constitution would not be cherished by the people and would not hold. For the people rightly feared a strong central government.[2] Because of the false preeminence he is often given in these matters, it should be recalled that during this period Jefferson was in France as ambassador.

Necessarily, then, the First Amendment was a work of prudence. Its passage by a reluctant Congress and then by a majority of suspicious state governments was no sure thing. Its very wording was carefully crafted under the pressure of intense debate. This was no academic exercise, no ideal statement for a theological manual. The final Bill was the product of serious Protestant minds, chastened by the lessons of the many experiments in religious liberty conducted in all the original colonies over some two hundred years. For them, it took a great deal of self-abnegation. In two vital areas they declared the lawmaking power of the Congress simply incompetent: Congress could pass no law establishing a religion ("*a* religion," Madison clarified in the constitutional debate) or inhibiting the free exercise of religion. They denied themselves the power to do these things.

Schindler and Baxter both complain of shortcomings in Murray's analysis of this historic and unparalleled achievement. And there are such shortcomings. Yet Murray had made some effort to acquire four demanding intellectual habits: theological, philosophical, political, and historical; in addition, he tried to put himself in the shoes of the statesmen who toil to give ideals flesh in institutions. To acquire all these habits requires many years of work, and even then no one can do everything. To a very large extent, Murray necessarily had to exercise these habits in the arena of ecclesiastical history, rather than in the arena of American political history, since it was in that arena that he was under the fiercest sort of attack.

In this respect, I do not think the criticisms of Murray by Schindler and Baxter advance the argument very much, although they do help us to look at it from a fresh angle. With one exception, Baxter captures well enough the difficulties Schindler faces and the practical self-contradiction into which Schindler falls. However, Baxter follows Schindler in accepting this generation's "liberal" interpretation of the Constitution (for example, in the American Civil Liberties Union, Harvard Law School, and the higher Courts) as essentially the same as the interpretation expressed by the Founding generation. This is a great blunder, both historical and strategic. It is historically false, and it unwisely grants to our theological enemies all the prestige and legitimacy that the Constitution rightly accrued during its first 160 years. (I exempt the period from 1947 on, the period of liberal revisionism.)

Based upon this inadvertence, Schindler argues that "liberalism" presents us with a scam, imposing under the guise of "neutrality" a form of liberal indoctrination. He is quite right about that. That is one reason, among several, why some of us moved in a different direction, which liberals spurned as "neo-conservative."

This new direction is that of Acton, Tocqueville, and Aquinas ("the first whig," as Acton called him), not to mention Pope John Paul II. This is the tradition for which, in political philosophy and in political statesmanship, practical wisdom or *phronesis* is the central natural virtue. (*Phronesis*, blown by the infusion of grace, becomes *caritas*.)

In the American Founding, which was far more religious than liberal scholars of the last fifty years have reported,[3] there are plenty of signs both of prudence and of *caritas*. One might consult, for instance, the great sermon of John Witherspoon, President of Princeton for 23 years, "the most influential professor in American history," signer of the Declaration of Independence, and teacher of James Madison (for an extended one-year tutorial), as well as of 29 congressmen, 21 senators, and 56 state legislators. The sermon in question was published in Philadelphia two weeks before the Declaration of Independence, appealing for self-denying love.[4]

One might also consult, simply, a favorite American hymn:

America! America! God shed his grace on thee
And crown thy good with brotherhood . . .

So recently after the religious wars of Europe, which many in America had experienced in their own flesh, and in a context in which a majority of the states already cherished established churches, what would have been the path recommended by prudence and charity for the formulation of the First Amendment for the Republic as a whole—a path also likely to win a majority of the necessary votes? The first task in the order of prudence was to secure religious peace, to prevent state control over religion, and to preserve the sphere of conscience, thought, speech, and action free for the pursuit and practice of virtue, widely recognized as the only true happiness. Given historical precedents, this was a great work of divine prudence. So, forty years later, Tocqueville recognized it. So also the Third Plenary Council of Baltimore, looking back on the nation's first one hundred years under the Constitution.

Schindler argues that the First Amendment not only allows for an oath of loyalty to the Constitution on the part of atheists but actually tilts in the favor of atheists and against religion. That the amendment is often so interpreted today, even by the Supreme Court, I concede. But it is also a desecration of the acts of the Founding generation, and a treason against the understanding of all generations prior to about 1950.

Moreover, Schindler's proposal—to put into the First Amendment an understanding of religious liberty as the divine *communion*—directly intrudes state power into consciences. I do not think Schindler has a ghost of a chance of writing Catholic trinitarian doctrine into a new constitutional amendment, to replace the First Amendment. Nonetheless, he could well argue that the best available, and most profound, explanation of the First Amendment is to be found in reflection upon the nature of the human person, invited through Jesus Christ to participate in the trinitarian *communio*. He might well cherish this view in his heart and offer it publicly to all who might be won over by it.

Both Orestes Brownson and Alexis de Tocqueville held that one day Catholics might be the Americans best placed to offer a profound and coherent defense of the American achievement, and to prevent it from eroding, crumbling, and losing its intellectual footing. Furthermore, Catholics might also supply (one day) a philosophical defense of the Constitution. Some might turn to Maritain and Murray, others to the phenomenology of the human person such as is found both in Karol Wojtyla's *The Acting Person* and in the not-yet-compiled collection of all Pope John Paul II's statements about the United States, reflecting upon the meaning of this nation in the current history of salvation.

Straussian political philosophers are fond of pointing to a supposed "gap" between the medieval and the modern world. To this argument, there are many partial rebuttals. But it must be said that Wojtyla has added a dimension of reflection on the person as "subject" that mediates the Thomistic tradition and modern preoccupations, and brings to light the connective tissue between older conceptions of "nature" and modern practices of rights. All this Schindler ignores. Although he often invokes the name of Pope John Paul II, it is surprising how thin are his references to Wojtyla's thought.

Baxter, as I understand him, turns away from the politics of prudence, and wants to build up the City of God with Scripture and the local communal church as his main supports. This is a radical view, and I applaud him for it. In every generation the Spirit raises up voices such as his, and calls the rest of us to listen well to his challenging complaints. Nonetheless, there are other vocations in the Church, including the vocation to carry the leaven of faith into the dough of ambiguous history, civic turmoil, and human striving. Moreover, in his radical fundamentalism, Baxter sometimes seems confused about the difference between dualism and distinctions. To distinguish in order to unite is not to practice dualism. In the light of eternity and of the trinitarian *communio* that is the proper life of the Church, neither democracy nor capitalism nor pluralism has more than a flickering temporal importance.

Nonetheless, it was in time—the fullness of time—that Jesus Christ under a particular political and economic regime was born, suffered, died, and rose again. So each of us also is called to incarnate the faith in a particular time, in the heat of its social battles, in the ambiguous arena of decisions of policy. We are called to suffer and die, and to allow Jesus Christ to live in us, in a manner worthy of saints and of the grace that is in us. But this, too, must be done with practical wisdom, and with as much knowledge as we can hungrily acquire and open ourselves to receive. Here, too, Thomas Aquinas is a saintly model; also the Chancellor to a problematic King, Thomas More; and many another. Christian humanism of this sort tends to get lost in the extreme ("radical") theologies of Schindler and Baxter.

The distinctions between *eternal* and *temporal*, *natural law* and *law of love*, *nature* and *grace*, and several of the others that Baxter holds up to mockery as signs of "dualism" *are* sometimes signs of dualism in the unwary imagination. I remember several preachers of retreats and professors over the years, the hardworking but less profound ones, using metaphors and examples that showed, indeed, a "two-story universe." But the best of them, even then (my seminary education, back in the Dark Ages, extended from 1947 to 1960), cautioned us not to allow our imaginations to trick us in that way. They had read their de Lubac, and made sure we did too. Of course, in those days, de Lubac was under a papal cloud and one was instructed to use de Lubac intelligently, as an explorer, not as the writer of a textbook to be memorized like Denziger. De Lubac on nature and grace can use language in quite ambiguous and even equivocal ways, as any attempt to map his ten or twelve different uses of these terms will soon show the attentive student.

Further, if what de Lubac says about the workings of grace within the only "nature" of which we have experience is true, then we would not expect Aristotle to speak of grace or the Gospels. Yet we would not be surprised to find intimations of precisely those realities, glimpsed perhaps only partially and with some distortion, in parts of his work. We do not expect that our fellow citizens who are atheists see in the First Amendment what we do. Yet we are not surprised when they come up with insights that give us a new way of reading old familiar passages, such as "Give unto Caesar." It would be wrong for us to put into the First Amendment such language as only committed orthodox Catholics can swear commitment to. As it happens, even God permits each individual soul the opportunity (even right?) to refuse the Light shining into darkness. God, too, for the sake of receiving the love of women and men who are free, practices self-abnegation. If it is without precedent or model in the earlier history of the City of Man, the First Amendment is not without analogue in the divine economy.

For those who love God, the First Amendment is better than the establishment of an official church, on the one hand, or of official atheism, on the other. While there is more that government has done, can do, and ought to do in order to strengthen in the public mind the beliefs and practices of Judaism and Christianity (on which the success of our form of government depends), the First Amendment provides a necessary barrier against coercion by state power. On their lower side, the sound virtues and solid commitments engendered by the Jewish and Christian sense of responsibility are necessary means for the success of the experiment in republican government. Beyond that, they are also the *end* for which freedom was so earnestly pursued in the first place. Under a system of self-government, such virtues are ends in themselves.

The vigor of the First Amendment depends, however, upon a sturdy set of historical and philosophical-theological understandings of certain "truths." It is just these understandings that were for at least three generations in this century allowed to atrophy. During this period, a "liberal" and often explicitly atheistic understanding of the First Amendment captured an influential segment of the law schools and the courts. This doctrinaire and authoritarian revisionism has been a disaster for the moral ecology of the nation. Concomitant with it have come a horrific rise in criminality and crimes of the absurd, and a highly visible decline in basic habits of work, discipline, and respect in the nation's schools.

Our nation's Founders warned us often that without the practice of a sound faith and the habits inculcated by the Bible, our form of government is neither possible nor worthwhile. Our form of government is made to serve certain "truths," revealed to us both in Scripture and in our very reasoning about certain self-evident relations; for instance, the relations among virtue, self-government (in personal as well as public life), and liberty. About such truths our Founders were exquisitely clear.

No doubt the Founders were Protestant, and our understanding as Catholics is rather different. Yet I know of no Catholic body before them that built better. Some comfort may be gleaned from the early efforts on behalf of religious liberty in Catholic Maryland. In sum, I hope that both Schindler and Baxter turn their still youthful energies toward mastering the materials of history, politics, and economics. Then, and only then, will their theology take flesh in the tissues of ideas, institutions, and practices that constitute a civilization moved by the Love that moves the sun and all the stars.[5]

Notes

Reprinted from *The Review of Politics* 60, no. 4 (Autumn 1998): 765–74.

1. Robert A. Goldwyn, *From Parchment to Power: How James Madison Used the Bill of Rights to Save the Constitution* (Washington, DC: AEI Press, 1997).
2. It is not by accident that contemporary abuses of religious liberty date from the centralization of government subsequent to the New Deal.
3. The Library of Congress unveiled priceless documents to this effect in its new exhibit of June 1998, called "Religion and the Founding of the American Republic." The interpretive text written as the exhibit's catalogue by historian James H. Hutson is a primary document in its own right.
4. "I could wish to have every good thing done from the purest principles and the noblest views. Consider, therefore, that the Christian character, particularly the self-denial of the gospel, should extend to your whole deportment. . . . This certainly implies not only abstaining from acts of gross intemperance and excess, but a humility of carriage, a restraint and moderation in all your desires. The same thing, as it is suitable to your Christian profession, is also necessary to make you truly independent in yourselves, and to feed the source of liberality and charity to others, or to the public. . . . [T]he frugal and moderate person, who guides his affairs with discretion, is able to assist in public counsels by a free and unbiased judgment, to supply the wants of his poor brethren, and sometimes, by his estate and substance to give important aid to a sinking country." ("The Dominion of Providence over the Passions of Men," *Political Sermons of the American Founding Era*, ed. Ellis Sandoz [Indianapolis: Liberty, 1991], 557.)
5. Incidentally, the distinction between the actual practices of liberal institutions and liberal doctrines which Baxter finds in a 1994 essay by Joseph Komonchak appears as the structural backbone of my earlier book, *Freedom with Justice: Catholic Social Thought and Liberal Institutions* (1984).

CHAPTER 15

Communio Ecclesiology and Liberalism

DAVID L. SCHINDLER

David L. Schindler (1943–) is Edouard Cardinal Gagnon Professor of Fundamental Theology at the Pontifical John Paul Institute for Studies on Marriage and Family at the Catholic University of America. He held a faculty position at Mount Saint Mary's College from 1976 to 1979 and in the Program of Liberal Studies at the University of Notre Dame from 1979 to 1992. His thought has long been associated with the "Communio" movement in Catholic theology, a school that has included theologians such as Hans Urs von Balthasar, Joseph Ratzinger (Pope Benedict XVI), and Henri de Lubac. Since 1982, Schindler has served as editor-in-chief of the North American edition of Communio: International Catholic Review. *From this standpoint, Schindler has been a strong critic of liberalism, not only in its theological versions but also in its political, economic, and intellectual manifestations. This critique is reflected in the book that is the subject of the present exchange,* Heart of the World, Center of the Church: Communio Ecclesiology, Liberalism, and Liberation *(1996).*

I

I begin with a discussion of Father Michael Baxter's reflections on my *Heart of the World, Center of the Church* (*HWCC*). I am deeply grateful for the evident care and thoroughness with which he read the book, and can suggest here only the beginning of a reply to his serious questions.

Appropriately for the audience of the *Review of Politics*, Baxter develops his reflections mostly in terms of my argument regarding John Courtney Murray. Granting a basic validity to my critique of Murray, Baxter nonetheless argues that, in the end, my own constructive proposal "gets vague," and he suspects that "it will turn out not to be substantially different from what has already been proposed by Murray and his successors."

(1) Baxter's criticism here goes to the core of why I undertook to write *HWCC*; it needs to be addressed at some length. Regarding Murray, my position is not only that he fails to build positive relation to God into the first meaning he accords the human act in his proposals for the public (constitutional) order. It is that he also fails to conceive the nature of that positive relation adequately on intrinsic grounds, despite his intentions to the contrary. Thus my criticism of Murray was (and is) not only that a nature-grace dualism (and the host of attendant dualisms) constitute "the conceptual core of his theory of liberal democracy" (as Baxter rightly highlights). The further and crucial point is that Murray's "abstract" sense of the order of nature results in an inadequate notion of the *creatureliness* of the human person. Creatureliness properly understood implies that our being is *constitutively related to God* (and indeed to other creatures in God), not by virtue of what the *self* first *does* but by virtue of what is first *done to* the self *by God* (the divine *Other*). Creatureliness just so far implies "receptivity" (to God) as the basic act of the human being, in contrast to the "creativity" or "self-determination" affirmed by Murray and the others criticized in *HWCC*. In short, we are "receivers" before we are "achievers."

Hence *HWCC*'s repeated appeal to Mary as archetypal for the human being. Mary's *fiat* ("let it be done unto me according to your word": Lk. 1:38) provides the archetype for understanding the relational structure of the creature as one whose most basic *mode of being and acting* is to receive from God. In Mary, we understand what it means for creaturely being to be constitutively a gift from God and, consequently, for the self to be more the fruit than the source of love. In short, Mary shows how creaturely being is structurally prayer.

This prayer is radically social, including all other creatures, especially the "poorest" and most vulnerable. This is clear in the *magnificat* that follows the *fiat*: "My soul magnifies the Lord. . . . He has scattered the proud in the imagination of their hearts, he has put down the mighty from their thrones, and exalted those of lowly degree; he has filled the hungry with good things, and the rich he has sent empty away" (Lk. 1:46–53; cf. the Sermon on the Mount: Mt. 5:1–12).

It is crucial to understand that nature in its integrity is not here confused with the order of grace (and sin). The point is simply that nature, from the first moment of its existence, is never neutral to its own creaturely *being-from-Another*.

It is in this context that *HWCC* gives its most basic definition of liberalism. In making "creativity" or "self-determination" primary in its (often unthematic) view of the person, liberalism—including its most benign forms—fails to take account of the receptivity implied in *being-from-the-divine-Other*, and thus slides ipso facto into a wrongly *self-centered* view of the person (into a kind of ontological "pelagianism"). This self-centeredness is by definition *a-theistic*: not so much because of an explicit exclusion of God as of a (largely unintended) failure to integrate the constitutive relation to God into the first meaning of all creaturely being and action. (Will Herberg's discussion of the American Way of Life and its peculiar form of secularism is helpful here.)

HWCC takes this ontology of creatureliness to be the main critique of American culture entailed by the integration of Christology and anthropology that Pope John Paul II notes as perhaps the most important teaching of the Second Vatican Council (*Dives in Misericordia*, n. 1; cf. *Gaudium et Spes*, n. 22). Nonetheless, Father Baxter suspects that the implications of this ontology will turn out not to be so different from what has already been proposed by Murray and his successors—or, in any case, that what I have proposed remains too "thin," "vague," or "general," and needs to be spelled out more concretely, in terms of discrete positions and practices. I offer four comments in response to Baxter's criticism.

(a) Interestingly, Baxter's suggestion that my proposal remains too "general" echoes criticisms made by many of Murray's contemporary followers. Here I would therefore turn the tables on Baxter, and ask whether his suggestion does not itself already imply that he shares with these critics certain proclivities of the Anglo-American—liberal—philosophical tradition. In contrast to a metaphysical tradition that supposes a sense of being as concrete, precisely in its interior depths, mystery, and implicit universality (cf., e.g., Pieper, Balthasar, Siewerth, Marcel), certain moderns reduce the concrete to observable bits of behavior and discretely identifiable events and practices (cf., for example, in their different ways, Bacon, Locke, Hume). Having conflated the concrete with the empirical and "particular," these thinkers see ontological claims as ipso facto "abstract" and "general." *HWCC* argues that an adequate sense of *communio* ecclesiology implies the former ontology, and that the latter ontology in fact already implies the "nominalist" reduction of creatureliness that is an essential part of the liberalism *HWCC* opposes. But the further relevant point here is that this "nominalist" sense of creatureliness signals not the absence but the presence of a definite ontology, a presence that Baxter needs yet to acknowledge and argue as such.

(b) Baxter refers to Balthasar and the need "to move from a theological aesthetics to a theological dramatics." But that is just the point: Balthasar's theological aesthetics precedes his "theo-drama" because, without sustained attention first to the *interior form*—the *spirit and form*—of being, human action would remain barren and unfruitful (that is, too "thin") in the requisite Gospel sense, even if impeccably "correct" at some ("external") moral and political and indeed "practical" level. (See, e.g., the discussion of being as love in *The Glory of the Lord*, V, 611–56.)

(c) What, then, is the significance of this "new" interior form of being? I invite Baxter to consider how the notions of "knowledge (and indeed being) as power," of self-interest, and of "rights" dominate current patterns of life and thought in America; and to consider in this light the main features of the "culture of death" as described in *Evangelium Vitae*, especially numbers 19–23. It is the contention of *HWCC*, in fact, that "knowledge (or being) as power," self-interest, and "rights" as understood in even the most benign forms of Anglo-American liberalism imply an ontological, (unconsciously) a-theistic, self-centeredness, which is also the source of what John Paul II describes as the "culture of death" and Balthasar as the culture that results from the abstraction of nature (human being) from its original creaturely context (see the statement in *Love Alone* [Herder, 1969], pp. 114–15, which sums up the thesis of *HWCC*). There is obviously a chasm between the two cultures indicated here. The point is that the difference, as ontological, is already much "thicker" than that suggested by discrete practices, productions, or programs: as a difference in the *form and spirit of being*, it goes to the core of all life, thought, and action.

Here, then, is the significance of the constellation of views proposed by the Catholic authors criticized in *HWCC*—their common defense of the religious neutrality of liberal institutions ("articles of peace") and the religiosity of the American people (atheism being reserved to the explicit sort more often present in the "new knowledge class"); the primacy of "creativity," the moral legitimacy of self-interest ("rightly understood": e.g., James Madison), the irrelevance of the Beatitudes in proposals for public life (save as matters of private inspiration), and the resistance to acknowledging the need to change consumerist lifestyles (on this, cf., e.g., *Centesimus Annus*, n. 52), and so on. This constellation of views leaves largely intact (to be sure, unintentionally) the ontological self-centeredness—hence the implicit a-theism—that underpins the "culture of death." Thus, however much I might agree with the authors criticized in *HWCC*, for example, regarding abortion, my contention is that their proposals leave largely undisturbed the very ontological patterns of power and self-interest that dispose the culture toward abortion in the first place. They propose, as it were, a civil containment rather than genuine spiritual transformation of "knowledge (being) as power" and self-interest as the *goal* of the Christian's engagement with the world, insofar as this engagement takes *public form*.

An excellent case in point here is Father Richard Neuhaus's defense of American liberalism in the April 1997 *First Things*. Eloquent and astute in many respects, the article leaves unexamined the core issue raised here and by *HWCC*: namely, liberalism's ontological self-centeredness and hence implicit a-theism. And again, by liberalism I mean to include precisely the "benign" sort defended by Neuhaus himself and the other Catholic authors discussed in *HWCC*. The point of *HWCC* is not to reject modern subjectivity, but to retrieve it now in terms of the creature's constitutive (hence radical) relation to God. (Perhaps it should be noted, for those who find such terms helpful, that the ontology of *HWCC* is intended to be more in the spirit of "post-modernity" than of "anti-modernity," as the language of "relation to the other" should suggest.)

(d) Baxter rightly suggests that I would answer yes to each of his questions regarding capital punishment, war, economic rights, and abortion. But I would insist, in light of the above, that these answers are made concrete in the first instance by being spelled out, not in terms of statecraft (to which I will return below) but in terms of holiness as a way of being present in the world. A good example here is Dorothy Day—who embodies in a concrete way the vision urged in *HWCC*—and the Catholic Worker Movement she co-founded (see the articles by Mark and Louise Zwick and others in the Fall 1997 *Communio*). Day understood well that moral-social "conclusions" in matters of capital punishment and the like already differ profoundly depending on whether or not they are integrated in and by a Gospel-ecclesial *(communio) spirit and form*. Indeed, the purpose of the Movement Day co-founded was to transform social-political activity into the *prayerful mode of being* required by the Gospel (hence the importance for Day of St. Thérèse of Lisieux, for example).

To summarize, then: the intention of *HWCC* was to diagnose the *spirit and form of being* implied in the *communio* ecclesiology of the Second Vatican Council and embodied in "saints" like Dorothy Day. Baxter is right that much detail needs yet to be worked out. The presupposition of *HWCC*, nevertheless, is (a) that the diagnosis already suffices to show the profound difference from top to bottom between a culture integrated by an adequate notion of creatureliness and one that is not—such as the liberal culture defended by the Catholic authors criticized in the book; and (b) that the required detailed application bears significant prudential dimensions that can be known only in the concrete historical situation by economists and politicians themselves (hence John Paul II's insistence that the Church has no models to propose in these fields). The purpose of *HWCC* is achieved in clarifying the fundamental way of being and acting that should inform the prudential judgments of these economists and politicians: in clarifying how and why a genuinely Catholic-creaturely way of being differs profoundly from a liberal way of being, even on the latter's best reading.

(2) Baxter may think that I have delayed too long the question of modern statecraft. Given present limits and in anticipation of further mutual discussion, it will have to suffice merely to record the principles of my response. (a) First, as should be clear from the above, the presupposition of *HWCC* is that a false appeal to power in our relations with others (what Baxter refers to as "brute force") is first a problem of theology and spirituality (understood ontologically). The more urgent and concrete problem in the modern liberal state is that of a (practical, implicit) atheism driven by "pelagianism" and "nominalism" in the sense indicated.

(b) If and insofar as this is the case, our cultural concern should be directed first, not to the state but to the communities which are most basic to the self and its formation: the Church and the family (the "domestic church").

(c) Our cultural critique should be directed, secondly, to the areas which most immediately and pervasively affect the formation of the self by the church and the family: modern technology and the academy and the schools. For it is technology—with its intrinsic relation to the market and its media (television, computers)—which most homogenizes the meaning dominant in the culture, by carrying that meaning across national-legal borders and into local communities and homes (by meaning I refer especially to the ontological pelagianism and nominalism undergirding the Western consumerist style of life). Regarding the academy: the argument of *HWCC* is again that we must first attend to the deep flaw in the *interior form* of the modern (liberal) academy, and show how this form—whose archetype is the machine, not love—has shaped the primitive meaning of objects and subjects, of objectivity and subjectivity, as these are presupposed in the various disciplines. I agree with the direction implied in each of Baxter's questions about the disciplines, but the burden of *HWCC* is that the question about knowledge and being as power (cf., for example, Bacon's *Novum Organum*) is more basic than questions of polity and economy and indeed "ethics," and needs to be faced first. Of course, as we deal with this more basic question, those of us who work in the academy need also to work out the "new" meaning of, and interrelations among, the disciplines (on this, see the principles and questions discussed in *HWCC*, pp. 159–76 and pp. 209–20). For this reason, a group of us established Arkwood Foundation four years ago, to ponder the meaning of intellectual inquiry (and of its implications for the "critical methodologies" of the modern disciplines) when conceived most basically as a form of prayer. (Incidentally, the point of analogy as discussed in *HWCC* was not to suggest that the influence of faith on all the disciplines should ever be extrinsic rather than intrinsic—a danger in much of the modern teaching on analogy and the "subalternation" of disciplines—but to sustain the respect required by faith itself for the creaturely *difference* on all levels.)

(d) Regarding modern statecraft, then: the implication of *HWCC* is that what first needs to change in the liberal state is its meaning. Contrary to liberal assumptions, neither can the state remain "officially" neutral regarding the destiny of the human person, nor is the purpose of law primarily coercive. On the contrary, the state cannot avoid being most fundamentally pedagogical in nature: willy-nilly, the state "teaches" about human meaning and destiny. Hence *HWCC*'s insistence, following Pope John Paul II, that the solution is not to abstract religious freedom from truth but to integrate religious freedom into the truth that is love. Is it worthwhile for Christians to seek to transform the meaning of the state in the way indicated here?

I offer three comments in response: first, I do not see how an authentic *communio* ecclesiology would permit us simply to abandon concern for transforming the meaning of statecraft. The implications of the Son of God's Incarnation and Redemption are meant to extend to ends of the cosmos itself (cf. Col. 1:15–18), and it is difficult to see how this catholic inclusiveness can, as a matter of principle, leave the political order uncared for, however "statist" and power-ridden and self-interested that order has become. The Church, furthermore, can never serve first and primarily as "God's *contrast* society" (emphasis added). Any *contrast* with the world must always be placed in light of the Son of God's *embrace of* the world: Jesus' being *against* the world (by virtue of its sin) is always-anteriorly a function of his being *for* the world. Secondly, I would at the same time insist, with Baxter, that we should not have any great expectations for sustained and wholesale "conversions" of established world power. On the contrary, Jesus's own universal love was met with crucifixion by the dominant powers. There are no Gospel warrants for thinking that there will ever come a time in history when this will not be the case also for the followers of Jesus. Thirdly, I would nonetheless suggest that efforts to uncover the state's inevitable involvement (even if only implicit) with questions of human destiny serve at least to help prevent the *a priori* reduction of all debates in a liberal society to issues of "procedure," as is now the case. (For further discussion of "procedural totalitarianism" and of all the issues raised here, see my "Reorienting the Church on the Eve of the Millennium," *Communio* 23 [Winter 1997]: 728–79.)

(3) Regarding Joseph Komonchak's argument that Murray did not ignore distinctively Catholic theological grounds for Christian discourse and action in the public arena: Baxter demonstrates convincingly that Komonchak's argument does not yet suffice to show that the nature or natural law proposed by Murray for the public arena was adequately integrated in light of the order of grace. But it seems to me important to complete Baxter's point in terms of the consequences of an integrated view of the nature-grace relation for the first meaning assigned creatureliness. Neither Komonchak's "John Courtney Murray and the Redemption of History" nor his review of *HWCC* (*Commonweal*, October 1997) deals with this issue in the precise form raised in *HWCC*; and, though it is not possible to show this in the present forum, I believe this failure raises significant questions regarding each of the conclusions offered in Komonchak's Murray article.

That the issue of creatureliness as raised in *HWCC* is crucial can be seen in Murray's important article on incarnational and eschatological humanism, to which both Baxter and Komonchak refer. In that article Murray sets forth the claim that the achievements of the American economy, political order, and technology all represent works of "nature." But Murray's sense of how the two humanisms contrast makes clear that these achievements are to be "perfected" mostly by the *addition* of a new and enriching horizon rather than by any deep reversal. As Komonchak shows, this does not mean for Murray that grace introduces no intrinsic difference with respect to these achievements. The issue is entirely one of the *depth* of that difference: of the depth of the reversal that may be required with respect to any achievement of nature in the *actual order of history* (e.g., with its sin). The issue is not *whether* the two humanisms need to be integrated—Murray himself clearly acknowledges that—but *how*. My own view is that an adequate integration would require a much more paradoxical, and less purely "additive," sense of how grace is to *perfect* (i.e., "complete") nature. (The emphasis on "paradox" I believe provides the key to Henri de Lubac's significant difference from Murray in interpreting the traditional view that grace "perfects" nature: but that must be argued elsewhere.)

I suggest that Murray misses the depth of the reversal required at the heart of America's most distinctive achievements because his own emphasis on the "creativity" of the human person tends to render invisible the ontological self-centeredness, and hence implied a-theism, present in those achievements, notwithstanding the undeniable significance of those achievements in other respects (in securing a certain kind of freedom and a certain level of material well-being). (For further development of this argument, see my "Christological Aesthetics and *Evangelium Vitae*: Towards a Definition of Liberalism," *Communio* 22 [Summer 1995]: 193–224, especially 206–24.)

Murray of course was increasingly alarmed by what he saw as a growing secularism in America. But the pertinent point is that he, like his contemporary followers, locates the source of this trend primarily in the moral-legal climate of America in the post–World War II period. *HWCC* insists that this characteristic claim of Murray and his followers overlooks the source of current problems in the ontological pelagianism and nominalism resident in America's political, economic, and technological orders from the beginning.

(4) Baxter asks why I do not treat more extensively those "public theologians" who follow Murray from an apparently "liberationist" perspective, and who are sometimes more favorably disposed toward "*ressourcement*" theologians like de Lubac. Although of course that is an important task, my simple answer for purposes of *HWCC* is that, unlike Neuhaus, Novak, and Weigel, many of these "liberationist" theologians expressly disagree with significant aspects of John Paul II's teaching—for example, regarding *Veritatis Splendor* and "proportionalism"—and are often critical of John Paul as an authentic interpreter of the Council. Thus, although I think Baxter is quite right that the "public theologians" to whom he refers typically leave Murray's dualistic conceptual framework intact—and that they are thus often more "liberal" (in the Anglo-American sense) than "liberationist" (in the Latin American sense)—the fact of the matter is that the neoconservatives have had more credibility and influence,

both here and abroad, in their claim that the "new order of the ages" introduced by the American polity and economy, by virtue of the teaching of John Paul II (cf. especially *Centesimus Annus*)—and given Murray's interpretation of *Dignitatis Humanae*—has now been authenticated by the Church and thereby acquired a kind of normative status for the rest of the world.

II

Providing a clear contrast to Baxter's careful reading of *HWCC*—as evidenced, for example, in his failure to cite or quote the book a single time—Michael Novak reconstructs my (critical) positions mostly in terms of a projection based already on the terms of his (and Murray's) own argument.

(1) Regarding the nature-grace relation: the entire argument of *HWCC* rests on the claim that, while the order of grace is intrinsic to nature (in the one real order of history), this entails, not a denial of nature, but rather a new and deepened sense of nature's integrity. The burden of de Lubac's lifework (and of *HWCC*) was that nature could best be seen in its integrity precisely *as nature*, in the saint. Novak's critical comments presuppose that we can somehow get a better glimpse of what nature "in itself" really is, and better appreciate nature's achievements, if we first abstract nature from the one graced historical order, or indeed if we look at nature first as found in the non-Christian. His comments, in other words, presuppose the contrary of what both de Lubac and I have argued, fundamentally and repeatedly, while taking no account of the qualified form of our contrary argument. His comments thus amount to a gross *petitio principii*. For the details of my argument in this matter, I can here only refer the reader back to my writings. For an interpretation of de Lubac (including his significance relative to the Second Vatican Council), see my "Introduction to the 1998 Edition" of de Lubac's *The Mystery of the Supernatural* (Crossroad), xi–xxxi.

(2) Regarding my interpretation of the American Founding, two main points: (a) my argument has never been that the Founders were not men of genius, many of whom were religious in their own way, and in any case respectful of those who judged religion necessary to sustain the moral virtue undergirding good citizenship. My argument, rather, was and is that they were ambiguous about whether government should concern itself directly with the meaning of the human person, above all the person's relation to God—ambiguous enough that

such a sophisticated thinker as John Courtney Murray could plausibly interpret the First Amendment as "articles of peace," by which he meant that the First Amendment was officially agnostic in matters of theological-anthropological substance. To be sure, Murray insisted also that American *society* was founded on, and could continue to be civil only on the basis of, a shared natural law philosophy.

The pertinent point is that any intrinsic appeal to theological or *anthropological substance* in government is precisely ruled out by his own "articles of peace" reading of the purposes of government. On what grounds do we then criticize a Supreme Court which favors agnosticism in its reading of the official meaning of the First Amendment? For reasons I develop at some length in *HWCC* and elsewhere, I believe it is the very ambiguity already in interpretations like Murray's of the official meaning of America that provide support in principle for America's increasing "proceduralism." All claims, like that of Novak, that the Supreme Court's "liberal revisionism"—its imposition of liberal indoctrination, in the guise of neutrality—begin only post-1947 beg just this argument of *HWCC* that the First Amendment, *granted Murray's "articles of peace" reading*, itself already gives us the first form of liberal indoctrination under the guise of neutrality.

Nor is it so easy to rescue Murray from the dilemma indicated here, since the uniqueness he claimed for America's liberal institutions hinged above all on his "empty," neutral reading of America's official-legal institutions: America's distinctive achievement lay in its purely juridical conception of religious freedom.

(b) This, then, is why *HWCC* follows Bishop Wojtyla in the discomfort he expressed already during the conciliar discussion of *Dignitatis Humanae*, regarding the Americans' (i.e., Murray's) primarily juridical conception of religious freedom. Following Wojtyla and indeed Pope John Paul II, *HWCC* holds that religious freedom is best conceived from the beginning (even by governments) in terms of truth rather than no-truth ("articles of peace"). Religious freedom is best protected, not by being placed first outside any claim of truth, but by being placed rather inside the truth adequately understood: hence Pope John Paul II's emphasis on the *communio personarum*—on truth as love (*imago trinitatis*)—as the context within which alone freedom can finally be realized. The point is not that we should expect any human society ever to embody this truth fully, and certainly not that we are justified ever in seeking to *impose* it (it would be odd indeed to seek to impose the truth whose content is love!). On the contrary, we can only *propose*, through the concrete witness of our lives, that the truth of the *communio personarum* coincides with precisely the deepest respect for the religious consciences of others. I would only emphasize in conclusion that an essential part of this witness must consist in showing clearly how and why no governmental institutions—including the liberal institutions of America—have ever been able to avoid claims (however tacit) bearing intrinsically on the substantive truth about human destiny. Only as we succeed in this will it be possible to have the public debate in America that truly is needed: the debate, namely, regarding which notion of the human person will best protect religious freedom in its truest and deepest and most comprehensive sense.

NOTE

Reprinted from *The Review of Politics* 60, no. 4 (Autumn 1998): 775–86.

CHAPTER 16

"The Crisis in Church-State Relationships in the U.S.A."

A Recently Discovered Text by John Courtney Murray

JOSEPH A. KOMONCHAK, JOHN COURTNEY MURRAY, SAMUEL CARDINAL STRITCH, AND FRANCIS J. CONNELL

Joseph A. Komonchack (1939–) was the John C. and Gertrude P. Hubbard Chair in Religious Studies at the Catholic University of America until his retirement in 2009. He received his Ph.D. in theology at Union Theological Seminary in 1976 and taught theology from 1977 onward at the Catholic University of America. He is a leading historian of the Second Vatican Council and is editor of the English edition of the five-volume History of Vatican II. *He is the author of* Foundations in Ecclesiology *and has published over a hundred articles in journals of theology and religion.*

Editorial Note: In October 1950, John Courtney Murray, S.J., wrote for the use of Msgr. Giovanni Battista Montini of the Vatican Secretariat of State a memorandum with the title "The Crisis in Church-State Relationships in the U.S.A." This chapter includes the text of Murray's memorandum and the responses to it written by Samuel Cardinal Stritch and Fr. Francis J. Connell, C.SS.R. The following introduction to these texts sets the memorandum in context and explains the Holy Office's actions against Murray.

Introduction: The Context
Joseph A. Komonchak

Between 1948 and 1954 the American Jesuit John Courtney Murray (1904–1966) attempted to effect a development in Catholic teaching on church-state relations and on religious freedom. In 1954 four propositions thought to sum up his views were declared "erroneous" by the Vatican's Holy Office, and a year later he was advised by his Jesuit superiors in Rome to refrain from further publication on the subjects. Ten years later the Second Vatican Council published its Declaration on Religious Freedom (*Dignitatis Humanae*), in whose preparation Murray played a major role and whose teaching incorporated central aspects of the position for which he had been silenced.[1]

To recently discovered material in various archives which illumines this story may now be added the text of a memorandum which Murray prepared in 1950 for the use of Msgr. Giovanni Battista Montini, the future Pope Paul VI and at the time substitute secretary of state at the Vatican. Written, it seems, at Montini's request at a moment in which the issues of religious freedom and church-state relations were very controversial both in the United States and in Europe, the memorandum, "The Crisis in Church-State Relationships in the U.S.A.," has an unusual significance. First, it provides a very convenient summary of Murray's views as he was developing his own thought, a summary which, given its addressee and the probability that it would be reviewed at the highest levels in Rome, we may be sure he prepared with great care and precision. Second, it is perhaps the clearest brief statement of what Murray wished to see by way of a development of the Church's teaching. Third, the responses to it both in the United States and in Rome throw great light on the state of the question in the 1950s and provide a way of measuring the distance traversed in the fifteen years between Murray's preparation of the text and the promulgation of *Dignitatis Humanae*. All these reasons make it appropriate to publish for the first time both the text of the memorandum along with two comments on it, solicited by Rome from Samuel Cardinal Stritch, Archbishop of Chicago, and Father Francis J. Connell, C.SS.R, dean of the School of Sacred Theology at The Catholic University of America.

Background

John Courtney Murray's interest in the social and political mission of the Church was first revealed in the early 1940s when he promoted interreligious cooperation among Catholics, Protestants, and Jews to meet the spiritual and cultural crisis that had resulted in the Second World War. But the idea encountered serious resistance both among his fellow Catholics and from Protestants. Among the Catholic opponents was Francis Connell, who feared that such cooperation would promote the religious indifferentism he thought endemic in American culture and lead Catholics to surrender their Church's claim to unique rights. To prevent this he published an article, later reprinted as a pamphlet, on the Catholic doctrine of religious freedom.[2] This presented in clear and simple language the classic doctrine on church and state, that is, the thesis or ideal of the Catholic state, in which the Catholic Church enjoys official recognition and the State may justly place limits on the public activities of other religious bodies. The hypothetical conditions of a religiously pluralistic society justify extending full freedom to non-Catholic religions, and this is the ground on which American Catholics may support the First Amendment to the U.S. Constitution.

The defense of the ideal of intolerance led many American Protestants to be wary of any kind of cooperation with a church which in theory maintained that one day they might be deprived of their religious freedom, and it was this impediment to cooperation in the temporal sphere that led Murray to undertake a study of the classic Catholic doctrine and to propose a development of it that would permit Catholics to endorse the First Amendment on grounds other than simple expedience. After aborting an initial effort and devoting himself to three years of study of the question, Murray began to articulate his matured views in an address at the 1948 convention of the Catholic Theological Society of America. Connell accepted Murray's invitation to be the official respondent to this paper and in his brief reply argued that Murray's views were incompatible with modern papal teaching on the legitimate claims of Christ the King to reign also over civil society.[3]

In the years that followed, as Murray continued to develop his ideas, Connell became alarmed that they were gaining popularity in the United States, and he engaged Murray in a public controversy in the *American Ecclesiastical Review*.[4] But even before this exchange, Connell had also initiated a long series of private letters to various Vatican officials asking for action to halt the spread of Murray's views. In the first of these, 1 August 1950, Connell sent a Latin memorandum on Murray's views to Joseph Cardinal Pizzardo, sub-secretary of the Holy Office, along with a copy of the Proceedings of the 1948 CTSA convention and of a recent article by Connell in the *American Ecclesiastical Review*. The memorandum contrasted Murray's CTSA paper to the teachings of Leo XIII and Pius XII and gave examples from the popular press of American sympathy for Murray's views.[5] A year later Connell urged his friend and Catholic University colleague, Father Joseph Clifford Fenton, to pursue the matter while he was in Rome. "If necessary, I believe that a declaration from the Holy Office might be advisable. The repercussions of this new idea are, I believe, very unfortunate in our land especially." Upon his return from Rome, Fenton, whose usual contacts there were with officials in the Holy Office and in the Congregation for Seminaries and Universities, was able to assure his colleague that Murray's "case is much more serious than most people realize." "Your reputation," he told Connell, "is soaring in Rome."[6]

In February 1952 Connell sent Archbishop Amleto Cicognani, Apostolic Delegate to the U.S., a copy of an article in the *Washington Evening Star* which further illustrated "a confusion of thought regarding the Catholic doctrine, a failure to perceive the distinction between the thesis and the hypothesis, with a tendency toward the opinion advocated by Father Murray. I feel that it emphasizes the growing need for an authoritative statement on this subject of Church and State from the Holy See." In his reply Cicognani informed Connell: "I wish to assure you that I have recently had occasion to send to the Holy See certain material on this question. I am sure that it will be seriously considered but we know that the investigation and study take time."[7] It now appears possible to identify some of this "material" sent by Cicognani to Rome.

The Memorandum

In 19–22 September 1950, Murray participated in a meeting of Catholic ecumenists in Grottaferrata, Italy.[8] Sponsored by Unitas, a semi-official Roman center for ecumenical study headed by Charles Boyer, S.J.,[9] the meeting was feared by many of those involved in the nascent Catholic ecumenical movement as a command performance intended to bring them into line and to associate them under Unitas. These fears, only slightly lessened by learning that the meeting was encouraged by Montini, proved to be baseless.

In the circumstances of the day, six months after the publication of a Holy Office instruction on ecumenism and a month after the issuance of the Encyclical *Humani Generis*, which had included a warning against "false irenicism," it was thought prudent for participants simply to give reports on the state of ecumenical relations in their countries. Murray later described his own report: "When it came my turn to speak, as the representative of the United States, I was obliged to report that practically no ecumenical activities were going on.... The atmosphere was one of mutual mistrust, suspicion, not to say hostility. There was very little even in the way of cooperation in the temporal concerns of the community."[10] A diary entry about the event by Fr. Yves Congar, O.P., gives a little more information: "Then Fr. Murray's conference, of a quite remarkable precision, quality, and intellectual rigor. Fr. Murray thinks that the question of tolerance and, more generally, of the relationship of the temporal order to the Church, is a decisive question now." Murray's views were taken into account in the preparation of a summary of conclusions, the seventh of which read:

> In the face of the present controversies over religious freedom and Church-State relations (controversies which constitute a serious obstacle to friendly relations among separated brethren), an historical and doctrinal study of these problems seems necessary. It seems desirable that Catholics in the various countries make an effort to reach a unity of thought and sentiment on these questions.[11]

Perhaps at the conference, perhaps in connection with the papal audience granted to participants on 22 September, Murray met with Montini. Three years later, when he knew his views on Church and State to be under criticism in Rome, Murray described the conversation to Fr. Robert Leiber, S.J., personal secretary to Pius XII:

> On the occasion of my visit to Rome in 1950 I took up the matter in some detail with His Excellency, Msgr. Montini. It seemed to me that he fully appreciated the delicate nature of the problem and the special difficulties which it creates in the United States. This was very encouraging to me and to many others who in this country and in Europe are investigating these questions in scholarly fashion and who have expressed their sympathy for the views which I have tried to formulate in various articles.[12]

Not long after, in a letter to John Tracy Ellis, Murray repeated the comment: "This subject came up in a conversation with Msgr. Montini in Rome in 1950. He was personally sympathetic with my 'orientations,' and rather wanted his hand to be strengthened–but . . . ."[13]

This meeting appears to have led Murray, perhaps at Montini's invitation, to compose the memorandum, "The Crisis in Church-State Relationships in the U.S.A.," whose text is given below. Till now its existence has been known only from Murray's letter of 24 April 1951, to Fr. Vincent A. McCormick, S.J., American Assistant at the Jesuit Curia in Rome:

> I have been wondering what happened to the memorandum that I wrote for Msgr. Montini on the Church-State problem. My only information was that it had been called to the attention of the Holy Father by Msgr. Montini himself, and had been committed to the hands of "experts". Heaven help it, and me.[14]

The whole letter, and Murray's concern about his memorandum, reflect the tense situation created for theologians by the issuance of *Humani generis*.[15]

The only other use by Murray of his memorandum can be inferred from the presence of a copy of it among the papers of Clare Booth Luce in the Library of Congress.[16] Murray was a close friend of Henry Luce and his wife and helped the latter prepare for her appearance before Congress upon her appointment as U.S. ambassador to Italy. "Before she left I did some briefing," Murray later wrote, "in fact, I prepared her statements for the Congressional, rather Senate, Committee before which she had to appear. On the 'double diplomatic corps,' on how a Catholic frames his support of separation of church and state, etc."[17] It would appear that Murray provided Mrs. Luce with this text as part of the background on a question of great sensitivity at the time both in the United States and in Rome.

Repercussions

Meanwhile, as Murray had been informed, the memorandum had been referred to "experts" both in the United States and in Rome. On 4 May 1951, Montini sent a copy of it to Cardinal Stritch with an accompanying request:

The attached memorandum submitted by the Reverend John Courtney Murray S.J., discusses a question of particular importance. It would be appreciated if Your Eminence would examine it and would kindly indicate any observations which you may judge opportune in this regard.[18]

Stritch did not reply immediately to this request and in fact had to be prodded a year later by the information that other responses to the Secretariat of State's request had already been received. Stritch's comments, sent on 15 May 1952, argued that Murray was exaggerating the novelty and the danger of the situation, disagreed with his call for a development of Church teaching beyond that of Leo XIII, but agreed with Murray on the danger of secularism and that any new papal document, instead of restating the Leonine teaching should show "that democratic institutions are not in any way uncongenial to the Church."[19]

How many other American experts were asked to comment on Murray's memorandum is not known. One of them, however, was Francis J. Connell among whose papers is a five-page transcript, undated and without indication of addressee, entitled "Comments on 'The Crisis in Church-State Relationships in the U.S.A.'"[20] From internal evidence it would appear that this text was intended for a Vatican official and that it was written in the late spring or summer of 1951. There is no clear evidence that Connell knew that Murray was the author of the text on which he was commenting, although the reference he makes to remarks of Murray published in the *New York Times* and to the spread of ideas similar to Murray's leads one to suspect that he did. In any case, Connell's reply denied that a new crisis existed in Catholic-Protestant relations, questioned whether the adaptation called for in the memorandum could be reconciled with revealed truth, and recommended instead a reaffirmation of the traditional Catholic doctrine on church and state.

Much more serious was the fact that Murray's memorandum for Montini was also referred to the Holy Office for evaluation. When it began examining it is not now known, but it is likely that it was already known to the Vatican congregation when on 5 March 1953, its pro-secretary, Alfredo Cardinal Ottaviani, gave a speech on church and state in which he referred to the public controversy on the matter in the United States and referred, without naming him, to Murray's views as "the liberalizing thesis."[21] At the same time the Holy Office was engaged in a systematic review of recent Catholic publications on church and state and there is evidence among the papers of Fr. Rosaire Gagnebet, O.P., the man entrusted with a preliminary investigation, that he was familiar with Murray's memorandum.[22]

Reassured by Fr. Leiber that Ottaviani's speech had neither official nor semi-official authority,[23] Murray continued to maintain his views, encouraged in particular by Pius XII's speech to Italian jurists on 6 December 1953, in which he believed the Pope had tactfully repudiated Ottaviani's rigid stance and opened the door to the sort of development for which he had himself been calling.[24] Murray made this case in a speech at Catholic University, 25 March 1954, in which he also indulged in some humorous and disparaging remarks about Ottaviani himself.[25] Informed of this by at least three friendly professors at Catholic University,[26] Ottaviani initiated a process against Murray which on 7 July 1954, resulted in a formal judgment of the Holy Office that Murray's most recent published essay contained errors which he was obliged to correct.[27] The Holy Office also identified in Murray's writings a set of four "erroneous doctrinal propositions," which not only were duly sent to Murray through the Jesuit Father General but were also given to Connell and Fenton by Cicognani along with instructions that they could not make them public but that they should report on Murray's fulfillment of the Congregation's instructions. No copy of these errors is found in Murray's own papers, but the diary of Fenton and the papers of Connell both contain the indicted propositions:

(a) The Catholic confessional State, professing itself as such, is not an ideal to which organized political society is universally obliged.
(b) Full religious liberty can be considered as a valid political ideal in a truly democratic State.
(c) The State organized on a genuinely democratic basis must be considered to have done its duty when it has guaranteed the freedom of the Church by a general guarantee of liberty of religion.
(d) It is true that Leo XIII has said "civitates . . . debent eum in colendo numine morem usurpare modumque quo coli se Deus ipse demonstravit velle" [states must follow that way of worshipping the divinity which God himself has shown that he desires] (Enc. Immortale Dei). Words such as these can be understood as referring to the State considered as organized on a basis other than that of the perfectly democratic State but to this latter strictly speaking are not applicable.[28]

None of these four propositions is found verbatim in the article of Murray criticized at the 7 July Holy Office session; but two of them closely resemble statements in Murray's memorandum for Montini. Compare the second statement above (b) to the statement on p. 12 of Murray's text as given below: "They [i.e., American Catholics] regard full constitutional and religious liberty as a valid democratic political ideal," and the third statement above (c) to the statement on p. 10 about "the democratically organized State," namely that it "may, and must, consider that it has done its political duty when it has guaranteed the freedom of the Church, by a general guarantee of the freedom of religion." A private document prepared by Murray for the Vatican Secretariat of State, then, had become part of the dossier used by the Holy Office to condemn Murray's views and to bring pressure on his Jesuit superiors to have him cease publishing on the matter.

The Holy Office continued to pursue its effort for some time. By 1958 preparations were well underway of a document that, after setting out the classic doctrine on church and state, would forbid Catholics to teach twenty-one propositions.[29] The fourteenth of these seems to have been drawn from Murray's memorandum for Montini:

> The public religious duties of the State, such as the acknowledgment of the true God, defense of the rights of the truth, the observance of divine laws, the right relationship between the temporal and the spiritual, etc. may not be fulfilled by the leaders of a democracy without the consent of the people. In a democracy the way in which harmony is established between Church and State and in which they are of aid to one another is not to be determined by treatises signed by the governors of both powers, but only by the civic actions of Catholic citizens in conformity with the laws of conscience and with political prudence.

Compare this to Murray's argument in his memorandum:

> For obvious reasons, in a lay democratic State of the American character, this *concordia* of laws can not be effected from the top down, by negotiations between the supreme rulers of the two societies. It must be achieved from the bottom up, by the layman acting under the guidance of his Christian conscience, and of the dictates of political prudence which must always preside over the formation of human law.

It appears that this condemnatory document was not formally approved before the death of Pius XII in October 1958, for the idea of such a text continued to be pursued in the early years of the pontificate of John XXIII. In fact, when the preparatory Theological Commission was preparing a draft of a dogmatic constitution on the Church for consideration by the Second Vatican Council, the first version of its chapter on church and state reproduced *verbatim* the expository part of the Holy Office's draft text, omitting, however, the condemnation of erroneous propositions. Severely criticized by the Central Preparatory Commission even before the Council opened, this text was rejected by the Council, which, with the considerable assistance of John Courtney Murray, who was appointed a conciliar expert in 1963, instead issued in 1965 its Declaration on Religious Freedom (*Dignitatis Humanae*), in which it presented that "vital adaptation of Catholic doctrine on church and state to the twentieth century political context" that Murray had proposed fifteen years earlier.

Editorial Note: It appears that neither of the two typed versions of Murray's memorandum is the original sent to Montini. The copy found in the papers of Clare Booth Luce is sixteen single-spaced pages, the one found in Cardinal Stritch's papers is only fourteen single-spaced pages; the difference is probably attributable to different type-sizes and to different page-sizes. There are a few minor typographical errors in the Stritch copy, corrected here without comment; but otherwise the texts are identical except for one point at which the Luce copy omits eight words on one line that are found in the Stritch copy, a proof, it seems, that the copy he gave to Mrs. Luce had been retyped after Murray sent the original to Rome. In Murray's memo below, I have inserted in square brackets the pagination of the Stritch copy, and I have provided translations of foreign words and phrases.

The Crisis in Church-State Relationships in the U.S.A.
John Courtney Murray, S.J.
29 October 1950

In this memorandum four points will be briefly made.

First, a grave danger confronts the Church in the United States, because the Church is the object of a newly intense fear, distrust, and hostility. At the same time a new apostolic opportunity is being offered to the Church, because the Church is now the object of a new interest, curiosity, and sympathy.

Second, one great obstacle hinders the Church in coping effectively with the danger confronting her. And the same obstacle also blocks her from making full use of the opportunity offered to her. This obstacle consists in the present state of development of the Church's doctrine on Church-State relationships. This doctrine has not yet been vitally adapted to modern political realities and to the legitimate democratic aspirations, especially as they have developed in the United States.

Third, there exists the urgent problem of effecting this vital adaptation. The situation is critical: if this vital adaptation is not immediately undertaken the result will be a progressive alienation of the American mind from the Catholic Church, with consequent damage to the apostolic activity of the Church.

Fourth, while the problem is indeed complicated and delicate, certain effective steps can be taken immediately. The conclusion of this memorandum will respectfully suggest these steps.

The Danger

The religious situation in the United States is very different today from what it was ten years ago. "The enemy" is no longer Protestantism, either orthodox or liberal. The enemy is a newly articulate, organized, and doctrinal secularism or naturalism. The majority of Americans, both among the masses and also among the leaders, are indeed unbelievers, in the sense that they no longer acknowledge allegiance to any of the traditional Christian churches. However, among these men a new quasi-religious belief has taken substantial form; it is a belief in "democracy." Democracy has become in a very true sense a widely popular "religion" in America.

This new secularist faith is not cynical, as was the French laicism of the last century. It is idealistic and it takes great account of what are called "spiritual values." It seems to meet certain fundamental aspirations of the American people. Its promises are many. It promises to fulfill the great American dream embodied in the Constitution of the [2] United States, which is "to secure the blessings of liberty to ourselves and our posterity." It promises to establish a social and economic order of justice and peace in which the dignity and rights of man will be respected and in which "the people" will be empowered to create for themselves the conditions of a full human life through a system of free institutions. It promises to be a "higher unity" that will resolve the conflict of divergent religious beliefs in American society. Consequently, this seductive naturalist faith has the power to attract the interest and adherence of important groups, and of influential men who must be considered "men of good will." And it continues to win multitudinous converts, especially in the field of education.

The intelligent Protestant also recognizes this naturalism as "the enemy," and he feels that he should make friends with the Catholic in a common struggle against it. However, he is definitely not willing to be friends with a Church that seems to him to be the political enemy of "the American way of life," with which Protestantism has historically identified itself.

The Obstacle

Here is the central point: In the United States there is a widespread belief that the Catholic Church does not fully and sincerely affirm the human and political values of a democratically organized political society; that American Catholic support of the principles of the U.S. Constitution is basically incompatible with certain tenets of Catholic faith; in a word, that Americanism and Catholicism are fundamentally in conflict.

Many Americans sincerely believe that the Catholic Church is prepared to support democracy only provisionally, and on the grounds of expediency, until what time she acquires sufficient power within society to do away with the forms and institutions of democratic government, and introduce some form of dictatorship subject to authoritarian, ecclesiastical control.

In particular, it is widely thought that the Catholic doctrine on Church-State relationships is in certain dynamic respects at variance with American constitutional principles of government. Concretely, the Catholic political ideal is considered to be inherently destructive of the institutions of freedom of religion, freedom of speech, freedom of the press, and freedom of association. These freedoms have historically been of the very essence of the American political system. Insofar as the Church seems to doubt or deny the validity and value of this political system, she is inevitably regarded with fear, distrust, and hostility.

This fear, distrust, and hostility of the Catholic Church is a central and critical fact of the contemporary religious and political scene in the United States. [3]

This hostile attitude towards the Church is being actively fostered by the secularist or naturalist. His attack is not directly launched against the theology of the Church. Indeed, he makes a point of distinguishing between the faith of the Church and the political implications of that faith, and deliberately confines his attack to the latter. He insistently points out that these political implications are in conflict with cherished and historic American ideas and institutions.

The most recent and ambitious attack was made by Mr. Paul Blanshard in his book, *American Freedom and Catholic Power*. This book has gone through eleven editions—more than 150,000 copies—in a little more than a year. Its indictment of the Church is the most impressive that has been produced in American Catholic history. And the impact of the book is a testimony at once to a great popular interest in the Church and to a great popular fear and distrust of her.

To repeat, the secularist thesis that the Church is the enemy of democracy is accepted by the great majority of Protestants. Moreover, the wide propagation of the thesis through all the media of communication, including education, has created considerable uneasiness in Catholic circles, especially among the laity. Here, the reaction sometimes takes the form of excessive and sentimental protestations of "Americanism"; sometimes, the form of a certain Catholic "integrism," a certain aggressive willingness to be "the enemy," with its consequent exclusion from a full participation in the national life. (This accounts often for the unwillingness of sensitive and devout Catholics to enter the arena of practical politics.)

The present fear, distrust, and hostility towards the Catholic Church constitutes, in six important respects, a serious obstacle to the apostolate in the United States.

First, a psychological barrier has been created that prevents Catholic access to the secular mind in America, which cherishes a sacred conviction as to the value of American political institutions.

Second, a barrier is created to positive and fruitful relationships with Protestant religious groups. For example, the public press increasingly quotes Catholics and Protestants speaking to each other in terms of mutual denunciation. (As between Catholics and Protestants, the danger in the United States is not an excess of eirenism but rather an excess of polemism.) However, Protestantism in the United States is presently able to assume a false prestige as the "bulwark of democracy" against the supposed "menace of the Catholic Church."

Third, an obstacle exists to individual conversions. Many thoughtful people, attracted to the Church by the richness and strength of her faith, feel repelled by her political theology.

Fourth, an obstacle is created to that effective Catholic participation in the world-wide intellectual movement of our times which was recommended by His Holiness, Pius XII, in his recent discourse to the Amsterdam Congress [4] of Pax Romana. In America, the distrust of the Church tends to carry over into a distrust of the intellectual integrity and even capacity of the individual Catholic.

Fifth, an obstacle is created to the conquest of the central adversary of the present moment, the secularism or naturalism mentioned above. The Church is not credited with having the intellectual resources to match the secular idealism of the naturalist movement.

Finally, and most important of all, the way is blocked to an equitable solution of the most serious question confronting the Church in the United States—the school question. Here, the adversaries of all kinds of State aid to Catholic schools offer as their main objection that such aid, granted even in small amount, would be the first step along a path that would lead to Catholic domination of the United States with consequent destruction of democratic institutions.

THE OPPORTUNITY

It is disastrous in this present moment that the Church's apostolate should encounter these needless obstacles. The paradoxical fact is that, alongside the fear and distrust and hostility towards the Church, there likewise exists a newly important interest in her. She is the object of much curiosity and sympathy. Hence, a "great door" is being opened to her, at the very time she is confronted by "many adversaries."

For instance, the problem of religion in American public education has become increasingly critical, and it urgently demands a solution. Hence, a potential sympathy for Catholic schools has been created; but this sympathy fails to materialize in public support because of fear of "Catholic power." Similarly, while there is much sympathy for the Church by reason of the persecutions launched against her beyond the Iron Curtain, it is negated by the belief that the Church herself is potentially a "persecuting power." Again, the contemporary challenge to religious liberalism has been largely successful, and movements are afoot towards a newly theological type of religion. The "free church" concept has been largely discredited, and religious men are realizing more and more the sacramental nature of the Church of Christ. And again, fear of the Church as a visible institution prevents men from fully examining her claims. Furthermore, people are realizing that Communism as a doctrine as well as an economic movement presents a serious challenge to the American way of life. They begin to see that this challenge cannot be met merely by opposing to Communism a concept of purely formal democracy. There must be opposed to it a total doctrine of the nature of man; for only out of this doctrine can there be evolved a genuinely substantial theory of democracy, more intellectually satisfying than the purely pragmatic concept prevalent in the United States during less challenging times. In seeking this theory students are being led to examine the political ideas of the Middle Ages, to whose development the Church powerfully contributed. But once more, this interest in the political achievements of the Catholic past is balanced by fear of "Catholic plans" for the political future. [5]

At this point, it is important clearly to have in mind that this present indictment of the Church cannot be dismissed as simply the product of "American bigotry" or of an innate hostility to the Church on the part of Protestants and secularists. The indictment troubles and concerns many Americans of good will, who are otherwise prepared to be friendly to the Church, to be sympathetic with her religious beliefs, even to embrace them. These men have been convinced by the world experience of totalitarianism in the last two decades that the best hope for a stable, free, and orderly society is to be found in the democratic ideal. They are among the men referred to by Pius XII in his 1944 Christmas message who regard the democratic form of government as being, under present circumstances, a dictate of natural law. But they still sincerely doubt whether the Catholic Church can adapt herself vitally, on principle, and not merely on grounds of expediency, to what is valid in American democratic development. These doubts and difficulties must be met squarely and on intellectual grounds.

The Need of Adaptation

It is certain that the American difficulty cannot be adequately met as long as Catholic doctrine in Church-State relationships remains in its present stage of development.

This stage of development was reached in the course of the 19th-century conflict between the Catholic Church and Continental liberalism. The concrete adversary was the Jacobin democracy that issued from the French revolution. It was formally anti-clerical, anti-Catholic, and even anti-religious. And against it the

Church was fighting for the cause of order against a false "freedom" that sought to undermine order.

This polemic state of the question naturally had consequences with regard to emphases in the Church's teaching. For instance, the Church's formal condemnation of the rationalist theories that lay behind the "democratic freedoms" in the Jacobin concept of democracy consequently cast doubt on the validity of these freedoms themselves as political institutions. This was the more inevitable inasmuch as these "freedoms" were being used as so many engines of war upon the freedom of the Church and the religious unity of the traditional Catholic countries. Engaged as she was in combatting the false revolutionary theories of popular sovereignty in Europe, the Church could not be concerned with exploring the merits of a system of popular rule, if it were to be based on a right philosophy of man and of political society.

Today, however, the state of the question has changed. The Church is now fighting for freedom against a false "order" that would destroy freedom. Her present enemy is the totalitarian order, especially in its communist form. Totalitarianism, the central fact of 20th century political experience, has put the value of the democratic development in a new light. Today the cause of the freedom of the Church herself is allied to the cause of political freedom. [6]

Consequently, the Church today has taken and can continue to take a far more positive and affirmative attitude towards the development of democratic political society than was possible in the 19th century. This is clear from Pius XII's 1944 Christmas radio-message—a document that could not have been written in the days of Leo XIII. In the 20th century, therefore, the ancient problem of Church and State is raised in a new form.

Adaptation to the American System

The problem is particularly crucial in the United States. The American Church has had a history different from her history in Europe, and she has lived through, and profited by, a political experiment different from any undertaken in the old world.

The American political experiment owed little to the principles which motivated the Jacobin democracy that was the European enemy of the Church. The American inspiration was not entirely pure; what political realizations ever can claim pure inspiration? Nevertheless, the essential American ideal derived from the Anglo-Saxon political tradition, whose roots go back to medieval political ideas and institutions, and even farther back to the politics of Pagan antiquity.

Scholars today agree that significant differences distinguish Anglo-Saxon democracy from Jacobin democracy, just as they agree that there is an important distinction to be made between the "Liberalism" of the 18th and 19th centuries and "the liberal tradition" which is the central political tradition of the Christian West. Continental Liberalism was a deformed version of the liberal tradition.

The American system, properly interpreted, embodies three basic political principles, which have roots in the liberal tradition.

It is the suggestion of this memorandum that these three American principles can be harmonized with the three corresponding essential principles of the Church's traditional doctrine with regard to her relations to the State. The affirmation of this harmony would not result in canonizing, as some sort of "ideal," a particular system of Church-State relationships. Rather, the result would be the assertion that the Church's traditional doctrine can be vitally adapted to the legitimate political exigencies of a democratically organized state.

American Political Principles

The three American principles may thus be briefly stated.

1. The State is lay in character, function, and end.

2. The State has the duty of cooperation with the Church; but this duty is limited, in the manner of its discharge, by the political fact that the State is a lay State. [7]

3. The lay State is subject to the sovereignty of God, and it recognizes that its acts and legislation ought to be in harmony with the law of God; but the political form of the State requires that this harmony be effected by the people. Through the medium of democratic institutions the people themselves bring the demands of their religious conscience to bear upon the acts and legislation of government.

A full development of these principles would necessarily be very lengthy. What follows are merely comments.

1. It was on the American continent that there was founded, by an act of the people, the first State that was lay, without being (like the third French Republic) laicizing.

The American State was not considered to be a person. It was considered to be simply a power, or more precisely, an action—the living action that is public order. This action was conceived to be limited to what concerns the temporal and terrestrial order of man's social life. The State was indeed to have a moral function. It was to establish and vindicate an order of justice and of human and civil rights and freedoms. It was to promote genuine human welfare. It was to assist the people in creating for themselves, through multiple social institutions, the conditions of order and freedom, within which the people might pursue their human ends and their eternal destiny.

However, since the power and action of the American State were of the lay order, it was not to have any charge over the religious orthodoxy or the ecclesiastical unity of its people. It was not indifferent to religion, but it was declared incompetent in the order of religious belief and practice, since this order is not lay but ecclesiastical. Its action and function were confined to the order of its own being and purposes—the order of civil society as such.

2. In the American sense the lay State is held to be "separate" from the Church. But it must be borne in mind that the formula of "separation of Church and State" has not had in the United States the same meaning and intent that was inherent, for instance, in the French Law of Separation of 1905. In the United States, the State was originally established as a lay power; it was never "separated" from the Church, because it had never been united to the Church, as in Europe. It did not presume to define the Church. It gave only a political definition of itself, and this definition was ratified by the people through a formal act of constitutional consent.

The people who created this lay State did not deny that part of its duty would be a duty of cooperation with the Church. They did, however, believe that there should be limits to the forms that this cooperation should take. And they believed that these limits were legitimately set by the nature of the State as a lay action.

Concretely, the American State was to cooperate with the Church in one major way, that is, by guaranteeing the freedom of the Church through an overall guarantee of the freedom of religion in society. [8]

The American ideal was not "libera Chiesa in Stato libero" [a free Church in a free State] in the sense of the Italian anticlericals. Nor has the phrase "the free exercise of religion" the same meaning in the American constitution that it had in Republican France, where it was an agency for the destruction of the historic liberties of the Church. In the American constitution it was, and is, an institution which has operated to protect the Church in her freedom, and enabled her to exercise her own powers, to fulfill her own function, and to be what she is.

For the rest, the State was to cooperate with the Church through the performance of its own proper task. This was to establish an order of justice, social peace, and human welfare, and to create and protect the conditions of freedom in society. This is indeed an indirect form of cooperation; but in our complex modern society its value cannot be exaggerated.

3. In asserting itself to be lay, the American State implicitly acknowledges that its processes are subject to a "higher law" not of its own making—the law of God. And as the servant of the people, the State recognizes the people's right to have harmony prevail between the human laws which organize their temporal life and this divine law which governs their consciences. However, in a democratically organized State wherein "We, the People" are sovereign, this harmony between the two laws is necessarily to be effected by the conscious political activity of the people themselves.

Here the assumption is the medieval one—that the sense of justice is resident in the people. And therefore, the responsibility for judging, directing, and correcting that living action, that public order which is the State and its government, is committed to the people. The people are empowered to discharge this responsibility through the democratic institutions of self-rule. In ruling themselves they stand under God, and are subject to His sovereignty. But the law of God can reach the processes of organized society only through popular participation in these processes.

The lay State, therefore, is open to moral and spiritual direction, but that direction is imparted to it from below—that is, from the broadest base—from all its citizens.

The way to harmony between divine law and civil law lies open, but it leads only through the constitutional path of the freedom of the people.

These three basic elements, affirmed in the American constitutional system as valid principles of modern political life, are also principles that the Church herself can affirm as valid. And having made this affirmation she can bring her own traditional doctrine on Church and State into vital relation with them. [9]

Catholic Principles

The Church's doctrine on her relation to the State is controlled by three essential principles. The first principle flows from the nature of the Church; the second, from the nature of [the last eight words were omitted from the copy in the Luce papers] man; the third, from the nature of political society.

(1) The first principle is that of "the freedom of the Church." The Church must be free fully to exercise her power to teach, sanctify, and rule, and to this end to "occupy ground" in this world. In more than sixty texts, Leo XIII used the phrase "libertas ecclesiastica" [freedom of the Church], or its equivalent, to express this fundamental demand that the Church, regarded as the spiritual power ruling an independent, divinely constituted society, makes on the State.

In the United States the Church has not had to make the complaint so often heard in Europe, that her freedom was violated by the American constitutional system. The fact that her freedom has been guaranteed only in a general guarantee of "the free exercise of religion" has not operated to diminish her freedom. This is a significant fact of American Church history.

(2) The second principle is that of the necessary harmony between "the two laws" whereby the life of man is governed—the divine law, both natural and positive, and the human law made by the political power. The word "concordia" [harmony] was the favorite word used by Leo XIII to express the essence of good relations between the Church as an order of law, and the State as likewise an order of law. He made clear that this *concordia* is a demand that flows from the nature of man and not from the nature of the Church. The human person is "civis idem et christianus" [at once a citizen and a Christian]. As a member of two societies the human person has the inherent right to demand that the two laws whereby he is governed should be in harmony with each other; if they are in conflict, the conflict is felt within him, and results in the destruction of his inner integrity. This *concordia* has never actually been realized in the United States; but the way to its realization lies open.

The American constitutional system asserts what the Catholic position likewise asserts, that as the human person is the final cause of this *concordia*, so he ought also to be its efficient cause, through his participation in the processes by which law is made and the acts of government directed.

For obvious reasons, in a lay democratic State of the American character, this *concordia* of laws can not be effected from the top down, by negotiations between the supreme rulers of the two societies. It must be achieved from the bottom up, by the layman acting under the guidance of his Christian conscience, and of the dictates of political prudence which must always preside over the formation of human law.

In this respect American political theory fits with the theology of the layman newly developed since the days of Pius XI. In this theology the layman bears the responsibility of seeing to it that the institutions and the laws of society are brought into harmony with the demands of Christian faith. [10]

(3) The third principle is that of the necessary cooperation between Church and State, each in its own order, towards the total good of man. The principle itself is always valid; but the forms of this cooperation have varied. They are not determined by the nature of the Church, or by the nature of man. Rather, they are determined by the special character of particular political societies as these exist in varying and changing historical contexts. The forms of political society, like the forms of private property, are subject to historical evolution, especially in what concerns the institutions of government. The modern lay democratic state can be regarded as a legitimate term of that progressive development of the distinction and relative independence of "the two societies" which is visible in political and ecclesiastical history.

The Government in the democratic state is not the "episcopus externus" [external bishop] of the early Christian empire. Nor is it the "Catholic Majesty" of the post-Reformation national State. It has not inherited all the functions historically assumed by those earlier institutions of rule.

Again, the people in a democratic society wherein universal popular education has been highly developed are not subject to the tutelage which "the Christian Prince" exercised over his subjects in feudal or monarchic societies. As the citizen's consciousness or his personal autonomy in the face of government grows, the areas in which governmental coercion may be applied correspondingly ought to shrink. In a democratic state the Catholic principle that the act of faith is free receives full emphasis.

Consequently, the democratically organized State, considering itself to be a lay action of limited scope may, and in obedience to the will of its people ought to, resign the special function exercised by "the Christian Prince" in historical frameworks different from today's—the function being "defender of the faith" and protector of the unity of the Church. This State may, and must—and does—consider that it goes beyond its proper competence when it undertakes to suppress dissident religious opinions by the force of law. It may, and must, consider that it has done its political duty when it has guaranteed the freedom of the Church, by a general guarantee of the freedom of religion. In enacting this constitutional provision, the lay democratic State, and its people, do not impose any limitations on the claims of the Church. They simply impose limitations on the authority of secular government.

The conclusion from the foregoing is that the affirmation of American political principles entails no denial or diminution of traditional Catholic principles regarding the relationship between Church and State.

On the contrary, only the manner of applying these principles need be different, in order that Catholic doctrine may be vitally adapted to this modern form of the democratic State. [11]

Some Practical Suggestions

(1) Catholic thought on Church-State relationships ought to show a greater awareness of the American scene—its political realities and the special history and situation of the Church in America. The Church in America is a massive part of world Catholicism. And at the present moment it is called upon to share in fullest fashion the opportunities and responsibilities that have been recently thrust in increasing measure on the United States.

All the material power, political wisdom, and spiritual strength of the United States are presently enlisted in defense of human freedom against the Communist threat. Americans in general believe that in this struggle great resources are to be drawn from the political concepts exhibited in the American Constitution, with its supporting principles. Hence, the extreme importance in the present world crisis of intelligent and firm Catholic affirmation of these concepts and these principles.

The Catholic Church cannot with full effectiveness oppose Communism as long as it is itself regarded as being in opposition to the American political system that today stands most strongly against the spread of Communism.

(2) European Catholic utterances on Church and State are particularly liable to misinterpretation in the United States. The most striking recent example was the article by R. P. Cavalli, S.J., in the *Civiltà cattolica* for April, 1948. One passage from this article (cf. ibid., pp. 33–34) has become a *locus classicus* [classic source] in the current campaign against the Catholic Church in America. This passage was widely quoted in both the public and Protestant press. After citing it in his book (referred to above), Mr. Blanshard states that if this article were translated and widely distributed the result would be a great wave of anti-Catholic feeling. (Actually the article was translated and distributed by a political agency, the Spanish Embassy in Washington.)

It would be difficult to exaggerate the fear of the Church and the hostility towards her that were aroused by the doctrine on religious freedom stated in this article. A distinguished Protestant theologian has said that this doctrine has "hardened the hearts of non-Catholics" against the Catholic Church. What is worse the article created difficulties in Catholic minds and divisions among Catholics.

The hostility to the Church was not aroused by the assertion that the Catholic Church is the one true Church, but by the suggestion that the Church must and will, wherever possible, make this tenet of her faith the premise for a program of political intolerance and civil inequality. The intelligent American understands that the Church herself cannot regard other religious beliefs as equally as true as her own. But he cannot be made to understand a determination on the part of the Church to use the coercive power of secular government to deny legal existence to beliefs which the Church regards as erroneous. [12]

The reason for the intolerance suggested in the article, namely, that "error has no rights," is unintelligible to the American thinker, who associates rights only with persons, and regards judgment on the truth or error of religious beliefs as beyond the competence of the State. The political implications of the "thesis" stated in the article have profoundly alienated the American mind from the Church. The general impression created was that the Church is inherently a persecuting power and that she is only held back from active persecution by considerations of expediency or lack of political power. Against this impression, the statement in the article that "the Church will not draw the sword" was certainly not reassuring to the American public.

In this connection, it might be suggested that discussions of the Church-State situation in Spain provoke strong repercussions in the United States. A very widespread impression has been created that only the Spanish religio-political system can in principle command the support of the Church; that any other solution is sheer "hypothesis," a reluctant and opportunistic acceptance of a situation of fact; that the Catholic Church essentially wants, and instinctively seeks alliance with, dictatorial political regimes; that consequently she is permanently uneasy within a democratic State and cannot in principle be at peace with it.

A sharp correction of this unfortunate impression is badly needed. And Catholic spokesmen must be put in the position of being able to appeal to Catholic principles and to official Catholic utterances when they argue for an interpretation of the Catholic doctrine on Church and State suited to conditions other than those which prevail in that historic entity, the "juridically Catholic nation."

For the Catholic it is not a question of criticizing the Spanish solution behind which lie a very special national history and a particular political tradition. But it is a question of being able to maintain, on principle, the equal validity of other solutions adapted to other historical situations and political traditions.

In the United States, for instance, it is and (as far as one can humanly see) always will be absurd to think of Catholics being, in P. Cavalli's words, "rassegnati di poter convivere là dove essi soli avrebbero il diritto di vivere" [resigned to have to live with others where they alone ought to have a right to live]; American Catholics do not consider themselves "costretti a chiedere essi stessi la piena libertà religiosa per tutti" [forced to request full religious liberty for all] *exclusively* because this full religious liberty is expedient for themselves as a minority. They regard full constitutional and religious liberty as a valid democratic political ideal. In holding this political position they do not consider themselves false to their faith in the Church as the one true Church.

(3) It is extremely necessary for our Holy Father to carry forward the line of thought so fruitfully begun in his 1944 Christmas Radio message, on the idea of the democratic state, the democratic citizen, and the democratic institutions. This discourse was received with much gratitude by American Catholics, and was studied with great attention by secular thinkers. The world events of the past five years, and the present Church-State crisis in the United States, call for further development of its affirmations and their implications. [13]

In the United States the prestige of our present Holy Father is very great, and his utterances command universal respect. The secular press prints the full texts of his major discourses, and they are widely read. The only regrettable thing is that at times their language and idiom, and even manner of translation, make their understanding difficult for the American intelligence, which is not accustomed to the *stylus curiae* [style of the curia].

Progress in this whole matter of the vital adaptation of Catholic doctrine on Church and State to the 20th century political context cannot otherwise begin than by the clarification, in the light of recent political experience and recent studies of political and sociological theory, of the whole idea of "the State" in Catholic thought.

The ultimate need is for a synthesis of the ethical idea of the State advanced by Leo XIII, the institutional theory of society developed by Pius XI, and the juridical theory of democracy, rooted in the human person as "the origin and end of social order," of which Pius XII has been the theorist.

The full constitution of this synthesis would take much time. But the first step towards it can and ought to be taken immediately, by developing more fully a positive theory of democratic government and institutions.

What is needed in this present moment is a correction of the impression that American political theorists frequently derive from reading Leo XIII, that the Catholic political ideal is really a *Polizeistaat* [police state], in which the Catholic hierarchy is the "policeman," who enforces his will through governmental officials as his instruments of rule.

(4) A larger work of scholarship needs to be undertaken. Both the historical and the theoretical dimensions of the Church-State problem require further exploration. The purpose would be the formulation of a unitary theory of Church-State relationships that would be capable of application to all the modern situations, without the suggestion of opportunism. The regrettable fact is that Catholic scholars, in different nations, are not in agreement with regard to certain important positions and orientations.

It is impossible here to discuss in detail the lines of this scholarly work; the following suggestions are offered without pretense of completeness.

A. First, the Church-State problem can no longer be fruitfully discussed in terms of the dichotomies, "thesis vs. hypothesis," or "union of Church and State vs. separation of Church and State." These categories are too reminiscent of a particular 19th-century polemic state of the question.

B. The controversy needs to be rescued from such facile solutions as are reached, for instance, by appeal to the statement, "error has no rights." This type of summary logic does not do justice to the full complexity of the problem of the function of State and government in the field of religion. [14]

C. The exact status in Catholic doctrine of the post-Reformation constitutional concept of "the religion of the State" needs to be determined by careful exploration of its history. It is from this concept, and not from the dogma of the Church as the one true Church, that there flows the political practice of intolerance, in some degree, toward non-Catholics.

D. In general, the influence of historical factors (national traditions, political facts and experience, cultural conditions, etc.) in fashioning solutions to the Church-State problem needs to be more exactly determined. Otherwise we cannot know what is principle and what is contingent application of principle, what is permanent demand and what is legitimate temporary expedience, what is required by the universal Church and what is required by the Church in certain nations.

E. It has to be decided whether the present conditions of *diaspora*, under which the Catholic people almost universally now lives, are to be considered mere brute fact, to which the Church only provisionally adapts herself, until what time she can see reconstituted a "closed Christendom" on the model of past eras, imperial and national; or whether these conditions are to be viewed as a fact which compels a return to a study of Catholic principles themselves, to see how they can be brought into vital, and not opportunistic, adaptation to the religious and political realities of the modern world.

(5) It has again to be emphasized that the present problem is critical and urgent. Events move fast today; so do ideas. The mass media of modern communications have made possible the rapid alteration of climates of opinion by quick assimilation of ideas. Hence, it is possible, as well as prudent, to move quickly towards a solution of the present problem. What is urgently needed is a clear statement of certain simple, fundamental, leading ideas that will meet and satisfy the legitimate demands of the democratic political conscience. This statement would lay the foundations for a Church-State doctrine that will not be an obstacle, but a help, in the Church's apostolate in the contemporary world.

Observations on the Memorandum "The Crisis in Church-State Relationships in the U.S.A."
Samuel Cardinal Stritch

After a very careful study of this memorandum and a study of the articles published on the questions discussed in it by its author and the French philosopher, Jacques Maritain, I submit the following observations.

I

The presentation of what the author calls a "grave danger" which confronts the Church in the United States in my judgment is not comprehensive. All through our history, we Catholics in the United States have had to face this same attack upon the Church from non-Catholics. The point of the attack has been the same all through the years: namely, that Catholics cannot be loyal to the Constitution of the United States and at the same time loyal to their Church. The notion of religious freedom in the non-Catholic mind in the English-speaking world derives from the Protestant doctrine upholding the right of the individual to interpret for himself the Sacred Scriptures. Generally the Protestant mind and those who are not Protestants but think in the Protestant mentality hold that the Reformation was a great emancipation of the intellect and the beginning of the day of freedoms. In England, about the middle of the 17th century, there was started a movement among Protestants for religious tolerance on the part of the State. The English philosopher, Locke (1632–1704) wrote his famous *Letters on Toleration*. He expresses in these letters the Protestant mind of his time when he excludes from his notion of toleration the Roman Catholic Church in England because of its allegiance to a foreign sovereign. It was this notion of religious tolerance which the colonists brought from England to the United States. A single exception was in the establishment of the colony of Maryland by Lord Baltimore, where the Catholic Church was included in the general grant of freedom of religion. However, when very early in the history of Maryland colony, the Protestants gained control, they immediately excluded Catholics from the enjoyment of full religious liberty and enacted penal laws against them. When, after the Revolution, our Federal Constitution, with the Bill of Rights, was framed, it seemed that it reflected the mind of the country and that there would be religious freedom for all religious groups in the United States. Despite the fact that in the discussions in some of the states, particularly in the New England States, before the ratification of the Constitution and the Bill of Rights, objections were raised to including the Catholic Church in the grant of religious freedom, the states did ratify the Constitution and the Bill of Rights. However, the Protestant tradition held on in Protestant minds, and Protestants questioned the loyalty of Catholics to the Constitution, on the grounds that they could not be loyal to the grant of religious freedom and at the same time be true to their Church. Catholics, of course, were a small minority in the United States in the beginning of our country, and they accepted wholeheartedly the grant of religious freedom to all groups. This was a practical arrangement which wise leaders saw was necessary for the good of our country. Time and time again, all through our history, we have had to face this same [2] sort of attack on the part of our non-Catholic fellow citizens. The Protestant mind simply will not admit that there is one true Church established by our Blessed Savior.

With the coming and the spread of secularism from out of our universities, this Protestant notion of religious freedom has been reasserted. The very growth of the Church has brought about this new attack on it. The growing activity of our government in the field of human welfare has brought new clashes between the rights of the Church and the asserted rights of the State in the field of welfare and education. In our non-Catholic schools of higher learning, many of which are supported from public funds, everything is dominated by an exaggerated notion of academic freedom. In these universities there is defended the proposition that professors and students must be unfettered in making their explorations for the truth. It is true that the attack on the Church today is widespread. The leaders of this attack assert that Catholics cannot be true to our democracy and at the same time true to their Church. They quote the papal encyclicals and papal pronouncements on Church-State relationships without giving the whole of the doctrine taught by the Popes. Actually their attacks center on the question of Church-State relationships. They will admit that Catholics today are loyal citizens, but they question the adherence of Catholics in the United States to the papal teachings on Church-State relationships. When that difficulty is answered by quotations from the encyclical letters and pronouncements of Pope Leo XIII, they pose this other question: "What if Catholics were a majority in the United States? Would they demand the constitutional abolition of the First Amendment? Would they be in favor of granting religious freedom to other religious groups?"

In my judgment this is a brief, comprehensive presentation of the question which confronts us.

II

A first principle in meeting this attack on the Church must be that we courageously and boldly and unflinchingly state Catholic truth. The author of the memorandum speaks of Catholic doctrine on Church-State relationships in its present state of development. He says that this stage of development was reached in the course of the 19th century conflict between the Catholic Church and continental liberalism. In other words, he seems to say, and in some of his published articles does say, that Pope Leo XIII in his Encyclical Letter, *Immortale Dei*, and in his many pronouncements on this question, simply applied Catholic principles to a particular condition which prevailed in the Europe of his day. The author of the memorandum asks for a further development of Catholic doctrine on Church-State relationships. He seems to indicate that the Popes in making their statements on this question have not had in mind the particular condition which obtains in the United States. I cannot subscribe to this position taken by the author of the memorandum. The wording of Pope Leo XIII's Encyclical, *Immortale Dei*, in my judgment makes very clear the fact that he is teaching Catholic doctrine. Clearly he teaches the doctrine on the independence of the Church in the field of its own competence as an independent society. He teaches that the State in its field is an independent society. He repudiates the [3] doctrine that the State is not subject to divine law. The Pope asserts that between these two supreme societies there must be cooperation and that in the field of "mixed matters" the State must recognize the rights of the Church. That Pope Leo XIII was fully cognizant of conditions in the United States is evident from the letter which he wrote to the Hierarchy of the United States on January 6, 1895. This Encyclical Letter, *Longinqua Oceani Spatia*, has this passage: "Moreover (a fact which it gives pleasure to acknowledge), thanks are due to the equity of the laws which obtain in America and to the customs of the well-ordered Republic. For the Church amongst you, unopposed by the Constitution and government of your nation, fettered by no hostile legislation, protected against violence by the common laws and the impartiality of the tribunals, is free to live and act without hindrance. Yet, though all this is true, it would be very erroneous to draw the conclusion that in America is to be sought the type of the most desirable status of the Church, or that it would be universally lawful or expedient for State and Church to be, as in America, dissevered and divorced. The fact that Catholicity with you is in good condition, nay is even enjoying a prosperous growth, is by all means to be attributed to the fecundity with which God has endowed His Church, in virtue of which unless men or circumstances interfere, she spontaneously expands and propagates herself; but she would bring forth more abundant fruits if, in addition to liberty, she enjoyed the favor of the laws and patronage of the public authority." Now in the United States, the Church has never been recognized and is not recognized as a supreme society. The practical arrangement which obtains here and is embodied in the First Amendment to our Constitution, granting religious freedom to all religious groups and individuals, is not a full recognition of the mandate of divine law. Moreover, in the field which the canonists call "materia mixta" [mixed matters], the rights of the Church are not always recognized. In the conditions which obtain in our country, where there are many religious groups, the First Amendment is a good practical arrangement. We Catholics accept it, and if it is rightly interpreted, we shall have in this arrangement a great measure of freedom. However, any attempt to make this arrangement an objective application of Catholic doctrine in my judgment is a mistake. Without detracting in any way from the teaching of the Church on Church-State relationships, we can give answers to the questions proposed to us. If Catholics were a majority in the United States, they would have no right and no desire to use political influence for bringing men to the Catholic Church. They would be fully cognizant of the facts of our history and in full loyalty to their Church and in obedience to its teachings, they would be just and fair towards all groups. What more can we say? We cannot give approval to the Protestant notion of religious freedom. We certainly must oppose the exaggerated notion of academic freedom which obtains in many of our institutions of higher learning. [4]

III

It is true that in the American political philosophy, those who hold office have only the authority given them in the Constitution and in our laws. Their position is not comparable to the position of the prince in the older forms of government. Only the people, acting in the manner prescribed in the Constitution, can make a change in our basic law. Since our officials are elected to office by the people, they will reflect the majority in their electorates in their official actions. Therefore, it is true that the apostolate of the Church in the United States must be directed towards bringing more and more into the Church. If the citizens observe divine law, they will see to it that divine law is not violated in their government. I fully agree with the author of the memorandum in his contention that to secure right governmental policies and right governmental action, we must direct our efforts towards inculcating truth in the minds of our fellow citizens. I would not go as far as the author of the memorandum goes in saying that the people of the United States do not think of their government as a juridical person. Actually in the laws of our country the government is recognized as a juridical person. However, the people of the United States do think of themselves as having the power to form to the doctrine of the Church on Church-State relationships. Our insistence should be rather on exposing the errors which are propagated among our citizens and prayerfully pointing out to them the authentic truth which the Church teaches. Through our history we mainly contended with the Protestant mind. Today our main contention is with secularism. It is true that our sort of secularism is not always inimical to religion. It is an abstraction in public and social life from religion and the placing of religion in the domains of the private lives of individuals. Many are seeing today the futility of secularism in our present crisis. They want something on which they can found their freedoms and their rights. Here we have a large opportunity.

IV

What our Holy Father, Pope Pius XII, said in his 1944 Christmas message on democracy was very helpful. It seems to me that if His Holiness deems it opportune, a further development of what he said in that important message would ease a great many minds. In such a development, stress could be placed on the duties of the citizens in a democracy and their obligation to work for the common good, under natural and divine law. It could be shown that when citizens recognize their responsibility to God and act in the light of the truths of the Gospel of Christ they can safeguard their freedoms and in reality promote the common good. Citizens could be urged to use their privileges as citizens according to the dictates of enlightened consciences. I do not think it would be opportune if such a statement were made by our Holy Father for him to restate the teaching of Pope Leo XIII on Church-State relationships. The great point of the statement could be that the Church is at home in a rightly ordered democracy and ready and anxious in such a political system to shower her benefits, from which there will come a greater and greater measure of common good. In making this suggestion, I have in mind that the Church cannot select for sole approval any of the [5] various forms of government which are of themselves capable of securing the good of citizens. Particularly in these times, considering the world situation, any serious rejection of any of these various forms of government would do much harm. I do think, however, that since in the world today the countries which are working against the powers who are fighting God and denying to men the enjoyment of their native rights are democracies, a statement of the Holy Father showing that democratic institutions are not in any way uncongenial to the Church would be helpful.

Comments on "The Crisis in Church-State Relationships in the U.S.A."
Very Rev. Francis J. Connell, C.SS.R., S.T.D.

1. The author seems to have no regard for the supernatural life and vigor of the Catholic Church. He proposes as the most necessary means of protecting the Church from grave harm in the United States something natural—the "adaptation" of a traditional Catholic doctrine to a naturalistic concept of the State. The

truth is that the most effective means toward preserving the Church from harm and promoting its apostolic activity will be found in a more ardent zeal on the part of bishops and priests and in a more faithful observance of God's law by Catholics. It should not be forgotten that Christ has promised to abide with His Church and to sustain it, so that the gates of hell shall never prevail against it. The author does not take this promise into consideration.

2. It is not correct to say that the religious situation in the United States is very different today from what it was in past (p. 1). For more than a century the Catholic Church has been attacked, time and time again, on the plea that it is opposed to the ideals of American democracy; yet, the Church has prospered. The recent attack by Paul Blanshard is essentially no different from many previous attacks; and it seems very probable that, like them, it will soon be forgotten. Even now the secular press is showing displeasure and disdain toward the most recent book of Blanshard, called *Communism, Democracy, and Catholic Power*. Thus, the news magazine *Time* (May 21, 1951) says of Blanshard: "He is not likely to convince anybody not already convinced." The *Washington Star* (May 20, 1951), in a review of this new book says:

> With the familiar reasoning of a certain type of muddled liberalism Blanshard argues that this country should not ally itself with "reactionary elements" in Europe, such as the Vatican and Franco, even if they are fighting Sovietism. Where we would get confining our friendship to leftwing factions he does not explain. He actually questions whether the Vatican "is a liability or an asset in democracy's war against Communism." Can he think that the Red flood could have been dammed in Italy or even in France without the Church?

It should be noted that much of the antagonism toward the Catholic Church in the United States is based, not on the Catholic doctrine of Church and State, but on the claim [2] of the Church to possess the one true religion, which all men are bound to accept. Other reasons for opposition are the stand of the Church on divorce, euthanasia, birth-control, therapeutic abortion, etc. Blanshard attacks the Church on all these grounds, and also with particular vehemence on the fact that ecclesiastical law forbids Catholic children to attend non-religious schools, such as the public schools of our land. Now, even if a doctrine on Church-State relations favorable to non-Catholics were propounded by the Church, there would still be opposition based on these other doctrines—and surely, the Church could never change or renounce these other doctrines.

3. It is difficult to see how the author's "adaptation" of the traditional Church-State doctrine can be harmonized with revealed truth. It has always been taught by the Catholic Church that civil rulers in their official capacity, as well as private individuals, are subject to the authority of Jesus Christ, and have been commanded by Him to recognize His one true Church. By virtue of this positive command of Christ the King all civil rulers are bound to acknowledge in the Catholic Church the right to preach and to conduct worship throughout the entire world (Can. 1322), the right to establish impediments for the marriage of baptized persons to the exclusion of any rights on the part of the State (Can. 1038), the *privilegium fori* (Can. 120), etc. Certainly, Pope Leo XIII clearly taught that *per se* [in principle] a government is bound to show special favor to the Catholic Church (e.g., Denz., 1874); and he enunciated this principle for all forms of government, including democracy. It is by virtue of this principle that a Catholic government, in order to protect the faith of the Catholic citizens, is *per se* justified in restricting heretical propaganda.

In this connection it should be noted that the author of this article seems to have confused two very different things—the *physical* freedom of the act of faith, and the *moral* freedom of that act (p. 10). A person is, indeed, *physically* free to make an act of faith or not; but no adult is *morally* free in this regard, since all are bound to elicit an act of supernatural faith as a necessary means of salvation.

Catholic bishops and priests in the United States have always explained this doctrine of the relation of Church and State as that which *per se* should exist by the law of [3] Christ. At the same time, they have pointed out that in the United States, because of the conditions existing therein, it is the most practical system for all religious groups to receive equal treatment from the government. Catholics in the United States have never asked any special favor from the government for their Church, and they do not hesitate to say that they would uphold the principle of complete freedom and equal treatment for all religions even if at any future time the Catholics of the United States became more numerous than the non-Catholics. Fair-minded Americans accept this explanation, realizing that it is entirely logical, and admitting that the Catholic Church, instead of being hostile to American ideals, is the staunchest defender of the principle of personal liberty. The loyalty which Catholics have always manifested to America, especially by giving their lives in defence of their country in war, is a convincing proof that the Catholic Church trains her members to be good citizens.

4. Even if, *per impossibile* [to take an impossible case], the Catholic Church proclaimed an "adaptation of the doctrine of Church-State relations to demo-

cratic ideals," as the author wishes, it would not make the apostolic activities of the Church any easier or any more effective. The enemies of the Church would boast that they had forced her to change her teaching; Catholics and fair-minded non-Catholics would not understand how there could be a modification in a doctrine that has been consistently taught by the Church for centuries. It is one of the Church's greatest sources of strength in the United States that she is unchangeable in her teaching, despite the changes going on in the world.

5. Instead of the suggestions made by the author as helpful to promote the welfare of the Church in the United States, I respectfully propose the following:

a. Bishops and priests should be urged to a more zealous and extensive apostolate to non-Catholics, in accordance with Canon 1350, 1. If all priests fulfilled their duty conscientiously in this matter, there would be three times as many converts in the United States annually as there are at present. However, in preaching to non-Catholics, priests must be warned to avoid the error of "eirenism" and to expound Catholic doctrine in its entirety, without compromise, in accordance with the principles laid down in the [4] Encyclical *Humani Generis* and in the Instruction of the Holy Office of December 20, 1949, on "ecumenism." Even if some non-Catholics will hate and persecute the Church in consequence of this open and honest exposition of Catholic doctrine, the clergy and the laity of the Church should realize that this is the fulfilment of the prophecy of Christ to His disciples: "If they have persecuted me, they will persecute you also" (John 15:20).

b. Instead of devoting their efforts to answering the charges made against the Church by persons like Paul Blanshard, Catholics would do better if they disregarded such writings and gave a positive explanation of the Church's teachings. The laity should be told that they will give a good argument for the Church by leading virtuous lives. A special effort should be made to persuade Catholics who hold posts of civil authority to be perfectly honest. It is a deplorable fact that many Catholics in public office in the United States today are a great source of scandal because of their dishonesty. Such persons are doing more harm to the Catholic Church than those who write against Catholicism.

c. Priests who are defending in print the theory of the "lay state" should be admonished to be silent, at least until the Holy See has given a decision. It is surprising both the Catholics and the non-Catholics of the United States to read that some Catholic scholars are upholding views on Church-State relationship that differ radically from the traditional doctrine. For example, in the *New York Times* for Sept. 8, 1949, Fr. John Courtney Murray, S.J., is quoted as saying that some Catholic scholars "are endeavoring to make a vital, not opportunistic adaptation of the Church's teaching, so that it will fit the political realities of democratically organized society. . . . A certain dissatisfaction has developed among Catholic thinkers regarding the adequacy of the formulation of the Catholic position on Church and State made in the nineteenth century. . . . The central operative concept of this school of thought is the freedom of the citizen in its relation to the freedom of the Church. One aspect of this concept is that the change from an authoritarian feudal state to the modern democratic nation has brought about a change in the relation of the Church to the people." Again, in *The Priest* for June, 1950, a writer argues that the civil government has the obligation to grant heretics full freedom of religious worship, as long as no harm is done to any individual, group, or society. (No mention is made of any harm that might be done to the rights [5] of God or Christ.) He argues thus: "The individual, though in error, has a right, not *per se* [essentially] but *per accidens* [accidentally], but a real right just the same, to what his conscience dictates. If, then, one in good faith is invincibly convinced that he is obliged in conscience to worship in the manner of an heretical sect, has he not the obligation and the right to do so? If so, then, since it is the primary purpose of the State to protect the natural rights of the individual, it is the duty of the State to recognize and to protect that right. . . . Thus is begotten, if everything so far is correct, the principle of the freedom of religion, not indeed on the basis that all religions are equally true and salutary, but on the strength of the fact that the immediate tribunal of man's responsibility to God is his own conscience and the further fact that man may in good faith err even regarding that which has been infallibly revealed." Again, in *The Sign* for October, 1949, we read: "Democracy is bound (as state religion governments, such as Spain or Sweden are not) to remain aloof from affiliation with any religious denomination, not in a spirit of indifferentism or agnosticism, but with benevolent neutrality."

The underlying idea of all such statements, which are surely influencing many American Catholics, is that the democratic form of government is not subject to the positive laws of Christ, and is not permitted to restrain heretical attempts to lead Catholics astray.

d. Catholics should be urged to obey more faithfully the *Monitum* of the Holy Office, June 5, 1948, and the Instruction of the same Holy Office, December 20, 1949; since there is a tendency on the part of some to favor indifferentism both in word and in practice.

These suggestions have been made in a spirit of profound respect and deference to any directives that may be issued by the Holy See.

Notes

Reprinted from *The Review of Politics* 61, no. 4 (Autumn 1999): 675–714.

1. See Donald E. Pelotte, *John Courtney Murray: Theologian in Conflict* (New York: Paulist Press, 1975); Dominique Gannet, *La liberté religieuse à Vatican II: La contribution de John Courtney Murray* (Paris: Éd. du Cerf, 1994); Joseph A. Komonchak, "The Silencing of John Courtney Murray," in *Cristianesimo nella Storia: Saggi in onore di Giuseppe Alberigo*, ed. A. Melloni et al. (Bologna: Il Mulino, 1996), 657–702 (a shorter version of this essay has been published as "Catholic Principle and the American Experiment: The Silencing of John Courtney Murray," *U.S. Catholic Historian* 17 [1999]: 28–45).

2. Francis J. Connell, "The Catholic Position on Freedom of Worship," *Columbia* 23, no. 3 (December 1943): 6, 24; reprinted as *Freedom of Worship: The Catholic Position* (New York: Paulist Press, 1944).

3. John Courtney Murray, "Governmental Repression of Heresy," *Proceedings of the Catholic Theological Society of America* 3 (1948): 26–98; Francis J. Connell, "Discussion of 'Governmental Repression of Heresy,'" ibid., 98–101; see also Connell, "Christ the King of Civil Rulers," *American Ecclesiastical Review* 119 (October 1948): 244–53.

4. John Courtney Murray, "The Problem of 'the Religion of the State,'" *American Ecclesiastical Review* 124 (May 1951): 327–52; Francis J. Connell, "The Theory of the 'Lay State,'" ibid., 125 (July 1951): 7–18; Murray, "For the Freedom and Transcendence of the Church," ibid., 126 (January 1952): 28–48; Connell, "Reply to Fr. Murray," ibid., 126 (January 1952): 49–59.

5. Connell to Pizzardo, Washington, 1 August 1950 (copy), Redemptorist Archives Baltimore Province (RABP), "Church-State Letters"; the accompanying memorandum, "Adnotationes de quadam nova theoria theologica," is dated 2 August 1950; RABP, Connell Papers, "Church-State Writings, John Courtney Murray."

6. Connell to Fenton, Washington, 29 June 1951 (copy); Fenton to Connell, 29 August 1951; RABP, Connell Papers, "Church-State Letters."

7. Connell to Cicognani, Washington, 23 February 1952 (copy); Cicognani to Connell, Washington, 27 February 1952; RABP, Connell Papers, "Church-State Letters."

8. On this meeting see Etienne Fouilloux, *Les catholiques et l'unité chrétienne du XIXe au Xxe siècle: Itinéraires européeens d'expression française* (Paris: Centurion, 1982), 705–9; "Catholic Leaders in Unionistic Field Meet at Grottaferrata," *Unitas* 2 (1950): 303; "A Conference on Christian Unity at Grottaferrata," *Eastern Churches Quarterly* 8 (Winter 1950): 494–97; Yves Congar, *Dialogue between Christians: Catholic Contributions to Ecumenism* (Westminster, MD: Newman Press, 1966), 38–39.

9. Boyer had been in touch with Murray in the planning stages of Unitas and had asked him to consider establishing "a national committee of *Unitas* for America" (Murray to Parsons, 13 December 1945, Woodstock, Woodstock College Archives (WCA), Parsons Papers, Box 11, File 40).

10. From an untitled, undated Chicago lecture, ca. 1965, after the promulgation of Vatican II's Decree on Ecumenism (WCA, Box 6, File 461). A year or two later, Murray gave a similar description of the event: "In my turn I had to report that there was no ecumenical activity in the United States, and that no one wanted any, least of all the Catholic bishops"; see John Courtney Murray, "A Memorable Man," in *One of a Kind: Essays in Tribute to Gustave Weigel* (Wilkes-Barre, PA: Dimension Books, 1967), 16–17.

11. For these two quotations from Congar's unpublished journal, which may be found in the archives of Le Saulchoir, Paris, I am grateful to Professor Etienne Fouilloux in his letter to me of 20 December 1991, and to Eric Mahieu in a communication, 8 April 1998; my translation from the French.

12. Murray to Robert Leiber, undated but before 12 June 1953, when Leiber replied to it; copy in my possession; my translation from the German.

13. Murray to John Tracy Ellis, Ridgefield, CT, 20 July 1953; Archives of the Catholic University of America (ACUA), Ellis Papers.

14. Murray to Vincent A. McCormick, Woodstock, 24 April 1951 (copy); WCA, Box 2, File 151.

15. It is possible that Murray already knew that his views were under examination in Rome and that Connell was among those who had prompted the interest. When in 1952 Connell had understood Murray's article of public reply to him to disparage Connell's intelligence, Murray's letter of apology included at the end an oblique criticism: "You will doubtless agree that it is more painful to a theologian to have his orthodoxy impugned than his intelligence. I can always try to meet public objections to my opinions. But it is particularly painful when suspicions of unorthodoxy are raised privately, by word of mouth in high places. Up to the present, no one, either in America or in Europe, has brought forward warrant for such suspicions"; Murray to Connell, New Haven, 25 January 1952; RABP, Connell Papers, "Church-State Writings, John Courtney Murray."

16. "The Crisis in Church-State Relationships in the USA," Library of Congress, Clare Booth Luce Papers, Box 703, Folder 14.

17. Murray to Vincent A. McCormick, Woodstock, 23 November 1953 (copy); WCA, Murray Papers. A copy of the transcript of Luce's statement on church and state during her appearance before the Senate Committee on Foreign Relations, 17 February 1953, can be found in her papers in the Library of Congress, Amb. File, B642, 2.

18. Montini to Stritch, Vatican City, 4 May 1951; Archives of the Archdiocese of Chicago (AAChicago), Stritch Papers, Box 4, File 10.

19. Msgr. Joseph F. McGeough to Stritch, Vatican City, 5 May 1952; Stritch to McGeough, Chicago, 15 May 1952 (copy); AAChicago, Stritch Papers, Box 4, File 10. Stritch's reply is entitled "Observations on the Memorandum 'The Crisis in Church-State Relationships in the U.S.A.'"

20. RABP, Connell Papers, "Church-State."

21. There are at least three versions of Ottaviani's speech. A typed copy of it as delivered can be found in the ACUA, NCWC/USCC. A significantly revised version was published as a pamphlet, *Doveri dello Stato cattolico verso la religione* (Rome: Ateneo

Lateranense, 1953), the basis for the English translation that appeared in *The Newark Advocate* in 1953 and for another translation published as a pamphlet, *Duties of the Catholic State in Regard to Religion* (Tipperary: "The Tipperary Star," 1954; republished Kansas City, MO: Angelus Press, 1993). Finally, there is a version, apparently shortened and altered at Ottaviani's direction, in "Church and State: Some Present Problems in the Light of the Teaching of Pope Pius XII," *American Ecclesiastical Review* 128 (May 1953): 321–34. There is reason to think that the revisions of the spoken text responded to Vatican criticism of the vigorous and unnuanced character of Ottaviani's remarks.

22. The relevant materials are found in the Gagnebet papers at the Istituto per le Scienze Religiose, Bologna, Italy.

23. Leiber to Murray, Rome, 12 June 1953; WCA, Murray Papers.

24. See *Acta Apostolicae Sedis* 45 (1953): 794–802; English translation in *American Ecclesiastical Review* 130 (February 1954): 129–38.

25. Murray spoke from handwritten notes, which he later typed out, he said, "exactly as I find them on my handwritten autograph." Both the notes and the typescript can be found in the Murray Papers, WCA, but, in fact, the transcription is not entirely exact.

26. Letters were sent to Ottaviani by Connell, Fenton, and, it seems, Fr. Maurice Sheehy, all professors at Catholic University.

27. The indicted essay was "On the Structure of the Church-State Problem," in *The Catholic Church in World Affairs*, ed. Waldemar Gurian and M. A. Fitzsimons (Notre Dame, IN: University of Notre Dame Press, 1954), 11–32.

28. Fenton, 1954 Roman Diary (in my possession); RABP, Connell Papers, "Church-State Letters."

29. There is a copy of this document in the Gagnebet Papers, Istituto per le Scienze Religiose, Bologna.

Chapter 17

Christianity, Magnanimity, and Statesmanship

Carson Holloway

Carson Holloway (1969–) is an American Catholic political scientist and associate professor of political science at the University of Nebraska Omaha. Holloway earned his Ph.D. in political science from Northern Illinois University in 1998 and began teaching at the University of Nebraska in 2002. In 2005–2006 he was the William E. Simon Visiting Fellow in Religion and Public Life at Princeton University's James Madison Program, and from 2014 to 2015 he was a visiting fellow in American political thought at the B. Kenneth Simon Center at The Heritage Foundation. Holloway is the author of The Way of Life: John Paul II and the Challenge of Liberal Modernity; The Right Darwin? Evolution, Religion, and the Future of Democracy; *and* All Shook Up: Music, Passion, and Politics. *He is the editor of* Magnanimity and Statesmanship *and coeditor of* Reason, Revelation, and the Civic Order: Political Philosophy and the Claims of Faith.

I

In the *Nicomachean Ethics* Aristotle presents the virtue of magnanimity or greatness of soul as a kind of summit of the moral life. The exercise of this particular virtue, he contends, presupposes the possession of all the others and at the same time "enhances" the "greatness" of all the others. Thus he characterizes magnanimity as "a crowning ornament of the virtues."[1]

This article investigates whether there can be a Christian magnanimity. More precisely, it inquires whether *Aristotelian* magnanimity is compatible with Christianity, a question that arises because of the apparent conflict between Christian morality and the specific excellence of the magnanimous man. According to Aristotle, the magnanimous man displays a certain praiseworthy disposition toward great honors: he claims great honors for himself believing, and believing rightly, that he is worthy of them because of his moral excellence. This awareness of his own superiority of character, moreover, necessarily leads the great-souled man to look down upon other men. He does this, Aristotle thinks, with perfect propriety. Thus he writes that "the great-souled man is justified in despising other people" and has "good ground" for doing so because "his estimates," both of others and of himself, "are correct."[2]

This is almost certainly not what most people would call the Christian understanding of the proper disposition toward great honors. Indeed, Aristotle's account of magnanimity appears almost diametrically opposed to the Christian moral teaching. What he calls a great virtue the Christian would likely call a great sin: pride.

This apparent opposition is also suggested by Aristotle's account of vanity and smallness of soul, the vicious dispositions opposed to magnanimity. The vain man errs on the side of excess, claiming more than he deserves, while the small-souled man errs on the side of deficiency, claiming less than he deserves. Not only is it on Aristotle's account a moral failing to claim less than one deserves, however. It is in fact a more serious moral failing than claiming more than one deserves. Smallness of soul, he argues, is more opposed to the virtuous mean than is vanity, the former "being both more prevalent and worse."[3]

Smallness of soul, however, would seem strikingly to resemble the Christian virtue of humility. Thus from the standpoint of Christianity Aristotle's moral universe seems topsy-turvy. He appears to condemn as a vice what Christianity holds up as a great virtue and to hold up as a great virtue what Christianity condemns as the greatest vice. It would therefore seem that Aristotelian magnanimity has no place in Christianity.

This article, however, argues that in spite of the seeming difficulties Aristotelian magnanimity is compatible with Christian morality. This argument takes the form of a response to Larry Arnhart's article, "Statesmanship as Magnanimity: Classical, Christian, and Modern," which contends that Christianity necessarily undermines magnanimity.[4] The article concludes with an account of the contemporary political importance of these issues. While Arnhart claims that Christianity's undermining of magnanimity is responsible for the lack of great statesmanship in the modern world, I argue that in the modern world Christianity alone can make magnanimous statesmanship possible.[5]

II

At the outset one must concede the considerable prima facie plausibility of Arnhart's contention that Christianity makes magnanimity impossible. The magnanimous man exalts himself, claiming for himself the greatest honors. In contrast, Christian morality appears as one of self-abasement rather than self-exaltation. Even for one who possesses only a passing familiarity with the New Testament, numerous passages come to mind that seem to suggest disapproval of Aristotelian magnanimity. "Learn from me," Christ advises his followers, "for I am gentle *and lowly* in heart."[6] "Whoever would be great among you," he teaches, "must be your servant, and whoever would be first among you must be slave of all."[7]

The Gospel of Luke offers what seems an even more direct repudiation of Aristotelian ethics. There Christ forthrightly tells his listeners to claim less honor than they deserve, thus apparently endorsing what Aristotle calls smallness of soul:

> When you are invited by any one to a marriage feast, do not sit down in a place of honor, lest a more eminent man than you be invited by him; and he who invited you both will come and say to you, "Give place to this man," and then you will begin with shame to take the lowest place. But when you are invited, go and sit in the lowest place, so that when your host comes he may say to you, "Friend, go up higher"; then you will be honored in the presence of all who sit at table with you. For every one who exalts himself will be humbled, and he who humbles himself will be exalted.[8]

The meaning of this parable would seem to be that those who claim less honor than they deserve in this life will be all the more honored in the next. And this meaning is made explicit when Christ says elsewhere that whoever "humbles himself" like a "child" will be "greatest in the kingdom of heaven."[9]

Nevertheless, that some reconciliation of Christian and Aristotelian ethics is possible is suggested by Christ's own actions as they are reported in the New Testament. According to the Gospel of Luke, upon his entry into Jerusalem Christ was greeted by "the whole multitude of the disciples," who were saying, "Blessed is the King who comes in the name of the Lord! Peace in heaven and glory in the highest." Luke continues, reporting that some Pharisees, hearing this, asked him to rebuke his followers. Christ's response: "I tell you, if these were silent, the very stones would cry out."[10] In this episode Christ displays magnanimity in the strict Aristotelian sense: he claims the great honors of which he is truly worthy. But since he claims elsewhere, as we have seen, to be humble, and since he commands his followers to imitate him, we must conclude—assuming that Christ's behavior and teaching are coherent—that for him as well as for them magnanimity and humility are somehow compatible, that humility is not smallness of soul and magnanimity is not sinful pride.[11]

This possibility of a compatibility between Aristotelian magnanimity and Christian morality is also suggested by Saint Augustine in *The City of God*. In book 5 of that work Augustine criticizes the Romans for their love of glory. Such criticism would seem to imply disapproval of Aristotelian magnanimity as well. After all, the magnanimous man's claiming of great honors for himself stems from a desire to enjoy them: he takes pleasure in the honors he claims and deserves.[12] If the Christian must renounce earthly glory, then magnanimity is incompatible with Christianity. Although Augustine's critique of Rome might at first glance seem to point to this conclusion, a more careful consideration of the argument of *The City of God* suggests that for Augustine it is not the love of glory itself that is blameworthy but the *excessive* love of glory.

Virtue, Augustine argues in *The City of God*, "is the order of love."[13] That is, virtue is loving each thing in the right proportion. Thus when he warns that physical beauty "is not fitly loved in preference to God" he implies that it is not wrong to love it to some extent.[14] This teaching would seem equally to apply to the love of glory. Augustine speaks of those Romans who "burned with an excessive desire of" human glory and recommends that "the desire of glory be surpassed by the love of righteousness."[15] Thus he suggests that glory or honor can be loved in right measure and that the desire for it need not be completely eradicated from the Christian's heart.

A similar position is advanced by Saint Thomas Aquinas. In the *Summa Theologica*'s account of magnanimity—in which he, following Aristotle, treats it as a virtue—Aquinas responds to the objection that "the virtuous are praised not for desiring honors but for shunning them."[16] In response he claims that the magnanimous man "strives to do what is deserving of honor" yet does not "think much of the honor accorded by man."[17] Thus he leaves open the possibility that, although a Christian must not set too much store by worldly honors, he may to some extent desire and enjoy them. That this is indeed Aquinas's meaning is suggested by his mentioning, in his response to this same objection, that Christian virtue requires that we despise riches, but only "in such a way as to do nothing unbecoming in order to obtain them" and not to "have *too great* a desire for them."[18] As it is with wealth, it would seem, so it is with honor: one may desire it so long as the desire does not become inordinate.[19] And, Aquinas later argues, such desire becomes inordinate when it undermines one's proper subjection to God.[20]

Further light is shed on Aquinas's understanding of the permissibility of some desire for honor by his suggestion in his account of magnanimity that "things external," including "money and honor," are "very desirable, as being necessary for human life."[21] It is worthwhile to pause to draw out the full implications of this statement.

The statement suggests that the things necessary to human life are by their nature desirable to human beings. God, it seems, has arranged nature in such a way that, although it does not simply provide man's good, it does facilitate the attainment of that good by making the things necessary to it desirable. According to Christianity, man is an embodied spirit. As such, his body is part of his nature: human nature is defined by neither the body nor the soul but by body and soul united.[22] Accordingly, the good of the body is part of the good of the whole man. And nature supports the attainment of the good of the body by making the things necessary to it, such as food and sleep, pleasant.

Man is also, according to Christianity, by nature a social being. And as Aquinas's comments indicate, the attainment of man's good as a social being is facilitated by the natural pleasantness of the external goods, money and honor, necessary to it. The enjoyment men find in gaining money is an inducement to the production of goods and provision of services required by the economic common good. Similarly, the enjoyment men find in honors is an inducement to the exercise of the virtues necessary to secure the political common good. Thus Christian ethics does not call for the utter renunciation of these things because to do so would be to resist and undermine the inducements God has provided to the attainment and preservation of man's good. Christianity therefore no more commands human beings to renounce honor and the enjoyment it provides than it commands them to renounce food and the enjoyment it provides. Rather it merely asks that those pleasures and the goods toward which they are directed be kept subordinate to man's final end: the enjoyment of God. Put simply, Christianity is not, Nietzsche to the contrary notwithstanding, opposed to life. It seeks not to deny this life but only to put it in its proper place.

Furthermore, and in relation to this argument that a Christian may legitimately desire honor since honor is necessary to the attainment of the *common* good, it is worth observing that on Aristotle's account the honors the magnanimous man claims for himself do not benefit himself alone, for those honors necessarily entail exertion on behalf of the political community. This is implied in Aristotle's discussion of the vices opposed to magnanimity, in which he states that the vain man's excessive claiming of honor takes the form of "undertak[ing] honorable responsibilities of which" he is "not worthy" and that the small-souled man's deficient claiming of honor manifests itself as the avoidance of "noble enterprises" of which he is capable.[23] We conclude, then, that the great honors rightly claimed by the magnanimous man also involve the shouldering of some great responsibility. This is made most clear in the *Eudemian Ethics*, where, as Arnhart points out, Aristotle states that the magnanimous man claims and is worthy of "the greatest 'offices' (*archai*)."[24] Yet in order to be truly worthy of such offices, the magnanimous man must conduct himself in them in a way that is proper. And Aristotle insists that the only proper use of political rule is with a view to the common good.[25] Thus the magnanimous man's desire for great honors redounds to the well-being of the city.[26]

What, then, are we to make of passages in the New Testament and in the works of Christian writers of great authority that seem to condemn not just inordinate love of honor but any concern with it at all? What are we to make of the parable, discussed above, in which Christ teaches his followers to take the "lowest place," or of Augustine's comment in *The City of God* that it is "doubtless far better to resist" than "to yield to" the desire for glory?[27] The answer to this question is suggested by Augustine's remark that the pleasure of glory is so powerful that the love of it "does not cease to tempt even the minds of those who are making good progress in virtue."[28] The Christian understanding may be that while it is possible and permissible to desire honor in a measured way, to do so is very difficult, for the pleasure of honor is so great that it powerfully tempts one to love it above all things. Perhaps, then, Christ and Christian writers state in a very strong and even exaggerated way the need to resist the desire for honor because almost all men are inclined to love honor far more than is fitting and therefore need to be pushed in the opposite direction.[29] Indeed, the use of such exaggeration by Christ is not unheard of in the Gospels. For example, at one point he says, "If any one comes to me and does not hate his own father and mother and wife and children and brothers and sisters, yes, and even his own life, he cannot be my disciple."[30] One would be hard pressed, I suspect, to find any serious Christian moralist who thinks that the word "hate" in this passage is meant to be taken literally.

One might respond to the preceding arguments as follows: Perhaps it is permissible for the Christian to desire honor, but surely the magnanimous man's contempt for other human beings is contrary to Christianity. In response to this point we may first observe that, on Aristotle's account, the great-souled man's contempt for others does not entail animosity toward them. On the contrary, the great-souled man is said by Aristotle to treat ordinary people with a kind of gentleness. He is "courteous" toward those of "moderate station," and he uses "ironical self-depreciation" to conceal his greatness from common folk.[31] His contempt, then, is simply a looking down upon others as beneath him. Moreover, that such looking down is, if well-founded, compatible with Christianity is indicated by Aquinas's teaching that humility regards more one's relationship to God than to other men.[32] Aristotelian magnanimity, in contrast, is concerned with the great-souled man's relationship to other human beings. Thus, insofar as their points of reference differ, the self-evaluations involved in humility and magnanimity need not come into conflict. A Christian outstanding in virtue, it seems, may look down upon other human beings so long as it does not distract him from looking up to God, may recognize his superiority to others so long as he does not allow it to obscure his recognition of God's superiority.[33]

It is true that Aquinas argues that humble submission of ourselves to God requires that we submit ourselves to other men, indeed *all* other men, for God's sake.[34] Yet this call for submission, for thinking others better than ourselves, is qualified in such a way as to still leave room for magnanimity. Aquinas distinguishes that which is in us that is God's and that which is in us that is our own. The former "pertains to man's welfare and perfection" whereas the latter "pertains to defect."[35] Humility, Aquinas contends, requires only that one submit what is in oneself and is one's own to that which is in others and is from God. It neither requires that one submit what is in oneself and is from God to what is in others and is from God nor that one submit what is in oneself and one's own to what is in others and is their own. Thus Aquinas's account leaves room for recognizing one's own superiority to others and thus looking down upon them, so long as it is well-founded, that is, so long as the virtues God has given one are really superior to those he has given others and the defects one has from oneself really are less than those others have from themselves. And one may claim the honors those virtues merit, including great honors if one's virtues are great, so long as one recognizes that ultimately those virtues are from God and thus that ultimately those honors belong to Him.

III

The preceding section argues that, despite first appearances, Christian morality does not make magnanimity impossible by demanding the utter renunciation of honor. The Christian, no less than the Aristotelian magnanimous man, may claim the honors he deserves. If, however, the magnanimous man not only claims honors, but is a lover of honor, that is, if he treats the winning of honor as the primary purpose of his activities, then greatness of soul is clearly incompatible with Christianity, and the demise of the former may rightly be attributed to the rise of the latter. For if our previous arguments show that the Christian may love honor, they also show that he must not love it above all else.

This, then, is Arnhart's argument.[36] He contends that the lack of great statesmanship in the modern world is due to the "political influence of Christianity," which condemns the magnanimous man as "too proud, too preoccupied with human glory, to be truly virtuous."[37] This argument depends upon Arnhart's presentation of the magnanimous man as one who is in fact preoccupied with human glory. Thus he treats as a description of magnanimity Hamilton's account in *Federalist*, No. 72, of those men who are moved by that "love of fame" that is the "ruling passion of the noblest minds."[38] He presents the magnanimous man's "devotion to the moral life" as if it is the same as a commitment to the pursuit of glory.[39] He offers Alexander the Great as an example of the political manifestation of Aristotelian magnanimity.[40] In sum, he contends that the aim of the magnanimous man's virtuous activity is the acquisition of glory, that he seeks self-sufficiency, the overcoming of chance, through the immortal fame accompanying great political achievement.[41]

Again, if this is indeed the true nature of magnanimity, if the great-souled man's "ruling passion" truly is "the love of fame," then magnanimity is clearly incompatible with Christianity. On Aristotle's account, however, the magnanimous man is not motivated primarily by the desire to acquire glory, and he does not seek immortality and self-sufficiency in the manner Arnhart suggests.

The *Nicomachean Ethics* suggests that the magnanimous man has in fact a moderate disposition toward the great honors he claims and deserves. This moderation, moreover, is reflected not only in the propriety of his claim—that is, his claiming only so much as he does in truth deserve—but also in his attachment to the honors of which he is worthy: he is not passionately attracted to them. Thus Aristotle writes that he gets only "pleasure in a moderate degree" from great honors.[42] He continues by saying that the magnanimous man "will also observe due measure" with regard to other external goods such a money, power, and fortune generally: "he will not rejoice overmuch in prosperity, nor grieve overmuch at adversity" since "he does not care much even about honor, which is the greatest of external goods."[43]

Moreover, the kind of honor sought by Aristotle's magnanimous man seems fundamentally different from that pursued by an Alexander the Great, whom Arnhart puts forward as an example of the political face of Aristotelian magnanimity.[44] Alexander's activity—worldwide conquest—would seem to have been motivated by a desire to rule and be honored by all men indiscriminately. Yet Aristotle suggests that the honors from which the great-souled man derives moderate pleasure are those bestowed by the morally serious (*spoudaion*), who, he implies by distinguishing them from "common people," are few.[45]

Indeed, if honor were the object of the magnanimous man's striving he would not, according to Aristotle's teaching in the *Nicomachean Ethics*, truly be morally virtuous and therefore would not be magnanimous. Again, magnanimity presupposes complete moral virtue, but true moral virtue, as Aristotle repeatedly asserts, requires that one choose what right principle dictates for the sake of its own nobility.[46] Hence, in his account of courage, Aristotle explicitly classes as a kind of false courage that which is practiced for the sake of "the honors awarded to bravery," later observing that a man ought to be brave for no other reason than that "courage is noble."[47]

In response to these arguments one might point to the fact that Aristotle remarks twice in his discussion of magnanimity that "honor" is the object with which the great-souled man "is especially concerned."[48] Surely this suggests that his love of honor outstrips his love of virtue? Yet these remarks are made in the context of Aristotle's treatment of the great-souled man's *moderate* enjoyment of the great honors he claims and deserves. In this light it would seem that Aristotle intends to say not that the magnanimous man is especially concerned with honors in the sense of being preoccupied with them, rather that his specific virtue is displayed with regard to honors. But that virtue, again, involves moderation with regard to honors. Similarly, the liberal man might be said to be especially concerned with money, since liberality is displayed "in relation to wealth." Yet it would plainly be mistaken to suggest on this basis that the liberal man is preoccupied with money, for, on the contrary, the disposition he displays toward money is moderate.[49]

Aristotle's magnanimous man does seek and achieve a kind of immortality through the practice of moral virtue. But this immortalizing, this participation in eternity, this conquest of chance and achievement of self-sufficiency comes not from the honors won as a result of morally excellent activity but from the activity itself. The noble (*kalon*), which again is the end and motive of moral virtue and hence of the magnanimous man's activity, is said by Aristotle to be one of the objects apprehended by intellect (*nous*).[50] Furthermore, Aristotle goes on to indicate that through the activity of *nous* man achieves a kind of immortality and thus that the objects of *nous* are eternal.[51] The magnanimous man, therefore, participates in this eternity, the *kalon*, and makes it present in his own soul, through the activity of moral virtue.[52] And such activity is, according to Aristotle, naturally pleasant in itself and, therefore, those who pursue such activity have no need for the pleasures provided by external goods—such as honor—as "a sort of ornamental appendage."[53] Hence his contention that one can achieve not inconsiderable happiness even in private life, absent the honors that accompany ruling.[54] The magnanimous man's moral excellence, it seems, is not directed toward the winning of glory as a means to an end. Rather it is itself the naturally pleasant end, and the magnanimous man's enjoyment of it is the basis of his moderate disposition toward honor and all other lesser goods.

Unlike the pursuit of immortality through political glory, moreover, this striving for a kind of earthly participation in eternity which, on my interpretation, Aristotle's magnanimous man pursues is compatible with Christianity. It is true that the Christian looks for immortality primarily in the next life. Nevertheless, the New Testament suggests the possibility of, and encourages the seeking of, a sort of participation in the eternal in this life similar to that achieved by the magnanimous man's actualization of the noble in his moral activity. Christ tells his followers: "He who has my commandments and keeps them . . . will be loved by my Father, and I will love him and manifest myself to him. . . . If a man loves me, he will keep my word, and my Father will love him, and we will come to him and make our home with him."[55] This suggests that through moral activity the good Christian attains a kind of earthly pre-experience of the beatific vision, the contemplation of God that is the source of perfect and eternal happiness in heaven.

With regard to the question whether the magnanimous man's love of honor is excessive according to Christianity, however, a final problem remains to be resolved. Aquinas suggests that the magnanimous man must acknowledge his greatness as a gift from God.[56] In this light he contends that a man displays an excessive love of honor when he "desires honor for himself without referring it to God."[57] Arnhart points to such passages as an attempt to "infuse the great-souled man with Christian humility," an attempt which he regards as ultimately destructive of magnanimity. Hence he says that Aquinas merely "*seems* in the *Summa Theologica* to adopt Aristotle's account of magnanimity."[58]

Such passages do indeed pose a difficulty, for there is little in Aristotle's account of magnanimity to suggest that the great-souled man recognizes any source of his greatness other than himself. Nevertheless, a case can be made that Aristotle's magnanimous man is capable of such acknowledgment of some external source of his excellence. On the basis of Aristotle's argument in book 2 of the *Nicomachean Ethics* one must conclude that the great-souled man does in fact owe his virtue in large part to someone else. There Aristotle contends that, with a view to the practice of virtue in our maturity, our training "from childhood" in a certain "set of habits" "is of very great, or rather of supreme, importance."[59] In this light the magnanimous man's moral excellence, and hence his worthiness of great honors, can be said to be to a great extent the work of his parents or whoever directed his early habituation in virtue. That the magnanimous man recognizes this debt is nowhere explicitly stated in the *Ethics*. Yet it is suggested by Aristotle's comment at the beginning of his account of greatness of soul in book 4 that to be "foolish or senseless" is incompatible with moral virtue and hence with magnanimity.[60] This debt is so evident that even people of mere ordinary decency are not so foolish or senseless as to fail to recognize it, so it would be strange if it were unacknowledged by one so outstanding in virtue as to be worthy of great honor.

Of course, acknowledging one's parents is not the same thing as acknowledging God, and it should be observed that the *Ethics* says very little about the gods or the proper relationship of human beings to them. Nevertheless, my argument is not that Aristotle's magnanimous man is a Christian but that his virtue, his disposition toward honor, is compatible with Christianity. Both the magnanimous man and the Christian can recognize that their virtues are not simply due to themselves, that in fact their virtues are for the most part due to someone else. Both, therefore, can refer the honors they claim to that external source of their goodness. Thus magnanimity is not incompatible with Christianity.

One might object that on this issue an incompatibility in fact still remains, for the great-souled man, while he may acknowledge that some or even most of his greatness is due to those who provided his moral education, does not go so far as the Christian, who seems to be required to refer *all* of his excellence to God and to renounce any credit for it. One might well conclude that this is the Christian position in light of Aquinas's statement that the magnanimous man's virtues are held as a gift from God. This is not, however, the last word on this subject. Aquinas holds that the magnanimous man rightly "despises others in so far as they fall away from God's gifts."[61] This implies that the virtues, though they are given by God, nonetheless require one's cooperation in order to be operative. Thus the Christian need not go so far as to attribute his virtues entirely to God; and just as Aristotle's magnanimous man must acknowledge his moral education but may justly take pride in his appropriation of it, so the Christian magnanimous man must acknowledge God's gifts but may innocently take satisfaction in his cooperation with them.[62]

IV

What are the contemporary political ramifications of Christianity's relationship to magnanimity? Arnhart holds that Christianity's undermining of magnanimity is responsible for the lack of great statesmanship in the modern world. He points to Tocqueville's argument that democratic men think too little of themselves and as a result "love success much more than glory," despising themselves to the point of believing that they are "made for tasting only vulgar pleasures." Tocqueville thinks that for such men "humility is never healthy": instead they are in great need of "pride," and Tocqueville admits that he would "willingly surrender several of our petty virtues for that vice."[63] It is, however, Christian moral teaching, Arnhart contends, that forces Tocqueville into the "awkward position" of endorsing a vice over "certain 'petty virtues.'"[64] Thus Christianity appears as an obstacle to the relief of democratic man's abject lowness, the amelioration of which therefore requires some "appeal to pre-Christian moral thought."[65] The promotion of "human greatness" in modernity requires a marked departure from Christianity, the revival of the "pagan virtue of magnanimity."[66]

This article has already offered an argument that in some measure responds to what Arnhart contends here. Christianity does not, as we have seen, condemn the pride displayed by the magnanimous man. His awareness of his own greatness, his claiming of great honors on that basis, and his accompanying contempt for others do not necessarily fall afoul of the Christian virtue of humility, which requires only that a good man acknowledge God's superiority to himself, not that he deny his superiority to others. It certainly does not teach him that he is "made for tasting only vulgar pleasures."[67]

In this section, I further argue that Christianity, far from being an obstacle to human greatness in the modern world, is in fact the only secure basis for it. Drawing upon Tocqueville, I contend that Christianity is the cure for the abject vulgarity of democratic peoples and that the application of this cure requires magnanimous statesmanship. Going beyond Tocqueville, I also argue that Christianity provides the only hope in a democratic world that such statesmanship will be forthcoming, that those capable of it will enter political life.

The "vulgar pleasures" for which democratic men believe they are made are, according to Tocqueville, physical pleasures. The "taste for physical well-being," he contends, dominates democratic society, in which "everyone is preoccupied caring for the slightest needs of the body and the trivial conveniences of life."[68] In an aristocracy the impossibility of social mobility results in a certain indifference to physical comforts. Aristocrats, secure in their possession of such comforts, enjoy them without being obsessed by them and then turn their attention to "some grander and more difficult undertaking that inspires and engrosses them."[69] Similarly, peasants, resigned to their poverty, do not think about physical comfort "because they despair of getting it." They are thus driven "to dwell in imagination in the next world."[70]

In contrast, the absence in democracy of fixed social classes and the resulting possibility of upward economic mobility unfetters and intensifies the longing for physical comforts.[71] In a democracy a large number of "middling fortunes are established," which provide "enough physical enjoyments" for their owners "to get a taste for them, but not enough to content them."[72] And because the human heart is most excited not by "the quiet possession of something precious but rather the imperfectly satisfied desire to have it and the continual fear of losing it again," democratic man is "continually engaged in pursuing or striving to retain these precious, incomplete, and fugitive delights."[73]

This democratic tendency, Tocqueville fears, ends in man's dehumanization. Democratic men pursue physical pleasures so single-mindedly that they "lose sight of those more precious goods" of the soul "which constitute the greatness and glory of mankind."[74] They dwell so much upon the "petty" objects of their desire that these finally "shut out the rest of the world" and "come between the soul and God."[75] Thus democratic inclinations, if unchecked, ultimately lower man to the level of the beasts. Physical pleasures, after all, are what we have in common with animals.[76] And it is to this brutish side of human nature that democratic society almost exclusively attends, neglecting that other, nobler, side by which "man is able to raise himself above the things of the body and even to scorn life itself," of which capacity "the beasts have not the least notion."[77]

Fortunately, the cure for this democratic malady is available: religious belief. Tocqueville observes that on Sunday in America trade and industry cease and are supplanted temporarily by a "solemn contemplation" of things spiritual. Turning to Holy Scripture, the American finds accounts not only of the greatness of God but also "of the high destiny reserved for men," of "the need to check" their "desires" in favor of "the finer delights which go with virtue alone."[78] Only the Americans' piety, Tocqueville suggests, is able to distract the people from the pursuit of material comforts and thus to elevate their lives by appealing to, and in some measure satisfying, the natural human "taste for the infinite and love of what is immortal."[79] Thus he asserts that he is "firmly persuaded that at all costs Christianity must be maintained among the new democracies."[80]

Tocqueville fears, however, that religion's hold upon the democratic mind is so weak that its influence must be actively supported if it is to act as a sufficient restraint on democratic materialism. Hence he advocates a kind of spiritual statesmanship the purpose of which is to "raise up the souls" of the citizens and to "turn their attention toward heaven." "There is a need," he insists

> for all who are interested in the future of democratic societies to get together and with one accord to make continual efforts to propagate throughout society a taste for the infinite, an appreciation of greatness, and a love of spiritual pleasures.[81]

This elevation of the people, Tocqueville further argues, can only be achieved if politicians lead by example, if they use their official duties as a means of educating the citizenry. In order "to make the immortality of the soul respected," he writes, statesmen must "act as if they believed it themselves. I think that it is only by conforming scrupulously to religious morality in great affairs that they can flatter themselves that they are teaching the citizens to understand it and to love and respect it in little matters."[82]

This statesmanship, however, calls for Aristotelian magnanimity. Since its aim is the moral improvement of the people, and not merely the maintenance of peace, it must respect the magnanimous man's claim to be worthy of office and honor because of his moral excellence. To teach the people the importance of virtue, Tocqueville suggests, the statesman must act virtuously in his political capacity. But to act virtuously, Aristotle insists, one must be virtuous. That is, one must have a settled disposition of habit to act virtuously. Possessing such a disposition more completely and securely than others, the magnanimous man can legitimately claim to be most worthy to conduct the statesmanship Tocqueville prescribes.

This statesmanship, moreover, requires the magnanimous man's contempt for others no less than his virtue. "Love of comfort," Tocqueville contends, is in a democracy the "dominant national taste."[83] That is, public opinion holds that the pursuit of physical pleasures is life's most important activity. Tocqueville's spiritual statesman must therefore resist public opinion. Resisting public opinion, however, is very difficult in a democracy, for two reasons. First, Tocqueville observes that in a democracy the majority enjoys an immense "moral authority." Democratic men, it seems, are powerfully inclined to believe that the majority can "do no wrong," that the opinions it holds are necessarily correct.[84] The basis of this inclination is the democratic belief in equality: Democratic men "think it not unreasonable that, all having the same means of knowledge, truth will be found on the side of the majority."[85]

Second, in the rare instances in which its moral authority is not acknowledged, the majority can bring to bear a subtle coercion that prevents the few who disagree with it from speaking their minds. Modern democracy, it seems, has given rise to a form of tyranny much more effective than that of princes. The latter made use of physical violence, clumsily and ineffectively striking at the body. The former, in contrast, "leaves the body alone and goes straight for the soul," threatening the dissident as follows:

> You are free not to think as I do; you can keep your life and property and all; but from this day you are a stranger among us. You can keep your privileges in the township, but they will be useless to you, for if you solicit your fellow citizens' votes, they will not give them to you, and if you only ask for their esteem, they will make excuses for refusing that.[86]

So powerful is this threat, Tocqueville suggests, that one finds very little "true freedom of discussion" in a democracy and among democratic politicians very little of the "virile candor and manly independence of thought" that are the "most salient feature[s] in men of great character."[87]

The magnanimous man, however, remains unmoved by both the majority's moral authority and its power of intimidation. He does not share the egalitarian presupposition that supports the former, and he does not much desire the things the denial of which is the instrument of the latter. Well aware of his own superiority to the many, he does not fall victim to the democratic delusion that what the many believe must be true. He is confident of the truth of his judgment that in its obsession with material comforts public opinion is mistaken and in need of the corrective influence of the education provided by his statesmanship. In acting on the basis of this judgment he is undeterred by the possibility that his unpopular course might so provoke the people that they will deny him their "votes" or even their "esteem" because he cares little for either. He is willing to risk the loss of public office in the pursuit of what is right because the natural pleasure of his virtuous activity makes the enjoyment of all such external goods seem small in comparison. Only such a man is fitted to undertake the very difficult statesmanship advocated by Tocqueville. Democracy, it seems, desperately needs the magnanimous man.

There is a problem, however. No matter how much democracy needs the magnanimous man, there is little reason to believe that he would even attempt to come to its rescue. Again, the great honors that the magnanimous man claims and deserves, and from which he derives moderate pleasure, are those bestowed by the morally serious. But, according to Aristotle, "honor rendered by common people and on trivial grounds he will utterly despise, for this is not what he merits."[88] Yet to involve oneself in democratic politics is necessarily to seek honors bestowed by common people and on trivial grounds, for, as Tocqueville points out, in a modern democracy the people's political power is "absolute" and they almost always select their leaders on the basis of "hasty judgments" and the "most prominent," though not the most salient, "characteristics."[89]

The magnanimous man, then, would experience participation in democratic politics as a kind of lowering of himself, and it is difficult to see what motive could induce him to endure this. One might suggest the prospect of winning high office as a possible inducement to his participation. The great-souled man, however, derives only moderate pleasure from even the greatest honors. It remains, therefore, unclear that any satisfaction he might gain from holding high office could outweigh the dissatisfaction he would necessarily encounter in courting the approval of people he knows to be his inferiors by addressing himself to their at best petty and at worst vicious concerns. Besides, we know from Aristotle's account that the great-souled man would not gain any pleasure from holding high office in a modern democracy because he would regard that office as an honor unworthy of him and would therefore despise it. For him, then, both the pursuit of the office and the achievement of it involve a kind of pain.

Alternatively, then, one might point to a desire for the people's well-being as a motive for the magnanimous man to endure this pain and enter politics. There is little evidence in Aristotle's account, however, that the magnanimous man feels such a desire. It is true that the magnanimous man's contempt for the people does not involve hostility and that he even treats them with a kind of gentleness, treating them courteously and speaking to them with ironical self-deprecation. Such actions, however, seem to stem less from care for the people than concern for the great-souled man's own self-respect. Hence Aristotle indicates that he does these things because he thinks it is "vulgar to lord it over humble people: it is like putting forth one's strength against the weak."[90]

For Aristotle's magnanimous man, it would seem, participation in democratic political life is all humiliation and no satisfaction. He will therefore eschew such participation. This problem is recognized by Tocqueville in his discussion of why democracy so seldom gives rise to great statesmanship. He observes that in a democracy a "strong instinct diverts" "men of distinction" from pursuing "a political career, in which it would be difficult to remain completely themselves or to make any progress without cheapening themselves."[91] Tocqueville's "new political science" designed to cure the ills of the new democratic world thus faces an apparently insoluble difficulty: the remedy for democracy's vulgarity can only be applied by the magnanimous man, but that vulgarity is so odious to the magnanimous man that he is unwilling to attempt to apply the remedy.[92]

This problem is solved by Christianity, which provides the magnanimous man with the motive he needs to lower himself by entering democratic politics. That motive is charity, or love of the people. The Christian believes that he is obligated to love his neighbor, no matter how vicious that neighbor may be, and his religion teaches him that even the vicious are in a way worthy of that love. Aristotle's magnanimous man looks at the people and sees the less-than-virtuous many, the multitude whose activities are not in harmony with the precepts of nature, who live a life that is not fully human, and whose defective habituation is probably so deeply ingrained as to foreclose the possibility of reform. The Christian magnanimous man looks at the people, and, in the light of the Christian revelation, sees something more. He sees, true enough, sinners, but sinners who are capable, with the help of God's grace, of being saints. More than that, he sees in each an immortal soul, infinitely beloved of God, destined for an eternal misery or felicity that will be the culmination and reward of its life on earth. Consider the following passage from the Christian writer C. S. Lewis:

> It is a serious thing to live in a society of possible gods and goddesses, to remember that the dullest and most uninteresting person you can talk to may one day be a creature which, if you saw it now, you would be strongly tempted to worship, or else a horror and a corruption such as you now meet, if at all, only in a nightmare. All day long we are, in some degree, helping each other to one or other of these destinations. It is in the light of these overwhelming possibilities, it is with the awe and circumspection proper to them, that we should conduct all our dealings with one another, all friendships, all loves, all play, all politics.[93]

The love that he owes his neighbor and the possibility of the great good that might be achieved through his statesmanship—the possibility that it might help some to avoid endless damnation and to achieve endless glory—provide the Christian great-souled man sufficient motive to endure the mortification he necessarily feels at lowering himself to participate in democratic politics. Yet even here such a man does not depart from magnanimity by being a good Christian. In loving the people and in lowering himself to help them he does not therefore lose his awareness of his superiority to them, does not cease looking down upon them. Like Christ he dines with sinners, but like Christ he knows who are the "sick" and who is the "physician."[94]

NOTES

Reprinted from *The Review of Politics* 61, no. 4 (Autumn 1999): 581–604.

I would like to thank the anonymous reviewers of this piece for their interesting and helpful comments.

    1. Aristotle, *Nicomachean Ethics* 1124a1–4. I have generally followed the translation of H. Rackham (Cambridge, MA: Harvard University Press, 1990) while occasionally supplying transliterations of certain key Greek terms.
    2. Ibid., 1124b5–6.
    3. Ibid., 1125a30–35.

4. Larry Arnhart, "Statesmanship as Magnanimity: Classical, Christian, and Modern," *Polity* 16, no. 2 (Winter 1983): 263–83. Arnhart's argument seems so far to have received no comment in the scholarly literature.

5. I should note that I owe Professor Arnhart many thanks for what I have learned not only from his insightful article but also from his always stimulating seminars at Northern Illinois University.

6. Matt. 11:30 (emphasis mine). All biblical references are to *The New Oxford Annotated Bible*, Revised Standard Version, ed. Herbert G. May and Bruce M. Metzger (New York: Oxford University Press, 1962).

7. Mark 10:43–44.

8. Luke 14:7–11.

9. Matt. 18:4.

10. Luke 19:37–40.

11. Of course, to say that Christians must imitate Christ is not to say that their behavior will be identical to his. Christian magnanimity obviously cannot manifest itself in the same way as Christ's magnanimity because no Christian can rightly claim the great honors that Christ claims for himself. Nevertheless, it may be that there are honors, less great than those claimed by Christ but still great according to human standards, that Christians may rightly, and without departing from the virtue of humility, claim for themselves. In so doing they would display magnanimity.

12. *Nicomachean Ethics* 1124a5–10.

13. Augustine of Hippo, *The City of God*, trans. Marcus Dods (New York: Modern Library, 1993), 511.

14. Ibid., 510.

15. Ibid., 167, 164 (emphasis mine).

16. Thomas Aquinas, *Summa Theologica* II-II, q. 129, a. 1. I have followed the translation of the Fathers of the English Dominican Province (Allen, TX: Christian Classics, 1948).

17. Ibid.

18. Ibid. (emphasis mine).

19. It is worth noting in this connection that Aquinas, in his discussion of magnanimity in his famous commentary, makes no mention of any incompatibility between greatness of soul and Christian morality. See Thomas Aquinas, *Commentary on Aristotle's Nicomachean Ethics*, trans. C. I. Litzinger, O.P. (Notre Dame, IN: Dumb Ox Books, 1993), 237–51.

20. *S.T.* II-II, q. 131, a. 1.

21. Ibid., II-II, q. 129, a. 2.

22. On this point see, for example, *The City of God*, 674.

23. *Nicomachean Ethics* 1125a25–33.

24. Arnhart, "Statesmanship as Magnanimity," 267.

25. Aristotle, *Politics*, trans. and ed. Carnes Lord (Chicago: University of Chicago Press, 1985), 1279a28.

26. In this light Aristotle's magnanimous man resembles less the man who takes the highest seat in Christ's parable of the wedding feast than the good servant who uses the talents given him to earn a great profit, and similarly the small-souled man resembles less the humble man who takes the lowest place than the worthless servant who buries his talent in the ground where it produces nothing good. On this point see *S.T.* II-II, q. 133, a. 1. Also, see the *Commentary on Aristotle's* Nicomachean Ethics, where Aquinas contends that the small-souled man "refuses to strive after great accomplishments and aims at certain petty undertakings" and that he does this "from a certain laziness," 238 and 251.

27. Augustine, *The City of God*, 164.

28. Ibid.

29. One might also observe that the context of the parable in which Christ advises his listeners to take the lowest place (Luke 14:1–11) indicates that his audience is a group of Pharisees, who are said repeatedly in the Gospels to have been much more concerned with their reputation for holiness than with holiness itself. Thus Christ may exaggerate the need to shun honor not only because of the general tendency of most human beings but also in view of the specific weakness of his immediate audience.

30. Luke 14:26.

31. *Nicomachean Ethics* 1124b17–25 and 1124b27–1125a1.

32. See *S.T.* II-II, q. 161, a. 1.

33. Aristotle says very little in the *Nicomachean Ethics* about man's relationship to the gods and therefore the Christian virtue of humility seems utterly alien to him. Nonetheless, that Aristotle's thought contains the basis for something not unlike humility is indicated by his comment that prudence, or wisdom about human affairs, cannot be the "loftiest kind of knowledge, inasmuch as man is not the highest thing" in the cosmos. See the *Nicomachean Ethics* 1141a21–23.

34. *S.T.* II-II, q. 161, a. 3.

35. Ibid.

36. This is in fact only the first of three distinct arguments advanced by Arnhart in support of his contention that Christianity undermines magnanimity. The other two are that Christianity does away with the need for magnanimous statesmanship by lowering the end of politics to the preservation of temporal peace and that it destroys the ground for magnanimity by undermining belief in nature as an autonomous order. In this article I respond only to Arnhart's first argument.

37. Arnhart, "Statesmanship as Magnanimity," 263, 272.

38. Quoted in ibid., 264.

39. Ibid., 269.

40. Ibid., 266–67. Arnhart contends that there is, in addition to the political manifestation, also a philosophic version of magnanimity exemplified in Socrates.

41. Ibid., 265–67, 271. Harry Jaffa also presents the magnanimous man as being preoccupied with honor. See chapter 6 of his *Thomism and Aristotelianism: A Study of the Commentary by Thomas Aquinas on the* Nicomachean Ethics (Westport, CT: Greenwood Press, 1979).

42. *Nicomachean Ethics* 1124a5–10.
43. Ibid., 1124a12–20.
44. Arnhart, "Statesmanship as Magnanimity," 267.
45. *Nicomachean Ethics* 1124a5–13.
46. Ibid., 1115b13, 1116b31, and 1120a22.
47. Ibid., 1116a20 and 1116b3–4.
48. Ibid., 1124a5–20.
49. Ibid., 1119b21–22.
50. Ibid., 1177a12–18.
51. Ibid., 1177b30–1178a1.
52. This interpretation of moral virtue as a participation in the eternal differs considerably from Harry Jaffa's contention that for Aristotle "morality is merely a human affair." See Jaffa's *Thomism and Aristotelianism*, 120.
53. *Nichomachean Ethics* 1099a7–21.
54. Ibid., 1179a3–8.
55. John 14:21–23.
56. *S.T.*, II-II, q. 129, a. 3.
57. Ibid., II-II, q. 131, a. 1.
58. Arnhart, "Statesmanship as Magnanimity," 273 (emphasis mine).
59. *Nicomachean Ethics* 1103b24–25.
60. Ibid., 1123b1–5.
61. *S.T.*, II-II, q. 129, a. 2.
62. One might object that the argument of this article, in relying so heavily on the thought of Aquinas, is distinctly Thomist or Catholic while there are other versions of Christianity that might not so readily harmonize with Aristotelian magnanimity. My intention, however, has been to show that some reasonable interpretation of Christianity can be compatible with Aristotelian magnanimity, not that every interpretation can be. In any case, those who suspect that this harmonization of Christianity and Aristotle can be accomplished only within the Thomist or Catholic framework would have to come to grips with the arguments the article advances based on passages adduced not only from Augustine, who is regarded as a profound interpreter of Christianity by many non-Catholic Christians, but also from the New Testament itself.
63. Quoted in Arnhart, "Statesmanship as Magnanimity," 264.
64. Ibid.
65. Ibid.
66. Ibid.
67. What, then, one may wonder, is Tocqueville thinking when he calls a "vice" the kind of pride necessary to democracy's elevation? It may be that Tocqueville simply misunderstands Christian morality, that he is speaking in light of what he mistakenly thinks is the Christian understanding. Alternatively—and, to my mind, more plausibly—it may be that such usage is forced on him not by Christianity but by democracy, the egalitarian sensibilities of which are necessarily offended by any claims of superiority.

68. Alexis de Tocqueville, *Democracy in America*, trans. George Lawrence (New York: Harper and Row, 1969), 530.
69. Ibid., 531.
70. Ibid.
71. Ibid.
72. Ibid.
73. Ibid., 530, 531.
74. Ibid., 534.
75. Ibid., 533.
76. Ibid., 546.
77. Ibid.
78. Ibid., 542.
79. Ibid., 534–35.
80. Ibid., 545.
81. Ibid., 543.
82. Ibid., 546.
83. Ibid., 532.
84. Ibid., 247.
85. Ibid., 435.
86. Ibid., 255.
87. Ibid., 255, 258.
88. *Nicomachean Ethics* 1124a5–15.
89. *Democracy in America*, 198.
90. *Nicomachean Ethics* 1124b23–24.
91. De Tocqueville, *Democracy in America*, 199.
92. Ibid., 12.
93. C. S. Lewis, *The Weight of Glory and Other Addresses* (New York: Collier Books, 1965), 18–19.
94. Matt. 9:10–12.

CHAPTER 18

Fides et Ratio

Approaches to a Roman Catholic Political Philosophy

JAMES V. SCHALL

James V. Schall, S.J. (b. 1928) is an American Catholic political philosopher and a Roman Catholic priest in the Society of Jesus. Schall joined the Jesuits in 1948, earned his Ph.D. in political theory from Georgetown University in 1960, and was ordained a priest in 1963. He taught at the Pontifical Gregorian University in Rome from 1964 to 1977 and at the University of San Francisco from 1968 to 1977 (alternating spring and fall semesters). From 1977 until his retirement in December 2012 he was Professor of Political Philosophy in Georgetown's Department of Government. Schall served as a member of the Pontifical Commission on Justice and Peace from 1977 to 1982 and a member of the National Council on the Humanities of the National Endowment for the Humanities from 1984 to 1990. The author of over thirty books, Schall is best known for titles such as Another Sort of Learning; The Church, the State, and Society in the Thought of John Paul II; Reason, Revelation, and the Foundations of Political Philosophy; Roman Catholic Political Philosophy; *and* The Regensburg Lecture.

"Philosophy could be employed, not indeed as a principle allowing one to pass judgment on the truth or falsity of Revelation, but as a tool with which to probe its meaning and counter any attack that might be leveled against it in the name of reason."

—Ernest Fortin, 1996[1]

"Revelation clearly proposes certain truths which might never have been discovered by reason unaided, although they are not of themselves inaccessible to reason. Among these truths is the notion of a free and personal God who is the Creator of the world, a truth which has been so crucial for the development of philosophical thinking, especially the philosophy of being. There is also the reality of sin, as it appears in the light of faith, which helps to shape an adequate philosophical formulation of the problem of evil. The notion of the person as a spiritual being is another of faith's specific contributions: the Christian proclamation of human dignity, equality and freedom has undoubtedly influenced modern philosophic thought. In more recent times, there has been the discovery that history as event—so central to Christian revelation—is important for philosophy as well."

—John Paul II, *Fides et Ratio*, 1998, #76[2]

"The emperor of the visible empire, 'sol invictus,' the invincible sun, has as his opponent and successor the vicar of the invisible empire, 'servus servorum Dei,' the servant of the servants of God. . . . We never understand more than the half of things when we neglect the science of Rome."

—Pierre Manent, *The City of Man*, 1998[3]

The Unexpected Combination: Political Philosophy— Roman Catholic

At first sight, "among the heathen," so to speak, if not also among believers themselves, the very idea of a "Roman Catholic political philosophy" is rather quaint, if not actually shocking.[4] Even to hint that there is an inner and coherent relation between the core of Roman Catholic thought and political philosophy requires a kind of Straussian "secret writing," something not mentioned in polite circles, as it were. Roman Catholicism, of course, prides itself on distinction, forthrightness, and clarity in the service of a knowledge of the whole. St. Thomas' refusal—his careful distinctions—to let intellectual confusion reign is central to its identification of itself. "Grace builds on nature; it does not contradict it."[5] Both grace and nature, while remaining what they are, can be intellectually explicated and, if necessary, both defined and defended. Therefore, reason, to be helpful to revelation, must be what it is, reason acting according to its own exigencies on its proper object, on *what* is. Reason itself is found in human nature as a real property or faculty. Reason is not itself constructed or given to this same nature by man himself who possesses this capacity but does not "invent" it.

But not just anything that calls itself "reason" is reasonable. Even "chaos" theory presents itself as reasonable, as does every form of skepticism. Claims to truth or to doubt can be tested. We must add, if it is not a tautology, we are concerned with "true reason," with reason that seeks to know the truth of things even when it denies, paradoxically, that truth can be known by this same reason. Thus, when some philosopher, implicitly or explicitly, denies, say, the principle of non-contradiction, we do not, as Aristotle said, have to believe him, even less, agree with him. We just have to watch what he does to see that implicitly he upholds in practice this basic principle he denies in theory. He invariably opens the door before he walks through it; he assumes that it cannot be there and not there at the same time and in the same place. And yes, we have to trust our senses when we see him open the door. Our minds and our sensory powers are connected.

Thus, we ask precisely "what is Roman Catholic political philosophy?" I deliberately use the term "Roman Catholic" here to distinguish it, benignly not polemically, from a more Protestant view as found in, say, Glenn Tinder's excellent *The Political Meaning of Christianity,* or Reinhold Niebuhr's famous *Moral Man and Immoral Society,* or C. S. Lewis's *Mere Christianity*, which latter seeks admirably to concentrate on those things all Christians hold in common, or an Orthodox view as in Nicholas Berdyaev's *The Destiny of Man*.[6] The things that are uniquely Roman Catholic are part of the argument I want to make, however much or little other branches of Christianity might agree with them. Or perhaps I should say that I am interested in the whole that it stands for. Still, I acknowledge that some of the most provocative incentives to Roman Catholic thought on political philosophy come today from outside its immediate circles. I think not only of the enormous influence of Strauss and Voegelin, each of whom I hold of particular importance for any consideration of reason, revelation, and politics.[7]

Of increasing importance is the work of Oliver O'Donovan, George Grant, Catherine Pickstock, Hadley Arkes, Robert Song, Henry Veatch, and others such as those associated with "Christians in Political Science."[8] On the Catholic side itself, we find a surprising number of young scholars doing political philosophy with full awareness of the import of revelation.[9] I am concerned in this reflection with what I would call basically mainline positions—say those who can read the *General Catechism of the Catholic Church* with no big problem. Things like "liberation theology," in its various incarnations, while interesting, I would consider mostly aberrations.[10]

Philosophy and theology, in any case, are both legitimate; both can articulate their foundations. The intelligible content of each is at least comprehensible to the other, even when not agreed upon. But they are *not* related to one another as reason to unreason respectively. Revelation is a grounded claim to truth, not to irrationality. Things can be beyond the power of particularly human reason fully to know without necessarily being beyond reasonableness as such. We are the lowest, not the highest, of the intellectual beings.[11] "Man is the best of animals ... [but] there are other things much more divine in their nature even than man," as Aristotle put it (*Nicomachean Ethics* 1141a35–b2).[12]

Revelation addresses itself to the same reason that philosophy considers. *Fides quaerens intellectum; intellectus quaerens fidem.*[13] Indeed, the very fact that reason brings up questions, legitimate questions, that it cannot fully answer on its own terms, means that it is not a complete account of all things, of the whole, even when it is *capax omnium*, even when it wants to know all things. This awareness of a quest to know the whole is the valid, if negative, insight of Strauss in his famous essay, "On the Mutual Influence of Theology and Philosophy."[14] Roman Catholic sources in theology and philosophy would put closer together what Strauss separated, without denying, indeed while affirming, the difference between the way of the philosopher and the way of the theologian.[15] These may indicate different ways of seeking the truth, but they do not find different, unrelated truths. In *Fides et Ratio*, John Paul II puts it this way: "Philosophy must obey its own rules and be based upon its own principles; truth, however, can only be one. The content of revelation can never debase the discoveries and legitimate the autonomy of reason. Yet, conscious that it cannot set itself up as an absolute and exclusive value, reason on its part must never lose its capacity to question and to be questioned" (#79).[16] Roman Catholic theology, at least, has a vested interest in the validity of philosophy as such.

Human reason does not "explain" everything. But it is curious about *all that is*. It proceeds step-by-step. What it first encounters is what is there; what is not caused by itself. This is to be explained. It is "philo-sophia," the friendship with or the love, not the cause, of wisdom. It therefore remains open to what it does not yet know, even, with Socrates, knowing that it does not know everything even when it knows something. "It is owing to their wonder that men both now begin and at first began to philosophize" (*Metaphysics* 982b13). And they began this effort, Aristotle notices, only "when almost all the necessities of life and the things that make for comfort and recreation had been secured" (982b23–24). The most important things are beyond comfort and necessity, even though, as Aristotle also said, an adequate amount of material goods is needed for most of us to practice virtue. In revelation, both faith and authority rest not on themselves but on the testimony of someone who does know, who does see, who does hear. In this sense, faith is not blind. Reason can reflect on itself; that is, once in the act of knowing, it can be luminous to itself.

Revelation, Philosophy, and the City

By any objective analysis, revelation appears to be much more conscious of reason than most philosophical reason is of revelation, though there are always Plato and his followers to caution us here. Philosophy has to be proper philosophy to hear revelation. An inadequate philosophy is deaf to the voice of revelation. Revelation, rather frequently, has to defend philosophy itself from itself. This is, in fact, what *Fides et Ratio* is about, that philosophy be philosophy. "Christian doctrine is primarily concerned with offering salvation, not with interpreting reality or human existence," Josef Pieper has written. "But it implies as well certain fundamental teachings on specifically philosophical matters—the world and existence as such."[17] Reason that illogically proclaims its own autonomy can, however, consciously choose to make itself into a closed system incapable of any openness to *what is*. Philosophy, and this is the dark side of its mystery, can choose to deny itself, deny its openness to truth, and still call itself "philosophy." Political systems can be built on this theoretical denial. Political philosophy seems inordinately susceptible to corruption by an ill-grounded philosophy, which is why political philosophers must also know philosophy.

This possibility of philosophy denying itself is no doubt at the origin of St. Paul's famous impatience with the philosophers: "Where is your wise man now, your man of learning, your own subtle debater—limited, all of them, to this passing age? God has made the wisdom of this world look foolish" (1 Corinthians 1:20). Much of modern philosophy—which surely considers itself as "the wisdom of this world"—can best be understood as the intellectual and logical consequences of this choice of denying to itself, frequently indeed "foolishly," some basic element of the proper "range of reason," to use Jacques Maritain's phrase.

The Bible, to be sure, is not immediately a "political" or "philosophic" tract. It is primarily an account of a way, indeed the way, as it maintains, of salvation, itself a word related to the "happiness" discussions of the philosophers and the political philosophers. Yet, for philosophers, if they set their mind to it, the Bible is neither incoherent nor unintelligible; it is not lacking in its own philosophical profundity.[18] "The Bible, and the New Testament in particular, contains texts and statements which have a genuinely ontological content. The inspired authors intended to formulate true statements, capable, that is, of expressing objective reality" (#82). Scripture can be intelligently read by philosophers, believed by the politicians, without making either philosopher or politician any less profound or, in spite of Machiavelli, any less competent or practical. Theologians and believers can likewise philosophize; they have in fact done so. *Ex esse sequitur posse.* To deny this possibility is itself unphilosophic, an unwillingness to consider *all that is*. The notion that philosophy and theology are two "contradictory" ways of life does not explain the fact that at least a few men, perhaps more than a few, are legitimately both the one and the other without confusing the one for the other.

Philosophers and believers, moreover, must, like everyone else, live in cities in this world, even when they call Augustine's "City of God" their true home. They are both aware—if we pass over certain types of utopians over the centuries—that we "have here no lasting city." The New Testament in particular has very little to do, directly, with politics.[19] In fact, it frankly acknowledges that the things of Caesar and the things of God are not the same (Matthew 22:22–23). Almost for the first time, we have here a revelational source affirming the validity of the state in its, the state's, own terms. The things of Caesar, however, still need to be explicated philosophically to show why it is "natural" that man is a "political animal."[20] Without the *polis*, he cannot "flourish," cannot practice all the virtues he discovers in himself, cannot have the leisure for things beyond politics.[21]

When Paul told Christians to be "obedient to the Emperor" (Romans 13:1–7), the emperor was Nero, a tyrant, as Tacitus graphically tells us in his *Annals*. Paul was not, however, approving tyranny, nor denying its obvious possibility or dangers. Nor was he an advanced Nietzschian who saw in "turning the other cheek" a sure sign of political ineptness and betrayal of worldly power. He was rather pointing out, something already found in Aristotle, that man was by nature a political animal, but one who often revealed his own inability, or better, unwillingness, to rule himself. Interestingly, revelation seems to have more to do with our inability or unwillingness to live the virtues than with our more successful efforts to define them.[22] But, to keep priorities straight, "I would rather feel compunction than know how to define it," as Thomas a Kempis remarked in a famous phrase in the *Imitation of Christ*. Therefore, at times, indeed often, Paul acknowledged that the ruler also possesses "the sword . . . to punish wrong-doing" (Romans 13:4).

Aristotle indicated much the same thing at the end of his *Ethics* when he spoke of the transition to the *Politics* (1179b31–80a4) about the need of law and coercion. Neither philosophy nor politics, however, could quite explain why this abiding wrong-doing, this "wickedness," as Aristotle called it (1263b23), persisted in all human polities. This very perplexity was something to which revelation addressed itself in the account of the Fall. There, the problem of human disorder is located not in things, nor in institutions, nor in human faculties as such but in the operation of the will, and therefore in personal choice (Genesis 3:1–24). The Philosopher, as Aquinas called him, did notice, without revelation, that human nature was in a kind of "bondage" (982b29). Philosophy had questions it could not quite answer.

This "unansweredness," as it were, was theoretically bothersome. It caused many a good philosopher to wonder if the world was not created "in vain," with no purpose or meaning, hardly a consoling alternative. Paradoxically, it was revelation's odd answer to this enigma that charged the universe, particularly the human universe to which all else seemed ordained, with risk, drama, uncertainty, and, yes, the possibility of love and glory. Such things are only possible if our choices make some ultimate difference, if we really do choose between right and wrong. The tractates on evil, thus, are aspects of the tractates on free will.

THE CITY AND HUMAN DESTINY

Evidently, there should no more be Roman Catholic politics than there should be Roman Catholic physics, however much the methods and subject matter of politics and physics, and, yes, theology, might differ. "It is the mark of an educated man," Aristotle tells us, "to look for precision in each class of things just so far as the nature of the subject admits; it is evidently equally foolish to accept probable reasoning from a mathematician and to demand from a rhetorician scientific proofs" (1094b25–27). The effort of modern sociology, by its own "methods," to investigate issues of faith or grace is thus replete with irony. Yet, perhaps it makes a difference what our philosophy is, what our understanding of the world is before we can have either physics or politics.[23] Both physics and politics claim to deal with reality. A politics without a metaphysics can itself be, and usually is, an unacknowledged metaphysics. Political science, however, is itself a valid, but limited "practical science." It considers a certain range of reality. This is the reality of free human beings in active exchange about what they are and choose in this world. Political philosophy, for its part, cannot, without bad will, refuse to consider revelation's insight into political things when politics does not solve its own problems in its own terms about its own subject matter.

"Although the teachings of Jesus as recorded in the Gospels have little to say about the proper attitude for Christians to adopt toward the social order and the state," Herbert Deane has written,

> certain fundamental principles are clearly established. On a number of occasions, Jesus warned His disciples against thinking of His kingdom as an earthly kingdom, to be established by a revolt of the Jews against Roman rule and maintained by ordinary political instruments.... Jesus not only insisted that His kingdom was not of this world and so discouraged his followers from thinking of Him as a Messiah who would be the temporal ruler of the Jewish people, but He also endeavored to draw His followers' attention away from interest in worldly matters such as the attainment of wealth or power over other men.[24]

Roman Catholic political philosophy would, thus, agree that the ultimate destiny of each human being, the political animal, is not located in politics, a conclusion also found in its own way in Plato and Aristotle. It would also recognize that in leaving politics relatively free, Christianity implied that the political order had its own worth and, indeed, its own dangers. It accepted, in other words, the teaching in Genesis that nature, including angelic and human nature, was good in its fundamental being. The origin of evil—the lack of something that ought to be present—was neither in God nor in nature as such. It was in a good and free faculty that could cause things to be otherwise—in brief, in the human free will.

The early Christians were primarily city dwellers, though some of the more pious ones began to flee the city's corruption into the desert.[25] Cities, if left to themselves, could and did, at times, become morally unliveable. A certain "exodus," individual or collective, always remained a possibility.[26] The founding of America itself, with its Old Testament overtones among the Puritans, is not unrelated to this sentiment. The city was, however, the scene within which the positive things that Christians were commanded to do—forgive, love, serve their neighbor, keep the commandments—were to be visibly carried out in a real, not abstract, world. The dictates of faith and charity, as well as the practice of the natural virtues, were expected to bear fruit in the world. The Good Samaritan was a real citizen, as was Paul of Tarsus a Roman citizen, as he insisted (Acts 25:8–13).[27] This is why Christian metaphysics has always insisted on defending the reality of the world itself, the reality of being. Augustine could thus argue that Christians were good citizens, good soldiers even.

The city was also the arena wherein Christians found themselves, in their own way, in the predicament of Socrates wherein they had to choose between the existing city and death. They were tried by the state for telling the truth and living as they were commanded—something as well true in the century just closed as in the first century.[28] Christians were often seen, however, as a-political, as not believing in the gods of the city. Like Socrates, they were considered to be "atheists." When they first appeared in any numbers, they were in one of the most powerful and indeed in one of the most decent of historical states, one that, to reform itself, thought, as did someone like Diocletian, that it should demand full allegiance to the city's gods. Much about Rome was indeed worth saving.

Philosophy and Revelation in *Fides et Ratio*

However esoteric or strange it may sound, the consideration of Roman Catholicism and political philosophy together, keeping the proper distinctions, is itself a worthy endeavor that betrays the deepest cultural and intellectual purposes. Lest there be any doubt, let me add these words of caution from *Fides et Ratio*: "To believe it possible to know a universally valid truth is in no way to encourage intolerance; on the contrary, it is the essential condition for sincere and authentic dialogue between persons" (#92). It is more philosophical, indeed more "ecumenical," to take important intellectual differences seriously since they too are arguments about the truth itself. Unfortunately the fear of political "intolerance" has become a justification of intellectual skepticism.

Roman Catholic political philosophy is obviously not simply "political theology," a description of exactly what Scripture may say about political things, however important the little that is said may be. It is not a discussion of civil religion. Nor is it an effort to compete with, say, Aristotle or political science about its own subject matter. Indeed, if anything via St. Thomas, it claims Aristotle as its own, even knowing his non-Christian origins and certain problems, like that of the eternity of the world, also happily resolved by St. Thomas, connected with his thought. *Fides et Ratio*, the 1998 encyclical of John Paul II, is not itself, as was, say, his *Sollicitudo Rei Socialis* (1987) or his *Centesimus Annus* (1991), directly social, economic, or political in content or inspiration. Yet, I wish to suggest, more than almost any other specifically Roman Catholic document, it addresses itself to the broad background questions that have surged through political philosophy in what is called modernity and even in what the Pope himself calls "postmodernity" (#91).

We thus do not call *Fides et Ratio* a tractate in political philosophy, but what it says about philosophy is pertinent to political philosophy:

> The Church has no philosophy of her own nor does she canonize any one particular philosophy in preference to others. The underlying reason for this reluctance is that, even when it engages theology, philosophy must remain faithful to its own principles and methods. Otherwise, there would be no guarantee that it would remain oriented to truth and that it was moving toward truth by way of a process governed by reason. A philosophy which does not proceed in the light of reason according to its own principles and methods would serve little purpose. At the deepest level, the autonomy which philosophy enjoys is rooted in the fact that reason is by its nature oriented to truth and is equipped moreover with the means necessary to arrive at truth. A philosophy conscious of this as its "constitutive status" cannot but respect the demands and the data of revealed truth (#49).

If we recall that among the academic disciplines, political science departments are the only ones with their own specific subdivision devoted to "philosophy," it will be clear that these same principles and admonitions apply in their own way to all endeavors claiming philosophical pertinence. It is worth adding that if we look at the number of doctoral theses in academic departments of philosophy devoted to what has to be called "political philosophy," as indicated in the annual review of theses published in the *Review of Metaphysics*, it is clear that political philosophy represents a wide segment of philosophic studies.[29]

The peculiarities and strengths of Roman Catholicism relative to political things are that it does not, following Scripture, have a specific political program or philosophy, something explicitly reaffirmed in *Fides et Ratio* (#49). Politics, as it were, is not one of the things revealed in Scripture, but it is not taken less seriously for all that. If, as we should, we are to know political things, we must largely rely on reason and experience, both of which can go wrong. It is necessary to read the philosophers and consult the constitutions, laws, and practices to know how peoples succeed and fail in political history. No doubt, certain scriptural passages and teachings can and should have political meaning. Christians were supposed to live in this world, "quietly," if they could, as "sojourners and wayfarers" (1 Peter 2:11). But perforce, they could never quite be completely passive. They were commanded to do too many things that related to others.

The fact that Scripture does not contain a systematic political teaching modeled on the *Republic* of Plato or the *Politics* of Aristotle—or even on Hobbes or

Locke or Rousseau, who in fact spend a good deal of time on Scripture—does not imply that there is something lacking in revelation. Not a few good books in political affairs, both ancient and modern, no doubt, have been written by Roman Catholics—perhaps the most pertinent these days is de Tocqueville's *Democracy in America*. But Scripture's, especially the New Testament's, lack of treatment of political affairs rather indicates that much is to be learned from Plato and Aristotle, from the philosophers ancient and modern, even for the sake of Scripture. The lack of attention to politics in Scripture implies that politics is, for the most part, adequate unto itself, unless perhaps politics claims something more than it is in itself or unless the personal lives of citizens in any given polity fall into moral chaos.

Christ says to Pilate, "you would have no authority at all over me if it had not given you from above" (John 19:11) That is, to draw an indirect principle, the Roman governor has authority, but neither he nor his polity invented what authority is. Its discovery and definition may be something reason could, and more importantly, should figure out by itself. Not everything, in other words, was necessary to be revealed. Human reality had the relative autonomy of its own finite being. But what was revealed had the indirect effect of freeing politics from the burden of answering certain higher questions that cannot be answered by politics. To burden politics with responsibility for answering questions that are more than political is a sure way to corrupt politics itself.

The first step in politics is to think of its form, that is, of its limits, of what makes it to be politics and not something else. A politics that conceives itself to have no limits is the main rival to revelation in any age, including our own, a view, ironically, already found in Scripture itself.[30] Politics is the highest practical science, not the highest science as such, as Aristotle also noted (*Nicomachean Ethics* 1141a20–22). When it claims to be the highest science, as it often does, it strives in effect to take the place of both reason and revelation, to become itself a metaphysics defining by itself a will-based "what is."

Early Christians first met politics when politicians wanted to get rid of them as being threats to the state, as they thought. They were even, as Augustine recounted at the beginning of the *City of God*, accused of being the cause for the decline of Rome—a perennial theme that later became famous with Gibbon and Nietzsche. The Augustinian answer to Rome, interestingly enough, was not to deny in principle legitimate political authority to Rome. Rather it was to point out, in the very name of its greatest minds, Varro and Cicero, that Rome itself did not observe its own philosophic standards which themselves were quite valid.

It does not take revelation to identify and observe moral and political corruption. Revelation, in other words, said to political reason that it was not reasonable enough.

Political Philosophy and Philosophy in Christian Thought

Fides et Ratio barely speaks of what would ordinarily be called political things. It speaks of philosophical things, of what is revealed, of how and why there is a relation between the one and the other. Theology, in the Christian sense, does not begin with, but presupposes, reason directed to reality, to *what* is. It begins with what is revealed. However, it soon discovers that to understand and render in intelligible order what is revealed, it needs to turn to issues of human knowing, human experience, to philosophy. "The chief purpose of theology is to provide an understanding of revelation and the content of faith" (#93). What is characteristic of Roman Catholicism is this "understanding," this effort to make clear and available in a coherent whole to the human mind as such what is revealed in the myriads of narratives in Scripture. Likewise, it endeavors to relate this knowledge to what we know by our experience and reason, among which latter are political things. It does not see this elaboration as a violation of the explicit words of Scripture, which it must respect as given. It sees it as an obligation to illumine the intelligibility that is found there. And this endeavor does not imply that somehow God was rather sloppy in not revealing Himself in a concise form that would not require, over the centuries and even today, much human theological and rational effort.

Rather what Catholicism suggests is that we are intended to use our minds even in revelation, or more exactly, we are to use them better because of revelation. It implicitly grants the possibility of a human historical order in which revelation never happened, even though such an order is not the actual one in which we live. In using mind to reflect on revealed things, the mind itself becomes more mind. "The Word of God is addressed to all people, in every age and in every part of the world; and the human being is by nature a philosopher" (#64). Not only is this sentence a delicate statement about the universality and equality of all men, but it is even more an affirmation of the primacy of Chesterton's "common man," of the fact that everyone can know basic truths. This position that "the human being is by nature a philosopher," not relativism, is the true basis of Catholicism's advocacy of democracy as a good regime. This preference is not a denial of the value of excellence and talent, but it is a deep-seated Christian and Catholic sentiment that each person does have the faculties and insights to enable him consciously to know his own meaning and destiny. The doctrines of eternal life, sin, resurrection of the body, and beatific vision, among others, have a definite communal flavor about them, which is, at the same time, anti-collectivist.

Strauss, among others, often stresses that philosophy is a quest for a "knowledge of the whole," a knowledge rooted in the capacity of human reason. This same reason cannot arbitrarily exclude what is understandable and claims intelligible content, particularly when revelation itself has turned to philosophy precisely to explain more fully what is revealed.[31] "It is necessary therefore that the mind of the believer acquire a natural, consistent and true knowledge of created realities—the world and man himself—which are also the object of divine revelation," John Paul II writes. "Still more, reason must be able to articulate this knowledge in concept and argument. Speculative dogmatic theology thus presupposes and implies a philosophy of the human being, the world and, more radically, of being, which has objective truth as its foundation" (#66). The point here is not that the nonbeliever, presumably closed off from this revelational knowledge, must live only in philosophy and therefore be unconcerned about these revelational questions. Rather it is to maintain that even the nonbeliever, genuinely aware of unanswered questions he shares with others, including believers, can appreciate that revelational arguments and positions can be seen as responses to genuine philosophic questions and enigmas. Even though such revelational responses can be rejected, it cannot be denied in some uncanny sense that they do present answers to philosophic questions as asked. The Pope has taken great pains in this encyclical fairly to present the case of various other religions and philosophies, even those most hostile to his enterprise. It is on philosophic, not revelational, grounds that he invites reciprocity and mutual respect.

Roman Catholic political philosophy, thus, does not think, whatever the distinction of faith and reason, that the subjects of political life and those who receive revelation live in different physical or political worlds. The "knowledge of the created universe" is also "the object of divine revelation." We must take the knowledge of the whole seriously. "It may well be," Josef Pieper has remarked, with some irony, "that at the end of history the only people who will examine and ponder the root of all things and the meaning of existence, e.g. the specific object of philosophical speculation—will be those who see with the eyes of faith."[32] It is not insignificant at the beginning of the twenty-first century that it is the pope, the "Philosopher-Pope," as the *New York Times* called him when *Fides et Ratio* was published, who speaks of the legitimacy and necessity of philosophy, who speaks of its own condition, a condition that is, often, anti-philosophical. It is not, after all, the pope but the Supreme Court, in the Casey decision, that embraces the anti-metaphysical position that each one's happiness and understanding of the universe is for him to define for himself, a position that implicitly denies any human common good, indeed any common world.

Contrary also to what we might expect, *Fides et Ratio* is not primarily concerned to relate philosophy to revelation, though it is quite frank about revelation's interest in and need of a sound philosophy. Its main purpose is to address itself to philosophy and its contemporary condition. Indeed, it argues that it is in the strongest possible interest of revelation for its own integrity that philosophy be itself. "It is an illusion to think that faith, tied to weak reasoning, might be more penetrating; on the contrary, faith then runs the grave risk of withering into myth or superstition. By the same token, reason which is unrelated to an adult faith is not prompted to turn its gaze to the newness and radicality of being" (#48). "Weak reasoning" is not an ally of revelation. The pope is at equal pains to reject a fideism that distrusts reason in the name of faith and skepticism or nihilism which, as it were, distrusts reason in the name of reason (#52–55; 87–89).

Revelation thus does not hesitate to engage the philosophic mind and examine its own proposed validity. This might annoy philosophers who want to claim the exclusive turf of reason for themselves. But they cannot maintain this position if the object of the mind is not the mind itself but *what is, all that is*. Philosophy cannot pretend or prove that revelation does not exist and exist as something also directed at itself. Catholicism takes the condition of the philosophic mind seriously because it sees clearly that its own truths depend for their integrity on the validity of a philosophy that can know, and know *what is*. That is, revelation defends both the mind's own reflective powers and the fact that those powers do not simply turn on themselves. They reach the world, reality, *what is*; they can speak or judge the truth of things.

John Paul II sees the necessity to clear the air, filled as it is with the predominance of what might be called "tolerance theory," which tolerates everything but efforts to state the truth (#92). The notion that tolerance is the first principle of political philosophy and not a practical principle for setting the ground rules for engagement in the highest things is itself a product of philosophic modernity. This "dogmatic tolerance," for fear of "fanaticism," must deny, it is said, the possibility of "universally valid truth." In other words, the very claim of a "universally valid truth" is said to be "fanatic," and thus not worthy of serious examination. This position is itself the product of a philosophy that must be examined for its philosophical integrity. It takes no genius to comprehend that if the principle of "dogmatic tolerance" is true, it is, by its own definition, false.

The pope draws out the consequence of this contradiction, namely, that it is itself intolerant to refuse to examine a philosophy or doctrine that claims to be true on the sole ground that it does claim to be true. Moreover, there are conditions in which this examination can and should take place—in "sincere and authentic dialogue between persons"—that is, in circumstances the very opposite of fanaticism or intolerance. This is something already found in Plato, of course. That widespread discussion of reason and revelation is not taking place, on the grounds that revelation has nothing to talk about or no opening to reason, is already, as it seems to many, a sign of unacknowledged "fanaticism." The contemporary polity itself reflects ideas proceeding from the "lowering of the sights" of virtue (Machiavelli) upon which much of modernity was originally built.

Clearly, classical political philosophy pointed to and in a sense brought human beings to friendship which itself depended on "the sincere and authentic dialogue among persons." Roman Catholic political philosophy cannot be unaware that the link between reason and revelation is most graphically attested to by St. Thomas's use of *amicitia* as the natural analogate for *caritas* (*Summa Theologiae* II-II, 23, 1). That is to say, tolerance at its best is a condition of manners and friendliness that enables the highest things to exist in conversation.

Understanding "Christian" Philosophy

John Paul II does not use the expression "Roman Catholic political philosophy." He does speak of "Christian philosophy," which is a reference to earlier discussions in neo-Thomism (#76). In this sense, he does not ask about the relation to philosophy of the various Christian denominations such as Luther's famous hostility to Aristotle. Christian philosophy refers to the fact that the content of revelation does address itself to truth and philosophy. It is clear that not every philosophy can sustain the realism that Christian theology requires if it is to defend the reality of its content. Moreover, certain questions such as the dignity of the person, the meaning of evil and history, have come to the fore through the influence of revelation. Once posed, these philosophic questions remain active in philosophy itself.

Fides et Ratio 439

This is how the notion of a "Christian philosophy" appears in *Fides et Ratio*:

> Christian philosophy therefore has two aspects. The first is subjective, in the sense that faith purifies reason. As a theological virtue, faith liberates reason from presumption, the typical temptation of the philosopher.... The philosopher who learns humility will also find courage to tackle questions which are difficult to resolve if the data of revelation are ignored—for example, the problem of evil and suffering, the personal nature of God and the question of the meaning of life, or more directly, the radical metaphysical question, Why is there something rather than nothing (#76).

It is worth remarking here that these "metaphysical questions" that are asked here and are often repeated by John Paul II, are similar to the ones that Eric Voegelin employs in his efforts to ground philosophy in being.

"The quest for the ground ... is a constant in all civilizations," Voegelin likewise observes. "The first question is, 'Why is there something; why not nothing?' and the second is, 'Why is that something as it is, and not different?' (If you translate those into conventional philosophical vocabulary, the first question, 'Why is there something; why not nothing?' becomes the great question of *existence*; and 'Why is it as it is and not different?' becomes the question of *essence*.)"[33] These metaphysical questions that John Paul II and Voegelin ask are the very ones that first establish the grounding of philosophy and the questions that it must ask of *what is*. The fact that there are both metaphysical and revelational answers to these questions, however complete or incomplete, itself prevents political philosophy from claiming an autonomy it does not possess. When the politician's will decides also the content of the metaphysical questions, political philosophy, in justifying such an aberration, itself claims to be its own metaphysics.

The second understanding of "Christian philosophy," John Paul remarks, is "objective" because it concerns "content." What is meant here?

> Revelation clearly proposes certain truths which might never have been discovered by reason unaided, although they are not of themselves inaccessible in reason. Among these truths is the notion of a free and personal God who is the Creator of the world, a truth which has been so crucial for the development of philosophical thinking, especially the philosophy of being. There is the reality of sin, as it appears in the light of faith, which helps to shape an adequate philosophical formulation of the problem of evil. The

notion of the person as a spiritual being is another of faith's specific contributions: The Christian proclamation of human dignity, equality, and freedom has undoubtedly influenced modern philosophical thought. In more recent times, there has been the discovery that history as an event—so crucial to Christian revelation—is important for philosophy as well (#76).

Notice that the status of these ideas, or many of them, are, in the pope's mind, indeed open to reason, but they were not in fact discovered by reason without the prior impetus of faith. This correlation or coincidence is itself a curious intellectual event of the first order. History, evil, equality, freedom, dignity—these are subjects of philosophy which are also addressed in revelation as if they were both investigating the same reality and the same notions on which they are based.

Strauss, in *Persecution and the Art of Writing*, moreover, had made an important point about the relation of Christianity to philosophy, something that made it distinct from the law emphasis of Islam and Judaism.

> For the Christian, the sacred doctrine is revealed theology; for the Jew and the Muslim, the sacred doctrine is, at least primarily, the legal interpretation of the Divine Law. The sacred doctrine in the latter sense has, to say the least, much less in common with philosophy than the sacred doctrine in the former sense. It is ultimately for this reason that the status of philosophy was, as a matter of principle, much more precarious in Judaism and in Islam than in Christianity: in Christianity philosophy became an integral part of the officially recognized and even required training of the student of the sacred doctrine.[34]

In *Fides et Ratio*, John Paul II spends a considerable amount of time reaffirming the importance of philosophy to students of theology. He even chides theologians for neglecting philosophy.

Interestingly enough, the pope's strongest words in criticism of the failure to study philosophy in the modern world are not directed at the professors but at theologians. "I cannot fail to note with surprise and displeasure that this lack of interest in the study of philosophy is shared by not a few theologians" (#60). He warns them that their own methods invariably contain philosophical suppositions which they ignore at their peril. Many of the aberrations in theology have arisen from precisely philosophical sources. "I wish to repeat clearly that the study of philosophy is fundamental and indispensable to the structure of theological studies and to the formation of candidates for the priesthood. It is not by chance that the curriculum of theological studies is preceded by a time of special study of philosophy" (#62). Strauss, in other words, had it right.

The most evident way that Catholicism might differ from Strauss's hesitation to say anything more than that theology could not disprove philosophy and philosophy could not disprove theology can be seen in the Pope's effort to reunite the two "ways" through what is in effect the basic principle of metaphysics. "This truth which God reveals to us in Jesus Christ is not opposed to the truths which philosophy receives. On the contrary, the two modes of knowing lead to truth in all its fullness. The unity of truth is a fundamental premise of human reasoning, as the principle of noncontradiction makes clear" (#34). Granting the contingency and freedom of political and moral affairs, there is still an awareness that moral truth, of which political life is an aspect, is open in a coherent and non-contradictory way to both reason and revelation.

The Incompleteness of Philosophy and the Political

Fides et Ratio is an explicit argument about why Roman Catholic understanding of itself needs philosophy. Reason and faith are everywhere directed at each other in such a way that they correct or better illuminate each other, without ceasing to be themselves. The biblical scholar who knows no philosophy is a dangerous man. The scientist who is unaware of the higher dimensions of philosophy locks himself into an autonomous ideology. The pope is particularly concerned with metaphysics, a concern that is of immense indirect importance to political philosophy.

> Here I do not mean to speak of metaphysics in the sense of a specific school or a particular historical current of thought. I want only to state that reality and truth do transcend the factual and the empirical, and to vindicate the human being's capacity to know this transcendent and metaphysical dimension in a way that is true and certain, albeit imperfect and analogical. In this sense, metaphysics should not be seen as an alternative to anthropology, since it is metaphysics which makes it possible to ground the concept of personal dignity in virtue of their spiritual nature. In a special way the person constitutes a privileged locus of the encounter with being, and hence with metaphysical inquiry (#83).

Ever since his own philosophical studies long before coming to the papacy, Karol Wojtyla concentrated his attention on the central place of the person as the ground on which both nature and grace stand firm.[35] It is to the special dignity of the human person that political philosophy is particularly attuned.

In *Fides et Ratio*, John Paul II directly but briefly touches on contemporary political philosophy by noticing the changes in the meaning of "democracy," changes that tend to relativize the special dignity of the human person. Speaking of "pragmatism," the pope writes,

> There is growing support for a concept of democracy which is not grounded upon any reference to unchanging values. Whether or not a line of action is admissible is decided by the vote of a parliamentary majority. The consequences of this are clear: In practice the great moral decisions of humanity are subordinated to decisions taken one after another by institutional agencies. Moreover, anthropology itself is severely compromised by a one-dimensional vision of the human being, a vision which excludes the great ethical dilemmas and the existential analyses of the meaning of suffering and sacrifice, of life and death (#89).

This understanding of "democracy," the pope observes, does not arise so much from political philosophy as from certain epistemological and metaphysical aspects of modern philosophy itself. This understanding of democracy is itself, like historicism, a consequence, not a cause (#87). What is of particular interest in this passage is how this relativist theory about democracy is seen to deprive us of genuine philosophical questions that stand behind all political life, those of ethics, suffering, sacrifice, life, and death.

Strauss, to recall, in a solemn address, explained the importance of Jerusalem and Athens to *political* philosophy, the background in which all discussions about the relation of reason and revelation are set. "It is a great honor, and at the same time a challenge to accept a task of particular difficulty, to be asked to speak about political philosophy in Jerusalem," Strauss began.

> In this city, and in this land, the theme of political philosophy—"the city of righteousness, the faithful city"—has been taken more seriously than anywhere else on earth. Nowhere else has the longing for justice and the just city filled the purest hearts and the loftiest souls with such zeal as on this sacred soil. . . . The meaning of political philosophy and its meaningful character is

evident today as it always has been since the time when political philosophy came to light in Athens.[36]

The theme of political philosophy—"the city of righteousness, the faithful city"—and its relation to the best regime in fact and in speech comes from revelation, yet Athens is present. No one in a Catholic tradition, of course, can read these likes without recalling Augustine and the question of the proper location of "the City of God."

The Pope has his own reflection on the relation of Jerusalem and Athens—perhaps a "Roman" view, to recall Pierre Manent's remark cited in the beginning of these reflections. John Paul II pointed out the difference of method between Eastern and Western theologians and philosophers. "Consider Tertullian's question," John Paul II writes in a manner redolent of Strauss's "Jerusalem and Athens":

> "What does Athens have in common with Jerusalem? The academy with the Church?" This clearly indicates the critical consciousness with which Christian thinkers from the first confronted the problem of the relationship between faith and philosophy, viewing it comprehensively with both its positive aspects and its limitations. They were not naive thinkers. Precisely because they were intense in living faith's content they were able to teach the deepest forms of speculation. It is therefore minimalizing and mistaken to restrict their work simply to the transposition of the truths of faith into philosophical categories. They did much more. In fact they succeeded in disclosing completely all that remained implicit and preliminary in the thinking of the great philosophers of antiquity. As I have noted, theirs was the task of showing how reason, freed from external constraints, could find its way out of the blind alley of myth and open itself to the transcendent in a more appropriate way (#41).[37]

Several things are worth remarking about John Paul II on "Jerusalem and Athens." (1) Faith was not an accident to, but an essential element in a consideration of the "deepest forms of speculation." (2) He not only includes Jerusalem and Athens, but the academy and the Church. This calls to mind Voegelin's thesis that after Athens, the city of philosophers, betrayed philosophy in killing Socrates, philosophy fled to the Academy. It also touches Dawson's thesis that the ancient civic culture was kept alive in the monasteries.[38] (3) The pope specifically relates revelational responses to the completion of philosophical, not theological, questions. What was implicit or uncertain was "completed." That is, reason and revelation were not seen to be at impossible loggerheads. The deepest forms of "speculation" could be further pursued. "Purified and rightly tuned, therefore, reason could rise to the higher planes of thought, providing a solid foundation for the perception of being, of the transcendent and of the absolute" (#41). The "perception of being" became the key metaphysical grounding that was needed to keep track of "the whole."

Conclusion

When I suggest, in conclusion, that *Fides et Ratio* provides an "approach" to a "Roman Catholic political philosophy," what I have in mind is to point out that, in almost an uncanny way, it addresses the very theoretical problems that were urged by philosophers like Strauss and Voegelin. I am not suggesting, of course, that the Holy Father intended to take up their profound works in any specific way. But the similarity of concern and topic is striking and ought to be reflected on. Indeed, *Fides et Ratio* includes, as does Voegelin in particular, a relationship with the ancient religions, particularly Hinduism (#72). While classical Greek and Roman philosophy does hold a special place for both intrinsic and historical reasons, revelation is conceived to be addressed to all men, granted its historical dimensions. All men, naturally described as philosophers in *Fides et Ratio*, are capable of understanding revelation's essential core and the common sense philosophy that is implicit in it.

The renewed consideration of philosophy is not a "political proposal" in the sense that it implies some particular political regime. But philosophy is addressed to political philosophy so that philosophy can present the highest things for consideration within any polity, no matter what its configuration. As the history of martyrdom, among other things, shows, revelation is not absent from history's worst regimes. The essential argument is that in fact, a personal or human incompletion exists in every historical polity. This "incompletion" is rooted in the transcendent destiny of each human being who has a right and duty to know what is revealed and how it relates to his reason. This revelation can personally be rejected, of course, and modern ideology is in many ways the political form of this rejection.

The central events in political philosophy are the deaths of Socrates and Christ. In his *Crossing the Threshold of Hope*, John Paul II remarked that "Christ is not simply a wise man as was Socrates, whose free acceptance of death in the name of truth nevertheless has a similarity with the sacrifice of the Cross."[39] The question of political philosophy is how to prevent the politician from killing the philosopher. When Socrates' death comes up in *Fides et Ratio*, the Pope remarks that "It is not insignificant that the death of Socrates gave philosophy one of its decisive orientations, no less decisive now than it was more than 2,000 years ago" (#26). The question of death can be avoided by neither "philosopher nor the ordinary person." What is at issue?

> The answer we give will determine whether or not we think it possible to attain universal and absolute truth; and this is a decisive moment of the search. Every truth—if it really is truth—presents itself as universal, even if it is not the whole truth. If something is true, then it must be true for all people and all times. Beyond this universality, however, people seek an absolute which might give to all their searching a meaning and an answer—something ultimate which might serve as the ground of all things. In other words they seek a final explanation, a supreme value, which refers to nothing beyond itself and which puts an end to all questioning (#27).

To such searching, political philosophy is surely related. It does not itself substitute for metaphysics or for revelation. But it does, as Strauss intimated, need to know enough about both to render the politician—hopefully better educated than Callicles who loved philosophy but only in his youth (*Gorgias* 485a)—sufficiently benign that the pursuit of the highest things, including the light given by revelation, be legitimate in any polity of our kind.

NOTES

Reprinted from *The Review of Politics* 62, no. 1 (Winter 2000): 49–75.

1. Ernest Fortin, "Faith and Reason in Contemporary Perspective," in *Classical Christianity and the Political Order: Reflections on the Theologico-Political Problem*, vol. 2 of *Ernest L. Fortin: Collected Essays*, ed. B. Benestadt (Lanham, MD: Rowman and Littlefield, 1996), 299.

2. John Paul II, *Fides et Ratio*, Encyclical Letter on the Relationship between Faith and Reason, Vatican Web site, September 14, 1998, http://w2.vatican.va/content/john-paul-ii/en/encyclicals/documents/hf_jp-ii_enc_14091998_fides-et-ratio.html, #76.

3. Pierre Manent, *The City of Man*, trans. Marc A. LePain (Princeton: Princeton University Press, 1998), 206.

4. "It is not sufficient for everyone to obey and to listen to the Divine message of the city of Righteousness, the faithful city. In order to propagate that message *among the heathen*, nay, in order to understand it as clearly and as fully as is humanly possible, one must also consider to what extent man could discern the outlines of that city if left to himself, to the proper exertion of his own powers" (Leo Strauss, *The City and Man* [Chicago: University of Chicago Press, 1964], 1, emphasis added).

5. "This also confirms the principle that grace does not destroy nature but perfects it." John Paul II, *Fides et Ratio*, #75.

6. Glenn Tinder, *The Political Meaning of Christianity: The Prophetic Stance* (San Francisco: HarperCollins, 1991); Reinhold Niebuhr, *Moral Man and Immoral Society* (New York: Charles Scribner's Sons, 1960); C. S. Lewis, *Mere Christianity* (London: Fontana, 1961); Nicholas Berdyaev, *The Destiny of Man*, trans. N. Duddington (New York: Harper, 1960).

7. See my *Reason, Revelation, and the Foundations of Political Philosophy* (Baton Rouge: Louisiana State University Press, 1987); *At the Limits of Political Philosophy: From "Brilliant Errors" to the Things of Uncommon Importance* (Washington, DC: Catholic University of America Press, 1996).

8. See Ernest L. Fortin, "Rational Theologians and Irrational Philosophers: A Straussian Perspective," in *Classical Christianity and the Political Order*, 287–96; James Rhodes, "Christian Faith, Jesus the Christ, and History," in "Eric Voegelin's *The Ecumenic Age—A Symposium*," *The Political Science Reviewer* 27 (1998): 44–67; "Philosophy, Revelation, and Political Theory: Leo Strauss and Eric Voegelin," *The Journal of Politics* 49 (1987): 1036–60; Oliver O'Donovan, "Behold the Lamb!," *Studies in Christian Ethics* 11 (1998): 91–110; Hadley Arkes, *First Things: An Inquiry into the First Principles of Morals and Justice* (Princeton: Princeton University Press, 1986); Catherine Pickstock, *After Writing: On the Liturgical Consummation of Philosophy* (Oxford: Basil Blackwell, 1998); Robert Song, *Christianity and Liberal Society* (Oxford: Clarendon Press, 1997); Henry B. Veatch, *Swimming Against the Current in Contemporary Philosophy* (Washington, DC: Catholic University of America Press, 1990).

9. These younger thinkers are often immediate or second- or third-generation students of Gerhard Niemeyer, Alasdair MacIntyre, E. B. F. Midgley, Heinrich Rommen, Charles N. R. McCoy, Francis Canavan, Ernest Fortin, John Hallowell, Charles de Koninck, Clifford Kossel, I. Th. Eschmann, Yves R. Simon, Jacques Maritain, Etienne Gilson, John Courtney Murray, Russell Kirk, Mary Nichols, Francis Graham Wilson, Waldemar Gurian, Jerome Kerwin, Josef Ratzinger, John Finnis, Josef Pieper, David Walsh, Charles Taylor, Henri de Lubac, Dietrich von Hildebrand, Robert Sokolowski, Hans Urs von Balthasar, G. K. Chesterton, Christopher Dawson, and a number of others.

10. See my *Liberation Theology in Latin America: With Selected Essays and Documents* (San Francisco: Ignatius Press, 1982).

11. See E. F. Schumacher, *A Guide for the Perplexed* (New York: Harper Colophon, 1977), 27–39.

12. Translations of Aristotle from *The Basic Works of Aristotle*, ed. Richard McKeon (New York: Random House, 1941).

13. [Roughly translated as "seeking to understand faith" and "faith seeking understanding." Ed.]

14. Leo Strauss, "On the Mutual Influence of Theology and Philosophy," in *Faith and Political Philosophy*, ed. P. Emberley and B. Cooper (University Park: Pennsylvania State University Press, 1993), 217–34.

15. I have discussed this point at further length in chapter 3, "On the Political Importance of the Philosophic Life," in *Jacques Maritain: The Philosopher in Society* (Lanham, MD: Rowman and Littlefield, 1998), 39–58.

16. See Robert Sokolowski, "The Method of Philosophy: Making Distinctions," *The Review of Metaphysics* 60 (1998): 515–32.

17. Josef Pieper, "Philosophy out of a Christian Existence," in *Josef Pieper: An Anthology* (San Francisco: Ignatius Press, 1989), 165.

18. On the curious philosophic order in Genesis itself, see Leo Strauss, "On the Interpretation of Genesis," in Susan Orr, *Jerusalem and Athens: Reason and Revelation in the Works of Leo Strauss* (Lanham, MD: Rowman and Littlefield, 1995), 209–26.

19. "The most striking feature of Christianity, as distinguished from the other great religions of the West, Judaism and Islam, is its almost complete indifference to questions of a properly political nature" (Fortin, "Natural Law and Social Justice," in *Classical Christianity and the Political Order*, 226).

20. The best explication of this philosophic reasonableness of political authority is still Yves R. Simon, *A General Theory of Authority* (Notre Dame, IN: University of Notre Dame Press, 1980), 31–49.

21. For a discussion of the term "flourish," see John Finnis, *Natural Law and Natural Rights* (Oxford: Clarendon Press, 1980), *passim*.

22. "Classical philosophy had failed, not because—by its stubborn refusal to take into account the all too deplorable human character of man's behavior—it makes unreasonable demands on human nature, but because it did not know and hence could not apply the proper remedy to man's congenital weakness" (Ernest Fortin, "St. Augustine," in *History of Political Philosophy*, ed. Leo Strauss and Joseph Cropsey, 3rd ed. [Chicago: University of Chicago Press, 1987], 182).

23. See William Wallace, *The Modeling of Nature: Philosophy of Science and Philosophy of Nature in Synthesis* (Washington, DC: Catholic University of America Press, 1996).

24. Herbert A. Deane, *The Political and Social Ideas of St. Augustine* (New York: Columbia University Press, 1963), 5.

25. See Christopher Dawson, *Religion and the Rise of Western Culture* (Garden City, NY: Doubleday Image, 1958).

26. "The rise of monasticism in the fourth century was no accident. It was rather an attempt to escape the Imperial problem, and to build an 'autonomous' Christian Society outside of the boundaries of the Empire, 'outside the camp.' On the other hand, the Church could not evade her responsibilities for the world, or surrender her missionary task. Indeed, the Church was concerned not only with individuals, but also with society, even with the whole of mankind" (Georges Florovsky, "Empire and Desert: Antinomies of Christian History," *Cross Currents* 9 [Summer 1959]: 237).

27. See Charles N. R. McCoy, *The Structure of Political Thought* (New York: McGraw-Hill, 1963), 117–18.

28. See Paul Marshall, *Their Blood Cries Out* (Dallas, TX: Word Publishing, 1997).

29. See *The Review of Metaphysics* 52 (1998): 221–48.

30. See Oscar Cullmann, *The State in the New Testament* (New York: Scribner's, 1956), 71–85; Heinrich Schlier, "The State in the New Testament," in *The Relevance of the New Testament* (New York: Herder and Herder, 1968), 234–38.

31. "Philosophy, as a quest for wisdom, is quest for universal knowledge, of the whole" (Leo Strauss, "What Is Political Philosophy?," in *What Is Political Philosophy? And Other Essays* [Glencoe, IL: The Free Press, 1959], 11).

32. Pieper, "The Possible Future of Philosophy," in *Josef Pieper: An Anthology*, 184.

33. Eric Voegelin, *Conversations with Eric Voegelin*, ed. R. Eric O'Connor (Montreal: Thomas More Institute, 1980), 2.

34. Leo Strauss, *Persecution and the Art of Writing* (Westport, CT: Greenwood, 1973), 19.

35. See John Paul II, *Person and Community: Selected Essays*, trans. T. Sandok (New York: Peter Lang, 1993). See also George Weigel, *Witness to Hope: The Biography of Pope John Paul II* (New York: Cliff Street Books, 1999), chaps. 4–6; Andrew Woznicki, *A Christian Humanism: Karol Wojtyla's Existential Humanism* (New Britain, CT: Mariel Publications, 1980).

36. Strauss, *What Is Political Philosophy?*, 9–10.

37. Strauss's famous essay on "Jerusalem and Athens" can be found in Orr, *Jerusalem and Athens*, 179–208. It is also in Leo Strauss, *Studies in Platonic Political Philosophy*, ed. T. Pangle (Chicago: University of Chicago Press, 1983), 147–73.

38. Eric Voegelin, *Plato and Aristotle*, vol. 3 of *Order and History*, ed. Dante Germino (Baton Rouge, LA: Louisiana State University Press, 1957), 3–23; Dawson, *Religion and the Rise of Western Culture*, 44–66.

39. John Paul II, *Crossing the Threshold of Hope*, ed. Vittorio Messori (New York: Knopf, 1994), 43.

CHAPTER 19

Is American Democracy Safe for Catholicism?

GARY D. GLENN AND JOHN STACK

Gary D. Glenn (1941–) is Distinguished Teaching Professor Emeritus in the Department of Political Science at Northern Illinois University. He earned his Bachelor's Degree from Loras College in 1962 and his Ph.D. from the University of Chicago in 1969. He published numerous articles and book chapters over the course of his career on the history of political philosophy, American political thought, the role of religion in the Constitution and in modern political philosophy, and the relationship of Catholicism to American democracy.

John Stack (1968–) teaches grade school at the East Lake Academy in Lake Forest, Illinois, whose faculty he joined in 2006. He has also taught full-time at Hiram College and at Concord University. He received his Bachelor's Degree from Northern Illinois University in 1991 and a Master of Arts in Political Science in 1993.

> The question is sometimes raised, whether Catholicism is compatible with American democracy. The question is invalid as well as impertinent; for the manner of its position inverts the order of values. It must, of course, be turned round to read, whether American democracy is compatible with Catholicism.
>
> —John Courtney Murray, S.J. (1960)[1]

The Traditional View That Catholicism Is Not Safe for American Democracy

The idea that Catholicism is not safe for American democracy already appears in the constitutional ratification debates (1787–89). Several reasons are given. Catholics "acknowledge a foreign hand, who can relieve them from the obligation of an oath."[2] Congress's Treaty power would allow the Catholic religion to be established in the United States "which would prevent people from worshiping God according to their own consciences."[3] And "no man is fit to be a ruler of [P]rotestants without he can honestly profess to be of the [P]rotestant religion."[4]

A century later the Blaine amendment, which had been proposed to deal with the problem posed by Catholics, came within one vote of passing Congress.[5] More particularly, the amendment was introduced because the growing Catholic population was succeeding in obtaining public money for its own schools. That Catholics were the particular aim of this amendment was made explicit in the debates.[6] The amendment sought to stop the spending of public money for "sectarian" schools which it defined as schools not under public control. Thus schools controlled by public bodies were permitted to read the King James Bible and teach Protestant ideas of conscience.

Twentieth-century formulations maintained that the Catholic Church is dangerous to American democracy because it sided with the Fascist side, and against the democratic side, in the Spanish Civil War;[7] because of its hierarchical ("clerical") structure;[8] because the mere existence of parochial schools is inimical to national unity, to say nothing of the attempt to secure public funding for them;[9] because it is intolerant;[10] because it "claims infallibility for itself and denies spiritual freedom, liberty of mind or conscience, to its members. It is therefore the foe to all progress; it is deadly hostile to democracy";[11] and because its opposition to legalized abortion is a violation of both the free exercise of religion and the establishment clauses.[12]

Catholicism's incompatibility with democracy is plausible partly because modern democracy arose within Protestant countries. And Tocqueville remarked that "Puritanism . . . was almost as much a political theory as a religious doctrine. . . . Most of English America . . . brought to the New World a Christianity which I can only describe as democratic and republican."[13] In contrast, from Constantine until the twentieth century, Catholicism was associated with monarchy. Whether there are decisive theoretical reasons for this historical connection, it seems historically plausible that Protestantism is somehow akin to democracy in a way that Catholicism is not.

Furthermore, the Encyclicals of Pius IX (*Syllabus of Errors* 1864), of Leo XIII (*Diuturnum* 1881 and *Immortale Dei* 1885), and of Pius XI (*Quas Primas* 1925) considered democracy anti-Catholic. They associated it with the French Revolution, anticlericalism, liberalism, public atheism, authority rooted in will rather than transcendent standards of right, and granting religious liberty as a matter of right to those whom the Church regarded as schismatics, heretics, and infidels.[14] Accordingly, as late as 1925 *Quas Primas* taught that the state should underwrite Catholicism's faith and moral teachings. And as late as 1940 Father John Ryan, the distinguished Catholic liberal, wrote that separation of church and state and religious freedom were acceptable expedients when circumstances prevented establishing the Catholic faith as the state religion.[15]

In light of this history, as late as the 1960 campaign, respected Protestant leaders could fairly ask:

> Is it reasonable to assume that a Roman Catholic President would be able to withstand altogether the determined efforts of the hierarchy of his [C]hurch to gain further funds and favors for its schools and institutions, and otherwise break the wall of separation of church and state?[16]

In one political sense, this fear that Catholicism is unsafe for American democracy was played down by the election of John Kennedy and by Vatican II's acceptance of religious liberty beyond mere toleration.[17] However, precisely in the aftermath of Kennedy's election, Murray questioned how deeply they settled this issue. His question "whether American democracy is compatible with Catholicism" not only strikingly reverses the traditional question, but is surprising given Murray's credentials as the leading Catholic exponent of their compatibility and his later role in persuading the Vatican Council to endorse religious liberty.

The 1991 nomination of Clarence Thomas to the Supreme Court suggests that Murray was onto something. Laurence Tribe criticized as "an extraordinary theological argument" Thomas's view that the Declaration of Independence's statement that rights are God-given means the Constitution could not be neutral on abortion.[18] Virginia Governor Douglas Wilder questioned "how much allegiance is there [in Thomas] to the pope"?[19] Columnist Ellen Goodman's more genteel formulation was:

> The concern is no longer the Pope as such. The problem is now the Catholic [C]hurch's institutional hierarchy which violates the separation of church and state by instructing its members on [C]hurch moral doctrine and tell[ing] Catholic officeholders how to vote on one issue: abortion.

The heat was apparently produced by Thomas's publicly thanking the nuns who had taught him in school; and by his acknowledged belief in natural law, "the principle that the Catholic [C]hurch used to underpin its opposition to contraception as well as abortion."[20]

As a passing political matter, the Thomas episode would have been striking if the Episcopalian Thomas had been a Catholic.[21] As a matter of enduring concern, these objections to Thomas suggest something deeper. It may be true, as Arthur Schlesinger Sr. once told a Catholic scholar, that "the prejudice against your Church is the deepest bias in the history of the American people."[22] But this bias has a theoretical root, namely, the democratic political thought of dissenting Protestantism, found most relevantly for us in John Locke's *Letter Concerning Toleration* (1689), James Madison's "Memorial and Remonstrance Against Religious Assessments" (1785), and Thomas Jefferson's "Statute on Religious Freedom" (1785). In this thought, Catholicism's "foreign allegiance," that is, its understanding of conscience as subject to Church and ultimately papal instruction, is incompatible with American democracy's dissenting Protestant assumption that there is no higher source of guidance in matters of faith and morals than individual conscience. With democracy so understood, how can Catholicism be safe unless it adopts this view of conscience and thereby ceases to be historic Catholicism?

The Transition from Civil Liberty to Civil Liberties

In the 1940s, while Father Ryan was both restating the Church's traditional objections to the secular liberal state and arguing that they could be prudentially accommodated to American democracy, the Supreme Court began intensively to secularize American democracy. The rubric was a new reading of the establishment clause which in principle, and eventually in practice, rendered all revealed religions, including the Protestantism which it partially resembled but which it displaced, incompatible with any significant place in public life. By "secularism," we understand "the doctrine that morality should be based solely on regard to the well-being of mankind in the present life, to the exclusion of all considerations drawn from belief in God or in a future state."[23] This is today thought to require excluding public support from religious schools and prohibiting both religious practices in public contexts and moral teachings based on revelation when those teachings cross secular morality or secular ideas of freedom. Post-1940s democracy, thus authoritatively articulated and fashioned by the Court, appears to regard secularism as the *sine qua non* of liberal democracy.

We argue this mandatory public secularism is part of a new constitutional regime which the Court instituted at this time. The new regime is verbally indicated by the Court's introducing, for the first time in our constitutional history, "civil liberties" in contrast to the traditional "civil liberty."[24]

"Civil liberty" is the language of Blackstone, common law, and *The Federalist*. The latter speaks of it in the context of the problem of maintaining "the order of society."[25] WESTLAW first finds "civil liberty" in a Supreme Court opinion in *Marbury* (1803),[26] but not until the *Slaughterhouse Cases* (1872) is it given explicit judicial definition. There, Justice Field refers approvingly to Blackstone's definition, given by Senator Trumbull in the debate on the Civil Rights Bill of 1866. "Civil liberty is no other than natural liberty, so far restrained by human laws and no further, as is necessary and expedient for the general advantage of the public."[27] Field quotes Blackstone's editor's gloss on this definition: "that state in which each individual has the power to pursue his own happiness according to his own views of his interest, and the dictates of his conscience, unrestrained, except by equal, just, and impartial laws."[28] Thus, "civil liberty" did not privilege individual power to the extent of requiring the laws to grant it as much latitude as possible. The laws only had to be "equal, just and impartial," thereby giving as much emphasis to the *restraints* of such laws on an individual's power as to his license to exercise that power. The modern idea that "rights are trump" is alien to "civil liberty" but is the cutting edge of the new "civil liberties" regime.

Under the old "civil liberty regime," religion was permitted in public life, including ritual public prayer, which survives to this day in the opening of each day of Congress and the Court, and the public school Baccalaureate Service and graduation prayer, found unconstitutional as late as *Lee v. Weisman* (1992).

The grounds for the old "civil liberty" regime's solution to the problem of the relation of religion and government were publicly advocated at the Founding by James Madison.

> In a free government, the security for civil rights must be the same as for religious rights. It consists in the one case in the multiplicity of interests and in

the other, in the multiplicity of sects. The degree of security in both cases will depend on the interests and sects; and this may be presumed to depend on the extent of country and number of people comprehended under the same government.[29]

This Madisonian regime publicly assumed that "religious rights" included influencing public policy through truck and bargaining among the multiplicity of sects. Speaking for the Constitution's advocates, he argued that this system would so limit any particular sect's influence as generally to produce "justice and the general good."[30]

This public religious pluralism permitted legislatures to work out pragmatically the relation between religious belief, churches, and government without conforming to a constitutional theory of what the outcome should be.[31] This regime, constitutionally in place from 1789 until the 1940s, also permitted public schools to have a character forming function which warranted "impartial governmental assistance of all religions."[32] Thus *McCollum*'s publicly supported religious instruction was consistent with the old public religious pluralism.

It was this traditional "civil liberty" regime which Murray in 1960 thought compatible with Catholicism because that democracy both permitted and presupposed "the coexistence within one political community of groups who hold divergent and incompatible views with regard to religious questions—those ultimate questions that concern the nature and destiny of man."[33] Murray further denied that the First Amendment religion clauses embodied any theory. Rather, he maintained that they are better understood as "articles of peace," that is, practical formulations the concrete meaning of which is negotiated from time to time in legislatures and school board meetings, and renegotiated as circumstances change—democracy as government by the people as one might once have conceived of it.

In contrast to this "civil liberty" regime, which permitted widely differing views of what religion is, as well as what its relation to government should be, the secular regime the Court began instituting in the 1940s attributed to the religion clauses a new substantive theory that seems to require all Americans to understand religion as a private matter lacking either public encouragement or consequence.[34] The seed of this secularism was planted by the Court's declaring in *Everson v. Board of Education* (1947), without evidence or precedent, that the establishment clause mandated government neutrality between religion and nonreligion.[35] The first blossoming was finding unconstitutional government-sponsored religious instruction in public schools as a means to combat growing juvenile delinquency in *McCollum* (1948).[36] The mature fruit became visible for all to see in finding unconstitutional publicly sponsored prayer and Bible reading in public schools in *Engel v. Vitale* (1962) and *Abington v. Schempp* (1963), respectively.[37]

The Court's replacement of constitutionally permitted public religious pluralism with constitutionally mandatory public secularism is part of the new "civil liberties" regime which the Court began instituting in about 1940. The novelty of this regime is indicated superficially by its name. Although now a preeminent category of constitutional law, WESTLAW shows "civil liberties" first used as a term of art in a Supreme Court opinion only in 1940.[38] It first occurred in a Supreme Court case as the proper name of the American Civil Liberties Union in 1938. However, "civil liberties" was not yet an accepted term of legal art, according to then Professor Felix Frankfurter. It was only "a very loose expression" used in communication with "the laity."[39] "Civil liberties" appeared only twice in Supreme Court cases prior to 1938 and in neither is it the Court's language. In the first case (1892),[40] it is part of a 1701 quotation from William Penn. In the second case (1904),[41] it occurs in a military order which was part of the evidence in the case.

"Civil liberties," as it developed after 1940, differs decisively from traditional "civil liberty" by intensified license to individual choices and desires as against other constitutional goods. "Civil liberty" had privileged "the general advantage of the public" (Justice Field [1872] citing Senator Trumbull [1866] quoting Blackstone [1776]) or "justice and the general good" (*Federalist*, No. 51 [1788]). "Civil liberties" privileges individual rights and that probably generates constitutional secularism. "Civil liberty" permitted governmental support for religion and relied on the competition between, and compromise among, the multiplicity of sects to prevent injustice. It did not define justice as requiring constitutional equality between religion and nonreligion. When the Court instituted that equality in *Everson* (1947), it redefined injustice to something like exposing an individual to government-supported religious activities with which that individual did not agree. Thus one atheist's right not to have to listen to the traditional Baccalaureate prayer is constitutionally superior to the community's determination that such prayer is for the "general advantage of the public" (*Lee v. Weisman*, 1992). If an individual's choice constitutionally trumps the legislatively determined "general good," then public secularism apparently, or at least plausibly, follows.[42]

Secularism may even more sharply contrast "civil liberties" with "civil liberty" than does the intensified individualism from which it springs. For while Professor Tribe thought "extraordinary" Clarence Thomas's reasoning politically on the basis of the Declaration's theological content, under the "civil liberty" regime even Jefferson thought it proper to state for America that we are "endowed" with rights "by our Creator." And elsewhere he asked "can the liberties of a nation be thought secure when we have removed their only firm basis, a conviction in the minds of the people that these liberties are of the gift of God? That they are not to be violated but with his wrath?" And because slavery violates them "I tremble for my country when I reflect that God is just; that his justice cannot sleep for ever.... The Almighty has no attribute which can take side with us in such a contest."[43] Nor did Lincoln think the Declaration's theological argument "extraordinary." Indeed, at Gettysburg he declared that America was dedicated to the Declaration's proposition "under God."[44] Similarly, Frederick Douglass cited the Declaration and quoted Psalm 137 "By the rivers of Babylon ... ," declaring "The existence of slavery in this country brands your republicanism as a sham, your humanity as a base pretense, and your Christianity as a lie."[45]

The "civil liberties" regime transformed secularism from at most a common social opinion[46] into a constitutionally obligatory theory.[47] Tocqueville had foreseen that, as equality becomes more absolute, "trust in common opinion will become a sort of religion, with the majority as its prophet."[48] However, "Christian morality" was still the common American opinion of his day and still "the first of their political institutions." Yet he foresaw that if Christian morality ceased to be an "impediment, one would soon find among them the boldest [moral and political] innovators and the most implacable logicians in the world."[49] He did not foresee that the justices of the Supreme Court would become the hierarchy of the new equality-inspired religion,[50] or so far mimic Catholicism as to claim "infallibility" in teaching doctrine. "We are not final because we are infallible, but we are infallible only because we are final."[51] Tocqueville may have foreseen better than he knew in finding Catholicism even more compatible with American democracy than is Protestantism.[52] Catholics' faith in papal infallibility need only be transferred to faith in the infallibility of "common social opinion" and the Supreme Court.

By 1960 the original Madisonian regime had not yet been completely overthrown by the new judicially created secular regime. The Court, in particular, had backed off from its 1947 *McCollum* decision under attack from many religious sectors, and even the *New York Times*. It did so in 1953 by finding constitutional an ever so slightly different plan for public encouragement of religious instruction.[53] However, the subsequent bans on governmental encouragement of prayer (1962) and Bible reading (1963) in public schools visibly established public secularism as authoritative. Public secularism's exclusion of religious practices as such from a place in public life has now worked its way through a score of subsequent cases.

Contemporary Liberal Theory on the Permissibility of Religiously Grounded Arguments in the Public Sphere

Originally, the Court's new secular regime excluded only such practices from public support as public school religious instruction, public prayer, and Bible reading. Recent liberal theory goes further in excluding religiously grounded moral arguments from political discourse. John Rawls, for instance, who discusses religion under the rubric of "comprehensive doctrines," thinks some comprehensive doctrines are unreasonable, and hence morally objectionable. Unreasonable comprehensive doctrines, according to Rawls, are those "that cannot support a reasonable balance of political values."[54] While he is ginger about identifying contemporary examples of such doctrines, he so identifies (albeit in a footnote) an opinion which excludes the right to abortion in the first trimester.[55] Adherents of such doctrines would seem to be required "to submerge or to set aside their comprehensive [i.e., revelation-based] doctrines when entering the public sphere."[56] Thus Rawls would morally exclude some revelation-based beliefs from having political consequence. He can even be plausibly understood as meaning that voting on the basis of such revelation-based beliefs is "illegitimate."[57]

We acknowledge Rawls's subtlety on this matter. In particular, he would not exclude *all* religiously grounded opinions from political discourse, but merely unreasonable ones. However, Goerner accurately captures the drift of what religious views Rawls excludes as unreasonable, namely, those that do not provide "support for a Rawlsian liberal regime," which Goerner thinks excludes at least some views of "most religious believers." Rawls would apparently include only those religious views that support *liberal* policies, such as Rev. Martin Luther King Jr.'s Civil Rights movement, Abraham Lincoln's Thanksgiving and Fast Day proclamations, and (quoting Rawls) Lincoln's "Second Inaugural with its prophetic (Old Testament) interpretation of the Civil War as God's punishment for the sin [of] slavery."[58] Thus Rawls can be defended against the charge of excluding religious opinions as such because he excludes only nonliberal religious opinions, such as opposition to abortion in the first trimester.[59]

The connection between "civil liberties" democracy and secularism is made explicit by Robert Audi, who thinks democracy requires "a principle of secular rationale" which denies a right to "advocate or support any law or public policy that restricts human conduct unless one has ... adequate secular reason." And a secular reason is "one whose ... status ... does not (evidentially) depend on the existence of God, ... or on theological considerations, ... or on the pronouncements of a person or institution *qua* religious authority."[60] Paul J. Weithman superficially disagrees with Audi, but on the basis of a more fundamental agreement, by following Rawls in permitting revelation-based arguments that support "economic justice and racial equality."[61] Thus there is a dispute within contemporary liberal theory whether democracy requires secularism simply or whether secularism is required only so far as necessary to prohibit nonliberal, anti–civil libertarian, policies. This suggests that secular/civil liberties democracy might be safe for liberal Catholicism.

Of course, contemporary liberal political theory has not gone unchallenged in its effort to remove, to whatever extent, religiously grounded moral convictions from political discourse. For example, Michael Perry has argued that to require a religious citizen to bracket her moral convictions in public discourse would "annihilate herself. And doing that would preclude *her* ... from engaging in moral discourse with other members of the society."[62] Moreover, William Galston has argued that liberal society simply cannot sustain itself without religiously grounded morality, especially concerning the family and the raising of children.[63]

Why did the new "civil liberties" regime come to require public secularism? In general, "civil liberties" signifies intensified license to individual choices and desires as against other constitutional goods. Evidently the political interests of this new constitutional category are better served by a secular rather than revelation-based public life. These political interests have sought to free individuals from many traditional, biblically rooted, legally enforced moral restraints: prohibitions against such speech as blasphemy, obscenity and pornography, libel and slander, and against such behavior as divorce, artificial birth control, abortion, adultery, sodomy, euthanasia, and gambling.[64] Such traditional prohibitions were believed to support the kind of self-restraint which made political freedom compatible with order and, in particular, which protected monogamous family life.[65] Tocqueville, who thought that "almost all the disorders of [European] society are born ... not far from the nuptial bed" but that America is the country in which "the marriage tie is most respected," had attributed this largely to religion's ability to "regulate the state" by "regulating domestic life."[66]

By liberating individuals from the moral and legal restraints which protect monogamous families, the foregoing contemporary liberal theorists seem to share with "civil liberties" jurisprudence the view that human beings are primarily individuals rather than primarily parts of such families. This view seems problematic for Catholics. According to Pope John Paul II, for Catholics, "Every man is his 'brother's keeper,' because God entrusts us to one another. And it is also in view of this entrusting that God gives everyone freedom, a freedom which possesses an inherently relational dimension." In contrast, "A culture of death ... betrays a completely individualistic concept of freedom, which ends up by becoming the freedom of 'the strong' against the weak who have no choice but to submit."[67]

How Secular Democracy Endangers Catholicism

One might doubt whether or the extent to which secular democracy threatens Catholicism. After all, Catholicism has coexisted with American democracy for over 200 years. And isn't secular democracy merely another belief about the grounds on which human beings ought to decide how they should live together? But secularism is now the constitutionally privileged public philosophy and hence legally dominates all public institutions. It thus politically marginalizes religious citizens except when they agree with secularism. Whether government may support a particular public policy seems to depend on that policy being defensible on nonreligious grounds. Citizens without religious faith may legitimately attempt to write into law their ideas about how we should live together. But religious citizens are constitutionally permitted to do so only if they can show their ideas square with secular convictions. As Murray said at the time of *McCollum* (1947), this "legal victory for secularism" is "hostile to the *interests* of religion."[68] However, hostility to the interests of religion is not necessarily dangerous to religion. Not all threats to one's interests also threaten one's rights or existence. Such threats might produce only fruitful and energizing, or at least tolerable, tensions. Why does the new constitutional privileging of secularism make it a "danger" to Catholicism?

The danger is primarily to the souls of Catholic political leaders who are tempted to sever the connection between their religious convictions and their political positions when the former are inconsistent with their political interests. This seems to be what John Kennedy said and did. "There is an old saying in Boston that we get our religion from Rome and our politics at home, and that is the way most Catholics feel about it."[69] Perhaps, understandably, he denied that he was "the Catholic candidate for President" but then further distanced himself from Catholicism by adding "I do not speak for the Catholic church on issues of public policy—and no one in that church speaks for me."[70] By opposing the official Catholic Church side on the two "Catholic interests issues," namely federal aid to parochial schools and appointing an ambassador to the Vatican,[71] he showed he spoke in earnest when he said, "the responsibility of the office-holder is to make decisions on these questions [public issues] on the basis of the general welfare as he sees it, even if such is not in accord with the prevailing Catholic opinion."[72]

In 1984, then Governor Mario Cuomo went further in the direction pointed by Kennedy in severing his Catholic moral convictions from his political life by publicly supporting the legal right to abortion while saying that personally he believed abortion was wrong. In many other matters, notably regarding public support for the poor, Governor Cuomo arguably acted in accordance with Catholic social teachings. But he apparently thought himself prohibited from acting publicly on those teachings when they contradicted secular morality. As a public official he thought himself required to approve, support, and even fight for what his religiously grounded moral convictions told him were wrong.[73] At the root of this position is secularism's view, shared with some dissenting Protestantism, that religion is a wholly private matter.[74] But Catholicism holds that its moral teachings are publicly relevant. Hence, Catholics must be torn between their religion and this new secular democracy.

This contradicting in one's public actions what one believes is sound morally is a danger to the soul. The secular psychologist, who deals with the mind not the soul, knows it as "cognitive dissonance" or perhaps schizophrenia. It creates at least stress as the divided personality is torn between the desire for integration and the need to maintain compartmentalization. The believer has it on God's authority that a city divided against itself, even a city in the soul, cannot stand.[75] The Kennedy and Cuomo examples show that contemporary secular democracy's danger to the souls of Catholics is neither imaginary nor marginal.

The Kennedy election may have settled that a Catholic can be elected president. However, it did not settle whether contemporary secular democracy will permit Catholics to act *legitimately* as public officials on the basis of Catholicism's moral teachings when their policies are seen as peculiarly deriving from those teachings. The Cuomo example suggests that contemporary American democracy does not permit Catholics to so act. "The values derived from religious belief will not—and should not—be accepted as part of the public morality unless they are shared by the pluralistic community at large."[76] "Should not" comes artfully close to saying "Catholics have no right." But it is ambiguous enough to mean only "as a practical matter of securing workable policy." Even if secularism allows Catholics such a right, acting on that right apparently requires more willingness to be a political outsider than might reasonably be expected of most politicians.

Catholicism takes seriously divine revelation, authoritatively interpreted by the Church, as a guide to how human beings ought to live. Contemporary secular democracy does not. Instead, it seemingly relies on a relativism respecting how one should live which rejects, as incompatible with democracy, any moral authority (except perhaps science) beyond individual conscience. The incompatibility of Catholicism and secular democracy surfaces when the two sources disagree. Commonly this disagreement involves some human passion, which secularists want to be free from restraint by civil law, and which the Church teaches is morally wrong and encourages civil law to reflect that view.

Secular democracy is dangerous for Catholicism because it prevents Catholics from acting in the public sphere when their views spring peculiarly from their faith. The theoretical rubric for this censorship is a particular interpretation of liberal democracy's teaching that government must refrain from interfering with the private sphere. The existence of a private sphere, which liberal governments exist to protect but not to penetrate and regulate, is surely necessary for both religious freedom and civil peace. However, is it legitimate to dispute, within a liberal order, exactly what aspects of human life should and should not be regarded as within the private sphere? Or to what extent should they be considered beyond public regulation? Or are these things decided in advance by liberalism, so as to preclude legitimate public controversy? The Kennedy-Cuomo syndrome suggests that the precise danger to the souls of Catholics is that secular democracy regards Catholicism's moral teaching, when it conflicts with secularism, as so "beyond the pale" as to be excluded from a place at the table in these debates. If so, then Catholics who try to live politically by their Church's moral teachings are politically marginalized.[77] The danger to their souls is the temptation to purchase entry into public life by leaving their Catholic views at the door. The danger to Catholicism is from a regime that excludes Catholic moral teachings from political influence.

Catholicism's New and More Favorable View of Democracy

After World War II, the Catholic Church came to a far more positive view of democracy than had been reflected in the encyclicals referred to earlier. A document of the Second Vatican Council praises the excellences of constitutional democracy.[78] Pope John Paul II has enthusiastically recommended constitutionally limited government, inalienable rights, and the free exchange of capital and goods, entrepreneurship, and participation in the "circle of productivity" within "a strong juridical framework," as most compatible with "the inherent dignity of the individual." He has stressed democratic capitalism as promoting the conditions which tend to foster the moral life for individuals, and justice and the common good for societies.[79]

John Paul II sees the constitutionally limited state as more compatible with the Catholic understanding of what is good for the human person than any available alternative. The state is to be limited by legally acknowledging the inalienable rights of human beings; and by the principle of subsidiarity[80] which, in the first instance, gives "primary responsibility" for securing economic rights and providing care for the needy "not to the State, but to individuals and to the various groups and associations that make up society."[81] Subsidiarity is partly a strategy for reminding Catholics that reducing the centralized state's economic functions requires them to provide more for those in need. His argument for decentralization of power and responsibility goes so far as to endorse, on pragmatic and experiential grounds, separation of powers as a means to the rule of law.

However, more recently the pope has begun to strongly criticize contemporary democracy's moral defects. In *Evangelium Vitae* (1995) he speaks of a "more sinister character" to the "new cultural climate." "Broad sectors of public opinion justify certain crimes against life in the name of the rights of individual freedom."[82] "The very right to life is being denied or trampled upon, especially at ... the moment of birth and the moment of death."[83] While carefully refraining from explicitly identifying his target here as either contemporary "democracy" or "democratic countries," at what else could this warning about "a veritable culture of death" be directed?[84] In order to be speaking about anything other than contemporary Western democracies, one would have to suppose that public opinion is as influential in other contemporary regimes (say China) as in Western democracies. Moreover, later in the encyclical he warns that "democracy cannot be idolized to the point of making it a substitute for morality or a panacea for immorality . . . democracy is a 'system' and as such is a means and not an end."[85]

Nor does the pope limit his criticism to corrupted "public opinion" and "culture," although these seem to be his preferred foci.[86] He also criticizes governments. In particular, he quotes Pope John XXIII: "any government which refused to recognize human rights or acted in violation of them, would not only fail in its duty; its decrees would be wholly lacking in binding force."[87] Though still not mentioning Western governments by name, in the context it is difficult to avoid the implication—but still and wisely only the implication—that contemporary Western democratic governments, insofar as they fail in this duty, make "decrees" that are not morally binding on citizens.

Evangelium Vitae suggests that Catholicism and secular democracy may speak the same rights language but mean incompatible things.[88] This seems to be a recent development arising from the new secular democracy established in *McCollum* (1948). Until 1972, the old religiously pluralist American democracy regarded abortion as a violation of God-given rights, hence a crime; while Catholicism regarded it as a violation of God-given rights, hence a sin.[89] Now the new secular democracy regards abortion—edging into infanticide—as a right; with euthanasia already on the judicial agenda. "The roots of the contradiction between the solemn affirmation of human rights and their tragic denial in practice lie in the notion of freedom which exalts the isolated individual in an absolute way, and gives no place to solidarity, to openness to others and service of them."[90]

John Paul II's implicit message for Catholicism seems to be that, to maintain itself within contemporary American democracy, Catholics will have to understand themselves as living in a political and cultural order increasingly hostile to the moral teachings of their [C]hurch. This is a hard message for American Catholics who have spent several generations seeking to become accepted in and acceptable to the American democratic culture. But that was in the old non-secular democracy, whose public policy generally took its bearings from generically Protestant morality with which Catholics were not fundamentally at odds. Hence, notwithstanding their separate schools, Catholics have not until recently had to live in a culture hostile to their moral traditions. *Evangelium Vitae* appears to suggest that, for their religion to survive here under the new secular democracy, Catholics will have to learn to think of themselves, to an uncertain extent, as moral and cultural outsiders. His argument for a constitutionally limited state might be a political strategy for persuading the new secular democratic state to allow that.

Conclusion

The souls of Catholics were never fully safe within the constitutional order established in 1789 because that Madisonian regime solved the problem of religious liberty by encouraging a multiplicity of sects which it appeared to regard as good. This strategy, while arguably politically salutary, nevertheless tended to undermine the conviction that any particular religion is true.[91] This endangers all religions which (like Catholicism) claim their beliefs are true. However, the old Madisonian regime did not exclude Catholic moral views from public life, either constitutionally, theoretically, or morally. It neither constitutionally required Catholics to live under a political or cultural regime indifferent or hostile to their moral traditions nor required them to renounce their truth claims in order to participate in public life. Its multiplicity of sects only practically constrained their ability to influence public policy.

In contrast, the new secular democracy excludes truth claims that conflict with its foundational religious and moral relativism.[92] It thus excludes Catholics *qua* Catholics as well as others whose religion rejects these relativisms. Thus, insofar as Catholics want to be good democrats now, they are required to act publicly like secularists, that is, to bracket, relativize, renounce, or be silent about at least some of their Catholic truth claims. Thus secularism strongly induces them to accept, or at least not speak against, the goodness (not merely the inevitability) of the relativism of religion and morality. The inducements are not limited to having policies overturned by the judiciary if they support religion rather than secularism. The chief inducement is inclusion, the punishment exclusion, from respectability in the culture. These are democracy's means of control which so awed Tocqueville.

> You are free not to think as I do; you can keep your life and property and all; but from this day you are a stranger among us. You can keep your privileges

in the township, but ... if you solicit your fellow citizens' votes, they will not give them to you, and if you only ask for their esteem, they will make excuses for refusing that ... when you approach your fellows, they will shun you as an impure being, and even those who believe in your innocence will abandon you too, lest they be shunned.[93]

Our thesis is not that Catholics cannot, in principle, be good democrats without becoming secularists. It is that contemporary American democracy, by constitutionally privileging secularism, offers Catholics in public life a strong inducement to abandon, relativize, or remain silent about their moral beliefs when they conflict with secularism. Catholics have to act like, not necessarily be, secularists. That makes it spiritually and politically unsafe, not to say impossible, for Catholics to be democrats now.

Notes

Reprinted from *The Review of Politics* 62, no. 1 (Winter 2000): 5–29.

1. The epigraph is from Murray's *We Hold These Truths: Catholic Reflections on the American Proposition* (New York: Sheed and Ward, 1960), ix–x.
2. "David," *Massachusetts Gazette*, 7 March 1788, in *The Complete Anti-Federalist*, ed. Herbert J. Storing, 7 vols. (Chicago: University of Chicago Press, 1981), 4:248. Major Lusk, in the Massachusetts Ratifying Convention, 4 February 1788, in *The Debates in the Several State Conventions on the Adoption of the Federal Constitution*, ed. Jonathan Elliot, 5 vols. (New York: Burt Franklin, 1888), 2:148. Henry Abbott, in the North Carolina Ratifying Convention, 30 July 1788, in Elliot, *Debates*, 4:191–92. This criticism follows Locke, who says, "We cannot find any Sect that teaches expressly, and openly, that men are not obliged to keep their Promise; ... But nevertheless, we find those that say the same things, in other words. ... [i.e.] that *Faith is not to be kept with Hereticks*? ... I say these have no right to be tolerated" (Locke's emphasis). Again, "That Church can have no right to be tolerated by the Magistrate, which is constituted upon such a bottom, that all those who enter into it, do thereby, *ipso facto*, deliver themselves up to the Protection and Service of another Prince" (*A Letter on Toleration*, ed. James Tully [Indianapolis: Hackett, 1983], 49–50).
3. Henry Abbott, North Carolina Ratifying Convention.
4. "A Friend to the Rights of the People" (New Hampshire), 8 February 1788, in Storing, *Anti-Federalist*, 4:242. William Lancaster, in Elliot, *Debates*, 4:215. Zachias Wilson, in Elliot, *Debates*, 4:212.
5. See Gerard V. Bradley, *Church-State Relationships in America* (New York: Greenwood Press, 1987), 9 and 30, esp. note p. 64.

6. See the debate between Senators Morton, Kernan, Bogy, and Edmunds, 14 August 1876, in 4 *Cong. Rec.*, 5585–89, 5590–91. See especially Sen. Bogy's remarks on 5589.

7. Paul Blanshard, *American Freedom and Catholic Power*, 2nd ed. (Boston: Beacon Press, 1960), 14. What this view of democracy calls the democratic side was also the Communist side. For a discussion see Philip Gleason, "Pluralism, Democracy, and Catholicism in the Era of World War II," *Review of Politics* 49, no. 2 (Spring 1987): 209.

8. Discussed in Gleason, "Pluralism, Democracy, and Catholicism," 214. Blanshard asserts, "It [the American Catholic hierarchy] is an autocratic moral monarchy in a liberal democracy" (*American Freedom and Catholic Power*, 14). Andrew Greeley notes, "Suspicion and hostility toward the Catholic hierarchy have always been a part of American life" (*An Ugly Little Secret: Anti-Catholicism in North America* [Kansas City, MO: Sheed, Andrews and McMeel, 1977], 23).

9. James B. Conant, *Education and Liberty* (Cambridge, MA: Harvard University Press, 1953), 80–81. Conant was then president of Harvard University.

10. Blanshard, *American Freedom and Catholic Power*, x–xi, 2.

11. Theodore Parker, *The Rights of Man in America* (1911), quoted in Blanshard, *American Freedom and Catholic Power*, 13.

12. This has been the public position of the American Civil Liberties Union since about 1977.

13. Alexis de Tocqueville, *Democracy in America*, ed. J. P. Mayer and trans. George Lawrence (New York: Harper & Row, 1969), 288. See generally Part I, chap. 2, 31–49, esp. 38.

14. The experience formative of this view is primarily with European democracies. Catholicism's American experience seemed to have been little noticed. Philip Gleason, *Contending with Modernity: Catholic Higher Education in the Twentieth Century* (New York: Oxford University Press, 1995), 278–79.

15. John A. Ryan and Francis J. Boland, *Catholic Principles of Politics: The State and the Church*, 2nd ed. (New York: Macmillan, 1940), 316–21.

16. Statement of the National Conference of Citizens for Religious Freedom, quoted in the *New York Times*, 8 September 1960, pp. 1, 25. Among the prominent signatories were the Rev. Norman Vincent Peale and the Rev. Dr. Billy Graham. See also Allen J. Matusow, *The Unraveling of America: A History of Liberalism in the 1960s* (New York: Harper & Row, 1984), 22.

17. "Declaration on Religious Liberty," *Dignitatis Humanae* (7 December 1965), in *Vatican Council II: The Conciliar and Post Conciliar Documents*, ed. Austin Flannery, O.P. (Northport, NY: Costello Publishing Company, 1987), 800–812.

18. *New York Times*, 15 July 1991, p. A15.

19. Quoted in *Chicago Tribune*, 17 July 1991, sec. 1, p. 17.

20. Goodman in *Chicago Tribune*, 14 July 1991, sec. 5, p. 6.

21. Philip Lawler says that Thomas "was raised a Catholic but eventually drifted away from the Church," *Catholic World Report* (July 1996). Thomas apparently returned to the Catholic Church only in 1996. At the time of his nomination he was an "evangelical

Episcopalian" (David G. Savage, *Turning Right: The Making of the Rehnquist Court* [New York: John Wiley & Sons, 1992), 426).

22. Quoted in John Tracy Ellis, *American Catholicism*, 2nd ed. (Chicago: University of Chicago Press, 1969), 151. See also Burton Dulce and Edward J. Richter, *Religion and the Presidency: A Recurring American Problem* (New York: Macmillan, 1962), vi–vii.

23. *Oxford English Dictionary*, 2nd ed. (Oxford: Clarendon Press, 1989), 14:849, definition 1.

24. We set aside, as not immediately relevant here, two other major elements of this new order, namely, the decreased constitutional protection afforded to property and the transfer of power from legislatures to courts.

25. See Jacob Cooke, ed., *The Federalist Papers* (Cleveland: World, 1965), no. 9, p. 51.

26. 5 U.S.137 at 163. Marshall here quotes Blackstone concerning the "settled and invariable principle in the laws of England, that every right, when withheld, must have a remedy, and every injury its proper redress." In light of the important distinction we draw between "civil liberty" and "civil liberties," we note that Marshall does not imply that individual protection by the laws trumps other goods which the law may also properly protect. "Civil liberty" appears in thirty-nine cases from *Marbury* (1803) to *Gobitis* (1940).

27. *Congressional Globe*, 1st Session, 39th Congress, Part 1, 29 January 1866, p. 474. See William Blackstone, *Commentaries on the Laws of England*, 1:121. Trumbull follows Blackstone (and Locke's *Second Treatise of Civil Government*, chap. 4, para. 22) in contrasting "civil liberty" to "natural liberty," which "consists properly in a power of acting as one thinks fit, without any restraint or control, unless by the law of nature." *Commentaries*, 1:121.

28. 83 U.S. 36 (1872). Citing "1 Sharswood's Blackstone,127, note 8" at 111 fn. 40.

29. Cooke, ed., *The Federalist Papers*, no. 51, pp. 351–52.

30. Ibid., 353.

31. "Religious pluralism" is the phrase Murray uses in *We Hold These Truths* (15ff). It does not mean that public schools were not predominately Protestant or that government was neutral between Protestants and Catholics. It means only that their situations were determined politically rather than constitutionally.

32. Defense counsel in *McCollum v. Board of Education* 333 U.S. 203 at 211 (1948).

33. Murray, *We Hold These Truths*, x.

34. Dissenting in *Everson* 330 U.S. 1 at 39 (1947), Justice Rutledge correctly finds this view in Madison's "Memorial and Remonstrance" (1785). But his argument that this view is required by the First Amendment is not persuasive. See Gary D. Glenn, "Forgotten Purposes of the First Amendment Religion Clauses," *Review of Politics* 49, no. 3 (Summer 1987): 340–67.

35. 330 U.S. 1 at 15–16. We abstract here from the Court's having earlier (*Gitlow v. U.S.*, 1925) assumed the First Amendment applied to the states.

36. 333 U.S. 203 at 211–12. Murray saw immediately both that *McCollum*'s theory mandated public secularism, that this was wholly new, and that it went together with the

Court's view of civil liberties and civil rights. John Courtney Murray, "Law or Prepossessions?", *Law and Contemporary Problems* 14 (Winter 1949): 1, 37, 39 [reprinted in *Essays in Constitutional Law*, ed. R. G. McCloskey (New York: Alfred A. Knopf, 1957), 316–47. Ed.]. The American Catholic bishops described *McCollum*'s understanding of church-state separation as a "novel interpretation of the First Amendment" and as "the shibboleth of doctrinaire secularism." "The Christian in Action," 21 November 1948, quoted in *New York Times*, 8 September 1960, pp. 1, 25.

37. 374 U.S. 203 and 370 U.S. 421. LEXIS finds "secular" or its cognates used 4 times in Engel and 55 times in *Abington*.

38. *Minersville School District v. Gobitis* 310 U.S. at 602 and 603.

39. Letter from Frankfurter to Chief Justice Stone, 27 April 1938, quoted in Walter F. Murphy, James E. Fleming, and William Harris, *American Constitutional Interpretation* (Mineola, NY: The Foundation Press, 1986), 491. As late as *Niemotko v. Maryland* (1951) Frankfurter (concurring) resisted the thought that "civil liberties" was a term of legal art. "Particularly within the area of due process colloquially called 'civil liberties' . . ." 340 U.S. 268 at 288.

40. *Holy Trinity Church v. U.S.* 143 U.S. at 467 (1892).

41. *Kepner v. U.S.* 195 U.S. at 111 (1904).

42. We consider in the next section why the political interests of the "civil liberties" regime prefer public secularism.

43. *Notes on Virginia* (1787), ed. Bernard Wishy and William E. Leuchtenburg (New York: Harper & Row, 1964), Query XVIII, p. 156. Perhaps this statement can be read as saying only that democracy requires *popular belief* that rights are God-given. But then how might divine retribution be possible?

44. Roy P. Basler, ed., *Abraham Lincoln: His Speeches and Writings* (New York: Da Capo Press, 1946), 734.

45. Speech at Rochester, New York, 5 July 1852, "The Meaning of July Fourth For the Negro," in *The Life and Writings of Frederick Douglass*, 2:189, 201.

46. John Courtney Murray, S.J., "Address to the National Federation of Catholic College Students," 23 April 1948, *Murray Papers* 7/538, Georgetown University Library, Special Collections Division, Washington, DC.

47. Murray, "Law or Prepossessions?" (see n. 36 above), 29.

48. *Democracy in America*, 436.

49. Ibid., 292.

50. Recall Frankfurter's reference to "the laity," above. Moreover, secularists called secularism a religion long before religious conservatives began to do so. Horace M. Kallen, *Cultural Pluralism and the American Idea* (Philadelphia: University of Pennsylvania Press, 1956), 206–7, says pluralism applies only to those who share the same "apprehension of human nature and human relations . . . this is how the American Idea is, literally, religion."

51. Justice Robert Jackson in *Brown v. Allen* 344 U.S. 443 (1953) at 540.

52. "One is wrong in regarding the Catholic religion as a natural enemy of democracy. Rather, among the various Christian doctrines Catholicism seems one of those most

favorable to equality of conditions . . . . Protestantism in general orients men much less toward equality than toward independence" (*Democracy in America*, 288).

53. *Zorach v. Clauson* 343 U.S. 306 (1952).

54. Rawls, *Political Liberalism* (New York: Columbia University Press, 1993), 243, 253.

55. Ibid., 243–44, fn. 32.

56. Andrew R. Murphy; "Rawls and a Shrinking Liberty of Conscience," *Review of Politics* 60, no. 2 (Spring 1998): 269. He plausibly understands Rawls to hold that such views should be "eradicated" from the public sphere (268).

57. Ibid., 273.

58. E. A. Goerner's review of *Political Liberalism*, "Rawls's Apolitical Political Turn," *Review of Politics* 55, no. 4 (October 1993): 715. The Rawls quote is from *Political Liberalism*, 254. Murphy argues that, "despite his [Rawls's] claims, this [privileging political values appealing solely to public reason] would likely rule out the theologically-laced rhetoric of Lincoln's Second Inaugural" and even "much of King's eloquent Letter from [a] Birmingham Jail" ("Rawls and Shrinking Liberty," 268, emphasis in original).

59. Since only nonliberal comprehensive doctrines are excluded, Murphy goes too far in accusing Rawls of "in effect eradicating comprehensive doctrines from the public sphere" ("Rawls and Shrinking Liberty;" 268).

60. Robert Audi, "The Separation of Church and State and the Obligations of Citizenship," *Philosophy and Public Affairs* 18, no. 3 (1989): 279, 278. Kent Greenawalt also presents this view in *Religious Convictions and Political Choice* (New York: Oxford University Press, 1988), 216–17. "The government of a liberal society knows no religious truth and a crucial premise about a liberal society is that citizens . . . can build principles of political order and social justice that do not depend on particular religious beliefs." Michael J. Perry doubts that Greenawalt consistently maintains this view. See Perry, *Love and Power: The Role of Religion and Morality in American Politics* (New York: Oxford University Press, 1991), 22.

61. Paul J. Weithman, "The Separation of Church and State: Some Questions for Professor Audi," *Philosophy and Public Affairs* 20, no. 1 (1991): 58.

62. Michael J. Perry, *Morality, Politics and the Law: A Bicentennial Essay* (New York: Oxford University Press, 1988), 72–73. Emphasis in original.

63. Galston, *Liberal Purposes: Goods, Virtues, and Diversity in the Liberal State* (Cambridge: Cambridge University Press, 1991), esp. chap. 12. Harry Clor agrees, though on explicitly nontheological grounds. See his *Public Morality and Liberal Society: Essays on Decency, Law, and Pornography* (Notre Dame, IN: University of Notre Dame Press, 1996), chap. 4.

64. Justice Potter Stewart noted (in dissent) that secularism replaces the biblical morality as the basis of public life when he argued that banning Bible reading establishes "the religion of secularism" (*Abington v. Schempp* 374 U.S. 203, 313 [1963]). This secularism is now so taken for granted by the Court that Richard John Neuhaus could plausibly say that *Romer v. Evans* 116 S.Ct. 1620 (1996) placed "religiously based virtue or moral judgment . . . beyond the pale of public discourse." See "Religion and the Shifting Center

in American Politics," *The Long Term View* 3, no. 3 (Boston: The Massachusetts School of Law, 1996), 77. We think it more precise to say that Romer so excludes from the public sphere only nonliberal religiously based moral judgments.

65. Clor, *Public Morality and Liberal Society*, chap. 2, esp. 61–62. His argument in defense of traditional morality is wholly secular.

66. *Democracy in America*, 291.

67. *Evangelium Vitae*, chap. 1, #19.

68. "A Common Enemy, A Common Cause." Speech to an interfaith audience at Wilmington, Delaware, 3 May 1948. Printed in *First Things*, October 1992, p. 34 (emphasis added).

69. 1947 Congressional hearings on federal aid to parochial schools, quoted in Berton Dulce and Edward J. Richter, *Religion and the Presidency* (New York: Macmillan, 1962), 123.

70. Speech to the Society of Newspaper Editors, Washington, DC, April 21, 1960, quoted in ibid., 143.

71. *New York Times*, 8 September 1960, pp. 1, 25.

72. Quoted in Dulce and Richter, *Religion and the Presidency*, 142, 130.

73. Cuomo, speech at the University of Notre Dame, 13 September 1984, "The Confessions of a Public Man." Printed in full in *Notre Dame Magazine*, Autumn 1984, pp. 21–30, esp. 25. Excerpts appeared in *The Washington Post*, Friday, 14 September 1984, p. A6.

74. As we argued in the second section above, "The Transition from Civil Liberty to Civil Liberties."

75. Matthew 12:25, Mark 3:24–25, Luke 11:18, Revelation 16:19.

76. Cuomo, speech in *Notre Dame Magazine*, 24.

77. And even, incipiently, socially discriminated against. See Hadley Arkes's discussion of the potential employment consequences and legal vulnerabilities of *Romer* for those opposed to homosexual actions. Arkes, "A Culture Corrupted," in *The End of Democracy: The Judicial Usurpation of Politics?* (Dallas: Spence, 1997), 36–37.

78. "Pastoral Constitution on the Church in the Modern World," *Gaudium et Spes* (1965), sec. 75, in Flannery, *Vatican Council II*, 982–85.

79. *Centesimus Annus* (1991), #49.

80. Ibid., in #48, 20, 15, and 49. "Subsidiarity" was first adopted by Pius XI in *Quadragessimo Anno* (1931), #79.

81. *Centesimus Annus*, #48.

82. *Evangelium Vitae*, Introduction, #3. This emphasis on a broad-based corruption of popular and elite opinion on these life matters is a recurring theme. See chap. 1, #14 and #17.

83. Ibid., chap. 1, #18.

84. Ibid., chap. 1, #12.

85. Ibid., chap. 3, #70.

86. George Weigel suggests that the pope thinks culture is more important than politics "as an engine of historical change." "John Paul II and the Priority of Culture," *First Things*, February 1998, p. 19.

87. *Evangelium Vitae*, chap. 3, #71. Quoted from *Pacem in Terris* (1963), chap. 2, #61.

88. "Precisely in an age when inviolable rights of the person are solemnly proclaimed and the value of life publicly affirmed [i.e., by the Western democracies], the very right to life is being denied or trampled upon [by these Western democracies]" (*Evangelium Vitae*, chap. 1, #18).

89. In *Evangelium Vitae*, Introduction, #4, the pope distinguishes "[t]he basic principles of their Constitutions [i.e., of many countries] which protect the right to life," from modern legislation which makes legal some practices that are against life.

90. Ibid., chap. 1, #19.

91. Walter Berns correctly argues that the liberal American Constitution follows Locke on religious toleration and Adam Smith on the desirability of commerce and multiplicity of sects. And religious toleration "probably does depend on a way of life from which weakened belief follows as a consequence." That way of life, he says, is commerce. Berns, *Taking the Constitution Seriously* (Lanham, MD: Madison Books, 1987), 180, 173ff.

92. John Paul II takes note of "those who consider such relativism an essential condition of democracy, inasmuch as it alone is held to guarantee tolerance, mutual respect between people, and acceptance of decisions of the majority, whereas moral norms considered to be objective and binding are held to lead to authoritarianism and intolerance" (*Evangelium Vitae*, chap. 3, #70).

93. *Democracy in America*, 255–56.

CHAPTER 20

The Core of Freedom

Public or Private?

GLENN TINDER

> Glenn Tinder (1923–) is Professor Emeritus of Political Science at the University of Massachusetts at Boston. His many publications include The Political Meaning of Christianity *(2000), as well as a widely cited article in the* Atlantic Monthly, *"Can We Be Good Without God?" (1989).*

As a protest, the argument of Professors Glenn and Stack is valid and important. That the realm of public debate is largely closed to those who stand explicitly on Judaic and Christian principles is an intellectual scandal. This closure, of course, is the doing not of the courts (even though it accords with attitudes quite evident in the courts) but of academicians, journalists, and various political activists who are quick to rule any appeal to religious premises, as well as any moral judgments thought to derive therefrom, such as the evil of abortion, out of order. Their ostensible justification is that public discourse must be based on premises common to all participants. Such a justification may be superficially plausible, but it is worse than dubious. It enables opponents of religion to narrow their minds without compunction and to constrict the public realm. In effect, contemporary secularists say to would-be religious interlocutors, "Yours are arguments we refuse even to face or consider."

The result is a drastic impoverishment of the public realm. Not only are participants in political discourse deprived of insights which might be vital in the resolution of moral issues; public debate is closed to transcendental considerations, such as the sacredness of every person, on which the morale and justice of public life ultimately depend. Among discernible consequences today are the establishment of nearly unrestricted abortion rights and, seemingly, a growing willingness to permit euthanasia and even infanticide.

A polity closed in this manner is certainly unsafe for the faltering and the dying. Is it, however, unsafe for Catholics, or for Christians of any sort? This is not clear. I suggest that while Glenn and Stack have made a true and significant argument concerning public debate, care must be taken that their argument not thrust into the shadows important truths which, although not major objects of their polemic, might seem to fall before it as more or less incidental victims.

One such truth is that Christians do not have quite so incontestable a right of entry into every part of the public realm as they do into the part reserved for political discourse. Prayer and Bible-reading in public schools, and Christian symbols in public places, are rather different from religious argumentation in political debate. Granted, they entail no serious threat to basic liberties, and are not manifestly in conflict with the First Amendment. By their very nature, however, they rule out any right of reply. In this sense, they do contain a slight element of coercion. Those most vocal in attacking them may be petty, but still they have a point. How strenuously need Christians dispute their point? Can any Christian imbued with the spirit of Saint Paul think that the vitality of Christianity depends on prayer in public schools or on crèches in the public square during the Christmas season? While Christians may justifiably protest the exclusion of religiously grounded arguments from political discourse, they might on certain other matters reasonably defer to secular sensitivities.

The underlying question here is what Christians can properly ask of the polity. This question suggests a more important truth than the one just discussed. Does even participation in political discourse matter fundamentally to Christians? Their exclusion is harmful to the polity. Is it, however, harmful to Christians? Glenn and Stack argue that it is. But perhaps there is more of Pericles than of Paul, and more of Aristotle than of Augustine, in their argument. The classical attitude of Christians is that they cannot, while holding to their faith, be at home in the world. Describing his own state, and that of his followers, Paul wrote, "To the present hour we hunger and thirst, we are ill-clad and buffeted and homeless, and we labor, working with our own hands. . . . We have become, and are now, as the refuse of the world, the offscouring of all things" (1 Corinthians 4:11). They were far, to say the least, from being recognized participants in political discourse. But Paul did not suggest that their circumstances in any way threatened their Christian fidelity. Given the assumptions Christians have traditionally made about the fallenness of the world and the radical imperfection of the worldly city, the authors of "Is American Democracy Safe for Catholicism?" ask for a lot. I suggest that American democracy is about as safe for Catholicism, and all kinds of Christianity, as a polity ever is. And the reason for this is that, even though public freedom is abridged, private freedom is secure.

Finally, there is yet another truth we should not allow ourselves, in pursuit of other truths, to forget. This is individualism, along with the necessity of individual choice. Again and again, nowadays, Christians assail individualism. For example, they speak disparagingly, as do Glenn and Stack, of the idea that "human beings are primarily individuals rather than primarily parts of... families." But Jesus said explicitly that families would fall apart upon his coming. "Brother will deliver up brother to death, and the father his child, and children will rise against parents" (Matthew 10:21). Isn't this individualism of a kind? Individualism is implicit in the very notion that justification comes through faith, rather than through obedience to the law. Righteousness must arise from personal depths and be freely affirmed. This is a central tenet of Christian doctrine, not a peculiarly Protestant principle. According to the latest catechism of the Catholic Church, "Man has a right to act in conscience and in freedom so as personally to make moral decisions" (Paragraph 1782). The inescapability of these decisions sets individuals apart from one another; I cannot decide for you, or you for me. Clearly, individualism does not necessarily entail secularism. There is a Christian individualism, even though it presumably pertains only to our fallen state and not to the kingdom of God. Social and political theorists who close their eyes to this individualism cannot but go seriously astray.

What, then, can Christians ask of the polity? They can certainly ask, as do Glenn and Stack, for public freedom, the freedom to participate in political discourse. It is something less than this, however, that they are compelled to demand, namely private freedom, the freedom to worship as they choose. For Christians, the one absolute political evil—if there is such an evil—surely is totalitarianism, the one absolute good constitutionalism. The latter means freedom for the Church and for the individual Christian. It enables Christians to inquire into and practice their faith, and to do this, if need be, in the cloister of individual solitude, in the conscience which, according to the Catholic catechism, quoting *Gaudium et spes* (Paragraph 1795), is man's "secret core" and "sanctuary," where he is "alone with God, whose voice echoes in his depths."

NOTE

Reprinted from *The Review of Politics* 62, no. 1 (Winter 2000): 36–38.

CHAPTER 21

Robust Tension over Safety

Clarke E. Cochran

Clarke E. Cochran (1945–) is Professor of Political Science and Adjunct Professor, Department of Health Organization Management at Texas Tech University. He received his Ph.D. from Duke University in 1971. Professor Cochran's primary fields of teaching and research are religion and politics, political philosophy, and health care policy. He is the author of Catholics, Politics, and Public Policy; Beyond Left and Right *(2003);* Religion in Public and Private Life *(1990); numerous articles and book chapters; and a co-author of* American Public Policy: An Introduction *(2012).*

Gary D. Glenn and John Stack advance two important claims; one explicit, the other implicit. Their *explicit* claim is that the "new regime of civil liberties" is dangerous to Catholicism. Here I am in qualified agreement, though important ambiguities cloud the argument. Their *implicit* claim is that it is a bad thing for Catholicism to be in danger. This proposition is flawed. Glenn and Stack cite (without irony) American Catholics "who have spent several generations seeking to become accepted and acceptable to the American democratic culture." A large part of the danger seems to be "the punishment of exclusion from respectability in the culture." This assumes that the "normal" mode for Catholicism is comfortable accommodation to political culture and institutions.

Glenn and Stack contend that American democracy has changed from a regime of "civil liberty" to one of "civil liberties," a regime dangerous for Catholicism. Their evidence is strong on the troubled relations between the Catholic Church and democracy in American history and on the considerable changes wrought by the modern civil liberties regime that insists on a sharp distinction between public life and private belief. Such a regime is indeed inimical to Catholic faith's insistence on inseparability.

Yet Glenn and Stack picture a sharp break between old and new liberalism. Their story is of a breach of faith, a falling away from a satisfactory old dispensation. Is this narrative, however, faithful to the old and lively debate among political theorists about the nature of liberalism? Might it not be that the new regime represents the working out of a logic implicit in early liberalism? Indeed, Glenn and Stack acknowledge this possibility in passing references to the "conflict between classical liberalism and revealed religion as such" and to Walter Berns's claim about tolerance and weakened belief (see their note 91). Yet their tale of fall from grace would look different if liberalism's roots in autonomous individualism were central to the plot. For example, the distinction between public life and private belief runs throughout liberalism. The old and new regimes merely draw it in different locations, just as American liberals and conservatives both accept the distinction, but make different uses of it.[1]

Moreover, although the claim that Catholicism and the new regime are incompatible might be accepted, an ambiguity in "Catholicism" bedevils the argument. What is "Catholicism?" Except for a brief reference to "liberal Catholicism" (safe in the new regime), Glenn and Stack refer only to Catholic politicians and to Catholicism in general. Given the size, diversity, and internal tensions within the Catholic Church in the United States, what is "Catholicism" sans adjective, and precisely how does the new regime threaten it? The term's abstraction obscures important distinctions among liberal Catholics, conservative Catholics, neoliberal and neoconservative Catholics, Catholic Worker Catholics, and many other flavors, including ordinary apolitical Catholics for whom these terms are merely confusing. The new regime differently affects different groups.

Catholicism could refer to the institutions of the Catholic Church. Yet the obvious internal tensions within these institutions do not stem solely or mainly from the new liberal regime. Despite important questions of identity, Catholic higher education and Catholic healthcare, for example, have flourished in recent decades.[2] "Catholicism" also could refer to Catholic social teaching, which is certainly at odds with the new regime. But the church's teachings were at odds with a good deal of the old regime as well. I do not doubt that there is difficult and dangerous terrain along the liberalism-Catholicism border, but I would urge Glenn and Stack to devise a more fine-grained description.

Even more problematic is the implicit claim that it is bad for Catholicism to be in danger. The deep assumption is that the normative position of Catholicism is acceptability and respectability. But this is a deeply problematic affirmation.[3] Glenn and Stack fear that the new regime of civil liberties is irresistibly seductive to Catholic politicians and to Catholicism itself, posing a danger to their salvation. But the old regime was equally seductive. If the new regime is to be dated from the late 1940s (or perhaps from the full flowering of civil liberties theorists such as John Rawls in the 1970s), then by their own account American Catholics sought acceptability and respectability in an old regime whose rituals of civil, public religion sanctified an economic order at odds with Catholic social teaching and legitimated structures of segregation, discrimination, and injustice all-too-tempting to many Catholics. Indeed, one might argue that the new regime, by placing itself so starkly in opposition to Catholic teaching on abortion, sexual ethics, and the family is less seductive than the old. The attentive Catholic cannot avoid knowing where she stands.

Despite the allegiance of most Catholics to the Democratic Party from the 1930s to the 1970s, the American two-party system and constitutional order never furnished a congenial venue for Catholics seriously committed to their obligations both as democratic citizens (obligations referenced in Glenn and Stark's citation of Pope John Paul II) and as believers faithful to the entirety of Catholic social teaching. The authors rightly criticize Mario Cuomo's accommodation on abortion. But can serious Catholics be fully at home in the Republican party or the nascent neopopulist Reform Party? Similarly, no ideological movement competing for allegiance—varieties of liberalism and conservatism, feminism, libertarianism, liberation ideologies, populism—tracks its roots to Catholic teaching. Each has its affinities and its divergences from the Catholic tradition.

The tension between the heavenly and the earthly cities is an old Christian story. The dangers inherent in their relation carry a salutary reminder to keep the Catholic pilgrim on his toes. Catholic politicians and Catholic citizens owe only a limited allegiance to party or nation. But loyalty and even active political life are possible. In a liberal democratic regime, Catholics who toil in the messy fields of political life must learn the distinction between moral compromise (a real and seductive danger pointed to by Glenn and Stack) and prudent, political compromise (an alternative they do not describe).[4] The former denies the applicability of moral principles; the latter keeps them in view while extracting what moral goods recalcitrant social and cultural matter yield to honest political labor. Is American democracy safe for Catholicism? No, but a safe democratic regime implies domesticated Catholicism. Robust tension is a better alternative.

Notes

Reprinted from *The Review of Politics* 62, no. 1 (Winter 2000): 39–42.

1. Clarke E. Cochran, *Religion in Public and Private Life* (New York: Routledge, 1990).
2. Clarke E. Cochran, "Institutional Identity; Sacramental Potential: Catholic Healthcare at Century's End," *Christian Bioethics* 5, no. 1 (1999): 26–43.
3. I should not want my argument to be misunderstood. My account applies only to the dangers implicit in any legitimate regime. I do not recommend the altogether different and deadly perils to Catholics in, for example, Sudan or East Timor.
4. John Paul II alludes to this distinction in *Evangelium Vitae*, #90.

CHAPTER 22

Democracy Unsafe, Compared to What?

The Totalitarian Impulse of Contemporary Liberals

MICHAEL NOVAK

I am sympathetic to the problem enunciated by Professors Glenn and Stack, viz., "that contemporary American democracy, by constitutionally privileging secularism, offers Catholics in public life a strong inducement to abandon, relativize, or remain silent about, their moral beliefs, insofar as these conflict with secularism. Catholics have to act like, not necessarily be, secularists. That makes it spiritually and politically unsafe, not to say impossible, for Catholics to be democrats now." However, while they have circled in on an important problem—the totalitarian impulse of contemporary liberals—they have not hit the bull's-eye exactly.

Let me begin by citing George Washington, a most reflective and deliberative man, on the prospects for the success of the American experiment in liberty:

> I would not be understood to speak of consequences which may be produced, in the revolution of the ages, by corruption of morals, profligacy of manners, and listlessness of the preservation of the natural and unalienable rights of mankind; nor of the successful usurpations that may be established at such a juncture upon the ruins of liberty, however providently guarded and secured, as these are contingencies against which no human prudence can effectually provide.[1]

Our Founders expressed strikingly similar fears about the natural moral entropy in human affairs. After brief periods of high morals and high morale, succeeding generations slip into decline, carelessness, corruption, and the ineradicable itch to tyrannize over others. As a precaution, though, we need to recall that *O tempora! O mores!* is a refrain that never goes out of date.

Second, it may be that the current American democratic regime is not safe for the souls of Catholics. Was there ever a regime that was? Thomas à Becket did not find it, nor Thomas More. Alexis de Tocqueville did not find it in the Terror of the French Revolution. The family of Thomas Aquinas was riven by conflicting choices between Frederick II and papal armies, and death threatened on both sides. In arguing that it is "impossible" for Catholics to be democrats now, one must ask, "compared to when?"

Third, the world, the flesh, and the devil—a slightly antique description of the essence of secularism—are in every age and under every form of government a menace to the souls of humans. They constantly offer humans, heroic and non-heroic, "inducement to abandon, relativize, or remain silent about, their moral beliefs." Moreover, they offer quite compelling practical reasons that to the unwary have a high patina of moral plausibility. The most secular of liberals also face, and often succumb, to these moral dangers. Those who observe politics closely are certain to have noticed moral backsliding among liberals. The danger is not only to Catholics.

Fourth, Professors Glenn and Stack shrewdly choose two prominent liberal Catholics, John F. Kennedy and Mario Cuomo, to make their case; but if they had chosen two other prominent exemplars, one liberal and one conservative, Eugene McCarthy and Henry Hyde, for instance, their case would have sagged a little. Eugene McCarthy always resented seeing John Kennedy (whom he knew well in the Senate) publicly described as a Catholic. In the relevant sense, he didn't think Kennedy knew enough to be a Catholic, one way or the other. He thought Kennedy's mind, at a level commensurate with his education, was almost innocent of Catholic culture. In other words, it was not the American regime, it was Kennedy's personal formation that made his a thoroughly secular mind. Under the same regime, Eugene McCarthy developed a well-furnished Catholic mind, perhaps because he was raised in the great Midwest where Catholics grew up with no inferiority complex, where there was no earlier entrenched establishment to look down on them. For McCarthy, being a Catholic was a matter of intellect and personal witness, not an ascription like being a Bostonian; it required intellectual exercise.

As a close observer of the Washington scene, similarly, I have never seen Henry Hyde flinch from acting according to his Catholic beliefs—with humor, with grace—and across party lines he is perhaps the single most respected member of the House. By his learning, his humility, his constancy, his outspokenness, and his good manners he honors all the rest of us who are Catholic. He demonstrates integrity and courage in an easy, low-key way that seems almost effortless (but, in fact, is not). To be sure, he is the object of rhetorically ugly and violent attacks, some private, some public, and not a few scary threats have been made. But other people in public life, not only in politics, can report the same.

The situation of the Catholic in political life looks different if one looks away from Kennedy and Cuomo. Even Cuomo, I am certain, would resent being lumped in as a Catholic in the same mental frame as Kennedy; like McCarthy, Cuomo has worked at his faith at a level of cultivated intellect that Kennedy never reached. I offer this hypothesis, however: It is somewhat easier for a person of more conservative leanings to resist the secular zeitgeist than it is for a liberal. The very act of being conservative is already politically incorrect, already a dissenting position. "Right-wing extremists" multiply in the press; there are no recorded instances of "left-wing extremists." There are no enemies on the left. In other words, a conservative begins public life being subjected to scorn in the media. So why not be a Catholic, too? It is not so hard as Glenn and Stack suppose to become used to name-calling and double standards. Many have done so.

Glenn and Stack, finally, leave out of their analysis the growing disdain for the liberal elite throughout the country. What has that elite done in the last thirty years that is worthy of respect? Which of the reforms they championed have worked out as promised? Not everyone, quietly watching their behavior, finds liberals tolerant of opinions on the right. They who in their youth lionized scruffy picketers who picketed for peace now put in jail those who picket for life. They who scream "choice" in defense of their own current passions ban smokers at the next table. They who descend from defenders of conscience object to any public expression of conscience not conformed to secularism. Liberals act like petty tyrants, while admiring themselves for being the most tolerant of humans. This elite is standing on a very thin crust above a very deep pit of public contempt.

In brief, Glenn and Stack attribute to our "regime" (an inappropriate name for humankind's greatest experiment in self-government) the accident of its having been in the hands of a secular liberal elite for the last two generations (following World War II). It is true, of course, that both the Depression and World War II had the effect of enormously strengthening the staffing and regulatory powers of the central state. They also summoned forth a new research elite, both to develop new technologies and to organize group activities on a scale never seen before in history. By this state-supported gate, the new liberal elite took national power. They achieved much good, and amassed unrivaled moral esteem. But that era is now passing. Too long a monopoly at the cultural heights has been thoroughly corrupting. Thus, it is the decaying liberal culture that led to the change of attitudes and rules that now afflict us, not the "regime" bequeathed to us by our Founders. Altering that culture is an intellectual and a political problem of the first order; but it is no cause for despair.

I believe, with George Washington, John Adams, and many others of the Founders, that Providence intended the destiny of liberty among other peoples to depend on the destiny of the American experiment. As a Catholic, I believe that the reason God created the universe in the first place is so that somewhere within it there would be as least one creature, the human being, able to respond to His creation with intelligence and love, in liberty. This faith gave our Founders confidence that, though their prospects against the mightiest army in the world seemed bleak, they were bound to prevail. If it is true that Providence intends the American experiment to succeed (although, of course, humans must live up to their end of the covenant), it is far too early for us today, after so many blessings, to give up on it.

Some, most recently certain Straussians, interpret the Founding as a thoroughly Lockean/Hobbesian experiment, and that approach does lead to gloom. Of themselves, Lockean/Hobbesian principles destroy Christianity and Judaism by strangling them in private straitjackets. But without religion as an additional energy for rebirth and renewal, the Founders (even Jefferson) taught that for most people the probability of maintaining over time the morals necessary for self-government is exceedingly low. Reading the Founders (aside from Jefferson) makes it impossible to believe that they were merely Lockean; even more, they were classically republican. Their "natural theology" was that of the Bible; their "Governor of the universe" was simultaneously Creator, Endower of inalienable rights, Judge, and Providence.

To put this sharply: I don't believe the Founders read Locke for his metaphysics, which are thin and shabby, and which was not their pressing need, but for his robust political practicality. The great preachers of the day, even the most orthodox preachers, found it useful to put this practicality to work with their deeper biblical commitments. They used both Locke (and Sidney and Cicero "and other books of natural liberty") and the Bible to mutual advantage. See, for instance, the Sermons on public occasions of Samuel Cooper at Harvard and John Witherspoon at Princeton.

The American experiment is of immense importance to the future of the Catholic peoples of the world, and Catholics in America have a great vocation yet to fulfill in articulating it, defending it, and restoring it to its proper biblical dimensions. The reigning liberal elite may be secularist and shallow, "religiophobic" and intolerant. But it is already in its last patriotic chapter.

Don't give up the ship, not now.

Notes

Reprinted from *The Review of Politics* 62, no. 1 (Winter 2000): 31–35.

1. Letter to Lafayette, 7 February 1788, quoted in Matthew Spalding, "Making Citizens: George Washington and the Founding of the American Character," in *Patriot Sage*, ed. Gary L. Gregg II, and Matthew Spalding (Wilmington, DE: ISI Books, 1999).

CHAPTER 23

Response to Our Critics

GARY D. GLENN AND JOHN STACK

We are grateful that the editors secured three thoughtful though critical responses to our essay. Such responses perform a service by calling to our attention matters we have insufficiently considered, pushing us to greater clarity, and perhaps revealing to us errors that we have overlooked.

Clarke E. Cochran, Michael Novak, and Glenn Tinder disagree with us about whether the danger to the souls of Catholics in contemporary American democracy is noteworthy. They rightly think there has always been, and will always be, some such danger in any regime. Cochran says we assume "that the 'normal' mode for Catholicism is comfortable accommodation to political culture and institutions." Novak asks us "Democracy Unsafe, Compared to What?" Tinder goes so far as to say that contemporary "American democracy is about as safe for Catholicism, and all kinds of Christianity, as a polity ever is." We would seem to be naively unaware that "the tension between the heavenly and the earthly cities is an old Christian story" (Cochran). We agree with Tinder's reminder that Christians "cannot, while holding to their faith, be at home in the world."

Though no regime has ever provided a completely safe haven for Catholics, and it would be utopian to expect that any regime ever will, some regimes are more dangerous for Catholics than others. The dangers to which secularism exposes the souls of Catholics are noteworthy partly because they are of a new and more subtle kind. The new "civil liberties" regime tempts Catholics to omit to mention or to subsume those parts of their moral convictions that are the objects of contempt by their secular fellow citizens. This is especially the case with Catholic public officials. If Governor Cuomo would say that the abortion he thinks necessary to accommodate as public policy is morally wrong for everyone, not just wrong for "me and Matilda," he would arguably be tolerating an evil he lacks the power to overcome rather than appearing to endanger his soul or risk scandalizing other Catholics by relativizing his Catholic ethics.

Novak objects that we selectively point out, as evidence for our position, the Cuomos and Kennedys while ignoring better witnesses to their faith, such as Henry Hyde. That some Catholics are willing to suffer secular obloquy for acting publicly on the basis of their faith shows only that some do not succumb to the temptations. Novak seems to grant that Hyde's example does not suggest there are no dangers, but he thinks this example weakens our argument, which he takes to be that the regime *causes* the Kennedy-Cuomo syndrome. He says that "it was not the American regime, it was Kennedy's personal formation that made his a thoroughly secular mind." But we never claimed that the new secular regime "made" Kennedy's outlook secular. We argued only that it offered strong inducements and pressures to adopt that outlook. It allows Catholics to practice their religion in private. In return, it discourages Catholics from trying to influence public policy when their religiously grounded ethics conflict with policies grounded on secularism. If Catholics willingly accept this bargain, one of two dangers follows. Either they implicitly withdraw their public claim that their ideas of good apply to all, not only to Catholics; or else they suffer a cognitive dissonance between what they believe as Catholics and what they believe as citizens of the new secular American democracy.

These are, we think, partly different dangers from any Catholic Americans have hitherto had to confront. Under the old regime, Catholics may have been socially and culturally outsiders but that regime permitted them to act publicly on the basis of Catholic ideas of good. This is precisely what the new secular regime would deny to them. Novak sees this: "they who descend from defenders of conscience [anti-Vietnam War picketers] object to any public expression of conscience not conformed to secularism." He recognizes the danger but, since there are always dangers, he seems not to think it particularly noteworthy. This is similar to a point Tinder makes and to which we respond next.

Tinder thinks it is enough for Christians if "civil liberties" secularism allows them to believe and worship in private. After all, says he, "even though public freedom is abridged, private freedom is secure." He is right that there could be worse dangers than those present in the new regime. Still, it is worth remembering that the old regime substantially protected both freedoms and also permitted Catholics to influence policy whether or not it comported with secularism. It is now in varying ways impermissible in America (objectionable in elite opinion, contrary to mainstream liberal theorists, and socially unacceptable)[1] to influence public policy on the basis of revealed truth that crosses secularism. If Catholics today may not argue in the public square that consenting to physician-assisted suicide violates the dignity of the person created in the image and likeness of God, then what stands between them and a regime that legalizes such suicide? And once legalized, does not the experience of the Netherlands suggest that it is soon done to people without their consent? It is already, in the one American state that has legalized it, on the way to becoming publicly encouraged by government financial support for the suicide drugs and rationing of funds for continued care.

"First they came for those who wished to die before their God appointed time, and I was not permitted to publicly oppose them, so I said nothing. Then they came for those whose heirs wished them to die before God's time, and my heirs did not wish me to die prematurely, so I remained silent. Then they came for those who it was financially burdensome for the public to keep alive, and I was not such a burden, so I said nothing. Then they came for me," to paraphrase Pastor Martin Niemöller's famous saying. We think this danger is noteworthy and that it endangers our souls to live in such a regime even if, as Tinder argues, private freedom is secure. Is not mankind a Christian's business, as the repentant ghost of Jacob Marley said to Scrooge? If so, then when does our noting these dangers stem from siding, as Tinder suggests, with Pericles and Aristotle against Saints Paul and Augustine?

Strikingly, in this regard, both Tinder and Novak find it instructive to speak in their responses of "totalitarianism" (a term we nowhere use). Novak speaks of "the totalitarian impulse of contemporary liberals" while Tinder says if there is "one absolute political evil," it "is totalitarianism." If the danger to which we call attention reminds two such thoughtful critics of such a danger, does that not partially answer Novak's question "Unsafe Compared To What?" Catholic Americans are safer in the new "civil liberties" regime than they would be in a totalitarian regime but their souls are more at risk in the new regime than they were in the old civil liberty regime, which merely permitted discrimination against Catholics in localities where they were a minority. Protestant dominated public schools were in some ways inhospitable to the Catholic *faith*; but they encouraged the *morality* of Catholic children. Moreover, neither the Court nor mainstream American democratic thinkers then suggested that Catholics had no right to try to influence public policy from a Catholic perspective.

Cochran agrees that the new secular regime is dangerous to Catholicism. But he thinks our assumption that it is bad for Catholicism to be in danger is "flawed" because "a safe democratic regime implies domesticated Catholicism." While he "does not recommend the altogether different and deadly perils to Catholics in, for example, Sudan or East Timor," where Catholics are slaughtered, he seems to think any danger short of that is "salutary" because it "keep[s] the Catholic pilgrim on his toes." Frankly, we thought Catholics had plenty to keep them on their toes under the old civil liberty regime. As we stated in our essay, "the souls of Catholics were never fully safe within the constitutional order established in 1789" because that regime dealt with the problem of religious liberty by undermining "the conviction that any particular religion is true." Also, in the early days under the Constitution, some state constitutions prohibited Catholics from holding public office, though such prohibitions disappeared by the early nineteenth century.

Catholic citizens need to be aware of and try to understand the nature of the dangers they confront in the new secular "civil liberties" regime because they are somewhat different from those Catholics faced in the old civil liberty regime. Cochran says we assume Catholicism should seek "acceptability and respectability" in the new regime. Not so. We assume rather that Catholics should be aware *that* and *why* they cannot be fully acceptable and respectable in this new regime. Catholics ought to reflect upon the extent to which the constitutional, political, and intellectual marginalization of part of their Catholic vision of society presents new dangers to their souls, as well as to their freedom. It would behoove them to know what, if anything, can be done, consistent with Catholicism, to reduce those dangers. They need to consider whether to expect their situation to be that which Tocqueville describes, in which those who oppose the current democratic regime will be "as a stranger among" their fellow citizens. If that is to befall Catholics, it would help them to know why it is happening. This would help to prepare them to learn how to deal publicly with the new situation of living among a once religious people whose public life, at least, is now secular.

Novak agrees that there is an important difference between America's old civil liberty regime and the new secular "civil liberties" regime. He further agrees that in important respects, the new regime departs from the Founders' Constitution. The new regime follows "Lockean/Hobbesian principles," which Novak rightly says "destroy Christianity and Judaism by strangling them in private straightjackets." He regards the Founders as "classically republican." Hence, he concludes it is an "accident" that our regime has "been in the hands of a secular liberal elite" since World War II.

In contrast, Cochran suggests that "the new regime represents the working out of a logic implicit in [the 'autonomous individualism' of] early liberalism." This suggestion is correct in itself but misdirected here. Civil liberties secularism does not inevitably follow from the Founders' Constitution because that Constitution, while informed by that liberalism and thus at least open to secularism, also permitted state governments to foster religion. The new secular regime works to abolish this state function by absorbing the originally nonsecular state governments into the intensified national regime the Court begins to create in the 1940s (what constitutional specialists refer to as the "incorporation" of the Bill of Rights). The Court simultaneously, and for the first time, groundlessly declares this more nationalized constitutional order to be *simply* secular. This is the meaning, for the whole constitutional, social, and cultural order (which is what we mean by "regime"),[2] of the way in which the Court applied the religion clauses of the First Amendment to the states. In *Everson*, the Court established secularism by mandating government neutrality between religion and nonreligion, thereby rejecting the religion fostering function of the states.

The Founders established a constitutional order in which, however secular the national government, the regime (which includes the state governments) was not simply secular. We think the Founders' Constitution instantiates a tension between a secular and a religious public life. That tension was destroyed when secularism became constitutionally privileged. If Novak means the domination of secularism since World War II is an "accident" in the sense that it was not inevitable, we would agree. But if he means that there is no basis for secularism in the Constitution, we would argue that goes too far. Secularism is one side of the foregoing Constitutional tension. We agree with Cochran's assertion that "robust tension" between the earthly and the heavenly city is better than "domesticated Catholicism." But the new regime would destroy the possibility of any tension at all by refusing even to consider distinctly Catholic arguments.

Notes

Reprinted from *The Review of Politics* 62, no. 1 (Winter 2000): 43–48.

1. "Of all the traditional religious stances, it is probably Roman Catholicism that has the hardest time at Harvard Divinity School. Anti-Catholicism is still the anti-

Semitism of the intellectuals. Certain positions that Catholicism regards as crucial to its vision of the just society cannot be easily advocated in the Divinity School. You try to take a pro-life position there, boy, you're dead. A Catholic has to be either dissident or silent on issues like these—or astonishingly courageous." Jon D. Levenson, Albert A. List Professor of Jewish Studies at Harvard Divinity School. *Harvard Magazine*, September–October 1999, p. 61.

2. Novak asserts parenthetically that "regime" is "an inappropriate name for humankind's greatest experiment in self-government." We use the term regime (*politeia*) nonpejoratively, as did Plato and Aristotle.

Chapter 24

Beyond the Nations

The Expansion of the Common Good in Catholic Social Thought

WILLIAM A. BARBIERI, JR.

William A. Barbieri, Jr. (1965–) teaches in the Religion and Culture and Moral Theology/Ethics programs in the School of Theology and Religious Studies and directs the Peace and Justice Studies Program at the Catholic University of America. He received his doctorate from Yale University in Religious Studies in 1992 and has held fellowships at Georgetown University and Humboldt University. A scholar of human rights, comparative ethics, peace studies, Catholic social teaching, and German studies, he is the author of Ethics of Citizenship: Immigration and Group Rights in Germany *(1998) and editor of* At the Limits of the Secular: Reflections on Faith and Public Life *(2014).*

THE BOUNDS OF THE COMMON GOOD

When one speaks of the common good, it always makes sense to inquire: The common good of whom? How the common good is demarcated is a matter of no small moment for any claims that are made in its name. For these claims stumble as soon as it becomes clear that the good referred to is in fact shared by only some members of the assumed collectivity and not the rest; and they likewise falter if they are revealed to rest on an inappropriate delimitation of the collectivity at the expense of others who, for the purposes at hand, should rightfully be included. To illustrate this one need only imagine, say, a federal toxic waste disposal policy that, while purporting to serve "the public good," distributes the risks involved in a manner that either ignores the health concerns of certain underprivileged internal minorities, or transfers the costs to foreign populations by exploiting their economic need. In either case, one may well be prompted to protest the exclusion of those most affected from the calculus of communal concerns. To do so—to raise the question of criteria for equal inclusion in the political community—is, more often than not, to challenge the very institutions of borders and citizenship that define the contemporary nation-state system.[1]

A hallmark of the political boundaries and distinctions that divide and order the world's people is, as Benedict Anderson for one has noted, their normative poverty.[2] The question of criteria for boundaries and gradations of membership is one that has in recent years begun to establish itself, somewhat belatedly, as a foundational concern in political theory.[3] Only in the wake of a growing awareness of the ways in which human agency subtly and not so subtly shapes what were previously taken to be given, more or less "natural" political institutions and categories have political thinkers begun to focus in a disciplined manner on the normative questions posed by boundaries.[4] At the same time, much of the history of modern states may be seen as a march toward greater equality for previously subordinated groups in various societies.[5] In many cases, these processes have taken the shape not of the promulgation of new principles applying to new classes of people, but rather of the extension of established principles to groups who, it came to be recognized, were improperly excluded in the first place.

The conception of the common good advanced in Catholic social teaching has been immune to neither the logic nor the social dynamic of inclusion. It is thus no surprise that the common good has experienced a steady broadening of its field of reference over the past several decades. In this regard it has kept pace with other comparable movements in what might be called the discursive construction of moral community: the creation of an international human rights regime,[6] the discussion of an emerging global civil society,[7] and, perhaps most significantly, the promotion of a "global ethic"[8] linked with a "Universal Declaration of Human Responsibilities."[9] From a prior orientation assuming the primacy of the nation-state, church teachings have shifted more and more toward envisioning the common good as international or global in scope. This burgeoning perspective has its roots, on the one hand, in egalitarian commitments and universalist strains that lie at the wellsprings of the Christian tradition. On the other hand its emergence has been occasioned by specific contemporary developments that have consolidated the material basis for speaking of the existence of a global community.

The broadening of the common good beyond the nation is, in short, a development whose time has come. What it means to speak of the common good in a supranational setting is, however, by no means clear, and thus far the notion has received little critical attention. Upon examination, the global common good quickly reveals itself to be a complex affair attended by problems both theoretical and practical. The aims of this article are, first, to trace the expansion of the common good in Catholic political theory; second, to explore some of the difficulties—and potential solutions—attending this process; and finally, to indicate some directions in which constructive reflection on the common good might fruitfully proceed. It is my belief that in the project of articulating a viable theory of the common good, Catholic social thought stands to gain much from its engagement with contemporary political theory. For this reason I attend throughout to the contributions of political theorists on the problem of the common good. In the end, it seems to me, the profit may be mutual.

The Political Common Good in Catholic Social Thought

As a political concept, the common good is by no means the exclusive preserve of the Aristotelian and Thomistic tradition that originally fostered it and that continues to form the horizon of Catholic social thought.[10] There are modern thematizations of the term—or of related phrases such as the general welfare, the common interest, the public good, and the common weal—in the liberal tradition, ranging from Locke's individualist formulation to T. H. Green's social conception;[11] in the utilitarian thought of Bentham and his heirs;[12] in Hegelian and Marxian thought;[13] and in non-Western traditions as well.[14] Understood, though, as (1) social, in the sense of being a value distinct from and not reducible to the good(s) of individuals, and (2) structural or institutional in character, the common good has received, in the last century, its richest development in Catholic social thought: in the various social encyclicals and other church documents, and no less in the contributions of Catholic theorists such as Jacques Maritain, Yves Simon, and John Courtney Murray.

While the Catholic conception of the political common good has by no means been strictly unitary,[15] the characteristic functioning of Catholic tradition ensures that certain generalizations can still be made about it. The notion marks off, to begin with, a sphere of meaning distinguished, in one direction, from the idea of private good, and in another from that of a higher, spiritual dimension of the common good rooted in God. The political common good functions, further, as the linchpin in the complex of interrelated principles—such as solidarity, subsidiarity, and the option for the poor—that constitutes the framework of the Catholic social discourse,[16] and its content is to a certain extent bound up with these other concepts.[17] In this theoretical context, the common good signals a commitment to certain crucial premises: that human beings are, in essence, social or political animals; that there are constraints on the conditions for human flourishing that are in some sense "natural"; and that these must be of vital concern in a community's adoption and maintenance of political structures. Strictly speaking, the common good is usually employed in two distinct, if related, senses: on the one hand, it refers to the *telos* of a given community—that goal or end-state toward which it aspires—while on the other hand it serves as a *criterion* for evaluating various courses of action considered in the here and now.[18] To speak of the global common good can hence mean to refer either to shared goals for all of humankind or to normative standards bearing on questions of global import. In its development over the last fifty years, and especially in the decades since Vatican II, Catholic political thought has come increasingly to incorporate both of these senses.

Mid-Century Catholic Thought

A notion of the common good as embracing all of humanity is hardly alien to a tradition of Christian political thought which, after all, has been nourished by the Stoic cosmopolitanism at the wellsprings of the natural law tradition. Thus one may note that Aquinas extended the notion of the *communitas perfecta*—and by implication the political common good—to the entire human family,[19] or point to the manner in which the natural law lawyers Vitoria and Suárez upheld the claim of all the varied peoples of the world to political status in the family of nations.[20] These strands of the tradition have, however, for the most part confined discussion of a global common good to a theoretical, highly speculative context. Only in this century, and particularly in the watershed years following World War II, did Catholic theorists begin tentatively to address in concrete terms what it might mean to apply the concept of the common good supranationally. In doing so, they at the same time reflected and helped shape the milieu in which official Catholic teaching about the common good has been articulated and interpreted.

A seminal figure in this process was Jacques Maritain, whose philosophy of personalism and conception of human rights have deeply conditioned contemporary readings of the common good tradition. In addressing the idea of a common good conceived in supranational terms, Maritain, following the trajectory of his basic distinction between individual and personal, temporal and spiritual, devoted his attention first of all to the universal society of the church. This did not, however, lead him to rule out the idea of global political community:

> [T]he development of the human person normally requires a plurality of autonomous communities which have their own rights, liberties and authority; among these communities there are some of a rank inferior to the political state.... Other communities are of a rank superior to the State, as is above all the Church in the mind of Christians, and as would also be, in the temporal realm, that organized international community towards which we aspire today.[21]

Strongly critical of both the idolatrous notion of national sovereignty and the various totalitarianisms to which it gave rise, Maritain spiritedly endorsed the idea of world government, pronouncing it "the perfect society required by our historical age."[22] He was at pains to emphasize, however, that what the times called for was not a theory of a world state, but rather a "full political theory of world organization" that took as its purview the entire global community and recognized the distinctiveness and relative autonomy of different levels of human organization.[23] A world state could not simply be created by force or even by democratic decision, he held, but could arise only from a deep-rooted process of "change in structures of morality and sociality" culminating in a pluralistic global polity united by civic friendship and possessed of a unified common good.[24] It was thus at best a long-term proposition, to be approached with circumspection and care.

This cautious assessment was largely shared by Oswald von Nell-Breuning, the German Jesuit so influential in the formulation and interpretation of papal teaching from *Quadragesimo Anno* on. An heir to the "solidarism" of Heinrich Pesch, Nell-Breuning sought in his work to mediate between communalist interpretations of the common good, such as that of Eberhard Welty, and more personalist perspectives, such as that of Gustav Gundlach.[25] The common good, he emphasized, is not contingent upon the imperatives of a community, but rather the other way around: communities are constituted through their sharing of a common good.²⁶ This relation provided the basis for his verdict regarding an international common good: "A collective human common good can exist only if all of humanity constitutes a social unity not only in theory, but in fact; which is today, if only in very incomplete measure, the case."²⁷

Among leading European systematicians of the common good nuances in this guarded perspective emerged, if in different ways. For the Austrian theorist of natural law, Johannes Messner, for example, the "community of nations" (*Völkergemeinschaft*), as a group rooted in the order of nature, possessed, along with other such groups—family, local community, profession, state, and subnational and regional political organization—as well as voluntary associations of various sorts, both a common good and a "relative autonomy" of its own.²⁸ Because, however, Messner's interpretation of society emphasized the centrality of the person and hence the ordering of social groupings to a help-function,²⁹ the principle of the common good (*Gemeinwohlprinzip*) became in his theory largely reducible to the principle of subsidiarity, understood, moreover, in a relatively restrictive way. This scaled-down model brought Messner to view the prospect of world government skeptically, and to link the supranational common good instead to a society of nations in which the autonomy of individual states, rooted in their "natural" ethnic, geological, historical and "spiritual" conditions, was firmly maintained.³⁰ A somewhat contrasting account was provided by the Swiss Dominican Arthur Utz, who, inspired by a theology of the mystical body,³¹ sought to articulate a social conception of the common good that corrected the tendency of personalist theories to envision the person (as opposed to the individual) as somehow transcending all forms of community. In his theory, a supranational conception of the common good embracing the entire species was portrayed as a historical inevitability, readily demonstrable metaphysically, even if only faintly to be discerned in practice, for example in such developments as the European Community.³²

An American perspective on the question was provided by John Courtney Murray. Murray, so influential in the development of official teaching on church-state relations, religious freedom, and pluralism, gave prominence in his writings to the distinctions between politics and religion, between state and society, and, accordingly, between public order and the broader category of the common good.³³ In this work his frame of reference remained for the most part the nation-state; for him, not global interdependence, but rather the disorder of the international scene was the "fact of the century."³⁴ Still, he recognized that a notion such as the national interest "today stands with historical clarity (as it always stood with theoretical clarity)" subordinate to the political ends of the international community.[35] In the task of serving these ends, the "consensus" he perceived at the heart of political life in the United States represented, for him, a "pattern in miniature" for a pluralistic global order—a model, that is, for an account of an international political authority entrusted with basic peacekeeping functions within the context of an expansive notion of the common good geared to the entire human community.[36]

The writings of these Thomistic commentators reveal a climate of Catholic thought in the postwar years poised to take on the challenge of articulating a nuanced supranational account of the political common good, but restrained by the absence of the material conditions required for a sufficiently robust global community. The sweeping technological, economic, and political developments of ensuing decades have done much to alter this situation.[37] As the basis for speaking of a "global village" has grown, so too has the imperative to address the implications for the common good. In this enterprise, in the wake of the decline of neoscholastic thought, official church teaching has taken the lead.

The Documentary Tradition

The notion of the common good is a consistent theme in the tradition of papal teaching dating back to the encyclical letter *Rerum Novarum* (1891, hereafter *RN*).[38] Yet while early writings exhibited a general concern with humanity and addressed certain international dimensions of the social question, usually through the lens of class relations, their talk of the common good was as a rule linked specifically to contexts defined by specific public authorities—to, in a word, states.[39] It was only beginning in the 1960s that the notion of the common good was systematically extended to, in the first place, considerations of relations among sovereign states, and ultimately, to an implied polity conceived along the lines of humanity as a whole.

John XXIII initiated this turn in *Mater et Magistra* (1961, hereafter *MM*) by explicitly assigning the promotion of international economic relations a place alongside the customary standard of national economic well-being.[40] Building on this step, *Pacem in Terris* (1963, hereafter *PT*) contained abundant reference to "the universal common good,"[41] which it linked with the need for the protection of human rights,[42] international solidarity,[43] and a global political authority.[44] The pastoral constitution *Gaudium et Spes* (1965, hereafter *GS*) then explicitly invoked the notion of interdependence to explain why its definition of the common good "today takes on an increasingly universal complexion and consequently involves rights and duties with respect to the whole human race";[45] in a concluding section on the promotion of international community, this global common good was closely linked with peace,[46] which Paul VI, in turn, set equivalent to development in *Populorum Progressio* (1967, hereafter *PP*).[47] *Octogesima Adveniens* (1971, hereafter *OA*), for its part, developed the idea of an individual responsibility to seek to bring about "both the good of the city and of the nation and all humanity."[48]

Beginning with *Sollicitudo Rei Socialis* (1987, hereafter *SRS*), John Paul II has introduced several innovations in this process of transition and translation. To begin with, he links the common good with the notion of overcoming structures of sin and, correspondingly, with the notions of conversion and sacrifice.[49] This explicitly Christian formulation is at the same time joined, in striking fashion, with a fortified account of the demand of the common good on all, believers and unbelievers alike.[50] In addition, John Paul expounds upon what one might call the affective dimension of the situation of interdependence undergirding the idea of the universal common good, pointing to the manner in which the experience of injustice is shared by others,[51] and citing a growing consciousness, especially through the experience of fear and anxiety, that humans share a common fate and are bound to common goods.[52] This affective aspect is reinforced by an account of solidarity as a virtue consisting in "*a firm and persevering determination to commit oneself to the common good,*"[53] and as ultimately ordered to the Christian ideal of communion.[54] A final contribution of the encyclical is its specification that the relation between the common good internal to societies and that of international society is to be understood *analogically*.[55]

Centesimus Annus (1991, hereafter *CA*) further develops a supranational conception of the common good. On the one hand, it elaborates on the common good as an economic, not solely a political concept. The economic aspect comes to the fore both in the document's portrayal of all work as oriented toward a structure of goods extending in stages from the family to "all humankind,"[56] and in its call for international efforts to ensure that the effects of globalization are brought in line with the common good of the entire human family.[57] On the other hand, the encyclical also bolsters the claim that the common good is in essence not a matter of laws or policies, but rather a question of values and conversion, in which the church has a crucial role to play through its presentation of the correct understanding of humans and their common good.[58]

Building on the fundament of the encyclicals, various national churches have helped contextualize the emerging teaching on the supranational common good. The U.S. bishops, for instance, have explicitly linked the notion of the international common good to the problematic of world peace, identifying both the just war and nonviolent traditions as legitimately oriented toward the common good.[59] Against the backdrop of the dynamic of increasing interdependence, they attribute to the state "a real but relative value" that stands, as they recognize, in tension with the identity of Catholics as "citizens of the world."[60] In their pastoral letter *Economic Justice for All* (1986, hereafter *EJA*), the bishops further urge U.S. citizens to develop a perspective going beyond their own welfare to that of the entire human family[61]—to recognize "a definition of political community that goes beyond national sovereignty to policies that recognize the moral bonds among all people."[62] Global solidarity and stewardship practiced by "all economic actors"—including local businesses, transnational corporations, individual citizens, food-producers, and not least of all the church—are necessary in light of the continued absence of effective international political institutions that might promote the global common good.[63] In Germany, meanwhile, the Catholic bishops, together with their Lutheran colleagues, have approached the problem of the common good in light of the process of globalization and its undermining of the power of states. Their response has been to develop an account of subsidiarity on a European scale, together with a principle of "one world" in which less developed nations in particular are to be extended a participatory role.[64]

The emerging picture of the supranational common good provided by the documentary tradition is not without its ambiguities. The official teachings are, indeed, remarkable for their endorsement of ideas which, if not contradictory, at least stand in tension with one another. Thus the community in question is portrayed as both a society of nations and a single global polity; the common good appears to be at once an affective reality and a structural task; it is presented both as a distinctively Christian concept and as a matter of reason accessible to all; and as a principle it appears to function in both a spiritual and a social scientific context. While the relations among these components remain to be resolved, the general thrust of Catholic social teaching on the political common good is, however, reasonably clear. The ascendancy of the supranational common good is a function of concrete conditions of increasing international interdependence and integration accompanied by the undermining of traditional state sovereignty. This new situation calls for a progressive prioritization of global concerns in political decision making and, correspondingly, a continuing relativization of the value and interests of (national) states. In the normative paradigm shift accompanying this change, however, traditional states hardly disappear. Rather, they are relegated to a place in a broader conceptual framework—the global polity—that integrates a wide range of levels of social organization, in a manner regulated by the principle of subsidiarity.

Problems and Prospects

To fill in this sketch requires considering a number of further questions. How wide is the net of the global common good to be cast, and what sort of entities does it properly encompass? How, on the one hand, does this notion fit with Catholic conceptions of the destiny of the entire human family? How, on the other hand, does it relate to more locally drawn conceptions of the common good, and how might potential conflicts be resolved? Through what sorts of processes might the requirements of a supranational common good be determined, and with what degree of specificity? And how might a politics of the global common good look in practice? In surveying the issues, I will address the problems posed by this concept under three headings—scope, organization, and application—suggesting along the way some possible avenues of response. In each case, as we will see, the sort of unity usually associated with the common good is balanced by a recognition of pluralism—a step that constitutes an important feature of the emerging theory.

Scope

To return to our initial question, what is the community imagined by recent Catholic teaching regarding the supranational common good? The problem of the scope of the common good bears several distinct facets. There is, to begin with, the issue of the breadth of the community whose good is at stake. The initial impulse driving the expansion of the common good is the imperative to combat the tendency to myopia, chauvinism, and violence inherent in an exclusive focus on the national state. But where does the process of inclusion stop? The tendency, as we have seen, is toward a global frame of reference. There are, however, practical reasons for questioning whether such a scope is feasible. In the Western political tradition, even when the notion of the common good has been loosed from the polis and projected onto the matrix of larger types of communities, the historical presumption has been that a certain degree of social cohesion, of shared values and commitments, of cultural homogeneity has been necessary in order to speak coherently of a shared moral stake in a communal good.[65] Another way to put this criticism is to cast it in the proposition that human communities, in order to function, require a sort of closure.[66] In this reasoning, the provenance of the common good in a tradition loosely classifiable as republican is brought to bear, challenging the liberal universalism that grounds the cosmopolitan ideal.[67] The criticism is a serious one. Can the common good be transplanted meaningfully to a community as diverse, divided, and dispersed as the entire human race?[68] In the end there is no compelling reason to think not, yet it seems advisable to acknowledge that the common good may become attenuated, the thinner the consistency of the collectivity in question. This adjustment allows one to speak, in principle, of the basic open-endedness of the common good as a historical category.[69]

This thesis then leaves open a response to a further boundary problem, involving the temporal dimension of the common good: To what extent do future generations weigh in judgments regarding the good of the community? A differentiated conception of the consistency or "thickness" of the common good enables us to recognize the claim of future generations to *some* consideration in judgments of the common good without allowing their prospective interests to overwhelm the goods of already existing persons. A similar sort of response might be directed at yet another question of scope raised, for example, by the arguments of proponents of animal rights or the "Gaia hypothesis."[70] Does the global common good include nonhuman animals or, indeed, nature as a whole? It is clear that nonhumans cannot participate as equals in the sort of moral community corresponding to conventional notions of the common good. This is not, however, to say that they bear no moral status, nor that one cannot speak of there being common purposes among living beings.[71] Beyond this, there also exists a basis for speaking of the good of the natural order, consisting—in the Catholic tradition—in the sacramentality of creation.[72]

To speak in this way about various types or degrees of moral community is to recognize a form of pluralism in regard to the supranational common good. One way to relate the multiple scales of the common good to one another, it seems to me, is to think of them as corresponding to narrative genres.[73] The extent to which a notion of the common good establishes new boundaries can be seen, I would suggest, as related to the presence of a common existential story and, by implication, destiny: as our well-being, and indeed our fate, become bound up with those of others, we enter willy-nilly into a common-good relationship with them.[74] Taking their place with the founding myths of states, with the cosmogonies of religions, and with the histories of tribes, peoples, and cultures, the past century's saga—of world wars, of crimes that shock the conscience of humanity, of the response of human rights—becomes the narrative context for addressing one genre of global common good; the story of our technological mastery of, our threat to, and our continued dependence upon nature becomes the basis for another, and so on.

The mention of religious narratives touches on another problem of scope for Catholic political theory. How are religious, cosmological conceptions of the common good related to the political sense of the term? The tendency among Catholic thinkers is to speak of the *universal* common good as the spiritual *telos* of all persons, consisting in a contemplative union with one another and in God—this in contradistinction to the temporal, political conception of the *international* or *global* common good. The relationship between these two types of common good, moreover, is frequently termed analogical, a usage signifying that the political common good and the universal common good correspond to two distinct orders.[75] This view has implications for a related problem, namely, that of the division of labor between the church and political agencies with respect to the pursuit of the "earthly" common good. Where, for some, a global political community would constitute the *communitas perfecta* in which the common good is to be sought, as others, such as Maritain, would have it, it is the church that most warrants this title. It seems clear that the church, in the end, is charged with a dual role of acting as servant of the universal destiny of humankind while, at the same time, teaching about and contributing to the political common good. It remains crucial, however, to insist that the distinctness of these orders be observed, in order to prevent the translation of any metaphysical hierarchy between heavenly and earthly goods into the direct subordination of the political common good to the "higher," spiritual common good.[76]

Organization

These considerations regarding boundaries reveal little about the relations among the various components and levels that constitute any community, which brings us to another set of questions regarding the internal structuring of the supranational common good. The custom in Catholic thought has been to speak of a plurality of human groupings—both "natural" (marriage, family, state) and constructed (labor groups, religious communities, civic associations)—each of which is said to be characterized by its own common good. This device is odd on its face. For how can competing common goods coexist? What is to prevent the common goods of various subgroups from coming into conflict with one another or with the common good of the broader community, in much the same way that individual goods can? Yet if, as has traditionally been the case, the common good of the overarching political community is, as a rule, given priority over the particular common goods of smaller communities, what is to prevent it from swallowing up and replacing these lesser goods? And in particular, what is to stop the common good conceived on global terms from dominating, and ultimately absorbing, the notion of the common good of particular states? The idea of dispensing with the notion of the national common good seems, for a pluralistic world in only a fledgling state of international cooperation and order, as impracticable as it does impolitic. In what way, however, might it be preserved? The question leads us to a related ambiguity in official Catholic teachings about the supranational common good, involving the sorts of subjects or agencies that are involved. Is the common good in question that of a society of equal and autonomous actors in the form of states? Or is what is at issue the good native to a global community of human persons?[77] Part of the difficulty involved in articulating a global conception of the common good is the problem of how to specify its relation to other groups and their respective goods.

The natural starting point for any such account is the time-honored formula that the common good is of greater value than the individual good.[78] Even this basic rule is complicated by the tendency of modern Catholic thought to conceive of the person, as distinct from the individual, as possessing a value transcending that of all earthly communities. When properly understood, however, the good of the person—the *bonum humanum*—does not stand against the common good of the political community. Rather, the social nature of the person renders the *bonum humanum* itself a common good, indeed one which remains to some extent reliant on the political common good, even though it is itself finally of a transcendent order.

We are next confronted with the task of relating the global common good to the array of diverse and overlapping groups—familial, cultural, social, and so on—that make up the human community as a whole.[79] The classic response to this issue has been to assign to the political community a special status as a "perfect community," an entity capable of providing for human flourishing in a manner unattainable by smaller sorts of groups.[80] On this account, the common good of humanity is truly achievable only in the context of the state; the goods common to lesser communities, meanwhile, relate to the good of the political community as parts to the whole.[81] Today, however, especially in light of ongoing shifts affecting international organizations and state sovereignty, there are reasons for doubting that the state can still be thought of as perfect in the sense traditionally supposed.[82] This prompts the question of whether the global community may be considered to have replaced the traditional state as a perfect community. That we may eventually reach this point is not to be ruled out in theory, but at present the conclusion is not compelling. In lieu of a single sort of perfect community, the good of which warrants preeminence over all other common goods, what we have instead is a complex, open-ended picture in which different goods exist, in different social contexts, both for individuals and for members of a broad range of types of community.[83] The vista is, in short, pluralistic, in the sense that more local conceptions of the common good—including that of the nation—retain a degree of autonomy with respect to the global common good.

If this is the case, is there then at least some principled way of distinguishing among the respective spheres of various common goods, and perhaps even of mediating among them in cases of overlap? The rudiments of an answer are provided in Catholic social thought in the form of the principle of subsidiarity, which stipulates that each level of social organization is responsible for helping all others, by performing certain tasks ordered to the common good while refraining from taking on other tasks that naturally devolve upon other levels.[84] The assumption behind this principle is that there is a functional diversification within human society that results in a sort of layering of the common good. The goods associated with different levels of social organization at once retain their distinctness and are capable of being harmonized in the overall project of realizing human potential, both personally and in toto. Placed within the context of the supranational common good, the principle of subsidiarity offers a means of coordinating the global level of community with lower-level groups, including nation-states.[85] On the one hand, it preserves the integrity of the goods of smaller groups by placing them beyond the legitimate purview of any global political authority. On the other hand, it establishes the primacy of the supranational common good over more local conceptions in any matters which can be shown to depend for their resolution on concerted global action.

The notion of subsidiarity reflects an optimism about the organization of the common good that should not prevent us from squaring off with another problem, namely, that of how to resolve potential conflicts between the global common good and other varying conceptions.[86] At issue are two possible types of collisions, pitting the supranational political common good against, first, the good of a smaller community, and second, the spiritual good of persons. Based on the view that the more general a good is, the higher it is, the basic maxim of the Thomistic tradition is "*Ceteris paribus bonum commune praecedit bono singulari*" ("All things being equal, the common good comes before individual goods").[87] While this rule would seem to favor the primacy of the supranational good, the qualification it contains introduces important limits to this conclusion. The *ceteris paribus* clause raises the possibility, in particular, that the global common good might under certain circumstances be forced to bow either to the good of a smaller community, due to the great intensity of its demands, or to certain sorts of personal goods, due to their ordering to a good that transcends the political.[88] In the end, the pluralist aspect of the common good dictates that there is always a contextual element involved in the process of mediating among the conflicting claims of different sorts of communities.

Application

These largely theoretical issues regarding the organization of the common good rapidly give way to a final set of problems concerning its application. What can be said in practice about the requirements of the global common good, and how might these best be realized?

In regard to the first question, the initial order of business is to observe some characteristic limitations attending the notion. Modern Catholic thought tends, on the whole, to subscribe to two sorts of qualifications on knowledge of the political common good. The common good is, first, its expositors agree, a dynamic concept that varies according to historical conditions.[89] Hence there can be no question of obtaining a blueprint for the ages of how human society ought to look. To recognize this dynamism is not, however, to deny that the theory of the common good is rooted in, and remains bound up with, the unfolding tradition of natural law that continues, even in the wake of the methodological changes attending Vatican II, to form the heart of Catholic social teaching.[90] It is this tradition itself that furnishes a second limitation, for a natural law perspective recognizes that in the ethical hierarchy of laws, principles and rules, there is a direct correlation built in between the degree of specificity of a prescription and the amount of indeterminacy, and hence the margin for error, that accompanies it.[91] In keeping with these limits, recent papal teaching has not hesitated to insist that it does not aim to promote any particular model or ideology with regard to the form social life should take. The tenor of these qualifications has come to produce, in short, a counsel of modesty when making concrete pronouncements about the common good. This is in no way to suggest, however, that the idea of the common good has been reduced to the point where we can no longer speak of it as bearing any particular meaning or requirements. With the requisite care, it is possible, even in a postmodern setting, to articulate a plausible normative theory of the political common good, one that begins with formal criteria but eventually extends some way in the direction of endorsing specific courses of action.

In this account, the common good stands, to begin with, simply for the proposition that certain central concerns must be given their due in any social order. This implies, however, at the very least that an institutionalized discourse on the common good should be an established feature of the political life of any community—including the global community.[92] This discourse, or practice, should moreover be oriented around certain guidelines. The language of the common good characteristically presupposes certain broad intellectual commitments: an anthropology that acknowledges the constitutive sociality of human knowing and being,[93] a sociology that gives due recognition to the complex social dynamics of life in common in modern societies, and an ethical theory that highlights the teleological structure of morality.[94] It follows that discussion of the common good should serve to direct our attention to a particular species of questions invoking concerns of social structure and their implications for human values. To place collective concerns such as racism, or xenophobic violence, or a lack of civic-spiritedness in the context of the common good, then, means to view them not simply as behavioral failures that require exhorting individuals and members of different groups to mutual friendship, benevolence, and aid, but rather as parts of an overall puzzle involving social structures and collective action.[95] The Catholic label for this normative genre is social, as distinguished from distributive or commutative, justice.[96]

Beyond this thematic guideline, the discourse of the common good involves further criteria that might be termed critical or directional. In the various fora in which social agency occurs—the sphere of formal politics chief among them—commitment to the common good involves employing a certain corrective bias in evaluating prospective courses of action. In this capacity the concept of the common good functions as a hermeneutical principle, a lens that sharpens our vision for certain features of the political landscape that, for various reasons, are often distorted or otherwise lost to view. It pushes us, for instance, to counteract an inbred tendency to favor individualist readings of politics—without, however, endorsing the opposite extreme of collectivism. It leads us to distance ourselves from particularistic conceptions of the good—without, though, engaging in the sort of drive to totalization that inevitably endangers a principled pluralism. It presses us to shift our focus from short-term calculations of rationality toward a longer-term view—yet without subscribing to a rigorism that sacrifices flesh and blood interests to the demands of an ultimately indeterminate future.[97] And it urges us to temper our deeply ingrained anthropocentrism with a strong dose of othercenteredness—without going so far as to deny the deep and lasting value of humans within the broader scheme of things.[98] In this critical role, the common good points us not in the direction of a static mean, but rather toward contingent, constantly shifting points of balance. As a result, it makes sense to speak of the primacy of negative arguments regarding the common good; epistemically, in other words, we will as a rule be able to identify what constitute affronts to the common good with greater authority than we will be able to name its precise demands.[99]

By applying these guidelines in light of prevailing political conditions, we may go so far as to draw some tentative conclusions with regard to the present content of the global common good. Of great significance here is the distinctive international dialogue on the idea of basic human rights and (more recently) human responsibilities that has arisen over the past few decades in response to systemic and widespread violations of human goods. This discourse bears the potential to serve as the core of a substantive conception of the political common good on a supranational scale. On this view, a concrete contribution to the good of all may be discerned in the institutionalization of interpenetrating processes aimed at (1) debating, promoting, and enforcing basic rights and duties; (2) ensuring that all people enjoy the basic requirements for social agency; and (3) providing for the amelioration of conflicts and the prevention, or at least limitation, of organized violence. These broad objectives are marked in the Catholic vocabulary by the terms order, development, and peace, each of which is understood as a crucial facet of the common good. On the first point, while some discursive room remains in working out formulations of the rights and responsibilities in question,[100] their outlines are already fairly well established: they cover the basic areas of subsistence, self-determination, and recognition.[101] Likewise, significant empirical and philosophical research has been done on the question of how to enhance the capabilities and participation of global citizens, even if present findings remain subject to empirical critique and revision.[102] In the field of peacemaking, finally, beyond the emergent mandate for the centrality of development assistance, there is an ongoing effort to establish collective criteria for humanitarian intervention—a category which is in the process of replacing the idea of just war in the idiom of the global common good.[103]

These goals are, of course, hardly exhaustive of the supranational common good, representing instead starting points for a political enterprise the progress of which will depend to a great extent on the ongoing dynamics of international integration. Even these basic projects, however, seem far from realization, which raises a question: Is some form of world government required in order to uphold the global common good? The answer to this depends, of course, on what one means by world government. If, indeed, basic human rights and duties are to be enforced, or wars effectively combated, then in some cases a centralized authority commanding coercive force will be called for to ensure that certain tasks are accomplished. Yet a global entity exercising all the powers displayed by today's nation states seems neither feasible nor, ultimately, desirable. It would, on the whole, be a mistake to conceive of a supranational order purely on the analogy of the nation state. What the idea of the global common good calls for, rather, is a new, diversified conception of sovereignty that reflects the pluralism of a polity made up not only of states, but of relatively independent actors such as NGOs, TNCs, and unions; various regional entities; overlapping religious and ethnic communities; and of course international organizations. In this normative landscape authority is diffused and organized according to a conception of subsidiarity that ensures that, in most matters, states or other subglobal organizations will retain their customary competency. Under this principle, much in human affairs can be left over to, in the place of an omnicompetent state, the global civil society at large.[104] At the same time, however, subsidiarity is in the end not merely a principle of decentralization, and it ordains that in the last instance, power in certain crucial spheres must rest with the most general level of authority. What form such a global authority might take—a confederation, a treaty organization, a limited constitutional entity—remains open in theory. What is crucial is that arrangements be sought through which international law and policy impacting upon distinctively global concerns may be effectively promulgated, applied, and enforced. Beyond these central tasks, pluralism should remain the rule.

A Plurality of Pluralisms

On the account I have provided of Catholic social thought, the political common good functions, at root, as a symbol. It is a discursive device that has accrued its own historical heft and penumbra of meaning, even as it ultimately points beyond itself to a *telos* of human flourishing-in-community. This symbolic character carries with it an invitation to interpretation, one that I have accepted in sketching an account of the common good writ on the scale of a global polity. The interpretive process is to an extent controlled by its context in a longstanding, authoritative tradition of thought, argument, and social engagement. The resulting interpretation must, all the same, vie with others in the give and take of political discourse; for a consequence of the epistemic limitations on our knowledge of the good is that no one version can claim a monopoly on the truth about how humans ought to live together.

In the theory of the political common good, this interpretive pluralism takes its place alongside the other varieties of pluralism we have encountered: of scales for the supranational common good and the communal narratives that ground them; of national cultures and their accompanying political systems; of levels and types of social organization and their respective goods; of acceptable outcomes in response to clashes between different common goods; and, ultimately, of orders of being. In the face of the pluralistic and analogical character of the common good, it would be overburdening our theory—or any theory, for that matter—to expect from it a comprehensive or final exposition of how the global community should be organized. We are better advised to focus on the common good's hermeneutical aspect, on the angle of vision it affords us, and to trust in its potential to unfold through conversation and further reflection.

On the other hand, we also would not want to ask too little of the common good. A supranational conception of the political common good represents a powerful rhetorical tool that can be of great value in characterizing and promoting the very sorts of institutions toward which such a notion directs us. Beyond this, the normative thrust of this idea sets it against a Promethean challenge. The existence of a global common good, as we have seen, in some measure presupposes the presence of material conditions instituting a world community. It would be a crucial mistake, however, to view these conditions as the results of inexorable, impersonal, and hence uncontrollable processes, for, to a considerable extent, they are produced by purposive human action. Rather than taking the emerging form of the global community for granted, we have a responsibility to subject its contours and outlines as best we can to critical guidance. The test of the supranational common good may well be its success in helping to shape the globalizing world in its own image.

NOTES

Reprinted from *The Review of Politics* 63, no. 4 (Autumn 2001): 723–54.

The research for this article was carried out at the Institute for Political Theory of the Humboldt University of Berlin under a grant from the Alexander von Humboldt Foundation. I am grateful to the Foundation and to Professor Herfried Münkler for their gracious support.

1. For views of this problem from the standpoints of law and international relations see Lea Brilmayer, *Justifying International Acts* (Ithaca: Cornell University, 1989); Justin Rosenberg, *The Empire of Civil Society* (New York: Verso, 1994).

2. Benedict Anderson, *Imagined Communities: Reflections on the Origins and Spread of Nationalism*, rev. ed. (New York: Verso, 1991), 5. Some recent attempts to provide philosophical justifications for limited preferential treatment of one's compatriots are Maurizio Viroli, *For Love of Country: An Essay on Patriotism and Nationalism* (Oxford: Clarendon, 1995); Robert Goodin, "What Is So Special about Our Fellow Countrymen?" *Ethics* 98 (1988): 663–86; Richard W. Miller, "Cosmopolitan Respect and Patriotic Concern," *Philosophy and Public Affairs* 27 (1998): 202–24. See also Martha Nussbaum et al., *For Love of Country: Debating the Limits of Patriotism*, ed. Joshua Cohen (Boston: Beacon, 1996).

3. The most important treatment is Michael Walzer, *Spheres of Justice: A Defense of Pluralism and Equality* (New York: Basic, 1983), 31–63; see also Charles Beitz, *Political Theory and International Relations* (Princeton: Princeton University, 1979), 105–15; Peter Brown and Henry Shue, eds., *Boundaries* (Totowa, NJ: Rowman and Littlefield, 1981); Robert Dahl, *Democracy and Its Critics* (New Haven: Yale University, 1989), 119–31.

4. In the case of liberal political theory, there is some irony in the manner in which a tradition dominated by the notion of social contract has, from Hobbes to Rawls, so consistently failed to justify, or even to focus on, the boundaries of the polity. Recent work on nationalism has helped focus attention on this issue: see Anderson, *Imagined Communities*; Eric Hobsbawm, *Nations and Nationalism since 1780* (Cambridge: Cambridge University, 1990); *Nationalism*, ed. John Hutchinson and Anthony D. Smith (Oxford: Oxford University, 1994). Noteworthy contributions on the ethics of community include Iris Marion Young, *Justice and the Politics of Difference* (Princeton: Princeton University, 1990); Joseph Carens, "Migration and Morality: A Liberal Egalitarian Perspective," in *Free Movement: Ethical Issues in the Transnational Migration of People and of Money*, ed. Brian Barry and Robert E. Goodin (University Park: Pennsylvania State University, 1992), 25–47;

Rainer Baubock, *Transnational Citizenship: Membership and Rights in International Migration* (Aldershot: Edward Elgar, 1994); Charles Taylor et al., *Multiculturalism: Examining the Politics of Recognition* (Princeton: Princeton University, 1994); Will Kymlicka, *Multicultural Citizenship* (Oxford: Oxford University, 1995); *Democracy and Difference: Contesting the Boundaries of the Political*, ed. Seyla Benhabib (Princeton: Princeton University, 1996).

5. Kenneth L. Karst, *Belonging to America: Equal Citizenship and the Constitution* (New Haven: Yale University, 1989); Judith Shklar, *American Citizenship: The Quest for Inclusion* (Cambridge, MA: Harvard University, 1991); Peter Riesenberg, *Citizenship in the Western Tradition: Plato to Rousseau* (Chapel Hill: University of North Carolina, 1992).

6. The literature on this development is vast. See, e.g., James W. Nickel, *Making Sense of Human Rights* (Berkeley: University of California, 1987); Jack Donnelly, *Universal Human Rights in Theory and Practice* (Ithaca: Cornell University, 1989); Abdullahi Ahmed An-Na'im, ed., *Human Rights in Cross-Cultural Perspective* (Philadelphia: University of Pennsylvania, 1992); Paul Gordon Lauren, *The Evolution of International Human Rights: Visions Seen* (Philadelphia: University of Pennsylvania, 1998).

7. *Toward a Global Civil Society*, ed. Michael Walzer (Providence: Berghahn, 1995); Reinhart Kößler and Henning Melber, *Chancen internationaler Zivilgesellschaft* (Frankfurt: Suhrkamp, 1993).

8. *A Global Ethic: The Declaration of the Parliament of the World's Religions*, ed. Hans Küng and Karl-Josef Kuschel (New York: Continuum, 1995); Hans Küng, *Weltethos für Weltpolitik und Weltwirtschaft* (Munich: Piper, 1997).

9. *Allgemeine Erklärung der Menschenpflichten*, ed. Helmut Schmidt (Munich: Piper, 1997).

10. On the development of the concept from Plato to Nicolas of Cusa see Peter Hibst, *Utilitas Publica–Gemeiner Nutz–Gemeinwohl: Untersuchungen zur Idee eines politischen Leitbegriffes von der Antike bis zum späten Mittelalter* (Frankfurt: Peter Lang, 1991).

11. John Locke, *Second Treatise of Government*, par. 131, 158, in *Two Treatises of Government*, ed. Peter Laslett (Cambridge: Cambridge University, 1970), 371, 391–92; Thomas Hill Green, *Prolegomena to Ethics*, ed. A. C. Bradley (New York: Kraus, 1969; orig. ed. 1883), 229–89; *Lectures on the Principles of Political Obligation*, ed. Paul Harris and John Morrow (Cambridge: Cambridge University, 1986), esp. 25–26.

12. Jeremy Bentham, *Introduction to the Principles of Morals and Legislation* II, chap. 5, in *The Limits of Jurisprudence Defined*, ed. Charles Warren Everett (New York: Columbia University, 1945), 113–18.

13. For a Hegelian interpretation see Anselm Min, "Hegel on Capitalism and the Common Good," *Philosophy and Social Criticism* 11 (1986): 39–61. The Marxian legacy is taken up in *Socialism and the Common Good: New Fabian Essays*, ed. Preston King (London: Frank Cass, 1996).

14. See, e.g., Whalen Lai, "The Public Good that Does the Public Good: A New Reading of Mohism," *Asian Philosophy* 3 (1993): 125–41.

15. Witness the heated discussion among Thomists in the 1940s over the primacy of the common good—a debate involving interpretations of Aquinas which point, ulti-

mately, to an unresolved issue in his own conception. See Charles de Koninck, *De la primauté du bien commun contre les personnalistes* (Quebec: Éditions de l'Université Laval, 1943), and "In Defense of Saint Thomas: A Reply to Father Eschmann's Attack on the Primacy of the Common Good," *Laval Théologique et Politique* 1 (1945): 1–103; Thomas Eschmann, "In Defense of Jacques Maritain," *The Modern Schoolman* 22 (1945): 183–208; Yves R. Simon, "On the Common Good," *Review of Politics* 6 (1944): 530–33; Jacques Maritain, *The Person and the Common Good*, trans. John J. Fitzgerald (Notre Dame, IN: University of Notre Dame, 1966). A helpful overview of the debate is Mary M. Keys, "Personal Dignity and the Common Good: A Twentieth-Century Thomistic Dialogue," in *Catholicism, Liberalism, and Communitarianism: The Catholic Intellectual Tradition and the Moral Foundations of Democracy*, ed. Kenneth L. Grasso, Gerard V. Bradley, and Robert P. Hunt (Lanham, MD: Rowman and Littlefield, 1995), 173–95. For careful and detailed analyses of Aquinas on the point in question (the priority of personal versus communal goods) see Antoine Pierre Verpaalen, S.C.J., *Der Begriff des Gemeinwohls bei Thomas von Aquin: Ein Beitrag zum Problem des Personalismus* (Heidelberg: F. H. Kerle, 1954), and M. S. Kempshall, *The Common Good in Late Medieval Political Thought* (Oxford: Clarendon, 1999), 76–129.

16. Commentators endorsing this view include Drew Christiansen, "The Common Good and the Politics of Self-Interest: A Catholic Contribution to the Practice of Citizenship," in *Beyond Individualism: Toward a Retrieval of Moral Disclosure in America*, ed. Donald L. Gelpi (Notre Dame, IN: University of Notre Dame, 1989), 58; Oswald von Nell-Breuning, *Soziallehre der Kirche: Erläuterungen der lehramtlichen Dokumente*, 3rd. rev. ed. (Vienna: Europaverlag, 1983), 24; Michael J. Schuck, *That They Be One: The Social Teaching of the Papal Encyclicals 1740–1989* (Washington, DC: Georgetown University, 1991), 180.

17. Thus, for example, solidarity may be viewed as the subjective dimension involved in the ordering of persons toward the (objective) common good.

18. The relation between these two senses stems from the normativity associated with the telos of the common good. English-language discussions of the term frequently obscure several distinct senses in which we speak of (the) (common) good: an object may, for example, *be* good, it may be *a* good, or it may be *for someone's* good, in each case in several different ways. Although one may speak idiosyncratically of *a* common good or of common *goods*, in conventional usage the common good is in its basic sense an abstract, indivisible substantive, comparable to "equality" or "peace." For a discussion contrasting the ideas of common good as goal and as means see Josef Endres, *Gemeinwohl heute* (Innsbruck: Tyrolia, 1989), 52–64; on the common good as both task and guideline see Roman Herzog, "Gemeinwohl," in *Historisches Wörterbuch der Philosophie*, ed Joachim Ritter (Darmstadt: Wissenschaftliche Buchgesellschaft, 1974), 256.

19. Thomas Aquinas, *Summa Theologicae* (hereafter *ST*) 1-2, q. 91, a. 1; *Sententia Libri Ethicorum* 1, 2, n. 11–12; and especially *Quaestiones Disputatae de Malo* q. 4, a. 1c: "The whole multitude of human beings is to be considered as like one community" (cited in John Finnis, *Aquinas: Moral, Political, and Legal Theory* [Oxford: Oxford University, 1998],

115 n. 60). Cf. Louis Dupré, "The Common Good and the Open Society," *Review of Politics* 55 (1993): 711.

20. Francisco de Vitoria, *De Potestate Civili*, par. 21. Francisco Suárez, *De legibus* 3, chap. 2, no. 4; *Defensio fidei* 6, chap. 4, no. 1. For a comparison of Vitoria's "organized" and Suárez' "inorganic" conceptions of the international community see James Brown Scott, *The Catholic Conception of International Law* (Washington, DC: Georgetown University Press, 1934), 181–83, 482–84. Two other prominent proponents of a universal conception of the common good were Leibniz and Wolff: see Albert Heinekamp, *Das Problem des Guten bei Leibniz* (Bonn: H. Bouvier & Co., 1969), 90–132; Nicholas Greenwood Onuf, "Imagined Republics," *Alternatives* 19 (1994): 321.

21. Jacques Maritain, *The Rights of Man and Natural Law*, trans. Doris C. Anson (New York: Charles Scribner's Sons, 1949), 21; cf. *Person and the Common Good*, 55.

22. Drafted by the University of Chicago's Committee to Frame a World Constitution. See Robert M. Hutchins et al., *Preliminary Draft of a World Constitution* (Chicago: University of Chicago Press, 1948).

23. Maritain, *Man and the State*, 202.

24. Ibid., 206–9. See also Emmanuel Mounier, *Personalism*, trans. Philip Mairet (London: Routledge and Kegan Paul, 1952), 109–11.

25. See Heinrich Pesch, *Die soziale Befähigung der Kirche*, 3rd ed. (Berlin: Germania, 1911); Eberhard Welty, *Gemeinschaft und Einzelmensch: Eine Sozialmetaphysische Untersuchung* (Salzburg: Anton Pustet, 1935); Gustav Gundlach, *Die Ordnung der menschlichen Gesellschaft* (Köln: J. P. Bachem, 1964), esp. 158–61; Georg Wildmann, *Personalismus, Solidarismus und Gesellschaft: Der ethische und ontologische Grundcharakter der Gesellschaftslehre der Kirche* (Wien: Herder, 1961).

26. Oswald von Nell-Breuning, *Gerechtigkeit und Freiheit: Grundzuge katholischer Soziallehre* (Munich: Europaverlag, 1980), 37. See also Oswald von Nell-Breuning, "Gemeinwohl," in *Zur christlichen Gesellschaftslehre: Beiträge zu einem Wörterbuch der Politik*, ed. Nell-Breuning and Hermann Sacher, vol. 1 (Freiburg: Herder, 1947), 1:47–48.

27. Nell-Breuning, *Gerechtigkeit und Freiheit*, 35 (my translation).

28. Johannes Messner, *Das Naturrecht: Handbuch der Gesellschaftsethik, Staatsethik und Wirtschaftsethik*, 5th rev. ed. (Munich: Tyrolia, 1966), 216.

29. Ibid., 190, 290.

30. Ibid., 695.

31. Arthur-Fridolin Utz, *Sozialethik, 1. Teil: Die Prinzipien der Gesellschaftslehre* (Heidelberg: F. H. Kerle, 1964), 136.

32. Utz, *Sozialethik, 3. Teil: Die Soziale Ordnung* (1986), 190.

33. John Courtney Murray, S.J., *We Hold These Truths: Catholic Reflections on the American Proposition* (New York: Sheed and Ward, 1960). Murray's distinctions continue to animate American Catholic thought, most notably in the work of J. Bryan Hehir; see, for example, his "Catholicism and Democracy: Conflict, Change, and Collaboration," in *Christianity and Democracy in Global Context*, ed. John Witte, Jr. (Boulder, CO: Westview, 1993), 15–30.

34. Murray, *We Hold These Truths*, 88.
35. Ibid., 287.
36. Ibid., 75.
37. The extent to which a "global community" may meaningfully be said to exist is, of course, partly a matter of semantics; beyond this it depends upon a complicated dialectic in which factors of cultural, political, economic, and social convergence stand over against continuing forms of division and difference. For purposes of the common good, however, we may define a community as a body constituted through the sharing of a goal or purpose. In this light, an account of developments that have attended the formation of a global community would have to include, *inter alia*, the confrontation with various *problems*, such as the prospect of world wars, genocide, and nuclear holocaust, and the specter of environmental degradation and overpopulation; the response to the *tasks* of protecting human rights and promoting development and, in the wake of the cold war, responsible political organizations; and the furthering of the *projects* of establishing global communication, trade, and cultural exchange. The technological ties, trade relations, international organizations, migration, transportation networks, mass media, sports tourneys, and so on are, in this respect, manifestations of a burgeoning moral community of global dimensions.
38. Unless otherwise noted, Church documents cited are in *Catholic Social Thought: The Documentary Heritage*, ed. David J. O'Brien and Thomas A. Shannon (Maryknoll, NY: Orbis, 1995).
39. This goes for the overwhelming number of references in early documents: e.g., *Rerum Novarum*, 26, 27, 28, 35; *Quadragesimo Anno* (1931, hereafter *QA*), 49, 58, 84, 85, 86, 110. Two references in *QA* (57, 113), however, admit of a more internationalist interpretation. For an argument linking the notion of the international common good to the "Leonine" period of papal teaching stretching between 1878 and 1958, see Schuck, *That They Be One*, 75.
40. *MM*, 71, 78, 80, cf. 40, 174, 202.
41. *PT*, 100, 133, 138, 140, cf. 7, 132, 134, 135, 146.
42. *PT*, 139.
43. *PT*, 98, 123.
44. *PT*, 84, 85, 137.
45. *GS*, 26; cf. 84.
46. *GS*, 78.
47. *PP*, 77.
48. *OA*, 46.
49. *SRS*, 36, 38, 45; cf. 35.
50. *SRS*, 38.
51. *SRS*, 38.
52. *SRS*, 26.
53. *SRS*, 38.
54. *SRS*, 40.

55. *SRS*, 39.

56. *CA*, 43, 51. The model here, which orders work to the needs of, in turn, family, community, nation, and humanity, differs from the earlier formulation in *Laborem exercens* (1981), 10, which focuses on person, family, and nation.

57. *CA*, 52, 58. This theme was rehearsed in John Paul II's address to the Pontifical Academy of Social Sciences on 24 April 2001: "Now that commerce and communications are no longer bound by borders, it is the universal common good which demands that control mechanisms should accompany the inherent logic of the market."

58. *CA*, 51, 58; cf. 60.

59. *The Challenge of Peace* (1983, hereafter *CP*), 243, 74. The German bishops have followed suit in *Gerechter Friede* (Bonn: Secretariat of the German Conference of Bishops, 2000), par. 61–62.

60. *CP*, 240, 237, 326.

61. *EJA*, 13, 97, 100, 251.

62. *EJA*, 258.

63. *EJA*, 116, 322 (on solidarity); 238 (on stewardship); 258, 324 (invoking all economic actors); 256 (regarding TNCs); 322 (on citizens); 231 (on food-producers); 363 (regarding the church); 261, 323, 325 (concerning existing international institutions).

64. *Für eine Zukunft in Solidarität und Gerechtigkeit: Wort des Rates der Evangelischen Kirche in Deutschland und der Deutschen Bischofskonferenz zur wirtschaftlichen und sozialen Lage in Deutschland* (Bonn: Secretariat of the German Conference of Bishops, 1997), par. 117–19, 237–42.

65. This presumption characterizes Hegel and Rousseau as much as it does Aristotle.

66. See Michael Walzer, "The Moral Standing of States," in *A Philosophy and Public Affairs Reader* (Princeton: Princeton University, 1979).

67. An important element of the perspective is its claim that the bonds and fellowship in smaller communities are a precondition for the development of civic virtue. For contemporary defenses of republicanism see Philip Pettit, *Republicanism: A Theory of Freedom and Government* (Oxford: Clarendon, 1997); Michael J. Sandel, *Liberalismus oder Republikanismus: Von der Notwendigkeit der Bürgertugend* (Vienna: Passagen, 1995). See also Herfried Münkler, ed., *Bürgerreligion und Bürgertugend: Debatten über die vorpolitischen Grundlagen politischer Ordnung* (Baden-Baden: Nomos, 1996).

68. Jürgen Habermas, a contemporary republican in the tradition of Kant's *Perpetual Peace*, has written interestingly on how to promote a "domestic politics" encompassing all of Europe and, potentially, the entire international society. Habermas, *Die postnationale Konstellation: Politische Essays* (Frankfurt: Suhrkamp, 1998). For a more critical view of globalization see Peter Sloterdijk, *Sphären II: Globen* (Frankfurt: Suhrkamp, 1999).

69. An argument regarding the incompleteness of states and the consequent openness of the logic of the common good is advanced by John Finnis, *Natural Law and Natural Rights* (Oxford: Clarendon, 1980), 149–56. Finnis goes on, however, to argue, in my view inconclusively, that the common good of the political community is not basic, but rather instrumental, in the sense of being in the service of the only three human goods

that count as basic: namely, friendship, marriage, and religion. John Finnis, "Is Natural Law Theory Compatible with Limited Government?" in *Natural Law, Liberalism, and Morality: Contemporary Essays*, ed. Robert P. George (Oxford: Clarendon, 1996), 1–26, esp. 4–9.

70. On animals, see Peter Singer, *Animal Liberation*, rev. ed. (New York: Avon, 1990); and Tom Regan, *The Case for Animal Rights* (Berkeley: University of California, 1983). On more universal conceptions of community including the Gaia hypothesis see Larry Rasmussen, *Earth Community, Earth Ethics* (Maryknoll, NY: Orbis, 1996); Rosemary Radford Ruether, *Gaia and God: An Ecofeminist Theology of Earth Healing* (San Francisco: Harper, 1992); James Lovelock, *Gaia: A New Look at Life on Earth* (Oxford: Oxford University, 1995).

71. William A. Barbieri, Jr., "The Rights of Animals," in *The New Catholic Encyclopedia*, vol. 19 (Washington, DC: Catholic University of America, 1996), 15–16.

72. See *Catechism of the Catholic Church* (Collegeville, MN: Liturgical Press, 1994), para. 1147; see also William A. Barbieri, Jr., "'Therefore the Land Mourns': Environmental Hazards and Catholic Social Teaching," *Chicago Studies* 38 (1999): 91–108.

73. On the narrative dimensions of morality Paul Ricoeur's work strikes me as particularly instructive; see *Time and Narrative* vol. 1, chaps. 2–3, and vol. 3, chap. 8 (Chicago: University of Chicago, 1988); "Life: A Story in Search of a Narrator," in *A Ricoeur Reader: Reflection and Imagination*, ed. Maril J. Valdes (Toronto: University of Toronto, 1991), 425–40; *Oneself as Another*, trans. Kathleen Blarney (Chicago: University of Chicago, 1992). For a particularly insightful interpretation of the common good in light of Bernard Meland's hermeneutical notion of the "structure of experience," see Douglas Sturm, "On Meanings of Public Good: An Exploration," *The Journal of Religion* 58 (1978): 13–29. The implications of the teleological character of practical reason for the common good are explored by Charles Sherover, "The Temporality of the Common Good: Futurity and Freedom," *The Review of Metaphysics* 38 (1984): 475–97. On the role of myths and stories in constructing a relatively universal narrative specifying the requirements for human well-being in general see Martha Nussbaum, "Aristotelian Social Democracy," in *Liberalism and the Good*, ed. R. Bruce Douglass, Gerald M. Mara, and Henry S. Richardson (New York: Routledge, 1990), 203–52.

74. This perspective bears some similarities to Dewey's account of "the consequences which call a public into being" (John Dewey, *The Public and Its Problems* [Athens: Ohio University, 1991; orig. ed. 1927], 26–27). Unlike the Aristotelian tradition, however, which roots the common good in friendship, Dewey contrasts these two forms of relation.

75. A classic point of reference here is Aquinas's distinction between earthly and heavenly goods: *ST* 1-2, q. 91, a. 5. For a cogent exposition of the analogical character of the common good which does not, however, directly address questions of scope, see David Hollenbach, "The Common Good Revisited," *Theological Studies* 50 (1989): 70–94, esp. 85.

76. On this point within the context of states see Charles E. Curran, "The Common Good and Official Catholic Social Teaching," in *The Common Good and U.S. Capitalism*,

ed. Oliver F. Williams and John W. Houck (Lanham, MD: University Press of America, 1987), 121.

77. Nell-Breuning points out this ambiguity, for example, in connection with *PT*, 84–85 (Nell-Breuning, *Soziallehre der Kirche*, 109).

78. Aristotle, *Politics* 1252a1–5, 1253a18–20; Aquinas, *ST* 1-2, q. 90, a. 2.

79. Michael J. Schuck has counseled a healthy skepticism regarding the viability of any notion of the common good in light of the ever-increasing diversity of today's societies ("Response to David Hollenbach's 'The Common Good in a Postmodern Epoch: What Role for Theology?'" in *Religion, Ethics, and the Common Good*, ed. James Donahue and M. Theresa Moser, R.S.C.J. [Mystic, CT: Twenty-Third Publications, 1996], 23–26). Interestingly, what social groups exist is itself a question of the common good, for groups—even those conventionally thought of as "natural" such as ethnic groups or the family—are themselves to some extent the products of purposive political action and to this degree must answer to common good criteria. On the family, see Susan Moller Okin, *Justice, Gender, and the Family* (New York: Basic, 1989).

80. Of course, virtually all social groups are to some extent *political*, in the sense that they are implicated in the uses of power that shape the lives of humans and impact on their chances to flourish. The designation of the state as a "perfect community" relies, however, on the distinctive character of government as the agent par excellence of the structuring of communal life.

81. *ST* 1-2, q. 90, a. 2 c; a. 3, ad 3.

82. Finnis, *Aquinas*, 114–15; Maritain, *Person and the Common Good*, 54.

83. On this point, Michael Novak is correct to urge a more complex conception of the common good. Michael Novak, *The Catholic Ethic and the Spirit of Capitalism* (New York: Free Press, 1993), 83–84.

84. The classic formulation of this principle in papal teaching is *QA*, 79. For a useful exposition in terms of political and legal theory see Otfried Höffe, *Vernunft und Recht: Bausteine zu einem interkulturellen Rechtsdiskurs* (Frankfurt: Suhrkamp, 1996), 220–39.

85. Cf. *PT*, 140; *GS*, 86. For an argument from an ecumenical perspective, see John Cobb's case for a conception of the global common good that attempts to tame the dynamisms of globalization by insisting on the maintenance of "communities of communities (of communities)" integrated by a principle of subsidiarity. John B. Cobb, Jr., *Sustaining the Common Good: A Christian Perspective on the Global Economy* (Cleveland, OH: Pilgrim Press, 1994).

86. See David Hollenbach, *Claims in Conflict: Retrieving and Renewing the Catholic Human Rights Tradition* (New York: Paulist Press, 1979), 142, on the tendency of Catholic thought to minimize conflict in its conception of society.

87. Valentin Zsifkovits, "Gemeinwohl," in *Katholisches Soziallexikon*, ed. Alfred Klose et al. (Wien: Tyrolia, 1980), 855; cf. Nell-Breuning, "Gemeinwohl," 48.

88. By the same token, considerations of the spiritual common good may in some cases be subordinated to particularly intense requirements of the global common good. On limitations of quality and quantity applying to the priority of the common good, see

Rudolf Weiler, "Gemeinwohl," in *Neues Lexikon der christlichen Moral* (Innsbruck: Tyrolia, 1990), 237–42. On Aquinas's view in regard to sacrificing personal goods for the sake of the common good, see Verpaalen, "Begriff des Gemeinwohls," 70.

89. See, e.g., Curran, "Common Good," 117; A. Nemetz, "Common Good," in *The New Catholic Encyclopedia*, vol. 4 (Washington, DC: Catholic University of America Press, 1967), 15–19. Michael Novak echoes this characterization, but sees it as applying only to the material, as opposed to the formal common good—a view based, to my mind, on a misinterpretation of Maritain's account. Novak, *Catholic Ethic*, 84; cf. Thomas R. Rourke, *A Conscience as Large as the World: Yves R. Simon versus the Catholic Neoconservatives* (Lanham, MD: Rowman and Littlefield, 1997), 78–81.

90. On the evolving role of natural law in Catholic teaching see, e.g., Bernhard Fraling, *Natur im ethischen Argument* (Freiburg: Herder, 1990); Ursula Nothelle-Wildfeuer, "Vom Naturrecht zum Evangelium? Ein Beitrag zur neueren Diskussion um die Erkenntnistheorie der katholischen Soziallehre im Ausgang von Johannes Paul II," in *Perspektiven christlicher Sozialethik: Hundert Jahre nach Rerum novarum*, ed. Franz Furger and Marianne Heimbach-Steins (Munster: Regensberg, 1991), 55–76; Klaus Demmer, "Naturrecht und Offenbarung," in *Brennpunkt Sozialethik: Theorien, Aufgaben, Methoden: Für Franz Furger*, ed. Marianne Heimbach-Steins, Andreas Lienkamp, and Joachim Wiemeyer (Freiburg: Herder, 1995), 29–44.

91. So, for example, while peace may be established as a general imperative with great certitude, for progressively more specific issues—e.g., the broad legitimacy of the use of violence in pursuit of peace, criteria for humanitarian intervention on behalf of the common good, whether a specific situation warrants armed resistance—ethical judgments become increasingly contingent and uncertain. The tendency in recent pastoral teachings to affirm both just war and pacifist approaches is another sign of the emerging acknowledgement of moral pluralism in Catholic social thought.

92. Dennis McCann makes a similar suggestion, but argues that the common good should be conceived purely in proceduralist terms, along the lines proposed in Jürgen Habermas' social theory. This seems to me to render the term unduly thin. See Dennis P. McCann, "The Good to be Pursued in Common," in *The Common Good and U.S. Capitalism*, 158–78. Two powerful attempts by German scholars to synthesize Christian social theory and the discourse ethics of Apel and Habermas are Christian Kissling, *Gemeinwohl und Gerechtigkeit: Ein Vergleich von traditioneller Naturrechtsethik und kritischer Gesellschaftstheorie* (Freiburg: Herder, 1993); and Hans-Joachim Höhn, *Vernunft–Glaube–Politik: Reflexionsstufen einer christlichen Sozialethik* (Paderborn: Schöningh, 1990). A noteworthy effort at articulating a conception of solidarity ("*Gemeinwohlorientierung*") rooted in discourse ethics is Lutz Wingert, *Gemeinsinn und Moral: Grundzüge einer intersubjektivistischen Moralkonzeption* (Frankfurt: Suhrkamp, 1993). On the pluralistic implications of a discursive practice of the common good see Gary J. Dorrien, *Reconstructing the Common Good: Theology and the Social Order* (Maryknoll, NY: Orbis, 1990); Christopher F. Mooney, S.J., *Boundaries Dimly Perceived: Law, Religion, Education, and the Common Good* (Notre Dame, IN: University of Notre Dame, 1990).

93. An intriguing transcendental phenomenological account of sociality and the common good is James G. Hart, *The Person and the Common Life: Studies in a Husserlian Social Ethics* (Dordrecht: Kluwer, 1992). For arguments as to why liberal individualist anthropologies cannot ground an authentic discourse of the common good, see Ulrich Matz, "Aporien individualistischer Gemeinwohlkonzepte," in *Selbstinteresse und Gemeinwohl: Beiträge zur Ordnung der Wirtschaftsgesellschaft*, ed. Anton Rauscher (Berlin: Duncker und Humblot, 1985), 321–57; Alasdair MacIntyre, *Whose Justice? Which Rationality?* (Notre Dame, IN: University of Notre Dame Press, 1988), 326–48. An excellent discussion of American debates is Brian Stiltner, *Religion and the Common Good: Catholic Contributions to Building Community in a Liberal Society* (Lanham, MD: Rowman and Littlefield, 1999); cf. David Hollenbach, "A Communitarian Reconstruction of Human Rights: Contributions from Catholic Tradition," in *Catholicism and Liberalism: Contributions to American Public Philosophy*, ed. R. Bruce Douglass and David Hollenbach (Cambridge: Cambridge University, 1994), 127–50.

94. In his illuminating study of the contemporary theory of the common good, Patrick Riordan shows how the language of the common good embodies a distinctive model of rationality. Patrick Riordan, S.J., *A Politics of the Common Good* (Dublin: Institute of Public Administration, 1996), 28–42.

95. On the difference between individual and social models of action see Axel Honneth and Hans Joas, *Social Action and Human Nature* (Cambridge: Cambridge University, 1988); Margaret Gilbert, *On Social Facts* (Princeton: Princeton University, 1992); Nick Crossley, *Intersubjectivity: The Fabric of Social Becoming* (London: Sage, 1996); Mary Douglas, *How Institutions Think* (London: Routledge & Kegan Paul, 1987).

96. Hollenbach, *Claims in Conflict*, 152–55. For a defense of the centrality of social justice in questions of the global common good, see Rafael Caldera, "The Universal Common Good and International Social Justice," *Review of Politics* 38 (1976): 27–39.

97. Cf. Walter Kerber, S.J., "Ordnungspolitik, Gemeinwohl und katholische Gesellschaftslehre: Der sozialen Marktwirtschaft zum Gedächtnis," *Jahrbuch für christliche Sozialwissenschaften* 31 (1990): 11–33.

98. What I term "other-centeredness" here may be interpreted in a variety of ways. A biocentric account is that of Rasmussen, *Earth Community, Earth Ethics*. An influential theocentric proposal is James M. Gustafson, *Ethics from a Theocentric Perspective* (Chicago: University of Chicago, 1981, 1984), esp. vol. 2, pp. 18–19. More broadly, John Hick elaborates on a notion of "Reality"-centeredness spanning the world's religions; see John Hick, *God Has Many Names* (Philadelphia: Westminster, 1986). Vaclav Havel, meanwhile, places "Being" at the center of ethical responsibility; see Vaclav Havel, *Gewissen und Politik: Reden und Ansprachen, 1984–1990*, ed. Otfrid Pustejovsky and Franz Olbert (Munich: Institutum Bohemicum, 1990); cf. David Hollenbach, S.J., "Tradition, History, and Truth in Theological Ethics," in *Christian Ethics: Problems and Prospects*, ed. Lisa Sowle Cahill and James F. Childress (Cleveland: Pilgrim, 1996), 60–75.

99. Cf. B. J. Diggs, "The Common Good as Reason for Political Action," *Ethics* 83 (1973): 292.

100. I follow here William O'Neill's suggestion, in his rich essay "Babel's Children: Reconstructing the Common Good," that human rights "are best viewed rhetorically, that is, as limning the possibility of rationally persuasive argument across our varied narrative traditions" (*The Annual of the Society for Christian Ethics* 18 [1998]: 164).

101. On the notion that certain human rights are basic see Hollenbach, *Claims in Conflict*; Christiansen, "Common Good," 75; Henry Shue, *Basic Rights: Subsistence, Affluence, and U.S. Foreign Policy* (Princeton: Princeton University, 1980); David Little, "The Nature and Basis of Human Rights," in *Prospects for a Common Morality*, ed. Gene Outka and John P. Reeder, Jr. (Princeton: Princeton University, 1993), 73–92. On the need to grant greater recognition to groups in rights discourse see Ronald Garet, "Communality and Existence: The Rights of Groups," *Southern California Law Review* 54 (1983): 1001–75; William F. Felice, *Taking Suffering Seriously: The Importance of Collective Human Rights* (Albany: State University of New York, 1996).

102. See, for example, the contributions in *The Quality of Life*, ed. Martha C. Nussbaum and Amartya Sen (Oxford: Clarendon, 1993). On the philosophical side, virtue theory is a particularly valuable resource in this endeavor insofar as it is concerned with the social foundations of virtue; for an overview see Lee Yearley, "Recent Work on Virtue," *Religious Studies Review* 16 (1990): 1–9. Also, to the extent that egalitarianism plays a role in this research program, Michael Walzer's conception of complex equality remains a still largely untapped source of insight. See Walzer, *Spheres of Justice*, esp. 17–20.

103. See Kenneth R. Himes, O.F.M., "Notes on Moral Theology: The Morality of Humanitarian Intervention," *Theological Studies* 55 (1993): 82–105; Brian M. Kane, *Just War and the Common Good: Jus ad Bellum Principles in Twentieth Century Papal Thought* (San Francisco: Catholic Scholars Press, 1997), 133–64. The recent conference on world peace in The Hague marks another milestone in the growth of a global discourse on the common good.

104. This is the presumption of Michael Walzer and his collaborators in *Toward a Global Civil Society*. See also Karl-Otto Apel, "Discourse Ethics as a Response to the Novel Challenges of Today's Reality to Coresponsibility," *Journal of Religion* 74 (1993): 496–513.

CHAPTER 25

MacIntyre, Aquinas, and Politics

THOMAS S. HIBBS

> *Thomas S. Hibbs (1960–) is Dean of the Honors College and Distinguished Professor of Ethics and Culture at Baylor University. He also taught for three years at Thomas Aquinas College and for thirteen years at Boston College, where he was a full professor and department chair. Hibbs received his B.A. and M.A. in philosophy from the University of Dallas and his Ph.D. from the University of Notre Dame. Hibbs focuses on the moral philosophy of Thomas Aquinas and is the author of* Dialectic and Narrative in Aquinas: An Interpretation of the Summa Contra Gentiles; Virtue's Splendor: Wisdom, Prudence, and the Human Good; *and* Aquinas, Ethics, and Philosophy of Religion: Metaphysics and Practice. *He also writes movie reviews for popular venues and is the author of two popular books on film:* Shows About Nothing: Nihilism in Popular Culture *and* Arts of Darkness: American Noir and the Quest for Redemption.

At the end of their "introduction" to a recent collection of essays on *Virtue Ethics*, Roger Crisp and Michael Slote assert, "virtue ethics needs to expand its recent moral horizons so as to take in larger questions of political morality."[1] As they note, some of the most telling objections to virtue ethics as an independent and comprehensive theory focus either upon the lacuna concerning politics or the implausibility of developing a viable political theory from the notion of virtue. The silence of virtue ethicists on political matters is especially disconcerting for the followers of Aristotle, who allies ethics with politics, the architectonic science.[2]

Since the appearance of *After Virtue* in 1981, Alasdair MacIntyre has been a vigorous proponent of an ethics of virtue. Yet through the 1980s and into the early 1990s, he had little to say about politics, except by way of reiterating and amplifying vituperations against modern liberalism. Even the sequel to *After*

Virtue, which bears the promising title, *Whose Justice? Which Rationality?*, supplies little in the way of political philosophy. Of course, much of MacIntyre's early writing was devoted to Marxist political theory, but with the abandonment of Marxism came a concomitant shift in attention from politics to ethics. In recent years, however, MacIntyre has had quite a bit to say about "the political and social structures of the common good," as he puts it in the title of a chapter in his latest book, *Dependent Rational Animals*.[3] In these recent writings, MacIntyre supplements his long-standing critique of liberalism with a defense of the politics of the common good as embodied exclusively in local communities, which are, as he puts it, "the only places where political community can be constructed, a political community very much at odds with the politics of the nation-state."[4]

Like his prophetic call at the end of *After Virtue* for a new St. Benedict, MacIntyre's advocacy of local communities has earned him rebuke and scorn, mostly from those who have failed to take the time to understand what he has actually written.[5] In what follows, we will look carefully at what MacIntyre has written recently on politics, especially on the politics of local communities. In the first section of the essay, we will examine MacIntyre's reasons for the promotion of the politics of local communities and the weaknesses in the standard objections to his position. Indeed, more than most contemporary Aristotelians or Thomists, MacIntyre highlights the distinctive features of a political theory that takes its bearings from a conception of the common good, most evident to us in local communities. In the second section, we will argue that, despite its virtues, the sort of small, fleeting, marginal communities MacIntyre promotes are sub- or prepolitical not just by modern standards, but even by the standards of the Aristotelian *polis*. In the third section, we argue that MacIntyre's attempt, in the wake of the failure of Marxism, to develop a politics of the common good by means of a fusion of elements from Marx, Aristotle, and Aquinas leaves him with a severely truncated and distorted political theory, whose dangers consist less in posing a radical, subversive threat to the conventional order than in restricting our ability to think about modern political orders in anything other than reductionist terms.

The Common Good as the Basis for Repudiating the Modern State

A series of faulty interpretations of his writings, especially of their political implications, prompted MacIntyre to write "Politics, Philosophy and the Common

Good," in which he responds to two misconceptions. The first concerns the accusation, voiced by Hilary Putnam, that, by "its attitude to alternative ways of life," MacIntyre's politics "immunize[s] institutional oppression from criticism." The second has to do with the tendency of friends and foes alike to align MacIntyre with communitarianism.[6] For all the alterations in MacIntyre's philosophical positions over the years, there remains a unifying thread: opposition to liberalism and the modern nation-state. Implicit in *After Virtue*'s discussion of practices as providing the indispensable communal setting for the understanding and cultivation of virtue, the notion of the common good has come to occupy an increasingly important place in MacIntyre's fashioning of a political alternative to the liberalism of the modern state. Indeed, the revival of a Thomistic understanding of the common good is at the heart of MacIntyre's recent political writings.

The problem with most critics who embrace Putnam's objection is that they typically ignore what MacIntyre has to say about the rationality of traditions, his repudiation of a Burkean conception of tradition, and his emphasis on the necessity of, and conditions for, debate between rival traditions of inquiry.[7] In "Politics, Philosophy and the Common Good," for example, MacIntyre distinguishes between a *Volk* and a *polis*, the latter of which is "always potentially or actually a society of rational inquiry and self-scrutiny." In fact, MacIntyre seems increasingly inclined to turn Putnam's objection against liberalism. Whereas MacIntyre advocates an active and engaged toleration that would take seriously the possibility of learning the truth from a rival, modern politics fosters passive tolerance, that is, public indifference to the good. Toward the end of "Politics, Philosophy and the Common Good," MacIntyre asserts that while inequality may involve oppression, the chief form of oppression consists in the deprivation of the possibility of learning about the good in and through inquiry with others. As MacIntyre sees it, modern politics systematically frustrates this type of inquiry.[8] The unstated conclusion would seem to be that modern politics is the true oppressor.[9]

MacIntyre himself suggests that "the revolutionary struggles" regarding slavery, suffrage, and organized labor "involved degrees and kinds of political participation that are quite as alien to the democratic forms of the politics of the contemporary state as they are to nondemocratic forms."[10] Although much more would have to be said about these matters, there are grounds for thinking that MacIntyre's account of oppression as a deprivation of opportunities for communal education about the good could help us to recover features of American history that we are increasingly in danger of forgetting. The tendency, for example, to depict African-American struggles exclusively as a civil rights struggle is reductionistic, presenting a version of American history that is suspiciously comforting to procedural liberalism.[11]

Part of what MacIntyre thinks we might recover from a more accurate history is a notion of the common good, irreducible to a summing of individual goods. Precisely because MacIntyre advocates a politics of the common good and thinks that the common good can be pursued only within the context of local communities, he has often been labeled a communitarian. One of the points of the essay "Politics, Philosophy and the Common Good" is to assure us that this is not so.[12] MacIntyre's depiction of the particular or local aspiration for the universal good cuts across the contemporary divide between particularists or communitarians, on the one hand, and universalists, on the other. Political reflection is at first, and to some extent always, local. Debates and issues are framed in local terms, but even here the answers given have universal import and, if followed to their logical term, engender questions about the human good, not just about the good for me as an individual or about the good of my community.[13]

Furthermore, whereas communitarians are relatively silent on the question of the common good, MacIntyre is committed to an account of the common good that sets him in opposition to the nation-state. MacIntyre's most concise formulation of this opposition and of the importance of recovering a notion of the common good can be found in the following passage from "Politics, Philosophy and the Common Good":

> We now inhabit a social order whose institutional heterogeneity and diversity of interests is such that no place is left any longer for a politics of the common good. What we have instead is a politics from whose agendas enquiry concerning the nature of that politics has been excluded, a politics thereby protected from perceptions of its own exclusions and limitations. Enquiry into the nature of the common good of political society has become therefore crucial for understanding contemporary politics. For until we know how to think about the common good, we will not know how to evaluate the significance of those exclusions and limitations.[14]

Of course, the modern nation-state is characterized by all sorts of cooperative endeavors, as individuals give allegiance to a host of common pursuits. But the justification of political authority is merely instrumental, "in so far as it provides a secure social order within which individuals may pursue their own particular ends, whatever they are."[15] In this context, the common good is nothing other than a summing of individual goods, a conception of the common good "at once individualist and minimalist."[16] No longer the architectonic practice organizing all other practices in light of the common good, politics becomes one specialized sphere among many.[17]

The common good performs the function in MacIntyre's political thought of the best regime in classical political theory; it provides a vantage point from which one can gauge a variety of political orders and perceive their "limitations and exclusions." To "limitations" and "exclusions," we should add "distortions" and "deceptions." Here MacIntyre turns to Marx as an indispensable analyst of modern liberalism:

> Even if the Marxist characterizations of advanced capitalism are inadequate, the Marxist understanding of liberalism as ideological, as a deceiving and self-deceiving mask for certain social interests, remains compelling. Liberalism in the name of freedom imposes a certain kind of unacknowledged domination which in the long run tends to dissolve traditional ties and to impoverish social and cultural relationships. Liberalism, while imposing through state power regimes that declare everyone free to pursue whatever they take to be their own good, deprives most people of the possibility of understanding their lives as a quest for the discovery and achievement of the good.[18]

MacIntyre's political thought has at least one advantage over what often now passes for Aristotelian and Thomistic political thought. His thought forces upon us a question that followers of Aristotle and Aquinas have rarely formulated, let alone answered: In what sense can modern politics be considered an Aristotelian craft? As MacIntyre explains, the various expressions of "good," such as "'good at,' 'good for,' the virtue words, the expressions which appraise performance of duty, and 'good for its own sake' are at once socially and semantically ordered." They have their primary sense and meaning in the context of practices, where we have clear standards of excellence, of progress and failure. Outside of such practices, especially in "social orders in which practice-based relationships have been marginalized . . . such expressions . . . inevitably degenerate into what appear to some as no more than generalized expressions of approval."[19] But if modern politics—because of its size, its impersonal modes of bureaucratic organization, its penchant for according preeminence to instrumental reason—no longer meets the criteria for a craft in Aristotle's sense, then our situation is grave indeed. Not because we shall have trouble knowing how to think about modern politics in Aristotelian or Thomistic terms, but because, if MacIntyre is right, our very usage of the terms good and its cognates will be rendered deeply problematic.

MacIntyre's response to the crisis of the good, the waning of our appreciation and practice of virtue, is a shift in attention away from the nation-state to local communities and specific practices, wherein the language of "good," the pursuit of common goods, and the fostering of virtues perdure. In these locations, we can discover the residual elements of premodern politics, a politics that is diametrically opposed to the modern political structures of the nation-state.

The Dilemmas of Local Government

In his boldest statements, MacIntyre is Kierkegaardian regarding the situation of virtue in the modern state. Either one accepts the communitarian attempt to invest the nation-state with the task of moral education, of providing an ethos for the cultivation of virtue, or one repudiates the moral legitimacy of the state entirely. MacIntyre's assertion that the "modern state can't advance any justifiable claim to the allegiance of their members" would seem to make opposition to the nation-state morally obligatory. Of course, a majority of citizens could not believe this about the modern state and go on serving it in the way they do. Hence, the modern nation-state must "masquerade" as a liberal democracy. His precise description of modern states is that they are "oligarchies disguised as liberal democracies." Given MacIntyre's persistent opposition to capitalist economics, it remains unclear why his goal should not be to undermine entirely the nation-state. We have already quoted the passage in which MacIntyre concedes that the "Marxist characterizations of advanced capitalism are inadequate." Since MacIntyre describes capitalism in the same sweepingly negative terms as does Marx, it remains unclear precisely where MacIntyre thinks Marx went wrong about capitalism.[20]

As Kelvin Knight suggests, MacIntyre has indeed continued the project some have criticized him for abandoning, namely, the project of articulating "emergent socialist consciousness within capitalist society," a consciousness evident in the "ways in which men and women seem to be more 'realized' as rational or moral agents, when acting collectively in conscious rebellion (or resistance) against capitalist process."[21] The reason the socialist and anti-capitalist features of MacIntyre's thought are not so evident as they once were is that MacIntyre has given up the hope of replacing or reforming the nation-state along socialist lines.

Yet, MacIntyre himself retreats from his dismissive attitude toward the nation-state, which, he concedes, has "massive resources and exercises coercive legal powers."[22] While remaining deeply suspicious of it, we should acknowledge that the nation is "ineliminable" and we should "not despise its resources."[23] But the reliance on resources and coercive power raises other sorts of difficulties. There is the question of the principles and procedures in light of which the nation-state should go about distributing its massive resources in a just and economical way. Every time the state supports the project of one local community, it takes potential resources away from other communities and other projects. MacIntyre might allow that the local community should articulate for itself guidelines regarding distributive justice, guidelines that it would follow in its competition with other local communities for the resources of the state. But he seems to think that any attempt to come up with guidelines for the state is pointless, since the nation-state's "distribution of goods in no way reflects a common mind." This once again raises the question of the moral legitimacy of the state. And that question becomes more pressing when we turn from the state's distribution of resources to its use of coercive power.

Now, MacIntyre frankly admits that political communities, even on the scale that he is advocating, must exercise coercive power. On behalf of the political nature of these local communities, MacIntyre can point to ranking and organizing an array of practices and to the engagement in deliberation about goods held in common. But what is absent is any reference to legislation, the key mark of politics for Aristotle and Aquinas. Indeed, in the *Summa Theologiae* Aquinas treats politics under the topic of human law. The only way that the natural law of Aquinas can become political is by becoming human law. Within the confines of the nation-state with its invasive and seemingly omnipresent legal apparatus, what sort of legislative self-determination can a local community have? Even if it decides how to allocate resources and enact local laws, its police force is still fundamentally committed to enforcing the law of the nation and its economy is largely dependent on the national and increasingly the international economy.

A related issue concerns war. In keeping with his focus on the local rather than the national, MacIntyre avoids references to war. While Aristotle famously argues that the ambition to empire is ignoble, he does seem to grant a priority (in the order of generation if not in the order of excellence or nobility) to war. Any nation that is insecure in its relationships with its neighbors is unlikely to have the time or the resources to pursue the higher goods, which constitute a truly good communal life. MacIntyre is not a pacifist; he is committed to Catholic just war teaching. But does not this entail some sort of discrimination between rival nation-states? One might respond that we could determine just wars on an ad hoc basis, by focusing on specific criteria of just war, for example, whether the cause is just and whether the means of executing the war are just. But this leaves aside another criterion: whether the government that wages the war has the just authority to do so. And if the nation-state's "distribution of goods in no way reflects a common mind," then it is hard to see how it could reflect a common mind in the most important matters of life and death.[24]

MacIntyre made a gesture in the direction of a response to these sorts of criticisms toward the end of *After Virtue*, where he cautioned that he was not offering an "anarchist critique of the state." By this he means that "certain forms of government" may well be "necessary and legitimate." But he adds quickly that the "modern state is not such a form of government." But this is hardly reassuring; it seems to leave open the possibility that fomenting anarchy in any modern state might well be legitimate and desirable. At this point, MacIntyre adds a long clarification that renders his position even more baffling:

> This does not mean that there are not many tasks only to be performed in and through government which still require performing: the rule of law, so far as it is possible in a modern state, has to be vindicated, injustice and unwarranted suffering have to be dealt with, generosity has to be exercised, and liberty has to be defended, in ways that are sometimes only possible through the use of governmental institutions. But each particular task, each particular responsibility, has to be evaluated on its own merits.[25]

There are two serious problems with this line of argument. First, MacIntyre in quick succession takes away and then reasserts the legitimacy of the modern state. It has no claim to legitimacy and yet we are to uphold its "rule of law," its correction of "injustice," its alleviation of "suffering," and its promotion of "generosity" and "liberty." But if the modern state can, even only occasionally, foster these virtues, then it is hardly worthy of the wholesale condemnation MacIntyre levels against it. Second, the admission that the modern state operates in better and worse ways, that it sometimes does and sometimes does not promote certain virtues, suggests that we should have a more complicated discussion of its strengths and weaknesses, its virtues and vices, than MacIntyre anywhere pursues or even encourages. Instead, MacIntyre suggests a piecemeal engagement of the modern state with "each task" evaluated on its own merits. But this would return us to the sort of sporadic, punctual approach to politics that virtue ethics has been set on removing from ethical theory.[26]

Indeed, some such reflection on modern states would contribute to MacIntyre's defense of the limited autonomy of local communities. Would it not be useful, for example, to examine various conceptions of the relationship between national and state governments and between state and local communities?[27] Would it not be necessary to have some sort of position on constitutional law? MacIntyre includes the establishment of "formal constitutional procedures of decision-making" as one of the goals of "deliberative participation" in local communities.[28] But if local communities are going to develop procedures for self-legislation, then other constitutional issues shall have to be settled, such as the proper relationship between local communities and the state and between both of these and national governments. Without such large-scale political theorizing and activity, it is hard to see how a local community, subject to the laws of the nation, could be a political community in any meaningful sense or at least in any sense countenanced by Aristotle or Aquinas.[29]

MacIntyre calls these communities "political" because they involve ranking of various practices and the communal pursuit of goods internal to the practices. Yet the term sovereignty is never used. Would not any local community, committed to the common good in the way MacIntyre describes it, aspire to the kind of self-determination that only sovereignty could provide? Would it not always have to be prepared, not just prepared but eager, to overthrow the dominant regime? Yet, MacIntyre's admission that the nation-state is "ineliminable" indicates that he no longer harbors revolutionary hopes.

His repudiation of this project involves more than the prudential judgment that the time is not right for revolution. He asserts: "Those who make the conquest of state power their aim are always in the end conquered by it."[30] The problem, as he now sees it, is not "to reform the dominant order, but to find ways for local communities to survive by sustaining a life of the common good against the disintegrating forces of the nation-state and the market."[31] Only in this sense and at this level does he continue to advocate a subversive and radical politics, a "politics of self-defense for all those local societies that aspire to achieve some relatively self-sufficient and independent form of participatory practice-based community."[32] In these passages, MacIntyre conflates "reform" and "conquest." As we shall see shortly, Aristotle has little patience for the sort of social engineering entailed by conquest, both because he was critical of the desire to rule over others as an end in itself and because he was suspicious of radical reform projects. But he, nonetheless, supposes that every regime presents opportunities for improvement. By contrast, MacIntyre provides no argument to demonstrate that the discussion of better and worse ways for the modern state to engage in a host of political activities is tantamount to "conquest."

The more timid hopes for politics correspond to a contraction in the scope and ambitions of his political theorizing. Even if MacIntyre's thought can be brought to bear upon the present questions, one wonders what fruits can come of the sort of politics MacIntyre recommends. Of course a certain formulation of this sort of question, which accuses MacIntyre of not providing the kind of political theory that would enable us to reform the modern state, misses the point entirely. And certainly MacIntyre is more honest, or at least more clear-sighted, than are most communitarians about the sort of common good required to cultivate virtue. MacIntyre notes that the society he is promoting "must be small-scale and, so far as possible, as self-sufficient as it needs to be to protect itself from the destructive incursions of the state and the wider market economy."[33] Here MacIntyre adverts to another of Aristotle's criteria for a political regime: self-sufficiency. But, given the pervasiveness of the modern state and its economy, how could any local community ever attain, let alone sustain, such self-sufficiency?

Another sign that something has gone awry in MacIntyre's current political writings is the disjunction between two senses of tradition-constituted practice. As we have seen, MacIntyre holds out hope for political life only in local communities existing at the margins of modern life, communities whose existence beyond a generation is tenuous. These are the communal contexts within which we can pursue the virtues. But there is another sense of tradition-constituted practice, the one to which MacIntyre devotes much attention toward the end of *Whose Justice? Which Rationality?*[34] He describes the initial development of such a tradition in three stages:

> A first in which the relevant beliefs, texts, and authorities have not yet been put in question; a second in which inadequacies of various types have been identified, but not yet remedied; and a third in which response to those inadequacies has resulted in a set of reformulations, reevaluations, and new formulations and evaluations, designed to remedy inadequacies and overcome limitations.

As MacIntyre makes clear at the end of *Three Rival Versions of Moral Enquiry*, for this sort of tradition-constituted inquiry to flourish in the modern world it would require a restructuring of university life and pedagogy. But this ambitious intellectual enterprise would not seem possible in the sorts of communities MacIntyre praises for embodying, however fleetingly, the tradition of the virtues. These communities are so pressed by the concerns of daily life that they barely have time for leisure, much less for the establishment of textual traditions and the patient engagement of the texts of rival traditions. Yet, if these are the only sorts of communities in which the tradition of the virtues can still flourish, MacIntyre's entire philosophical project of tradition-constituted inquiry would be otiose indeed.

MacIntyre responds directly to the accusation that he is recommending a "politics of Utopian ineffectiveness."[35] His rejoinder is that since "the state and the market economy are so structured as to subvert and undermine the politics of local community," local communities will from "time to time" have to deal with nation-states and their economies. He adds that in so doing local communities will "always" have to be "wary and antagonistic." The most troubling part of the response is the phrase from "time to time." If the antagonism were as sharp as MacIntyre depicts it as being and if the state were as pervasive as it seems, then would not any local community serious about its integrity end up being consumed by its wrangling with the state? And would not the long-term survival necessitate so many compromises with the state that the community's self-sufficiency would be undermined? Some of the local communities MacIntyre cites as embodying the politics of the common good have survived for no more than twenty-five years, barely a generation.[36] Can we call such communities, which are unable to perpetuate themselves from one generation to another, "political"?

Rival Authorities, Conflicting Accounts of Politics

MacIntyre is fond of putting to himself the objection that he is advocating utopian politics, but his current position marks such a retreat from Marxism or even Aristotelianism that, contrary to being utopian, it fails even to rise to the level of politics, at least as it is conceived by Aristotle, Aquinas, or Marx. Indeed, the problems with MacIntyre's recent political writings concern not just their coherence or practical viability, but also their relationship to the authorities and traditions MacIntyre invokes.

In the course of elaborating his rival conception of politics, MacIntyre draws upon Aristotle, Aquinas, and Marx. An important question for MacIntyre's present political views concerns the relative weight he attaches to the political positions of each of these authorities and what he thinks we need to learn from each of them. This is more than an exegetical or historical question. MacIntyre advocates a conception of rationality as rooted in tradition-constituted inquiry and holds that a sign of the flourishing of a tradition is its ability to overcome conflicts between rival traditions.[37] So, it is a serious and substantive philosophical question: How well does MacIntyre navigate these various sources and integrates them into his argument?

In his account of the virtues, MacIntyre regularly refers to Aristotle; yet MacIntyre almost wholly neglects Aristotle's politics, in spite of the fact that Aristotle offers a politics of the common good. Human beings naturally desire "to live together," both to achieve the goods necessary for survival and to pursue a common life of excellence through the practice of the virtues. Indeed, Aristotle's two basic criticisms of existing regimes are that they aim too low and that they aim for only a part of the common good. The political order provides more than "security from injustice" and an arena for "exchange and mutual intercourse" (*Politics* 1280a35–39).[38] These are indispensable but insufficient ingredients of the political order. The true goal of the political order, whose origin is the "will to live together" in "friendship," is a "perfect and self-sufficing life," whose centerpiece is "noble actions, not mere companionship" (*Politics* 1280b30–1281a10). When Aristotle turns his critical eye to actually existing regimes, he finds that each embodies "a part of justice only" (*Politics* 1281a10). Every regime is organized around a constitution that specifies the principles of merit, the particular conception of justice, and who takes "part in the deliberative or judicial administration" in the regime (*Politics* 1275b18–19).

The most obvious division among regimes is a quantitative one, concerning whether one person, or few, or many exercise such power. But Aristotle introduces a more fundamental consideration, namely, whether those who rule do so for the sake of the common or the private interest. These two principles—one quantitative, the other qualitative—generate six possible types of regimes: kingship, aristocracy, constitutional government, on the one hand, and tyranny, oligarchy, and democracy, on the other (*Politics* 1279a17–1279b10). Aristotle calls the latter set of three, those that regard the private interest, "defective and perverted forms" (*Politics* 1279a17–22). Nonetheless, Aristotle does not dismiss these forms of government; instead, he investigates their partial apprehension of justice. Equality, which is the principle of democracy, and wealth, which animates oligarchy, are legitimate claimants to acknowledgment and honor in the political order. Aristotle's strategy is to unveil the limits of each of these "perverted forms" of regime, to exhibit the way in which a neglect of other goods, especially virtue, is deleterious not just to the flourishing but to the very survival of the regime. How do these arguments figure in MacIntyre's politics?

Although MacIntyre nowhere offers a sustained reflection on Aristotle's analysis of regimes, he does describe "the societies of advanced Western modernity" as "oligarchies disguised as liberal democracies." Now, MacIntyre's resistance to oligarchy certainly reflects in some measure Aristotle's criticisms of oligarchy as elevating wealth above virtue and other constitutive goods of a regime. Yet, in contrast to MacIntyre's grim and hasty dismissal of modern oligarchies, Aristotle seeks to engage oligarchies in light of their peculiar and partial apprehension of the good. Aristotle treats the oligarch as making a legitimate claim to office and power in the political order; all such claims are based upon the "possession of elements which enter into the composition of the state." Thus, the "noble or free-born or rich may . . . with good reason claim office," since "wealth and freedom are necessary" (*Politics* 1283a14–18). Although Aristotle would clearly share MacIntyre's worries about the elevation of the market above other constituting elements of the political order, especially virtue, there is good reason to doubt that his judgment would be as quick or sweeping as MacIntyre's.

Another way to put the difficulty concerning MacIntyre's relationship to Aristotle's politics is this: what replaces the analysis of the regimes? Has Aristotle's differentiated and prudential assessment of a variety of legitimate regimes been suppressed in favor of the one regime of virtue? Something like the latter position seems operative in MacIntyre's Marxist opposition between "civil society" and some sort of community that transcends the standpoint of civil society.[39] If there are types of regime here, there seem to be only two: the regime of civil society with its abstract individualism and the regime of the common good with its construal of individuals as always already related to one another. Yet, MacIntyre's conception of the rationality of traditions, of the dialectical encounters between rival traditions, and his insistence on the particularist aspiration for the universal good would seem not only to allow for, but to require, a differentiated and prudential engagement of specific communities, indeed of types of regime. But the question remains: is Aristotle's focus on regimes helpful for our current predicament or not? What are its specific strengths and weaknesses? So far as I can tell, MacIntyre nowhere directly addresses these issues. Leo Strauss captures Aristotle's dialectic thus:

> Political life is characterized by conflicts between men asserting opposed claims. Those who raise a claim usually believe that what they claim is good for them. In many cases they believe, and in most cases they say, that what they claim is good for the community at large. In practically all cases claims are raised, sometimes sincerely and sometimes insincerely, in the name of justice. The opposed claims are based, then, on opinions of what is good or just. To justify their claims, the opposed parties advance arguments. The conflict calls for arbitration, for an intelligent decision that will give each party what it truly deserves. Some of the material required for making such a decision is offered by the opposed parties themselves, and the very insufficiency of this partial material—an insufficiency obviously due to its partisan origin—points the way to its completion by the umpire. The umpire par excellence is the political philosopher.[40]

MacIntyre's considered opinion about the political activities of the nation-state must be that it furnishes none of "the material required for making . . . a decision" about justice. MacIntyre continues the dialectic only with respect to those residual premodern elements of our political life. For anything distinctively modern, there is only repudiation.

But this forces MacIntyre into an odd position in relationship to Aristotle. He wants Aristotle's ethics without his politics, in spite of the fact that Aristotle presents them as complementary. In his reaction against the modern separation of ethics from politics, MacIntyre seems at times to go to the other extreme, to fuse his politics to an ethical conception of the good life. How Aristotelian is such a fusion? While closely related, politics for Aristotle is not simply an elaboration or expansion of ethics. The *Ethics* depicts the model of the good man, whereas the *Politics* operates with the distinction between the good man and the good citizen. No such distinction seems to be operative in MacIntyre's political thought. This distinction is closely allied to another distinction in Aristotle, between the best regime and legitimate regimes. Indeed, the crucial, dialectical encounter in the third book of the *Politics* concerns precisely a conversation between oligarchy and democracy, regimes that by their very nature risk subordinating the common to the private good of a portion of the citizenry. If Aristotle shares MacIntyre's exalted conception of politics as the pursuit of the common good of virtuous living, he appears more willing to countenance imperfect realizations, even distortions, of this ideal.

As Mary Nichols shows in her study of Aristotle's *Politics*, Aristotle argues that the best possible regime is polity, which combines elements of oligarchy and democracy.[41] Aristotle wants his audience, the legislators or statesmen, to be "acquainted not only with that which is best in the abstract, but also with that which is best relatively to circumstances." He urges an investigation of how each regime "is originally formed, and, when formed, how it may be longest preserved" (*Politics* 1288b27–30). He wants what is possible or attainable; but this is not a slavish conformity to tradition, to what is, rather than what might be. The sense of the possibilities for improvement latent within any regime is precisely what leads Aristotle to study in detail the varieties of regime, how many there are and in how many ways they are combined (*Politics* 1289a7–11). The prudential assessment of what is given in actually existing regimes, of their complexities and internal conflicts, and of the forces that provide for their amelioration and longevity—these are the central preoccupations of Aristotle's politics. Yet these have little or no place in MacIntyre's political thought.

MacIntyre's neglect of the analysis of regimes and his focus on the opposition between civil society and the virtuous community raise the question of whether his allegiance in political matters is not closer to Marx than to Aristotle. The presence of words such as "utopian" (in "Politics, Philosophy and the Common Good"), "revolution" (MacIntyre refers us approvingly to Kelvin Knight's piece on "Revolutionary Aristotelianism"), and "subversive" (see "Natural Law as Subversive") trace their lineage to Marx rather than Aristotle. This in itself is certainly not a criticism, much less an unmasking of MacIntyre, who readily admits that contemporary Aristotelianism must learn from Marx.[42] MacIntyre urges a critical reappropriation of Marx, one that takes its point of departure from Marx's fatal error, his repudiation of philosophy after his encounter with the inadequate philosophies of Hegel and Feuerbach. In his precipitate abandoning of philosophy, MacIntyre argues, Marx deprived himself of the philosophical resources for articulating the common good, resources that MacIntyre finds in Aristotle and Aquinas. MacIntyre deploys Aristotelian language to articulate Marx's contrast between civil society and objective activity:

> In activities governed by the norms of civil society there are no ends except those which are understood to be the goals of some particular individual or individuals, directed by the desires of those individuals....

By contrast, the ends of any type of practice involving what Marx calls objective activity are characterizable antecedently to . . . the desires of particular individuals. . . . Individuals discover in the ends of any such practice goods common to all who engage in it, goods internal to and specific to that particular type of practice, which they can make their own only by allowing their participation in the activity to effect a transformation in the desires which they initially brought with them to the activity.[43]

The passage covers what are by now familiar themes and includes a familiar contrast. What I want to suggest is that any attempt to reconstruct MacIntyre's mediation of Aristotle and Marx would do well to focus on Aquinas's natural law doctrine. Since MacIntyre embraced Aquinas after having already made the shift from Marx to Aristotle, this would not be a genetic reconstruction. Instead, it would be a teleological reconstruction, one which finds in the doctrine of natural law the most adequate expression of what MacIntyre wants from both Aristotle and Marx: a political theory based on the insights of Aristotle's ethics, capable of marshalling a critique of advanced capitalism, and independent of Aristotle's politics. But how could natural law, which at least on the surface seems alien to both Aristotle and Marx, help?

What MacIntyre finds in Aquinas's doctrine of natural law is a set of precepts specifying the "preconditions of rational inquiry," for a communal life organized around the pursuit of goods held in common. In this way, Aquinas's natural law doctrine becomes the basis for MacIntyre's politics. The most explicit statement of the political character of the natural law occurs in the essay "Natural Law as Subversive: The Case of Aquinas," an essay devoted to showing that natural law is equally at odds with local prejudice and centralizing power. MacIntyre writes,

The exceptionless precepts of the natural law are those which, insofar as we are rational, we recognize as indispensable in every society and in every situation for the achievement of our goods and of our final good, because they direct us toward and partially define our common good.[44]

In "Politics, Philosophy and the Common Good," he urges that the key political question is: "what form of social and political life" provides the conditions for individuals to "learn about their individual and common goods, so that questions about the justification of political authority can be asked and answered through rational inquiry and debate?"[45] Such a community would have to possess three characteristics: first, it would have to be small-scale and, second, it would have to find ways of resisting the domination of the market. But, third, it would also have to be a community "whose members . . . recognize that obedience to those standards that Aquinas identified as the precepts of the natural law is necessary, if they are to learn from and with each other what their individual and common goods are."[46] Natural law provides precepts for structuring political life without recourse to Aristotle's own political doctrines.

MacIntyre repeatedly describes the precepts of the natural law as constitutive of practical, communal deliberation. Aquinas famously argues that the precepts are underived, first principles. MacIntyre interprets this to mean that they are presuppositions of the very activities in which we must engage if we are to make progress in the life of virtue. MacIntyre underscores the pedagogical character of law in Aquinas. Conformity to the precepts provides an initial formation of the passions, whose education is crucial to the cultivation of virtue.[47] Aquinas himself responds in pedagogical terms to the question whether it is useful for human beings to frame laws (*ST*, I-II, 95, 1). Human beings, he states, attain the "perfection of virtue by training" and law supplies a crucial part of that training. For example, whenever Aquinas addresses the issue of private property, he justifies it not in terms of rights antecedent to civil government, but in light of the common good. The role of laws regarding property is to "accustom men to give of their own readily" (*ST*, I-II, 105, 2).

Aquinas, MacIntyre notes, does not construe human law as mapping the precepts of the natural law onto existing societies. The limits to human law derive from prudential principles concerning moral education. The attempt to forbid all vice frequently engenders unanticipated outbreaks of greater evils. Human law seeks to lead human beings gradually from the imperfect to the perfect. MacIntyre writes,

> Aquinas thus disagrees with both later puritans and later liberals. Like those puritans and unlike those liberals he understands law as an instrument for our moral education. But, like those liberals and unlike those puritans, he is against making law by itself an attempt to repress all vice.[48]

MacIntyre is right to insist that Aquinas is no liberal. He would resist the privatization of the good. If human law should not settle for the low aims of modern liberal regimes, it can certainly make do with much less than what is urged by the entirety of the natural law. Sometimes Aquinas writes that human law forbids only the most grievous vices, especially those that are harmful to others, such as murder and theft (*ST*, I-II, 96, 2). Any attempt to reform the character of a people by the enactment of law must take its cue from the existing customs of the society. Custom itself, Aquinas writes, has the force of law, abolishes law, and is the interpreter of law (*ST*, I-II, 97, 3). In situations where the people are free to make their own law, custom "has greater authority than the sovereign" (*ST*, I-II, 97, 3, ad 3). MacIntyre concludes, "one . . . would need the strongest of reasons to interfere with local custom." On MacIntyre's interpretation, Aquinas's account of custom protects the local community from the incursions of centralized power.[49]

But Aquinas nowhere limits himself just to "local" customs; he speaks of the difficulty of setting aside the "customs of a whole people" (*ST*, I-II, 97, 3, ad 2). Indeed, the ineradicable role of custom leads Aquinas in the direction of a sustained, detailed prudential engagement with particular regimes. In his discussion of the "utility" of human law, his principal authority is Isidore, who speaks principally of the negative function of law, its checking of "audacity" through "fear," its providing safety for the innocent in the "midst of wickedness" through the "dread of punishment" (*ST*, I-II, 95, 1). In circumstances where the people is not virtuous, law forbids only "the most grievous vices" and its goal is to move the people to virtue, "not suddenly but gradually" (*ST*, I-II, 96, 2, ad 2).[50]

Aquinas repeatedly gives evidence of being committed to Aristotle's focus on the regime in political theory. The "precepts of the law," Aquinas writes, "are diversified according to the various kinds of community" (*ST*, I-II, 100, 2). Aquinas understands different kinds of political community in terms of different constitutions or regimes. For example, in response to the question whether the old law provided fitting precepts concerning rules (*ST*, I-II, 105, 1), Aquinas argues that the regime established by God for the Jewish people at the time of Moses was a mixed regime, the best realizable, constitutional structure. It combines elements of kingdom or monarchy (in the rule of Moses) with elements of aristocracy (in the function of the 72 elders) with elements of democracy (in the elders being elected by the people). Commenting that "this form of constitution ensures peace, commends itself to all, and is guarded by all," he refers us to Aristotle's *Politics*, book two. Similarly, in another passage, this one on human laws being framed by those who govern (*ST*, I-II, 95, 4), he runs through the types of regime and concludes that the best government is one that is made up of all the others.

For Aquinas as for Aristotle, an analysis of regimes brings to light the multiple ways of embodying and pursuing the goods of political life, especially justice. MacIntyre himself grasps the importance of this point. He writes, "Every political and social order embodies and gives expression to an ordering of different human goods and therefore also embodies and gives expression to some particular conception of the human good."[51] Yet, MacIntyre ignores regimes entirely, focusing instead on local communities, communities even smaller than that of the ancient *polis*. By contrast, Aristotle and Aquinas describe the political order as a "composite," a complex mixture not just of goods but of levels and parts. The defense of a mixed, constitutional regime requires careful analysis of conflicts of goods and interests and of the levels of participation and degrees of allegiance. Second, the analysis of regimes provides a sense of the limitations to any particular, political order, as embodying only a part of justice. Conversely, of course, every regime embodies some part of justice and thus contains within itself principles, however unarticulated, that can operate as dialectical starting points in the movement toward a more adequate conception and practice of justice. A corollary of the second advantage is a lesson about how an excessive emphasis on the dominant good of a regime can exclude from practice, and occlude from theoretical analysis, other goods. Thus does the emphasis on regimes allow for a prudential assessment of the virtues and vices, the inclusions and exclusions, of particular political orders.

By way of conclusion, I would like to consider briefly two possible, MacIntyrean rejoinders, concerning political theory and regimes. First, there is the problem of the notion and nature of political theory. Although MacIntyre is not the anti-theorist he is often taken to be, he does insist upon the primacy of certain kinds of practice for effective theorizing. In "The *Theses on Feuerbach*," he notes that what Marx rejected in his predecessors was a particular understanding of the relationship between theory and practice, which supposes that the theoretical analysis of the incoherence of various practices is sufficient to bring about, or at least initiate, social change. Moreover, such abstract, detached theorizing rests upon an unwarranted gap between the self-understanding of the theorists and how the theorists understand the "subjects of their inquiries." The theorists see themselves as "rational agents," while they see "others in terms of a determinist theory."[52] This gap invites theorists to think that it is legitimate to "impose their conception of the good" onto the subjects of their inquiries. Thus is born the bureaucratic, modern state with its hierarchical division of "managers and managed."[53] To all this, MacIntyre opposes the primacy of a "particular kind of practice . . . informed by a particular kind of theory, rooted in the same practice." Only in the context of such communal practices can theorists themselves be "transformed" by the practice of the intellectual and moral virtues. Now,

MacIntyre might say that the political theory of Aristotle and Aquinas is susceptible to the Marxist critique. Is it? The distinction between best and legitimate regimes would seem to presuppose some sort of distinction between theory and practice, but precisely what sort is unclear. It is certainly not the case that Aristotle or Aquinas thinks that the theoretical exposing of incoherence or contradiction in an existing regime will resolve anything at the level of practice. Nor do they suppose that the political theorist can operate as a social engineer. The dialectical relationship between nature and custom in classical political theory is not an anticipation of Descartes's repudiation of all received opinion as a means of arriving at clear, unadulterated ideas. Aristotelian and Thomistic political theory takes its point of departure from, and never fully transcends, the opinions about the good already operative in existing regimes. As MacIntyre himself notes, laws, even those informed by the ideals of the natural law, must be applied prudentially to the existing customs of a society.[54]

Second, however central to Aristotelian and Thomistic political thought is the notion of the regime, such an inquiry might now seem to be of no more than antiquarian interest. We may not be at the end of history, but we no longer witness a rich variety of regimes. The phenomena themselves may warrant MacIntyre's neglect of the dialectic of the regimes. And yet—here I can do no more than gesture in the direction of a response—precisely because of the nearly universal dominance of the democratic idea, the dialectic of the regime may still be useful to us. One of the most important lessons that we are to learn from Aristotle's dialectic of regimes is that no existing regime is perfect and that each can be diminished if not destroyed by an excess of its dominant tendencies. Serious thinking about the nature of regimes can provoke a sense of alternative possibilities, a sense absent from conventional liberal theorizing about conventional liberal politics.[55] This is the traditional Aristotelian and Thomistic way of overcoming the "unphilosophical politics" and "unpolitical philosophy" to which MacIntyre objects.[56]

NOTES

Reprinted from *The Review of Politics* 66, no. 3 (Summer 2004): 357–83.

This essay is an expanded version of a piece I composed as respondent to Alasdair MacIntyre's lecture "Politics, Philosophy and the Common Good," delivered as part of the Bradley Lecture Series in Politics and Religion at Boston College on February 25, 2000.

I am grateful to Professor MacIntyre for his responses to the questions posed to him on that occasion. I am also grateful to John O'Callaghan, Jay Bruce, Walter Nicgorski, and two anonymous reviewers at *The Review of Politics* for helpful comments on previous drafts of this essay.

1. Roger Crisp and Michael Slote, Introduction to *Virtue Ethics*, ed. Crisp and Slote (Oxford: Oxford University Press, 1997).

2. The problem is not a dearth of available material on politics and virtue. See, for example, William Galston, *Liberal Purposes: Goods, Virtues, and Diversity in the Liberal State* (Cambridge: Cambridge University Press, 1991); Quentin Skinner, "The Republican Ideal of Political Liberty," in *Machiavelli and Republicanism*, ed. G. Bock, Q. Skinner, and M. Viroli (Cambridge: Cambridge University Press, 1990); Amy Gutmann, *Democratic Education* (Princeton, NJ: Princeton University Press, 1987); Richard Sinopli, *The Foundation of American Citizenship: Liberalism, the Constitution, and Civic Virtue* (Oxford: Oxford University Press, 1997); Richard Dagger, *Civic Virtues: Rights, Citizenship, and Republican Liberalism* (Oxford: Oxford University Press, 1997).

3. See Alisdair MacIntyre, "Politics, Philosophy and the Common Good," *Studi Perugini* 3 (1997): 9–30, reprinted in *The MacIntyre Reader*, ed. Kelvin Knight (Notre Dame, IN: University of Notre Dame Press, 1998), 235–52; "The *Theses on Feuerbach*: A Road Not Taken," in *Artifacts, Representations, and Social Practice: Essays for Marx Wartoftky* (Hingham, MA: Kluwer Academic Publishers, 1994), reprinted in *The MacIntyre Reader*, 223–34; "Natural Law as Subversive: The Case of Aquinas," *Journal of Medieval and Early Modern Studies* 26 (1996): 61–83; *Dependent Rational Animals: Why Human Beings Need the Virtues* (Chicago: Open Court, 1999). To these, we might add, "The Privatization of 'Good': An Inaugural Lecture," *Review of Politics* 52, no. 3 (1990): 344–61, and the preface to the 2nd edition of *Marxism and Christianity* (New York: Duckworth, 1995).

4. MacIntyre, "Politics, Philosophy and the Common Good," in *The MacIntyre Reader*, 248.

5. But perhaps not as much scorn as his embrace of Catholicism and Thomism. See the vitriolic reactions of Martha Nussbaum, "Recoiling from Reason," *New York Review of Books* 36, no. 19 (1989): 36–42, and Annette Baier, "What Women Want in a Moral Theory," in *Moral Prejudices: Essays on Ethics* (Cambridge, MA: Harvard University Press, 1995), 17.

6. For criticisms of MacIntyre's accounts of tradition and of liberalism, see Gary Gutting, *Pragmatic Liberalism and the Critique of Modernity* (Cambridge: Cambridge University Press, 1999), 69–112; Jean Porter, "Tradition in the Recent Work of Alasdair MacIntyre," in *Alasdair MacIntyre*, ed. Mark Murphy (Cambridge: Cambridge University Press, 2003), 38–69; and Jeffrey Stout, *Democracy and Tradition* (Princeton, NJ: Princeton University Press, 2003), 118–39. The best criticisms can be found in Stout, who argues that, in his hasty and sweeping dismissal of modernity, MacIntyre falls short of his own standards for debate with rival positions. Stout writes, "The result is utterly unsympathetic caricature at the very point where the narrative most urgently requires detailed and fair-minded exposition if it means to test its author's preconceptions with any rigor at all"

(127). For a lucid discussion of MacIntyre on tradition and modernity, see Terry Pinkard, "MacIntyre's Critique of Modernity," in *Alasdair MacIntyre*, ed. Murphy, 176–200.

7. See, for example, Alasdair MacIntyre, *Whose Justice? Which Rationality?* (Notre Dame, IN: University of Notre Dame Press, 1988), 349–69. For a response to the charge that MacIntyre is a political conservative, see Kelvin Knight's "Revolutionary Aristotelianism," in *Contemporary Political Studies 1996*, vol. 2, ed. I. Hampsher-Monk and J. Stanyer (Nottingham: Political Studies Association of the United Kingdom, 1996), 885–96.

8. In this, modernity, according to MacIntyre, fails on its own terms. "Instead of the ever-widening educated public of the democratic intellect," which Enlightenment theorists had predicted would be the result of liberalism, "we have the mass semiliteracy of the television audience" ("An Interview for *Cogito*," in *The MacIntyre Reader*, 272).

9. Even more powerfully, the argument of *Dependent Rational Animals* is that philosophical biases, rooted in a distinctively Western celebration of rational autonomy and a Lockean conception of the person, have led certain strains of contemporary liberalism to defend policies of unjust exclusion. In this book, MacIntyre retracts his earlier rejection of natural teleology and depicts the virtues as constituting the "form of life" appropriate "for beings biologically constituted as we are." The book seeks to recover a greater sense of the "animal conditions" of human agency and of the "nature and extent of human vulnerability and disability" (p. x). If the turn to natural teleology seems a novelty to readers accustomed to MacIntyre's defense of an historicist, social teleology, it is nonetheless something of a return. In "Notes from the Moral Wilderness," first published in *The New Reasoner* in 1958, MacIntyre argued that the bridge between morality and desire, severed in a variety of ways on modern thought and life, is the Marxist conception of human nature. He writes, "Capitalism provides a form of life in which men rediscover desire in a number of ways. . . . One meets the anarchic individualist desires which a competitive society breeds in us with a rediscovery of the deeper desire to share what is common in humanity, to be divided neither from them nor from oneself, to be a man" ("Notes from the Moral Wilderness," reprinted in *The MacIntyre Reader*, 46–47).

10. MacIntyre, *Dependent Rational Animals*, 142.

11. Contemporary liberal political theory may itself be at odds with important features of the African-American struggle. In "Rawls and Liberty of Conscience" (*Review of Politics* 60, no. 2 [1988]: 247–76), Andrew Murphy cogently argues that underlying Rawls's liberalism "is, at best, a belief-action split that has historically worked against liberty of conscience; at worst, a scheme of repression and self-censorship which renders comprehensive doctrines meaningless" (250). I am currently working on an essay on MacIntyre and African-American Thought, the thesis of which is that something very much akin to MacIntyre's account of rationality and cooperative inquiry is operative in the writings of Frederick Douglass and W. E. B. DuBois.

12. As MacIntyre sees it, "communitarianism . . . is a diagnosis of certain weaknesses in liberalism, not a rejection of it" ("Politics, Philosophy and the Common Good," in *The MacIntyre Reader*, 244).

13. Ibid., 249.

14. Ibid., 239.
15. Ibid., 241.
16. Ibid., 242.
17. MacIntyre is quite clearly aligning himself with those Thomists, such as Charles De Koninck, who advocated a strong sense of the priority of the common good. For a discussion of a variety of Thomistic conceptions of the common good and for helpful clarification of the meanings of "common good" in Aquinas's own thought, see Greg Froelich, "The Equivocal Status of the Bonum Commune," *New Scholasticism* 63, no. 1 (1989): 38–57. On Thomist debates over the common good, see Mary Keys, "Personal Dignity and the Common Good: A Twentieth-Century Thomistic Dialogue," in *Catholicism, Liberalism, and Communitarianism*, ed. Kenneth Grasso, Gerald Bradley, and R. Hunt (Lanham, MD: Rowman and Littlefield, 1995), 173–96.
18. MacIntyre, "An Interview with Giovanna Borradori," in *The MacIntyre Reader*, 258.
19. MacIntyre, "An Interview for *Cogito*," ibid., 273–74.
20. In "The *Theses on Feuerbach*," MacIntyre traces Marx's failures to his precipitate abandoning of philosophy, but this is a failure in Marx's attempt to articulate a viable alternative to capitalism, not in his analysis of capitalism itself. For MacIntyre's account of the inadequacies of Marx as an economist, especially in his prophetic predictions about the imminent and inevitable collapse of capitalism, see *Marxism and Christianity*. A recent attempt to apply MacIntyre's thought to economics and social theory is Peter McMylor's *Alasdair MacIntyre: Critic of Modernity* (London: Routledge, 1994).
21. Knight, "Revolutionary Aristotelianism," 885. Knight is quoting E. P. Thompson's lament that MacIntyre abandoned this line of inquiry. See E. P. Thompson, "An Open Letter to Leszek Kolakowski," in *The Socialist Register*, ed. Ralph Miliband and John Saville (London: The Merlin Press, 1974), 58–59.
22. MacIntyre, *Dependent Rational Animals*, 142.
23. Ibid., 133. In this context MacIntyre praises those responsible for passing the Americans with Disabilities Act.
24. Ibid., 131.
25. MacIntyre, *After Virtue*, 237.
26. In the context of the passage just quoted, MacIntyre adds that "modern systematic politics, whether liberal, conservative, radical or socialist, simply has to be rejected" (ibid., 237). MacIntyre does not say precisely what he means by "systematic politics," although in the immediately preceding pages he has criticized the political theories of Nozick and Rawls. Between their approaches and that of MacIntyre stand a host of other political theorists, including a number of Thomists, who can hardly be said to be naïve about the prospects for virtue in the modern state. I am thinking of Yves R. Simon, Russell Hittinger, and Anthony Lisska, among others. Toward the end of this essay, I will take up MacIntyre's objection to a certain kind of political theorizing. This much is clear—MacIntyre has clearly not shown that all types of theorizing about politics in the modern state are vulnerable to his objections.

27. MacIntyre does precisely this, if only briefly, when he sides with liberals against communitarians in holding that the nation-state "should remain neutral between rival conceptions of the human good" and that "shared visions of the good" should be articulated in "the activities of subordinate voluntary associations" ("A Partial Response to My Critics," in *After MacIntyre*, ed. John Horton and Susan Mendus [Cambridge, MA: Polity Press, 1994], 302). Among the essays in this volume that address MacIntyre's political views, see especially Charles Taylor, "Justice After Virtue," 16–43, and Philip Pettit, "Liberal/Communitarian: MacIntyre's Mesmeric Dichotomy," 176–204.

28. MacIntyre, "Politics, Philosophy and the Common Good," in *The MacIntyre Reader*, 248.

29. One might argue that MacIntyre's defense of local communities has been the centerpiece of at least one influential modern, political theory, namely, that of Alexis de Tocqueville, who praised the New England townships as the very model and source of a robust democratic politics. But the comparison fails in three respects. First, the townships were much more accommodating of certain kinds of economics than MacIntyre's communities would be. Second, Tocqueville describes the citizens of the townships as transferring their allegiance from the local community to the nation, whereas the members of MacIntyre's communities must see themselves in a state of undeclared war with the nation-state. Third, the emphasis in Tocqueville on the primacy of the township for the practice of self-government does not preclude reflection on, and taking positions about, issues of modern constitutions, national politics, and so forth.

30. MacIntyre, *Marxism and Christianity*, 2nd ed. (Notre Dame, IN: University of Notre Dame Press, 1995), xv.

31. MacIntyre, "The Spectre of Communitarianism," *Radical Philosophy* 70 (1995): 35, quoted in Knight, "Revolutionary Aristotelianism," 894.

32. MacIntyre, *Marxism and Christianity*, xxvi. MacIntyre would undoubtedly defend the commitment to local communities not just or primarily on the basis of a radical politics but as the appropriate response for anyone committed to thinking about politics in the tradition of the common good. As he puts it, an "adequate sense of tradition manifests itself in a grasp of those future possibilities which the past has made available to the present" (MacIntyre, *After Virtue*, 223).

33. MacIntyre, "Politics, Philosophy and the Common Good," in *The MacIntyre Reader*, 248.

34. MacIntyre, *Whose Justice? Which Rationality?*, 326–88.

35. MacIntyre, "Politics, Philosophy and the Common Good," in *The MacIntyre Reader*, 252.

36. See, for example, his discussion of hand-loom weavers in Lancashire and Yorkshire at the end of the eighteenth century ("The *Theses on Feuerbach*," in *The MacIntyre Reader*, 231–32).

37. See MacIntyre, *Whose Justice? Which Rationality?*, 349–69.

38. All quotations from Aristotle's *Politics* are from the Benjamin Jowett translation (Oxford: Oxford University Press, 1941).

39. MacIntyre, "The *Theses on Feuerbach*," in *The MacIntyre Reader*, 225–28.

40. Leo Strauss, "On Classical Political Philosophy," *The Rebirth of Classical Political Rationalism: An Introduction to the Thought of Leo Strauss*, ed. and intro. Thomas Pangle (Chicago: University of Chicago Press, 1989), 51.

41. Mary Nichols, *Citizens and Statesmen: A Study of Aristotle's Politics* (Savage, MD: Rowman and Littlefield, 1992), especially 85–123.

42. See MacIntyre, "Politics, Philosophy and the Common Good," 251, and "An Interview with Giovanna Borradori," 265 (both in *The MacIntyre Reader*).

43. MacIntyre, "The *Theses on Feuerbach*," in *The MacIntyre Reader*, 225–26.

44. MacIntyre, "Natural Law as Subversive: The Case of Aquinas," *Journal of Medieval and Early Modern Studies* 26 (1996): 68.

45. MacIntyre, "Politics, Philosophy and the Common Good," in *The MacIntyre Reader*, 247.

46. Ibid.

47. MacIntyre, "Natural Law as Subversive," 80.

48. Ibid., 66.

49. See Mark Murphy, "Consent, Custom, and the Common Good in Aquinas's Theory of Political Authority," *Review of Politics* 59 (1997): 323–50. Also see Murphy's "MacIntyre's Political Philosophy," in *Alasdair MacIntyre*, ed. Murphy, 152–75.

50. Aquinas also addresses the regimes in *On Kingship, to the King of Cyprus*, Book I, chapters 1–6, trans. Gerald B. Phelan and intro. I. Th. Eschmann (Toronto: PIMS, 1978). This treatise is, in its examples and style, less Greek than Roman. The examples of political life are not from Greek city-states but from the Roman Republic. On the debates surrounding the manuscripts and authenticity of *On Kingship*, see Jean-Pierre Torrell, *Saint Thomas Aquinas*, vol. 1, *The Person and His Work*, trans. Robert Royal (Washington, DC: Catholic University of America Press, 1996), 350. Torrell also discusses the incomplete *Commentary on the Politics* (344).

51. MacIntyre, "Politics, Philosophy and the Common Good," in *The MacIntyre Reader*, 247.

52. MacIntyre, "The *Theses on Feuerbach*," in *The MacIntyre Reader*, 230.

53. Ibid., 231.

54. Furthermore, one might wonder whether MacIntyre's own thought fits his model of effective theorizing. That is, one needs to ask, out of what concrete, communal practice does MacIntyre's own theorizing arise? He tends to cite as admirable examples local communities with which he is clearly very familiar but not ones in which he has been an active participant. Is not his theorizing in some ways exactly parallel to the sort engaged in by Aristotle and Aquinas?

55. At least this is the thesis advanced by the contemporary, French political philosopher, Pierre Manent, whose two most important books are *The City of Man* and *The Nature of Democracy*. But the elaboration of that position must await another day.

56. MacIntyre, "Politics, Philosophy and the Common Good," in *The MacIntyre Reader*, 236–37.

CHAPTER 26

Render Unto Caesar ... What?

Reflections on the Work of William Cavanaugh

PAUL S. ROWE

Paul S. Rowe (1972–) is Associate Professor in the Department of Political and International Studies at Trinity Western University in British Columbia, Canada. He earned his Bachelor's Degree from the University of Toronto in 1995 and his Ph.D. from McGill University in 2003. He has published widely on religion and global politics, Middle Eastern politics, and Christian groups in the Middle East and the developing world.

The past decade has seen significant growth in interest surrounding religion at the transnational level, from notions of civilizational clash to castigations of the dysfunctions of organized faiths.[1] Religion has assumed increasing centrality in discussions of state policy and global order.[2] In a challenging piece published in *World Politics* in the wake of September 11, 2001, Daniel Philpott explored the extent to which the assault of transnational religious organizations on America was, in fact, a challenge to the Westphalian synthesis that underpins the modern state. Philpott argued that out of religious beliefs, radical networks are able to "construct a political theology as well as a social critique that measures the distance between that theology and contemporary social conditions and prescribes action accordingly."[3] The broad range and depth of these organizations likewise call into question the continuation of the secular international system, either by replacing it entirely or by creating dueling ideological-cum-theological systems at the global level.

In the midst of the military response that has driven the putative challengers to the status quo into hiding, it would appear that this attack on the Westphalian state is in some ways overstated. Osama bin Laden and his al-Qaeda network and their affiliates have been driven underground and seem unlikely to create a unified challenge to the international order. Their influence seems rather limited to portions of northwestern Pakistan and the inspiration of collected groups of radicals. Their would-be followers in the Middle East are torn between the poles of Sunni and Shi'i sectarian leaders. While they seem every bit as capable of launching another suicide operation that will claim the lives of thousands as they were in 2001, they are just as limited in their aim of replacing the secular world order with an eschatologically Islamic one.

A more serious question, however, is whether a more generic religious objection to the modern state system is likely to erode the confidence of the world's population in the authority and legitimacy of the state. While perhaps al-Qaeda militants do not have the power to overthrow Western civilization or the U.S. military, or even succeed in recreating the Caliphate, one does wonder to what extent developments in religious awakening worldwide will threaten the secular state system that has evolved since Westphalia. Clashes of civilizations might take a Huntingtonian or other form, but it is clear that basic substantive debates over values have taken center stage in transnational discussions. Distrust of the modern nation-state is by no means confined to the likes of Osama bin Laden or Sayyid Qutb.

Political scientists who are used to looking for challenges to world order from ideological radicals in the mold of Che Guevara or Abu Musab al-Zarqawi might miss those coming from bespectacled or overlooked quarters of academia and society. This is true even though intellectuals have had important roles to play in the establishment of important changes in the state system, from the Treaty of Westphalia to the end of the Cold War. So far, the work of William Cavanaugh, an American Roman Catholic political theologian, has not been well remarked. However, it is interesting to explore Cavanaugh's work as a deliberate and deliberately nonviolent attack on the Westphalian state.

As a postmodern critic of the state and proponent of a reinvigorated church, Cavanaugh is correct to take aim at the unquestioned place of the state. Still, Cavanaugh's arguments against the legitimacy of the state and in support of a religiously inspired ordering principle seem to provide strong ammunition for all opponents of the state. Does Cavanaugh's work only provide a Christian rationalization against the Westphalian state that runs the danger of being taken up by religious radicals of other bents who would agree with his attack on the secular nation-state while dropping his Christianity and pacifism? Does Cavanaugh set up a religious alternative to the state that is just as fraught with the potential abuse of temporal power and even authoritarianism as the state itself? Perhaps most importantly, does Cavanaugh dismiss the very vital and important role that religion plays as both an intermediary and critic of the state in civil society?

In the following article, I will explore these and other considerations. The review takes Cavanaugh's work at face value as both political theory and theology and, therefore, considers it from both angles. It comes from an analyst with shared roots in the Christian tradition, albeit grafted outside Cavanaugh's Roman Catholic arboretum. It serves as an attempt both to introduce his thought to a wider audience in political theory and political science as well as to serve as a critique from the perspective of a political scientist. I follow three lines of questioning. First, what are we to make of Cavanaugh's argument against the state, and in particular, the coercive nature of the state? Second, is Cavanaugh correct to challenge the independence of civil society as a part of the state apparatus? Third, is Cavanaugh creating a fulsome critique of the modern international system from a Christian perspective? In light of these assessments, I suggest that Cavanaugh has unduly criticized the state and even more civil society and that his view of the church speaks in a limited way to Christians but even less to non-Christians. I conclude with some reflections on the implications of Cavanaugh's thought.

SEPARATING CHURCH AND STATE?

With close associations with a new theological movement toward radical orthodoxy,[4] Cavanaugh's work displays an unusual combination of the conservative and the radical. In bold strokes, he seeks to champion cultural primacy of religion over that of an artificial and incorrigible state in the modern international system. One might suggest that this channels Pope Benedict XVI's assertion of the primacy of Western reason through Noam Chomsky's equation of pirates and emperors.[5] Cavanaugh has an expanding opus of work in peer-reviewed articles and full-length books, including his strongly constructed critique of Chilean authoritarianism, *Torture and Eucharist*, and his broad treatise on political theory, *Theopolitical Imagination*. Building on the work of Alasdair MacIntyre,

Cavanaugh stands as a colleague in the virtue-based political theology of Stanley Hauerwas. However, as a Roman Catholic who would have a natural bent toward the scholastic convergence of theology and polity, he has created a new style of theorizing that combines the liberationist's skepticism of authority with a faith in the institutions of the universal church. Furthermore, he has combined this perspective with the neomedieval analysis of modern globalization identified by Hedley Bull, in which "modern states ... share their loyalties, on the one hand with regional and world authorities, and on the other hand with sub-state or sub-national authorities, to such an extent that the concept of sovereignty ceased to be applicable."[6] Cavanaugh thereby presents a critique of our modern understanding of the state as the repository of social goods. He sees the state as a primary modern rival to the church as a place of reverence and legitimacy, one that is, however, artificial and contrived. In consideration of Jesus' words to render unto Caesar the things that are Caesar's, it would suggest to us that Caesar has little to demand of Christians beyond the mere payment of a few denarii.

Cavanaugh begins with a common assertion of studies of politics and nationalism: that the state as we see it today is a modern construct, dating, in fact, to the late medieval period in which the principle of royal sovereignty was gradually extended to the boundaries of the territorial entities that we now identify as the core of the state system. The state as an administrative apparatus arose, according to Cavanaugh, as a means of consolidating the power of a small royal elite, and not to promote a common good, as is often portrayed in modern philosophizing over the authority of the state. It overrode more time-honored local and traditional forms of political organization, a process that "took place to serve the particular interests of dominant groups, and not as the expansion of common space."[7]

In contradiction to the traditional view of the so-called wars of religion of the 1500s and early 1600s as the ultimate outcome of dueling transnational religious forces, Cavanaugh posits that they were "in fact themselves the birth pangs of the State."[8] In other words, far from being the curse of religious fundamentalism, the wars of the 1500s and 1600s introduced us to the martial flaws of modern statecraft. The creation of the modern state system ushered in the era of modern warfare, but secularized it, so that the state might arise as the primary repository of social power. It created a justification for the use of war as a means of extending authority and thereby consolidated the state's mediation of just war doctrine as against that of prior moral and cultural communities.

In becoming the primary fulcrum of political order in the post-Westphalian age, the state increasingly took upon itself an all-embracing totality that had never obtained previously. Civil society as a cultural form independent of the authority of the state effectively disappeared as the state penetrated all aspects of society, regulating, streamlining, legitimating, and otherwise controlling it. The state perpetuated the myth of an independent civil society even though it effectively bounded and controlled civil society so that it might claim sovereignty over a social and territorial entity coterminous with the nation. Thus Cavanaugh's critique of civil society is as strong as his critique of the state—a view of civil society as benign and foundational to the state is dismissed as naive and counterintuitive.[9]

Furthermore, the nation-state as a territorial and cultural device arrived with the emergence of the phenomenon of nationalism in the early modern age. Cavanaugh points to the absence of a national common good in the work of Hobbes and Locke, arguing that, in fact, the state arose in the 1700s and 1800s absent a societal base, civil or otherwise. Law here is based on will, order, and ownership, not upon a shared notion of the good.[10] Calling upon the well-developed tradition of scholars of nationalism from Hans Kohn to Benedict Anderson, Cavanaugh taps into the notion that nationalism is an invention of the industrializing and modernizing period. The state was, thereafter, a colonizer of the nationalist impulse, not the responsive institutional expression of common beliefs and opinions. It differed markedly from prior political organization in that it did not "grow organically out of the self-government of social groups," but instead consolidated its control over preexisting social and cultural institutions.[11]

As a result, Cavanaugh views the state as an organization that has (improperly) absorbed and defined civil society as a part of its own ambit. Since the modern state is a collection of unalike interests and serves as the arena for mediation among such groups, it would be overly indulgent to assume it is the repository of the values of all. "The sheer size of the nation-state precludes genuine rational deliberation; deliberation is carried on by a political elite of lawyers, lobbyists, and other professionals. For the same reason, the unitive community that the idea of the nation offers is an illusion."[12] It is a strong illusion, however—one that competes directly with religion for legitimacy.

While Cavanaugh clearly takes aim at the state, it is not the modern welfare state or the expansion of state bureaucracy that vexes him (in distinction to many modern religious neoconservative, and even Catholic, critics of the state such as Richard John Neuhaus or Michael Novak). From the standpoint of political theory, the primary issue for Cavanaugh is the Weberian notion of the state as the "human community that claims the monopoly of the legitimate use of armed force."[13] Cavanaugh takes aim at the legitimacy of the state as a purveyor of violence in the name of order, in particular targeting state use of torture and military force. He contends that "torture is a kind of perverted liturgy" used by the state to eliminate alternative social bodies.[14] The expansion of concern over state use of torture in recent years seems only likely to reinforce the extent to which the state is singularly defined in the Weberian sense by its use of violence. This critique of the state as the bearer of the sword has situated Cavanaugh well as an apologist for the Roman Catholic cynicism toward American actions in the war on terror and the invasion of Iraq, as well as the arbitrary use of torture and imprisonment in the campaign against radicals.[15]

Calling upon the nationalistic imagery of civil religion in America, where "the nation competes with the church on the same religious grounds,"[16] Cavanaugh challenges the state's claim to secular legitimacy as against the sacred as a false dichotomy. To divest the sacred of the secular and to invest the secular state with a status significant enough to justify murder in war is, in fact, impossible.

> Nation-states are fetishes. They have power because people believe in the need for their security. They have power because people will kill and die—and sometimes torture—for them. Christians in modernity have often bought into a devil's bargain in which the state is given control of our bodies while the church supposedly retains our souls. This arrangement would be bad enough if it stopped there. But the state cannot be expected to limit itself to the body; it will colonize the soul as well.[17]

The state inevitably creates a comprador civil society that it uses to maintain its imperial, even totalitarian role.

According to Cavanaugh, the Christian approach would be to deny the state the transcendent political role it has arrogated to itself. Cavanaugh views the ideal of the separation of church and state as an artifact of the creation of a notionally secular state in the years following the Treaty of Westphalia. Prior to the creation of the modern state system, according to Cavanaugh, "the civil and ecclesiastical powers were different departments of the same body, with the ecclesiastical hierarchy of course at the head."[18] The definition of religion as a domain apart from the state is, therefore, a modern contrivance: "The creation of religion, and thus the privatization of the Church, is correlative to the rise of the State."[19] If Cavanaugh's critique of the state is correct, the argument for the separation of church and state has wrongly extended Jesus' words to the modern state. Caesar's demands went no further than the denarius, but the modern state requires much more of us: loyalty, legitimacy, commitment, sacrifice, social engineering, surrender to a set of rules and demands, and (perhaps most egregiously according to Cavanaugh) service in war. Instead, the proper community for these efforts would be the sacramental community, for Christians the church community represented in the Eucharist.

The Nation-State as Historical Artifact

Having considered Cavanaugh's theoretical positions, let us first consider his contentions against the state. Cavanaugh brings to the topic of the state an impressive grasp of European history, political theory, and theological reflection. His marriage of the three is largely unparalleled. In particular, his points about the artificiality of the state and its roots in the close of the feudal system are well made. He is certainly correct to point out that the wars of religion of early modern Europe were only euphemistically driven by religion. While the Lutheran and Calvinist Reformations and their intellectual predecessors such as Hus and Savonarola brought revolutionary social change to Europe, this only predated the Enlightenment and Romantic periods, each of which has a great deal of blood to commend its own role in international warfare. A survey of the history of anticlericalism will demonstrate that irreligion is at least as lethal as religion, a point that Cavanaugh returns to again and again.[20] Additionally, the very secular city-states of Italy had already long developed a states system that was very effective as a template for power relations among the squabbling kings and princelets of Europe in the years leading up to the conflagrations of the 1500s and 1600s. When the Thirty Years' War began in 1618, only the Hapsburg Holy Roman Emperor could press the claim that it was a war of religion. Within a very few years, the defection of France to the side of the northern European Protestant kings was sufficient to reveal the paucity of confessional solidarity as a motivating force for war.

I am, therefore, sympathetic to the way in which Cavanaugh presents the origins of the state. However, his contention that the concept of the state is new and that local entities prevailed before the nation-state is stretched. This argument is based on the assumption that the nation-state as a territorial and sovereign entity did not exist prior to the period of state consolidation in the sixteenth and seventeenth centuries. To a point this is factually correct—it is true that modern bureaucratic and secular theory of the state dates to this time. But the ancient empires *were* nation-states in that they created an embryonic notion of the nation, complete with national gods associated with their success. The first conflict in recorded history pitted the nation-states of Lagash and Umma over a water boundary known as Gu-Edin. Assyrian palace inscriptions celebrated the exploits of their military for foreign audiences to consolidate their rule. Egyptians defined themselves quite clearly against their foes among the Asiatics, Hyksos, and others. Jesus' own statement "render unto Caesar that which is Caesar's" pointed to the existence of an authority apart from locally conceived communities.

What is more, territoriality in the ancient world was conceived differently only insofar as sovereignty could not be consolidated in the modern sense of defended borders. Often, however, it reflected the very geographic notion of the state that we know today. Thucydides' Greece contended over quite clearly defined spheres of influence, and the division of Greece among city-states was similar to our modern understanding of the state boundaries. Babylonians delineated internal boundaries using standing-stones known as *kudurru*. Roman power in Britain extended only as far as Hadrian's Wall. Likewise, the Great Wall of China illustrates that the Chinese conceived of frontiers of their own national control. In general, then, the state is not so modern a notion after all. While the medieval conception of the state was very much tied into the feudal system, underpinning it was the imperial concept as an ideal from the past. The European Empire of the day did not simply derive its authority from that of the universal church, as Cavanaugh contends. It was not simply the *holy empire* but the *Holy Roman Empire*, implying origins in an early version of the nation-state.

One might also suggest that Cavanaugh's strength as a historian is his weakness as a theorist. Most scholars agree with Cavanaugh, to one degree or another, that the notion of the nation-state has evolved and that the consolidation of the state system arose in the midst of the conflagrations of the seventeenth century. Kenneth Waltz, for example, argued that the rise of nationalism imbued ancient loyalties with a new "loyalty to the state that overrides their loyalty to almost any other group." He went on to presage Cavanaugh by suggesting that this loyalty replaced that of the church at this time in history.[21] It is also clear that the state arose in many ways to justify the very secular power of royal factions, republican revolutions, and military dictatorships rather than to seek the common good.

But just because the state arose as an artificial concept does not mean that it is just as artificial today. The historic origins of the state are of relevance to history, but they are not necessarily binding upon the contemporary state. Nor do the sins of the father condemn all states to behave as did the states of the Enlightenment. True, the state arose as a means of consolidating the authority of monarchs and to an extent the very idea of the nation-state was a myth back in the seventeenth century. But myths in themselves may have a reality in that they are accepted as prevailing justifications for norms of behavior. Likewise over time, an institution such as the state may evolve to exceed its original mandate. Modern constructivists do not argue that international regimes are necessarily established for the common good, but this does not rule out the possibility that they may be used for the common good.

Conceptions of the state evolve over time and relate as much to the way the state behaves today as they do to its putative history. Realist and Weberian notions of the state have in large part given way to more nuanced definitions. Liberal theorists would suggest to us that there are significant differences between liberal-democratic and coercive states.[22] Even Alexander Wendt, one of the principal defenders of the Weberian notion of the state in international relations today, argues that nation-states have developed different "cultures of anarchy" over the years. Wendt suggests that the "Hobbesian" cultures of the past are being replaced by the "Lockean" and "Kantian" cultures of the present.[23] His point is that structures that constrain and control the nature of the state are changing, and changing in progressive ways: "In fact, it seems obvious that today's international system represents considerable progress over that of 500 or even 1500 A.D.; progress there has been."[24] Liberal and alternative theorists typically picture the state as a secondary or derivative force in world politics, a Gulliver held down by the ropes of thousands of Lilliputians.[25] Recent liberal assessments of international society have stressed the extent to which the rise of democratic norms, interdependence, and intergovernmental institutions has tamed the martial instincts of the state.[26] To the extent that the state reflects an array of contending forces and voices in civil society, it resists categorization as a modern analogue of the secular nationalist replacements for the religions of the past. It is instead a much more complex creature, reflecting both anti- and pro-social behavior.

As to the coercive apparatus of the state, the modern liberal-democratic state has proven less and less likely to demand the participation of its citizens in warfare or to engage in torture against its people, notwithstanding recent concerns over the conduct of the "war on terror," to which we shall return. While government in the United States has been increasingly perceived as a coercive state in the wake of the invasions of Afghanistan and Iraq and the concomitant expansion of domestic and international military presence, this is by no means a universal phenomenon. Given the budgetary limitations increasingly placed upon the United States, going into the future, and the tendency among its allies to resist foreign adventurism, there might even be reason to believe it to be a temporary development. Be that as it may, in places such as Europe, Latin America, and Canada, the military impulse of the state has dramatically waned since its high point in the earlier portions of the last century such that praetorian rulers like Hugo Chavez are a distinct minority. In most of the developed world, the state has largely become a mediator of contending social forces, many of which use its institutions as means of making themselves heard. Modern developed states have, therefore, become more like a social contract than those of the past, and arguably this process of evolution may continue as states seek new and innovative ways to engage their citizens.

The evolution of the Western tradition is, therefore, ignored by Cavanaugh in an effort to demonstrate the militant secularism demonstrated by its founders. Yet it is important as well to note that the Western tradition has much to credit the Christian tradition out of which it evolved. Philosophers of the state did not arise simply to grant unconditional authority to the state but to find ways in which the state might serve as a means of Christian charity for those with whom we disagree. Theorists such as Grotius, Hobbes, Locke, Mill, and even Hegel arose out of a Christian civilization and spoke to a Christian society even as they sought to create a secular sphere in which those Christians might interact.[27] It is not until the Romantic period of the early nineteenth century that philosophers such as Marx and Nietzsche began to theorize out of avowedly secular and even pagan principles. Cavanaugh himself is dialoguing with a society that shares much of his Catholic heritage.

These philosophers emerging from the Christian tradition of the state did not create the state as a rival for the legitimacy of the masses. In a sense, they were serving the independence and authority of the church every bit as much as they supported the secular state. Detaching the church from the state (even as an intermediate) was a way to create the church as a separate and unbounded entity.

For example, in England, the collusion of church and state led to the creation of a new state church that, in turn, engaged in the persecution of Roman Catholic and nonconformist sects. As a result, the Reformation created a state designed to protect the people from clerical authority combined with that of the monarchy. Ultimately the state's ambitions were tamed to get out of the business of religious persecution entirely, as in the case of American disestablishmentarianism, and only later the modern secular state. Surely, the eighteenth-century Enlightenment philosophers were seeking to create space for the ultimate authority of challengers to the state in places such as Britain where the state had improperly overstepped its bounds. In other words, the state rising out of the traditions of the European Reformation and later Enlightenment, pace Cavanaugh, was in effect created to avoid the very crisis of legitimacy that Cavanaugh decries. If it has failed to achieve these ends, it is likely the fault of application rather than design.

Violence, the State, and the Expanding Role of the State

I have stated previously that Cavanaugh's primary complaint against the state is that it has arrogated to itself power over life and death, that modern society has taken too seriously the Weberian proposition that it boasts the monopoly over the legitimate use of force. For Cavanaugh the state is flawed because it is a martial state. But the modern liberal-democratic state is increasingly defined by its very reticence to use armed force. Cavanaugh's interest in the state arose in Chile, where the Pinochet regime used torture and violence as a matter of course. But Chile has shed bureaucratic authoritarianism and embraced a more democratic form today. What is more, South American states have not gone to war in more than a century, with the one exception of Argentina's war over the Falkland Islands. Notwithstanding the American incursions in Iraq and Afghanistan, postcolonial wars of this sort have generally been on the wane. The past decade has been replete with explorations of the democratic peace, and while the jury may remain unconvinced, liberal-democratic capitalist states seem very unlikely once again to pick up the swords of war among themselves.

Admittedly, war has not ceased, and some would argue that the past decade has been as warlike as any in the history of humankind, in spite of the unprecedented growth of liberal-democratic principles. But warfare has been confined largely to areas of the nondemocratic periphery. What is more, since 1945 warfare has increasingly pitted substate elements in contestation over the direction of the state rather than states against one another in a pattern Holsti calls "people's wars."[28] The concerted response of Western states to September 11th and the ill-begotten 2003 invasion of Iraq are not particularly representative of the modern pattern of warfare. Yet even among NATO allies in Afghanistan, developed nations have displayed their reticence to engage in armed conflict, many of them bound by caveats that keep them out of combat roles, with publics at home fretting that the price of young soldiers' lives is too high a price to pay. The development of fearsome technologies of warfare have certainly increased the lethality of war, but at the same time states are often taken to be less likely to use a nuclear device than would nonstate elements with a radical agenda.

It may seem utopian to suggest, but if scholars such as Francis Fukuyama or Bruce Russett and John Oneal are correct to suggest that there are zones of peace in international politics that will grow as democracy spreads, the state may someday get out of the business of warfare entirely.[29] Americans have recently come to question the likelihood of a peaceful realm emerging from the end of the Cold War, but modern conflicts have continued to pit the liberal-democratic states individually and together in an increasingly familiar pattern. Outside the United States, the primary preoccupations of many Western industrialized states have moved beyond war and peace toward more vexing issues of social management. Government intervention in favor of social rights has been the primary point of polarization for religious activists in North American and other societies, yet Cavanaugh does not generally address the limitations of the state in regulating or controlling these questions. This is so in spite of the fact that transnational organizations are increasingly affected by these concerns, as demonstrated in debates over the wording of the European Union constitution and direction of expansion or in periodic controversies over family planning initiatives, such as at the 1994 UN International Conference on Population and Development. A recent issue of *The Economist* explored the expanded role of government in providing a "nanny state" for its citizens, encouraging their use of green technologies, access to exercise, provision of child care, and discouraging social vices and unhealthy behaviors.[30] One would assume that such soft paternalism would also run afoul of Cavanaugh's limitations on the state. But consigning these issues to the management of global civil society would also run the risk of compromising with these authorities. Cavanaugh provides us with no general model for temporal management of these affairs other than his vaunted Church.

Even if the state remains first and foremost the purveyor of war, does Cavanaugh's challenge to the legitimacy of the state extend beyond this moral fault? Does a state that engages in warfare either abroad or against its own citizens thereby give up the legitimate right to administer social programs, to build roads, to encourage citizen activism, to print and circulate currency, or any number of other services and projects? In Western societies, the state has shed much of its coercive apparatus and become a service provider. If the state is perverted by its aspirations to rival the faith, is it an institution to be trusted at all? Again, it is unclear where Cavanaugh's assessment will lead us.

The State and Civil Society

I have considered Cavanaugh's critique of the state, but what of his consideration of civil society? Cavanaugh has learned well some of the lessons taught to political scientists over the past few decades. These include that the state is not homogenous nor is it the simple repository of the collective authority of a nation, that the state should not be understood apart from the interests in which it is embedded, and that the state is one of many prominent actors in world politics.[31] He sounds a proper cautionary note about the extent to which the state has permeated much of modern civil society. While he does not always use the terms of political analysis, what Cavanaugh is arguing is that the state has risen to permeate, colonize, and dominate the society in which it is embedded. His critique of the state comes at a time when the future of the state is a matter of significant debate. On one side are political economists and others pronouncing the retreat or the end of the state.[32] On another side are many suggesting that the state has only found new ways to reassert its authority.[33]

Yet even if we accept Cavanaugh's argument that the state is an artificial construct of modernity, his contention that the "public realm outside the State is, however, largely a fiction, as is therefore the ideal of a noncoercive public marketplace of ideas" seems to be an overstatement.[34] Indeed, the work of several prominent social scientists has reinforced the extent to which religion and politics reflect the noncoercive public marketplace of ideas that Cavanaugh denies.[35] The choices that citizens make for identification with religious and nationalist movements seem to contradict the premise of Cavanaugh's all-consuming state. Many modern political scientists see the erosion of state power as one of the most important developments of the post–Cold War era. In many areas of the world, such as Somalia, Afghanistan, or Haiti, state failure has given way to anarchy. Elsewhere structural adjustment, neoliberalism, and budget crunches have limited the capacity of the state to achieve many of its aims. In the midst of the retreat of state capacity, states may take new forms and use non-governmental agencies and civil society actors to reinforce their authority, functioning as hegemonic blocs (to use a Gramscian turn of phrase).

On the other hand, civil society actors may increasingly present an insurmountable obstacle to the state and may operate increasingly in ways that ignore the authority of any one given state. In the words of Robert Cox, "Civil society is itself a field of power relations; and forces in civil society relate, in support or opposition, to powers in state and market."[36] Civil society seen in this way is not solely the penetrated space described by Cavanaugh but instead a field over which state and social forces may do battle. Cavanaugh's use of the term *civil society* seems closer to the notion of civil religion in the sense of the cultural trappings and underpinnings of the state in society. On the other hand, the typical use of the term in political science today tends instead to refer to the various plural groupings that contend with the state. Often they do so as veritable equals to the state, far from Cavanaugh's "intermediate associations." If, as Cavanaugh states, the church must "promote the creation of spaces in which alternative economies and authorities flourish,"[37] how would this be done outside the assertion of its role within civil society, as understood by analysts such as Cox? By using this artificially narrow notion of civil society, such that civil society cannot even be conceived outside its relationship to the state, Cavanaugh unfortunately seems to miss the power of his church in civil society fearing that it might be compromised by simple semantics.

In the field of civil society, it is not just the state with which the church must contend—there is a constellation of actors that vie for the loyalties of citizens. If the state is indeed "a source of an alternative soteriology to that of the church,"[38] it is certainly not the only one. Obviously, other religious movements present a challenge to the logic of the nation-state: sometimes these movements even overtly boast the language of alternative soteriology.[39] Islamist movements boast that "Islam is the solution"; others foster ideals of an Islamic economic system; an Algerian group is even known as the Islamic Salvation Front (*front Islamique du salut*). Elsewhere, organized crime syndicates, sometimes coupled with resistance movements such as the Revolutionary Armed Forces of Colombia (FARC), have arrogated to themselves the role of ultimate arbiter of life and death. In spaces such as these, the church has often viewed the state as (at worst) the lesser of two evils as an interlocutor or protector. For example, in my own study of the church in Egypt, I have found that Christians have largely internalized a distrust of the state in keeping with Cavanaugh's critique, but they also tend to place greater trust in the state than they do in some of the radical elements of civil society. None of this detracts from the centrality of the Coptic Orthodox Church to the regulation of social affairs within the country. In this case, the church has not necessarily surrendered to the logic of the state so much as it has enjoyed the protection of the state when it turns a blind eye.

But Cavanaugh is generally interested in the role of the Christian church in the Western (and notionally Christian) traditions of political discourse. He bemoans the gradual surrender of the power of traditional authorities in European civilization, accepting for themselves the role of "intermediate associations" defined by their relationship to the state. For example, he cites the experience of the university: the level of transcendent independence enjoyed by the university in the medieval period came to be undermined by its subordination to the nation-state during the Enlightenment.[40] Similarly, civil society institutions, and even the church itself, have come to accept the geographic and social boundaries of the state as definitive.[41]

In the developed world, the surrender of the church (and of other actors) to the logic of the nation-state is uneven in its application. Two general models are posited for representation of organized interests: the corporatist model and the pluralist model. In the pluralist model, groups are self-constituted and are granted the autonomy to represent interests as citizens see fit. In the corporatist model, the state initiates the process of interest aggregation through gathering and classifying interests, creating peak organizations through which various societal interests are filtered. The corporatist model is most common in European states whereas the pluralist model is the more typically North American approach, although almost all states allow some mixture of pluralist and corporatist models.[42] The application of these models to religion suggests under pluralism that religion shapes interests, which then are represented to the state through domestic civil society; under corporatism, interests are defined by pre-existing religious groups recognized by the state.

Clearly, Cavanaugh's fear that the state has colonized society comes closer to the corporatist approach. In Scandinavian states, labor unions, cultural societies, and indeed churches have been granted special relationship to the state for consideration in discussions surrounding their interests. The state recognizes, funds, and helps to legitimize and empower such groups. The corporatist model has had an enormous impact in Germany over the years. During the 1930s, the Nazis famously sought to bring the Protestant and Catholic Churches into a patriotic union under the Nazi banner, while a small but heroic Confessing Church movement defied the union. Corporatism has not always been so egregiously used to penetrate civil society. But it does create a mechanism by which the state may seek to manage religious practice, among other forms of social organization. Today, Germany maintains the role of the state in directly taxing citizens so as to fund state-recognized churches. A movement critical of the state role has arisen in the Free Church. The permeation of the church under state auspices in these cases may well constitute a mistaken surrender of the church.

In pluralist systems, by contrast, the church remains a free institution and is less likely to be colonized by the state. In Canada and the United States, churches survive on the private donations of churchgoers, and though the state may regulate the zoning of church locations and the registration of weddings, or require proper accounting procedures of the church, the level of financial and regulatory control is far less significant. Instances in which the state follows a more corporatist philosophy in these states have typically been controversial in the extreme, as in the case of American funding of faith-based social services. What Cavanaugh envisions appears to be pluralism in its extreme—perhaps a pluralism that only applies to the church. However, no matter how he envisions the representation of interests within or among states, it seems rather unnecessary to rule out the very useful place of organized religious discourse in a civil society, whether corporatist or pluralist in its foundations.

Theopolitical Concerns: The Political Significance of Church

Beyond his assessment of state and society, a third consideration is Cavanaugh's particular take on political theology. It is rather unclear where Cavanaugh's critique of the state should lead believers. His conclusions are generally euphemistic in that he requests Christians to rediscover the ways in which the temporal and spiritual authority of God may be promoted. In one place, he suggests that Christians accept more deeply the discipline of the church, a discipline that "will more often resemble martyrdom than military victory."[43] But religious institutions of this sort cannot be promoted as mere interests, given that he negates the church's role as intermediary. Instead, Cavanaugh chooses to emphasize the exalted nature of the church as God's provision for world order. He disavows modern notions of citizenship as a sort of idolatry, for "citizenship has displaced discipleship as the church's public key."[44] But given the existence of the modern state as an organizing principle, even a flawed one, this perspective limits the ability of the church to provide ministry and service to the present political order.

Here Cavanaugh, like Hauerwas, overstates the ability of the church as a socially and ethically constructed polity. Even given a commitment to the Christian faith, his exalted understanding of the church does not anticipate the venality of temporal authorities within the church or the potential for sin among its members. Faced with criticisms of the church's role in torture during the Inquisition, Cavanaugh admits that it is "one of the many sins of the Church for which Catholics should do penance," but he is rather dismissive of the possibility that these errors may be repeated.[45] A church that accepts the discipline of external accountability need not be one that sacrifices its claim to universal truth and the authority of the almighty.

No matter one's perspective on the veracity of the Christian faith, Cavanaugh's faith in the church as the body of Christ does not fully acknowledge the diversity of spiritual and existential experiences of its members. There is here potential for monism. The church affirms its unity through a creed, but the insistence that this is a unitive fiction stronger than that of the modern nation-state stretches the traditional notion of the church as Christ's body, potentially justifying acts that seek to impose conformity. As one theologian has noted, "Cavanaugh's account seems to suggest a partial misconstrual of our possession of shared humanity as implying *unity rather than community*. Is our created and redeemed destiny not better depicted as a relational communion among individually distinct persons, rather than as participatory union?"[46] If this is true, the church is ultimately the sum total of the actions of individuals that lead and participate in it, either consistent or inconsistent with the Christian worldview.

Cavanaugh, instead, reposes in the church all the authority of God to discipline the believer. Individuals do not find their authority in relationship to God but in relationship to the church; in one place, Cavanaugh argues that "religious symbols are . . . embedded in bodily practices of power and discipline whose regulation belong to the authoritative structure of the Church, or at least did until modern times."[47] The individual's role is subsumed within the power of a collective unit, the church, rather than in one's own convictions or relationship to the Almighty. Christian theology holds that the church is the "body of Christ," but does this imply a homogenization of interests, or the necessary construction of a divine polity emerging from it?

Commonality of purpose in a mystical sense does not imply, nor should it, that all Christians are unified in their personalities, their style of worship, or even their preferences for getting things done: hence the existence of an array of local churches and denominations. From the Christian standpoint, such apparent disunity results from both the fallen nature of human beings and from the mere existence of God-given diversity among Christians. Similar critiques of organized and centralized religion may be distinguished in other religious traditions: disputes over leadership in Islam between Sunni and Shi'i and over transcendence between fundamentalists and Sufis; the absence of centralized authority or dogma in Hinduism or Buddhism; diverse schools and sects of Judaism. Within each tradition, one can justify a certain suspicion of attempts to create a temporal order based on the unity of the faith. Beyond that, it goes without saying that Cavanaugh's perspective does not really provide Christians with a platform for interacting with those who do not hold to their faith.

In this sense, Cavanaugh does not identify the artificiality of national churches that consistently engage in rivalries with upstart denominations supposed to be of foreign origin. Arguments for the universality of the church are less often invitations to ecumenical understanding and more often attempts to solidify orthodoxy contrary to the freedom of the Christian faith or to create apologetics for the unchallenged authority of one group or another. For example, established churches in Russia, the Middle East, and even parts of Europe have jealously guarded their prerogatives against modern reformist movements, sects, and cults, perceiving them, rightly or wrongly, as challenges to their inherited authority. The unity of the church may well be a proper doctrine of the Christian faith, but this need not translate into an unremitting need to homogenize or institutionally unify Christians under a temporal banner. Indeed, history is replete with examples in which this attempt to cement religious unity itself became a source of political tensions and violent sectarianism.

Here we arrive at an important point about Cavanaugh's ecclesiology that, in turn, ties into his critique of civil society. If the state was not formed for the common good, neither was the church, by its own admission. Humanity's chief purpose, according to the Westminster catechism, is to "glorify God and to enjoy Him forever." Roman Catholic doctrine gives the church a more central role as the City of God on Earth, but even so, the aim is spiritual beneficence rather than temporal. The primary reference to Jesus' use of the term *church* is in his response to Peter's declaration at Caesarea Philippi that "on this rock I will build my church, and the gates of Hades will not prevail against it" (Matt. 16:18). This referred to a spiritual gathering of disciples committed to the teachings of Jesus, not a set of institutional responses to present problems. By the same token, the church is not a political institution, though by all means its teachings will have direct political import. "My kingdom is not from this world," Jesus himself stated under Pilate's questioning, "if my kingdom were from this world, my followers would be fighting" (John 18:36).

The church was to become the standing witness of Jesus' *spiritual* kingdom in the world. The fact that this had political and institutional implications was evident in the perceived challenge to existing authorities, Pilate included. It would provide alternative principles for leadership, reverse relationships of enmity, and create new conceptions of mercy, grace, and justice. As such, it devised new patterns for political thinking, which have challenged and will challenge the nature of the modern nation-state. But it did not create an alternative temporal order. Attempts to do so have been woefully inadequate, not because of the failures of the church as a spiritual entity but because the institutional church is by definition something more than that spiritual church to which the scriptures refer.

Of course, Cavanaugh's exalted notion of the church does not follow from this Protestant tradition, but rather from an assumption of the church in some way as a continuation of the theocratic polity of the Jewish Old Testament. In one place, he argues that the use of the word *ekklesia* in ancient Greek for the church of the New Testament indicates its identification with the assembly of all Israel in the Old. "In calling itself an *ekklesia*, the church was identifying itself as fully public, refusing the available language for private associations (*koinon* or *collegium*)."[48] The point Cavanaugh is making here is that the church is not a mediating influence between state and society, that it is properly an alternative locus of authority and tradition with a firmer grounding than the state itself. Insofar as it describes the *spiritual* gathering of the church universal, this is persuasive. It suggests that the Christian needs to filter the ideals of the state through a mind transformed by the power of Christ. But the *ekklesia* is not, nor should it be, conflated with the temporal institutions of the church, many of which have proven as tragically artificial and unfocused on the common good as the modern nation-state itself. One must remember that the wheat grows up with the tares.

This vision of the church as a continuation of the temporal community of Israel runs into the danger of creating a justification for theocratic rule not via the spiritual authority of the church universal but through its institutional and incompletely sanctified auspices. It is interesting to note that Cavanaugh disavows such theocracy, stating that the church is not a "polis," nor is "the call for the Church to be 'public' . . . a call for the church to take up the sword once again."[49] By comparing the *ekklesia* of the New Testament Christians to that of the Old Testament, Cavanaugh does not seem to imply that the church is the representative of the nation. It is a public institution, certainly, but not constitutive of a polity as a whole—and hence, once again, may be a functioning part of civil society.

There is an element to which Cavanaugh is simply providing an apologetic for the continued supremacy of the Roman Catholic Church as a transnational religious order, even if it is a significantly reformed and chastened authority. His argument that the state is an artificial contrivance of the modern age dovetails conveniently with a contention that the separation of church and state was a mistake of the Reformation.

> Luther rightly saw that the Church had become worldly and perversely associated with the wielding of the sword. His intention was to prevent the identification of any politics with the will of God, and thus extricate the Church from its entanglement in coercive power. In sanctifying that power to the use of secular government, however, Luther contributed to the myth of the State as peacemaker which would be invoked to confine the Church.[50]

There seems to me a sort of circular reasoning here. Nation-states were formed to control the venal power of the church. These nation-states became artificial and venal contrivances themselves, and the church must come to the rescue. Is it not possible that the problem is institutionalized and unchecked power rather than the state per se?

Conclusions

William Cavanaugh has engaged in an important and interesting convergence of theology and politics. He has identified the relationship between religion and politics in bold terms. "To identify politics and religion as acts of the imagination is to recognize their historical contingency and thus give hope that things do not necessarily have to be the way they are. It is also to put the political and the theological imaginations on an equal footing."[51] For many political scientists and theorists, this equation of the religious and the political is likely to be disconcerting. For others, it will only echo contentions they have been making for many years.

Nevertheless, Cavanaugh's exaltation of the Christian church over and above the state argues for the higher levels of legitimacy contained in the neomedieval model of world organization. It suggests that when people organize themselves around the poles of loyalty created by the higher plane of religion there is a pull to a higher power that transcends interstate relations and calls them to more pacific and constructive relations. Indeed, it does stand to reason that people are most likely to accept calls to solidarity and mutual help through the language of their own sacred tradition. Furthermore, these sacred traditions are far more likely to be constructive and enriching to modern society than they are to be divisive or injurious. Far too often has the modern state sought to be, in T. N. Madan's phraseology, secular*ist*, rather than secular.[52]

There is a danger, however, that Cavanaugh fails to address—the extent to which these transcendent ties are likely to talk past one another. As Hedley Bull pointed out many years ago:

> It is conceivable that a universal society of this kind might be constructed that would provide a firm basis for the realisation of elementary goals of social life. But if it were anything like the precedent of Western Christendom, it would contain more ubiquitous and continuous violence and insecurity than does the modern states system.[53]

Of course, Cavanaugh disputes the ubiquity of violence in the medieval past, but he does not seek to consider the ways in which the Europe of 1600 was far less plural in its societal dynamics than the modern international system, which includes diverse traditions, from Christian to Muslim, from materialist to particularist. Is it not possible, even for the true believer, to accept that such intellectual diversity is enriching, if only due to its role in helping modern society to explore issues of ultimate value, especially issues of peace and conflict?

Returning to the larger constitutive questions of international relations theory, the fear that religious traditions seeking to challenge the place of the nation-state will inevitably clash with one another and with modernity suggests that the diversity of religion represented by Cavanaugh's devotion to the Eucharist will inevitably be destabilizing. I hope to suggest otherwise: that the international stage is, indeed, a place for contending values to play themselves out, and often in political ways, but that this need not translate into uncontrolled conflict. What is necessary here, however, is a category of social relations in which such relations can play out. Cavanaugh may be right that the state is the wrong category. But he may also have ruled out more promising venues. His counterparts in other religious traditions have too often done the same.

The Christian tradition has had to deal with this level of diversity for two thousand years in many locations around the world. The very Eucharist that Cavanaugh describes as the ideal archetype of unity is a source of disunity for the various sects of Christendom. Without the state, or its attendant civil society, how do modern religious organizations of this sort seek some sort of common ground? By eliminating the secular state and civil society, Cavanaugh has left us with precious little space to construct common ground with the *Other*. If nation-states are indeed fetishes, so too can faith groups become cults gathered around esoteric minutiae, condemning and excommunicating those who disagree, or looking askance at them as alien intruders. Cavanaugh creates a strong notion of Christian solidarity, but no notion of how relations with other sacred communities can work—and have worked in the past. Where would this take place, if not in an arena of debate and discussion such as a modern global civil society? Cavanaugh is unhappy with the term, but his alternative political model of the church in the Eucharist does not provide us with a strong alternative. The church remains a prophetic voice, one challenging authority through its own perfectionist logic, a voice of alternative theology and politics—but it is still a member of a civil society distinct from the state.

William Cavanaugh's critique of the state also leaves modern Christians in an uneasy place. How does the modern Christian interpret Jesus Christ's injunction to render unto Caesar that which is Caesar's? If the state is an artificial construct of the wars of the 1500s and 1600s, and has unjustly usurped, constrained, and colonized the universal church, how far does it have the right to assert its authority? Was Jesus referring to the state when he made this claim? Was he not in fact declaring the separation of church and state or was he making a pronouncement in the absence of the modern state? Or is it simply that the state must be constrained against the wanton use of violent means?

I have suggested here that Cavanaugh's coverage of the state suffers on a few counts. His theory of the state assumes that the state remains what it was originally created to be. He gives little attention to the evolution of the tradition of separation of church and state out of the theoretical perspectives of Christians themselves. He takes aim primarily at the coercive apparatus of the state without answering important questions about the myriad of other responsibilities that states take on. His theory remains concerned primarily with the state but leaves out the many contenders for legitimacy that reside outside the state. It is also founded on an exalted notion of the church as a sacred community that is not particularly well suited to the history of the church universal on earth. In the final analysis, Cavanaugh thus eliminates the state and, more importantly, civil society from their constructive roles in the world. He replaces them with an exalted notion of the church that is not likely to be attractive to nonbelievers and may not match up to the experience of believers either.

Still, Cavanaugh is right to give us pause about the permeation of the state throughout modern society. It is certainly possible that the extension of the modern state into the management of social life in deeper and deeper ways sows the seeds of its own crisis of legitimacy. These challenges do not simply come from Islamist radicalism but from citizens who share much of the Western liberal heritage and its motivations. I have suggested that the statist and corporatist approach may need reassessment. As liberal-democratic states increasingly take on postmodern aims that are not seemingly as ethically dubious as warfare and internal enforcement, the problematic that Cavanaugh has opened up for us becomes more complex but equally significant.

NOTES

Reprinted from *The Review of Politics* 71, no. 4 (Fall 2009): 583–605.

1. Samuel Huntington, *The Clash of Civilizations and the Remaking of World Order* (New York: Simon and Schuster, 1998); Christopher Hitchens, *God Is Not Great: How Religion Poisons Everything* (New York: Twelve, 2007).

2. A broad array of texts have arisen since the mid-1990s, including Douglas Johnston and Cynthia Sampson, eds., *Religion: The Missing Dimension of Statecraft* (Oxford: Oxford University Press, 1994); Susanne Hoeber Rudolph and James Piscatori, eds., *Transnational Religion and Fading States* (Boulder, CO: Westview Press, 1997); John Esposito and Michael Watson, eds., *Religion and Global Order* (Cardiff: University of Wales Press, 2000); Douglas Johnston, ed., *Faith-Based Diplomacy: Trumping Realpolitik* (Oxford: Oxford University Press, 2003); Scott M. Thomas, *The Global Resurgence of Religion and*

the Transformation of International Relations: The Struggle for the Soul of the Twenty-First Century (New York: Palgrave Macmillan, 2005).

3. Daniel Philpott, "The Challenge of September 11 to Secularism in International Relations," *World Politics* 55, no. 1 (2002): 92–93.

4. Radical orthodoxy is a broadly based ecumenical movement in Christian theology that combines postmodern analysis with a return to the earlier church traditions to provide a critique of modern Enlightenment reason. It tends to stress the Christian roots of various political concepts and theories as a means of assessing how in modern society they have departed from their original meanings. The term for this perspective arose with the publication of John Milbank, Catherine Pickstock, and Graham Ward, eds., *Radical Orthodoxy: A New Theology* (London: Routledge, 1999). See also James K. A. Smith, *Introducing Radical Orthodoxy: Mapping a Post-Secular Theology* (Grand Rapids, MI: Baker Academic, 2004).

5. For Benedict XVI, see the (in)famous Regensburg address, Benedict XVI, *Faith Reason, and the University: Memories and Reflections, Lecture of the Holy Father*, September 12, 2006, available at http://w2.vatican.va/content/benedict-xvi/en/speeches/2006/september/documents/hf_ben-xvi_spe_20060912_university-regensburg.html. For the reference to Chomsky, see Noam Chomsky, *Pirates and Emperors, Old and New* (Cambridge, MA: Southend Press, 2002), vii. It is perhaps noteworthy that Chomsky's image comes originally from St. Augustine.

6. Hedley Bull, *The Anarchical Society: A Study of Order in World Politics* (London: Macmillan, 1977), 254.

7. William T. Cavanaugh, "Killing for the Telephone Company: Why the Nation-State Is Not the Keeper of the Common Good," *Modern Theology* 20 (April 2004): 247.

8. William T. Cavanaugh, "'A Fire Strong Enough to Consume the House': The Wars of Religion and the Rise of the State," *Modern Theology* 11 (October 1995): 398.

9. William T. Cavanaugh, *Theopolitical Imagination* (New York: T. and T. Clark, 2002), 70ff.

10. Cavanaugh, "Killing," 251–54.

11. Ibid., 256.

12. Ibid., 263.

13. Max Weber, "What Is a State?" in *Comparative Politics: Notes and Readings*, 9th ed., ed. Bernard E. Brown (Fort Worth: Harcourt College Publishers, 2000), 147.

14. William T. Cavanaugh, *Torture and Eucharist* (Oxford: Blackwell Publishers, 1998), 12.

15. William T. Cavanaugh, "How to Do Penance for the Inquisition," *Review of Faith and International Affairs* 5, no. 2 (2007): 13–16.

16. William T. Cavanaugh, "The Liturgies of Church and State," *Liturgy* 20, no. 1 (2005): 25–30.

17. Cavanaugh, *Torture and Eucharist*, 195–96.

18. Cavanaugh, "A Fire," 400.

19. Ibid., 403.

20. Jose Sanchez, *Anticlericalism: A Brief History* (Notre Dame, IN: University of Notre Dame Press, 1972). See also Michael Burleigh, *Sacred Causes: The Clash of Religion and Politics, from the Great War to the War on Terror* (New York: HarperCollins, 2007).

21. Kenneth Waltz, *Man, the State, and War: A Theoretical Analysis* (New York: Columbia University Press, 1959), 177.

22. See, for example, Ted Robert Gurr, "War, Revolution, and the Growth of the Coercive State," *Comparative Political Studies* 21, no. 1 (1988): 25–65.

23. See Wendt's "Three Cultures of Anarchy," in *Social Theory of International Politics*, ed. Alexander Wendt (Cambridge: Cambridge University Press, 1999), 246–312.

24. Ibid., 311–12.

25. This has been the chief claim of many liberal and neorealist arguments against the autonomy of the state in the international system at least since the publication of Robert O. Keohane and Joseph S. Nye's *Power and Interdependence: World Politics in Transition* (Boston: Little, Brown, and Co., 1977).

26. Bruce Russett and John Oneal, *Triangulating Peace* (New York: W. W. Norton, 2001).

27. It is perhaps important to note that I don't mean to suggest that these philosophers were seeking to engage in Christian reasoning or to engage in religious discourse: indeed, Hobbes and others were seeking to do quite the opposite. However, these foundational philosophers cannot be separated from their dialogue with the Christian tradition, and they largely understood the world through the lenses of Christian thought. Mark Lilla has recently argued that this was a long process "opened up by a unique theological-political crisis within Christendom" whereby political theology was largely replaced by political philosophy. Mark Lilla, *The Stillborn God: Religion, Politics, and the Modern West* (New York: Knopf, 2007), 308.

28. K. J. Holsti, *The State, War, and the State of War* (Cambridge: Cambridge University Press, 1996).

29. Francis Fukuyama, *The End of History and the Last Man* (New York: Free Press, 1992); Russett and Oneal, *Triangulating Peace*.

30. "The Avuncular State," *The Economist*, April 8, 2006, 67–69.

31. Along these lines, see Peter Evans, Dietrich Rueschemeyer, and Theda Skocpol, eds., *Bringing the State Back In* (Cambridge: Cambridge University Press, 1986); and Peter Evans, *Embedded Autonomy: States and Industrial Transformation* (Princeton: Princeton University Press, 1995).

32. Following Susan Strange, *The Retreat of the State* (Cambridge: Cambridge University Press, 1996).

33. For example, Adam Harmes, *The Return of the State* (Vancouver: Douglas and McIntyre, 2004).

34. Cavanaugh, "A Fire," 414.

35. Jelen and Wilcox use personal choice in the midst of a market of ideas as a template for the operation of religious groups in liberal-democratic societies. They present several case studies in areas throughout the world to support their contention. Ted Jelen

and Clyde Wilcox, eds., *Religion and Politics in Comparative Perspective: The One, the Few, and the Many* (Cambridge: Cambridge University Press, 2002).

36. Robert Cox, "Civil Society at the Turn of the Millennium: Prospects for an Alternative World Order," *Review of International Studies* 25 (1999): 25.

37. Cavanaugh, "Killing," 267.

38. William Cavanaugh, "The City: Beyond Secular Parodies," in *Radical Orthodoxy*, ed. Milbank, Pickstock, and Ward, 182.

39. For an excellent exploration of the broader concept of religion as an alternative to the modern international system, see Philpott, "The Challenge of September 11th."

40. William T. Cavanaugh, "Sailing under True Colors: Academic Freedom and the Ecclesially Based University," in *Conflicting Allegiances: The Church-Based University in a Liberal Democratic Society*, ed. Michael L. Budde and John Wright (Grand Rapids, MI: Brazos Press, 2004), 41–42.

41. Cavanaugh, *Torture and Eucharist*, 74ff.

42. Note here that pluralism is used solely in the neoinstitutional sense, rather than the sense of *cultural pluralism*. A useful study of pluralism as a model as against established churches and strict separation of church and state is provided by Stephen V. Monsma and J. Christopher Soper, *The Challenge of Pluralism: Church and State in Five Democracies* (Lanham, MD: Rowman and Littlefield, 1997). However, Monsma and Soper refer to pluralism as a mode of state neutrality, whereas pluralism as a model of interest representation could be used in a state with or without the application of strict neutrality.

43. Cavanaugh, "A Fire," 415.

44. Cavanaugh, *Theopolitical Imagination*, 83.

45. Cavanaugh, "Penance," 14.

46. Jonathan Chaplin, "Suspended Communities or Covenanted Communities? Reformed Reflections on the Social Thought of Radical Orthodoxy," in *Radical Orthodoxy and the Reformed Tradition*, ed. James K. A. Smith and James H. Olthuis (Grand Rapids, MI: Baker Academic, 2005), 166.

47. Cavanaugh, "A Fire," 411–12.

48. Cavanaugh, "Killing," 267.

49. Cavanaugh, *Theolopolitical Imagination*, 85.

50. Cavanaugh, "A Fire," 399.

51. Cavanaugh, *Theopolitical Imagination*, 2–3.

52. "Secularism is the ideology that argues the historical inevitability and progressive nature of secularization everywhere" (T. N. Madan, *Modern Myths, Locked Minds* [Delhi: Oxford University Press, 1998], 5–6).

53. Bull, *The Anarchical Society*, 255.

CHAPTER 27

If You Render Unto God What Is God's, What Is Left for Caesar?

WILLIAM T. CAVANAUGH

William T. Cavanaugh (1962–) is Professor of Catholic Studies and Director of the Center for World Catholicism and Intercultural Theology at DePaul University. He received his Bachelor's Degree from the University of Notre Dame in 1984, his Master's Degree from Cambridge University in 1987, and his Ph.D. in Religion from Duke University in 1996. Before taking up his position at DePaul University in 2010, he taught at the University of St. Thomas, beginning in 1995. Cavanaugh has become a major voice in debates within American Catholicism and is known for his argument that the Catholic Church has become co-opted and redefined by the modern state and contemporary capitalism. Among his many books, two particularly representative of his thought are Migrations of the Holy: God, State and the Political Meaning of the Church *(2011), and* The Myth of Religious Violence: Secular Ideology and the Roots of Modern Conflict *(2008).*

I must begin by expressing my deep appreciation to Paul Rowe for bringing my work on theopolitics before a different audience than the ones to which I am accustomed and for bringing his own expertise in political science and political theory to bear on my writings. The depth and incisiveness of his critique provide me an opportunity to rethink and clarify my ideas. It also gives me the opportunity to prove that I do not deserve being mentioned in the same sentence as Che Guevara and Abu Musab al-Zarqawi!

To a political scientist, I grant that I must appear as an odd figure, a Catholic theologian mounting a critique of the basic political structures of Western society, based on theological resources. If I am taken as trying to reconstruct the world political system to be based in the Christian church, then my project would seem absurd and antiquated, like a member of the Flat Earth Society mounting an assault on the current state of geography. For this reason, I must clarify my audience from the outset. I am a Christian theologian, and I write in the first instance for other Christians. My principal concern is to help Christians to be realistic about what they can expect from the powers and principalities of the present day, especially the nation-state and the market, and to urge Christians not to invest the entirety of their social and political presence in these institutions. My goal as a Christian theologian is to help the church be more faithful to God in Jesus Christ. In the present day, I think that faithfulness means taking a hard look at political and economic structures many Christians take for granted. Rowe criticizes me for providing "no general model for temporal management" of global civil society, but I am not in the business of setting forth models for a new global order. I tend to think such global models are inherently problematic. If my work, therefore, seems rather too parochially Christian, it is not because I think non-Christians are unworthy of consideration; it is rather that I do not consider myself competent to tell Muslims and Jews and others what the ideal polity would look like. Christians and Muslims and Jews and others do have plenty to say to each other and can cooperate in creating alternative social spaces. But a true pluralism, I believe, consists in each community being more, not less, faithful to its own traditions. My work can be understood as an attempt to mine what is good in the Christian tradition for the purpose of resisting some of the idolatries of the modern era and thus contributing to a more just and peaceful world.

Whether my work contributes to such a world or provides ammunition for some of the unsavory characters Rowe mentions in the introduction to his essay depends on whether my analyses of political structures hold water. After introducing my work, Rowe criticizes my views of the state, civil society, and the church. I will respond to each of these in order.

State

Christians in the modern era have tended to take the state as a permanent and natural feature of God's creation for granted. Scripture is read through a modern lens so that Jesus' statement about rendering to Caesar is read as a theory of church and state. Some things belong to God—spiritual things—and some things belong to Caesar—temporal things. The eventual separation of church and state in the modern era is thus seen as the final outworking of the Christian liberation of the spiritual from the temporal, or religion from politics. Implicit in this common view is often a Whiggish Protestant narrative of history— Christ's kingdom that is not from this world (John 18:36) and Martin Luther's Two Kingdoms are the liberation of the spirit from both Jewish and Catholic legalism and entanglement with temporal affairs.

I have tried to show that the state is a modern idea, as are the binary categories of religion/politics and spiritual/temporal. Neither Jesus nor the writers of Scripture would have had any conception of the state as we know it, nor would they have dreamed that God's concerns could be cordoned off into a distinct *spiritual* or *religious* category of life. Contrary to what Paul Rowe implies in several places, I am not against the separation of church and state; I think it is an advance from the church's point of view to rid it of access to coercive power. I am, however, opposed to the separation of religion from politics, if that means the privatization and marginalization of the church's public witness.

Rowe questions my genealogy of the state, claiming that "ancient empires *were* nation-states in that they created an embryonic notion of the nation" and that ancient Greece with its city-states was similar to the United States of America divided into states. Rowe cites Hadrian's Wall and the Great Wall of China as examples of markers of ancient territorial sovereignty. But Rowe is able to use the term *nation-state* for ancient empires only by stretching the term to mean any type of translocal government. I have no doubt that translocal governments existed before the modern era, but they are not what political scientists call nation-states. The governments of ancient empires had very little regular administrative access to the lives of ordinary people outside centers of power; most people in conquered territories were not citizens; most conquered peoples did not identify themselves as members of, for example, the nation of Rome, but maintained local identities; and ancient empires, as Anthony Giddens says, had vaguely defined frontiers, not borders.[1] In feudal Europe, law was defined by fealty, not by territoriality, and overlapping loyalties at the local level kept power largely decentralized. The Holy Roman Empire was an extraordinarily complex and weak ideal in which civil authorities had to contend with ecclesiastical authorities for power. The advent of the sovereign territorial state at the dawn of modernity was not just a new twist on the same old thing. The further transformation from state to nation-state depended on the creation of heretofore unknown national identities; as patriot Massimo d'Azeglio said in 1860: "We have made Italy, now we have to make Italians."[2] Even the scholars who give the earliest origins for nationalism (Adrian Hastings[3] and Liah Greenfeld[4]) only find antecedents in late medieval England and France. One can only suggest that the nation-state is ancient by distorting the term beyond recognition.

The reason I think the newness of the nation-state matters is that it allows us to reconsider the naturalness and inevitability of the nation-state. Today devotion to one's country is often considered within the churches as a Christian virtue with biblical roots. But as Rowe concedes, borrowing from Kenneth Waltz, loyalty to nation and state replaced loyalty to the church in the early modern period. As Rowe acknowledges, "It is also clear that the state arose in many ways to justify the very secular power of royal factions, republican revolutions, and military dictatorships rather than to seek the common good." But, argues Rowe, just because the state arose in this fashion does not mean it continues to function this way today. Rowe argues that we have moved from Hobbesian to Lockean states, that "the state's ambitions were tamed," that it no longer substitutes for the church and can, in fact, be used to promote the common good.

It is, of course, true that the nation-state continues to change and is not the same as it was several centuries ago. I am willing to grant, as I do in one of the articles that Rowe cites, that nation-states can and do provide useful services and protect and promote a certain order. I agree that certain forms of ad hoc cooperation with nation-states can be laudable.[5] Nevertheless, I find the standard progressivist narrative to be inadequate to empirical fact and also inadequate to deal with the theological insight that idolatry is a constant temptation. One version of the progressivist narrative begins in the so-called Wars of Religion and sees the rise of the state as our salvation from the violent fanaticism of *religion*. The story of these wars serves as a kind of creation myth for the modern state, because it indicates that the modern state was born as peacemaker between warring religions by relegating religion to private life and uniting people around loyalty to the sovereign state. In my new book, I demonstrate by examining the historical record that the very creation of religion was at stake in the wars, and that the rise of the sovereign state was a cause, not solution, of the wars in question.[6] Although Rowe does not accept the Wars of Religion narrative, he nevertheless tells a progressivist story of the "process of evolution" of the modern state, the taming of its ambitions, and the ever-expanding inclusion of citizens in the social contract. I think there are good reasons to be wary of such a happy story. Not only has the sheer size of the state continued to increase, but the nation-state as repository of sacred value and loyalty still provides a temptation to idolatry. As E. J. Hobsbawm has pointed out, ours is an unliturgical age in most respects, with one enormous exception: the public life of the citizen of the nation-state. Citizenship in secular countries is tied to symbols and rituals that have been invented for the purpose of expressing and reinforcing devotion to the nation-state.[7] The extensive work that has been done by Robert Bellah and others on civil religion makes clear that, from a Christian point of view, the replacement of the church by the nation-state is not a phenomenon of the early modern era alone. According to Carolyn Marvin and David Ingle, "nationalism is the most powerful religion in the United States, and perhaps in many other countries."[8] For Marvin and Ingle, the transfer of the sacred from Christianity to the nation-state in Western society is seen most clearly in the fact that authorized killing has passed from Christendom to the nation-state. Christian denominations still thrive in America, but as optional, inward-looking affairs. They are not publicly true, "[f]or what is really true in any community is what its members can agree is worth killing for, or what they can be compelled to sacrifice their lives for."[9]

Violence is clearly one of my central concerns about the modern state, though not the only one. Rowe attempts to allay my concerns about the violence of the nation-state by arguing that "[i]n Western societies, the state has shed much of its coercive apparatus and become a service provider." Of the recent adventures of the United States in Afghanistan and Iraq, Rowe claims "there might even be reason to believe it to be a temporary development." Outside the United States, Europe, Latin America, and Canada are said to have largely demilitarized; South American states have not gone to war in a century, excepting the Falklands War. Rowe even suggests that "the state may someday get out of the business of warfare entirely." Again, I find good empirical reasons to be wary of such progressivist cheer. It may be possible to find reason for optimism in Europe where peace has reigned over the last few decades, with the notable exception of the breakup of Yugoslavia. In Latin America, the calm is more recent and comes after a brutal century of countries using their bloated militaries not against each other but against their own people. Elsewhere, Rowe offers no hard evidence that militarism and military spending is on the wane, nor could he. Although Rowe claims that we have more to fear regarding nuclear weapons from non-state actors than we do from states, it remains the case that states are the only actors so far that have developed, tested, and used nuclear weapons, and their number is growing.

The case of the United States concerns me most as an American, and I find it very difficult to accept the idea that the wars in Afghanistan and Iraq are merely recent, temporary aberrations. The myth of America as reluctant superpower has been shown by Andrew Bacevich to be false. Bacevich's book *American Empire* shows the continuity between the foreign policies of Bush I, Clinton, and Bush II, on the one hand, and the expansionism at the heart of American foreign policy since the late nineteenth century, on the other.[10] Contrary to Rowe's notion of the inherent peaceableness of liberal democracy, Bacevich has shown that American expansionism is based on the necessity to spread liberal notions of open markets and open societies. This is Woodrow Wilson's idea that the peace and prosperity of the world depends on the extension of liberal principles of government—along with open markets—to the entire world. Liberals are opposed by realists in American foreign policy debates, but Americans tend to favor military action, as Colin Dueck says, "either for liberal reasons, or not at all."[11] Despite the frequency with which the Bush Doctrine is seen as a radical departure from traditional American foreign policy—especially for its apparent expansion of the idea of preemptive war—many scholars emphasize the continuity between the foreign policy of George W. Bush and the Wilsonian tradition.[12] As Bush said, "Every nation has learned, or should have learned, an important lesson: Freedom is worth fighting for, dying for, and standing for—and the advance of freedom leads to peace."[13] I think there is very good reason to be wary of this missionary imperative in liberalism.

As we witness Pentagon budgets soar past the half-trillion-dollar mark annually, it is clear that American militarism is not on the wane.[14] In the American case especially, but by no means exclusively, I think there is good empirical reason to reject Rowe's presentation of the modern nation-state as bland and benign service provider. It has a dual aspect, on the one hand, as bureaucratic provider of services that, as Alasdair MacIntyre says, "is always about to, but never actually does, give its clients value for money," and, on the other hand, as repository of sacred value for which citizens are sometimes asked to kill and die. As MacIntyre quips, "It is like being asked to die for the telephone company."[15] To maintain social coherence in a liberal social order, and to get people to be willing to kill and die for a bureaucratic service provider, the liberal nation-state must provide a sense of transcendent meaning, a civil religion of freedom or love of country. The kind of utopian eschatology that Rowe suggests, following Fukuyama and others, in which liberalism is just about to vanquish war for good is an important element in this kind of civil religion. From a Christian theological point of view, such civil religion is a temptation to idolatry. Liberal eschatology is a substitute for the real thing. Carl Schmitt was right when he wrote: "All significant concepts of the modern theory of the state are secularized theological concepts not only because of their historical development—in which they were transferred from theology to the theory of the state, whereby, for example, the omnipotent God became the omnipotent lawgiver—but also of their systematic structure, the recognition of which is necessary for a sociological consideration of these concepts."[16] From my point of view, if you're going to have a utopian eschatology, you might as well have a real one, a Christian theological one, that is. The problem with the modern nation-state is that it often offers an ersatz version, theology without God.

CIVIL SOCIETY

In the twentieth century, the Catholic Church finally broke off its centuries-long romance with state establishment. Pope Pius XI accepted the terms of formal separation of church and state in Catholic countries, and at Vatican II *Dignitatis Humanae*, the Declaration on Religious Liberty, upheld freedom of conscience for all. One of the architects of *Dignitatis Humanae* was the American Jesuit John Courtney Murray, who had for several decades been trying to make the Catholic Church's peace with liberal democracy, despite opposition from within the church. Civil society was a key concept for Murray because it identified a way that the church could be released from binding ties to the state and yet avoid privatization. Civil society was the public space in which the church could interact with other free associations. Murray applauded the American system because it established a state whose power was limited to vigilance for public order. The state was the creation and servant of civil society. The genius of liberalism was to free the intermediate associations of civil society by limiting the state.[17]

Given my emphasis on the independence of the church from the state, I should be expected to embrace Murray's attractive picture of a church that is fully public yet free from the state. Rowe is frustrated with me because I seem to refuse the promise that civil society has to offer, and "rule out the very useful place of organized religious discourse in a civil society." I do so, according to Rowe, based on an exaggerated vision of an all-consuming state that has wholly colonized civil society. Rowe indicates that my criticisms apply to corporatist models such as those that obtain in Scandinavia and other European countries, but not to more pluralist systems, such as that of the United States.

Rowe is right to criticize some of my statements on this question for being overstatements. He is right to say that civil society is a contested field, not a monolithic site of state hegemony. It is also true that there are examples, especially in Africa, of weak states whose power to penetrate civil society is very limited. Even where the state is more powerful, there would be little sense in encouraging the church to help foster alternative spaces if state discourses were so thoroughly dominant.

Nevertheless, I have tried to caution the church not to take Murray's attractive model of free civil society and limited state as a description of empirical fact. Political scientist Michael Budde says of Murray, "No testing of reality seems to have affected his assessment of American political institutions."[18] Talk about the limited state must be qualified by recognition of the fact that the federal budget for the current year exceeds 3.5 trillion dollars, a sum that is difficult to fathom. The current government bailout and partial assumption of ownership of financial institutions and other enterprises make it increasingly difficult to talk of a limited state. With the growth of the state, many have pointed to the atrophying of the intermediate bodies that make up a robust civil society: the decay of unions, the loss of church membership, the fragmentation of families, the decline of civic organizations, and the loss of autonomy of universities. Recognition of the decay of civil society in the United States is hardly idiosyncratic; Robert Bellah and Robert Putnam have documented the trend, Michael Hardt writes of the "withering of civil society," and the Council on Civil Society— including such diverse figures as Cornel West and Francis Fukuyama—was formed to combat the decay.[19] According to Robert Nisbet, the great conflict of modern political history is not between state and individual, but between state and social group, as the state moved to absorb rights and responsibilities formerly belonging to those groups.[20] My point, however, is not that an enormous and totalitarian state threatens to crush the organs of civil society. It is rather that state and civil society have become increasingly fused, such that little significant social action takes place wholly outside the funding, direct implementation, or regulation of the state.

Rowe is right to point out that the church in the United States is not as subject to direct government involvement as is the church in Sweden, for example. Nevertheless, the social presence of the church is often diminished. Sometimes this happens through the direct intervention of the state. For example, the social action of the churches on behalf of the poor has been largely either assumed by the state or made subject to state funding and regulation. Likewise, the once extensive church-related hospital system is threatened with disappearance, having also been made subject to state funding and regulation; whether church-related hospitals may legally refuse to perform procedures they deem morally repugnant is currently in question. Often, however, it is not direct state intervention, but the colonization of the social imagination of Christians that is the problem. If economic structures breed injustice and environmental degradation, we can think of little else to do but ask the state to fix it. If the ranks of the homeless increase, all we can think to do is to ask the state to house them. Most significantly, we have been so captivated by the rhetoric of national interest that we will go and fight in wars that most church leaders condemn as unjust on the assumption that it is our patriotic duty. The church has not disappeared, but Christianity has often taken on the status of a hobby. Christians consider it true, but only privately. As Marvin and Ingle write, "For what is really true in any community is what its members can agree is worth killing for, or what they can be compelled to sacrifice their lives for."[21] And this ability to generate truth, Marvin and Ingle point out, has largely passed to the nation-state in the modern West.

It is possible to exaggerate the extent to which the church has disappeared as a social body in the contemporary West. I do not wish to ignore the many kinds of social action that church groups and other groups undertake. In my 2008 book *Being Consumed*, I hold up many concrete examples of Christians creating and supporting alternative economic spaces.[22] In that sense, I do not at all "rule out the very useful place of organized religious discourse in a civil society" as Rowe fears, if what "civil society" denotes is anything that happens outside the direct purview of the state. I resist the language of civil society, however, if it is used to ignore the real pervasiveness of the nation-state or if it confines all types of social groups, including the church, to mere intermediaries between the individual and the state, if civil society is constructed as an arena of interest groups vying for influence within the state. I am interested in a more radical pluralism; I have certain sympathies with the English pluralists of the early twentieth century, people like John Neville Figgis and G. D. H. Cole. From a Christian point of view, I think that resisting modern idolatries requires something more robust than the confinement of the church to one more lobbying group within the nation-state. When facing the economic crisis, for example, the church can act more creatively, in concert with other non-state actors, to support economic practices that escape the dominance of the state-supported corporate paradigm. There are even times when the church must be a bit more unruly, when it cannot, for example, let the president decide for it what is a just war and what is not.

Church

But the question, of course, is What do I mean when I say "church"? Do I want a return to the Middle Ages? Do I believe in the "exalted nature of the Church as God's provision for world order"? Am I advocating some kind of Christian version of the Taliban?

Rowe acknowledges that I explicitly disavow the idea of theocracy. Modernity has liberated the church from most of its pretensions to have access to the means of violence, and I wholeheartedly endorse that movement. Despite what Rowe says, I do not believe that the separation of church and state was a mistake. How could I, given my critique of the state? I do, however, want to retain the reality of the church as a social body in its own right, and here Rowe finds a multitude of problems. His critiques are as follows: I do not deal with the inherent sinfulness of the church's members. I overemphasize the need for unity and conformity within the church and seek to impose conformity by means of ecclesiastical hierarchy. I have no way of dealing positively and ecumenically with those outside of the church. And I ignore the fact that the church is meant to be a spiritual gathering and not an institutional response to temporal problems.

With regard to the sinfulness of the church, Rowe cites my article "How to Do Penance for the Inquisition" but claims that I am dismissive of the possibility that church sins like the Inquisition may be repeated. I am not sure how Rowe comes to that conclusion; it was certainly not my intention. The point of the article is that the church can do penance for the Inquisition by speaking out and resisting the use of torture today. The use of torture in the West has passed from medieval inquisitors to modern secular intelligence operatives. To recognize this fact is not to say that the church no longer sins, but to call Christians not to give tacit approval to the violence that is currently done in our name by the state. As I have argued elsewhere,[23] the church's resistance to violence should not be based on a romanticization of the church as the gathering of the sinless, but rather on the recognition that we are deeply sinful and, therefore, incapable of using violence justly. To call the church to be faithful to the Gospel is a claim of the holiness of God, not the subjective holiness of the church.

Rowe's second complaint is about church imposition of conformity in political matters. In my first book, *Torture and Eucharist*, I endorsed the excommunication of torturers by a group of Catholic bishops under the Pinochet regime in Chile. In the Catholic Church, bishops have an important role to play in safeguarding the integrity of the Body of Christ; where there is the scandal of torturers and tortured approaching the same altar, excommunication can and did bring the scandal to light. I believe excommunicating torturers was an important and prophetic gesture, but it was an extraordinary gesture. I do not endorse excommunication in general as a common tool for the imposition of uniformity in the church. The quest, as Rowe points out, is not for conformity but for community. A healthy community will have a great deal of diversity within it. Certain kinds of diversity, however—torturers and tortured, for example—are not healthy. In Pinochet's Chile, some Catholics had clearly put allegiance to the nation-state and its security above their allegiance to the Body of Christ. The call for community, the call to live eucharistically, is not a call for uniformity, but a call to put loyalty to Christ before other types of loyalty and allegiance.

My earliest published work was based on my experience in Chile, where an exercise of discipline by the church hierarchy operated positively in the theopolitical arena. Rowe's analysis is based on a rather limited selection of my work, mostly from this early period.[24] Even in Chile, the other two concrete examples I give of church resistance to the military regime besides excommunication were grassroots initiatives of laypeople, priests, and nuns. After my first book, I have written little about the actions of the Catholic hierarchy, and primarily about the actions of everyday Christians, Catholic, Protestant, and Orthodox. Even where I discuss the action of the hierarchy, such as in the denunciation of the Iraq War,[25] I do not think the solution is simply for the pope and bishops to tell us what to do and for the laity to obey. I look instead to the laity, especially those in the military, to say "This war is unjust, and I'm going to sit this one out." I describe my book on economics, *Being Consumed*, as a "contribution to a kind of theological microeconomics."[26] Likewise, I am far more interested in a Christian micropolitics than in the imposition of uniformity from above. When I say "church," I primarily mean "us Christians," though I don't discount the legitimate role of the hierarchy.

I am increasingly concerned as I see some vocal Catholic bishops become involved in electoral politics in the United States, often giving de facto support to the Republican party based on some (usually empty) Republican promise to push the legislative agenda of the bishops. Not only is such involvement often counterproductive—support for a euthanasia law in Oregon actually increased once the Catholic bishops entered the fray on the opposing side—but the bishops' involvement is often based on a mentality that sees state enforcement as the only solution to any given cultural problem. As my critique of the state should make plain, I am opposed to any nostalgia for Constantinianism. I believe that a Christian should feel politically homeless and refuse to regard the choice between voting for Democrats and voting for Republicans as the summit of our social witness. I favor instead the formation of real communities of witness.

Such communities cannot be closed in upon themselves, but must attend to all in need. There is nothing in my view of the church, to answer Rowe's third objection, that limits its reach beyond church and denominational boundaries. To the contrary, I have tried to make clear that the boundaries of the church are porous, and Christians should cooperate with non-Christians in creating alternative economic and political spaces.[27] I don't think that my critique of the reality of civil society leaves us "with precious little space to construct common ground with 'the Other.'" On the contrary, I think a more radical pluralism opens the possibility of a greater variety of such spaces that are not simply subject to the disciplining imagination of the nation-state.[28]

Though I find much agreement with Rowe's concerns, his fourth objection to my view of the church is based on spiritual/institutional and spiritual/temporal dichotomies that I question. Rowe is right to say that the Body of Christ is not simply to be conflated with the sinful institution of the church, with its checkered history. Nevertheless, I do not think it is sufficient to reduce the social gathering of the church to a spiritual gathering or to suggest "that the Christian needs to filter the ideals of the state through a mind transformed by the power of Christ." In my book on Chile, I show how this type of model had negative consequences in Chile. The prevailing model of Christian social action in pre-Pinochet Chile, derived in part from Jacques Maritain, was of individual Christians absorbing the Gospel message and then entering as individuals into one of the various political parties. This individualization of the Christian message left the church with no social body to resist when the military regime began to employ its strategy of atomization on the body politic. Gradually, however, the church did recover its social body under persecution, and the church became the only effective institutional resistance to the Pinochet regime, the only social space where resistance could gather. What this shows is that, despite anti-institutional sentiment in some forms of Protestant Christianity, the church as institution, that is, as tangible social body, is sometimes necessary to resist the depredations of unchecked power. Rowe is, of course, right to say that there is no guarantee that human abuse of power will not affect the church institution itself. But the disappearance of the church as social body is the disappearance of the hope that Christ's redemption can have tangible effects in this world.

The spiritual/temporal binary as a spatial distinction is also problematic. Before modernity, the temporal was a time, not a space, the interval between the first and second comings of Christ, when coercive civil authority was temporarily necessary to stave off chaos.[29] The temporal did not indicate some realm of merely mundane concerns, such as business and government, that were fundamentally separate from spiritual concerns, or the things that pertain to God. To read this modern distinction back into the Gospels—to divide the world into what is Caesar's and what is God's—is anachronistic. What would Jesus have thought belongs to God? Psalm 24 begins, "The earth is the LORD's and all that is in it, the world, and those who live in it." If this is so, what is left for Caesar? It is quite unlikely that Jesus had in mind the modern separation of spiritual and temporal, a tidy division of labor between God and Caesar. The title to which Jesus refers on the denarius used to pay the temple tax in Jesus' time read, "Tiberius, son of the Divine Augustus." It is unlikely that Jesus meant to hand much of life over to a rival son of god. For this reason, Scripture scholars tend to be quite skeptical of attempts to read modern Western political institutions back into the episode of Caesar's coin.

The modern nation-state is not Caesar, but the problem of idolatry has not disappeared. What should Christians render unto the civil powers of our day? Many kinds of ad hoc cooperation with civil government are possible and necessary. My work is meant as a reminder to Christians, nevertheless, that before we are Americans, Britons, and so on, we are followers of Jesus Christ.

NOTES

Reprinted from *The Review of Politics* 71, no. 4 (Fall 2009): 607–19.

1. Anthony Giddens, *The Nation-State and Violence* (Berkeley: University of California Press, 1987), 35–60.
2. Quoted in E. J. Hobsbawm, *Nations and Nationalism since 1760: Programme, Myth, Reality* (Cambridge: Cambridge University Press, 1992), 44.
3. Adrian Hastings, *The Construction of Nationhood: Ethnicity, Religion, and Nationalism* (Cambridge: Cambridge University Press, 1997).
4. Liah Greenfeld, *Nationalism: Five Roads to Modernity* (Cambridge, MA: Harvard University Press, 1992).
5. William T. Cavanaugh, "Killing for the Telephone Company: Why the Nation-State Is Not the Keeper of the Common Good," *Modern Theology* 20, no. 2 (April 2004): 266–67.

6. See William T. Cavanaugh, *The Myth of Religious Violence: Secular Ideology and the Roots of Modern Conflict* (New York: Oxford University Press, 2009), chap. 3.

7. Eric Hobsbawm, "Introduction: Inventing Traditions," in *The Invention of Tradition*, ed. Eric Hobsbawm and Terence Ranger (Cambridge: Cambridge University Press, 1983), 12.

8. Carolyn Marvin and David Ingle, "Blood Sacrifice and the Nation," *Journal of the American Academy of Religion* 64, no. 4 (Winter 1996): 767. It is worth noting that Marvin and Ingle wrote this before the surge in patriotism following the attacks of September 11, 2001. This article is a brief synopsis of Marvin and Ingle's fascinating book *Blood Sacrifice and the Nation: Totem Rituals and the American Flag* (Cambridge: Cambridge University Press, 1999).

9. Marvin and Ingle, "Blood Sacrifice and the Nation," 769.

10. Andrew J. Bacevich, *American Empire: The Realities and Consequences of U.S. Diplomacy* (Cambridge, MA: Harvard University Press, 2002).

11. Colin Dueck, *Reluctant Crusaders: Power, Culture, and Change in American Grand Strategy* (Princeton: Princeton University Press, 2006), 26.

12. See for example, ibid., 1–2; Bacevich, *American Empire*, 198–244; Robert Singh, "The Bush Doctrine," in *The Bush Doctrine and the War on Terrorism: Global Responses, Global Consequences*, ed. Mary Buckley and Robert Singh (London: Routledge, 2006), 13.

13. George W. Bush, "Remarks by the President at the Twentieth Anniversary of the National Endowment for Democracy," Washington, DC, November 6, 2003.

14. See Andrew J. Bacevich, *The New American Militarism: How Americans Are Seduced by War* (Oxford: Oxford University Press, 2005).

15. Alasdair MacIntyre, "A Partial Response to My Critics," in *After MacIntyre: Critical Perspectives on the Work of Alasdair MacIntyre*, ed. John Horton and Susan Mendus (Notre Dame, IN: University of Notre Dame Press, 1994), 303.

16. Carl Schmitt, *Political Theology: Four Chapters on the Concept of Sovereignty*, trans. George Schwab (Cambridge, MA: MIT Press, 1985), 36. It should be obvious that I do not share Schmitt's conclusion that the state should enhance its divine character and marginalize the divisive influence of the Church.

17. See John Courtney Murray, *We Hold These Truths: Catholic Reflections on the American Proposition* (New York: Sheed & Ward, 1960), 5–24, 45–78.

18. Michael Budde, *The Two Churches: Catholicism and Capitalism in the World-System* (Durham, NC: Duke University Press, 1992), 115.

19. Robert Bellah et al., *Habits of the Heart* (San Francisco: Harper and Row, 1985); Robert Putnam, *Bowling Alone* (New York: Simon and Schuster, 2000); Michael Hardt, "The Withering of Civil Society," *Social Text* 14, no. 4 (Winter 1995): 27–45; Council on Civil Society, *A Call to Civil Society: Why Democracy Needs Moral Truths* (Chicago: Council on Civil Society, 1998).

20. Robert Nisbet, *The Quest for Community* (London: Oxford University Press, 1953), 102–9.

21. Marvin and Ingle, "Blood Sacrifice and the Nation," 769.

22. William T. Cavanaugh, *Being Consumed: Economics and Christian Desire* (Grand Rapids, MI: Wm. B. Eerdmans, 2008).

23. William T. Cavanaugh, "Pilgrim People," in *Gathered for the Journey: Moral Theology in Catholic Perspective*, ed. David Matzko McCarthy and M. Therese Lysaught (Grand Rapids, MI: Wm. B. Eerdmans, 2007), 88–105, and William T. Cavanaugh, "The Sinfulness and Visibility of the Church: A Christological Exploration," in *Proceedings of the 2007 Leuven Encounters in Systematic Theology* (Leuven: Peeters, forthcoming).

24. Rowe cites my first two books and six articles or chapters, two of which are wholly incorporated into the second book. In 2008, when his article was submitted to the *Review of Politics*, I had published twenty-five articles in scholarly journals, and another seventeen chapters in edited volumes, in addition to dozens of articles and interviews in less academic venues.

25. See William T. Cavanaugh, "At Odds with the Pope: Legitimate Authority and Just Wars," *Commonweal* 130, no. 10 (May 23, 2003): 11–13; and "From One City to Two: Christian Reimagining of Political Space," *Political Theology* 7, no. 3 (July 2006): 299–321.

26. Cavanaugh, *Being Consumed*, viii.

27. See for example, William T. Cavanaugh, "Church," in *The Blackwell Companion to Political Theology*, ed. William T. Cavanaugh and Peter Scott (Oxford: Blackwell Publishers, 2003), 393–406, and "From One City to Two," cited above.

28. It should be obvious as well that I am just as averse to national churches as is Rowe.

29. For a genealogy of the temporal, see William T. Cavanaugh, *Torture and Eucharist: Theology, Politics, and the Body of Christ* (Oxford: Blackwell, 1998), 216–21; and "From One City to Two," 308–15.